FROM: The President

RICHARD NIXON'S SECRET FILES

TO: Gabs Mor...

FROM: The President

Richard Nixon's Secret Files

Edited by Bruce Oudes

90-149

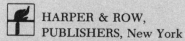

HARPER & ROW,
PUBLISHERS, New York

Cambridge, Philadelphia, San Francisco, London, Mexico City, São Paulo, Singapore, Sydney

FIRST EDITION

Copyeditor: Karen P. Mitchell

Designer: Barbara DuPree Knowles

Indexer: Maro Riofrancos

LIBRARY OF CONGRESS CATALOGING-IN-PUBLICATION DATA
Nixon, Richard M. (Richard Milhous), 1913–
    From: the president.
    Includes index.
    1. United States—Politics and government—1969–1974.
2. Watergate Affair, 1972–1974.   3. Nixon, Richard M.
(Richard Milhous), 1913–   .   I. Oudes, Bruce.   II. Title.
E838.5.N52   1989| 973.924   88-45050
ISBN 0-06-015953-7

89 90 91 92 93 CC/RRD 10 9 8 7 6 5 4 3 2 1

To the memory of Jacob Scher
and the future of his dream

ACKNOWLEDGMENTS

Given the circumstances under which Richard Milhous Nixon came to resign the office of President of the United States, it would seem inevitable that there always will be a tendency to focus attention on what's missing from the record, what may be covered up. However, an important aspect of Richard Nixon's lawyerly love of documents is his propensity to generate them himself—and to require his staff to do the same. One who examines the documents of the Nixon administration seriously cannot fail to be impressed by the efficiency and thoroughness with which H. R. "Bob" Haldeman, Nixon's chief of staff, and his colleagues generated and filed the memoranda that were so much the stuff of their daily routine in the White House. Casual as well as serious students of the Nixon presidency should praise President Nixon and his associates for the extent of the record they generated and preserved. To fail to do so would not only be ungracious but also unfair.

Alison Picard, my literary agent, and Craig Nelson, Jennifer Hull, and Anne McCoy of Harper & Row have been most enthusiastic, hardworking supporters of this project and have my special thanks.

This book never would have been possible without the cooperation and support provided by James Hastings, Director, Joan Howard, Supervisory Archivist, and the entire staff of the Nixon presidential materials project of the National Archives. They all deserve recognition for the professionalism with which they performed the extraordinarily demanding task of preparing the Nixon papers for public use. They include Bonnie Baldwin, Mark Fischer, Myrna Geselbracht, Raymond Geselbracht, Frederick Graboske, Stephen Greene, Paul Guité, Anita Happoldt, Linda Jones, William Joyner, Janet Kennelly, Maarja Krasten, Richard McNeill, Wanda Overstreet, Walton Owen, Byron Parham, Ronald Plavchan, Edith Prise, Thomas Redard, Paul Schmidt, Janis Wiggins, and Mary Young. Special commendation for valor goes to Jennifer Edwards, Jodi Fernandez, and Sue Ellen Stanley, who photocopied the more than 30,000 pages of Nixon materials from which this final selection was made.

My parents, Helen and Joseph Oudes of El Sobrante, California, helped make it possible for me to attend Northwestern University three decades ago, and their love and encouragement always have been a greater inspiration to me than words can express. We three and my brother, Terry, expect much from his sons, my studious nephews, Asa Joseph and Orrin Starr Oudes. One who is blessed with friends too numerous to mention must not be remiss in letting them know the importance of their thoughtfulness and interest.

Jacob Scher was a pioneer in the evolution of professional journalism. He completed his undergraduate work and law degree at the University of Illinois, studied history at the University of Chicago, and worked on newspapers in Chicago and Oakland, among other things, before joining the faculty of the Medill School of Journalism at Northwestern in 1947. In the ensuing decade and a half Professor Scher did a great deal to enhance the intellectual credentials of a course of study traditionally reviled by both the purists of academe and the ink-stained wretches of the trade. He was the workhorse of Medill's undergraduate program. The typical student took Professor Scher's courses in press history, press law, and press ethics, among others. In recommending him for tenure in 1956 Dean Kenneth Olson called Scher "one of the ablest and most inspirational men on our faculty," and added that "the students love him." Dean Olson was right on the mark on both counts. Scher taught an ideal of the journalist as renaissance intellectual. He saw no reason why serious journalism should take a back seat to history or the law. In the 1950s Scher became increasingly absorbed by the problem of developing lawful means by which journalists could examine the very stuff of government, its documents, to convey a complete portrait of government to the public. He slowly arrived at the conclusion that there should be laws that would provide procedures for the orderly review and release of materials so that the public might come to know the *reality* of what government was doing, which then could be compared with what government *said* it was doing. At the federal level the motive in circumscribing the latitude traditionally accorded our President, the elected king, and his hundreds of thousands of servants was not partisan. The goal was the enhancement of trust between the government and the people, perhaps even leading to consensus and a modicum of national unity. It was a blend of quintessential idealism with quintessential democracy.

As the 1950s progressed Jacob Scher moonlighted as counsel to the newly formed House Government Operations Subcommittee on Government Information and as counsel to the National Editorial Association. In 1959 he also became special counsel on freedom of information affairs to the American Society of Newspaper Editors (ASNE). In an article in *Journalism Quarterly* in early 1960 he discussed, among other things, the Eisenhower administration's use of the "executive privilege" rationale to withhold information from Senator Joseph McCarthy's investigation of the U.S. Army and quoted a clarifying statement on March 8, 1958, by Attorney General William P. Rogers setting forth the following principles:

1. While the people are entitled to the fullest disclosure possible, this right, like freedom of speech or press, is not absolute or without limitation. Disclosure must always be consistent with the national security and the public interest.

2. In recognizing a right to withhold information, the approach must be not how much can legitimately be withheld, but rather how little must necessarily be withheld. We injure no one but ourselves if we do not make thoughtful judgments in the classification process.

3. A determination that certain information should be withheld must be premised upon valid reasons and disclosure must promptly be made when it appears that the facts justifying nondisclosure no longer pertain.

4. Nondisclosure can never be justified as a means of covering mistakes, avoiding embarrassment, or for political, personal or pecuniary reasons."

In spring 1960 a fellow graduate student and I joined Jacob Scher for dinner at a restaurant not far from the White House. He spoke with humility and quiet pride of his recent admission to practice before the Supreme Court. It was the achievement of a lifetime. He joked about his case of "Potomac fever." He had taken a leave of absence from Northwestern that spring quarter to work on freedom of information issues for ASNE in Washington. Scher was back at Northwestern during the fall and winter quarters of the 1960–61 academic year, and was asked by Eugene S. Pulliam, the ASNE's freedom of information chairman, to deliver the committee's report at the 1961 meeting. Just before his scheduled departure for Washington, he became ill. He died of cancer in a Chicago hospital in September 1961, at age 53, an incalculable loss.

Everything Jacob Scher taught was in one way or another a sermon for fairness, so there is every reason to believe he would have had mixed emotions about the events involving presidential papers in the past two decades. He would have been thrilled by the movement to make presidential papers public property but appalled by the awkwardness with which the progress came about. He would have been stunned perhaps most of all, however, by the cavalier treatment given Richard Nixon's Special Files by the press. When a student of his noted what was happening at the Nixon research room at the National Archives in 1987, or more precisely what was not happening, there could be no doubt about what had to be done.

Jacob Scher concluded his 1960 article in *Journalism Quarterly* with these words:

Perhaps the crucible of experience, which is democracy, will provide in the future the proper tests so that the right [to government information] becomes fully recognized. A problem so important in big government's relation to the people cannot long remain unsolved. The first 10 years of the movement for access to information have brought major breaches in "the paper curtain." If the news media persist, more significant advances are bound to come.

It is a profound joy and privilege to dedicate this collection of papers, formerly classified U.S. government documents, to Jacob Scher.

INTRODUCTION

[. . .] Only those items that are placed in burn bags are destroyed here and burned. Anything that goes in your trash basket is placed in a bag—taken to FOB #7 where it is compressed into bales—and then the papers are sold to the highest bidder.

With all the additions and [im]provements we make to the building [the White House], I would think one of the things we would want to consider as a top priority would be some way of disposing of all papers that are used here on the first floor, be they carbons, notes scribbled, etc.

Between now and the time that something is done on something like this, I can only hope that the highest bidder isn't the USSR or the DNC.

LARRY HIGBY TO ALEXANDER BUTTERFIELD,
APRIL 16, 1970, HRH60

In today's political world, Tony, you need more shredders and not fewer.

RAYMOND PRICE TO ANTHONY LEWIS,
MARCH 24, 1988, "MACNEIL/LEHRER NEWSHOUR"

Documents. Classified U.S. government documents. Documents that Whittaker Chambers found in a pumpkin in the late 1940s helped catapult a young California lawyer to the vice presidency of the United States in just seven years. More than two decades later his reaction to the publication of another collection of classified documents eventually drove Richard Milhous Nixon to become the first President in the history of the United States to resign.

At that time, Congress, with his successor, took the unprecedented step of seizing the documents of a President's administration. In tradition dating from George Washington, such documents had been regarded as personal property. The seizure was the only formal punishment Nixon received for his alleged crimes.

In the wake of that seizure, the Congress enacted and President

Jimmy Carter signed into law a statute which made presidential documents and other materials public property. This process begun by Richard Nixon was one of the traps in which Oliver North ensnared himself in 1986. When Richard Nixon's secretary erased the famous 18½ minutes of presidential recording during the Watergate imbroglio, she destroyed what was then private property. However, when Colonel North shredded the paper trail of his activities, there was no question that the documents he shredded were the property of the U.S. government and not that of Ronald Reagan.

The classified documents of the executive branch especially trace dramas of global significance as well as episodes of banality, baseness, and humor. They are evidence that can be used to build a portrait of a given period—or to build a case for prosecution or persecution. Whether balanced or adversarial, a portrait painted by documents cannot be the whole picture. Documents are snapshots of a continuing communications process among human beings. Notes, jottings, and memoranda to oneself can be of exceptional value as evidence of the thought processes of an individual—or, when expressly produced for the record, can serve to mislead those who might read them.

Richard Nixon was a member of the largest special interest group in the American government—lawyers. If there is to be any serious headway in understanding his thought patterns, especially during the crises of his presidency, the starting point is the fact that he was a lawyer with a lawyerly love of documents. And he felt himself uniquely qualified to pass political judgment on documents. His appetite for, consumption of, and ability to command the production of intelligence in documentary form seems limitless. At the same time, he was a news junkie. Intelligence is news, and news is intelligence—as he knew so very well. Where Richard Nixon got into trouble, however, was in attempting to shape media opinion and reform American journalism as he produced his own files.

At the outset of Richard Nixon's political career, journalists seemed for the most part very helpful. They helped the young congressman become famous during his investigations of Alger Hiss, a former bureaucrat. In *Six Crises* (New York: Doubleday, 1962), Nixon is careful to depict the role of several journalists in the Hiss affair. However, when the print press proved troublesome during the 1952 vice presidential campaign, Nixon triumphed by going over their heads directly to the people through the then-infant medium of television in his famous Checkers speech. During the balance of the decade, television became politically famous for its role in the downfall of Senator Joseph McCarthy, but both television and newspapers generally treated Vice President Nixon in a professionally objective manner. The problem, in Nixon's view, arose during his 1960 presidential campaign. He discussed it at length in *Six Crises* in the context of a conversation he said he had with Willard Edwards of the *Chicago Tribune* on the morning after the election.

"Although a majority of the nation's publishers were Republican, an overwhelming majority of the reporters covering Kennedy and me during the campaign favored Kennedy," Nixon said.

I am sure that no candidate is ever completely satisfied with the press coverage given his activities. And I am the first to grant that the candidate is the least objective of critics in this kind of appraisal. But I completely reject the theory, expressed by some since the campaign, that I might have received better treatment from the press had I "courted" them more, or had Herb [Klein] provided the more elaborate facilities for entertainment that [Pierre] Salinger, with greater funds at his disposal, was able to provide.

I told Edwards that morning that I doubted if any official in Washington had greater, more sincere respect for the press corps than I, or had tried to be more fair in his treatment of them. Kennedy, Salinger, and several top members of the Kennedy staff followed the practice during the campaign of complaining to individual reporters about the fairness of their stories. In several instances, Kennedy himself and members of his staff went over the heads of the reporters to the publishers and to the top officials of the radio and television networks, when they felt they were getting less than fair treatment in news stories or on TV and radio reports. Never once during the course of the campaign did I resort to such tactics, regardless of what opinion I had of the coverage of my activities. . .

Typical of the problem was the attitude of one of the most highly regarded of the Washington corps—James Reston, chief of the New York Times Washington bureau. He had, for example, given me very generous treatment when he covered my Russian trip. But ten days before the election, one of my supporters—Henry Arnold of Philadelphia—had written him, complaining about his coverage of my activities. Reston wrote back: "I'm afraid we differ about Korea, Radford, Nixon, Knowland, Bridges, etc. You like their policy, and I don't."

As Edwards was leaving, he asked me what I thought was the answer to this problem. I expressed my honest opinion: "Republicans will get better treatment in the press only if and when more reporters, like their publishers, take a more favorable or at least a more tolerant view of Republican policies and principles— and not before. (p. 469–71)

Nixon's words masked deep emotion. Just twelve days before the election the *New York Times,* which had supported Eisenhower in 1952 and 1956, endorsed Kennedy in its lead editorial, which it reprinted in the same position three days later. The endorsement undoubtedly had considerable impact on opinion leaders across America. James Reston was at that point both chief of his paper's Washington bureau and a columnist, a purveyor of opinion. According to *Six Crises,* Reston in the 1940s had recommended Alger Hiss to John Foster Dulles for the position with the Carnegie Endowment which Hiss held at the time of the House hearings. Six days before the 1960 election columnist Reston had written that Eisenhower was engaged in a great "rescue operation" on Nixon's behalf, words that Nixon quoted in *Six Crises.* "Maybe even now his popularity can turn the tide, but it is very late in the game to reverse the forces now moving with Senator Kennedy," Reston concluded. With four days to go columnist

Reston was even stronger: "There is general agreement here that Senator Kennedy is going to win the election, but nobody knows for sure, and nobody quite agrees on the reason."

Six Crises was published in the spring of 1962 as Nixon was running hard to become governor of California. In reviewing the book, Tom Wicker, who had covered Nixon for the *Times* in 1960, described him as "that Kafkaesque figure so prominently and yet so elusively in the public eye." The off-year elections were held in the wake of the Cuban missile crisis, arguably the greatest triumph of John Kennedy's presidency. This no doubt made Nixon's mood grimmer as he struggled vainly in California. On the morning after his defeat, obviously fatigued and distraught, he held one of the most memorable press conferences of his political career. He spoke with considerable emotion and repeated some of the points about the press he had made in *Six Crises:*

Now that . . . all the members of the press are so delighted that I have lost, I'd like to make a statement of my own. I appreciate the press coverage in this campaign. I think each of you covered it the way you saw it. . . . I don't believe publishers should tell reporters to write one way or another. I want them all to be free. I don't believe the FCC [Federal Communications Commission] or anybody else should silence [word indistinct]. I have no complaints about the press coverage. I think each of you was writing it as you believed it.

I congratulate Governor [Pat] Brown. . . . I believe Governor Brown has a heart, even though he believes I do not. I believe he is a good American, even though he feels I am not. . . . I am proud of the fact that I defended my opponent's patriotism. You gentlemen didn't report it, but I am proud that I did that. I am proud also that I defended the fact that he was a man of good motive, a man that I disagreed with very strongly, but a man of good motives. I want that—for once, gentlemen—I would appreciate if you would write what I say, in that respect. I think it's very important that you write it in the lead, in the lead. . . .

And as I leave the press all I can say is that for sixteen years, ever since the Hiss case, you've had a lot of—a lot of fun—that you've had an opportunity to attack me, and I think I've given as good as I've taken. It was carried right up to the last day. I made a talk on television, a talk in which I made a flub—one of the few that I make, not because I'm so good on television but because I've done it a long time. I made a flub in which I said I was running for governor of the United States. The Los Angeles Times duly reported that. Mr. Brown the last day made a flub—a flub, incidentally, to the great credit of television that was reported—I don't say this bitterly—in which he said, "I hope everybody wins. You vote the straight Democratic ticket, including Senator [Tom] Kuchel." I was glad to hear him say it, because I was for Kuchel [a Republican] all the way. The Los Angeles Times did not report it. I think that it's time that our great newspapers have at least the same objectivity, the same fullness of coverage, that television has. And I can only say thank God for television and radio for keeping the newspapers a little more honest. . . .

The last play. I leave you gentlemen now, and you will now write it. You will interpret it. That's your right. But as I leave you I want you to know—just think how much you're going to be missing. You won't have Nixon to kick around any more because, gentlemen, this is my last press conference, and it will be one in which I have welcomed the opportunity to test wits with you. I have always respected you. I have sometimes disagreed with you. But, unlike some people, I've never canceled a subscription to a paper, and also I never will. I believe in reading what my opponents say, and I hope that what I have said today will at least make television, radio, the press first recognize the great responsibility they have to report all the news and, second, recognize that they have a right and responsibility, if they're against a candidate, give him the shaft, but also recognize if they give him the shaft, put one lonely reporter on the campaign who will report what the candidate says now and then. Thank you, gentlemen, and good day.

Asked if he thought that Richard Nixon's political career was finished, the victorious governor-elect Pat Brown replied, "I don't think so." In the *New York Times,* however, Tom Wicker wrote in the lead story that Brown's victory had "probably" ended Nixon's political career. Taking his cue from Wicker rather than Governor Brown, James Reston wrote his first political obituary of Richard Nixon. Nixon "never seemed to understand the difference between news and truth," Reston concluded. "To him what he said was 'news' and should be left there. Maybe he was right. It could be that the 'real Nixon' was the one on stage, but that is beyond journalism now and will have to be left to the historians and the psychological novelists."

Six years later, almost to the day, James Reston wrote an overview of the issues that American voters would face two days hence in choosing between Hubert Humphrey and Richard Nixon for President in 1968. "Seldom in this century have the voters had a more difficult or important decision to make," Reston concluded. However, elsewhere on the same page the *Times* editorial endorsement of Hubert Humphrey was unequivocal.

In an interview early in that political season David Frost, the British television personality, asked Nixon if there was any particular remark made in his political career that he now regretted. Nixon responded,

When I finished that campaign for governor of California I didn't have any idea that I would ever be sitting where I am today, being interviewed as a potential candidate for the presidency of the United States. A private citizen has a right to express his views when he thinks he's being put upon. However, as a public figure, I would say that was a mistake, and I can also assure you that as far as getting in an argument with the press, it won't happen again as long as I'm a public figure."[1]

When Richard Nixon won, however narrowly, he could hardly be faulted for a profound sense of exultation, vindication, and determination—a determination to be not just an adequate leader but a great President in a period that already was being described as the most divisive since another lawyer, Abraham Lincoln, came to Washington. Nixon under-

[1]David Frost, *The Presidential Debate, 1968* (New York: Stein and Day, 1968).

stood perfectly well the narrowness of his margin of victory and the bizarre constellation of political forces that made it possible. Those forces included the hippies, Leonid Brezhnev, the yippies, Sirhan Sirhan, Eldredge Cleaver, James Earl Ray, Lyndon Johnson, Lee Harvey Oswald, and a cast of thousands. Sirhan had murdered the Democratic Party's probable nominee Robert Kennedy just minutes after his triumph in the California primary had made his nomination seem probable. Two months later Leonid Brezhnev gave Nixon a boost by sending Soviet troops into Czechoslovakia.

Even with this assistance, Nixon had received only 500,000 votes more than Humphrey, just two-thirds of one percent of all the votes cast, and he would be the first President since Zachary Taylor to enter office with both houses of Congress in the hands of the opposition. He certainly could not be faulted for planning to win a much stronger popular mandate in 1972. Nor could he be faulted for feeling more than a little cold toward the *New York Times* and other members of the media that had lobbied the public in a vain attempt to defeat him.

What evolved, as we shall see, was essentially a two-track strategy. On the one hand, President Nixon courted the press by improving the conditions under which they worked; he had news prepared and supplied for them in an orderly manner, followed the product of their efforts carefully as he had promised in 1962, invited them to White House receptions, and made TV stars of them by scheduling news conferences in prime time. On the other hand, those televised news conferences were a way of going over the heads of the reporters directly to the voters—a variation on the Checkers technique. Carrot-and-stick tactics were regularly used on owners and management to keep them under control, as much as possible, as well as on the pollsters to make their results as favorable as possible. White House writers prepared letters to the editor and to key television personalities that were disguised as coming from some member of the public.[2]

[2]On June 24, 1969, H. R. Haldeman told Patrick Buchanan in a memorandum: "The President feels very strongly that we need to develop a 'Letters to the Editor' and 'Calls to Broadcasters' program somewhere within the Administration. He is not sure how this should be set up, but he wants a thorough and efficient Nixon network whose task will be to really raise hell with the people who unfairly take us on, and pour praise on those who take a more productive viewpoint. The President feels this might be something that could be done within the framework of the [Republican] National Committee [. . .] The President wants you and Tom Huston to take direction of this project [. . .]" On July 2 Buchanan visited the RNC to discuss the matter and then wrote a memo outlining the program: "The girl at the National Committee would keep on file the names of some dozen to fifty who she could get to write letters on a moment's notice to either national publications or to the networks as soon as word came from the White House. I would hope and expect word to come from the White House quite infrequently, but I can't guarantee this. If word comes to me, for example, I could get in touch with this girl, who could work immediately writing a half a dozen letters herself and who could phone up a number of her correspondents around the country to do the same." Buchanan told Haldeman on July 21 in a "very confidential" memo that a letter had been sent "special delivery to the [*Washington*] *Post* early this afternoon for which we have a volunteer signer, an old friend of mine from Bethesda." The letter signed by John S. Toland begins: "Your whitewash Monday of the episode involving Teddy Kennedy in which a young woman's life was lost is the worst kind of col-

All this was carried out in a highly businesslike manner. For years the Washington press corps had been jokingly referred to as a "herd." Now they were formally recognized by the White House and identified as animals of various kinds, many species of which did not deserve to be on the Ark. Those who were deserving were fed morsels of news. They were the herbivores, the ones who got the "plants," the prepackaged news that is a traditional staple of the journalistic diet. It could all be regarded as rather amusing, except Nixon forgot that even herbivores need water—leaks, that is—to survive. And that became the bone of contention which choked his business, the business of politics. Secrecy drained banter from the dialogue between the press and the White House politicians.

Nixon knew from the outset that he, as President, held a trump card: documents, classified government documents. He and those in his employ could create and then edit them, classify them, destroy them, or feed them to the press. The man whose political career once had hung on the Pumpkin Papers had moved on to a much richer trove.

When George Washington left the White House, his papers were packed into several trunks and taken to Mount Vernon, where in his spacious study on the south side of his home he could peruse them, leaving what he wished for posterity. In 1834 the U.S. government purchased a major part of Washington's papers. As historian Raymond Geselbracht has noted, during the nineteenth century such purchases were "few and always dependent on special congressional appropriation." While the papers of John and John Quincy Adams were in the hands of a family with a sense of history, the papers of others were not treated so well. The bulk of Franklin Pierce's papers, Geselbracht notes,

have simply disappeared. Those of Zachary Taylor and John Tyler vanished almost in their entirety in the flames of the Civil War. . . . The papers of many of the nineteenth century presidents were seriously damaged, and almost every collection suffered from neglect. . . .

In 1903, the several collections of presidential papers in the custody of the government were transferred to the Library of Congress, which immediately began a program to augment those collections and to acquire new ones—most importantly, those of outgoing presidents. By the late 1930s the Library held the principal collections of the papers of twenty-two presidents. . . . Although Theodore Roosevelt and William Howard Taft were cooperative, as was Woodrow Wilson's widow, the widows of Warren Harding and Calvin Coolidge were not; and Herbert Hoover decided to deposit his papers at the Hoover Institution on the campus of his alma mater, Stanford University.[3]

---

laborationist journalism." At the same time a letter written by Buchanan and signed by a volunteer was sent to the *Washington Star* complaining about a Mary McGrory column. HRH51
[3]Raymond Geselbracht, "Archivist's Perspective: The Four Eras in the History of Presidential Papers," *Prologue* (the National Archives journal), spring 1983, pp. 37–42.

By the late 1930s the Library of Congress held about two million pages of presidential papers at a time when Franklin Roosevelt's administration was producing about a million pages a year.

Richard Nixon was fresh out of Duke University law school, an attorney in Whittier, California, his hometown, when Roosevelt announced in December 1938 his intention to house his papers at a facility at Hyde Park which would be administered by the National Archives, a step which Congress subsequently approved. The research facility was opened to the public in May 1946. By early 1950 about 85 percent of the Roosevelt administration's eleven million pages were open to the public. In 1955 the law was amended to permit Harry Truman and subsequent presidents to establish libraries and museums similar to Roosevelt's, also under the aegis of the National Archives.

Although Richard Nixon's concern with the papers and decisions of his immediate predecessors was anything but disinterested, his appetite for that history was, on the whole, quite laudable. The public cannot but applaud a politician who makes every effort to get his facts straight. The regular, comprehensive summary of news and comment that evolved on Nixon's orders was also progressive. One of the more memorable images of the Johnson administration is the series of television sets permanently installed in the President's office; they seemed to symbolize the horizon from which Lyndon Johnson did his policy planning. Nixon wisely banished the television sets and relegated TV monitoring to staff members who could provide him far more of substance in fifteen minutes of reading than he could glean from an hour in front of the tube. The news summaries, of course, represented a monumental effort. Theodore White provides a memorable description of the operation in the Executive Office Building:

> News tickers clacked; video-tape monitors stood by to record the television news shows; newspapers and magazines piled up from all over the country, stacked on tables, desks, wastebaskets, shelves, until the offices looked like a paper-baling operation in a junk shop.[4]

These summaries gave Nixon a strong sense of knowing what the press knew and when they knew it.

When the *New York Times* began to print documents about a quarter-century of Vietnam policy "planning" on Sunday, June 13, 1971, tension between selected segments of the American press and the Nixon White House had had more than two years to build. Nixon had been outraged at leaks in the *Times* in the spring of 1969, and things generally went downhill from there. After Vice President Spiro Agnew delivered, on behalf of the President, a blistering attack on the media in the fall of 1969, FCC Chairman Dean Burch, a Nixon appointee, suggested to Nixon's aides that "a monitoring system [for television and radio] be set up outside

[4]Theodore White, *The Making of the President 1972* (New York: Bantam, 1973), p. 350.

of the administration and the RNC[.] [T]hen, if evidence of bias [is] found [. . .] the findings should be presented to the FCC which then could demand that the networks take measures to correct the situation."[5] When the *New York Times* published in March 1970 the texts of memoranda written by Daniel Moynihan to Nixon, the President took several steps, one of which was to issue instructions that Punch Sulzberger, publisher of the *Times,* be invited to a White House dinner. Another was to investigate the source of the leak.[6] The *Times* published an editorial on March 11 that echoed Nixon's views. "Not since Whittaker Chambers exhumed the 'Pumpkin Papers' at the height of the McCarthy spy scare two decades ago have confidential documents been leaked with so obvious an intent at political annihilation. A Presidential adviser, even one so given to indiscreet utterance as Mr. Moynihan, is entitled to protection in the privacy of his communication with the man he serves. The nation will be the poorer if men of talent fear to serve in Washington because they cannot tell the President what they believe."

To Nixon the Pentagon Papers were "the most massive leak of classified documents in American history."[7] In his memoirs Nixon faults the *Times* for not developing a channel of communication with the White House before publication, but by spring 1971, as we shall see, *Times* editors and reporters had good reason to suspect that the informal channels of communication the newspaper had traditionally maintained with the administration of the day might not work in this matter. They also knew the Supreme Court to be clearly opposed to prepublication censorship since its historic *Near v. Minnesota* (283 U.S. 697) decision in 1931. Moreover, there was widespread belief within the journalistic community that the *Times* had been too cozy with government in the past, particularly in 1961 in failing to report what it had known of plans for the Bay of Pigs invasion. Had those plans been reported more widely, President Kennedy would have been forced to expand the size of the operation to ensure success or else to abort it.

[5]See Nofziger memo of 11/17/69 meeting and Magruder to Haldeman of 11/21/69. HRH54
[6]See Haldeman to Woods of 3/9/70 and Haldeman to Mollenhoff of 3/5/70. HRH58
[7]Richard Nixon, *RN: The Memoirs of Richard Nixon* (New York: Grosset and Dunlap, 1978), p. 508. (Further page references to this work are given in the text.) See Murphy to Haig and Eliot to Kissinger, both dated 6/17/71, in JDE22 for a description by the Defense and State departments of previous incidents of the unauthorized publication of classified information. The State Department memo begins by generally citing Drew Pearson, then the publication by the *Chicago Tribune* in December 1941 of the latest U.S. strategic war plan as "the result of interservice rivalry," and finally the *Amerasia* magazine case of 1945, which involved hundreds of classified documents although "only one secret document was actually published before the FBI moved in." The Pentagon's memo begins by citing the December 1941 *Tribune* leak and another in June 1942 published by the *Trib* of the fact that the U.S. had broken the Japanese military code. The memo refers Haig to David Kahn's description of the episode on page 602 of his book, *The Codebreakers* (Macmillan 1967). The Pentagon memo also cites the publication of the minutes of the meeting between Truman and MacArthur on Wake Island in 1950 as well as articles published by the *New York Times* in December 1953 on the Pentagon's "New Look" program and on July 15, 1956, concerning discussion by the National Security Council of a "proposed military manpower out of 800,000 men."

Whatever the rights and wrongs of the etiquette followed in the weeks before the Pentagon Papers' brouhaha, it does seem clear in hindsight that had Hubert Humphrey won in 1968, he too would have been faced with the leaking of Johnson-era papers on Vietnam, and perhaps earlier than 1971. To liberals and conservatives alike the papers were evidence of incompetence. For the doves the incompetence lay in the decision to get into the war in the first place; for the hawks the incompetence lay in the failure to use sufficient force to achieve a rapid victory from the outset of the war.

Richard Nixon had proper reason for deep concern as the *Times* began to publish the papers. He needed to know as rapidly as possible the extent of the cache, to understand the impact of the publication on his own policy options, to do what he could to make sure the leaks were truly limited to the papers of previous administrations, and to be sure that the sources and methods of U.S. intelligence were protected. He might have used a carrot by establishing communications with the *Times*, but instead he chose the biggest stick he could find. He saw his options in the starkest of terms:

On consideration, we had only two choices: we could do nothing, or we could move for an injunction that would prevent the New York Times *from continuing publication. Policy argued for moving against the* Times; *politics argued against it . . . [Defense Secretary] Mel Laird felt that over 95 percent of the material could be declassified, but we were all still worried about whatever percent— even if it were only one percent—that should not be. If we did not move against the* Times *it would be a signal to every disgruntled bureaucrat in the government that he could leak anything he pleased while the government simply stood by. The* Times*'s decision to publish the documents was clearly the product of the paper's antiwar policy rather than a consistent attachment to principle. (p. 509)*

Although U.S. attorneys successfully obtained a temporary injunction, the Supreme Court quickly ruled in favor of the newspaper, 6 to 3. Thus, Nixon's action against a newspaper in the name of sending a signal to disgruntled bureaucrats resulted in major strengthening of a principle, the ban on prepublication censorship, with which Nixon did not agree. It was a logic which Americans sympathetic to him and concerned about the problems that had been raised would long find baffling.

Meanwhile, Nixon took a quiet step inside the White House. He established an investigative working group which was given a number of assignments, most of them designed to stop government leaks. This, of course, was the group eventually known as the Plumbers.[8] While a President Humphrey likely would not have hauled the *New York Times* into

[8]Although it is not yet certain who first used the word "plumber" to describe someone charged with stopping leaks, the credit may be due the late Murray Chotiner in a memo to Donald Rumsfeld, then director of the Office of Economic Opportunity (OEO) on May 29, 1970. Chotiner was upset that news of some OEO grants in New Mexico had first appeared

court, he, like any President in that situation, probably would have established a White House working group of some sort.

Richard Nixon had many ideas for reorganizing the executive branch of government, some of which seem worthy of close scrutiny. Among these was an idea which first appeared in *Six Crises* and may be applicable to his thinking about the Plumbers as well as, more recently, the late CIA director William Casey's concept of "stand alone" covert action in the Reagan administration. Nixon said he had told John Kennedy in 1960 that "it had been my plan, had I been elected, to set up a new and independent organization for carrying out covert para-military operations" outside the CIA (*Six Crises*, p. 484).

The first target of the Plumbers was Daniel Ellsberg, the man the President said he believed had "stolen" the Pentagon Papers. On June 28, 1971, a Los Angeles grand jury indicted him on one count of theft of government property and one count of unauthorized possession of writings related to national defense. In his memoirs President Nixon provides an important description of the scope and nature of the mandate given the Plumbers:

During his years at the Defense Department, [Ellsberg] had had access to some of the most sensitive information in the entire government. And the Rand Corporation, where he had worked before he gave the Pentagon Papers to the Times, *had 173,000 classified documents in its possession. I wondered how many of these Ellsberg might have and what else he might give to the newspapers. . . .*

Ellsberg was not our only worry. From the first there had been rumors and reports of a conspiracy. The earliest report, later discounted, centered on a friend of Ellsberg, a former Defense Department employee who was then a Fellow at the Brookings Institution. I remembered him from the early days of the administration when I had asked Haldeman to get me a copy of the Pentagon file on the events leading up to Johnson's announcement of the bombing halt at the end of the 1968 campaign. I wanted to know what had actually happened; I also wanted the information as potential leverage against those in Johnson's administration who were now trying to undercut my war policy. I was told that a copy of the bombing halt material and other secret documents had been taken from the Pentagon to Brookings by the same man. I wanted the documents back, but I was told that one copy of the bombing halt report had already "disappeared"; I was sure that if word got out that we wanted it, the copy at Brookings might disappear as well.

In the aftershock of the Pentagon Papers leak and all the uncertainty and renewed criticism of the war it produced, my interest in [a Pentagon file on Johnson's announcement of a bombing halt] was rekindled. When I was told that

in the press attributed to a New Mexico Democratic senator up for reelection. "It will be appreciated if you can have someone call a plumber and plug the leak in the office," Chotiner told Rumsfeld. HRH60 *it was still at Brookings, I was furious and frustrated. In the midst of a war and with our secrets being spilled through printing presses all over the world, top-secret reports were out of reach in the hands of a private think tank largely staffed with antiwar Democrats. It seemed absurd. . . . I said I wanted it back right now—even if it meant having to get it surreptitiously. My determination only increased when I learned of a 1969 Brookings circular announcing a new study of Vietnam, due in 1971, to be based in part on "executive branch documents." The director of the study was Dr. Daniel Ellsberg. . . .*

In early July, John Mitchell reported that the Justice Department had continuing indications that Ellsberg had acted as part of a conspiracy; we received a report that the Soviet Embassy in Washington had received a set of the Pentagon Papers before they had been published in the New York Times. . . . I was told that some of the documents provided to the newspapers were not even part of the McNamara study [Pentagon Papers]. Once again we were facing the question: what more did Ellsberg have, and what else did he plan to do?

Even as our concern about Ellsberg and his possible collaborators was growing, we learned that J. Edgar Hoover was dragging his feet and treating the case on merely a medium-priority basis; he had assigned no special task forces and no extra manpower to it. He evidently felt that the media would automatically make Ellsberg look like a martyr, and the FBI like the "heavy," if it pursued the case vigorously. Mitchell had been told that Hoover was sensitive about his personal friendship with Ellsberg's father-in-law. Finally, other agencies, principally the Defense Department, were conducting simultaneous investigations, and Hoover strongly resisted sharing his territory with anyone.

I did not care about any reasons or excuses. I wanted someone to light a fire under the FBI in its investigation of Ellsberg, and to keep the departments and agencies in active pursuit of leakers. If a conspiracy existed, I wanted to know, and I wanted the full resources of the government brought to bear in order to find out. If the FBI was not going to pursue the case, then we would have to do it ourselves. (pp. 512–13)

On July 23 and again on August 13 the *New York Times* published stories that Nixon said were based on leaked information and which therefore angered him even more. The first was about the administration's fall-back position at the strategic arms limitation talks with the Soviets; the second was based on a CIA report received at the White House only a few days earlier, according to Nixon. "The information in the story was traceable to a highly secret CIA intelligence source. By fall the CIA reported that we were in the midst of the worst outbreak of leaks since 1953." The Plumbers were asked to track both of those leaks as well.

On September 3 the Plumbers organized a break-in at the office of Ellsberg's psychiatrist in an attempt to get information from his files on his motivation and intentions. The original idea for the break-in came from among the Plumbers, not the President, according to one of the group, Gordon Liddy, who said the proposed operation was then authorized from above. In his memoirs Nixon wrote:

I do not believe I was told about the break-in at the time, but it is clear that it was at least in part an outgrowth of my sense of urgency about discrediting what Ellsberg had done and finding out what he might do next. Given the temper of those tense and bitter times and the peril I perceived, I cannot say that had I been informed of it beforehand, I would have automatically considered it unprecedented, unwarranted, or unthinkable. . . . Today the break-in at Ellsberg's psychiatrist's office seems wrong and excessive. But I do not accept that it was as wrong or excessive as what Daniel Ellsberg did, and I still believe that it is a tragedy of circumstances that [my aides] went to jail and Daniel Ellsberg went free. (p. 514)

Although no information on Ellsberg was found during the break-in, the operation was a success from the White House point of view in that no one was caught. To those who knew about it, the mission demonstrated something even more significant, an off-the-shelf, stand-alone, in-house capability to penetrate covertly any chosen target, for tasks ranging from the implantation of listening devices to the photography of documents. The documents obtained from this trial run were meaningless, but in less than three months the focus of attention had begun to shift to political targets.

"In hindsight," Nixon wrote,

I can see that, once I realized the Vietnam war could not be ended quickly and that I was going to be up against an anti-war movement that was able to dominate the media with its attitudes and values, I was sometimes drawn into the very frame of mind I so despised in the leaders of that movement. They increasingly came to justify almost anything in the name of forcing an immediate end to a war they considered unjustified and immoral. I was similarly driven to preserve the government's ability to conduct foreign policy and to conduct it in the way that I felt would best bring peace. I believed that national security was involved. I still believe it today, and in the same circumstances, I would act now as I did then. History will make the final judgment on the actions, reactions, and excesses of both sides; it is a judgment I do not fear. (pp. 514–15)

In one important sense the involvement of Gordon Liddy in the break-in at the office of Ellsberg's psychiatrist is evidence corroborating Nixon's description of his attitude about the episode. The press was tracking Liddy's activities weeks *before* the break-in, and the administration had even used Liddy as a spokesman. The *Washington Post* described Liddy this way on August 2, 1971:

This spring, at the National Rifle Association's annual convention, the spokesman for the Nixon administration was a man named G. Gordon Liddy, appointed in 1969 as special assistant to the Secretary of the Treasury.

Liddy, who was formerly an FBI agent and later an upstate New York prosecutor, offered the NRA anniversary congratulations from the Nixon administration and went on to say that the decline in support for gun-control legislation during the two years of the Nixon administration "did not come by accident." . . .

On July 20, Liddy was transferred out of the Treasury Department to the

White House Domestic Council. A Treasury Department spokesman says the transfer was a promotion [. . .] Liddy himself declined to be interviewed by the Washington Post.*"*[9]

The next day Liddy crowed in a memo to his boss, Egil "Bud" Krogh, "It is not every staffer who is attacked by name in the *Washington Post* within ten days of coming aboard!"

On August 24, just before going to California for the break-in, Liddy told Krogh about the possibility of running again for a House seat from Dutchess County, New York, in 1972. While using such a public figure as Liddy in the California break-in was dumb tradecraft in the eyes of intelligence professionals, it bolsters the argument that Nixon and/or his senior aides did not feel they were doing anything wrong by organizing a White House burglary team.

In October Krogh turned down a proposal by Liddy that he and Howard Hunt be sent to Latin America on a mission to gather intelligence on the cocaine trade. Liddy cited his expertise in drug smuggling and Hunt's "language ability, singular familiarity with the Latin American underworld in general and his contacts and relationship with the Cubans. As you know, the cocaine trade is dominated by the pre-Castro Cubans. It is this element with which Hunt is so intimately familiar."[10]

At the beginning of the 1972 presidential campaign the political rules most in the public eye were those governing campaign financing. It was a subject which long had absorbed Richard Nixon. His concern about financing the 1972 campaign began, in fact, in late 1968 even before he was inaugurated. When the 1972 political season rolled around the press was having a jolly time with fat-cat contributors said to be skewing the American political process. No one in the press ever dreamed that political burglary would be an issue before the season was over.

As Richard Nixon noted in his memoirs: "My reaction to the Watergate break-in was completely pragmatic. If it was cynical, it was a cynicism born of experience. I had been in politics too long, and seen everything from dirty tricks to vote fraud. I could not muster much moral outrage over a political bugging" (p. 628).

Numerous observers, including Jimmy Carter, have called Watergate simply a domestic matter, but the affair had broad implications for American foreign policy and, therefore, the world. Nixon has said that the revelations of 1973 prevented him from carrying out a Middle East initiative he was planning that year. Could the Yom Kippur War and the subsequent oil embargo have been avoided had there not been a Watergate? Could the Congress have denied a request from a strong, internationally successful Richard Nixon for support for South Vietnam in 1975? The list of implications is very long. Certainly among the most important is that the lust for stolen papers in the short term resulted in a massive disclosure of U.S. government documents, one comparable in size to the

[9]"Odd Alliance Forms After Gun Raid" by Jim Mann. JDE21
[10]Liddy's memos to Krogh are in JDE21.

Pentagon Papers, and in the long term, of course, created new laws and rules governing presidential papers. Although the irony is nothing short of extraordinary, those struggling for an accurate, nonpartisan, and informed American journalism should forever be grateful to Nixon and/or his associates for what they did.

More than fifteen years after the event it is still not certain whether Nixon or one of his close aides pulled the trigger. The available evidence suggests that the process may have been comparable to bad investment decisions made after looking at the upside potential but without considering the downside risk.

June 12 was, according to Gordon Liddy, the day he received approval for the second covert penetration of the Democratic National Committee offices at the Watergate complex. John Mitchell, Liddy's boss, met with President Nixon from 4:09 to 5:40 P.M., with H. R. Haldeman, Nixon's chief of staff, participating in the final hour. In his memoirs Nixon says that at that meeting he asked Mitchell to tell Vice President Spiro Agnew "that I had made the decision definitely to have him on the ticket again as my running mate." At the time, Liddy chose to go to jail rather than reveal what he knew. However, in his book published in 1980 Liddy said that it was on June 8 that he passed the first envelope containing intelligence obtained as a result of the first break-in to Jeb Magruder to be passed to Mitchell.[11] White House records show that President Nixon spoke with Mitchell on the phone that day from 10:30 to 10:51 A.M. On Friday, June 9, Magruder asked Liddy whether he could organize a second break-in. After Liddy responded positively, Magruder said he would have a decision for Liddy by the following Monday. President Nixon, meanwhile, phoned Mitchell twice that June 9. They talked from 10:34 to 10:47 A.M. and again from 4:55 to 5:07 P.M. On Sunday, June 11, Nixon again called Mitchell, and they talked from 10:41 to 10:54 A.M.

On the fateful Monday, June 12, Magruder stressed the importance of photographing *"everything"* (Liddy's emphasis) in the Democratic Party's files, according to Liddy. Moving and replacing the electronic surveillance devices was a secondary objective. Liddy therefore instructed the burglars to take two cameras and fifty rolls of film with them, enough to photograph 1,800 pages of "classified" documents of the political enemy. Liddy also said that on June 12 an aide to Haldeman, Gordon Strachan, expressed knowledge of the intelligence product of the first entry, and Liddy told him of the plans for the second break-in. Liddy did not disclose the times of his conversations with Magruder and Strachan that day, so it is not yet clear when they took place in relation to the afternoon conversation in the oval office between the President, Mitchell, and Haldeman.

On June 14 Liddy told his colleague, Howard Hunt, of the plans, and Hunt immediately was skeptical. "Looks like high risk, low gain to me," Hunt replied. On June 15 Liddy, Magruder, and others met with Mitchell. Liddy sat immediately to the right of Mitchell and placed a thick envelope

[11]Gordon Liddy, *Will* (New York: St. Martin's, 1980).

containing more transcripts on the right rear corner of Mitchell's desk, saying, "That's for you." Mitchell nodded his head. "The problem we have will be corrected this weekend, sir," Liddy said he told Mitchell. Mitchell again nodded his head slowly. Mitchell never touched the envelope while Liddy was present. In the wee hours of Saturday morning—June 17—the White House burglars were caught red-handed by police in the Democratic Party headquarters in the Watergate building complex.

In the uproar that followed there was, of course, little coherent discussion of the steps and the underlying motive(s) that led from the break-in at the office of Ellsberg's psychiatrist to the historic blunders of mid-June 1972. There was much effort to suggest that the actions were those of patriots who simply had been misguided and overly zealous. This essentially was the theory of noble motive. Nixon himself outlined the strongest version of this rationale in a 1973 conversation with John Dean, his counsel, in which he said that what had happened should be considered "not only [to] be legal but that it was totally necessary because of the violence, the demonstrations, the kind of activities that we knew were threatened against us in our [1972] convention and in our campaign and in all of our appearances. We had to have intelligence about what they were going to do [so] that we could in turn issue instructions." In this view, in other words, the patriots were not even misguided or overly zealous. However, since those who planned the operations believed themselves to be following orders down a chain of command that began with President Nixon, it is reasonable to examine motives that were geared to political survival. With benefit of hindsight Gordon Liddy himself raises such a question about the marching orders he received June 12. *"The purpose of the second Watergate break-in was to find out what* [Democratic Chairman Lawrence] *O'Brien had of a derogatory nature about us, not for us to get something on him or the Democrats,"* Liddy says with emphasis. Was there any political skeleton, real or imagined, in Richard Nixon's closet in 1972 that could have persuaded him the Democrats might have some political dynamite? Although the answer is yes, the emphasis to this day has to be on the possibility that the skeleton was, from a hard-nosed Washington point of view, largely imaginary. It is a story that begins in Richard Nixon's first term as Vice President, one that Gordon Liddy was trying to understand as he was preparing the Watergate break-ins.

The Howard Hughes Medical Institute of Miami Beach, Florida, filed for tax-exempt status with the Internal Revenue Service on June 1, 1955, according to a 1972 John Dean memorandum. The IRS denied the exemption on the basis that the institute was merely a mechanism contrived to siphon off otherwise taxable income into a tax-exempt organization. The institute filed an appeal on March 26, 1956. On December 10, 1956, a month after Nixon was reelected Vice President, Howard Hughes, a Southern California entrepreneur, loaned Richard Nixon's brother Donald $205,000 through indirect means. This loan was placed on the public record through a deed of trust filed in the office of the Los Angeles County recorder. On March 1, 1957, the IRS not only reversed its ruling and gave the institute tax-exempt status but also made the ruling retroactive to the date of the institute's formation in 1954, saving the institute $482,697 in back taxes.[12]

On October 1, 1957, the Los Angeles bureau of the Associated Press sent to its members a brief account of the fact that Donald Nixon was selling five restaurant–gift shops he owned in order to satisfy creditors. Had the press done its job properly, an investigation might well have exonerated Richard Nixon of impropriety. In theory, had the IRS and the Nixons cooperated with an inquiry, the whole matter could have been wrapped up in one article. That, however, was not what happened.

In judging the relative scandal potential of the affair, it is well to keep in mind that President Eisenhower's chief of staff, Sherman Adams, was forced to resign after the public learned he had accepted a vicuña coat as a gift from a businessman.[13]

As the presidential campaign was heating up in the fall of 1960, word of a mysterious loan to Donald Nixon began making the rounds of the Southern California rumor mills and was apparently originally insti-gated by one of the attorneys marginally involved. The press began inves-tigating, but no one opened up the subject until Peter Edson, a syndicated columnist, did so on October 24, just two weeks before the election. The account apparently was given to him by the Nixon camp, but it did not mention the Hughes connection. Edson's column persuaded Drew Pear-son, another syndicated columnist, to put out what he knew about the Hughes connection.[14] That opened the floodgates, and journalists were off and running in a flash. On October 28 Anthony Lewis reported in the *New York Times* that the deed of trust linking the loan to the Nixons was on parcel one of lot ten, tract 3359 in Whittier. The reporting in that two-week interval noted that Trans World Airlines, of which Hughes was the majority owner, had some favorable rulings from the Civil Aeronautics Board in the late 1950s, and that a Justice Department antitrust suit against another Hughes company had been resolved by consent decree; there was no mention of the Hughes Medical Institute or the IRS reversal. Once the story was in the press the Democrats used it against Nixon at will. Shortly after the election Robert Kennedy reportedly said that the loan stories probably had hurt Nixon at the polls. No doubt the affair made a major contribution to Nixon's conclusion that the press had cost him the 1960 election.

[12]See Dean to Ehrlichman, February 3, 1972.
[13]In 1970 Nixon's friend Robert Abplanalp gave him a pool table, which created logistical problems described by Haldeman in a memo on April 30 to Higby: "It apparently will not fit in the solarium on the third floor of the Residence which is where they had originally planned to put it, and therefore he'd like to find another place for it. Mrs. Nixon had suggested the Map Room after we remodel it, but the President feels he'd rather keep that as an office. He wonders if there is a room in the EOB that could be set up as the President's Pool Room." HRH59
[14]The *New York Times*, November 1, 1960, p. 24.

In 1961 Robert Kennedy, then the attorney general, ordered an investigation of the loan which concluded that no laws had been violated, but the investigation apparently did not include the IRS reversal, which had not yet been called to public attention. Kennedy and his aides, however, did not disclose to the press either the fact of the investigation or its result, a step which in fairness to Nixon they should have taken once they had reached their conclusion. Certainly the results of that investigation would have been extremely helpful to Nixon during his campaign for governor of California in 1962; at that time questions about the Hughes loan were a regular feature of his encounters with the press.[15] In the end the Hughes loan affair played an important role in his defeat, probably second only to the Cuban missile crisis, which, of course, dominated the news in the final days of the campaign.[16]

Given the trouble the Hughes loan had caused him in 1960 and 1962, it was not at all surprising that Richard Nixon as President would want to keep a weather eye on Howard Hughes and on Drew Pearson, whose reporting on the Hughes connection had opened the press floodgates in 1960. In 1969, five days before he was sworn in, Nixon reminded Haldeman "to see that someone is assigned to read the Pearson columns for the purpose of determining whether anyone in the Administration has violated my counsel for them not to talk to his people." This was just a week after the President-elect had reminded Haldeman to begin beating the bushes for funds for the 1972 campaign.

Meanwhile, the election of a Republican President and a Democratic Congress in tandem for the first time in more than a century was no small cause for concern among the corporations pursuing their interests in Washington. They would have to double the size of their lobbying staffs or else hire those skillful enough to navigate both sides of the political street. After all, what would Richard Nixon and his staff think about a cause being pursued by a prominent Democratic lobbyist? In one case the lobbyist also happened to be chairman of the Democratic National Committee, Lawrence O'Brien, and the corporate interests were those of none other than Howard Hughes. One can only imagine Nixon's reaction when he learned that O'Brien, a close associate of the Kennedys, was working for Hughes at the same time he publicly condemned Nixon's policies. If Richard Nixon had the IRS reversal of 1957 on his conscience as of early 1970, he might have been especially astounded to see a Hughes representative, of all people, complaining publicly about the possibility of political influence being used on the IRS. Such astonishment, if it existed, might contribute to a decision to be aggressive in a political approach to the Hughes empire rather than keeping one's distance, a far more prudent strategy, which would seem logical given the unhappy memories of 1960 and 1962.

[15]"The Nixon Family and the Hughes Loan" by James R. Phelan, *The Reporter,* August 16, 1962, helped spark a revival of press interest in the loan. The 1961 investigation of the loan was first reported in the *New York Times,* January 24, 1972.
[16]Nixon, *Memoirs,* pp. 242–43.

"A serious power struggle erupted within the Hughes empire" in 1970, Nixon writes in his memoirs, one "marked by vicious infighting among several factions" (p. 965). The record suggests that the President may have helped create the "power struggle." Nixon's fund-raisers took a bold approach toward Hughes no later than March and early April 1970. Meanwhile, the President ordered an investigation into Larry O'Brien's business connections. It is not yet clear whether he realized from the outset that there was a connection between O'Brien and the Hughes empire.

On March 9 H R. Haldeman instructed Lyn Nofziger: "In moving ahead on Operation O'Brien, we should push hard to get demands made that he disclose his clients and the nature of his affiliation with each. We should look for every opportunity to keep the heat on the DNC and O'Brien" (HRH58). A copy of the memo went to Murray Chotiner, who told Haldeman in a March 12 memo: "I have matters that are being checked very carefully concerning Illinois, Indiana, Maine, Massachusetts, Missouri, New Jersey, North Dakota, Ohio, Wisconsin and activities of O'Brien. I will *not* be sending you memorandums concerning any of these, but if at any time you wish to know the status, I will be glad to give you an oral report."

Meanwhile, in March John Mitchell asked the Antitrust Division of the Justice Department to look into the possible purchase by Hughes of the Dunes Hotel in Las Vegas. In 1968 the Antitrust Division had prevented Hughes from acquiring another Las Vegas hotel, the Stardust, after he had acquired four other hotels on the Las Vegas strip in the previous thirteen months.[17] On March 23 FBI Director Hoover told the Antitrust Division that his Las Vegas field office had been told that the Dunes had been told by Hughes officials that Hughes had been assured by the Antitrust Division that there would be "no objection" to the purchase of the Dunes by Hughes.[18] On April 3 a Hughes official made a major contribution to the Nixon political coffers during a meeting at Nixon's home in San Clemente, California.[19] However, apparently no one told Nixon about the contribution until after the 1972 campaign. Bebe Rebozo kept that contribution and a later one from the Hughes organization, a total of $100,000, in a safe-deposit box in his Miami bank. "He wanted to make sure that I was not embarrassed again by any connection with Howard Hughes," Nixon writes in his memoirs, "so he decided not to mention the money to me and simply to hold on to it until after the [1972] election, when he thought it could either be used to help pay any deficit the campaign had incurred or for the 1974 Congressional election" (p. 965).

On April 13, 1970, Lawrence O'Brien issued a press release criticizing the fact that Clark Mollenhoff, a White House aide and former journalist, was reviewing IRS records, a criticism which Nixon promptly rejected.

[17]Senate Watergate Hearings, vol. 26, p. 12876.
[18]Senate Watergate Hearings, vol. 26, p. 12878.
[19]Senate Watergate Hearings, vol. 20, p. 9531.

The President, Rebozo, and Attorney General Mitchell apparently did not learn for some months that O'Brien was connected with the Hughes organization and that the connection was through the head of the Hughes operations in Nevada, Robert Maheu. In the national uproar following the killing of four students during an antiwar protest at Kent State in May, O'Brien was among those publicly critical of the Nixon administration, a criticism the President did not forget. O'Brien "virtually accused me of killing the four students," Nixon writes in his memoirs. On May 12 Murray Chotiner, a Nixon political aide for more than two decades, told H. R. Haldeman in a memorandum that he had begun to look into O'Brien's activities systematically.

In August Lawrence Higby, Haldeman's deputy, wrote a memorandum to John Dean expressing concern about a case being pursued by the IRS against one of the parties involved in the Hughes–Don Nixon loan: "The prosecution of this case could reopen that entire issue which could be very damaging politically." While such a decision coming to Dean, the President's lawyer, through the political chain of command was favorable to the Hughes interests broadly speaking, it also constituted explicit recognition at a senior level that anything the Nixon administration did for or to the Hughes empire that caught the public eye could have serious political consequences.

One result of the war within the Hughes empire in 1970 was that the "emperor," Howard Hughes, chose his new ambassador to Washington from among the ranks of the Nixon officeholders rather than from the career bureaucracy of his organization. The new Hughes envoy was Robert Bennett, the son of a Republican senator from Utah, Wallace Bennett, who was on especially good terms with the Nixon White House. In December 1970, one aide to President Nixon described Bennett as "a good friend of ours [who] has volunteered to do anything we want at any time with the Hughes people." The White House expectation was that Bennett would be an ambassador (and intelligence agent) from the White House in the Hughes empire rather than an ambassador (and potential agent of penetration) from Hughes.

The fact that Bebe Rebozo apparently chose not to tell his friend the President about the $100,000 contribution from Hughes did not mean that Rebozo did not discuss matters involving Hughes, including the Hughes-O'Brien relationship, with Nixon. In a memorandum dictated on January 14, 1971, Nixon told Haldeman that on the basis of information he had received from Rebozo it was time to plant stories in the press about the relationship between O'Brien and Hughes once Rebozo's information was verified, perhaps by Charles Colson. Maybe hoping for a less passionate investigation, Haldeman initially steered the assignment to John Dean, but that merely delayed the inevitable. Keeping Colson from pursuing O'Brien was about as easy as keeping Paul Revere from his midnight ride.

During the Nixon years Charles Colson appeared to the public as a rather opaque presidential aide compared to the Germanic trio, H. R.

Haldeman, John Ehrlichman, and Henry Kissinger. Colson, however, was one of Nixon's favorites, and with good reason. He was eager, loyal, energetic, aggressive, efficient. But of his many traits perhaps the most important were his scathing sense of humor and his storehouse of political lore, centered on New England in general and the Kennedys in particular. It has often been said that Richard Nixon had no hobbies, but that is not true. His idea of relaxation was shooting the breeze about politics, and from 1970 to 1972 there was no one Nixon enjoyed talking politics with more than Charles Colson. Colson was an ex-Marine as well as a talented court jester. He was Nixon's loyal political viceroy, as well as Mark Russell and Rodney Dangerfield rolled into one. Colson also engendered a distinctive loyalty among his own staff. One of them, Douglas Hallett, expressed it this way: "When I first learned I was going to be placed with him, I must confess I was rather alarmed. In some quarters I know, he has the reputation for being a mean, ornery, hard-line son of a bitch who never uses a razor blade when he has available a two-ton howitzer. Although I find myself in frequent disagreement with Mr. Colson and feel that the instant-response-to-any-and-everything mentality over here can be very counterproductive, I've never enjoyed working for anybody more and am learning one hell of a lot from him. And besides, he's such a lovable mean, ornery, hard-line son of a bitch that it's impossible to dislike him even when I think his ideas are utterly insane."[20]

Charles Colson was born in Brookline, Massachusetts, of Swedish ancestry somewhat after John and Robert Kennedy but a bit before Michael Dukakis. He graduated from Brookline High a couple of years ahead of Dukakis and then went to Brown University, where he became a Nixon Republican. "The more the professors damned him, the more I liked him," Colson once wrote a friend. As a Marine, Colson was among those who waited offshore in vain for a signal to invade Guatemala in 1954. After migrating to Washington to work for the Massachusetts Republican Senator Leverett Saltonstall in the late 1950s, Colson crossed party lines for the only time in his life to vote for Harry Byrd, Sr., in Virginia in 1958. From 1958 to 1962 Colson was Secretary of the New England Senators Conference, an innocent conservative, as he would tell it, in a Washington then dominated by the Democratic jackals. In 1962 Colson was "deeply involved" in the campaign to beat Edward Kennedy in Massachusetts. In 1964 as a Washington lobbyist he made "by my standards a very healthy contribution" to the Barry Goldwater campaign and a contribution to the unsuccessful effort to defeat Senator Edmund Muskie in Maine. After a conversation with his political hero, Richard Nixon, Colson worked in Nixon's 1968 campaign before joining his staff late in 1969, where he quickly caught the President's notice and moved upward in authority and influence.

On January 26, 1971, John Dean confirmed that O'Brien's connec-

[20]Hallett to Chapin and Colson, August 27, 1971, CWC129.

tion with the Hughes organization had been through Maheu, by now no longer the head of the Hughes operation in Nevada, and that the friendship dated from their Boston years. Two days later Haldeman gave Dean these further instructions:

You should continue to keep in contact with Bob Bennett, as well as looking for other sources of information on this subject. Once Bennett gets back to you with his final report, you and Chuck Colson should get together and come up with a way to leak the appropriate information. Frankly, I can't see any way to handle this without involving Hughes so the problem of "embarrassing" him seems to be a matter of degree. However, we should keep Bob Bennett and Bebe out of it at all costs.

At the beginning of February CBS's "60 Minutes" aired a story about the Hughes empire which included an interview with Robert Maheu. The timing, perhaps, was coincidental, but the report came just three weeks after the President gave instructions to begin leaking information about Hughes and O'Brien. Maheu, a former FBI agent, was in the middle of that relationship.

By the summer of 1971 Robert Bennett began to act like a Hughes agent rather than a White House envoy to Hughes. It was inevitable and, at least from the Hughes standpoint, by no means necessarily improper. Charles Colson carefully laid out the problem in a memorandum to John Dean on July 16:

Bob Bennett saw me yesterday with respect to a matter I understand he had already discussed with you. That is, the tax status of the principal stockholder of Hughes Aircraft Co., a private medical research foundation [apparently the Howard Hughes Medical Institute].

I am sure you are familiar with the facts of the case. Treasury is attempting to impose regulations requiring medical research foundations to spend at least 4% of their endowment value per year. The entire endowment of the Hughes medical research foundation is the common stock of Hughes Aircraft. Hence, Hughes Aircraft must produce dividends of at least 8 percent a year which is a pretty tall order for any private corporation.

I can fully understand why the Treasury is taking the attitude it is. Obviously the Congress deliberately left a loophole in the law. Nonetheless a loophole that many private foundations might try to use. On the other hand, I could see no good argument for not including a grandfather clause that would not virtually put out of business the Hughes medical research foundation.

Yesterday the general manager of Hughes Aircraft met with Charlie Walker [of Treasury]. Walker seemed interested in a grandfather clause approach but his tax experts indicated that might put into question the validity of the entire regulation and I can't conceive of why that would be the case.

Because of some possibilities that we have been working on with respect to Hughes, this is a matter of considerable importance and I wonder if you could pursue it to see if there isn't some possible way to work a resolution. Could you advise me, please?

On August 4 Dean sent a memorandum to Walker about the Hughes Medical Institute, attaching a recent letter from Robert Bennett and requesting a draft response from Walker. The businesslike tone of those memoranda suggests that Colson and Dean did not yet appreciate the size of the snake pit into which they were falling by opening up the question of the Howard Hughes Medical Institute. However, presumably they began to hear rattling with the publication of a column by Jack Anderson on August 6. After years of working for Drew Pearson, Anderson had taken over the column upon Pearson's retirement. Anderson reported that in 1968 Maheu, acting on orders from Hughes, had contributed $100,000 to the Nixon campaign. The money allegedly had been skimmed from the Silver Slipper, a Hughes casino, and delivered to Bebe Rebozo by Richard Danner, another Hughes aide. With the 1968 contribution essentially public knowledge, lawyers like Colson and Dean had to appreciate that any decision on the grandfather clause proposal favorable to Hughes now could reasonably be construed as the result of a bribe. This would be particularly true of any funds contributed by Hughes since the President's inauguration in 1969.

On December 7 McGraw-Hill announced plans to publish the memoirs of Howard Hughes, allegedly written in collaboration with novelist Clifford Irving, an expatriate American resident in Ibiza, a Spanish island in the Mediterranean. *Life* magazine was to publish excerpts of the book. Hughes spokesmen immediately charged that the book was a hoax, but it was weeks before the press was able to confirm that the denial was accurate.

Howard Hunt was among those under the Hughes umbrella who were assigned the task of convincing the press that the Irving book was a hoax. Hunt had been a career officer in the CIA. During World War II Hunt served in the armed forces, worked as a correspondent for *Life*, began a career as a novelist, and worked for the OSS. After the war, he joined the CIA. His last overseas posting was to Madrid in 1965 and 1966. Back in Washington in the late 1960s Hunt met Charles Colson at the Brown University Club in Washington. By 1968 Colson had become the club president and Hunt the vice president. After Colson went to the White House, he offered Hunt a job. Hunt, however, chose to retire from government service and draw his pension. In May 1970 Hunt went to work for Robert R. Mullen and Company, a public relations firm across the street from the White House. Late that year Mullen sold the company to Robert Bennett, which put Hunt in the position of working for the Hughes empire while also having a close connection to the White House.

In his memoirs Hunt writes that early in 1971 he told Colson of his "dissatisfaction" with the turn of events at the Mullen Company.[21] Colson, however, expressed optimism that Hunt would be able to work with Robert Bennett. At the same time, White House documents show, Colson was

[21]E. Howard Hunt, *Undercover: Memoirs of an American Secret Agent* (New York: Berkley, 1974), p. 142. Further page references to this book are given in the text.

developing plans to use Hunt in a new public relations organization conceived in the White House which would support American policy in Vietnam. It was also in early 1971 that Clifford Irving began work on his Hughes hoax, which in the intelligence community would be considered a classic disinformation campaign. Hunt recalls that in late 1971 he did his best on behalf of Hughes to convince *Life* that the Irving book was, in fact, a hoax. "As a former *Life* correspondent, I was in an excellent position to argue the matter . . . on professional terms." Hunt says he spent "long hours . . . arguing the pros and cons" of the Irving book with a *Life* reporter (p. 180).

Later in his book Hunt carefully records his friendship with Irving when both were together in the same federal prison, Irving on charges related to the hoax and Hunt on Watergate. Hunt says, "we frequently ate together, discussing the publishing business, agents and our plans for the future. . . . The fact that both of us had lived in Spain provided another conversational link" (p. 313). The only pertinent point which Hunt does not discuss is just precisely when it was that he first met Irving. It may be entirely coincidental that Irving began his work on Hughes in early 1971 not long after the President of the United States ordered his staff to plant stories in the press about Howard Hughes, and the President's chief of staff ordered Colson to "come up with a way to leak the appropriate information" about the Hughes empire.

On Sunday, January 16, 1972, CBS ran another story on Howard Hughes on its "60 Minutes" program—a bombshell. Noah Dietrich, who had been the chief executive officer of Hughes Tool when that Hughes subsidiary had been involved in the loan to Donald Nixon, said on camera that not long after the loan was made in late 1956, the IRS had reversed an earlier ruling against the Hughes Medical Institute. Dietrich added that it was possible that the timing of the reversal had been purely coincidental; apparently he had never pursued the matter. In general, however, the CBS report emphasized the Hughes connections with the Democrats and also said that the loan eventually had been repaid. Richard Nixon read about the CBS report in his White House news summary of January 18, and his initial impression apparently was favorable. "Not bad!" he wrote in a marginal note for Haldeman.

On January 24 the *New York Times* prominently featured a story describing the Kennedy administration's investigation in 1961 of the Hughes loan to Donald Nixon. The timing of the story was rather curious. It had been more than four years since Richard Nixon returned to the national political scene. Presumably an enterprising reporter could have tracked down that investigation at any point. In this instance, however, the story appeared just eight days after the revelation of the IRS reversal on "60 Minutes" and left the impression that the Kennedy investigation had included the reversal, which apparently was not the case. The story was attributed to "government files" that had "come into the possession" of the *Times*. On January 16 the *Times* had given front-page treatment to a story by Wallace Turner saying that the Clifford Irving book would reveal a great deal about the relationship between Howard Hughes and Richard Nixon. Therefore the thrust of the January 24 story, also written by Turner, was not only to dissuade the press from pursuing the IRS reversal but also to throw cold water on both the Irving saga and the notion that there was anything worth pursuing in the relationship of the President to the Hughes empire. In a recent telephone conversation, Turner said he could not recall how he came upon the "government files," but he was certain it had not been from sources in the White House. He said he could not be certain that the information had not been planted with him, "but as far as I know, it was not."

On Thursday, January 27, Gordon Liddy presented his proposals for Operation "Gemstone," the Plumbers' plan, to Attorney General John Mitchell in a meeting also attended by Jeb Magruder and John Dean. The following afternoon Mitchell and Haldeman met with the President for forty minutes, in the first of only three meetings between the three to discuss political action in the first six months of 1972. White House logs tend to support Nixon's claim that he didn't pay enough attention to political matters in the first six months of 1972. In the last six months of 1971 Mitchell and the President met a total of thirty-two times, but there were only six such meetings in the first six months of 1972, including the three in which Haldeman was present. If the President did discuss Gemstone in a positive light with the attorney general and his chief of staff on January 28, it represented a sharp reversal of his views since 1968. According to one highly knowledgeable participant in Nixon's 1968 staff meetings, a suggestion was made to then candidate Nixon that the Democratic campaign's telephones be tapped, and he emphatically rejected it.

The following Monday, January 31, John Dean informed Haldeman and Ehrlichman that Jack Anderson was on the trail of the 1956 loan. "I learned today that Jack Anderson has his leg man, Les Whitten, looking for information on the Hughes loan to Don Nixon." In a blind note for the files Dean added: "Ed Cohen, Treasury Department, called to inform me that a Mr. Olscher—former staff man with Putnam—had been contacted by Whitten. It appeared like a fishing expedition." It is not difficult to imagine the tremor that ran through the White House. In December and January the White House and apparently the FBI were investigating the leak to Jack Anderson of top secret documents on the India-Pakistan war.[22] Haldeman called them the Anderson Papers. Relations between the White House and the press were, if anything, even worse than during the "credibility gap" of the Johnson administration. On Tuesday, February 1, the President and John Mitchell met with California Governor Ronald

[22]For example, John Dean told Fred Malek on December 15, 1971, that an attached Jack Anderson article "suggests a need to re-review our leak crackdown. This story would appear to contain an incredible leak, including what I would presume would be considerable amounts of classified information. You may want to consult with Bud Krogh on this one as he has also been working in this area, but I don't know if he has been specifically working on this case." JWD4

Reagan for close to half an hour, after which the meeting, listed as a discussion of the West Coast dock strike, was expanded to include other participants.

On Thursday, February 3, John Dean essentially corroborated Noah Dietrich's allegations about the sequence of events leading up to the March 1, 1957, IRS reversal of its position on the Hughes Medical Institute in a memorandum for John Ehrlichman. The memo did not discuss Richard Nixon's role, if any, in bringing about the sequence of events. Nevertheless, it was a job of investigative reporting that would have won Dean an award had he been in the newspaper business. It outlined what might be around the corner if Anderson and his associates were as determined as they appeared to be. Also on February 3 the *New York Times* carried a story that Hank Greenspun, a Las Vegas journalist friendly with Robert Maheu, had a cache of what were described as 200 memoranda by Howard Hughes. The following day, February 4, Gordon Liddy discussed a now scaled-down version of his Gemstone plan with the attorney general, John Dean, and Jeb Magruder. Again, however, no clear-cut decision from Mitchell was forthcoming.

Although the President's attention that February was focused on his trip to China, other wheels involving political intelligence continued to turn. In one operation called "Sedan Chair" an operative posing as a chauffeur loyal to Senator Edmund Muskie, the early Democratic front-runner, surreptitiously photographed documents given him for delivery or mailing. Another was a "pranks" operation which, it later emerged, included the mailing of fictitious letters to newspapers in an effort to undermine Muskie. Howard Hunt told Robert Bennett about the Muskie penetration, and Bennett helped him recruit a college student to penetrate the Muskie headquarters. Bennett also proposed consideration of what amounted to a joint venture, a break-in at the office of Hank Greenspun, and introduced Hunt and Liddy to the chief of security for the Hughes empire.[23] Nothing came of that, but in the process the Hughes empire gained an excellent understanding of the extent of the White House's black-bag capability as well as of the operations penetrating the Democrats. According to Liddy, he and Hunt discussed in oblique terms a project to assassinate Jack Anderson one day over lunch. Liddy also passed along the information that Hunt, who was quoting Charles Colson, said a top U.S. intelligence source abroad would be dead in days because of an Anderson story. They concluded that the best tradecraft to use would be to make it look as if Anderson had been a victim of street crime.

By the end of February, Charles Colson had fresh reason to wish Jack Anderson dead. On February 28 he circulated advance copies of a forthcoming column charging that ITT had received favored treatment from the Justice Department in return for a major campaign contribution. At the White House it was believed that Lawrence O'Brien had fed Anderson the story, which rapidly became a major focus of public attention and

[23]Hunt, *Undercover*, pp. 193–94.

a major headache for the President and his staff. On March 3 Steve Karalekas, an aide to Charles Colson, passed along a tip that O'Brien "and two cohorts were involved in very shady dealings with LBJ," namely, "an extremely lucrative leasing arrangement" connected with the headquarters building of the Department of Transportation. On March 7 the President told Haldeman to find out where the financial support for the Democrats was coming from.

As March unfolded, the White House, under the pressures created by the ITT disclosures, was forced to begin to think defensively. Jack Anderson, meanwhile, continued to pursue the 1956 Hughes loan matter. On March 21 he went to see William Ridgely, the financial clerk of the Senate, who immediately relayed the essence of the conversation to Rose Mary Woods, who typed it up in a memo to John Ehrlichman. Anderson had a copy of a document that Ridgely had notarized for Richard Nixon's mother on October 12, 1956. "I took the document from him [Anderson] for a minute to look at the signature," Ridgely told Woods, "and it was mine. It was something about Union Oil Co. It was a copy of an official record and Anderson said they went out to California and dug it up. It has something to do with the Hughes loan. He kept asking me whether Mrs. Hannah Nixon was in Washington on that date. I told him that she had to have been there—that otherwise I would not have notarized the signature." Woods told Ehrlichman that the 1956 campaign file showed that the Vice President had been on a campaign tour from October 9 to 19 (JDE23).

In response to a request from above, on March 30 Charles Colson carefully assessed the potential damage from the ITT matter. In a memorandum to Haldeman, Colson pointed out that Herb Klein's memorandum of June 30, 1971, to Haldeman had spelled out "the $400,000 arrangement with ITT," and a copy of that memo had been sent to Attorney General Mitchell, who at the time was responsible for putting together a settlement with ITT. "This put the AG on constructive notice at least of the ITT commitment at that time and before the settlement, facts which he has denied under oath. We don't know whether we have recovered all the copies," Colson told Haldeman.[24] In a phrase that was not yet in common use, Colson had described a "smoking gun." The Senate was already wondering whether the man chosen to succeed Mitchell as attorney general, Richard Kleindienst, should be confirmed; the President's chief of staff was now being advised that Mitchell may have committed perjury.[25]

On that same day, March 30, 1972, Mitchell gave Jeb Magruder the green light to go ahead with Gemstone. If the ITT matter had not already given him enough to worry about, Mitchell could ponder what the Democrats, particularly O'Brien, might be planning to make of the Hughes connection. For the moment the ITT affair had drawn the press away from the Hughes link, but sooner or later it would come up again. There were so many aspects to the connection that it was hard to know where to begin.

[24]8 Senate Hearings 3375.
[25]Nixon discusses the ITT affair in his memoirs, pp. 580–83.

Certainly the Howard Hughes Medical Institute's taxes were one logical question the Democrats and the press could study. However, the only place that Mitchell could know for certain that an illegal action was about to take place was in the matter of the $100,000 contribution from Hughes that was in Bebe Rebozo's bank in a safe-deposit box. Under the new federal campaign financing law that was to take effect on April 7, all political contributions had to be reported and placed on the public record. But to do so was to risk the possibility that the press would then have confirmation of the Hughes contribution. Apparently, the only strategy that seemed to make sense was to leave the contribution in the safety-deposit box and approve a plan which promised to produce intelligence on just how much the Democrats knew and what they were planning.

In his memoirs Gordon Liddy recalls that he received authorization to undertake Gemstone from Magruder "about" April Fool's Day. One phase of the operation, code-named "Opal," called for four clandestine entries—one each at the campaign headquarters of Muskie and George McGovern, a third at the Democratic convention that summer, and a fourth at a target yet to be selected—in order to install bugs. "Topaz," the title of a recent movie, was the code word for the document photography to be undertaken at those sites.

On April 4 McGovern won a major victory over Muskie in the Wisconsin primary, effectively terminating the Muskie campaign. McGovern's triumph was also a major victory for the Nixon White House, which believed, correctly, that McGovern would be much the easier of the two to defeat in November. From that point on the election was Nixon's to lose. On April 12 Mitchell and Haldeman met with the President from 3:29 to 4:40 P.M. in Nixon's office in the Executive Office Building adjacent to the White House. It was the only meeting of the three between January and June 12. The task now was to pin the label of "radical" on McGovern, who had been associated with the controversial Progressive Henry Wallace in 1948. McGovern, meanwhile, was returning the compliment by calling Nixon a "fascist." That was the level of the national political dialogue that spring. As the season progressed anti–Vietnam War demonstrations bloomed in Washington and elsewhere across the country as the President moved toward his decision to mine Haiphong harbor, while the planned Moscow summit meeting in May hung in the balance. Notes taken that month in meetings with various members of his staff indicate that Nixon was in an especially determined mood. While there is no doubt that the original approval of Gemstone in late March was made in a purely domestic political context, foreign policy and ideological issues were rapidly becoming intertwined with politics. Liddy recalls that it was "near the end of April" that Magruder informed him that the first target in the Opal series was to be the Democratic National Committee headquarters at the Watergate complex. "It was clear from [Magruder's] facial expression and manner of speech that he was just relaying orders," Liddy added. After months of waiting for his plan to be approved, Liddy was now under pressure to produce on an accelerated timetable. The selection of the

DNC headquarters as the first target did not mean there was to be any less emphasis on getting into McGovern headquarters. The two projects were to go forward in tandem.

In early May, as the nation's attention was centered on the passing of J. Edgar Hoover and Nixon's decision to mine Haiphong harbor in North Vietnam, a curious suit was filed in Los Angeles Circuit Court against a book, *The Nixon-Hughes Loan,* by Nicholas North-Broome, published by the American Public Affairs Institute. On May 12 Desmond Barker told Charles Colson in a memo that the plaintiff, Victor Shaub, "is considered to be a shill for the publisher to pump some life and interest back in a waning enterprise." The suit sought to prevent further distribution of the book on the grounds that it lessened the dignity of the President. When Colson inquired how the matter should be handled, H. R. Haldeman replied in a handwritten note: "Do *nothing* [without] consulting Ehrlichman first." Three days later Gordon Liddy sent John Mitchell a memo on the suit offering more details. Liddy described the matter as a "conspiracy." He reported that Robert Bennett had told him that Hughes had established "that both the complaint and the answer were typed on the same typewriter." Liddy repeated to Mitchell Bennett's assurances that Nixon was "far from vulnerable" on the loan, but his rationale was vague, largely based on the Robert Kennedy investigation of the early 1960s, and made no mention of the 1957 IRS reversal of its stance on the Hughes Medical Institute. On May 18 an aide to Haldeman, Gordon Strachan, following instructions, passed a copy of Liddy's memo to John Ehrlichman (HRH96). While Liddy was apparently not yet fully up to speed on the Hughes loan, the exercise of producing the memo helped prepare him for the kinds of information he should be on the lookout for in Larry O'Brien's office.

On the evening of the 18th, President Nixon, as was his habit, watched a movie. In the previous month he had seen a dozen films, among them *The Godfather, There Was a Crooked Man, Funeral in Berlin, The Carpetbaggers,* and two James Bond classics—*Diamonds Are Forever* and *Goldfinger.* That night it was another Bond movie, *From Russia with Love,* which he watched with his old friend Bebe Rebozo at Camp David. Soon the President was off to Europe en route to Moscow. His travels abroad, of course, were always carefully scripted. But there were some twists in the script of this trip that no screen writer could possibly have imagined.

On May 25 President Nixon had dinner at the country estate of General Secretary Leonid Brezhnev outside Moscow and then returned to the city to attend a performance of *Swan Lake* at the Bolshoi. After Nixon retired for the evening, Liddy back in Washington personally shot out the floodlights at the rear door of George McGovern's headquarters in preparation for a clandestine entry at a later date.

On the following evening, May 26, Nixon hosted a dinner for the Soviet leadership at the residence of the American ambassador in Moscow. Afterward he went to St. Vladimir's Hall in the Grand Kremlin Palace for the signing of the SALT treaty at 11 P.M. Moscow time, which was in fine time for the evening news back in the United States. At 2 A.M. Moscow time, Nixon telephoned Bebe Rebozo in the United States from his quarters in the Kremlin Palace Annex. Meanwhile, back in Washington the White House burglars had checked into the Watergate Hotel, posing as representatives of a fictitious company called Ameritas. An attempt that night to penetrate the DNC headquarters was foiled when the burglars could not defeat an electric alarm on a door leading from the hotel to the office complex. Howard Hunt found himself locked into one of the banquet rooms overnight.

After spending May 27 in Leningrad, Nixon returned to Moscow that same evening. In Washington a second attempt failed. This time the trouble was the door of the DNC offices.

On Sunday evening, May 28, Nixon spoke to the Soviet people in a live television address.

Most of you know our country only through what you read in your newspapers and what you hear and see on radio and television and in motion pictures. This is only a part of the real America. . . . Above all, we, like you, are an open, natural and friendly people. We love our country. . . . We Americans are idealists. We believe deeply in our system of government. We cherish our personal liberty. We would fight to defend it if necessary, as we have done before. . . .

Through all the pages of history, through all the centuries, the world's people have struggled to be free from fear. Whether fear of the elements, or hunger, or fear of their own rulers, or fear of their neighbors in other countries. And yet time and again people have vanquished the source of one fear only to fall prey to another. Let our goal now be a world free of fear. . . .

Back in Washington a few hours later the White House burglary team successfully penetrated the Democratic National Committee offices, shot two 36-exposure rolls of film, took Polaroid shots of the desk and office of Chairman Lawrence O'Brien, and planted the eavesdropping devices. As the sun was rising in Moscow on Monday morning, Liddy, Hunt, and their colleagues enjoyed what Liddy later described as "a small victory celebration in the command post before going home."

When President Nixon returned home from the Soviet Union, he saw a review of Irving Kristol's new book *On the Democratic Idea in America,* told Haldeman about it, and requested a copy of the book for himself on June 6.[26] On the same day John Ehrlichman wrote a letter to William H. Morris, the director of the National Conference of Bar Examiners, recommending Gordon Liddy for the Bar in Washington, D.C. "He was a very effective member of the staff [in 1971] and undertook numerous difficult assignments with great skill. He possesses a keen legal mind and is certainly highly qualified for the practice of law. He has approached all problems, even the most sensitive, with the highest sense of integrity. He

[26]Kehrli to Haldeman, June 6, 1972. ss84

would be a very able member of the Bar here in the District of Columbia" (JDE21).

George McGovern's victory over Hubert Humphrey in the California primary June 6 removed the last shred of doubt as to whether he would be the Democratic nominee. On June 7 James Reston opened his column by saying, "The question now . . . is whether the American voters are ready for a radical change in U.S. foreign and domestic policy." Reston used the word "radical" to describe McGovern eight times in just twelve paragraphs. President Nixon, by contrast, was knifed just once, and that was in harness with Lyndon Johnson for "political expediency" and hucksterism, comparatively mild stuff. The column's message was so pointed that his readers across the country, including Richard Nixon, could not fail to notice. Never before had Reston been so favorably disposed toward a Nixon candidacy. Although the impact the column made on Nixon's thinking is not fully clear, it was one of a number of subjects that Charles Colson discussed with the President on June 8, according to Colson's notes. June 8, it must be remembered, marked the opening of the window of decision to undertake the second Watergate break-in, a decision apparently taken no later than June 12.

In his memoirs Nixon quotes Haldeman as saying "half-jokingly" on June 20 "that maybe it would be better if we just said that yes, we were spying on the Democrats . . . because we were scared to death that a crazy man was going to become President and sell the country out to the Communists!" The other "half" of Haldeman's intent may well have been, if not serious, at least wistful. Had the burglars been caught in McGovern's headquarters rather than the DNC offices, there is little question that the option of going public would have been considered very carefully. Reston's column of June 7 could have been used as part of the justification for the operation. Moreover, it might have been yet another "crisis" from which Nixon would have emerged triumphant. Nixon argues so strenuously, in his memoirs and elsewhere, about the stupidity of breaking into Democratic headquarters rather than McGovern's that he must be mourning the loss of an opportunity.

As Gemstone evolved through March, April, and June, three distinct justifications emerged. First was the quest for attack material showing O'Brien or others to be corrupt. Second was the rapidly growing fear that O'Brien might have enough on the Nixon-Hughes relationship to make the ITT scandal seem trivial. Third was the national security notion, which was in one sense heartfelt and in another sense thoroughly cynical, to be used if necessary for a cover story. If it is eventually established that Nixon himself gave the green light for the second and fatal Watergate break-in, then historians can reasonably conclude that it was his love for documentary intelligence that finally prevailed over any sense of prudence. If, on the other hand, it can be persuasively established that Mitchell and Haldeman did not, in fact, give the President that opportunity to choose, then one might ponder what he would have decided.

A few days before the voters went to the polls that November, James Reston gave his readers another of his periodic assessments of Nixon. In place of the tacit endorsement of June 7, however, Reston had only scathing indictments. Nixon's supporters then, as now, believed that he was being victimized by a "press witch hunt," and they were absolutely correct. The witch hunts pursued within the White House for quite some time finally spawned witch hunts in the press, which only intensified after Nixon won the election by a landslide, 61 to 38 percent. It often became difficult to tell, in the immortal phrase, which witch was which.

In 1972 "The number of actual voters fell to the lowest percentage of eligible voters in a quarter of a century," observed Theodore White. "Millions of Americans rejected both national candidates. And in 23 states of the Union, despite the enormous number of potential new voters from 18 to 21 years of age added by the youth amendment, the total vote for President was actually *less* than it had been in 1968."[27]

In the spring of 1973 one of the burglars, James McCord, told what he knew in court. Then John Dean appeared before the Senate committee headed by Senator Sam Ervin. Nixon fired Haldeman and Ehrlichman. Others, including Colson and Magruder, already had left. When Nixon himself resigned in 1974, James Reston wasted no time producing his second obituary of Richard Nixon: "The journalists have now written his political obituary and passed him on to the historians—who will probably treat him more kindly—but he remains a tragic tangle of contradictions, and will have to be left in the end to dramatists, novelists, and psychologists."[28] Reston did not explain why he felt historians might look more favorably on Nixon than the journalists who, as a profession, claim they write at least the first rough draft of history. Nor did he explain why journalists should automatically relegate a President to "history" upon his departure from office, especially a President who would have such a lasting impact on the country.

If Watergate seemed to confirm McGovern's charge that Nixon was a fascist, then it was a charge that Nixon refuted by the simple act of resignation from office. Richard Nixon had long imagined himself as the American Churchill, someone who could clearly distinguish between acceptable conservatism and fascism. That was what made Watergate especially painful to him philosophically. He was forced to admit that he did not have an unerring ability to make correct distinctions. Watergate, Nixon observed in 1988, "was a great mistake. It was wrong, as I've pointed out over and over again. But . . . people, as they judge that period, have to see what we accomplished and what we did wrong."[29]

From today's perspective it seems quite possible that ultimately Richard Nixon may be remembered as the most significant American

[27]Theodore White, *The Making of the President 1972* (New York: Atheneum, 1973), pp. 399–400.
[28]*New York Times*, August 9, 1974, p. 33.
[29]"Meet the Press," NBC, April 10, 1988.

President of the second half of this century. When Leonid Brezhnev invaded Afghanistan in 1979, months after visiting Jimmy Carter, he made Richard Nixon's insistence on "bargaining chips"—a steady stream of new weapons systems—seem prudent in spite of the chicanery in the defense-contracting business. Meanwhile, the constellation of laws that should be known historically as the Watergate Statutes have helped make White House political tricksters at least a bit nervous from time to time. But the overriding significance of Nixon is the simple fact that as Vice President and President he was the one who made the right wing of the Republican party politically respectable for the first time since the Depression. That is something his critics on the right, thinking of his China opening and the treaties with the Soviet Union, tend to forget. Like many on the left, they have tried to make something of a non-person of Richard Nixon. Even Patrick Buchanan dismissed Nixon's conservative credentials in one television documentary on the conservative movement.

Nixon's political mentor, Dwight Eisenhower, was basically a centrist who in effect endorsed the dreams of Franklin Roosevelt. Ike was uncomfortable with, for example, Senator Joseph McCarthy's sweeping villifications of federal employees. In contrast, Nixon included among his closest advisers men like Buchanan and Charles Colson, who openly admired McCarthy. Could there have been a Reagan presidency had Richard Nixon not paved the way?

Whatever history's judgment on Nixon, the punishment he received from Congress, the seizure of his documents, has been in his mind perhaps the unkindest cut. On September 6, 1974, less than a month after resigning as President, Nixon signed an agreement with the government administrator supervising the National Archives under which he would retain control of his presidential materials. He could withdraw any or all of them from deposit after three years. The White House tapes were to be destroyed in the event of his death or in 1984, whichever came first, and the destruction of some tapes could begin as early as 1979. The country was in no mood to swallow that as a plan for the disposition of Nixon's papers, however, and in the following three months Congress passed and President Gerald Ford signed the law seizing the Nixon materials. It was a condemnation proceeding, usually used by the government to seize land for some public purpose such as a road or dam. Citizen Nixon did what any irate farmer would like to do: he challenged the constitutionality of the step. But the Supreme Court in 1977 upheld the right of Congress and the President to seize Nixon's property.

Chief Justice Warren Burger and Justice William Rehnquist, both appointed by President Nixon, dissented. Justice William Brennan, appointed by President Eisenhower, said in the opinion on behalf of the majority of the Court:

Congress acted to establish regular procedures to deal with the perceived need to preserve the materials for legitimate historical and governmental purposes. An incumbent President should not be dependent on happenstance or the whim of a prior President when he seeks access to records of past decisions that define or channel current governmental obligations. Nor should the American people's ability to reconstruct and come to terms with their history be truncated by an analysis of Presidential privilege that focuses only on the needs of the present.

At the same time, however, the Court agreed that materials of a private nature should be returned to Nixon. While the Court did not spell this out in any great detail, it was a general conclusion which seemed fair under the circumstances. Afterward, however, attorneys for Nixon and the United States found themselves unable to agree on much of anything, certainly not on enough to produce the kind of cooperation between the government and former President that had resulted in the presidential libraries and museums created for other modern American presidents. A paper curtain, so to speak, had fallen between Nixon and his country.

After four wilderness years of self-imposed political exile, Richard Nixon reemerged in 1978 with the publication of his memoirs and an address at the Oxford University Union which was telecast in the United States. At the same time the Congress wrote a new law which was to govern the disposition of the materials of future presidents. It was one of a family of statutes which also include the Independent Counsel Act, the Ethics in Government Act, the Campaign Financing Act, and the Foreign Corrupt Practices Act. These are the Watergate Laws. Their historical derivation was in a direct line from the Magna Carta; their aim was to limit the power of the king and his cronies. The concept underlying the Presidential Records Act had been around for a quarter-century. In fact, had it become law in the 1950s when journalism organizations were urging it upon Congress, it would have simplified Nixon's access to the papers of John Kennedy and Lyndon Johnson, in which he was so interested. Moreover, Nixon would have been under no illusion that he might some day at his leisure be able to choose the documents he wished to be destroyed.

However, Congress made the exceptions that the Supreme Court had given Nixon an integral part of the Presidential Records Act. These included "materials relating to private political associations" as well as "materials relating exclusively to the President's own election to the office of the presidency, and materials directly relating to the election of a particular individual or individuals to Federal, State, or local office. . . ." Ironically, a Democratic Congress and a Democratic President had thereby made sure that future political campaign tactics, particularly by incumbent Presidents, would not be subject to the same degree of scrutiny as that accorded Nixon's 1972 campaign. Presidential candidates could now breathe easier. In 1980 Richard Nixon filed suit against the United States for compensation for the seizure of his presidential materials. There was a bit of risk involved: although Nixon had a strong *prima facie* case, the courts might agree in principal with his claim but decide to award him only nominal compensation.

In 1981 the National Archives moved the seized Nixon materials from a federal records center in Suitland, Maryland, to a facility in the industrial section of Alexandria, Virginia. Some visitors were amused by the Nixonian flavor of the neighborhood. The nondescript structure was directly across the street from the headquarters of the Boat Owners Association of the United States, a reminder of the evenings on the yacht *Sequoia* and the vacations at Key Biscayne. Next door was an indoor softball field, and just down the street was an Asian import firm identified as Saigon Foods. The selection of such an unprepossessing locale for what archivists call the "Nixon Project" increased controversy. To the keepers of the Nixon flame it seemed a site that could only be chosen by some pinko bureaucrat.

Meanwhile, the Nixon era continued into the 1980s, much as FDR's era had lasted through the 1960s. Scores of midlevel administrators, cabinet members, and even Reagan's Vice President had first learned the ropes of Washington while working in Nixon's administration. Reagan apparently considered carefully the advice Nixon offered in person or on the phone. Nixon was careful not to upstage the publicists for a "Reagan Revolution," but no one could deny that he would have relished an opportunity to slash taxes even more during his administration, had the political atmosphere been right. To many of an aging generation of political pundits the very idea of seriously comparing FDR to RN was nothing short of sacrilege. Nonetheless, the Republican penetration of the South that Nixon had begun was a genuinely historic reshaping of the Republican Party into a Conservative Party, in the British sense.

As the Reagan White House in 1985 attempted to imitate some of the more innovative techniques of government introduced a decade and a half earlier, a series of briefs and reply briefs filed in Nixon's compensation suit moved at a snail's pace through the U.S. District Court.

Back in September 1972, the Nixon staff had begun transferring the most sensitive White House files to a new unit called the Special Files, which could be far more closely supervised and tightly held. As the Watergate scandal unfolded, the existence of these extremely secret files eventually became known, but Nixon used all the powers at his command to prevent disclosure of their contents. This was the core of the collection eventually seized by the United States. These papers, not surprisingly, were the ones the press was chafing at the bit to see; for that very reason, it was widely assumed Nixon would use every legal means at his disposal to keep them closed for as long as possible.

Late in 1986 the United States opened an eclectic assortment of materials from Nixon's Central Files. These, understandably, did not draw much public attention, although this was the first time the U.S. government had opened presidential papers that had not been deeded. To the surprise of reporters, historians, and archivists, however, in early 1987 Richard Nixon did not go into court to block the release then being planned by the Archives of the vast majority of the papers in the Special Files. He limited himself to filing a claim that 150,000 of the 3,200,000 pages to be released should be withheld. Materials relevant to Watergate had been specifically excluded by the law and the courts from those categories of documents subject to Nixon's wishes. When the Archives decided to comply with his request pending the outcome of a re-review of the 150,000 pages, the stage was set for what promised to be an archival version of the Oklahoma land rush.

However, when the day came on May 4, 1987, and the Archives began opening the bulk of Richard Nixon's secret Special Files, the press, confronted with a mountain of material to review, instantly discounted its significance, on the grounds that the most newsworthy in all likelihood was surely the 150,000 pages. The stories that followed generally featured a juicy quote from one memorandum, reported that the best material was being withheld, and conveyed the erroneous impression that research lay behind that conclusion.

There was not a lot that Archives personnel and Richard Nixon agreed on about Nixon's papers, but at that point they were tacitly in accord that the press had botched the story. Nixon was known to be unhappy about frivolous stories, and James Hastings, director of the Nixon papers project at the Archives, described the conduct of the press at the opening as that of a "mob."

The *New York Times,* not surprisingly, approached the Nixon papers more seriously than most, but its conclusion was, if anything, even more disappointing. Its attitude was perhaps best conveyed in a letter of thanks to the Archives written on May 7 by John Finney, a veteran reporter. "My own impression," he gracefully concluded, "is that the papers now are of more interest to historians than journalists. But for a day when the journalists were interested, your staff succeeded in making an unruly lot mannerly and studious."[30] This consignment of Nixon to historical assessment was consistent with the editorial position—particularly exemplified by James Reston—taken by the *Times* over the preceding quarter-century. It was, however, wrong on a number of counts.

In fact, a good deal of news could be culled from these files. The moment itself was one of considerable historic import, one that deserved to be recorded. Access to presidential papers at long last was a right of the people, not a privilege conveyed by a retired elected king. The opening of the papers of Richard Nixon was also reason to review the attitudes and practices of the press in relation to government, issues still facing the American democratic experiment. George Bush's link to all this should have given added impetus to serious inquiry. The Vice President, who owed the salvaging of his political career to Nixon, was already a leading candidate for the 1988 Republican presidential nomination. Zeal in the investigation of Nixon's papers could have been balanced by zeal in the study of Jimmy Carter's papers, which also began to be opened in 1987.

[30]Letter of May 7, 1987, from John W. Finney to Frank Burke, acting archivist, National Archives, released by National Archives pursuant to a Freedom of Information Act request for materials pertinent to the opening of the Nixon papers.

The conduct of the press was especially shameful when juxtaposed with the central and valid rationale for its conduct in the Pentagon Papers case. In that instance the press argued that it was interested in all materials illuminating the conduct of government. Indeed, the behavior of the "mob" in 1987 bolstered Nixon's argument that the only documents the press is interested in are those whose release is unauthorized—leaked.

Perhaps the principal news to come out of the Nixon papers is the unintentional and inadvertent release by the Archives of hundreds, perhaps several thousand, pages of the 150,000 that Richard Nixon had requested be withheld. Included in this "covert" cache were memoranda dictated by Nixon as well as staff papers of all sorts. This inadvertent release was primarily due to the efficiency of Nixon's White House staff and the existence of rapid photocopying technology during the Nixon years. A copy of any given document might be found in any number of places in the files, not all of them readily traceable. Since the documents withdrawn were all identified by date, author, recipient, and subject matter, it is a simple matter for a patient researcher to match documents released against the withheld list and determine with a high degree of probability that a document released in one part of the files is one described as having been withheld in another. Also highly newsworthy was the fact that when the Special Files were opened, some 230 folders of Bud Krogh's materials could not be located. These were files of the White House Plumbers, which had been seized by the Watergate Special Prosecutor but never returned to the Archives. According to Krogh, the files were "the hot stuff" of his operations. Archivists suspected that the files might be somewhere in the vast federal records storage center in Suitland. However, more than a year after they were due to be released along with the rest of the Special Files, the Justice Department had yet to locate them. A Freedom of Information Act request addressed to the attorney general in December 1987 was routed to the Federal Bureau of Investigation, which passed the buck back to the Justice Department in September 1988. The FBI said that it had delivered nine cartons containing Krogh's files "on April 15, 1974, at 2:30 P.M., to the office of Mr. James A. Wilderotter, Room 4208, U.S. Department of Justice for appropriate disposal." No further trace of the documents has been found.

Mystery also surrounds the disposition of the voluminous records of the Committee for the Re-Election of the President (CREP). These records had been in U.S. government custody and in legal limbo ever since the conclusion of the 1972 campaign. By 1987 American taxpayers had invested some $120,000 in storing the materials, which also had been processed by Archives personnel in anticipation that they would some day be opened. In August 1985 the Archives notified trustees of the 1972 Campaign Liquidation Trust that the records "are not considered to be presidential historical materials" as the term was defined by statute. In July 1986 Paul Barrick, a trustee who had worked for CREP in 1972, wrote the Archives that the Republican National Committee would "accept" the CREP records and "direct the Trustees to forward these records to former

President Nixon's office in New York." Six weeks later the Archives notified Barrick that they would have to be removed as soon as possible. In early June 1987 the CREP files were removed from the Archives by personnel employed by Nixon's attorneys and delivered to an office building in the West Park section of McLean, Virginia.

Most of the material apparently was destined for the Nixon Library, which was being planned privately for a site in Yorba Linda, California. Although the library was being developed by Nixon and his friends without any formal participation by the United States because of Nixon's continuing legal battle with his government, the hope of most serious observers was that some day this library might become part of the system of presidential libraries administered by the Archives. As a serious facility, the Nixon library could ill afford a new round of "cover-up" allegations. But that was what Nixon and/or his aides invited by removing these papers from government custody at a time when Nixon was deeply apologetic for the Watergate cover-up and otherwise cooperative with the press. The situation is all the more puzzling in that the United States continues to store a vast trove of other undeeded materials belonging to Nixon on a courtesy basis in anticipation that they someday will be consigned to a facility authorized by the government. In March 1987 an attorney for Nixon informed the Archives that "Mr. Nixon demands the immediate return to him of all personal and private materials now in the possession of the Archives. . . . The only thing the Archives should retain concerning these materials should be those records necessary to document the fact of the existence and return of the materials; not any information regarding their contents." However, two years later, Nixon's aides had not removed any materials other than the CREP records.

One incident during the 1988 presidential campaign amply demonstrated the enduring news value of the Nixon papers and the problems that the press can create for itself by failing to promptly and systematically review new releases of presidential materials. Fred Malek, deputy chairman of the Republican National Committee, resigned his post immediately after a front-page story in the *Washington Post* on September 11 by Walter Pincus and Bob Woodward used documents from the Nixon Special Files to provide details of a 1971 incident in which Malek, under instructions from Nixon and Haldeman, estimated the number of Jews and Democrats in the Bureau of Labor Statistics (BLS). Woodward had first reported the incident in his 1976 book *The Final Days* (pp. 177–78) in a much broader context centered on Nixon's alleged anti-Semitism. In the second paragraph of their article, Pincus and Woodward intimated that the timing of the article was dictated by the discovery of memoranda "found last week in the archives of Nixon's presidency." In the next-to-the-last paragraph the story noted that when Malek had been named to the position in August, George Bush had been asked by reporters about Malek's activities in the Nixon years and that he had replied that time had healed those wounds. The article carefully noted that scores of Malek's memoranda remained withheld at Nixon's request.

The Republicans, of course, immediately charged the *Post* with playing dirty pool,[31] and some prominent Jews leaped to Malek's defense. Indeed, the *Post*'s handling of the Nixon papers had been such that its belated discovery of news therein made it vulnerable to the charge of political bias. Had *Post* reporters systematically reviewed the papers in 1987, the series of articles that presumably would have been published that year as the product of such an effort would have left Bush under no illusion in 1988 that the press had forgotten either his role or that of Malek in the Nixon years. 1971, of course, was also the year in which the Kurt Waldheim nomination at the United Nations slipped past Ambassador Bush, President Nixon, and others for reasons still not clear.[32] While Nixon, Bush, and Malek might not have liked the substance, a series could have been handled in a demonstrably fair manner well before the 1988 primaries. In this instance, however, *Post* reporters were conspicuously absent from the Nixon papers research room for nearly a year before returning to look for material on Bush and eventually Malek. By rehashing the Malek story *after* Bush had suggested these wounds had been healed, the sequence of events made it appear that the *Post*'s story was a partisan response to Bush's comment.

As the "comprehension gap" about Nixon and his documents, classified and otherwise, grew wider, in 1987 and 1988, it became evident that decisions were shaping themselves into yet another of those crises that have so characterized his career. During this period, the National Archives also disclosed plans to release in 1989 several dozen hours of Nixon's White House tapes, materials subpoenaed and transcribed during the Watergate crisis. Late in the year it is expected to release the portion of the 150,000 pages withheld in 1987 regarding which its judgment differs from that of Nixon—likely a substantial part of the whole. The Archives

[31]See "Low Profile or Not, Nixon Gives Advice," *New York Times,* September 15, 1988, p. B11; "Who Will Believe Bush As a Nazi?" a column by Wesley Pruden, the *Washington Times,* September 12, 1988; "McCarthyism?!" a *Washington Times* editorial, September 13, 1988.
[32]In passing on the suitability of Waldheim, then the Austrian foreign minister, to become U.N. secretary general, Richard Nixon and his advisers apparently failed to ask a key question: Did the biographical data on Waldheim put together by the State Department and the Central Intelligence Agency for decision by the president consider any possible mention of him in the German war records, which were widely known to be available in the National Archives on microfilm? It was a question that should have especially fascinated World War II veterans such as Richard Nixon, Henry Kissinger, William Rogers, and George Bush. As ambassador to the United Nations, Bush had a direct responsibility to ask such a question of the bureaucracy to protect both himself and the President. It will take considerable effort to sort out the details of the answer to this question, so much so that it would be appropriate for Congress to lend a hand. It is important to note on Nixon's behalf that it appears he had no particularly deep commitment to Waldheim as secretary general. Nixon's comments to his staff about Waldheim's initiatives in 1972 were by no means uniformly complimentary. It just may be that Nixon would have welcomed an excuse to veto Waldheim in 1971, had he been given one. In that case the weight of historic responsibility for that blunder may fall most heavily on George Bush.

also has advised Nixon that it plans to begin the systematic release of the balance of his White House tapes starting in 1991, the twentieth anniversary of the installation of the White House taping system. It is not unreasonable to believe that Nixon, if he wishes, could string out the legal processes surrounding his materials into the next century.

He also must decide whether to structure the Nixon library in Yorba Linda as a facility to be taken seriously by serious people.

While his enemies undoubtedly would think his behavior appropriate to one of the great political cover-up artists, others might find deep irony in such behavior by someone whose determination not to destroy his White House tapes probably cost him the job of President.

In 1983 Nixon spent a pleasant summer afternoon touring the Franklin Roosevelt museum and Roosevelt's home at Hyde Park. However, he turned down the offer of a briefing on the organization of the Roosevelt papers with an airy comment. "They're only documents," he reportedly said.

Nixon's latest crisis is one that cries out for some glasnost. Does Richard Nixon really wish to be remembered as a man who went to China and the Soviet Union in search of peace but engaged his own government in cold war? Both Nixon and the United States could save a great deal of time, energy, and money and the interests of history could be well served by a peace that met the test of public acceptability. Were Nixon to drop his legal fight and deed his undeeded materials to the Archives, the Archives—with congressional approval—could accept the Yorba Linda facility as a part of its presidential library system and, if Nixon so requests, could agree to some reasonable delay in the opening of sensitive non-Watergate materials that he might specify. Certainly there would be some advantages for some researchers in the permanent establishment of separate Nixon research centers on each coast. However, on the whole there is little question that the public interest is best served by one library per president, not two.

In December 1987 Tom Wicker delivered the banquet address at a conference on Richard Nixon at Hofstra University. It was a gracious memoir centered on the 1960 campaign, which praised Nixon for not having demanded a recount, as he might easily have done. Wicker did not suggest that Nixon was anything like "that Kafkaesque figure" he had described exactly a quarter-century earlier.

Throughout the 1988 campaign Richard Nixon was a pervasive figure on the American political scene. He published yet another book, wrote numerous articles, granted dozens of interviews, made speeches, remained in frequent touch with President Reagan, visited at the White House, and watched as his former aides dominated the Republican Party and were major players in the media game.[33] The Maryland farm on

[33]For a quick look at Nixon's skills as a pundit see Andrew Sullivan, "Richard Nixon, Prophet: He's Wrong!" *New Republic*, August 29, 1988.

which the Pumpkin Papers had been stored during the 1940s was declared a National Historic Landmark. An opera about Nixon's first visit to China was performed in New York, confirming James Reston's 1974 prophecy that "dramatists" would find him of interest. Two hours after Reston was warmly applauded at the annual convention of the American Society of Newspaper Editors, Nixon received a warm ovation. Reston treated Nixon gingerly and only briefly in his introduction to a new edition of Theodore White's book on the 1960 campaign. He twice noted that Nixon is the sole survivor of the central figures of that campaign, and he confessed that on election night in 1960 "I very nearly made the greatest blunder of my professional life by proclaiming Kennedy's victory shortly after midnight on the front page of the *New York Times* before I had the results from Michigan and Illinois to justify that result, forcing the *Times* to stop the presses until later in the morning."[34] In July the Democrats selected Reston's neighbor, Lloyd Bentsen, as their vice presidential nominee. "I can testify that he is a gentleman and a good neighbor, which is more than can be said about some Vice Presidents I've known," Reston wrote.[35] The *Times* gave front-page treatment to a memorandum from Nixon to George Bush analyzing the 1988 campaign. When it came time to choose his own running mate, Bush tacitly paid tribute to Nixon by selecting a conservative senator who had made a meteoric rise in American politics by defeating incumbent opponents and was only a tad older than the conservative senator from California, Nixon, had been when picked by Eisenhower in 1952 after a similarly meteoric ascendancy against incumbent opponents. When questions were raised about the record of J. Danforth Quayle of Indiana, it was not long before the press made the expected suggestion. "Schedule your own Checkers speech. Even bring the dog, if you like. It worked before, and just might again," wrote Haynes Johnson in the *Washington Post*.[36] Senator Quayle quickly adopted Nixonian positions on both the Soviet Union and State Department personnel. "Perestroika is nothing more than refined Stalinism," Quayle said. "I always have had a lot of problems from time to time getting the State Department to put American policy and American interests first." America's career diplomats often "have a fundamentally different idea of what makes America tick than the average man and woman."[37]

Key elements of the Nixon philosophy dominated the Republican Party and its approach to the 1988 campaign. Until Nixon's bold thrust into the South in 1968, the differences between the two parties were not easily defined. The regional origins of each were significant; the conservative wing of the Democratic Party and the liberal wing of the Republican Party were both important elements within their respective parties. Although there was an obvious logic and neatness to Nixon's realign-

[34]Theodore White, *The Making of the President 1960* (New York: Atheneum, 1988).
[35]"Bentsen: A Solid Boost for a Needy Party" by James Reston, *New York Times*, July 13, 1988.
[36]"What Quayle's Revealed" by Haynes Johnson, *Washington Post*, August 26, 1988.
[37]*Washington Post*, September 6, 1988, p. A16; *Washington Post*, September 4, 1988, p. A5; the *New York Times*, September 4, 1988, p. 31.

ment of conservatives and liberals on opposite sides of the fence, it was an arrangement which in the long haul could foster stereotyping and paranoia in a country in which many people realize that they harbor liberal as well as conservative views at the same time on almost any given question. Bush pursued the Nixon approach to American political organization by suggesting liberalism was a dirty word and repeated two other tenets of the Nixon credo: the press is dominated by liberals, and only conservatives have the political gravity to decide the acceptability of Communist actions and policies.

There was a time when the Democrats thought it axiomatic that the role of determining the acceptability of Communist behavior belonged to the heirs of FDR's legacy, much as it had remained to Churchill the right to draw the line on fascism. By 1988, however, it had become traditional for them to come under routine and serious attack from the Nixonian Republicans (including George Bush) questioning even the foundations of their patriotism. 1950s terms like "comsymp" and "stooge" and "soft on communism" were not in vogue in 1988, but the thrust of the Nixonian charge remained the same.

While Nixon's views about Communists and liberals are politically partisan, there is a nugget of nonpartisan truth in his assertion that the press, especially reporters, are considerably more liberal than he believes appropriate. The nugget was a good bit larger in 1960 and 1968 than it became by 1988, but it is worth examining.

In the 1960s most reporters, particularly those under fifty, did tend to believe that the permissible range of the American presidential spectrum ran from Roosevelt on the left to Eisenhower on the right. That was all reporters of Nixon's generation had ever known. Given the historic association of far right policies with racism, the Depression, and fascism there seemed little likelihood that the American public would ever again look to the far right for leadership. After the tumult of 1968, it took time for even the most centrist and careful of reporters to understand that the movement to the right then beginning was not an aberration but rather the beginning of a long-term shift in American politics. Once that shift became widely reported and accepted, however, it was time for reporters, chameleons that they are, to adopt to the new "reality" that Nixonian Republicanism was centrist; on the whole, they did it rather well by the 1980s.

In the controversy over the military record of his choice for running mate, George Bush used Nixon dogma about the press. They were "blue-fish" in a feeding "frenzy." He refrained from calling them sharks. In 1988 Nixonian Republicans still took as an article of faith the notion that there was a good deal of political mileage to be had in bashing the press. Had the press, however, done its homework on Nixon's White House papers in a timely fashion, the herd might have decided it worthwhile to probe whether the protests it received about its 1988 campaign reporting might have been orchestrated by those originally trained in politico-journalistic warfare in the Nixon White House.

In sum, Nixon's influence on American politics remained so strong in 1988 that it was difficult to believe that the country might move beyond the Nixon Era during the rest of the century—even with a string of Democratic election victories from here on. The reforms needed to mark that passage would be ones of style as well as substance, perhaps chief among them a change in the triangular relationship between television, politics, and journalism. The year 1992 will mark the fortieth anniversary of Nixon's pioneering use of television to go over the heads of the press and the politicians to the people. For Nixon it was a simple, natural fusion of the techniques of debate in which he had been trained with those of the new telecommunications medium. However, in the four decades since then, the country has yet to insist that it is time to move to the next logical step in the conduct of the office of President—televised conversation.

Over the years many Americans have complained about the absence of a Westminster-style question period in the American political system. However, few are enthralled by the idea of obliging the President to go to Capitol Hill periodically to take the questions of Congress. But what if the President periodically were to invite the opposition to send its leaders to the White House for, say, 90 to 120 minutes of conversation televised live in prime time? Conversation is the basis of all politics, at least all democratic politics. It also is the basis of trust, an important commodity all too frequently in short supply.

That such televised presidential conversations are not yet an accepted practice is hardly the fault of Richard Nixon. It was perfectly logical for him to hone the simple technique that saved his political career overnight. Yet, as Walter Cronkite told the ASNE in 1988, Americans are in a "communications crisis." We are, he said, "being communicated at and not communicated with."

When introducing Richard Nixon to the ASNE in 1988, Herb Klein, who bears with dignity the scars of the knifings he took in the Nixon White House,[38] observed that "few men I've known in public office have understood the press . . . as has Richard Nixon." There was a time during the Watergate period when that remark would have brought an explosion of laughter from the Washington press corps. (Prior to 1969 the Washington press was routinely described with the upstanding, patriotic, and ringing term "corps.") However, in 1988 the suggestion that Nixon understood the press drew nary a howl in a hall packed with reporters. During the Watergate era Nixon erred in believing the press would not be as tenacious as it was and in believing that in any event he could always rely on a Checkers speech to save the day. With that historic exception, how-

[38]See, for example, Klein's memo to Haldeman of March 31, 1972, complaining about news articles saying he was planning to leave the White House staff. "As I told you the last time we discussed rumors such as this, I have made no such plans and again I am baffled at the source of these rumors. When I make plans in the next few years, I'll discuss it with you directly before I do anything. There's not time to even think about such things in 1972. I would appreciate anything you can do to kill off the rumors if they pop up with you." HRH96

ever, there was, in fact, considerable truth in Klein's observation. Indeed, Nixon had gone a long way since his freshman year at Whittier when, according to investigative historian Stephen Ambrose, he suffered a C in a journalism course while otherwise enjoying an A in French and seven Bs.[39]

Given the lack of press interest in 1987 in his Special Files, Nixon has reason to think that the press, including its elder statesmen, have done the traditional thing and for the most part consigned him to the historians—as James Reston recommended so long ago. At the same time he has a clear idea of just how voluminous the record of his administration is and how intimidating that will be for serious historians. (His White House generated an average of roughly 20,000 pages a day from all sources. The log of the 4,000 hours of his White House tapes itself runs to 27,000 pages.) And he knows that he has created an impressive postpresidential record that historians will be obliged to examine closely. He cannot erase the stain of Watergate, but serious historians will have to put it in context. If the press refuses to do so because of the myth that Richard Nixon is peripheral to an understanding of contemporary America, then it will be up to historians to uncover the extent of his influence on more recent presidents and events. While Nixon may not be able to rewrite history as much as he might like, he knows that not even the humiliation of his resignation from office stripped him of the ability to influence it.

What remains is for the press and historians alike to understand the scope of the challenge presented by those portions of Nixon's critique of the press that are thoughtful and deserve to be taken seriously. Americans will never forget the lawyer who rose to high office on the strength of a perjury conviction and who later lost high office by committing what amounted to perjury. They will also do well never to forget that lawyer's challenge to journalists to conduct themselves with the seriousness and the thoroughness of the finest lawyers. But how can journalists conduct themselves responsibly if they cannot have access to government documents— what lawyers call the discovery process?

When the leading newspapers and networks finally assign reporters full time to the National Archives, an increasingly significant source of information on government, they finally will be recognizing an important aspect of the Nixon legacy: documents. Declassified U.S. government documents can tell a story at least as important as any gathered by the traditional oral means from sources who invariably have motives invisible to reporters.

Yet, while some Americans think it high time for a President to order acid-free paper for government records, others think the acid levels should be high enough to cause presidential materials to disintegrate into powder on the day a President leaves office. Indeed, how could a President *not* pardon a career bureaucrat like Oliver North who went the last mile

[39]Ambrose, *Nixon,* p. 54.

for him by destroying apparently embarrassing presidential documents?

In 1968 David Frost asked Richard Nixon how he would like to be remembered: "It's a long way ahead, but what would you like the first line of your obituary in the *New York Times* to say?"

Nixon replied: " 'He made a great contribution to the peace of the world.' This probably goes back to a family situation. My mother and my grandmother were very devout birthright Quakers and I became, as a participant in World War II and as an antagonist and a very vigorous one in political campaigns, very un-Quakerish in their eyes. But deep down, there runs through me, as there does I think in most Americans, a deep desire for a better world in which we can really have peace. If I don't make a contribution to it, my life will have been a failure."[40]

Asked a similar question in 1988 by John Chancellor, Nixon bashed historians as he had bashed the press. "History will treat me fairly. Historians probably won't because most historians are on the left, and I understand that. . . . The China initiative hasn't brought peace to the world. We can't be sure that will happen. But without it, we would be in a terrible shape."[41]

Surely history will treat President Richard Nixon fairly, and surely his contribution to peace will be closely examined in the process. Not just world peace, but peace within the country that was so historically divided when he was in office. Real peace cannot exist in American democracy without confidence and trust among those of opposing political views. It is doubtful there can be confidence and trust in a society as large as ours without, to borrow a phrase, technical means of verifying that our leaders are abiding by the rules of law and the social contract. One of those means is the ability of the public to have access to the records of its presidents. In the years just ahead, the decisions and policies pursued by Nixon with respect to the records of his presidency will, in one way or another, have considerable impact on long-term domestic peace and tranquility. He has to decide whether in the long run history will conclude that the cause of domestic harmony is best served by continuing political war with the United States over his presidential materials or by an active search for peace. Either way it is an important question for the press to watch. Former President Nixon is still influencing history; Citizen Nixon is now making history.

[40]Frost, *The Presidential Debate, 1968,* p. 22.
[41]"Meet the Press," NBC, April 10, 1988.

EDITOR'S NOTE

MARCH 16, 1970

TO: **Bob Haldeman**

FROM: **Lyn Nofziger**

It is obvious some of our appointees are collecting memos for use when:

1. they are fired.
2. they quit.
3. they want to embarrass the President or members of his Administration.

I suspect we will have a great wave of these in about September or October and more in the fall of 1972.

The answers are, it seems to me,

1. Use the phone more and memos less.
2. Order a tightening of security.
3. Fire the people in this Administration who are opposed to the President.

If this leaks, it proves my point.

HRH58

The story of the incumbency of every President is something like a novel: it has a beginning, a middle, and an end. Drama at the highest level. In fact, the President often concludes that not only does what is being reported as the truth *read* like fiction, it *is* fiction.

For the past several decades, of course, the President has had at his disposal the perfect solution to that problem—a television camera in each presidential office—but, as Richard Nixon learned, even modest experiments in electronic recording can be fraught with political peril. However, the intense public fascination with Nixon's tapes as the repository of Ultimate Truth should not overwhelm the fact that the conversations can only be understood in a larger context, that is, the paper flow that provides the basis for so many of the recorded verbal comments. Moreover, as considered statements of fact and opinion designed to be read, documents, including those of Richard Nixon, deserve to be accorded more historical weight than oral comments that are figuratively as well as literally off the wall. At the same time, documents are far better suited to the book format than transcripts of conversations.

When the story to be told is Richard Nixon's, without doubt the most informative way to begin is to simply lay out the voluminous documents generated by him and his aides. The fairest way to reproduce the documents is, of course, as nearly as possible in the order in which they were written. That way they can convey a story—from beginning to end.

However, when the menu of documents from which to choose runs to some four million pages, the editor is instantly set against limits of technology and time. The bigger the book, the greater the amount of truth revealed and the stronger the editor's shield against those who may be afflicted by the documents' publication. Where is the line drawn?

The first strong feeling of any Nixon researcher is joy at finding a substantial volume of memoranda dictated by the President himself. It is vastly larger than that produced by any of Nixon's predecessors, and it must be assimilated by all serious students of the Nixon presidency. Drawing the line here, at Nixon's own memoranda, is a first, logical thought. It is logical, that is, until one also obtains a sense of the richness of the staff memoranda, which are crucial to a deeper understanding of the Nixon White House and, therefore, to a larger and more intimate truth. This, the first published volume of the Nixon papers, is therefore a blend of several possible approaches.

The selection of Nixon documents contained here is the product of more than 100 days spent researching in 1987 and 1988 and more than 700 hours spent reviewing several hundred thousand pages primarily in Nixon's personal and office files and in the vast files of H. R. Haldeman and Charles Colson, as well as in other, smaller collections.[1] More than 30,000 pages of document photocopies were generated. The pages selected ranged from arcane aspects of foreign affairs to the most human and trivial of comments by the lowest of staff members. There was a strong bias in

[1] The only other work of comparable scope undertaken during this period was that of University Publications of America, which is producing segments of the Nixon papers on microfiche so that academics unable to spend much time at the Archives can still have access to the papers. Interested parties should write to Dept B-NIXWH987, 44 North Market Street, Frederick, MD 21701, or call 1-800-692-6300. Researchers who wish to contact the National Archives Nixon Project directly should phone 1-703-756-6498, or write Nixon Presidential Materials Project, National Archives and Records Administration, Washington, D.C. 20408.

favor of documents that were readable and with broad potential interest. Whether any given document might portray Nixon favorably or unfavorably was most emphatically *not* a factor in selection. However, to determine those pages that might already have been in print, all the Nixon White House documents reproduced in Nixon's memoirs and in the twenty-six volumes produced by the Senate Watergate Committee were photocopied and added to the collection.[2] Then the whole caboodle was placed in chronological order.

Two rounds of pruning brought the remaining material down to 5,000 pages. Eliminated in these rounds were duplicates and a number of documents on specialized topics, which were either too long to merit further consideration or else not of sufficiently broad interest.

In this process I discovered that hundreds of pages of material that Nixon had requested be withheld from the public record had been inadvertently released by the National Archives. This was done by the simple process of checking the sheets identifying the documents withheld against the documents in hand. Documents withheld are identified by date, author, recipient, and subject. While it is conceivable that a given author might have produced more than one memorandum on precisely the same subject for the same recipient on the same day, the probability is slight.

At the 5,000-page level the choices were far more difficult. One technique was to select two or three of the most descriptive memoranda on a given subject out of a longer series. Although I favored reproducing memoranda in their entirety, in the handful of instances where this was impossible the excisions have been indicated as [. . .]. Another method of assisting evaluation was to write an introduction that covers far more ground than initially intended. The original plan was to reproduce in full all the Nixon documents in the body of the book. However, when in the course of the production process this became impossible, a decision was made to cite in the introduction references to significant memoranda that would not be printed. Readers puzzled by the fact that certain memoranda in the introduction are footnoted as to collection and box number within the Special Files while others are not should understand that those not footnoted are found in the body of the book while those that are so designated are not.

It also has not been possible to publish all the memoranda that Nixon requested be withheld, copies of which appear in the files nevertheless. Scores of these in the staff memoranda category appeared to be especially arcane or inconsequential. Among the publicly available presidential memoranda Nixon requested be withheld but which are not otherwise cited in this book are:

[2]Hearings before the Select Committee on Presidential Campaign Activities of the United States Senate pursuant to Senate Resolution 60, Sam J. Ervin, Jr., chairman, Howard H. Baker, Jr., vice chairman. Documents reproduced in this book that have appeared in the Ervin volumes are identified simply as having come from "Senate Hearings" or the "Senate Committee Final Report."

DATE	RECIPIENT	SUBJECT	WITHHELD FROM	FOUND IN
11/12/69	Kissinger	USIA	PPF1	SS85
1/31/70	Haldeman	JFK, LBJ TV press conferences	HRH229	PPF2
1/31/70	Woods Haldeman	press guests	HRH229	HRH138, 229*
2/9/70	Haldeman	press, business lists	HRH229	PPF2
5/25/70	Haldeman	congressional relations	PPF2, HRH229	HRH138, 140
11/22/70	Haldeman	Cliff White, Robert Finch	HRH138	PPF2, HRH229
12/11/70	Haldeman	unemployment	HRH164	HRH138
12/18/70	Haldeman	"nondescript" guest list	HRH138	HRH138*
3/4/71	Haldeman	staff friction	HRH140, 164, 230	HRH140*
3/8/71	Shultz	Secor Browne	HRH140	HRH230
4/27/71	Ehrlichman	housing projects	PPF3	HRH140, 230
4/27/71	Shultz Ehrlichman	appropriations freeze	PPF3	HRH140, 230
4/30/72	Haldeman	press war	HRH230	HRH162
8/9/72	Ehrlichman	price freeze	PPF4	HRH230
8/9/72	Colson	Pierre Rinfret	PPF4, CWC1	HRH162, 230
3/15/73	Ziegler Haldeman	press & Mrs. RN	PPF4	HRH162, 230

*Apparently this box contained more than one copy of the memorandum designated to be withheld.

A few memoranda identified as among the thirty-three linear feet of documents returnable to Nixon also were discovered in the research process. Most are from the weeks before his first inauguration, but two were generated while Nixon was President. Both were for Haldeman on April 13, 1970. One is reprinted in full. The other, located in HRH138 and 229, concludes "We must use our influence more effectively in the future to get our 70 year old people to retire gracefully. [Senator Hugh] Scott and [Senator] Margaret Smith are cases in point—both are 70. [Senator] George Murphy, of course, will have the age problem plaguing him in this campaign and we only hope he will survive it. Effective party leadership requires that we examine all of these cases and be ready for a contingency plan to deal with them in the future." These memoranda have been determined to be returnable to Nixon according to Nixon's right of private political association as intrepreted by the Supreme Court despite the fact that they were transcribed at government expense and directed to a government employee, Haldeman. Students of the rules of presidential document release may wish to study especially closely these rare examples available in the public domain.

Readers should remember that Richard Nixon did not personally decide which pages should be withdrawn from public release in 1987. This was done by employees of the Washington law firm of Miller, Cassidy, Larroca & Lewin, which he retained to represent him on the documents matter. Should President Nixon choose to personally review this book, he will be seeing for the first time numerous staff memoranda of his administration and others that he may not have seen for many years. Hence, all readers, including President Nixon, can participate in the process of judging whether there was good reason to request that many of the memoranda in this book be withheld from the public eye and of determining which memoranda might have been destroyed had the collection as a whole not been seized by the United States.

To increase readability all memoranda are reproduced in a "To:/From:" format. Many, though not all, marginal notes are reproduced. Minor spelling and punctuation errors as well as obvious typos apparently not intended by the author but which result from a typist's transcription have been corrected in the interest of fairness. For instance, the first sentence of a memo from Nixon to Alexander Butterfield on November 12, 1971, reads this way in the original: "I would like to make another purchase for long range plans of the 1966 French Bordeaux, Chateau Margot, Lafite, Rothschild and Hoitbrian." To reproduce what were most certainly secretarial errors would subject Nixon to unfair ridicule. This is an especially important point, given that Nixon did not personally review his memos.

In the same way, misspelled names have been routinely corrected except when a misspelling appears to have significance. For instance, in a March 7, 1972, memo from Charles Colson to Nixon, Colson twice spells Don Regan's name as "Reagan"; apparently, at this point he did not know how to spell Regan's name. (Interestingly, Nixon himself spelled Colson's name as "Coulson" until at least mid-1972.) All editorial notes or interpolations are enclosed in brackets. Initials and numbers below each document identify the box in the Special Files where the material can be located. In a couple of instances where it seemed of interest, file identifications, such as the Committee for the Re-election of the President and Material Removed from the President's Desk, have also been provided. The latter refers to materials removed from the President's desk following his resignation in 1974.

Within the general chronological framework, the documents have been organized in the following manner. First are the notes or other descriptions of meetings in which the President participated. Next come the memoranda either directly or indirectly *from* the President. These are followed by the memoranda *to* the President. Next appear memoranda from and to Haldeman, the chief of staff, who was succeeded by Alexander Haig. Following those are memoranda to and from Larry Higby, Haldeman's deputy. Next come the communications between or among other members of the staff or cabinet. Last is the correspondence with private individuals.

Nixon routinely made comments in the margin of his daily news summary, which were passed to the intended recipient(s) in the form of memoranda that did not mention Nixon by name but conveyed the substance of his comments. These were handled by a succession of aides over the years, including John Brown, Alexander Butterfield, Jon Huntsman, and Bruce Kehrli. Readers should be in no doubt as to the correct provenance of the comments and instructions thus conveyed.[3]

As the pace of activity picked up in the Nixon White House, Haldeman developed the habit of generating memoranda to himself derived from comments and instructions from President Nixon. These are usually called Action Memorandum, Action Memo, or Action Paper. As time wore on, some were called Talking Paper, Fresh Notes, or Political Strategy. At least one was called Thoughts on *New York Times* Strategy. Essentially, however, all were Haldeman's memos to himself carefully paraphrasing the President's own words—another form of presidential memorandum. When Haldeman was too busy to dictate these memoranda himself, he turned over his yellow pad notes to Higby, who completed the job.

The documents chosen for this book are roughly proportionate to the volume in which they were generated in the Nixon White House. The document production rate grew, together with staff size, to a crescendo in 1972. The Watergate revelations and resignations in the spring of 1973 had a dramatic impact on the number of documents turned out. Nixon, for instance, all but stopped dictating memoranda after James McCord began to disclose what he knew. This volume includes all the memoranda Nixon is known to have generated in his final fifteen months in office, according to Archives personnel, except, of course, those that he might have dictated for his personal diary, which were not transcribed and which he took with him when he left the White House.

Virtually all the documents reproduced here are from the White House Special Files. However, a few do come from other sources. In the instances where an important Nixon document, not yet located in the

[3]President Nixon took a deep interest early in his first term in developing the most efficient possible system for reacting to items in his news summaries. The procedures went through intensive refinement in the summer of 1969, when the machinery was established that was so effective through 1972. In the following memo Haldeman conveys to Patrick Buchanan on July 10, 1969, just how the President wanted the components of the procedure to fit together: "I believe that I have covered this subject with you at some point in the past, but apparently not with any results; therefore, I raise it again. The President insists now that when items appear in his news summary that obviously should have a reply or some other overt action by our side, a note should be made in the margin of the news summary as to what action is being taken. This puts on you the burden of determining what action should be taken and of implementing that action, and it should be clearly understood that you do have this burden. The point here is—as was discussed before—that the President now feels that he has to make margin notes himself on things that should be done rather than being told by the staff what *is* being done [emphasis in original]. This, of course, ties closely into the letters to the editors project which you are also supposed to be establishing, since that is one of the principal means of reaction to some of the items that appear in the news summary. He is particularly concerned with a reaction by us to anything in the news that appears to be slanted, and this, of course, applies even more importantly to television." HRH51

Archives files, appears in the Report of the Senate Watergate Committee, the document appears with appropriate reference. A few documents have been selected from the White House Central Files and are identified by the initials WHCF before the category and box identification.

The first of these describes the visit of Elvis Presley to the White House just before Christmas in 1970. Not long after the first portions of the Central Files were opened in late 1986, Archives personnel began to receive a significant but relatively modest stream of requests from Presley's fans for copies of these documents in a packet that sells for $7.35. By the spring of 1988 the Archives had mailed out a few hundred such packets. There was particular interest in the Nixon/Presley photographs, which actually had been available to the public since 1980. However, in mid-1988 syndicated columnist Bob Greene picked up the story and used it on three separate occasions. The result was a deluge of interest that quickly made the photographs the most-requested item in the history of the National Archives—far ahead of the previous leaders, a portrait of Abraham Lincoln and a photo of Pearl Harbor during the Japanese attack. Then Greene wrote an article on the documents for *Esquire*. The *Washington Post* magazine also got into the act, and MTV used the photos. The Presley documents are reproduced, therefore, as a service to those Presley fans who have yet to see them and to those Archives personnel who silently pray this might help stem requests.

Another selection from the Central Files is the request of CIA Director Richard Helms in January 1972 for permission to move a statue of Nathan Hale to CIA headquarters. At least as amusing, but unpublished, are the replies of John Ehrlichman and Rogers Morton. Bob Greene may wish to tell his readers about these gems.

Final selections from the Central Files are two examples of the President's Daily Diary, a log carefully put together outlining his meetings, movements, and telephone calls. Other materials used include excerpts from Nixon's May 1972 speech in Moscow. Readers who wish to experience the full and unanticipated historic irony of his visit to the Soviet Union should use as a companion text pages 224–240 of Gordon Liddy's *Will* (St. Martins, 1980), especially p. 229, which deals with the events of May 25 and 26, p. 231 (May 27), p. 232 (May 28), p. 234 (May 29), p. 236 (June 8 and 9), p. 237 (June 12), p. 238 (June 14), p. 239 (June 15), and p. 240 (June 16).

With his letter to Jay Lovestone of May 26, 1972, Charles Colson sent an article of September 8, 1948, on George McGovern from the Mitchell, South Dakota, *Daily Republic,* as well as pp. 58–61 of Robert Sam Anson's *McGovern: A Biography,* published in 1972 by Holt. Those pages deal with McGovern's activities in 1948. Anson's portrait of McGovern was one of the few serious examinations of the career of the Democratic nominee in that hectic year, and its contribution to the White House climate at that time should not be overlooked. (Anson, more recently, is also the author of *Exile: The Unquiet Oblivion of Richard Nixon,* Simon and Schuster,

1984.) Senator McGovern describes his postwar career in chapter 3 of *Grassroots: The Autobiography of George McGovern,* Random House, 1977. McGovern writes that during World War II he had considered himself a Republican.

Materials used from neither the Special nor Central files include the transcript of the famous "smoking gun" conversation of June 23, 1972, the release of which was the final straw that brought about Nixon's resignation; the Articles of Impeachment voted by the House Judiciary Committee, which will help readers ponder whether Richard Nixon deserved to be impeached; and excerpts from Nixon's comments on "Meet the Press" in 1988, which furnish some of his recent reflections on his administration.

The paucity of White House documents from the spring of 1973 onward raised a further editorial question. Many readers, especially those of a younger generation, may have no personal memory of the national furor of the early 1970s and, therefore, may have difficulty fully appreciating the depth of President Nixon's emotion as well as that of those who despised him. The first time Richard Nixon accepted the nomination of his party for President was on the centennial of the election of Abraham Lincoln of Illinois, and his speech at the Chicago Stockyards in 1960 was studded with references to the Great Emancipator. Nixon's great-grandfather served with the Ohio Infantry and is buried at Gettysburg. An analogy between the Civil War era and the Vietnam War period already was being widely drawn by the time Nixon took office in 1969. In the summer of 1988 a small news item was a reminder of the deep-seated distrust that remains at Kent State University as the result of the killing of four students there on May 4, 1970, by Ohio National Guardsmen. It was an announcement that some 110 crates of documents and photographs about the shootings were to be shipped to Yale University because the wounded and the families of those who died do not trust the state of Ohio. "Ohio might take some of the stuff and destroy it to destroy some of its unpleasant history," commented Dean Kahler, one of the wounded students, now a county commissioner in Athens, Ohio.[4]

To select for reprinting here editorials from the Washington or New York newspapers of 1973 to convey how deeply torn the country was by the revelations of that year would only duplicate what is readily available on microfilm and miss the point that Nixon was forced to resign when he lost Republican support. The task was to find editorial comment from a Republican paper in an area steeped with Lincolnian tradition. Then I remembered that I had first fully appreciated the profundity of Richard Nixon's trouble in 1973 when reading the editorials of the *Grant County Press* of Petersburg, West Virginia. Petersburg was a Union outpost during the Civil War. Lincoln's mother, Nancy Hanks, was born nearby, according to some sources. To this day the *Press* loves to print articles or commentaries about the area's heritage. In the context of the late nineteenth

---

[4] *Washington Times,* June 22, 1988.

century it was not especially surprising that Grant County politics became Republican. However, the fact that the phenomenon has persisted into the late twentieth century in a state where Democrats outnumber Republicans two to one is almost incredible, but true. The Republican primary settles all local and county offices; the Democrats usually don't bother to put up a candidate.

Alice Welton took over the *Press* in 1955, following the death of her husband, and ran the paper for the next three decades. She has never met Katharine Graham, who, under similar circumstances, took over her own family newspaper down the Potomac River in Washington. Many differences could be found between their newspapers, not the least of which was that Mrs. Welton wrote her own editorials in a Republican weekly in a Republican bastion. There was every reason why she could have been expected to remain silent on Richard Nixon's problem. However, to the consternation of many in Grant County, Mrs. Welton laid her views on the line, her anguish there for all to see. For a time the local controversy in Grant County over Alice Welton's editorials was more intense than that over the events down in Washington. While the editorials were not much noticed outside that part of West Virginia, they certainly were signals to the Democrats who represented Grant County in Congress that the Watergate investigation had bipartisan support.

This book is an interim progress report on the Special Files. Hundreds of thousands of important documents have yet to be evaluated. A few final notes as addenda:

—RE: *President to Flanigan of September 22, 1969.* Nixon's decision eventually led to the Newspaper Preservation Act of 1970, which permits competing newspapers to combine certain operations. The act was a reflection of Nixon's attitude toward antitrust and the press, and it was hailed as a measure to promote freedom of the press and preservation of newspapers that are failing economically. One of its consequences was to increase presidential leverage over the newspaper industry. Joint operating arrangements under the act, as of 1988, were in effect in Miami, Pittsburgh, San Francisco, Seattle, and elsewhere. A proposal to permit a joint operating arrangement in Detroit was under consideration. See, for example, "On the Road to Monopoly" by Albert Scardino, the *New York Times*, September 18, 1988, p. 1F.

—RE: *President to Haldeman of November 24, 1969.* On page 447 of his memoirs Nixon describes his daughter's attitude toward his attendance at her graduation in this way: "Although I knew how much Pat and Julie were counting on it, I canceled our plans to attend David's graduation from Amherst and Julie's graduation from Smith later in the spring. [. . .] She tried to hold back her tears, and she pointed out that only a few small radical groups were involved, and that everyone she knew—including students who opposed the war and my administration—felt that I should be able to attend the ceremony." It is not clear whether she might have changed her mind between November 1969 and the time of Nixon's decision, which he describes in his memoirs as having been taken in March 1970.

—RE: *President to Kissinger of November 24, 1969, and Andrews to President's File, June 16, 1972.* Vann's career is examined in *A Bright Shining Lie: John Paul Vann and America in Vietnam* by Neil Sheehan, Random House, 1988.

—RE: *Colson to Haldeman of February 13, 1970, regarding funding of the American Enterprise Institute.* Those interested in the evolution of the President's policy toward the establishment of private conservative foundations between March and July 1970 should consult memos in HRH61 and HRH62.

—RE: *President to Haldeman of March 10, 1970, on Robert McNamara.* Clark Mollenhoff's report to Haldeman of March 12, 1970, on McNamara's sale of his Ford stock in the 1960s is in HRH58.

—RE: *President to Haldeman of March 10, 1970, on the new press facilities.* Ziegler's prompt response to Haldeman of March 10, 1970, is in HRH58.

In conclusion, the extract on the facing page is reproduced exactly as it appears on an undated sheet of paper in box 48 of Haldeman's files. Its location suggests it was typed from Lord Robert Blake's biography *Disraeli* sometime between February and October 1972. The emphasis (those parts printed in roman type) is from underlining by an as yet unknown hand. At the beginning of Nixon's administration Daniel Moynihan gave him a copy of the book, which made a deep impact on him. In his memoirs Nixon writes that he read it twice. He apparently thought about what he had read with considerable frequency. Readers should keep this quotation in mind as they ponder Mr. Nixon's attitudes and actions.

Bruce Oudes
Rough Run, West Virginia

Where Disraeli excelled was in the art of presentation. He was an impresario and an actor manager. He was a superb parliamentarian, one of the half dozen greatest in our history. He knew how much depends upon impression, style, colour; and how small a part is played in politics by logic, cool reason, calm appraisal of alternatives. *This is why politicians appreciate him. They realize that* a large part of political life *in a parliamentary democracy* consists not so much in doing things yourself as in imparting the right tone to things that others do for you or to things that are going to happen anyway.

FROM: The President

RICHARD NIXON'S SECRET FILES

1969

JANUARY–APRIL

I would say the major mistake I made as President was . . . not doing in early 1969 what I did on May 3rd of 1972, and on December 15th of 1972, and that was to bomb and mine North Vietnam. I wanted to do it. I talked to Henry Kissinger about it. But we were stuck with the bombing halt that we had inherited from the Johnson administration with the Paris peace talks. I knew that, just like the cease-fire talks down here in Nicaragua, I didn't trust them at all, and they proved to be, of course, phony. But if we had done that then, I think we would have ended the war in Vietnam in 1969 rather than in 1973. That was my biggest mistake as President.

—RICHARD M. NIXON ON NBC'S "MEET THE PRESS," APRIL 10, 1988

JANUARY 8, 1969

TO: **Haldeman**

FROM: **RN**

You will recall that I asked for a check to be made on the effectiveness of our telephone campaign and on some of the other programs that we used. I know you are pretty tied down now with the White House responsibilities. I do, however, want some group to undertake this analysis so that it will be available to us within the next four or five months. Perhaps you can use Sears, under Ehrlichman's direction, to follow through from the White House level but with the primary responsibility either in the new National Committee set-up with Len Garment or possibly with a committee of both.

I have a feeling that we probably wasted a considerable amount of money during the campaign and that in certain areas we were grossly over-staffed. Some of this, of course, is inevitable but now a good, cold study of it can keep us from making such mistakes in the future.

On the same subject, I think it is important now for us to develop a plan for campaign funds for 1972. Johnson had enormous amounts col-

1

lected in the first year after he became President so that when 1964 rolled around he had all the money he needed. In this connection, as I have emphasized to you, funds should now be collected to take care of our deficit and transition expenses from those who failed to contribute before the election and, between now and 1972, we should get substantial contributions in the bank so that we will not have to make a major drive at the beginning of the election year.

JANUARY 9, 1969

TO: **Ehrlichman and Haldeman**

FROM: **RN**

This is not for you to write yourself but simply to take charge of and to find other people to do the work. I think an election analysis should be made answering these questions:

1. What was the effect of RN's not debating?

2. What was the effect of the HHH winner psychology which was built up by the press?

3. How much did Agnew hurt us?

4. What about the attacks on RN; how effective were they?

5. What about the anti statements in press and TV which reached a crescendo just before we left for Florida for our last swing, two and one-half weeks before the election?

What I am really trying to get at here is to get someone to study the last campaign in an objective way and to find out what happened. We know the bomb pause had a massive effect in shifting votes—Lou Harris is our best evidence on that score, according to Teddy White. On the other hand, again I think because of the total inadequacy of our staff in analyzing the *content* and *pictorial* slant, we do not really know what happened to voter sentiments. Perhaps what we need is an analysis of the TV coverage. How about Kevin Phillips as one of several to work on this.

JANUARY 15, 1969

TO: **Bob Haldeman**

FROM: **RN**

I want you to ride herd on Klein to see that someone is assigned to read the Pearson columns for the purpose of determining whether anyone in the Administration has violated my counsel for them not to talk to his people. The one exception here, of course, is Rogers who is smart enough to handle his situation.

The time to deal with this kind of problem is right at the outset of an Administration rather than waiting until we get burned.

HRH229

W/RN from PPF1

JANUARY 15, 1969

TO: **Bob Haldeman**

FROM: **RN**

What progress has been made in setting up a method where we can do some polling in depth on issues?

It was my understanding that we might get this done by some outside organization or foundation without cost to ourselves. I doubt if we want to expend a large amount of money on such a project but at least I would like a report within a couple of weeks after the Inauguration as to what Garment et al. have planned in this direction—if anything.

PPF1

JANUARY 16, 1969

TO: **Bob Haldeman**

FROM: **RN**

(This was on a tape prior to LBJ's State of the Union message.) RMW

Would you speak to Harlow with regard to Dirksen's project of making his own "State of the Union" speech, setting forth—in objective and not extremely partisan terms—just what we inherited as a contrast to the rosy picture Johnson will state in his State of the Union message.

My guess is that Dirksen will not follow through on this and that Harlow may have to find somebody else to do it. Perhaps this is a good project for a group of the young Congressmen, like Rumsfeld, to undertake.

A good example is Johnson's statement that balance of payments is better off than at any time since 1957. One economist at the Task Force Dinner said "That's just a lie" and Arthur Burns agreed that the figures had been juggled and that we actually faced a very desperate situation within the first year of our own Administration due to unfavorable trade balances. Johnson, of course, has obtained a good balance of payments figure by juggling the over-all statistics.

I cannot emphasize the importance of this project from a long range political standpoint and *I want a complete report from Haldeman within a week after the Inauguration* as to who is in charge of this activity and what I can expect to hear on carrying it out.

HRH229

JANUARY 16, 1969

TO: **John Ehrlichman**

FROM: **RN**

In considering appointments to prestige committees which do not require full time service, be sure that John Johnson, the publisher of *Ebony,* is high on the list. Incidentally, he also could be considered for a top ambassadorial post or a high level full time position if he would consider it.

Just as a further reminder to you—I have invited Jimmy Byrnes to the White House for his birthday which I think is sometime in May. This should be a formal dinner at night and will give us an opportunity to have good representation from the South—some high level Democratic representation—as well as some of our people from the VIP list.

Along the same lines, since this is the 10th anniversary of my trip to Russia we will have a reception for those who are members of the "Kitchen Cabinet." I have included this in a previous memorandum but wanted to put it in as a reminder now so that it could be worked into our schedule. The "Kitchen Cabinet" date can be anytime during the period I was in Russia which gives us about two weeks to play with in late June and early July.

PPF1

JANUARY 17, 1969

TO: **Bob Haldeman**

FROM: **RN**

What happened on Agnew's project with regard to the Brooklyn Navy Yard?

PPF1

JANUARY 21, 1969

TO: **Bob Haldeman**

FROM: **The President**

Would you put all the staff available to that task and get it done—let me see the forms and the letters, of course, will be signed by auto pen.

They should include letters to those who are the key men of the Inaugural Committee. I am referring to Bill Marriott, and any others who should be included in that category of some importance.

They should also include the Ministers who participated in the Inauguration itself, as well as in the morning ceremony. They should include letters to the artists that appeared at the Gala and at the Inaugural Concert, and letters should also go to each of the bands and marching units. I am referring, of course, to a letter to the head of the band or marching unit who happened to be in the Parade.

One of our difficulties in the past is that our thank-you notes have been bogged down because of lack of staff and go out two or three weeks, if not a month later. We will be held to a different standard now, and I want these to get out in 48 hours since we have enough staff to do it.

I am going to give a little guidance with regard to the form in the dictation now.

To the Ministers: something like this (and, incidentally, it can be the same letter to the people who participated in the morning affair as well as those who participated in the noon affair, with slight changes as far as the description of the event is concerned):

Dear _____:

I want to express my deep appreciation to you for participating in the _____ (whatever the morning prayer thing was).

The problems facing the United States and the world are so serious that we shall all need Divine Guidance if we are adequately to meet the challenge of our times.

Your words, as well as your presence, on that occasion will be a source of strength and inspiration to me in the years ahead.

Sincerely,

Now, with regard to the Inauguration—just "your participation in the Inauguration ceremonies at the Capitol" or something like that.

To entertainers:

Dear _____:

I want you to know how much I appreciated your participation in the Inaugural Ball at the (whichever hotel it was) or whether it was the Inaugural Gala or the Inaugural Concert.

Your presence at the occasion, as well as your performance, meant a great deal to the thousands of visitors who had come from all over the United States.

If it was the Gala, then go on to say:

I only regret that I was unable to attend the event personally, but through my daughters and their friends, I received a vivid eyewitness account which made me realize how much I had missed.

I shall look forward to hearing (seeing or whatever) you perform either on television or in person sometime in the days ahead.

Where it was the other two things (Concert or Ball):

Your magnificent performance was one of the highlights of the whole Inaugural program.

Where I did not meet them personally:

I only regret that I did not have an opportunity to express my appreciation personally.

I hope that I may be able to hear you again at some time in the future.

These are all just alternate lines depending upon where they fit.

Rose will have a pretty good idea, or somebody who was with me, Hughes, as to which lines would be effective or right.

Now, in the case of the pianist, and also in the case of the singer at the Inaugural Concert, and with regard to Roger Williams and any others (Rose and whoever is most knowledgeable, perhaps Ehrlichman, with regard to the quality here), you can add a note:

I hope that on some occasion in the future I shall have the opportunity of hearing you in the White House.

You can't say that with all because some of them, of course, we can't do that with.

Now, with regard to bands and marching units, these letters are very important and should go to the head of the band or marching unit. Don't make it "Dear Friend" or anything like that, but find out who the head of the band is from the Inaugural Committee and write it, "Dear Mr. _____:"

I wish you would express my appreciation to the members of the (Ohio State Marching Band) for their participation in the Inaugural Parade.

If it was a special unit:

It was a great sight as it came by the Reviewing Stand (or as the unit came by the Reviewing Stand), and I shall always be proud that they played such a significant part on the occasion of my Inauguration as President of the United States.

Here, again, variations may be necessary.

To Members of the Inaugural Committee:

I would naturally have liked the inauguration program in any event, but I am sure you must be gratified by what seems to be the universal opinion that this was one of the most efficiently organized and executed inaugural programs in history.

I know what a tremendous burden is placed upon the members of the Inaugural Committee (or describe whatever they are), and I shall always be grateful for the time and effort you devoted, far beyond the call of duty, to making the event such a success.

With every good wish

Something like that will do it.

This is to each of the Congressional Medal of Honor Winners who were in attendance at the Inauguration:

Dear (Mr., Sergeant)

I want you to know how honored I was that you attended my Inauguration as President of the United States.

Your magnificent service to the cause of peace and freedom as so eloquently demonstrated by the honor you have received will be a constant source of inspiration and strength to me in the years ahead.

Sincerely,

To each of the astronauts:

Dear (Mr. or Commander)

(This is not just the three that went around the moon, but all of them.)

It was a special honor for me that you and your colleagues were able to attend my inauguration as President of the United States.

Like millions of Americans I have had an immense interest in the space program from its inception, and I shall look forward not only to following your activities in the years ahead but in giving them my full support.

With every good wish,

Sincerely,

To the three that went around the moon put a P.S. on:

I want you to know also that from all reports (names of other two other than the one you are writing to) and you have made an immensely favorable impression on the nation in the various appearances you have made since the completion of your mission. You are a great source of inspiration to the youth of America as well as some of us who are probably a bit old to contemplate taking that first trip to Mars!

PPF1

JANUARY 23, 1969

TO: **Don Hughes**

FROM: **The President**

In the White House tour yesterday some very interesting descriptions were given of the rooms by the man who took us around. This was not West but the younger fellow.

I would like for you to ask him to prepare for me, not at too great length (perhaps one paragraph each), the salient facts about each room that he showed me on the first and the second floor. What I want is the history of the room. For example, the fact that the State Dining Room was, up until the War of 1812, used as the office of the President, and any other colorful facts that he thinks might be pertinent.

Tell him to use his judgment as to how much material to include. I do not want a whole book because I will not have time to read it.

PPF1

JANUARY 24, 1969

TO: **John Ehrlichman**

FROM: **Bud Krogh**

RE: **Inaugural Parade Disturbance**

Question 1: When the President ordered the militant protesters arrested, what specific action was taken by the Secret Service and other authorities involved?

Answer: A reconstruction of the events at and before the time of the disturbances—based upon inputs from the Secret Service, Deputy Attorney General Kleindienst, and the Executive Command and Communications Center for the District of Columbia—reveals the following:

1. Before the motorcade left the Capitol, Deputy Assistant Director Bob Taylor advised the President that there was some disorder along the parade route. The President, according to Bob Taylor, said words to the effect that people should not be allowed to break the law and that the police should be advised that the law should be enforced.

2. Taylor informed Chief of Police Layton that he had instructions on the best authority that the police should enforce the law. Chief Layton assured Mr. Taylor that as was the usual policy of the Metropolitan Police, all violators would be arrested.

3. As the motorcade approached 10th Street and Pennsylvania Avenue, Bob Taylor had been advised by radio that some smoke bombs had been thrown in the vicinity of 14th Street and Pennsylvania Avenue. He told the President that some smoke bombs had been thrown. The smoke was visible. According to Bob Taylor, the President told Taylor to tell "them" that anyone who throws a smoke bomb should be arrested. I was advised by Mr. Kleindienst that from his vantage point on the 3rd floor balcony, there was not sufficient provocation or any "overt acts" prior to the time the Presidential motorcade passed the central point of disorder at E Street and Pennsylvania to warrant mass arrests. Bob Taylor, after receiving the President's instructions, transmitted them over the radio to the Secret Service Command Post. By this time, the motorcade was approaching the area of disorder.

4. Immediately after the motorcade passed the main disorder point at E Street and Pennsylvania, the demonstrators left that area and began to walk up 14th Street. Kleindienst received word that the demonstrators were headed towards Lafayette Square. He ordered that they should be stopped.

*5. Immediately after the President's order was transmitted over the radio, and as the motorcade was approaching and proceeding through the main disturbance area, the Secret Service reported that the situation was such that it was not practicable to make many arrests. Police and enforcement officers were extremely busy preventing the crowd from entering the Street and preventing the thrown missiles from hitting the car. According to both the Secret Service and the Executive Command and Communications Center of the District of Columbia, several arrests were made in the area. Secret Service advised that none of the arrests can be said "to have resulted precisely from the orders given by the President. . . ." However, a number of arrests were made prior to the arrival of the motorcade at the scene and shortly thereafter. The Secret Service feels that these arrests would have been made even if the order had not been given. The conclusion as stated by the Secret Service: "We do not feel that DAD Taylor's radio order precipitated any arrests."

6. Relevant to the question of why arrests were not made earlier *before* the disturbance occurred are the following facts:

a. The more militant demonstrators, members of SDS and the Yippies, had met in Franklin Park at about noon on the 20th. Verbal permission was granted for a rally to be held at Franklin Park by Mr. Nash Castro of the Park Service—Interior Department at 10:00 A.M. Mr. Castro advised me that he felt it was necessary to issue the permit to avoid a confrontation at the Park which would have precipitated mass arrests.

b. Accordingly, when the militants met at the Park, few arrests could be made because the group had been granted permission to be there. The Park Service Police did make a few arrests for destruction of government property; some militants broke down barrels to make staves and clubs.

c. After noon, groups of militants proceeded down 14th and 15th Streets towards Pennsylvania Avenue in an *orderly* manner. The Metropolitan Police Department reported to their Command Center that the militants broke no local ordinances en route to Pennsylvania Avenue.

d. On reaching Pennsylvania Avenue, the militants merged into the crowds, thus making it difficult to isolate them. According to Mr. Kleindienst, the protesters assembling on the corners of 13th, 14th, and 15th Streets and Pennsylvania Avenue were not doing anything which would have justified mass arrests. This opinion was shared by Attorney-General Designate John Mitchell at this point.

e. After the motorcade passed the disturbance area, and as the militants surged towards Lafayette Square, Mr. Kleindienst's order to stop them was carried out. Numerous arrests were made for disorderly conduct. According to the Metropolitan Police Department's record of arrests, 4 arrests were made on January 20 for throwing missiles and a total of 87 arrests were made on that date.

NOTE: The most serious problem discernible in the present system for controlling civil disorders within the District is: operational decision-making takes place without sufficient liaison with all units involved with a need to know. The Secret Service advised me that they have consistently opposed the granting of permits to militant groups,* and they would like an opportunity to explain their position fully. Secret Service was not informed of the fact that verbal permission was granted to the militants to rally in Franklin Park. While it may have been a wise choice politically to issue the verbal permit, the fact that the final result was to create a heavy burden on those directly involved with security of the President along Pennsylvania Avenue suggests that it would be advisable to alter the system so the opinion of the Secret Service is requested before a permit is granted.

The decision may well be to go ahead and issue the permit, but the Secret Service will know in advance exactly what the legal status of the protesters is, how much pressure can be expected from a rally area, and add police or troops as deemed necessary. Also, it was suggested by Secret Service that a more direct line of communication be established whereby the Secret Service Agent with operational responsibility can call in troops for quick security if necessary.

Question 2: When Deputy Attorney-General Designate Kleindienst suggested through the Justice Department Communications Center that the motorcade should increase speed at approximately 12th Street and then move to the south side of Pennsylvania Avenue to bypass the disturbance area, what follow-through was there?

Answer:

1. Secret Service reported that Mr. Kleindienst's instruction to move to the south side of Pennsylvania Avenue was never received by the Secret Service Command Post. Mr. Kelley reported to me that even though the instructions were received, the decision to move to the south side of the Street would be DAD Bob Taylor's to make and it would be based on intelligence received from Secret Service Personnel in the area. Neither Assistant Director Kelley nor Mr. Rundle, who were both in the area of E Street and Pennsylvania Avenue, made such a recommendation.

2. The order to accelerate between 12th and 14th Streets was received by the Secret Service from the Justice Department. This suggestion

was similar to the one received from the Secret Service Agent in the area who recommended that the speed be increased between 12th and 15th Streets. Both instructions were coordinated with Bob Taylor who gave the order to the driver to increase speed between 12th and 15th Streets. Secret Service estimated that the motorcade was accelerated from four to seven miles per hour.

Recommendation: That a thorough review of the procedures used in Washington, D.C., during times of civil disorders and mass protests be made very soon with particular emphasis on the position of the Secret Service. Secret Service is dissatisfied with the "permissive" "liberal" attitude which has flourished in the District.**

*HANDWRITTEN NOTE BY RN: "I question the advisability of permits. They seem to aggravate the situation by making it lawful and easier to congregate."
**HANDWRITTEN NOTE BY RN: "RN agrees. On balance, however, it seems a good job by those in charge considering the orders they had."

POF1

JANUARY 25, 1969

TO: **Mrs. Nixon**

FROM: **The President**

In talking with the GSA Director with regard to RN's room, what would be most desirable is an end table like the one on the right side of the bed which will accommodate *two* dictaphones as well as a telephone. RN has to use one dictaphone for current matters and another for memoranda for the file which he will not want transcribed at this time. In addition, he needs a bigger table on which he can work at night. The table which is presently in the room does not allow enough room for him to get his knees under it.

PPF1

JANUARY 25, 1969   1:35 P.M.

TO: **Bob Haldeman**

FROM: **The President**

I want a report by noon today on what action we have taken with regard to the Mississippi tornado and what action we could or should take. In the future, I need to be better briefed on such matters so that I can personally indicate an interest—for example, by a telephone call to the Governor, etc. We dropped the ball here and I do not want this to happen again.

Let me make it very clear that this is the kind of action where whatever we may be doing at lower levels—I note, for example, that

Hardin indicated that some Agriculture Department emergency credit programs may be used to aid victims—the President should be the one who immediately reacts to a wire such as the one we received from Williams and makes a public announcement. I saw the wire in my file last night with no indication of what, if any, action had been taken on it. Don't let this happen again.

PPF1

JANUARY 25, 1969

TO: **John Ehrlichman**

FROM: **The President**

RE: **The Five O'Clock Group**

I noted some favorable quotes in the international press with regard to the Inaugural. I imagine too that there were some favorable editorial quotes in the U.S. papers. I am sure it will occur to the five o'clock group that a pretty good collection of one-line quotes—such as appears in the advertisement of a hit play or on the cover of a book—could be attached to the mail-out of the RN Inaugural Address when one is made.

PPF1
W/RN from PPF1 [correct]*

JANUARY 25, 1969

TO: **John Ehrlichman**

FROM: **The President**

For the five o'clock group, I again emphasize my desire to have someone do an effective job on the RN come-back theme. Some way I just don't feel we have adequately presented this case and that we have generally been too defensive on our whole PR approach.

PPF1

JANUARY 25, 1969

TO: **Dr. DuBridge**

FROM: **The President**

I have long favored a dramatic escalation of our testing program for the peaceful uses of atomic explosives. I recognize this is controversial but when it comes to the building of harbors, canals, etc., I think we should be very aggressive in going forward. I covered this, you may remember,

*[Mistakes in archival handling in cases such as this were apparently the result of more than one copy of a memorandum designated for withdrawal appearing in a given box.]

in a major speech in the 1960 campaign in Toledo. You might dig out this speech just as a reference point.

I note the news report with regard to the first industrial nuclear explosion in Australia. I think we ought to develop a forward position on this and see what applications can be made, for example, in the construction of a new Panama Canal and in other fields. I recognize the controversy involved—that some believe that using atomic explosives for peaceful purposes does not provide enough advantage over conventional explosives to be worth the potentially bad publicity we get in national news as well as the potential of spreading the "art" in ways that other nations might quickly develop a military capability.

I would like a briefing by Dr. DuBridge on this subject, and if you think well of it, we might go beyond that and give far greater impetus to this program.

cc: Henry Kissinger

PPF1

JANUARY 29, 1969

TO: **Bob Haldeman**

FROM: **The President**

Any progress on the California land purchase for the summer residence?

PPF1

JANUARY 29, 1969

TO: **Bob Haldeman**
        John Ehrlichman

FROM: **The President**

Would you give me a report on the progress of the official picture?

As you recall, I mentioned that I saw pictures hanging in the Defense Department that I thought were much too severe.

If that is the one that has been selected I want it changed.

PPF1

JANUARY 29, 1969

TO: **John Ehrlichman**

FROM: **The President**

As Jim Fulton came through the line in the House yesterday he mentioned that he had talked to someone, I assume you, with regard to Ed Nixon becoming a member of one of the Congressional Staff Committees that has to do with environmental problems. I don't know what was involved, but this might be a pretty good assignment in the event that you are thinking in that direction.

Give me a report.

PPF1

FEBRUARY 4, 1969   10:30 A.M.

TO: **John Ehrlichman**

FROM: **The President**

There are three items that I need a report on today (and I am writing this memorandum on Monday).

What have you found out with regard to how I can handle the announcement of using the $100,000 increase for presidential salary for White House expenses?

What is the situation with regard to *Six Crises*—do I own the rights to further sale of paperbacks or hardcovers and, if so, how will this be handled? My guess is that with the interest in the presidency and a bit of promotion by Klein and his group we might make this a pretty good asset in the months ahead. (I am not thinking, of course, financially, but in terms of the political effect.)

What action did you take with regard to the honorarium we were to receive from *Ladies' Home Journal* on the preface to *Six Crises*? I would like to have the *Ladies' Home Journal* pay the money directly to my favorite charity or charities. On reflection, I think if half of it could go to the Boys Clubs of America and the other half to the organization which supports the singer we had at the Sunday service, Jimmy McDonald, that would be most useful.

Would you follow up and give me a report.

PPF1; HRH228

FEBRUARY 5, 1969

TO: **Bob Haldeman**

FROM: **The President**

I would like to get Eugene McCarthy down for a visit at some appropriate time. This possibly could be scheduled before the trip abroad, but preferably probably should be afterwards. In discussing this with Harlow, point out that I think it would be well to worry Teddy a bit in renewing my acquaintance with McCarthy.

PPF1

FEBRUARY 5, 1969

TO: **Bob Haldeman**

FROM: **The President**

You will recall that I suggested we ought to get TV tapes recording the major events of the Administration. I do not want a full-time television crew but I do want these tapes made available. I am sure that USIA must be doing taping of our press conferences, and I think that we should direct Shakespeare to cover all future press conferences and to be present in every instance when the commercial TV is allowed to cover an event.

My TV library generally, incidentally, is pretty skimpy. Somebody ought to start going now to the networks to obtain if we can the tapes of everything we have done on TV over the years.

When Ollie Atkins comes in, for example, the USIA TV guy could also be asked to take a shot.

In carrying this out I definitely do *not* want to do it if it requires putting on an expensive TV crew full-time, unless the 5 O'clock Group determines that this would be useful to us in terms of disseminating our information to stations across the country who might not be covered by networks.

Also, in this respect, getting this TV record will be very helpful in developing documentaries as we go along which we will find very useful in the years ahead.

PPF1

FEBRUARY 5, 1969

TO: **Bob Haldeman**

FROM: **The President**

Will you give me a report on what letters went out to the bands that played at the Inaugural Ball and the celebrities who participated in the inaugural ceremonies. I specifically remember that we covered those who were in the Gala and the Concert, but I cannot recall letters which should have gone to Art Linkletter, Les Brown, et al. If they did go I want to be sure that they were properly first names.

With further reference to that subject, I still believe that the top celebrities who appeared at the Inaugural Ball should receive the Inaugural memento which we sent to the top contributors. As I recall the inscription would fit them just as well as it would a top financial contributor.

Give me a report.

PPF1

FEBRUARY 5, 1969

TO: **John Ehrlichman**

FROM: **The President**

To be passed on to the 5 O'clock Group:

I still have not had any progress report on what procedure has been set up to continue on some kind of a basis the letters to the editor project and the calls to TV stations.

Two primary purposes would be served by establishing such a procedure. First, it gives a lot of people who were very active in the campaign a continuing responsibility which they would enjoy having. Second, it gives us what Kennedy had in abundance—a constant representation in letters to the editor columns and a very proper influence on the television commentators. As a starter, some letters thanking those who have written favorable things about the Administration might be in order and expressing agreement with the views they have indicated. In addition, individuals can express their own enthusiasm for the RN crime program in Washington, the RN press conference technique and the Inaugural, and the general performance since the Inauguration. Later on, letters can be written taking on various columnists and editorialists when they jump on us unfairly.

I do not want a blunderbuss memorandum to go out to hundreds of people on this project, but a discreet and nevertheless effective Nixon Network set up.

Give me a report.

PPF1

FEBRUARY 5, 1969

TO: **Research**

FROM: **The President**

Winston Churchill had a quote which, in essence, said that criticism is good for the soul, and that he had never been lacking in receiving it.

Will you get this Churchill quote for me before the press conference Thursday.

PPF1

FEBRUARY 13, 1969

TO: **Bob Haldeman**

FROM: **The President**

The *Baltimore Sun* had a story indicating that the Ford Foundation had provided travel and study awards to 8 former aides of Senator Robert Kennedy, totaling $131,000.

With McGeorge Bundy heading up the Foundation this is a pretty good indication of how they scratch each other's backs.

The point of this memo is to suggest that if we have someone who is oriented our way and whom we are unable to place, we might have considerable leverage with the Ford Foundation in view of this historical record.

They probably will feel obligated to balance the thing out to an extent.

rrrl

FEBRUARY 14, 1969

TO: **Henry Kissinger**

FROM: **The President**

Jim Linen also leaned hard on the fact that Graham Martin was now "in pasture" as Dean of the School of Foreign Service at Georgetown. He says that Martin fell out of favor because of his opposition to McNamara's positions and because he was not in step with some of the State Department's Asia hands.

I have great personal confidence in Graham Martin and believe he should be brought back into the foreign service. I think he would be an excellent appointment for Tokyo, Bonn or Pakistan if he would accept one of these. If you think well of this suggestion put this in the form of a memo from me to Rogers. My purpose here, among others, is not to let the State Department play its usual game of promoting their favorites and kicking out those who may disagree with their policies from time to time.

PPFl

FEBRUARY 17, 1969

TO: **Bob Haldeman**

FROM: **The President**

When the oval room is re-done I would like to have the coffee table in front of the fireplace replaced by one that does not block the view of the fireplace from the desk.

PPFl

FEBRUARY 17, 1969

TO: **John Ehrlichman**

FROM: **The President**

This shockingly smug "retraction" of a viciously false misquote in the marked editorial from the Sunday *Washington Post* indicates a problem

I want you to zero in hard on with Herb Klein and the 5 O'clock Group. I know it is our general policy to let false statements by everyone from Pearson up to the *Times* go uncorrected on the ground that we can't get a retraction and that all we do is to make the one who published the falsehood an even worse enemy.

I agree with this appraisal, but also there is an even greater danger in allowing a false statement to go by without having a correction demanded promptly so that it is on the record. Have all the members of the 5 O'clock Group read this editorial and see what happens when this is the case.

The policy of this Administration, and this includes all Cabinet officers, should be to set the record straight whenever there is a misrepresentation. Usually the publication involved will not make the correction and if it does it will simply repeat the libel. On the other hand, prompt action may result in the false statement not being used by others who are innocent with regard to its inaccuracy. Have Herb Klein follow up with the Cabinet officers, and Ziegler should handle it wherever anything involves the White House or the White House staff.

PPF1

FEBRUARY 17, 1969

TO: **Ray Price**

FROM: **The President**

I think that Tom Wicker's column in the February 16 *New York Times* may be useful in preparing the statement on the student demonstrations. However, I would strongly question his brushing off some of the outrageous actions which have taken place with the idea that "they are trying to tell us something" and "listen to them and treat them as adults." As you well know from the campaign, the extremists do not want to be listened to and do not want to discuss their problems rationally. Some simply want to disrupt and others want nothing less than complete capitulation to demands that would destroy the higher education system.

PPF1

FEBRUARY 17, 1969

TO: **RMW**

FROM: **The President**

I would like to have Richard Rodgers for a very early White House dinner. On that occasion my plan would be to have the entertainment consist of a medley of his works. When John Ehrlichman returns from Paris bring this memorandum to his attention and he will follow through.

In that connection we need as a basic research document the names of all artists and orchestra leaders, etc. who supported us in the campaign. They should come before others who did not, assuming, of course, that their quality is high enough. Under no circumstances can we have in the White House, no matter how good a supporter, an artistic group which is sub-par because this would reflect on both the group and the White House.

PPF1

FEBRUARY 17, 1969

TO: **RMW**

FROM: **The President**

The silver Parker Pen that was given to me on Election Day, November 5, 1968, is such a good one that I would like to get one other exactly like it as a spare.

Will you check it out and arrange for a purchase.

PPF1

FEBRUARY 17, 1969

TO: **RMW**

FROM: **The President**

Would you check to see whether Miss Burum, my 5th grade teacher, and Mrs. Dargatz, the daughter of the doctor who took care of me when I fell out of the buggy as a child, received answers to their letters. If they did not answers should be prepared. Let me know.

Miss Burum, incidentally, was a remarkably good teach as I recall.

PPF1

MARCH 13, 1969

TO: **John Ehrlichman**

FROM: **The President**

I was impressed at both the Congressional receptions to note the number of good ideas that members of Congress had—particularly for domestic programs and some foreign ones—ideas that had imagination and emotion and were not as routine as most of those that seem to come up from our White House and Cabinet teams.

I realize that about 75 percent of these ideas are unworkable, but now and then one of them really has the quality that should be considered. What happens here is that White House staffers and Cabinet members— not being responsible to any constituency and not getting out to the country or reading any significant amount of mail from the country—get very much out of touch with the country and become pretty ingrown and incestuous intellectually. I want you to put some very sensitive person on the project of seeing what programs are advocated in the Congress to which we might give some consideration in the Executive branch. I know that many Congressmen and Senators send their bills to the Executive Branch for consideration, and many of them are simply for home consumption with no thought that they might work. On the other hand, Clarence Brown has a suggestion for bonds which would give private citizens a chance to participate in the rebuilding of cities, etc., which might have an immense amount of moxie in it. And several others of this type were suggested.

What is needed here is to take this out of the Harlow group who are frankly too busy and who look upon their jobs, properly, simply to respond in a way requiring the least possible action to Congressional pressures—and put it in some place in the executive group. Perhaps Bud Wilkinson's office is the place to put this project. Some young fellow there, like the young fellow from UCLA, might be a potential candidate, although this will take perhaps more than one and maybe two people to implement on a part-time basis. Follow through and see what you can do. What I am interested in here now—I wish to emphasize not to massage the Congressmen and Senators on their pet ideas, many of which are simply too far out to even consider—but to feed into our own executive organization a little more imagination and ingenuity. I sense that we seem to be pretty short on such ideas due to the very good reason that we are simply too busy fielding the balls that are being knocked our way. Let's correct this.

PPF1

MARCH 13, 1969

TO: **Herb Klein**

FROM: **The President**

It is vital in the next five or six weeks before the ABM votes are taken that we get a better than even break in seeing that those who support ABM get on all the programs. This not only means "Meet the Press," "Face the

Nation," "Issues and Answers," but the "Today" show, the radio talk shows and their counterparts at local levels.

I want you to use every possible method to see to it that articulate supporters of ABM get their fair amount of time on these shows. This will be difficult because, as you know, Huntley-Brinkley, Cronkite and most of the ABC staff are opposed to our decision, but I want you not only to see that our people get on, but these programs are to be carefully monitored, and every time one of these opponents opens his mouth calls should flood the station. But even more important, I want you to get on personally and arrange for equal time for somebody from our side.

Apart from this reaction, of course, I would like for you to game plan a scheme whereby we, on a positive basis, see that Packard, Laird, any scientists that Kissinger can dig up that might go our way, and other people (for example, Rockefeller who will speak out for us) get equal time on this subject and that they are properly briefed before they go on.

cc: John Ehrlichman

PPF1

(Copy of a handwritten letter)

Dear President Nixon:

Thank you so much for the lovely and rare Boehm bird—my first such treasure! It brings us all great joy.

We were delighted to see you in Paris. You and your family must be very proud of the unanimous opinion in France and in America that your visit was a personal success as well as of enormous benefit in helping France and the United States to understand each other so that they work more efficiently together.

Quite frequently I see a more positive attitude in my own everyday contacts.

I read in the paper today that Boehm birds were so different and that only last week one valued at $250 was sold for $18,000.*

You'd better hold [on] to those birds!

Thank you so much again.

Sincerely,

[s/Eunice K. Shriver]
18 March 1969

*HANDWRITTEN NOTE BY RN: "Show Mrs. N"

PPF188:
MATERIAL REMOVED
FROM PRESIDENT'S DESK

APRIL 7, 1969

TO: **Mr. Haldeman**

FROM: **Alexander P. Butterfield**

RE: **Notes from the President**

The President has expressed deep concern over two separate but related items. The first has to do with the abrupt decline in the Administration's domestic activities and news stories . . . a decline which started a week ago and has continued unabated to date. He read in his daily news analysis that "the week did not produce a single domestic story worthy of prominent attention from all networks for two consecutive days." There appears to be a vacuum on the domestic front (where opportunity for news is the greatest), and it has given a virtual open field to the opposition. "While we've been sitting on our hands, or seemingly so, they have been hitting us from all sides on the Safeguard System and Vietnam." The President believes that you should hold a meeting with Herb Klein, et al. and see what can be done immediately to reverse the trend.

The President's second concern pertains to our campaign to support his modified Safeguard System decision. He would like a report explaining who is in charge and why no action took place during the past week. (It may be that Bryce Harlow's briefing of earlier this morning came after the President wrote these notes to you.)

POF1

APRIL 10, 1969

TO: **Mr. Bryce Harlow**
      Mr. Herb Klein

FROM: **Alexander P. Butterfield**

The President noted a piece in his morning news summary which referred to former astronaut John Glenn's opposition to the antimissile Safeguard System because "nobody can tell us if the doggone thing will positively work."

With reference to Glenn's "rationale," the President wonders if he knew in advance that America's first manned space shot would "positively work." He went on to suggest that it would be a good idea to line up a few people like Glenn (i.e., astronauts and others of that general type) who could speak out *in favor* of the system.

cc: Mr. BeLieu
    Mr. Keogh

HRH50

APRIL 14, 1969

TO: **Bob Haldeman**
John Ehrlichman

FROM: **The President**

April 30 will mark the first 100 days of the Administration. Within a week I want on my desk a complete battle plan with regard to what the National Committee, Harlow's staff, Klein, et al., plan to do to see that a number of Senators, Congressmen, Governors, etc. make appropriate statements on the first 100 days.

We can, of course, assume now that the opposition will be yelping at our heels on that date. I do not want to come into that date without having a very effective, affirmative program covering speeches, television appearances, etc. pointing with pride with regard to what the first 100 days have really accomplished. Perhaps what we need here is to look at Dirksen's speech of a couple of weeks ago and see that several of that type are prepared and delivered from all sources—the National Committee, a prominent Governor or two, as well as the RN task forces in the House and Senate which I understand have now been set up.

I know what I personally will do with regard to dealing with this problem, and I am not interested in what the five o'clock group has to suggest with regard to my own activities. What I want to see is what will be done apart from what I say or do to make the most of this date through all the media, on the floor of the House and Senate, etc.

PPF1; HRH229

APRIL 14, 1969

TO: **John Ehrlichman**

FROM: **The President**

Tricia has agreed to go to California to appear for Goldwater. I want you to personally take charge of this project and see that one of our best advance men handles it. She says that she prefers not to make a speech, although she will be glad to participate in a big reception (probably one for Goldwater Jr.'s women workers might be in order).

On the other hand, she is perfectly willing to have any type of Q & A session or press conference. I believe that an appearance on the major independent television show—not the Chief of Police but the conservative who is presently making $300,000 a year, might be the best way she could appear. What is most important is to put the emphasis on television and not on newspaper appearance. Goldwater is going to win it, in any event, so what I am interested in is getting Tricia on a good television night-time show.

Haldeman can give you advice as to what would be the best one for her to appear on. Give me a report on it.

NO DIS

APRIL 14, 1969*

TO: **The Secretary of State**
       The Secretary of Defense
       Henry Kissinger
       Robert Ellsworth

FROM: **The President**

I was frankly quite disappointed there was no follow-up on the part of our representatives on the speech I made at NATO and the three positive recommendations (which should cause no problem for anyone). In reading all the newspapers, and particularly in reading the *New York Times* editorial, it appeared that the NATO representatives brushed them aside and decided not to give them consideration because of internal problems.

In the future I want it understood that when the President of the United States makes a major speech of this type I shall expect all representatives of our government to go all out in seeing that there is some implementation and some support of the President's position. There was no statement whatever from any person in our government indicating support of the proposition, praising the recommendations, or any other action of this type. I recall that during the past 8 years Kennedy or Johnson could burp and the whole administration establishment went into action saying what a "great and imaginative proposal" this was.

I want some action taken beginning immediately to see to it that the three recommendations are implemented by NATO. I think taking some rather strong positions, going beyond the toasts, the nice dinners, the "consultation ad infinitum" might bring us a little respect in the organization which we currently do not seem to enjoy.

This memorandum is not written in anger, but only with some dismay that we looked so inept and frankly made the President look so rather foolish in making a major statement and then getting no backing from the people in his own Administration. I want to see a battle plan as to what is to be done specifically on this score.

*THE FOLLOWING HANDWRITTEN NOTATION IS FOUND ON THE UPPER RIGHT CORNER OF THE FIRST PAGE: "file memo not sent"

24   FROM: THE PRESIDENT

APRIL 16, 1969

TO: **Colonel Hughes**

FROM: **H. R. Haldeman**

Per our conversation today, the President has given instructions that the *Julie* and *Tricia* should be decommissioned and put out of service, and the *Sequoia* should be turned back to the Secretary of Defense for his use.

This should be done as quickly as possible and confirmed back to the President because in his own way he intends to get the word out that he has taken these actions.

He also wants to be sure that Bebe knows of this plan so that he will know the *Julie* will no longer be available in Florida.

HRH50

APRIL 21, 1969

TO: **Colonel Hughes**

FROM: **H. R. Haldeman**

Here it comes again—more Haldeman nitpicking I'm afraid.

I do think, however, that it is important to cover these things—as we have agreed—when and as they come up rather than letting problems build up.

The subject this time is movies at Camp David. My feeling is that if we are going to the trouble of providing the service of movies at Laurel and especially at Aspen, we should do it right.

Starting at the beginning, there is some level of confusion as to the selection of films. Taking this past weekend as an example, the President asked for a list of available films so that Mrs. Nixon could select a movie. The first list we got was the list from the Navy Library, or something like that, which consisted of (I would guess) about a dozen films, almost all of which were identified on the list itself as being poor. A little later, a list came along of six or eight other films which were apparently available from some other source, some of which I guess were pretty good, and one of which—*Dr. Zhivago*—Mrs. Nixon selected.

Our first problem then is the selection of films. In my opinion, there is absolutely no reason why the President of the United States should not have available for his selection the very latest and the very best films on the market. He also should have available the best of films of earlier years so that he can select truly great pictures which he might have missed at the time of their release. There is also no reason why a more orderly process of film selection cannot be established so that we could set up ahead of time a half dozen or a dozen films that, over a period of time, the

President and the rest of the First Family would like to see, and then these could be programmed in as they wish at Camp David and at the White House.

It occurs to me that perhaps the film selection process is not a rightful function of the Aide's office, and that someone else should take on this part of the chore. If you agree, I would be happy to assign it to some other appropriate office.

Assuming we have licked the film selection problem and now have a good movie to show, there are a number of other problems in the actual presentation which should be considered.

We come very close to having an ideal film projection setup in Aspen. We have 35 mm projectors, a separate projection booth, built-in screen, communication system between the viewing area and the projection booth, and theoretically this should work pretty well. In fact, as evidenced by both this weekend and the past weekend, it does not.

On Saturday night, for example, the picture never did get fully on the screen because the projector was aimed a little bit to the side, so one edge of the picture ran on the curtain through the entire evening. That was on projector #1. Also on projector #1, the zoom lens was never properly adjusted so as to have the picture fill the screen area although this was done properly on projector #2. So as they switched projectors, the size of the picture jumped up or down which is, to say the least, somewhat disconcerting.

The solution to this problem would seem to be simple although maybe there is some mechanical problem involved. Why can't the projectors be permanently bolted down to their mountings so that the operator can't move them out of alignment no matter what he does? Also, why can't the zoom lenses be adjusted precisely to the screen size and shape and then locked with a set screw so that the operator, again, can't inadvertently knock them out of adjustment? (I have set up several projection facilities in our offices back when I was a civilian and this is the procedure we followed—it worked extremely well.)

Another problem is the projector noise and the talk of the projectionists coming from the booth. In most projection facilities, this is solved by a double pane of glass in the porthole between the booth and the viewing room so that sound does not travel between the two rooms either way. It would seem to me that this would be especially desirable in the case of the President's facilities at Aspen since the projection booth is adjacent to the dining area, and the projectionists are frequently setting up for the film showing while the President is at dinner. I think that it is undesirable for the projectionists to be able to hear the dinner conversation and it is certainly undesirable for the audience to have to listen to the projectionists' conversation during the film.

There were numerous times during the running of *Dr. Zhivago* when the loop apparently slipped in the projector and the picture started jumping, and the projectionist had to stop it, reset his machine and start it up again—another very disconcerting activity, especially in an absorbing movie. (This, incidentally, happened quite frequently the week before during the movie that was shown that weekend.) The problem here would appear to be inadequate training of the projectionists and, if this is the case, I would urge that a sufficient number of the permanent crew at Camp David be sent to projectionist school so that they are fully competent to handle the machinery. This should not be too difficult; movie theaters throughout America manage to project films night after night without this kind of problem, and there is no reason why it can't be done at Camp David.

There was also some problem in the volume level and this is probably at least somewhat unavoidable, but there should be some way to get the volume pre-set if the projectionist knows before the arrival of the President what the film is to be since he could then set it up and test the volume before the Family arrives at Aspen. On the other hand, if the film is selected too late to do this, there will probably have to be some volume adjustment when the actual projection starts. This can be handled by the telephone communication from the viewing room to the movie booth using facilities that are already there.

There was also some problem in focusing this week and a great deal of problem in focusing last week. It is imperative that the projectionists watch this carefully since there seems to be some dropping out of focus from time to time. Here again, a pre-running of the film to get the focus established properly on both projectors would be desirable. If this can't be done, the projectionist must be very alert to the focusing problem at the beginning of the first reel on each projector so they are sure to get things into tight focus. This also can be worked on via the telephone connection when necessary, but it should not be necessary. This is another factor of proper projectionist training.

We have already talked a little about the possibility of setting up better projection facilities at Laurel for staff movies. In looking at the thing quickly, it seems to me there would be no major drawback to building a small projection booth outside the window of the dining room, which would certainly make movie viewing at Laurel more enjoyable. The ultimate here, of course, would be to install 35 mm projectors instead of using 16 mm projectors, but this may be unreasonable in cost. I do think that it ought to be at least investigated.

I know that Jack Valenti and the Motion Picture Association would be delighted to be of any help they can to the White House in this whole area—especially in making good films available. I personally feel that we should use their services and that by doing so we can greatly upgrade the quality of film material to select from—and I would think they would be able to help us in getting the projectionists trained in ironing out all the technical difficulties.

I would be glad to discuss any of this with you that you want. I am sure that if you check with Major Brennan you will find that he went through considerable agony Saturday evening and that putting these things into effect would be very much welcomed by him.

APRIL 29, 1969

TO: **Mr. Higby**

FROM: **H. R. Haldeman**

When we redo the Oval Office the floor, as you know, will be replaced.

The President wants to be sure that the cork segments in the doorway leading out to the terrace, which bear the marks of President Eisenhower's golf shoes, are carefully removed and preserved.

These will then be made up in small pieces and mounted to be presented to old friends and golfing buddies of President Eisenhower's plus other selected people.

The President would like to have Freeman Gosden handle the preparation of a list of names of people to whom these plaques should be presented. Will you please make a note to follow up on this and, as soon as the project is actually under way, contact Freeman Gosden and get a list of names from him. Also, talk with Rose and assemble other names of people who would particularly appreciate these, such as Tkach, Harlow, etc., who have worked with President Eisenhower, and give me a complete list plus an estimate of how many plaques will be available.

28 FROM: THE PRESIDENT

MAY 1, 1969

TO: **Mr. Whitaker**

FROM: **H. R. Haldeman**

Will you please make a check as quickly as possible with each of the Cabinet Officers to find out, as completely as possible, what outside foundations and institutions they are using for staff studies, etc. They, of course, are using a wide range of groups, such as the Rockefeller Foundation, Brookings Institution, Rand Corporation, etc.

Also, while it is outside of your bailiwick, I realize, will you please make a similar check within the White House staff, especially with Dr. Burns, Dr. Moynihan, Dr. Kissinger, and Jim Keogh.

The President has asked for a report on this as quickly as possible, and I would appreciate your following up on it as fast as you can.

HRH50

MAY 1, 1969

TO: **Mr. Cole**

FROM: **H. R. Haldeman**

Re the attached, after the report comes in from Whitaker the President wants to issue an order to all White House staff people (I will have to do this verbally) as well as to Cabinet people (also have to be done verbally) that they are not to use Brookings Institution. Don't do anything on this until we get the report from Whitaker and find out what use is actually being made of Brookings at this time.

HRH50

MAY 21, 1969

TO: **Mr. John Brown**

FROM: **H. R. Haldeman**

The President indicated to me in a note recently that he had directed that a Drew Pearson file be assembled. I don't recall doing anything on this. Would you check through the various areas, including Rose, to see if we have somewhere started to assemble a Pearson file. Also check to see if you can find any directive from the President regarding this. Other possible sources would be Ehrlichman and Higby.

HRH50

MAY 31, 1969

Dear Rose Mary:*

    Will you put this on the Boss's desk first thing . . . I would like for the note to receive his personal attention.

    Thank you. Am looking forward to seeing you again soon and hope you will give me a chance to repay the many kindnesses you've shown.

Personal regards,

[s/Claude]

*[Letter to Rose Mary Woods, President Nixon's personal secretary, from Claude R. Kirk, Jr., governor of Florida]

HANDWRITTEN NOTE BY RN: "get Mitchell to advise the reply"

PPF188:
MATERIAL REMOVED
FROM PRESIDENT'S DESK

MAY 31, 1969

My Dear Mr. President:

    Your selection of the man to be the new Chief Justice of The United States Supreme Court is one which has met with resounding acclaim here in Florida not only for his ability and his reputation but also for the method which you used and the category from which he comes. Of course, it gives me great personal satisfaction, after the years of labor with you and Bob Finch, to be a part of the system that you are creating and improving. I am following here in Florida the same method to create a "bench" that has the confidence of all of our citizens.

    In regard to the replacement of Justice Fortas, I want to bring to your attention a federal judge in this district who meets what I believe are your criteria for experience, philosophy, and personal character. His name is Judge Harrold Carswell. Though still a young man he has been a strong

Republican leader here in Florida, beginning at a time when there were no Republicans in North Florida. He has been a man who has, with drive and determination, operated in the spirit of building, without personal avarice, a strong party in this area. His wife, Virginia, is an outgoing soul of kindness and charm, and they are raising a lovely family.

Mr. President, you will have many excellent candidates, I am sure, but I don't believe that you can make a better selection. To paraphrase the play entitled *A Man For All Seasons,* I can tell you that Justice Carswell is a man for all "regions" as well as for all seasons. My best personal regards.

Sincerely,

[s/Claude]*

P.S. As you know this is my first letter to you as President. I don't like to ever abuse a privilege and want any letter I send to have the full weight of my concern in it. Therefore, there won't be many in your tenure as President. This is just a note so that you will understand my sincerity.

[s/CRK]

*[Letter from Claude R. Kirk, Jr., governor of Florida]

PPF188:
MATERIAL REMOVED
FROM PRESIDENT'S DESK

JUNE 16, 1969

TO: **H. R. Haldeman**

FROM: **The President**

I have an uneasy feeling that many of the items that I send out for action are disregarded when any staff member just reaches a conclusion that it is unreasonable or unattainable. I respect this kind of judgment. On the other hand, I want to know when that kind of decision is made. In the future, I want you to keep a check list of everything I order and I want you to indicate what action has been taken (and I want no long memoranda indicating why it can't be taken) and particularly I want to know when the action that I have ordered has *not* been taken.

PPF1

JUNE 16, 1969

TO: **Bob Haldeman**

FROM: **The President**

I have decided to take positive action with regard to cutting personnel abroad. I am not satisfied with the reports I have been receiving on this project. I want you to assign somebody with top rank who has this sole responsibility to follow up on my orders that there should be a one-third cut in AID, USIA, U.S. military missions except in Vietnam and Korea, and CIA (the latter in particular must be cut). Give me a report on this by the end of this week.

PPF1

JUNE 16, 1969

TO: **Bob Haldeman**

FROM: **The President**

What is the situation with regard to redecoration of the Oval Room and the West Wing? Pending the decision, I would like something done immediately with regard to the George Washington painting over the fireplace. It should either be moved up or the clock should be moved out. I think the clock is probably not the most appropriate one for the room, even on a temporary basis. Check with Mrs. Nixon to see whether she has another clock in mind at this time, pending the time when the room is redecorated.

PPF1; HRH229

JUNE 16, 1969

TO: **Bob Haldeman**
       John Ehrlichman

FROM: **The President**

I have noted an increasing number of instances in the news reports of columnists indicating that "White House staffers privately" were raising questions about some of my activities. One of these instances was the Chamber of Commerce speech on student revolt. The other on the Air Force Academy speech. I want the whole staff in the strongest possible terms to be informed that unless they can say something positive about my operations and that of the White House staff they should say nothing. I also would like to get your report on who has been responsible for this kind of statement.

PPF1

JUNE 16, 1969

TO: **John Ehrlichman**

FROM: **The President**

On an urgent basis I need the press list before the press conference on Thursday. I intend to start following the practice used by Roosevelt and Eisenhower—calling on those press men who are not anti rather than constantly calling on those who are trying to give us the hook. Ziegler and Klein will disagree with this. I don't want you to consult with them. This is my decision and I intend to follow it up. All I need is the information with regard to which are the men who attend our press conferences who are definitely out to get us and which ones are either neutral or friends.

PPF1

JUNE 16, 1969

TO: **John Ehrlichman**

FROM: **The President**

I want you to get from Cy Laughter and whoever was in charge of our sports group—Bud Wilkinson et al.—the RN supporters list. When they do something that is effective in sports I think we ought to be in touch with them. For example, today I called Arnold Palmer when he made a very good showing but failed to win the Open and also called Mooney when he won the Open. I don't know where Mooney stands but it was probably a good idea in any event.

PPF1

JUNE 16, 1969

TO: **John Ehrlichman**

FROM: **The President**

There is an excellent musical group at Chez Vito. They are not ultra sophisticated but they are in a class of their own and would give an audience a good lift. They could be included in one of the state dinners that is not at the highest level but where we want everybody to have a good time.

PPF1

JUNE 16, 1969

TO: **Ron Ziegler**

FROM: **The President**

On the color side, you might tell the Sidey types that RN has become a regular bowler at Camp David on weekends, and I hope next week even in the EOB. His average is around 130 to 140 and his best game to date is 204. He has never bowled before except for a couple of occasions at Camp David in 1960.

PPF1

JUNE 16, 1969

TO: **Mr. Dent**

FROM: **Alexander P. Butterfield**

The President had a chance over the weekend to read your June 10th memorandum concerning Governor Laxalt's report on Reagan. He would like you to get together with John Ehrlichman and Henry Kissinger and see if, among the three of you, you can come up with an appropriate mission on which Governor Reagan might be sent. (He added that you might want to give special consideration to Eastern Europe.)

cc: Mr. Ehrlichman
    Dr. Kissinger

HRH50

JUNE 30, 1969
(dictated June 29, 1969)

TO: **Bob Haldeman**

FROM: **The President**

There was a woman reporter from the *Washington Post* at the church service this morning who was obnoxious to everybody who was there. She is not to be included in any further events at the White House under any circumstances. Inform Ziegler, Klein, Van der Heuvel and carry out this order without further discussion with me. Give me a report as to how you have executed the order.

HRH229

JUNE 30, 1969

TO: **Bob Haldeman**

FROM: **The President**

I don't think my memorandum with regard to state gifts was understood. I knew that they were in the archives. What I want clearly understood is that these state gifts are to be transferred to the Nixon Library at my direction when I decide where the Library will be. The State Department may give you some flak on this on the ground that all state gifts are simply to be left in the Archives. But this is my decision and I want this followed up. Give me a report on what the situation is.

PPF1; HRH229

JULY 9, 1969

TO: **John Ehrlichman**

FROM: **The President**

Without consulting anybody on the NSC staff I want you to get for me before the day is over the following information.

1. How many employees who are United States nationals does the State Department have abroad.

2. How many employees who are United States nationals does AID have abroad.

3. How many employees who are United States nationals does CIA have abroad.

4. How many employees who are United States nationals does USIA have abroad.

I want everybody included whether they are in Europe, Vietnam or other areas. The only people not to be included are those in the military. I will get this information with a different question.

How many U.S. military do we have abroad, exclusive of those stationed in Vietnam, the division complement for NATO and Korea. Give me that total amount with the top six or seven countries specifically given.

Incidentally, I want this same breakdown as far as countries are concerned with the top five or six given where the civilian employees are concerned.

I need this information by two o'clock today. It should not be difficult to obtain.

PPF1

JULY 9, 1969

TO: **Rex Scouten**

FROM: **The President**

Regardless of who happens to be the guest, the President is served first. I do not like the custom and hereby direct that it be changed. The following rules will apply.

    1. If it is a stag dinner or lunch, with no guest of honor, the President will be served first.

    2. If it is a stag affair, with a guest of honor, the guest of honor will be served first and the President next.

    3. If it is a mixed dinner, with no guest of honor, Mrs. Nixon will be served first.

    4. If it is a mixed dinner, with a guest of honor, the wife of the guest of honor will be served first simultaneously with Mrs. Nixon, and then the guest of honor and I will be served second.

    If it is one of those rare occasions where it is a mixed dinner and the guest of honor is not accompanied by his wife, serve Mrs. Nixon first and simultaneously the woman who is assigned as my dinner partner, and then serve me and the guest of honor second.

    These rules are to be followed explicitly from this time forward.

cc: John Ehrlichman

PPF1

JULY 21, 1969

TO: **Mr. Ehrlichman**
      Mr. Ziegler
      Mr. Klein
      Dr. Kissinger
      Mr. Harlow

FROM: **H. R. Haldeman**

As each of you is aware, the President reads quite closely his daily news summary and he has directed that each of you be provided with a copy of that news summary by 9 A.M. in the morning. That directive has been sent to Pat Buchanan, as well as other instructions concerning future distribution of the summary and analysis.

    Almost without exception, the President issues daily instructions on the basis of stories and articles within that summary, instructions for action on the part of the White House Staff. He now feels that each of your offices should read that news summary as early as possible in the morning and that action should be taken on those items which are within the scope of your department, and which quite obviously call for remedy of some kind.

After this memorandum is received, the President *will assume* that you have read Buchanan's news summary by 10:00 o'clock and that you have taken action on issues affecting your department, by at least noon. Buchanan has, in turn, been instructed (on a daily basis) to follow up with your department in submitting a report each evening to the President on what action has been taken in each area.

If at times you feel you are too pressed to read the entire summary—it is often quite long—a trusted staff member should be designated to read and mark it for you—or to initiate the necessary action himself. One of the great needs of the Administration is for quicker action and reaction to events on the part of the staff—independent action, which the President does not direct, but which is taken automatically.

In addition, the President feels that in the past the confidential news and TV analysis has been distributed far too broadly for security's sake. He has thus directed Buchanan's shop to cut back sharply on the number receiving it. However, your office will continue to receive it and, as mentioned, it should be in your office before 9 A.M. If not, please contact Pat Buchanan.

HRH51

AUGUST 6, 1969

TO: **The President**

FROM: **Patrick J. Buchanan**

The Soviet propaganda organs have been dumping the worst kinds of vilification on our heads ever since we've been in office—despite all the nice things Dobrynin has been telling us in Washington. Why not have the USIA start the damndest ideological offensive against the Soviets they have ever seen; drag in the Czech thing on the first anniversary; start dealing with the backgrounds of the leaders of the Soviet Union, in the Stalin period; turn the heat on them with every propaganda vehicle we can. If we can't outdo them in this area, we ought to punt. Erich Hoffer once wrote that one of the great failures of the West is that we have allowed this band of cutthroats and party hacks to masquerade as the great humanitarians of all time. Stalinism is in vogue in the Soviet Union and the American propaganda organs in my own simplistic view ought to pour the heat on them in every area of the world—then we might haul Dobrynin in and tell him that if they stop telling all these lies about us—we'll stop telling the truth about them.

HRH51

AUGUST 7, 1969

TO: **H. R. Haldeman**

FROM: **The President**

Will you give me a report as to how Buchanan, Nofziger et al. are coming along on the project I directed on letters to the editor and even more importantly, contacts with TV people where they are pro or anti.

HRH51

AUGUST 11, 1969

TO: **Mr. Higby**

FROM: **H. R. Haldeman**

The President wants his phone redesigned; he would like to have a direct dial line (an outside line) on the phone so that he can dial numbers directly when he wants to. I want a report on the degree of security that such a line would have compared to a line through the White House Board. He also wants direct PL's to Ehrlichman, Kissinger, and Haldeman.

Please work out a phone plan for this and let me see it before we take any action.

HRH51

AUGUST 12, 1969

TO: **Mr. Ehrlichman**

FROM: **H. R. Haldeman**

Huston's memo, while perhaps a bit strong, does make some valid points. I attach it for your information and consideration.

AUGUST 12, 1969

TO: **H. R. Haldeman**

FROM: **Tom Charles Huston**

The attached UPI story relates the testimony of a youthful FBI informer who testified yesterday before the House Internal Security Committee that there will be stepped-up campus disorders this fall, and the Communist party will be actively involved through its clandestine support of the Students for a Democratic Society.

On October 16, 1968, in a nationwide radio broadcast, the President spoke of "Today's Youth: The Great Generation." In that speech, he pledged that if elected he would "establish a Youth Service Agency (which) would have the mission of bringing together the separate and often duplicating functions dealing with the problems of youth that are now scattered all across the Federal system."

While it is not necessary that this particular pledge be implemented precisely as indicated a year ago, some gesture should be made to redeem the substance of the commitment. At the present time the Administration does not have a youth program; it has manifested no particular interest in youth problems; it has made no effort to convince young people that their problems are of interest or concern. Most particularly, we have made no gestures to indicate support for those young people who supported us, to encourage the vast majority of young people who reject violence, but who seek reform.

I recognize the dangers of shouting "wolf," but I am willing to state unequivocally that we will witness student disorders in the fall which will surpass anything we have seen before. Student militancy will sweep major campuses and flow into the streets of our major cities as the competing factions of SDS strive to prove that each is more "revolutionary" than the other and as antiwar protest organizations seek to escalate the fervor of opposition to the Vietnam war. You will see it most likely by October 15, certainly by November 15.

I recognize that youth problems are always low priority whether in a campaign or in an administration. But the point which should be recognized is that we are confronted with more than a youth problem. On no other domestic issue is the President's credibility more at stake than on the issue of law and order. Widespread student disorder will further polarize the country, the people will insist on prompt action to quell it, and we will be faced with the sole alternative of repression once the crisis is at hand. It is possible to contain if not prevent future student disorder. But this will not happen by wishing for it. Action is required, and time is running out.

The President recognizes inflation as a serious domestic problem, and he would not for a minute think of assigning it a priority somewhere between arranging church services and planning for the Bicentennial Celebration. Campus disorders and student unrest is perhaps the second most pressing domestic issue in the country today, yet it is receiving little serious attention. Young people constitute a significant and volatile portion of our population, a group which we can ill afford to ignore. I urge you to consider this problem and evaluate whether, in your opinion, we are doing as much as we should.

HRH51

AUGUST 15, 1969

TO: **Larry Higby**
John Brown

FROM: **Dub O'Neill**

RE: **Interim Report on Pearson Research**

There is no Pearson collection, and access is not available at his office. The only way to obtain a compilation of his columns on Nixon is to go through the microfilms of a paper carrying the column day by day. The D.C. Public Library has agreed to lend us these films as we need them. They come with half a month of the *Washington Post* on each roll of 35 mm. microfilm. Since each roll takes about twenty minutes to view and the time span involved is over twenty years, the physical task involved is fairly formidable. About 150 man hrs. of work remain to complete this task which has been finished through 1948. Thus far there have been only seven columns which have made reference to RN. There have been no major articles devoted to him and only 2 critical articles.

Columns that have a reference to RN are being noted for: Date, page, article title and subtitle under which the reference appears, and a notation indicating whether the article was favorable, unfavorable, or nondescript. Once the catalogue is complete copies of the desired issues will be available either from the Library of Congress or on machines that produce copies from microfilm within the EOB.

I am forced to leave this weekend to return to school, but I will give all the help I can to the intern who is taking over the job. Two people, working hard, should be able to finish the project in another week or ten days.

cc: John Campbell

HRH53

AUGUST 19, 1969

TO: **Lucy Winchester**

FROM: **H. R. Haldeman**

The President mentioned the other day that California red wine was served at the Kiesinger Dinner. It is his standing instruction that California wine is never to be served at State dinners—especially those for Europeans—without his specific personal O.K.

He did of course agree to the use of California wines here in California, but they should not be used at the White House except under unusual circumstances and with the President's prior approval.

cc: Mrs. Nixon

HRH51

SEPTEMBER 9, 1969

TO: **Mr. Buchanan**

FROM: **H. R. Haldeman**

Further on the President's views re News Summaries, etc., he was talking again about the TV analysis and what he wants here is a weekly analysis on Friday of how we came out over the whole week's time on each of the networks on an overall basis.

He does not want us just to react to each day's story, but rather to view this thing as editors instead of reporters, and look at the overall picture over a period of time rather than each day's flurry.

For example, a friend of David's had a summer project of doing some news analysis over the entire summer and, as a result of that, on a long range basis, he concluded that Huntley-Brinkley shafted us regularly by making all of their major coverage very negative. It is this kind of general impression over periods of time that he is seeking in these weekly TV reports rather than just a factual summary of what was covered last night on the news.

HRH51

SEPTEMBER 10, 1969

TO: **Mr. Buchanan**

FROM: **H. R. Haldeman**

The President referred your August 6th memorandum regarding a USIA ideological offensive to Henry Kissinger and it has been carefully reviewed with the recommendation now that this is not the time to take this kind of approach because it would be inconsistent with some other approaches currently underway.

I did want you to know, though, that your suggestion had received serious consideration and review.

HRH51

SEPTEMBER 13, 1969

TO: **Herb Klein**
      Pat Buchanan

FROM: **Ken Cole**

In his September 12 news summary, the President focused on Conrad's pictorial cartoon that appeared in the *Los Angeles Times* September 5th edition.

He thought this was an especially good one and requests that the two of you "get some complimentary letters to this fellow. (He's usually against us.)"

Would each of you please advise the President by memorandum of the number of letters that are finally generated in response to his request.

WHSF/SUBJECT-
CONFIDENTIAL 10/CO165

SEPTEMBER 17, 1969

TO: **Ken Cole**

FROM: **Pat Buchanan**

LOG # **1182**

We were a little late getting this, based on a September 5th cartoon; but I have batted out the attached two letters myself to Conrad using the following names. If we send any more from Washington, D.C. to L.A., it is certain to look organized. So, on this one I didn't bother informing the letters operation at the RNC—on which I do not lean very heavily in times of stress.

WHSF/SUBJECT-
CONFIDENTIAL 10/CO165

SEPTEMBER 16, 1969

Dear Mr. Conrad:*

RE: Your cartoon of September 5 "The Ho Chi Minh Trail"

Thanks for being one of the editorialists with guts enough to remind folks that "gentle, wispy Uncle Ho who smokes Salems" is the same ruthless little S.O.B. responsible for the death of hundreds of thousands of his countrymen—soldiers and civilians alike. Your cartoon was worth a thousand of the kind of editorials that disgraced the pages of the *New York Times* and *Nation* magazine.

Keep calling them as you see 'em.

Sincerely,

Jack Toland
Bethesda, Maryland

*[Letter to Paul Conrad of the *Los Angeles Times*]

WHSF/SUBJECT-
CONFIDENTIAL 10/CO165

SEPTEMBER 17, 1969

TO: **Mr. H. R. Haldeman**

FROM: **Dwight L. Chapin**

RE: **Appointment Request for Congressman Bush and Mr. Everett Collier**

As you know, the President approved seeing Congressman Bush and Mr. Everett Collier, Editor, *Houston Chronicle*, sometime in the near future.

Congressman Bush and Mr. Collier were both notified; however, they do not feel that there is a pressing reason to see the President at this time. According to Bill Timmons, they were very happy with the President's willingness to see them.

HANDWRITTEN HRH NOTE: "We need more Congressmen like Bush!"

DLC18

SECRET

SEPTEMBER 19, 1969

TO: **John Ehrlichman**

FROM: **Colonel James D. Hughes**

Carl Wallace asked me to call Dita Beard since I have known her personally for a number of years, in an effort to relieve her pressure on Secretary Laird reference the IT&T mergers. I did this and explained to her that this was out of my element, but since she was an old friend, I would pass on her request to the proper people.

Her pitch was long and involved, but basically boiled down to this: IT&T has not been able to discuss with McClaren the rationale behind the law suit. The Attorney General has disassociated himself from the case because of his law firm's interest in a subsidy of IT&T. The IT&T position is that they have done nothing wrong and in particular have violated no policy of this administration. On the emotional side, Dita cites a heavy financial support given by IT&T to the President's election.

In short, she requested that if the injunction were not granted by Monday, that Justice drop the entire matter.

I repeat, my role was simply a hand holding one and no commitment whatsoever was made. If you have a salving comment I'll pass it on. If not, I'll just ride it out.

PPF186:
MATERIAL REMOVED
FROM PRESIDENT'S DESK

SEPTEMBER 22, 1969

TO: **Mr. Haldeman**

FROM: **The President**

In memoranda in the future, I shall use the letters PR whenever I am referring generally to a project I want carried out in the PR front. Until we get a full-time man I think we need in this field, you will have responsibility for seeing that these decisions are implemented.

What is particularly important is that I be informed as to what action has been taken and, if action is not taken, why the decision has been made not to take it.

PR. The subject in this paragraph should be discussed only orally. It involves the attack Teddy made on our Draft Statement and on our Troop Withdrawal Statement which most critics, I think, would agree was totally irresponsible. Any sophisticate, however, would also agree that it was very clever for him to launch this attack. He is trying to divert attention from other subjects which could be quite embarrassing to him. The way for him to do it is to enlist the McCarthyites and all the far left on Vietnam, leading up to the October 15 mobilization date for the college campuses.

We, however, ought to have the good sense to take this on in a very effective way. I would suggest that one Senator with plenty of guts should hammer him along the lines that Griffin did a few days ago, and should quote directly from Hanoi's reaction to our troop statement in which they used the Teddy quote against us with devastating effect. In fact, Buchanan's prudent primary group might get a major mailing out to editors and columnists in Massachusetts and perhaps even nationally, just setting forth the Hanoi quote or, better still, an editorial which takes that line. The devastating cartoon in the *New York Daily News* could be used with good effect in this respect. The best place from which this could be mailed would be, of course, from Boston. Buchanan also should be able to get a columnist or two (and Nofziger could help in this respect) to pick up this line. I think Teddy's is the first round of Federal syllables we are going to get on Vietnam leading up to October 15th. It is absolutely essential that we react insurmountably and powerfully to blunt this attack. We cannot continue simply to leave this to Kissinger; he is overworked and the few people that he can meet in a backgrounder don't cover enough ground. And, in addition, I don't want him to get into the Teddy Kennedy fight. I want this followed up by one of our best people and a report given to me on its progress.

PR. Every Monday, I want a week's projection as to what we anticipate will be the major opposition attacks so that we can plan our own statements with those in mind. I realize that we sometimes may not have such information, but on the other hand, a careful checking with the offices of Kennedy and McGovern et al. will yield us some pretty good information as to what their plans are. Any newsman—maybe Mazo or somebody like that to build up his force and keep us informed. In this connection, I wonder if you might game plan the possibility of having some pro-Administration rallies, etc. on Vietnam on October 15, the date set by the other side. Inevitably, whenever we plan something, they are there to meet us; perhaps we can turn the trick on them. Give me a report as to what you think is possible.

PR. I have completed a very thorough analysis of the reports made by HK, E and Harlow which were submitted to me at San Clemente. On the four PR fronts I asked for coverage. In general, I think I could sum up my reaction in this way—the only area where we really came through with a better-than-average grade (and here it was considerably better than average) was on Family Assistance and Welfare and the New Federalism. This was due to a plan executed and followed through. On the Foreign Policy front, on the Nixon Big Charge front, our record in the Congress and the others are performances considerably lower than average. The reasons are obvious. K is simply too busy to be charged with the responsibility for seeing that our actions are publicized. The same is true of Harlow on the Congressional front. I have reached the conclusion that we simply have to have that full-time PR Director, who will have no other assignments except to bulldog these three or four major issues we may select each week or each month and follow through on directives that I give but, more importantly, come up with ideas of his own. I think the Cliff Miller participation is better than what we presently have, but it will be inadequate on a part-time basis. I think that H is simply too busy on the Operational front to carry out this assignment. The same is true of E and K.

While I do not think it will be the best answer, perhaps we ought to enlist Safire in this respect. He seems to have a long-range view and although his PR ideas are not usually in tune with my own, he at least will have us do something and will be watching for all of the curves. I know this is a subject that troubles all of us, but I do not want to continue to slide along with what I fear is an inadequate response, and an amateurish response to what will be an enormous challenge in the next two or three months. This could be a subject for discussion and decision next weekend at Camp David, among other subjects.

HRH164, 229

SEPTEMBER 22, 1969

TO: **Mr. Haldeman**

FROM: **The President**

RE: **PR**

Would you give me a report by the end of the week on how our Letter-to-the-Editor project on the *New York Times* and in other respects is being handled.

A weekly report on this assignment would be very useful.

HRH229

SEPTEMBER 22, 1969

TO: **Mr. Haldeman**

FROM: **The President**

The State Department Briefs are interesting, but they do not have enough priority to deserve my personal consideration.

I would suggest that they be discontinued and that whoever does them (and they are done well) be transferred to another Department.

The same goes for Bryce Harlow's daily report on Congressional Statements with regard to the Administration. This may be of some use to him, but I do not find it of enough use to me to have it prepared for my purposes. I think Bryce is so overwhelmed with work anyway that it would be just as well to discontinue this project unless he needs it for the purpose of keeping up with what is going on in Congress.

In any event, in the future do not send either of these reports to my office.

Some odds and ends on my scheduling:

It is not too likely that I will be playing golf very often. In any event, with the winter months coming on, I will be playing golf in Washington rarely, if at all. When I do play in Washington, I will be playing only at Burning Tree. Burning Tree is very proud of the fact that for over 50 years they have never allowed a photograph to be taken on the course. During the eight years that Eisenhower was President, there were many pictures of his playing golf, but never one at Burning Tree. Apparently this information was not available to Ziegler and Dwight because Dwight raised the point as to whether or not a couple of photographers could be allowed to take a shot of Hope, Laird and me before we teed off on Sunday. Simply inform all hands that this is a closed matter and that it is the decision of Burning Tree, and we, under no circumstances, want to change their policy. This, incidentally, will also be my policy whenever I play in the future. If I do play, I will generally go to clubs which do not allow photographs to be taken. Blindbrook in New York, incidentally, is one like this, and the same practice is also followed by Riviera in Florida. Where clubs do allow photographs, I will not play there. Also with regard to the golf routine, in the future will you instruct the Secret Service that I do not want any caddies; I prefer to play with a cart, without caddies, and that only one Secret Service cart travel with me and everybody else out of sight.

We have had a policy of Military Aides riding with me whenever I happened to be going some place alone. I want to discontinue this policy unless it is to a formal event. A man in uniform attracts attention to the car, and I think it is not a good idea unless it has been an advertised formal event, like an appearance at Congress or at some place where I'm supposed to make a speech. Have Chapin check with me before each event to see whether I want anybody to be riding with me, and explain the new policy to Hughes.

I want you to make a survey of the White House staff to see whether we can implement Moynihan's recommendation that we cut the staff by a third. My feeling is that we had too few people at the beginning and now far too many. This is a natural development, but the time to cut out the fat is right now before people get a lot [of] make-work projects which freeze them in. There is nothing worse than to have people on the staff without enough to do, because they are the ones who inevitably will begin to complain about not having "access." Give me a report on this within a couple of weeks as to how many we are able to cut. There should be no exceptions insofar as cuts are concerned, except with regard to Kissinger's operation (he needs everybody he can use to lessen his own burden) and Harlow's operation (he needs perhaps even one or two more to handle complaints that otherwise would land in my lap).

When you are writing to Kalmbach, I think it would be a nice gesture if you were to suggest to Don Nixon that Clara Jane would be welcome to come down to San Clemente any time she wants and cut some of the flowers there for her personal use or for gifts to old friends. This is particularly true of the roses, and I imagine will also become true of some of the other plantings which were put in just before we arrived in California. Also, along that same line, would you remind Kalmbach that I would like for him to send two or three dozen figs (fresh) from our trees if it can be worked out without too much trouble. Don't do it if he believes they may not hold up in shipment (of course, they would have to be sent Air Freight) or if there are other problems.

When I played golf with Tony Penna in Florida, he said that he was going to make up a set of clubs for me. My guess is that he has done so and, while I have no present need for them, I just want to be sure that he is thanked for them and that they are delivered here so that I can let certain VIPs use them, just as I let them use other sets that have been given to me. Would you check this out with Bebe or with the mail office here to see whether or not the clubs have been sent. If they have not been received, let Bebe make a discreet inquiry. I do not want Penna to think that we are asking for them, but he was so positive about his decision to send them that my guess is that they are on the way. The way Bebe might check it is to simply tell Penna where I would like to have them sent.

Also, would you check with whoever is in charge with bread-and-butter letters to see whether there was a follow-through on thanking the man who made up a set of clubs for me and left them at Burning Tree with Max Elbin. He was here with the Ryder Cup team and at the time I asked Elbin if he had received a note of thanks, and he had not—probably because Elbin had not delivered the clubs to me until a couple of weeks ago. Please follow up and see that a very gracious note is sent to him, to the effect that I shall be "proud to play with such superb clubs, and I only hope my game eventually may approach the magnificent workmanship and style of the clubs."

Mrs. RN does not like the procedure we followed at the New Zealand dinner of standing at the door as guests go into the dining room. I am inclined to agree with her for [a] reason which should have occurred to me earlier. While the most spectacular view is of the four people coming down the steps, the difficulty is that only eight or ten people at the most are able to see it. The press and the Marine Band blocked the view in front and, at the New Zealand dinner, there were only a half dozen people who caught us as we came down and made the turn at the second landing. I want her to make the decision as to how this receiving line should be set up. I think she prefers the East Room procedure and, if so, we will go forward with that. In any event, I would like the Guests of Honor to be invited for 7:45 so that we can meet them at the door and get them upstairs so that the guests are not held up downstairs, and also so that we will be able to come down and start the receiving line by 8:05 or 8:10. At the Israeli dinner, have one Aide (Lucy Winchester or anyone else Mrs. RN chooses) for the purpose of bringing people up to her. Either you or Ehrlichman should bring people up to me. If there are very special people present, have three or four Military Aides available for the purpose of giving them a quick 5-minute tour of the second floor. They can do this while we are shaking hands with the after-dinner guests. Also, let us be sure, because of the fact that the after-dinner guests this time will have within their numbers some fairly high-ranking people, that they are not invited too early and consequently have too long a time to wait before they come upstairs.

With regard to the reception we had for student government leaders, we dropped the ball on one point which I would like for you to check very carefully in the future. You may recall that I raised with someone the question as to whether there were to be women's college representatives as well as men's. I did not find until we arrived back from Camp David that that was the case. Mrs. RN would have liked to have been there to receive them, and I think should have been. As it was we substituted Tricia for her. In the future, whenever both men and women are present at any kind of a reception that I have, I would like for her to be included unless she has something else scheduled at that time.

At the reception, a number of Negro students from Negro colleges raised the question about funds for their teachers and students, etc. They apparently felt there should be some sort of Federal aid. I have no idea as to what the status is, but we had no one at the affair to whom I could refer the matter. Would you have whoever was in charge check into it and see that Finch's office follows up if there is anything we can do on the subject.

Would you get for my file Gallup's popularity rating starting with Eisenhower and running through Kennedy and Johnson. I do not want trial heats with other people, but simply the popularity rating—do you approve or disapprove of how he is doing the job as President? If a major event (and only a *very* major event) has occurred immediately before one of these figures comes out, like the Cuban missile confrontation, or an off-year election, put that into the Summary—don't go to too much trouble, however, I am more interested to see the trend lines over the eight-year period.

Bob Hope made a very strong plea for me to be an Honorary Chairman for the dinner he is having for the Eisenhower Memorial Hospital in Palm Desert, which is to be held in New York next month. This is a violation of our policy, just like the Eisenhower College one, but in this case, not because of the Eisenhower relationship, but because Bob Hope has been such a good friend, I will want to give him permission to use my name. If anybody raises a question on other requests of this type, we can always, of course, say that the only exception we make is for functions honoring Eisenhower.

HRH138, 164, 229

SEPTEMBER 22, 1969

TO: **Henry Kissinger**

FROM: **The President**

What, if anything, did Garment report to you on the absolute failure of the American Jewish community to express any appreciation by letter, calls or otherwise for RN's over-ruling both State and Defense in sending the Phantom jets to Israel?

Get me an answer before I see Mrs. Meir Thursday.

PPF1

SEPTEMBER 22, 1969

TO: **Dr. Kissinger**

FROM: **The President**

Will you make sure that we follow up on all of the commitments we made on our Asian trip. I want to be sure when I meet with foreign Heads of State that I make very few promises, but those that I make are always honored.

HRH228

SEPTEMBER 22, 1969

TO: **Dr. Kissinger**

FROM: **The President**

As you will recall, one of my first long-range projects before the Inauguration was to cut down on the number of reports required from abroad. There is just too much paperwork and it may be that we are adding to that paperwork by some of the requests we send from the White House.

Without urgency but over the next 30 days, would you get Richardson and others to see what they can do to cut down the massive amount of reports which are required. This should include all the Agencies, USIA, AID, Defense, etc. I know this is a mess, and I intend to do something about it. Put a real tiger on this job.

HRH228

SEPTEMBER 22, 1969

TO: **Dr. Kissinger**

FROM: **The President**

I have still not had a report on how we are going to cut contract personnel abroad. This is one area in Vietnam where personnel can be cut. What is even more important, I want to know how many contract personnel various Government agencies, including AID, have abroad. I still think the figures with regard to Americans abroad have been fussed up deliberately so as to cover up the true number we have abroad.

I would like to have this figure by the end of the week.

HRH228

SEPTEMBER 22, 1969

TO: **Dr. Kissinger**

FROM: **The President**

With no urgency but as a continuing assignment, you will recall that I want as complete a report as we can possibly get on the Bomb Halt from all vantage points[—]what we learned in the campaign, what we heard during the campaign, what the records show, the conversations of Rusk, etc. I know that much of the information is not available, but I want to be sure that we have this record as complete as we possibly can get it. The same goes for the Cuban missile crisis and the Diem murder; the latter two I realize are ancient history, but someone on your staff should be able to dig up information on these subjects. Perhaps Tom Huston might be a good candidate or Clark Mollenhoff, although I realize we do not want to risk too much publicity.

HRH228

SEPTEMBER 22, 1969

TO: **Mr. Ehrlichman**
      Attorney General Mitchell
      Dr. Kissinger
      Secretary Richardson (in Rogers' absence)

FROM: **The President**

I feel very strongly that we have to tackle the heroin problem regardless of the foreign policy consequences. I understand the major problem is with Turkey and to a lesser extent with France and with Italy.

In any event, I want the group included in this memorandum to give me a recommendation as to what we can do.

HRH228

SEPTEMBER 22, 1969

TO: **Peter Flanigan**

FROM: **The President**

For very practical political reasons I have decided to take the Commerce Department's position rather than that of the Justice Department on the Newspaper Preservation Act. The Justice Department is technically correct in its position but looking at the larger public interests of maintaining more newspapers with different editorial viewpoints in our major cities the Justice Department's position is completely unrealistic. In your discussion of this matter with John Mitchell it would not be inappropriate to point out that the Senators and Congressmen who are against the Act are liberal *Washington Post*–type Democrats, and that those who are for it are for the most part on our side.

cc: John Ehrlichman

PPF1

SEPTEMBER 22, 1969

TO: **RMW**

FROM: **The President**

When we were at "21" on the evening of the U.N. speech, we saw Gina Lollobrigida and she asked for an autographed picture. I think the best one to send her would be the Color Family picture. Send it to 35-B, The Waldorf, saying to Gina Lollobrigida, With Best Wishes From Richard Nixon.

HRH228

SEPTEMBER 22, 1969

TO: **RMW**

FROM: **The President**

Would you include Mrs. Longworth in one of the early dinners at the White House. I think she might enjoy the Shah of Iran more than others.

HRH228

SEPTEMBER 22, 1969

TO: **The President**

FROM: **Herbert Klein**

RE: **Action Memorandum #1182**

Twenty-three letters from major southern California figures were generated to Conrad regarding his effective cartoon on Viet Cong deaths.

On the day this was done, Conrad had another negative cartoon.

One letter writer mentioned this and we urged [him] to get others to follow through on this.

I have written Conrad asking for his original of the Viet Cong death cartoon for you.

WHSF/SUBJECT-
CONFIDENTIAL 10/CO165

SEPTEMBER 30, 1969

TO: **John Ehrlichman**

FROM: **Ken Cole**

Attached is a copy of Safire's memorandum regarding organizing support for the President's programs.

The President has reviewed this memorandum and likes the idea. He takes issue, however, with the name "middle Americans" because he doesn't think people like to be known as such. He thinks that perhaps a more positive action word is needed such as "working Americans" or at least that is his suggestion.

I recommend that in addition to working at a new name for the group, action be started quickly to develop a plan for the implementation of this concept.

CWC97

OCTOBER 1, 1969

TO: **Bob Haldeman**

FROM: **The President**

One subject I would like for you to discuss with Herb Klein was raised by Ted Lewis with Henry Kissinger.

He felt that Herb was spending too much time with the liberal press people (including the *New York Times*—I find this hard to believe) and not enough time with our friends. This I think makes it imperative that we get that hard list of people that are really worth our time and concentrate on them and not overlook our friends in the process. Once you get such a list perhaps we can get in Klein, Buchanan and Ziegler and give them their marching orders.

PPF1; HRH229

OCTOBER 7, 1969

TO: **The President**

FROM: **Alexander P. Butterfield**

RE: **News Media Monitoring Program**

Persons listed below have been assigned to monitor news media as indicated.

Al Snyder (Klein's staff)	CBS News . . . Ch 9 . . . 7:00–8:00 A.M.
Elizabeth Burke (RNC)	The "Today" show . . . only when political figures are scheduled to appear
Pat Buchanan, Mort Allin and Tom Huston alternately . . . backed up by Ed Jacobi (Dir. Media Relations, RNC), Al Snyder, and Rob Odle (Klein's staff)	NBC News . . . Ch 4 . . . 6:30–7:00 P.M. ABC News . . . Ch 7 . . . 6:00–6:30 P.M. CBS News . . . Ch 9 . . . 7:00–7:30 P.M.
James Hogue (RNC)	The "Tonight" show . . . only when political figures are scheduled to appear
JoAnn DiBella (RNC)	The "Merv Griffin Show" . . . only when political figures are scheduled to appear
Ron Ziegler and/or Nancy Turck (Ron's staff)	The *New York Times* The *Washington Post*
Robert Grannis (RNC—former Editor of the *Brooklyn Eagle*)	*Time* magazine *Newsweek* magazine

The recommendations of these individuals as to the most appropriate counter actions we might take to significantly pro- or anti-Administration news will be transmitted to my office at the earliest daytime opportunities following observance of the particular news items. I will assume responsibility for reviewing and coordinating with Herb Klein the recommendations received—and insuring that appropriate action is taken. (Mr. Jeb Magruder, recently assigned to Bob Haldeman's staff, will assume this responsibility in my absence.) Refinements are in the mill already, but the program will begin tomorrow.

HRH138

OCTOBER 7, 1969

TO: **Alex Butterfield**

FROM: **H. R. Haldeman**

During our meeting yesterday morning we discussed having an individual
who would work with the DAR, Boy Scouts, VFW, etc. when we wanted
them to support one of our programs. Bryce Harlow suggested that Chuck
Colson be given the responsibility for this task. He did this during the last
campaign.

    Would you follow through to see if Bryce has had any discussions
with Colson on this subject and also what Colson's qualifications are, etc.?

HRH53

OCTOBER 7, 1969

TO: **General Schulz**

FROM: **H. R. Haldeman**

In your capacity as liaison with former Presidents, would you please assume the responsibility connected with the declassifying of classified documents that are currently in the Johnson Library.

    In addition to this classified material, former President Johnson has
given to the United States some 30 million papers accumulated during his
presidency. This material, while not classified, is of a highly sensitive
nature and should be reviewed before being made available to the public
through the Johnson Library.

    Attached are memoranda that have already gone to [the] Depart-
ment of Defense and State Department, plus recent correspondence between my office and Tom Johnson, former President Johnson's assistant.

    This whole subject was covered in extensive conversation in August
between Presidents Johnson and Nixon. The President is most anxious to
see that this project is followed up with all possible speed and requested
that I forward a report of your progress to him by October 17.

    It is especially important that properly qualified people be assigned
to this project—and that it be done quickly since there has already been
a long delay.

cc: Colonel Hughes

HRH53

TO: **H. R. Haldeman**

FROM: **Tom Charles Huston**

The attached article from Sunday's *Evening Star* relates to my earlier memo on planning ahead for the President's library.

LBJ somehow arranged for 12,000 volumes of surplus (?) government publications, whose value is estimated at over $1,000,000, to be donated to the LBJ Library. When Joe Kilgore says these volumes can't be purchased and thus it is difficult to put a value on them, he is exactly correct. Yet, they form a nucleus of any serious Presidential Library.

You may wish to make a mental note and after plans are formalized for the Nixon Library have someone look into this situation and see if another set can be rounded up—that is, if LBJ didn't loot the government of its entire stock.

HRH53

OCTOBER 8, 1969

TO: **The President**

FROM: **Daniel P. Moynihan**

Mr. Haldeman has asked that I list for you what I would consider "the eight major goals on which Administration should make, or have made, its record in the first year."

FIRST-YEAR GOALS OF THE ADMINISTRATION

1. *Peace.* By year's end we should have made it clear that *you* are the leader of the peace movement. There are conditions for a cessation of hostility which you will not accept because they will not bring peace, but merely a temporary cease fire. But that must not obscure the fundamental thrust of your administration which is to bring an end to an ill advised, badly conducted, and shockingly misrepresented war. You will do what Eisenhower did: get us out of a land war on the Continent of Asia.

2. *Draft Reform.* By year's end we will by legislative enactment or administrative fiat [have] brought about the first fundamental change in Selective Service since its enactment as a permanent feature of the Cold War. The seven-year period of suspense and uncertainty which has driven a generation of American youth half mad will be a thing of the past.

3. *Deflation Without Depression.* By year's end we will—hopefully—be able to show that the fever has gone out of the economy, that we are well on our way to bringing off—for the first time in history—a success-

fully managed downturn in an economy that had been on the verge of a calamitous sequence of boom and bust. Simultaneously, we will have made clear that we are not going to buy price stability with men's jobs. *You* personally are determined not to. *You* know what it will mean. This becomes a pressing matter in view of the Treasury testimony yesterday.

4. *The first fundamental reform of government since Woodrow Wilson will have commenced.* At year's end, although few reform bills are likely to have passed, we will nonetheless have succeeded in getting through to the nation what it is you are about: namely a massive, concerted, determined and informed effort to restructure the Federal system so that government in the 1970s will once again become an effective instrument of democratic decision making. Electoral reform would be a powerful symbol of this new era, and might just have passed the Congress by December. D.C. Home Rule, Postal Reform, Revenue Sharing, Grant Consolidation—these and a dozen similar measures will be seen as part of a legislative pattern that will define the era.

5. *The growing antagonism between White and Black will have begun to recede.* At year's end the Administration will have succeeded in establishing its bona fides with black America, while reassuring white America, especially the white working class, that an administration is in office which understands that gains for blacks must not be automatically translated into losses for whites. The ill informed, often insensitive, and frequently crude manner in which Administration officials have handled black issues in the early months of the Administration will have been succeeded by positive programs in the hands of positive men who understand, among other things, that the great need is for reassurance among *all* weak and exposed groups in the society.

6. *Law and order will be seen as on the ascendancy.* By year's end the nation will feel the downward spiral into a nihilist nightmare of violence and disorder has stopped, and an upward spiral could now begin. Not the end, nor yet the beginning of the end, but the end of the beginning will have occurred. Some legislation may have passed. Far more importantly, the initiative of the President with respect to the drug traffic will have impressed the nation with the fact that those in high office really know, and really care, about what is going on. Hopefully, we will have resolved the present apparent mess on the Mexican border. Without establishing an image of the United States as a high-handed and assertive giant concerned only with its own interests, and not at all with either the interests or sovereignty of its Latin neighbors. Hopefully the far more urgent problem of heroin addiction will have been the subject of public international undertakings. If possible, some symbolic measures may have been taken against organized crime, although the effort to counter the heroin traffic will have largely served that purpose.

7. *The Family Assistance Program achieves a consensus.* By year's end the Family Assistance Program, the most important piece of social

legislation sent to the Congress in a generation, one of the ten great bills in the history of the American nation, will have won the support of a clear majority. This is already the case in the public opinion polls (i.e., at the beginning of Autumn). By the end of the year the general good will of the public will have been translated into specific support and endorsement of the great citizen groups which so much influence public action. (N.b. This might take the form of a broadly based, bi-partisan citizen's group supporting the legislation.)

8. *Tax Reform and a measure of further legislative measures.* By year's end the first major reform and revision of the Internal Revenue Code will have become law. The first significant proposal in this direction—exempting the poor from income tax—was taken by the Administration, and the administration will have every reason for pointing to the (hopefully) major substantive achievements incorporated in the bill. The essential point will be that the Federal government in the Nixon era is achieving things thought impossible in previous times.

In addition to tax reform, a number of important legislative measures will have been enacted, such as the hunger program, the population commission, and the extension of the Economic Opportunity Act.

These legislative achievements will have been accompanied by important Administrative advances such as the reorganization of the regional offices of the Federal government, the establishment of a vital minority business program, the Postal Academy program for minority youth, the reorganized and redirected Peace Corps, the new National Goals Research Staff in the White House, and many others.

Hopefully, the White House Conference on Food and Nutrition will have proven a landmark in American social history: a national gathering simultaneously concerned with the remnant of pre-industrial problems, such as hunger and malnutrition, the onset of post-industrial problems such as overeating, and the industrial era problems such as the toxic effects of prepared foods.

HRH138

OCTOBER 10, 1969

TO: **Mr. Haldeman**

FROM: **The President**

In talking with Ehrlichman, I was concerned about the fact that we apparently have not been getting across the theme which I have been emphasizing to you for four or five months—the long hours, hard-working image which we deserve and on which we have a really good case to sell.

I recall that you told me that this theme had been covered and that an adequate job had been done. Ehrlichman feels that there is an urgent need for a more effective job to be done on this score. I do not want to get into the nuts and bolts, but there are so many things that could be covered—no lunches or breakfasts, working in the office after dinner, calls and appointments which do not appear on the official schedule, etc., etc. Obviously, this has been an area where we have dropped the ball in a grossly inept way. I would like to see a game plan as to how this can be corrected, both as to the past where Ehrlichman has an idea or two that might be useful, and particularly as to the future. Here again, this shows why the Ziegler operation is deficient; he just can't get across what we do day by day, because he cannot sell . . . he can only report. Somebody constantly has to be telling the press until it runs out of their ears that the President is working hard, even though he may be at Camp David, Florida or in California. Johnson was away from the White House almost more than any other President and yet his staff got across the fact that he was the hardest working President in our history. I have probably spent less time away than any President in recent history—very little golf and no vacations without work, yet this story has not been told except, I understand from Ehrlichman, by Thimmesch who, of course, is not read by too many people.

I am really quite disappointed that, since I have mentioned this on at least a dozen occasions over the past four months, we apparently have not followed up. I hope you will get me an action plan that will reverse the situation, since on this issue I know we have a good case to sell.

HRH138, 164

OCTOBER 10, 1969

TO: **The President**

FROM: **Alexander P. Butterfield**

RE: **Media Monitoring Report**

NBC Evening News, Oct 9 (PJB et al.):

Resume included in Buchanan's morning television report to you. No counter action required.

ABC Evening News, Oct 9 (PJB et al.):

Resume included in Buchanan's morning television report to you. No counter action required.

CBS Evening News, Oct 9 (PJB et al.):

Resume included in Buchanan's morning television report to you. (Eleven minutes on Mollenhoff's emphatically expressed views re the farcical nature of the attacks on Haynsworth.)

"Merv Griffin Show," Oct 9 (JoAnn DiBella):

Nothing significant pro or con. (Entertainers only)

"Tonight" Show, Oct 9 (James Hogue):

Nothing significant pro or con. (Entertainers only)

CBS Morning News, Oct 10 (Al Snyder):

Senator Hollings (Dem.-S.C.) presented an exceptionally smooth and effective 5-minute defense of Haynsworth.
Recommendation: That he be telephoned and highly complimented by Bryce Harlow or Ken BeLieu. This was done at 10:20 A.M. by BeLieu.

"Today" Show, Oct 10 (Elizabeth Burke):

Nothing significant pro or con.

New York Times, Oct 10 (Ron Ziegler):

Highly critical editorial re Administration progress on draft reform and the President's "indifference." (Editorial entitled "Draft Evasion in High Places.")
Recommendation: That Ron Ziegler take the opportunity offered today during his announcement of news on Hershey to put the needle deeply into the *Times* for its unfair slant on Administration efforts to meet head-on the urgent issues of Selective Service reform. Ron has the plan and this will be done.

Washington Post, Oct 10 (Ron Ziegler):

Nothing which warrants special action on our part at this time.

HRH138

OCTOBER 16, 1969

TO: **Peter Flanigan**

FROM: **H. R. Haldeman**

Attached is a resume on Charles W. Colson. He is being brought aboard as an organizer of group support. His job would be to organize VFW groups, Boy Scouts, American Legion, etc., to support various programs and act as pressure groups for various programs. Apparently Colson did a similar job during the campaign.

Bob asked that I forward this to you requesting that you take a brief look at it and give him any reading you would feel appropriate on Colson.

Thank you very much.

HRH53

OCTOBER 17, 1969

TO: **The President**

FROM: **Alexander P. Butterfield**

RE: **Daily News Plan Critique and Media Monitoring Report**

I am attaching the new comprehensive report which provides the more
pertinent information included previously in the Press Office's "White
House News Recap" and my "Media Monitoring" summary.

We will continue to revise the format as new requirements are
brought to our attention.

DAILY NEWS PLAN CRITIQUE AND MEDIA MONITORING REPORT

. . . as of 11:15 A.M. daily, except Sat. and Sun.

. . . covers past 30-hour period Tues. thru Fri., and past 78-hour period on
Mon.

I. DAILY NEWS PLAN CRITIQUE

A. Events programmed to be major White House news items yesterday
and this morning . . . each followed by reviews of coverage received.

1. *Bi-Partisan Meeting on Inflation*

a. NEWSPAPERS: This story received good play across the nation
. . . ranking about 4 or 5 in order of impact. The articles centered mostly around the President's radio address scheduled for
today . . . and speculation on same. Much of the material written
on this meeting included Chairman McCracken's news conference.

b. TELEVISION: Received very good coverage from White House
correspondents, and played halfway into the 3 major network
news shows.

ABC 1:30 min.—Tom Jarriel (live)—"White House says that
breaks are beginning to work . . . politically unpopular to solve
inflation problems."

10 sec.—Comments and speculation on the President's
speech scheduled for today.

NBC 1 min.—"Administration economic advisers say that interest rates are to decline."

CBS 45 sec.—"Dr. Burns and Chairman McCracken say that

inflation measures are taking effect . . . GNP jumped . . . Housing starts increased."

      10 sec.—Announcement of the President's Friday afternoon speech.

2. *Chairman McCracken's Press Briefing*

    a. NEWSPAPERS: Dr. McCracken's news conference was pretty well wrapped up in the story on the bi-partisan meeting on inflation. It was a front-page item in the East coast newspapers. The story also moved on the wires.

    b. TELEVISION: Received fair coverage. Most of the story was covered in the TV comments outlined above.

B. The leading Administration news items were:

—*Secretary Laird's news conference* . . . U.S. to keep more than 7,000 non-combat troops in Vietnam after the war ends. This story played #1 in many national papers and received wide coverage on TV.

—*Draft Lottery* . . . News re Armed Services Committee approval. Although played lightly on TV it was the #1 or #2 story in newspapers nationwide.

—*The Paris Talks* . . . Ambassador Lodge declined to meet unilaterally with DRV representatives. This was one of the top items on all network TV news programs and played the front pages of most newspapers.

C. The single leading news item:

—A close race between Laird's conference, the draft lottery, and a recap of the moratorium.

II. MEDIA MONITORING REPORT

A. Of eleven news publications and TV programs monitored regularly,* only one reported information in a manner justifying counter action.

    1. *The "Tonight" Show*—for continually allowing (in fact, encouraging) long interviews of persons professing strong anti-Administration views . . . to the near-exclusion of those who are behind the Administration. Last night George McGovern and Robert Ryan were teamed up against us for nearly twenty minutes. They spoke out for immediate and unconditional withdrawal of U.S. forces and for public demonstrations against Administration policies. *Action:* Another letter-writing campaign to the network will

*[NBC, ABC, CBS Evening News; "Merv Griffin" and "Tonight" shows; CBS Morning News; "Today" show; *NY Times; Washington Post; Time* and *Newsweek* magazines]

begin today ... and thus follow on the heels of letters sent Wednesday and Thursday in protest of Shirley MacLaine's diatribe of Tuesday night.

B. Results of counter and/or follow-up actions previously reported:

1. *CBS Morning News*—Although interviewer John Hart's incisive questions somewhat counter balanced author-historian Barbara Tuchman's strongly anti-Administration remarks yesterday morning, she clearly had her impact on listeners and viewers. Therefore, Al Snyder (on Herb Klein's staff) called Bill Crawford, the Washington, D.C., program producer, and arranged for Don Rumsfeld to appear today. Rummy was great, and for 6 minutes went right down the line re our progress and current position on the Vietnam issue.

HRH138

OCTOBER 17, 1969

TO: **Mr. Higby**

FROM: **H. R. Haldeman**

The President is concerned by the fact that an increasing number of birds seem to be plummeting to their death against the windows of his oval office; specifically, the door out to the portico.

He wonders if there is some device that has been developed by modern science that will keep birds away from there so that they won't fly headlong into the glass, breaking their necks, and piling up on the pavement below.

Please investigate this and give me a report as quickly as possible.

HRH53

OCTOBER 20, 1969

TO: **The President**

FROM: **Peter M. Flanigan**

You should know that Don Kendall called to express his exceedingly high regard for the way Secretary Finch handled the Cyclamate matter over the past weekend. While he and the others in the industry for whom he spoke suffered a severe setback by virtue of the disclosures of the dangers of Cyclamate, he feels that Finch's strong leadership and judicious handling of all concerned minimized the damage done. He was particularly fulsome in his praise of the way Secretary Finch handled the adverse criticism from certain sections of the press.

HRH138

OCTOBER 20, 1969

TO: **Peter Flanigan**

FROM: **H. R. Haldeman**

RE: **Brookings Institute**

I attach a report by Clark Mollenhoff on the Brookings Institute and their connections with the Administration. I direct your attention specifically to page 2 of his report which I'm sure you'll find of interest.

Are we developing any realistic or effective plan to hit this particular issue hard, or is it something that we more or less put on the back burner.

As I'm sure you know, as long as it is on the back burner, we'll continue to have problems similar to the leaks that came forth this weekend.

HRH53

OCTOBER 21, 1969

TO: **Dr. Kissinger**

FROM: **The President**

On page 2 of the New Draft, below the bottom of the page, I see a point which clearly illustrates what the approach should and should not be. To say that our departure would inevitably invite "cruel retribution" means nothing to three-fourths of the American people, who haven't the slightest idea what retribution means. Also, to talk about the massacre at Hué means nothing except to the 15% of the American people who know where and what Hué stands for.

What I want here is how many people in North Vietnam were killed by Ho Chi Minh and his colleagues when they took over. Also, how many people in South Vietnam (civilian) have been murdered by the VC. This is the kind of stark, cold figures we need, rather than this kind of indirect reference which only the intellectuals understand.

HRH228

OCTOBER 26, 1969

TO: **Bob Haldeman**

FROM: **The President**

It occurs to me that for one of the "Evening at the White House" affairs we might invite the top 300 people in the Administration. This could be in lieu of the meeting we were talking about in which they would be briefed on Administration policies in the various departments. It may be that the working meeting is a better idea although we might consider even doing both. The affair for 300 would be a nice thing to do sometime in the Holiday Season.

HRH53

OCTOBER 28, 1969

TO: **Mrs. Constance Stuart**

FROM: **H. R. Haldeman**

How are we coming on a plan for the "Evenings at the White House"? The President suggested another possibility for entertainment at one of these affairs, which would be the new Hamlet in England who is such a great hit.

HRH53

NOVEMBER 12, 1969

TO: **The President**

FROM: **Alexander P. Butterfield**

RE: **Game Plan for Post-Speech Activities—Second Post-Speech Updating . . . Covers Period Nov. 10–Dec. 31**

The Game Plan for the period indicated is attached.

GAME PLAN FOR THE PRESIDENT'S PURSUIT FOR PEACE SPEECH

(Second Post-Speech Update . . . Covers Period Nov 10–Dec 31)

Nov 10–16   1. National Unity Week begins . . . increased display of American Flag (offices, homes, automobile bumpers and windshields, lapel pins, etc.), increasing display of porch lights and automobile headlights during daylight hours, and beginning of series of patriotic rallies throughout the country.

Nov 10–16   2. Beginning of second barrage of wires and letters to the President.

Nov 10–16   3. Continued public support given to the President's Vietnam stand by such spokesmen as Governors, Senators and Representatives, Mayors and County officials, business leaders, and officials of veteran and patriotic organizations.

Nov 10–16   4. Series of short TV spots highlighting theme of President's speech and pointing toward Perot's half-hour TV special scheduled for Sun, Nov 16.

Nov 10–11   5. Series of short (Washington, D.C. area only) TV spots and handbills advertising Veterans Day Freedom Rally at the Washington Monument.

Nov 10   6. Distribution of RNC's "Monday" . . . featuring President's pursuit for peace speech and the Gallup poll results (77% supporting the President) as well as the tremendous response to the speech as indicated by wires and letters received.

Nov 10   7. Local marches of policemen and firemen . . . on a nationwide basis . . . all in support of the President. ("March of Confidence" scheduled for noon local time in all areas.)

Nov 11   8. Veterans Day activities.
—President visits Veterans' hospital
—Local armistice ceremonies held nationwide
—Washington, D.C. Freedom Rally (Washington Monument, 2:00 P.M.)

Nov 11–13   9. Publicity given to Justice Department's release re undesirable character of certain groups participating in the New Mobe Committee's "March Against Death."

Nov 12   10. (Possible) injunction against demonstrators' use of names of those killed in Vietnam.

Nov 12 or 13   11. (Possible) advertisement in San Francisco and Washington, D.C. papers protesting demonstrators' use of names of Vietnam dead (by 5–7 incensed wives and mothers—or by entire Association of Gold Star Mothers with membership totaling 18,000).

Nov 12–16   12. Continued display (after Veterans Day) of American Flags throughout Washington, D.C. . . . agreed to by Mayor Washington.

Nov 12–15   13. Continued light pressure applied to key Congressmen re early passage of House and Senate resolutions (Ford's in the House—Dole's in the Senate) supporting the President's Vietnam peace plan.

Nov 13	14. Distribution of 1 million handbills to college campuses throughout the nation . . . all bearing the "Support the President" theme.
Nov 13	15. Booklets on President's speech back from printer.
Nov 13–14	16. Publicity given to "National Unity" and "Support the President" themes by GOP leaders at Des Moines meeting.
Nov 13–14	17. Publicity given to Apollo 12 launch and associated activities.
Nov 14	18. Apollo 12 launch and President's attendance.
Nov 14	19. Circulation by Herb Klein's office and State Department of President's speech in finished booklet form.
Nov 17	20. Full-page ad in *New York Times* and *New York Daily News* featuring picture of the President and George Romney and the Oval office desk loaded with telegrams responding to the "pursuit for peace" speech . . . and the Gallup poll's reported figure of 77% supporting the President. (Same as cover of current issue of *Monday*.)
Nov 14–15	21. Continuation of activities by college Republican leadership's "Tell It to Hanoi" program. —Circulating of "Support the President" and "Put the Pressure on Hanoi" petitions and Vietnam fact sheets . . . as well as excerpts from the President's pursuit for peace speech. —Writing of letters to editors of newspapers and magazines. —Encouraging of U.S. Flag display, automobile and porch lights, lapel buttons, visiting hospitalized Vietnam veterans, etc.
Nov 14–15	22. National Unity Week Committee press conference (Washington, D.C.) and planned activities in nation's capital. —Making public selected letters to the President from supporters of his Vietnam policy. —Possible appeal before both houses of the legislature for resolution proclaiming second week in November National Unity Week . . . henceforth.
Nov 14–15	23. TV camera crews and still photographers at work.
Nov 14 or 15	24. (Possible) public announcement of support for the President's position on Vietnam by the Vatican.
Nov 14–15	25. (Possible) heavy publicity re injunction against demonstrators, or public protest against demonstrators, for using

	the names of those killed in Vietnam to enhance effectiveness of moratorium.
Nov 14–15	26. Circulation of 30 million "Support the President" coupons via Junior Chamber of Commerce, American Legion and VFW. (Perot—IBM cards)
Nov 14–15	27. Congressional spokesmen and others publicize selected extracts from foreign press . . . indicating aid and comfort given to the other side by dissenters.
Nov 15	28. Publicity given to President's peace crusade via loudspeaker and radio and TV commentary at all NCAA football games nationwide . . . and as a part of some half-time ceremonies.
Nov 15–16	29. Publicity given to the President's peace crusade and the "importance of unity" (by National Unity Week Committee) at all NCAA and professional football games nationwide. Program will call for patriotic theme and each person in the stands shaking hands with those next to him.
Nov 16	30. Full-page ad in 103 leading newspapers. (Perot)
Nov 16	31. One-half hour TV spectacular . . . and reading of selected letters and wires received by the President in response to his Nov 3rd speech. (Perot)
Nov 16	32. Dr. Norman Vincent Peale to use selected letters and wires received by the President. (Some publicity)
Nov 17–18	33. Apollo 12 message. (Conrad)
Nov 17	34. Half-page ad ("a statement of support for the President's position on Vietnam") in the *New York Times, Washington Post, Cleveland Plain Dealer* and *Christian Science Monitor.*
Nov 17–23	35. Passage of resolutions supporting the President . . . locally throughout the nation by various groups.
Nov 17–23	36. Continued publicity given to numbers of letters and wires received by the President.
Nov 17–23	37. Continued support given to the President's Vietnam position by spokesmen (Governors, Senators, etc.)
Nov 17–23	38. Series of short TV spots by National Unity Week Committee pointing toward November 23rd TV spectacular.
Nov 22	39. (Possible) proclamation (official or unofficial) of "Solidarity Day."
Nov 17–23	40. Appropriate use of *Human Events* magazine.
Nov 23	41. National Unity Week Committee's one-hour TV spectacular . . . and reading of selected letters and wires received by the President.

Nov 27	42. Possible program (to be planned) in conjunction with Thanksgiving day.
late Nov	43. Announcement of red, white and blue Volkswagen mail motorcade . . . to travel from West to East to Nation's Capitol and to the White House.
Dec 1	44. Publication and circulation of December issue of *Reader's Digest* . . . containing a story of response to President's "pursuit for peace" speech and samples of letters and wires received by the President.
Dec	45. Appropriate use made of TV camera crews' film.
mid-Dec	46. Plan for bringing to Washington a representative group of POW wives for call on the President.

HRH138

NOVEMBER 24, 1969

TO: **Bob Haldeman**
John Ehrlichman
Bryce Harlow
Henry Kissinger

FROM: **The President**

I have been giving some thought to how we ought to handle the Senators who have voted against us on both ABM and Haynsworth. Here are some ideas that I would like to have implemented.

1. There should be no change in the relations with Williams. He is vital to us in the tax field.

2. Even though Griffin supported us on ABM, we should maintain a proper but not too close relationship with him due to the strong feelings that people like Dole, Baker, Cook et al. have developed on this score. In other words, let us be sure that our friends and supporters on both issues get some preferred social and other treatment for a while. The same, of course, applies to Scott.

3. I think that Goldwater et al. should be discouraged from having a confrontation with Scott and Griffin at this time. It is doubtful if they could win it but beyond that it would leave scars that would be very difficult to heal. I think the better plan is to lay the foundation for what needs to be done after the elections of 1970.

4. With regard to all those who opposed, I want one general rule followed without deviation. You are undoubtedly going to have instances where people like Jordan, Griffin, Schweicker, Percy et al. may contact

members of the White House staff indicating their willingness to support us in the next nomination or on some other issue which may be coming up. They will, of course, do this only when we are sure to win it. I want the answer in each case to be along these lines: "Thank you very much but the President wants you to feel free to vote your politics on this issue. He doesn't need you on this one." This will be quite effective and very hard for them to respond to.

5. We will have a definite policy from now on of having leadership meetings every other week and will try to have [as] subjects for discussion only those where we really have to bring matters up to the leadership for their assistance. On the alternate week, we will have in groups of our friends and I would occasionally mix some of our Democratic supporters into those meetings.

6. Since several Senators like Jordan, Saxbe, Schweiker et al. have complained about "White House pressure" I think the best line to follow in the future with them is not to discuss anything with them and if they complain simply say we didn't discuss it with them because we wanted to honor their request that we not exert White House pressure.

7. It goes without saying that those who are in this group should be given completely proper treatment so they cannot have anything obvious to complain about but none of them should get in to see me until I have gone through the list—one by one—of seeing all of those who supported us on these issues. I anticipate that this will take me several months!

HRH229

NOVEMBER 24, 1969

TO: **Bob Haldeman**

FROM: **The President**

It occurred to me that one way you could see that the Agnew poll got a good ride would be for Buchanan or Nofziger to get in 15 of the more conservative columnists and give them a little preview on it. The main point I wish to emphasize, however, is that this must *not* be treated as a poll which we took but simply one that came to our attention. Perhaps you could discuss this with the PR group and come up with a better idea. I am inclined to go harder on his own popularity rating and not quite so hard on the agreement with him on what he said about the TV commentators although the second point can be made as a second lead. I wouldn't put out the last two questions that you read to me over the phone.

PPF1; HRH229

W/RN from PPF1

NOVEMBER 24, 1969

TO: **Bob Haldeman**

FROM: **The President**

RE: **Public Relations—General**

In the development of themes, I think we should keep going back to the
"come-back theme." No one has been written off more than RN—in the
Hiss case; the Fund; several times during the Vice Presidency and, of
course, before the convention in 1968. Point out RN's resiliency in the way
he seems to do best when the going is toughest.

Another theme should be the effectiveness of RN in using the television medium. This is the point I particularly want emphasized on the
November 3 speech. It is not the substance which, of course, was all
important but the method—the hours of preparation involved. I think it
probably could be said that with the exception of Theodore Roosevelt,
Woodrow Wilson and Herbert Hoover, RN is the only President in this
century who still sits down from time to time and completely writes a
major speech. Building up the idea of RN being effective using the television medium will have an additional dividend—it tends to keep our critics
in the press and in TV off-balance.

It was interesting to note that the Gallup Poll showed the biggest
shift in the East. This, of course, could be due to the fact we were lower
in the East and had further to come back. I, however, imagine that there
is another factor which is even more important—the broadcast was carried in the East at a much better time than on the West Coast. My guess
is that the Nielsen in the East was forty to fifty higher than on the West
Coast. This would be an interesting bit of analysis to make for future
reference.

PPF1; HRH229

NOVEMBER 24, 1969

TO: **Bob Haldeman**

FROM: **The President**

When I went to the dentist Saturday it was a four-ring circus due to too
much security. I recall that Eisenhower used to go to Burning Tree in a
lead car without any security being present simply to avoid spectators, etc.

For your private information only, I am going to go to the dentist
Thursday morning (Thanksgiving Day). Let Chapin and others on the staff
think that it is going to be done here in the White House medical office.
I don't want it done here because I think Chase will work better in his own
office. However, this time I do not want to use the big car—just get one
of the regular limousines and have them drive me over without an escort

and with no Secret Service outside the building or in the halls or at the elevator. The press is not to be informed. I want them to cover the Thanksgiving Dinner and not a picture of me coming out of the dentist's office. Ziegler is not to be informed until after I return.

Let me try it my way once because late in December I may have to have another bridge repair job completed and I am simply not going to do it if I have to have 30 Secret Service men going ahead of me with the whole press corps there to take pictures.

PPF1; HRH229

NOVEMBER 24, 1969

TO: **Bob Haldeman**

FROM: **The President**

For your long-range planning, it will be necessary for me to plan some sort of trip out of the country at the time of Julie's graduation. She insists that she does not want us to come to the graduation ceremony because of the attitude of the faculty and students, and I believe she is probably correct. However, we could not justify not being there unless we were gone at that time on some sort of a special trip. If we were gone, of course, we would take her with us. Perhaps that is the time for a trip to Mexico or North Africa. At least, see what the date of the graduation is and then block off some time so that we will be able to accede to her wishes in this respect.

HRH229

NOVEMBER 24, 1969

TO: **Henry Kissinger**

FROM: **The President**

I am still waiting for a report on how we can cut the civilian and military presence in Saigon. We have been in almost a year now and there is no cut of significance. The place has swollen to the bursting point with Americans falling all over each other. I want some drastic action taken, both in the civilian and the military front in this respect. Give me a report in a couple of weeks.

PPF1

NOVEMBER 24, 1969

TO: **Henry Kissinger**

FROM: **The President** .

Sam Yorty told me on the phone that John Vann was the best man on pacification in South Vietnam. I haven't heard of him and it is possible that Yorty doesn't know what he is talking about, but if you agree with Yorty's proposal we might get him back and talk to him to get another view from the Thompson report.

WHSF/SUBJECT-
CONFIDENTIAL 10/CO165

W/RN from PPF1

NOVEMBER 24, 1969

TO: **John Ehrlichman**

FROM: **The President**

I wonder now if the time is not ripe for us to submit a bill to Congress requiring disclosure by all members of the judiciary of outside income. I think this is a subtle and effective way to get at some of the real crooks on the highest court and in some of the other federal courts and that it also would have considerable public appeal. You might discuss the matter with Mitchell when it is convenient and give me a recommendation. There is, of course, no urgency on this.

PPF1

NOVEMBER 24, 1969

TO: **Peter Flanigan**

FROM: **The President**

Is there still no feasible way to get multi-national participation in some of our future space flights? I have raised this with Paine and Borman and I know there are some technical problems but it is a pet idea of mine and I would like to press it. Raise it with Borman and see whether we can jog the bureaucracy in that direction.

PPF1

DECEMBER 1, 1969

TO: **Mr. Haldeman**

FROM: **The President**

One of our most important projects for 1970 is to see to it that our major contributors funnel all their funds through us except for nominal contributions to the campaign committees. I am referring to Clem Stone, Mulcahy, and any others of that category. Rollins of Delaware is another example.

What we need to do is to see that these funds are sent to the right people; but beyond that, we can also see that they are not wasted in overheads or siphoned off by some of the possible venal types on the campaign committees. This has generally been the case, incidentally. (This is not a joke. Unfortunately, this has more than often been the case in off-year elections.)

If we can get funds channeled through our hands, we can also see that they are used more effectively than would be the case if the candidates receive them directly.

HRH138, 229

DECEMBER 1, 1969

TO: **Mr. Haldeman**

FROM: **The President**

I noted in the News Summary some quote to the effect that I was concerned about Martha Mitchell's comments on the TV program. I have not expressed any concern to anybody, and I would hope that at one of your intimate staff meetings you would again urge upon all involved that Ziegler only is to be the expert on whether I'm concerned about anything. I will tell him what he can say. I simply don't like these constant notes in the columns, which are supposed to be inside dope, as to how I feel. If I determine that we want something like that in a column, I will let you know and we will handle it accordingly. Otherwise, White House staffers should refer all such questions to Ziegler. Be sure you let John Mitchell know that I have never expressed any criticism of Mrs. Mitchell to members of the staff. When I have such criticisms, I will tell him before I tell anybody else!

HRH229

DECEMBER 1, 1969

TO: **Mr. Haldeman**

FROM: **The President**

With regard to our future Congressional relations, I want to emphasize a bit on what I told you earlier with regard to my future activities on issues like ABM and Haynsworth. In both of these cases, Presidential prestige was called upon far too often and I will not let it happen again. I think we are becoming too "common" with our letters and phone calls to members of the House and Senate, and I want you to watch these things closely to see that, with our new setup, I make such calls when they really matter, but not just routinely every time something happens on the House or Senate floor which we like. Above everything else, however, I want it clearly understood by the entire Congressional Staff that I cannot and will not intercede with individual Senators in order to enlist their votes for Administration programs. I will see some of them in a group only when the stakes are high and when we feel there is a reasonable chance we can succeed.

HRH229

DECEMBER 1, 1969

TO: **Mr. Haldeman**

FROM: **The President**

I would like for you to discuss the conclusions I will be presenting in this memorandum [with] Klein, Ziegler and whoever else may be advising Administration or Cabinet people with regard to their relations with the press. It is important that you use this only as a Talking Paper because I do not want any distribution of my thoughts among the staff.

I have noted that within the staff and among some Cabinet people there has been criticism of Martha Mitchell for her appearance on TV, and also criticism of CBS and Maria McLaughlin, who was the interviewer. Both of these criticisms completely miss the mark. Neither Martha Mitchell nor the interviewer is to blame. The responsibility rests with those who advise Cabinet people and their staffs and families with regard to the press.

It is essential that some fundamental principles be borne in mind.

1. Before talking to any member of the press, remember that a great majority of the press are opposed to the Administration and, therefore, will subconsciously or consciously be after a story which will be harmful to the Administration.

2. Clearly apart from whether individual members of the press may be "friends" or not, it is vital to remember that virtually all members of the press, including those we may think are friends, owe their first loyalty to the story. As a matter of fact, we really wouldn't want to have it any other way.

3. This means, in other words, that it is vital always to be on guard regardless of what protestations the member of the press will make with regard to his or her friendship when he or she is after a story. As a matter of fact, that is the time to be most suspicious . . . when they come in and say "I want to do something that will be helpful" or "This story is going to be written anyway, and I wanted to be sure you got your side into the

story" or "You can count on my not using anything that is harmful." These are the oldest dodges in Washington, but people, particularly new people, and even some of the old timers, have to be reminded of them or they will fall into the traps.

4. Another rule that I want followed for all of my family, including Pat, Tricia, Julie and David and myself, and that I would advise for everybody else, is *never tape more than the interviewer is going to use.* Mrs. Mitchell answered 83 questions. Of course, I know that in many cases the interviewer will say that they will submit the part they are to use as they did when they interviewed Tricia and Julie for that President's Daughters series. This, however, is a bad deal. In any event, first we should not be in the position of having to "censor" a script and, second, when these interviewers go on too long, the person being interviewed inevitably will not be at his best toward the end and slips are bound to occur. It is vitally important that Ziegler, Klein and Connie Stuart carry out my instructions on this with regard to the RN family, and I would strongly urge that Klein give this advice to Cabinet people. If they are not bright enough to understand it, then that's just too bad. Just keep this one fundamental rule in mind: Over-taping is *always* in the interest of the interviewer; it is very seldom in the interest of the person being interviewed. Therefore, never over-tape regardless of how good a "friend" is doing the job.

HRH229

DECEMBER 1, 1969

TO: **Mr. Haldeman**

FROM: **The President**

I think last week illustrated my point that we need a part- or full-time TV man on our staff for the purpose of saying that my TV appearances are handled on a professional basis. When I think of the millions of dollars that go into one lousy 30-second television spot advertising a deodorant, it seems to me unbelievable that we don't do a better job in seeing that Presidential appearances always have the very best professional advice whenever they are to be covered by TV. Over the last week, for example, I signed the Non-Proliferation Treaty at my desk, I announced the Germ Warfare Proposal on Tuesday in the Roosevelt Room, and then signed the Draft Reform Bill in the Roosevelt Room on Wednesday. On Thursday, I made an appearance at the Thanksgiving luncheon in the White House. In each of these cases, I had excellent background briefing as to how many people would be present and how many pens I should use. I had, however, no professional advice as to where the cameras would be and how I could make most effective use of the TV opportunity. I should add to this list, even more importantly, the telephone call to the Astronauts. Even the question as to whether I should have held the phone with my right hand or my left hand is quite pertinent.

I think that each of these TV shots probably came off adequately. My point is that they should always be absolutely top-rate in every respect, and I should spend at least five or ten minutes with whoever is the TV producer to get his suggestions as to how I should stand, where the cameras will be, etc. In any event, give this some thought and perhaps we can come up with either a man or an idea to deal with the problem more adequately. I feel it is really worthwhile if we can get even a relatively good young man who doesn't come at too high a price and have him available for only one two-minute shot a week, if that is all I happen to be on that week. Let's be sure that two minutes is the very best that can possibly be. The President should never be without the very best professional advice for making a television appearance.

As a matter of fact, the advice for the two-minute shot is probably more important than for the 30-minute appearance. Over a period of 30 minutes, the audience will forget the technical difficulties if the subject is engrossing enough. In 2 minutes, the impression of the picture is fleeting but indelible.

HRH229

DECEMBER 1, 1969

TO: **Mr. Buchanan**

FROM: **The President**

You will recall Fulbright's book on *The Arrogance of Power*. It occurred to me that a good essay or speech subject might be the "Arrogance of Intellect."

Somebody should have a pretty good time with this theme!

HRH228

DECEMBER 1, 1969

TO: **The President**

FROM: **Clark R. Mollenhoff**

RE: **The Political Explosiveness of the Minutes of the Urban Affairs Council Kept by John Price and Daniel P. Moynihan**

A *Look* magazine article written by Nick Kotz demonstrates the serious problem that can arise from publication of quotations reported to be from the President that are taken out of context by persons antagonistic to the

Administration to embarrass the President in connection with the "hunger issue."

Mr. Kotz has quoted the President as saying: "Use all the rhetoric . . . so long as it doesn't cost . . . money."

A quotation somewhat similar to this was apparently made by the President in jest near the conclusion of an Urban Affairs Council meeting. It should never have been recorded in the minutes for it was simple light banter. Even this comment was taken out of context by Kotz to give the impression that the President of the United States lacked a sincere concern for the hungry of America, when the whole meeting in proper context demonstrated the most genuine concern.

There should be an immediate effort to obtain all copies of the minutes of the Urban Affairs Council. Also, immediate steps should be taken to determine why Mr. Price is keeping records on such comments and to determine how this closely held record was made available to Kotz in circumstances that could only be harmful to the President and the Administration.

This quotation from the December 2, 1969, *Look* magazine has already been used by Senator George McGovern for attacks on the President and it will be used constantly in the months ahead by McGovern, Kotz, and others of similar viewpoint to embarrass the Administration.

I am sure that this quotation, and many others, are probably a part of a Kotz book entitled *Let Them Eat Promises,* to be published in January.

The serious damage this quotation can do to the Presidential image is only a sample of the serious problem inherent in the minutes kept by the Urban Affairs Council meetings.

This entire problem should be discussed immediately and within the smallest group possible, if effective action is to be taken.

HRH55

DECEMBER 1, 1969

TO: **H. R. Haldeman**

FROM: **Pat Buchanan**

The plot thickens. Sunday morning, after an evening of debauching, I awoke to read my *Washington Post.* Mr. Jack Anderson quoting from the "confidential minutes" of the September 30th legislative meeting said that even Senator Tower had expressed " 'reservations' over Haynsworth business conflicts." True. What stood my hair on end was that *I* am the fellow who dictated the supposedly official minutes.

However, on reviewing my minutes as sent to you—I see that I did not indicate any such "reservations," that the word was not used; further, that these were not Tower's sentiments as I captured them in the September 30th dictated memo. Which seems to mean that either Anderson is feeding us and the country a measure of bull about seeing "confidential minutes" (he may just have a "source" or someone else kept "confidential minutes," which talked of Tower's "reservations").

In any event the upshot of this column is to make any of our people at these meetings gun-shy of speaking their minds.

HRH55

DECEMBER 3, 1969

TO: **The President**

FROM: **Clark R. Mollenhoff**

RE: **Effective Control of Government Operations**

My experience in the first four months shows there is no effective Administration control of government operations in many important areas This lack of control is frustrating the programs and policies of the Administration and is creating some serious personnel problems among the most loyal Nixon Administration people.

This condition is providing a continuing conduit for leaks of information to hostile magazine and newspaper writers, as well as to political opponents in the Senate and the House who have a primary allegiance to the Kennedy or Humphrey organizations. It is my view that it is best to meet this problem while the Nixon Administration popularity is at a high mark rather than to be faced with the issue in the midst of the chaotic trouble it can cause later.

This problem has already manifested itself in a number of ways that have been highly embarrassing to the Administration. The most recent was the incident in which the Presidential quotations on hunger were taken out of context and distorted in a book and in a magazine article. There have been a number of other problems arise dealing with civil rights as well as military and foreign affairs. Conditions continue to exist that can have disastrous consequences in the months ahead. The issue can be met only by the most careful planning by a small group with authority for direct action from the highest level. Those involved must be limited to persons with a total commitment to the success of the Nixon Administration. Broad general reorganization studies and plans, conducted under the jurisdiction of men of doubtful loyalty, can only confuse the issues and cause delays that cannot be afforded.

President Johnson could have been successful if he had fired Robert S. McNamara and others at an early stage and relied more upon his own basic political instinct for handling Vietnam. He could have had effective social programs if he had given control of the poverty war to men who wanted his Administration to succeed and who were practical in making Government programs operate efficiently.

This government can be made to operate in an efficient and an effective manner by careful handling of a few key problem areas at an early stage. Some political turmoil can be expected, even if these problems are handled carefully, for effective action will necessarily disrupt the communication lines of some anti-Nixon forces. However, careful planning and execution can keep the repercussions at a minimum. The alternative is to permit present problems to build to highly explosive levels.

Good government can be good politics but it takes organization geared to see potential problems and to take swift corrective action. The basic White House operation is sound but there is a need for this additional mechanism. The Administration has the personnel presently in place to do this job with only a few properly coordinated moves. Prompt initial action can make later moves effortless.

Discussions should be limited to no more than Dr. Arthur Burns, Bryce Harlow, John Ehrlichman, Robert Haldeman and myself. There should be no record kept of any conversations except where specific actions are agreed upon that can be explained publicly, if necessary, as essential to better management of government. If handled properly, there will be no need for those mentioned above to delegate authority or actions except on the basis of a single project area and for a specific purpose. My role would be confined to fact-finding and recommendations of alternatives to you and those named above.

HRH55

DECEMBER 3, 1969

TO: **Chuck Colson**

FROM: **Larry Higby**

As a result of yesterday's meeting, I understand you'll be following up in making sure that the name "Silent Majority" is incorporated and that we have the rights or some of our people have the rights. Is this correct?

CWC48

DECEMBER 8, 1969

TO: **Jeb Magruder**

FROM: **H. R. Haldeman**

With regard to your attached memo, we have, as you know, already contacted Ross Perot on this project. Through Perot we already have far more than 500,000 names available to put on tape as you suggest in your memorandum. Before proceeding let's make sure that you, Alex, Keogh, John Brown, and EDS are all on the same track. Alex supposedly had taken on this project about three weeks ago.

What I would like to see is a proposal of exactly how the project is going to be set up and how the financing will take place.

Thank you.

HRH55

DECEMBER 9, 1969

TO: **H. R. Haldeman**

FROM: **Jeb Magruder**

RE: **Names for our Outside PR Organization**

Enclosed is Lyn Nofziger's memorandum regarding names for our PR organization. He feels that "Americans For Responsible Action" has too right wing a sound to it. Consequently he has recommended a number of other names. After looking at his list, it would seem to me that either "American News and Editorial Service" or "American Information Service" would serve the same purpose without the connotation Lyn is concerned about.

Agree _____
Disagree _____
Comment:

HANDWRITTEN NOTE BY HRH: "His names tip our hand more than ARA does. Also—it depends on the overall position the organization takes. This needs to be decided first.   H 12/10/69"

HRH55

DECEMBER 9, 1969

TO: **Jeb Magruder**

FROM: **Chuck Colson**

RE: *National Journal*

I would like very much to order a copy of the *National Journal* for my use here in this office and I think that we should order at least nine other copies for use around The White House. I am sending this to you instead of John Brown because you know and understand the background of why we consider these subscriptions to be desirable.

I think Dan Hofgren can get for you or for John Brown, as the case may be, the necessary order forms. I would like, in view of what the publisher of the *National Journal* is going to do for us, to place these orders as soon as we possibly can.

cc: Dan Hofgren

CWC122

W/RN from CWC126

DECEMBER 15, 1969

TO: **Jeb S. Magruder**

FROM: **Chuck Colson**

RE: **Outside Public Relations Effort**

You asked for my thoughts on how the outside public relations effort should be structured. The enclosed memorandum is rough and quick but at least sets forth some of the options and possibilities.

RE: **Organization of Public Relations Activity**

The public relations activity will be incorporated in the District of Columbia. Its name could suggest that it is a foundation, an institute or a committee; in fact, from a legal standpoint it will be a corporate entity.

Depending upon the wishes and needs of the donors, it will either be a taxable corporate entity or organized as an educational foundation under Section 501(c)(3) of the Internal Revenue Code. The basic determination will depend upon the impact of the gift tax to the donor as well as the donor's desire to have a tax shelter.

If the operation is to be a tax free foundation under 501(c)(3), its activities will be more restricted. It will have to restrict its activities to public education although this definition has historically covered a wide range of permissible activities.

It would obviously be preferable to have a taxable corporation. The principal focus of the activity should be public relations and organization. Much of the substantive work—research, writing and analysis—could be performed by other outside groups which have a tax free status.

I believe that the most effective method of financing is to create a trust of an amount certain, with the annual income from the trust paid to the corporation to support its operating expenses. It would be possible, of course, to draw upon principal so that the trust could continue in effect for ten years but the money could be used in a shorter period. The ten year and one day trust has significant tax advantages to the donor. If the trust is unacceptable for any reason the donor can simply make annual gifts to the corporation to support its operating expenses, although clearly the donor will have to pay gift taxes.

cwc126

DECEMBER 30, 1969

TO: **Bob Haldeman**

FROM: **Richard Nixon**

Would you give me a report on what polls the RNC, or any other source we have, can undertake in our behalf. I have the impression that one of the reasons that our Democratic friends ducked out on the My Lai debate so quickly and also let up on the moratorium support was because of bad reactions they had from private polls they had taken.

On the other hand, it seems to me that we get very little information of this type and that we almost exclusively rely on Gallup or Harris. I think polls on issues have a great deal more meaning than trial heats on candidates. I don't want to duplicate what Gallup does and perhaps we can get a lot of this done by planting questions with him. I think that Joe Bachelder (Chilton Poll) could give us very valuable information with his telephone quicky polls on some of these key issues as we go along through the years. The purpose will not be to help us work out our policy but let us know what obstacles we confront in attempting to sell a policy. I would like to have a study made of this and a game plan submitted to me early in January.

I particularly don't want the RNC to waste a pile of money on trial heat polls taken months before an election for the House and Senate. They mean absolutely nothing.

ss84

W/RN from PPF1 and HRH229

JANUARY 2, 1970

TO: **Ken Cole**

FROM: **Chuck Colson**

RE: **National Women's Party**

The National Women's Party has requested that the President allude in the State of the Union Message to the issue of equal rights for women. As you will see from the enclosed, the President has publicly supported this amendment, as has every other politician down through the years. Fortunately the good sense and ultimate wisdom of Congress has always kept this ridiculous proposal from being enacted. It is good politics to talk about this, I must admit. Could you please advise me so that I can be in touch with the National Women's Party?

CWC126

JANUARY 9, 1970

TO: **Mr. Haldeman**

FROM: **The President**

I assume you are still looking for my anecdote man. As you may recall, what we need is somebody who will find the kind of anecdote that I used in the Guild Hall speech at the conclusion and also the Sophocles quote. It isn't just the question of quoting lines from famous men, but a question of getting one that fits into the mood and tempo of the speech. The best man presently working on this is Huebner, but he has difficulty in preparing things for the spoken word. Until we get somebody better, it is good, however, to keep him on it, but continue your search.

HRH164, 229

W/RN from HRH138

JANUARY 9, 1970

TO: **Mr. Haldeman**

FROM: **The President**

I think we will be missing a bet unless we assign someone now to a special project preparing a book, which I will eventually do under my own by-line, on special letters which are written to a President. I have read some of the letters from the mothers and widows of servicemen who died in Vietnam, as well as some of those we received after some of our speeches, particularly the one on November 3rd, and they are eloquent beyond belief. Also, some of the letters from young people, which I understand Art Linkletter will be looking into, have this same quality.

I want you to set up a project whereby these letters are not destroyed, and to the extent that our limited staff can do so where those which really have some special quality are set aside for my later use.

Of course, if in the process I can once a week or so get one of these letters which might be useful in some of the remarks or speeches that I make, this would be most helpful.

HRH138, 164, 229

JANUARY 9, 1970

TO: **Mr. Haldeman**

FROM: **The President**

Will you give me a report sometime this week on what we are doing to sanitize the White House staff. You will recall my concern with regard to one of the offices where big pictures of Kennedy were in the office in a rather sensitive area where some form letters are prepared to send out.

HRH229

JANUARY 9, 1970

TO: **Mr. Frank Shakespeare**

FROM: **The President**

What is the situation with regard to the horrible modern art in some of our embassies? I realize we can't censor this stuff, but I would like a report as to what embassies have some of these atrocious objects. I know that Keating cleaned out the embassy residence in New Delhi which was in disgraceful shape, and I wonder what some of our other Ambassadors are doing in this respect.

I don't mind if an Ambassador likes modern art provided he is doing a good job in other respects. I simply don't want our embassies abroad to be unrepresentative of the country.

HRH229

JANUARY 9, 1970

TO: **Peter Flanigan**

FROM: **H. R. Haldeman**

The President noted in a recent report that came in to him from some-where that we've appointed approximately 2,000 people (I believe it was 1,907) of which only 1,000 or 50% are Republicans and this, as you can well imagine, he found to be a bit of distressing news. Is there an explanation of this that would be helpful to him and is there a way to remedy this situation?

HRH56

JANUARY 9, 1970

TO: **Jeb Magruder**

FROM: **H. R. Haldeman**

Ed Nixon in talking with the President pointed out to him the fact that auto racing is the largest spectator sport in the United States, way out-drawing football, baseball, basketball, or anything else including horse racing.

Ed further pointed out that Andy Granatelli and Mario Andretti, two of the greats of auto racing, are strong Nixon supporters. The President requests, therefore, that we think about a way to recognize auto racing as a sport, and Granatelli and Andretti particularly as a way for the President to identify with the millions of people who find this a happy way to spend their Sunday afternoons.

Will you please develop a plan for recommendation to the President.

cc: Dwight Chapin

HRH56

JANUARY 14, 1970

TO: John Ehrlichman

FROM: John R. Brown III

The Media Memorandum for the period December 15 to January 10 reported that the Attorney General has replaced the Vice President as the radix malorum of American society. There is an identifiable nastiness to the articles being written about John Mitchell. On reading this the President noted that this shows that the press have to take their hate and frustration out on somebody.

ss83

JANUARY 14, 1970

TO: Dr. Kissinger
       Pat Buchanan

FROM: H. R. Haldeman

RE: Press Conference Material

The President feels that many of the press conference answers prepared for him have been, in essence, directed to the writing press, rather than the television viewer at home. We must remember what we're actually trying to do here is make a statement to the television viewer at home.

The President wants you to realize and emphasize to all appropriate members of your staff that a press conference is a TV operation and that the TV impression is really all that matters. Therefore, what is most important in developing material for a press conference is developing an answer that the TV viewer at home will understand.

He urges that all future answers that are prepared for him use the vernacular that he used in his November 3rd speech. He has asked that all those working on briefing books study this speech carefully.

HRH56

JANUARY 16, 1970

TO: Pat Buchanan

FROM: H. R. Haldeman

The President would like you to keep a constant check on the balance of the news summary, making sure that we don't overload it too much with non-representative material. In particular he wants to make sure we don't inject too much from either the extreme Right or extreme Left. He realizes that it is hard to get stuff from out of the eastern seaboard, but feels that we should try to get editorial comment from the South, Midwest, and West.*

*[Haldeman sent a similarly worded memo to Jerry Warren. See ss86 in the Archives.]

HRH56

JANUARY 16, 1970

TO: **Lyn Nofziger**

FROM: **Chuck Colson**

RE: **National Education Association**

You are very good at turning a phrase. How about preparing an answer which I would be glad to sign if you want me to. If I were to answer them, I would tell them they should go piss up a rope.

CWC90

JANUARY 17, 1970

TO: **Mr. Klein**

FROM: **H. R. Haldeman**

The President feels it is extremely important that Mitchell et al. get the word out to Congressmen and other leaders on what the Black Panthers actually stand for.

He was concerned by the recent report that most of the blacks support the Black Panthers, and feels that this could only be the case if the blacks were not aware of what the Panthers were really trying to do.

Will you please get something underway on this and let me know what kind of results we can get.

HRH56

JANUARY 20, 1970

TO: **Dr. Kissinger**

FROM: **John R. Brown III**

The January 16 News Summary contained a Marvin Kalb report that a command decision has been made in Washington to channel aid for Biafra through the Nigerian government. Many may starve first, and the U.S.

regrets the possibility but this is part of our low-key policy not to meddle in internal affairs.

In reading this the President directed the following remark to you: "We must not be too gentle with Nigeria."

Thank you.

ss85

JANUARY 20, 1970

TO: **Dr. Kissinger**

FROM: **John R. Brown III**

The January 14 *Washington Post* reported the Swedish reactions to the appointment of Holland as U.S. Ambassador "have been both sarcastic and reserved." Swedish officials do not disguise in private that they would have preferred a career diplomat.

On reading the above the President asked that you tell their ambassador here that if they don't like it we will be glad to leave the chargé there.

ss85

JANUARY 26, 1970

TO: **Bob Haldeman**

FROM: **The President**

I think the man who sang at the Ormandy concert might be a good one to have at one of our after dinner White House performances. My guess is that he probably has no political background although, of course, this should be checked out to see if there is anything particularly sensitive on that point.

HANDWRITTEN NOTE, APPARENTLY BY H. R. HALDEMAN: "Placido Domingo—was the gentleman's name."

HRH56

JANUARY 31, 1970

TO: **Bob Haldeman**

FROM: **The President**

I think it would be well to get out a story, and this time not just through a columnist but probably through Merriman Smith of the UP since the AP ran the story on the cost of our Florida helicopter pad, with regard to the expenses of the White House staff.

These points should be emphasized.

First, that we have taken the whole budget for the White House and put it in one bag and that the total for the White House staff has actually been reduced under the Nixon Administration.

Second, I want it pointed out that the helicopter pad in California and the one in Florida were not on RN's property and were not put in at his request. Point out that RN has very strongly objected to the number of Secret Service men and has asked that they be reduced but to no avail.

Point out that the purpose of the helicopter pads which the Secret Service insists on along with the National Command Authority is that the President must always have immediate access to his command plane in the event of a crisis and that both Secret Service and the National Command group consider it essential to have a helicopter pad available near his residence in California and also near his residence in Florida.

The main point to emphasize is that these decisions were made without RN's request and, as a matter of fact, over his objections since he prefers as much privacy as possible.

Also, make the point and do it quite specifically, that the cost of RN's international travels is approximately $115,000 less per week than those of his predecessor. This is due to the fact that RN likes to go with a lean staff and has cut down on the number of briefcase carriers, briefers, staffers, etc. This is a case which can be made and should be made very strongly and I think it is one that Smith might write a good story on.

Other than Smith another option would be to give it to Herb Kaplow, John Jarrell or Pierpont as an *exclusive*. Obviously, a major television coverage would be more important than having it appear in some column or even on a wire service.

I want you to follow up on this and give me a report on what you have been able to do. While these points may seem to be insignificant just remember that the press murdered Eisenhower for the expenses on his farm and also Johnson for all the work that was done *on his property* in Texas. Don't put out the story for the purpose of embarrassing either Eisenhower or Johnson but only for the purpose of putting out the facts with regard to RN's own procedures and the fact that RN has deliberately tried to keep expenses of the White House staff, and particularly those that relate to his own activities, at the minimum necessary in order to conduct the office.

You might also point out that RN has strenuously objected to having too much Secret Service and other protection on his trips within the United States and that what protection he does have is less than what was the case previously and has only been furnished due to the absolute insistence of the Secret Service and other people responsible for his security. It is vital that this story get out and get out fast and accurately.

PPF2

W/RN from HRH229

TO: RMW and Bob Haldeman

FROM: The President

I would like for you to check to see when Ormandy is going to be playing at Constitution Hall. He told me that he had three concerts scheduled during the month of April.

Pick a date which would fit in with my schedule and see whether I could attend. If you do pick such a date I would like for a check to be made with his secretary to see if on that occasion he would consider playing in addition to his usual repertoire, especially for me, *Victory at Sea*, Act II, Beethoven's 9th Symphony and anything from Tchaikovsky— *Swan Lake, Sleeping Beauty* or the *Nutcracker Suite*. Another number that I particularly would like to hear would be the *Grand Canyon Suite*.

Of course, if there is any problem on this just skip it and I will attend the concert for whatever he has scheduled on that evening.

I think, however, he might welcome the opportunity to play some things that I particularly like.

HRH229

FEBRUARY 2, 1970

TO: Mrs. Stuart

FROM: H. R. Haldeman

A couple of questions regarding the first Evening at the White House which, overall, was a smashing success. [. . .]

How did the Agnews happen to end up in the receiving line and upstairs afterwards?

The President has raised the question of the problem of press control at parties. His concern is that they look so awful, and they tend to degrade the party as they descend upon the guests and badger them in the corners. What is your thought on how we can improve this? I'm afraid that if we don't do something, we will end up with a Presidential decision that press is not to be allowed in. This, if you will recall, was the position he took about a year ago.

HRH57

FEBRUARY 3, 1970

TO: John Ehrlichman

FROM: John R. Brown III

On reviewing the unfavorable portion of the summary of editorial and column reaction to the State of the Union message the President noted that the following newspapers and columnists are individuals who are beyond appeal. He notes that we simply shouldn't have our people spend any time with them.

The *New York Times*

The *Washington Post*

The *Courier*

The *Louisville Courier-Journal*

The *Nashville Tennessean*

Martin Nolan of the *Boston Globe*

Richard Dudman of the *Post-Dispatch*

ss83

FRESH NOTES

FEBRUARY 3, 1970

RE: "Leaks"

First, it is important to realize that the President is very sophisticated on the subject of "leaks." He understands them, and the reasons that they come about; he realizes that sometimes they are not harmful; and he realizes that it is undesirable to run too tight a ship, which would be necessary in order to avoid all leaks.

Second, there is a problem, however, if important leaks do occur in that this will inevitably result in the President acting in a detrimental way. The prime example of this is the LBJ syndrome where he took the position that if something leaked he automatically reversed the impending decision so as to make the leak untrue. This, of course, can seriously affect policy adversely. The President's reaction will be different, but might also be quite detrimental; that is, he will usually react by refusing to talk about things which might leak, and this would mean we can't have the kinds of meetings that we have been having.

Up to now the President has been sympathetic to the leak situation; no one has been fired; there have been no FBI investigations, etc.

The point is, though, that the President generally thinks that the meetings he is required to sit in are a waste of time as far as he is concerned. He recognizes their value as therapy. Because, however, he is basically not favorably inclined toward the meetings to begin with, he will use leaks as the basis for eliminating these meetings and thereby will eliminate free and frank discussion of a matter before a decision is made.

We are, therefore, treading on very thin ice. If anything leaks, there will be no more meetings. The President is perfectly capable of making the decisions alone, and prefers to do so; but he is willing to bring people in and occasionally he recognizes that to see them helps.

The main problem here . . . or at least a main problem . . . is in debriefing of civil servants who don't have loyalty to the Administration.

Also, many leaks are, of course, on purpose in order to sell a case, and it should be clearly understood that the President does not act on this kind of pressure and that this is absolutely the wrong way to try to get something taken care of and might even result in the LBJ-type of reaction eventually.

HRH

HRH48

FEBRUARY 4, 1970

TO: **John Ehrlichman**

FROM: **John R. Brown III**

In the February 2 *Chicago Tribune* Walter Trohan reported that the new White House Police uniforms are a "frank borrowing from decadent European monarchies which is abhorrent to this country's democratic tradition." They belong on stage or in novels. They are more comical than splendid and "because police are not masters of close order drill, the ludicrous is emphasized."

On reading the above the President reacted with a large exclamation point.

ss83

FEBRUARY 4, 1970

TO: **Mr. Flanigan**

FROM: **H. R. Haldeman**

As I think back on it, I fear that you dismissed lightly and humorously a memo I sent you sometime back regarding the President's very firm feeling that we should be recruiting our new people—especially the young people—in the Government from the Midwest, Far West, and South, rather than from Harvard and the Northeast complex.

He was completely serious about this point and has again raised the question and feels that we are not following his guidance on it. The point here is that he feels, and I'm sure with some justification, that we are way over-balanced toward Harvard, the Ripon Society, and New York in terms of our personnel sources, and that we should be making a very strong, continuous and conscious effort to recruit from the rest of the country and from schools other than the Ivy League.

Trust you will get on Flemming and any others on this and that we can show the President some results in this direction as the months go by.

HRH57

FEBRUARY 5, 1970

TO: **H. R. Haldeman**

FROM: **John R. Brown III**

Upon reviewing the February 4 News Summary comments concerning the coverage on the new White House Police uniforms the President noted that he wants our staff to take the President's position on this *regardless* of their own views. He suggests that you remind them of Dr. Kissinger's line that "a White House staff member does not have independent views on White House matters."

The President also requested that you have Herb Klein or someone take the offensive on this pointing out the condition of the White House staff we found upon taking office.

ss84

FEBRUARY 9, 1970

TO: **Bob Haldeman**

FROM: **The President**

When I talked to Billy Graham he emphasized again that Johnny Cash was a great supporter of ours and enormously popular. I recall that you had suggested that he come to the White House for one of our nights at 8:30. I think he would be a good one to follow up *1776*.

On that occasion, we should probably allow television if he is willing to do so, and I would suggest that we deviate from the usual guest list by inviting 150 VIP older types and asking each of them to bring a younger person—somebody in the 15 to 25 age group. In other words, what we might well end up with here is a mix of people who would appreciate Cash. I think it might be better to let them bring their younger people rather than for us to select people from the White House staff and from the administrative assistants' group at the Hill to provide the sympathetic audience that would be required.

When you do have Cash I would like for you to ask Billy Graham and his wife to attend since they are very close friends.

PPF2; HRH229

FEBRUARY 9, 1970

Dear Dave:*

I do not wish to intrude on your vacation time but I would like you to have an opportunity to read over the enclosed before you return to Chicago. As you will learn from a telephone call I intend to make to you tomorrow, all hell is about to break loose on the Vietnam front and time is now of the essence. We are also prepared to go ahead with Peter White and a No. 2 man, Howard Hunt, if you approve. Hunt is available immediately. White is 99% certain that he would like to take the job.

I can't emphasize too strongly the urgency of the need. Obviously, the enclosed must be kept completely secret as should this letter.

Best personal regards.

Sincerely,

Charles W. Colson
Special Counsel
to the President

*[Letter to David Bradshaw, Palm Springs, California]

cwc120

w/rn from cwc39

FEBRUARY 10, 1970

TO: **Dr. Kissinger**

FROM: **John R. Brown III**

The February 6 *Philadelphia Inquirer* reported that middle-class Indians are puzzled over the U.S. support of Mrs. Gandhi during her struggle with conservatives in the Congress Party. One Indian said, "Mrs. Gandhi is bent on destroying private enterprise which you Americans value so highly." She is also delivering India to the Soviets, he said. But Americans seem to be supporting Mrs. Gandhi, whether they agree with her or not, simply because she is "doing something."

On reading this the President directed that we should not give her more than token support as an elected head of government.

ss85

FEBRUARY 10, 1970

TO: **John Ehrlichman**

FROM: **John R. Brown III**

The February 9 News Summary reported that a poll of Negroes living in urban areas places Julian Bond first among possible black candidates for President. 27% selected Bond. 23.5% chose Reverend Abernathy, 17% Wilkins, 12% Powell, and 12% Brooke.

On reading the above the President noted that Brooke is too responsible for them. This shows why they talk all right privately and then lash out in public.

ss83

FEBRUARY 10, 1970

TO: Dr. Kissinger

FROM: John R. Brown III

The February 9 News Summary contained a report by Steve Rowan of CBS that Secretary Laird has "long since made up his mind that we should be pulling out faster"—20,000 per month rather than 12,500.

On reading the above the President directed the following comment to you: "His (Secretary Laird's) clever game!"

ss85

FEBRUARY 13, 1970

TO: H. R. Haldeman

FROM: Chuck Colson

I called Harold Boeschenstein. He will be happy to work with the AEI in financing its operations. He said he thought he could be most helpful. He viewed it as an important project and will treat my call and the President's interest, which I transmitted to him, with great discretion. He asked me to assure the President that he would exert every effort to provide AEI with the financing it needs.

bcc: Lyn Nofziger
     Paul McCracken
     Dan Hofgren
     Jeb Magruder

cwc1

FEBRUARY 19, 1970

TO: John Ehrlichman

FROM: John R. Brown III

The February 18 News Summary contained several comments concerning the environment. The President noted that he thinks interest in this issue will recede.

ss83

FEBRUARY 19, 1970

TO: **Mr. Higby**

FROM: **H. R. Haldeman**

Find out quickly for me from someone what the Subversive Activities
Control Board does.

See if it would be within their appropriate area of authority to
investigate the Chicago Seven and the Black Panthers, and these other
related conspiracy groups, to find out whether they are involved in subversive activities and specifically what their funding sources are. Also, let
me know who controls and directs the activity of the Subversive Activities
Control Board, and what their current projects are, etc. Do this quickly
. . . I've got to get a report to the President on it.

                                                                        HRH57

FEBRUARY 20, 1970

TO: **H. R. Haldeman**

FROM: **John R. Brown III**

The February 12 Summary of Mail Trends reported that there has been
an increase in the volume of correspondence opposing U.S. policy in
Vietnam. The President noted that it seems that our silent majority group
has lost its steam. They probably need another demonstration.

                                                                        HRH57

FEBRUARY 20, 1970

TO: **Dr. Kissinger**

FROM: **John R. Brown III**

The February 19 News Summary reported that *Newsweek* quoted an aide
to Secretary Rogers saying that if Vietnam were left to the Secretary,
"We'd be out of there tomorrow."

The President asked that you take note of this.

                                                                        ss85

FEBRUARY 21, 1970

TO: **Harry Dent**

FROM: **H. R. Haldeman**

The President feels we need to be working strongly to pick up all the
money we can in building our kitty for 1972. To do this we need to broaden

the base of financial supporters we now have, especially in the $1,000 category but also in the big money groups.

He wants a scientific study of the people who have *real* money. Work with Colson on this. Don't just use the standard RNC lists—try to break out of the standard mold and look for *new* sources. Both in the establishment that haven't supported us yet—and in the new rich who haven't been tapped.

Please submit to me a report for the President by next Wednesday on what you're doing on this problem.

cc: Chuck Colson

HRH57

EYES ONLY

MARCH 2, 1970

TO: **Mr. Haldeman**
       Mr. Ehrlichman
       Dr. Kissinger

FROM: **The President**

For discussion with the group and implementation.

After a great deal of consideration of our performance during the first year, I have decided that our greatest weakness was in spreading my time too thin—not emphasizing priorities enough. This may sound strange in view of the fact that I did arrange my time to do the November 3rd speech and the State of the Union adequately; but the balance of this memorandum will demonstrate what I want implemented for the future. Also, while this applies primarily to my time, I want Ehrlichman and Kissinger to apply the same rules to allocating their time to the extent that they find it possible.

What really matters in campaigns, wars or in government is to concentrate on the big battles and win them. I know the point of view which says that unless you fight all the little battles too that you do not lay the ground work for winning the big ones. I do not agree with this point of view to the extent that it means that I will have to devote any significant part of my time to the lower priority items, or to the extent that Ehrlichman and Kissinger have to do so.

This means that there must be delegation to the Departments and within the White House staff of complete responsibility for those matters which are not going to have any major effect on our success as an Administration.

Applying this general rule to specifics, in the field of Foreign Policy, in the future all that I want brought to my attention are the following items.

1. East-West relations.

2. Policy toward the Soviet Union.

3. Policy toward Communist China.

4. Policy toward Eastern Europe, provided it really affects East-West relations at the highest level.

5. Policy toward Western Europe, but only where NATO is affected and where major countries (Britain, Germany and France) are affected. The only minor countries in Europe which I want to pay attention to in the foreseeable future will be Spain, Italy, and Greece. I do not want to see any papers on any of the other countries, unless their problems are directly related to NATO. At the next level out where I am indicating policy toward the Mid-East and then finally in the last is policy with regard to Vietnam and anything that relates to Vietnam, Laos, Cambodia, etc. As far as the balance of Asia is concerned, that part of Africa which is not directly related to the Mid-East crisis, and all of Latin America and all countries in the Western Hemisphere with the exception of Cuba and anything else that may be concerned with the East-West conflict, I do not want matters submitted to me unless they require Presidential decision and can only be handled at the Presidential level.

This is going to require a subtle handling on Kissinger's part. He must not let members of his staff or members of the establishment and the various Departments think that I do "not care" about the under-developed world. I do care, but what happens in those parts of the world is not, in the final analysis, going to have any significant effect on the success of our foreign policy in the foreseeable future. The thing to do here is to farm out as much of the decision-making in those areas to the Departments, and where Kissinger does not have confidence that State will follow up directives that I have previously laid down with regard to Latin America, Africa and the under-developed countries of Asia, he should farm that subject out to a member of his staff but he, himself, should not bother with it. I want him to concentrate just as hard as I will be concentrating on these major countries and these major problem areas.

In the future, all that I want to see with regard to what I consider the lower priority items would be a semiannual report indicating what has happened; and where a news conference is scheduled, of course, just enough information so that I can respond to a question, although it is interesting to note that we have received very few questions on the low priority items in news conferences to date.

Haldeman, in the arranging of my schedule, have in mind these priorities. Great pressures will build up to see this and that minor or major official from the low priority countries. All of this is to be farmed out to Agnew. For example, the Minister of Mines from Venezuela is a case in point; he should not have been included on the schedule, and I do not want this to happen again.

With regard to domestic affairs, our priorities for the most part will be expected but a couple will be surprising for reasons I will indicate.

I want to take personal responsibility in the following areas:

1. Economic matters, but only where the decisions affect either recession or inflation. I do not want to be bothered with international monetary matters. This, incidentally, Kissinger should note also, and I will not need to see the reports on international monetary matters in the future. Problems should be farmed out, I would hope to Arthur Burns if he is willing to assume them on a confidential basis, and if not Burns to Houthakker who is very capable in this field. I have no confidence in the Treasury people since they will be acting in a routine way. International monetary matters, incidentally, are a case in point in making the difficult decision as to priorities. I feel that we need a new international monetary system and I have so indicated in several meetings. Very little progress has been made in that direction because of the opposition of Treasury. I shall expect somebody from the White House staff who will be designated who will keep the pressure on in this area. The man, however, who could really be the lead man is Arthur Burns because he feels exactly as I do and it might be that he could exert some influence on the others. Ehrlichman, of course, could be helpful on the staff side but he is not familiar enough with the intricacies of the problem to assume the lead responsibility.

2. Crime: I feel that we have really failed in this area, not perhaps so much in what we have done but in publicizing it adequately. I am going to take charge and start pressuring some people and I want a lead man, either from the White House staff or in Justice, whom I can call daily if I feel like it and ask what is being done. The emphasis here must be more on crime in the street and narcotics. The attack on organized crime is important but not politically except as it affects the Democratic political machines in places like New Jersey and Missouri. Here, of course, we can count on Mitchell going ahead full-steam.

3. School integration: I must assume the responsibility here because it will be the major issue of controversy for the foreseeable future. Here again, I hope we can find one man to whom I can turn and on whom I can rely. This man should not be Garment because of his bias in one direction, or Buchanan, because of his bias in another direction.

You will note that I have excluded the environment. I consider this to be important from the standpoint of the nation and from the standpoint of the Administration making a good record in a vital field, but I have every confidence in Whitaker and believe that he can assume the lead responsibility and I don't want to be bothered with the details. Just see that the job is done. Of course, to the extent Train shapes up as an in-house Administration man he can work in tandem with Whitaker to carry out our objectives.

I have also not included family assistance, revenue sharing, job training, the whole package making up the "New Federalism." I consider this to be important but here again I think that our team is adequate to carry out our policies and I am going to count on them to do so without submitting to me the day-to-day decisions. In such fields as this I am only interested when we make a major breakthrough or have a major failure. Otherwise, don't bother me.

In the fields of education, housing, health, transportation, Post Office, agriculture and labor I want lead men, either within the Administration or within the Department, to assume the responsibilities. I consider each important but they are not the kind of matters which should require my attention. Here I think you could give Harlow a good batch of these, but tell him at the time that he has the responsibility and that I cannot be called upon unless it is something that requires Presidential decision.

The actions of the various agencies fall into the same category of lower priority items—lower priority not because of their not being important but because they do not need my attention. They can and should be handled by White House personnel or by a good Agency man who knows he has the responsibility.

In writing this memorandum I failed to include under the Kissinger section the national defense positions. Here I am interested only in those positions where they really affect our national security and East-West relations. That means that in the case of ABM I, of course, will consider that a high-priority item as long as it is before us. Where an item like foreign aid is concerned I do not want to be bothered with it unless it directly affects East-West relations. I have already indicated in my meeting with Pedersen (?) that I want some reform here and I shall expect that reform to be accomplished in some degree or the other.

A lot of miscellaneous items are not covered in this memorandum but I think you will be able to apply rules based on what I have already dictated.

For example, trade policy is a case in point. This is something where it just isn't going to make a lot of difference whether we move one way or another on the glass tariff. Oil import is also a case in point. While it has some political consequences it is not something I should become deeply involved in. A recommendation should be made and responsibility given at other levels and I will then act without getting involved at lower levels of the discussion.

One final note as to an area where I do feel Presidential involvement is necessary is in government reorganization. Here, however, I do not want to sit down in long haggling sessions but I do want the pressures kept on for a complete reorganization. I will expect Haldeman et al. to assume the lead responsibility, calling upon me only when I have to give it a push.

HRH164, 229

W/RN from PPF2

TO: **Mr. Haldeman**

FROM: **The President**

I have decided to initiate a program for teachers, judges, policemen, and others who take a strong stand against demonstrators and other militants when they engage in illegal activities. I am not satisfied with our program on this to date. It is too low key. I want information to be fed in from all over the country, and then I want letters to go out which will be publicized. In some cases [words indistinct] . . . in short . . . with local stations . . . and whenever possible, I want to bring individuals here to the White House to commend them. One place to start is in the Mafia. Whenever you find a teacher, policeman or principal publicized for standing up against these people, bring them in.

I do not want you to tell Garment or any of our liberal group of this matter. I recall years ago when Judge Medina took terrible abuse from the Communists in the Smith Act trial in New York that all liberal [media opinion] was on the side of the Communists. The country was on Medina's side. (And, incidentally, I was too. I supported him strongly at the trial, in public statements when I was a Member of Congress.) The same was true when the so-called "[Hollywood] 10" came before the Un-American Activities Committee. I was not on that subcommittee, but I recall the press was almost unanimous in condemning the committee for even asking them questions [words missing] supported them when they insulted the committee. The country, however, turned out to be on their side. I have decided to embark on this course of action in order to try to put some backbone and education in officials and in order to separate ourselves very clearly from the militants.

I know that Garment, et al. would strenuously object on the ground that we would be [throwing] down the gauntlet to the militants, and that they would suggest that the way to get at this is to invite them into the White House and try to "reason" which was their line, of course, before the October 15th Moratorium and after the Moratorium up until November 3. As you know, my reaction to this whole matter has been along these lines, and I have not adequately responded to it. From now on, we are going to take a very aggressive "militant" position against these people, not simply because the public is probably with us, but because we face a national crisis in terms of this disrespect for law, etc., at all levels. A very good example of it was when this silly Yale coed disrupted an alumni meeting in New Haven yesterday. Most of the alumni will, of course, blame themselves and the faculty for failing to "communicate" with the young. I know this is Moynihan's line and Garment's . . . and it used to be Price's. I have just been re-reading some memoranda on this subject which they submitted several months ago. It is, however, not my position, and has never been, and from now on I intend to follow through regardless of the consequences along the lines that I have indicated in this memorandum.

In this same vein, I want our guest lists for all events checked more carefully to see that none of this kind of individual is on any committee or is invited to the White House for some function. I know that, for example, on the Volunteer Action case, Wilkinson and Romney and Fisher had the radical student types there because they thought they could "win them" as far as the Committee on the Volunteer Armed Forces was concerned. I know they had the long-haired law school students there because they thought they could help us "appeal to the left." There is a slight bit of evidence to support this position. On the other hand, the evidence on the other side is overwhelming. Every time we bring one of these clowns into the White House or appoint him to a Commission, whether it's on Hunger, the Environment, or anything else, all we do is to reward those who resort to what I consider to be completely improper methods which sometimes are illegal and sometimes even go up to violence to accomplish their goals. It is time that the majority of this country, which does not believe in those methods, is rewarded by White House attention. Everybody will [consider] them square, etc., when we get students of that type, but that's what I want. Of course, I am not suggesting that we go to the Young Americans for Freedom for our people either; they are about as nutty on the other side as the militants are on our side. Somewhere in the heartland of student America and young America are some decent types, who would like to help out. What they probably are are the Junior Chamber of Commerce types in the medium or small cities, and they will come from the big corporations and the law firms and the big firms in the larger cities. In other words, they are our advance man types. As far as universities are concerned, just rule out the east even though there are some good ones here and go to the Midwest to try to find some decent people.

I consider this new direction as being of the highest priority. I want absolutely no deviation from it, and I want you to put somebody on it who will follow through just as I have directed. I am not interested in discussing the matter with anybody on our staff. Further, I have thought it through, and this is my conclusion. I would like for you to personally ride herd on whoever is the "lead man" you select to be in charge of this program.

I have mentioned to you the need to see whether the Subversive Activities Control Board, which is now dormant, could make itself useful by investigating some of the sources of funds for these organizations. Also I want you to see whether anything can be done in the two committees in the Senate and House to see if some younger member up there has the guts to take this problem on. They will catch a lot of heat, but I think the country is ready for some outspoken confrontations on this issue, even though the witnesses will come in and raise hell and cause disturbances in the committee rooms. This in itself will help our cause.

HRH164, 229

W/RN from HRH138

MARCH 2, 1970

TO: **Bob Haldeman**

FROM: **The President**

In thinking about the finance situation, I think what we ought to do is to get the names of 20 men in the country who can give $100,000 or more. We should concentrate on them. Have them in for a small dinner, let them know that they are RN's personal backers and take it on from there. The 20 men should include, of course, two or three who may not be able to give a hundred thousand but who will definitely raise a hundred thousand. Several names come to mind: Clem Stone, possibly Elmer Bobst, John Rollins, the South Carolina textile man, and a few others that will come to mind once you consider it.

What I have in mind here is that we tend to spin our wheels with a lot of people who mean very well but who can't do very much for us. I am inclined to think that if we really concentrate on 20 to 25 people of this group—$100,000 or above (the Olins might be in this class)—we will do much better.

PPF2; HRH138, 229

MARCH 2, 1970

TO: **Bob Haldeman**

FROM: **The President**

I think Colson, in his working with the volunteer groups, has failed adequately to get the women's clubs, service clubs and some of the broader areas of club activity involved. Will you talk to him and have him talk to the fellow from the Freedoms Foundation to see if we can't begin to mobilize a much broader spectrum of clubs and get away from the veterans organizations and the cow punchers which is about all we have been able to touch so far.

PPF2; HRH138, 229

MARCH 2, 1970

TO: **Bob Haldeman**

FROM: **The President**

What happened to the Eisenhower cleats?

HRH229

MARCH 2, 1970

TO: **Bob Haldeman**

FROM: **The President**

It occurred to me that someone might give Reagan a call and tell him that he could use the Western White House for a meeting when he found it desirable.

PPF2; HRH138, 229

EYES ONLY

MARCH 4, 1970

TO: **Mr. Krogh**

FROM: **H. R. Haldeman**

I have reviewed your memorandum concerning the financial support of the various revolutionary groups and would like you to do some additional digging for the following groups:

> Black Panther Party
> The New Mobilization
> Student Mobilization
> SNCC
> SDS
> YSA

As you'll note, many of the sources are not determined. We should be able to get a much better rundown on who the sources are and the amounts given. This would be particularly true in the case of the New Mobilization and Student Mobilization Committee. Also, I was surprised to learn of the lack of funds associated with the Students for a Democratic Society and would request that you re-check those figures and do more digging there to find if that is really the whole story.

Also in relation to the groups above, any additional, pertinent information that you could provide on them would be appreciated.

HRH70

HIGH PRIORITY

MARCH 10, 1970

TO: **Mr. Haldeman**

FROM: **The President**

As you know, under our new procedure, I do not want to see the reports of action on various orders that I may send out. I do, however, want to see reports where orders are not carried out for one reason or another, or are delayed unreasonably.

I want these memorandums covering such items to come to me weekly, and to be quite precise and limited. It should not, for example, carry lists of items that are simply delayed because a staff member hasn't been able to get around to them . . . for example, where I have asked for a research in a certain field. On the other hand, three weeks ago I ordered that Clark Field's personnel be cut by one-third. I realize that this order is one that will be opposed both by Defense and State, and not approved by the National Security Council staff. On the other hand, I made this decision deliberately because of recent developments in the Philippines in which the students rioted against Marcos and Marcos himself had used the United States as the whipping boy where Americans have been engaged in activities per the Filipino law.

I have had no report on this order and assume that it is placed in the bowels of the bureaucracy. I want a report within 48 hours as to why the order was not carried out or, if it is being carried out, what progress is being made.

HRH57, 138, 164, 228, 229;
SS84

MARCH 10, 1970

TO: **Mr. Haldeman**

FROM: **The President**

In view of the flap over Flanigan, I suppose it has occurred to you to have someone check McNamara's blind trust. Did he have Ford stock when he went into it? Did Ford stock go up after he put his stock in trust? I am sure there are Cabinet Officers and others within the previous Administration who were in exactly the same situation as Flanigan. As far as Ford stock is concerned, there would be very little difficulty in finding not only that the stock went up, but that Ford received several hundred million dollars in Government contracts during the period that it went up. At least have the matter checked out.

HRH164, 229

MARCH 10, 1970

TO: **Mr. Haldeman**

FROM: **The President**

The more I think of it, setting up a special group, including Nofziger, Buchanan, Mollenhoff and Huston, for the purpose not of cheering but solely of attacking and defending, is of the highest priority. Out of this group could come speech material for not only Congressmen and Senators, but Cabinet Officers, Agnew and Morton. Will you give me a report within a week as to what progress you have made in this direction.

HRH138, 164, 229

HIGH PRIORITY

MARCH 10, 1970

TO: **Mr. Haldeman**

FROM: **The President**

I understand, according to some of the workmen last night, that they now think it will be May 15th or June 1st before the new press facilities are available. I hope we can get an earlier deadline than that and keep them to it. There has simply been too much malingering on this job, and I also believe that, from walking through the facilities, we have gone overboard in terms of the elaborate individual cubicles and other areas that have been set up. This is likely to get us some pretty tough Congressional criticism.

HANDWRITTEN NOTE FROM HALDEMAN TO RON ZIEGLER: "You better give me a damn good answer on all the above—*fast!*"

HRH164, 229

MARCH 12, 1970

TO: **H. R. Haldeman**

FROM: **Murray Chotiner**

I have matters that are being checked very carefully concerning Illinois, Indiana, Maine, Massachusetts, Missouri, New Jersey, North Dakota, Ohio, Wisconsin and activities of O'Brien.

I will *not* be sending you memorandums concerning any of these, but if at any time you wish to know the status, I will be glad to give you an oral report.

HRH57

MARCH 16, 1970

TO: **Mr. Haldeman**

FROM: **The President**

Will you pass to both Ziegler and Connie the fact that I am paying for David and Julie's trip to Asia. I have made all the arrangements through Bebe for paying their airplane tickets and their expenses, and I want to be sure that this story gets out early so that there is no question raised on it as a reaction.

HRH228, 229

MARCH 16, 1970

TO: **Mr. Haldeman**

FROM: **The President**

Would you please have the Bordeaux years checked? I know that '59 is an excellent year, even with my unsophisticated taste; but my recollection is that '66 is one of the poor years. The reason I ask is that we seem to have a huge stock of '66 Bordeaux on hand, and I wondered why. It may be that the real experts consider '66 to be a good year; but have it checked out. I would like to see, from a wine expert, what they consider to be the best years for French Bordeaux, starting with '59, which most consider to be the best year in the last 25.

HRH138, 164, 229

MARCH 19, 1970

TO: **Mr. Ehrlichman**
        Dr. Kissinger

FROM: **John R. Brown III**

In the March 18 issue of the *Wall Street Journal* David Anderson reported that a disillusioned minority of returnee Peace Corps Volunteers have formed a group which purports to show that the Corps is deeply embedded in the U.S. foreign policy–foreign aid establishment. They regard their training as a graduate school for imperialism which is more concerned with furthering the aims of the U.S. government than solving problems of development abroad. One member of the group has written a book which "is sure to add substance to the anti–Peace Corps charges." It paints a picture of Corps officials who are more interested in their status within the agency than in the welfare of the volunteers or the people the Corps is there to help. The State Department insists that volunteers are not required to act as diplomats who always support U.S. policy. The agency itself defends the curbs on dissent by saying volunteers should spend their time on their jobs. Many people are skeptical of the JFK idealism that conceived the Corps, but the Corps is identified with that concept of human idealism and evolution away from the concept is a powerful problem.

On reading the above the President noted that he feels a quiet phasing out of the Peace Corps and VISTA is in order. He notes that the place to begin is to get the appropriations cut. He requests that you have Mr. Harlow begin to work quietly on this.

Please submit a report to the President on what actions are taken to comply with the above request.

Thank you.

HRH57

MARCH 20, 1970

TO: **The President**

FROM: **H. R. Haldeman**

RE: **Crime Increases**

1965	6%	
1966	11%	
1967	16% }	Two highest years
1968	17% }	since 1945
1969	11%	

HRH4

MARCH 23, 1970

TO: **Assistant Attorney General Antitrust Division**

FROM: **Director, FBI**

RE: **Dunes Hotel / antitrust**

Information was received by the Las Vegas, Nevada, office of this Bureau that on March 19, 1970, a representative of Howard Hughes contacted officials of the Dunes Hotel, Las Vegas, Nevada, and stated that Hughes had received assurance from the Antitrust Division of the Department of Justice that no objection would be interposed to Hughes' purchasing the Dunes Hotel. Hughes reportedly offered $46,500,000, and assumption of all debts of the hotel, which approximate $26,000,000.

It is noted that the Dunes Hotel is owned by Continental Connector Corporation; however, the majority of stock in Continental Connector Corporation is owned by the former owners of the Dunes Hotel, who are still operators thereof.

Reportedly Hughes has indicated that he might raise his price to $55,000,000, plus assumption of the $26,000,000 debt, which would make the total price $81,000,000. The Dunes officials advised Hughes that other negotiations were under way, that the Dunes accountants had not yet completed their projection of the tax position of the various officials in the event of a cash sale, and that it would take some time to reach a definite decision. Hughes' representative indicated that Hughes wanted the hotel and intended to buy same.

The above is furnished for your information.

26 SENATE HEARINGS 12878

MARCH 24, 1970

TO: **Dr. Kissinger**

FROM: **John R. Brown III**

The press reports concerning Senator Kennedy's recent trip to Ireland noted that he encountered some 200 anti-Kennedy demonstrators at Trinity College shouting "imperialist," banging on his car, and demanding that he get out of Ireland. There were some 300 pro-Kennedy demonstrators who engaged the antis in a tussle.

The President noted that he finds this very disturbing. He takes no comfort in this regardless of who is the target. There is a feeling of international anarchy in the air and it began in the U.S. (like Coca-Cola it has spread).

ss85

MARCH 24, 1970

TO: **Alex Butterfield**

FROM: **John R. Brown III**

On reviewing your memorandum regarding Bordeaux wines the President requested that we try to get some of the '59, '61 and '62 wines, particularly the '59 which he considers the best of these three.

In addition he requested that we attempt to get a few of the best years since 1945 ('45, '49, '55, '59 and '61) for special family use.

He noted that we seem to have a large supply of '66 which is a very bad year. He asked that we see if we can trade this wine in for another year.

Thank you.

ss81

MARCH 26, 1970

TO: **The Attorney General**

FROM: **Richard W. McLaren,**
       Assistant Attorney General, Antitrust Division

RE: **Howard Hughes—**
       Proposed Purchase of Dunes Hotel, Las Vegas

Earlier this month, you will recall that you asked me to check into the antitrust aspects of a possible purchase by Howard Hughes interests of the Dunes Hotel in Las Vegas. As I understand, the Nevada State Government has concluded that the Dunes is presently hoodlum-owned and operated and it has reason to believe that Howard Hughes would buy it.

I checked on earlier antitrust activity and found that in 1968 the Antitrust Division prevented Hughes from acquiring the Stardust. This came about because in the period April 1, 1967, to May 1, 1968, Hughes had made four acquisitions of resort hotels on the Strip, giving him 22% of all resort hotel accommodations on the Strip and 20% in the greater Las Vegas area.

Considering new capacity, we calculate that Hughes' market share is now approximately 20%. Acquisition of the Dunes would make this 26%.

On March 12th, you and I discussed the situation and I pointed out that, based on our prior experience, the proposed transfer to Hughes would evoke substantial interest, comment, and probably opposition. Some of the people on the Nevada Gaming Commission are very much concerned over Hughes' present market share in the resort hotel business, particularly because he seems to have bought up most of the vacant land in the area also. I pointed out that the Gaming Commission can get the hoodlums out by starting license revocation proceedings. I also suggested that if the Gaming Commission found in connection with such a proceeding that there were no other legitimate and reasonable bids, we would have no great difficulty in going along with Howard Hughes' acquisition of the Dunes.

We also discussed the possibility that Parvin-Dohrman, Levin-Townsend and Kerkorian were reputed to be in financial trouble and that we might have a real problem if they should also want to sell and Hughes should want to buy. In this connection, we have some indication of interest in the area by Hilton and Holiday Inn.

I trust that the attached FBI report inaccurately records the understanding which the State Government received from the Department.

26 SENATE HEARINGS 12876

APRIL 1, 1970

TO: Jeb Magruder

FROM: Pat Buchanan

I talked with Paul Simpson about the Vice President's forthcoming article in *TV Guide,* from which we deleted mention of that Vanderbilt project. Can you give me some idea of the current status of it; I get conflicting reports.
          Thanks.

————————————————————————
                                                                        cwc118

APRIL 6, 1970

TO: Bob Haldeman

FROM: The President

I would like a quiet check made with regard to the chairs in the Cabinet Room, without saying anything to anybody else. I have a distinct feeling that these chairs, probably because of their style, are pretty uncomfortable. For one thing they do not leave enough leg room beneath the table and, as I told you before, at least insofar as my chair is concerned, it is stiff and hard and pretty uncomfortable after a meeting goes as long as an hour or more.
          I realize that they represent a substantial investment, but a lot of important decisions will be made around that table and if my reaction is shared by others who have tried the chairs, perhaps we ought to meet the problem immediately and have them quietly rebuilt or exchanged for a different model. I emphasize "quietly" because we don't want to give the press a chance to have another "police hat" incident.

————————————————————————
                                                              HRH138, 164, 229

APRIL 7, 1970

TO: General Hughes

FROM: H. R. Haldeman

As I mentioned to you in the Residence today, the President would like to decommission both the *Patricia* and the *Julie.*
          In doing this he wants to get the maximum PR benefit out of the move, by making a maximum story out of the cost or present value of each of the boats, the number of men involved in the crew, compliments for each, etc.
          He also would like to get out the word on the closing down of the Army helicopter operation in Florida as soon as you are ready to do it.

He wants to keep the *Sequoia* in service and hold it always for Presidential use. He feels he hasn't used the other boats enough to justify their continuation, but does think he will make more use of the *Sequoia* than he has in the past.

As I mentioned to you earlier, he would like to look into the overnight possibilities on the *Sequoia* and, if he doesn't feel he wants to sleep on it, has in mind that he might cruise down to Quantico and sleep in quarters there, or go down to Annapolis and attend church at the Academy, then chopper back, etc.

He wants the running times for some of these trips and also for the trip to Mt. Vernon.

In announcing the retirement of the *Patricia* and the *Julie,* he wants to make sure we give Ziegler the full facts—the history of each boat, the names they sailed under, the Presidents that used them—a little background so as to make as much of a story out of it as possible.

As to the use of the *Sequoia,* in the future he doesn't want to be so free with Cabinet and staff on the use of it. He wants it held for Presidential use. It will, therefore, have to be operated on a totally preemptable basis even at the last minute, because he wants to be able to feel he can whip out whenever he feels like it. I think this is probably important to make possible.

In the promotion of the closing, he also wants to be sure Ziegler makes a strong story on this to the TV people, and that they have an opportunity to take film of the boats, etc., so as to make the maximum story out of it as we can.

As I also mentioned, he wants to be sure that State visitors staying at Camp David all receive Camp David jackets.

cc: Ron Ziegler
Dwight Chapin

HRH59

APRIL 13, 1970

TO: **Bob Haldeman**

FROM: **The President**

When the Blackmun nomination is sent down it is vitally important that somebody like Hruska praise the nomination as being that of a man who has the same philosophy on the Constitution as Haynsworth and Carswell. This line must be gotten out, not only by Hruska, but must be of the highest priority with our whole Congressional and PR staff. The attempt of the liberals will be to find shades of difference between Blackmun and Haynsworth and Carswell. As a matter of fact, Blackmun is to the right of both Haynsworth and Carswell on law and order and perhaps slightly to their left, but very slightly to the left only in the field of civil rights. I know the argument will be made that we ought to give the liberals a chance to save face, but there are much higher stakes—my pledge to name strict constructionists to the Court and the inevitable charge that I was forced to back down by the Senate and name a liberal or even a quasi-liberal. Take this on as a project of the highest urgency, discuss it with the Congressional group, the PR group, John Mitchell, etc. so that we get the right set on it at the earliest possible time.

RN HANDWRITTEN NOTE: "Just as strong a constructionist as Haynsworth and Carswell."

PPF2; HRH138, 229

APRIL 13, 1970

TO: **Bob Haldeman**

FROM: **The President**

The Hugh Sidey article in *Life* got across exactly one of the points I have been emphasizing and indicates that whoever talked to him hit the mark. This kind of column doesn't have any significant impact on public opinion in the short run but in the long run it can be most helpful provided there is follow-up and repetition. If he or some other reporter wants to write another article along this line in the future Rose has good material for them—the letters that I write and the calls that I make to candidates, sports figures and others who lose as well as those who win; calls during the Christmas season to parents of men killed in Vietnam and to old friends across the country who are sick; inviting the widows of Senators and Congressmen like Mrs. Dirksen and Mrs. Lipscomb to White House functions; and, of course, the major point that my treatment of both Johnson and Humphrey has been 180 degrees different than the way I was treated while I was out of office—the fact that in 8 years I was never invited to a lunch or a dinner at the White House, and that we have had Humphrey at the Astronauts' dinner and the Johnsons, of course, on numerous occasions. Rose is probably the best one to give out some of this material in case someone does a story in the future along these lines.

Another color point that could be emphasized is the practice we have of trying to invite the families of all former Presidents to the White House at some time while we are in office including the Cleveland sisters, John Coolidge, etc. [which] has never happened before. The invitation to Charles Lindbergh is also a case along the same line. Perhaps a good talking paper could be developed with all these "acts of civility" as Sidey might call them and distribute it to a very select group of people who may be talking to the press.

HRH59

APRIL 13, 1970

TO: **Bob Haldeman**

FROM: **The President**

I was rather surprised to note that in our conversation on the Senate races that no one had talked to Jack Olson. He is the Nixon man in Wisconsin and is going to be the next Governor and has some very strong ideas as to who might be the Senate candidate. This shows rather unusual stupidity for us to have failed to have talked with him. Will you see that whoever has responsibility for Wisconsin talks to him immediately and gets his views as to what would best serve his interests as far as a Senate candidate is concerned. He also may have some views as to what we should do on Knowles. On several occasions I have suggested that we ought to find out what Knowles might want to do and make some offer to him. I think our problem here is that our people are dealing with Laird. Laird really has no interest in the state at large and it is time to start talking directly to Olson and take him as the leadership man in that state.

HANDWRITTEN NOTE BY HALDEMAN: "Memo to Chotiner."

HRH 138, 229:
APPARENTLY WITHDRAWN
FROM PPF2 IN PREPARATION
FOR RETURN TO RN
ACCORDING TO THE RIGHT
OF PRIVATE POLITICAL
ASSOCIATION

APRIL 13, 1970

TO: **Bob Haldeman**

FROM: **The President**

Anita Bryant might be asked to come to a White House church service to sing on some occasion. As you know, she is very active in religious work and could be the soloist at the time we have a speaker.

PPF2; HRH229

APRIL 13, 1970

TO: **H. R. Haldeman**

FROM: **John R. Brown III**

It is requested that you find out as soon as possible from Hobe Lewis what Hubert Humphrey plans to do. If he is going to go for the Senate seat we should start causing him some problems.
    Thank you.

ss84

APRIL 13, 1970

TO: H. R. Haldeman

FROM: John R. Brown III

The April 13 News Summary reported that Larry O'Brien wants a ruling on whether Clark Mollenhoff can view IRS records. The DNC Chairman is not at all pleased with the idea.

It is requested that:

1. You insure that Clark continues his review of these records.

2. We get out a story on *their* review of our people.

ss84

APRIL 13, 1970

TO: Harry Dent
       Jeb Magruder

FROM: Lyn Nofziger

RE: Meeting with Allison, Wade

The purpose of this meeting is to gain for the White House policy control of the Republican National Committee's press and p.r. apparatus.

Obviously, we can't tell them to quit putting out self-serving puff pieces and little announcements that nobody uses, but we can demand that our interests be of first priority.

This means that if any of our three offices wants something put out, it should be done.

For instance, if we find a Republican spokesman to attack Birch Bayh, the National Committee should write the story and distribute it.

If I want some information leaked out, they ought to know how and be willing to do it.

In other words, we need to take them beyond the mechanical mass distribution of goodies and into the attack and defend area. This must be controlled from here. I hope you agree. And I hope we can make that plain to them.

cc: H. R. Haldeman

HRH59

TO: **The President**

FROM: **Clark Mollenhoff**

RE: **The Urgent Need for Continued Access to Federal Tax Returns**

It is vital to my operation that there be a continued access to federal tax returns and that there be public affirmation of that story.

It would appear there is a strong possibility that the Commissioner of Internal Revenue, Randolph Thrower, may seek to cut off my access to federal tax returns. If he accomplishes this, he will have played into the hands of certain Democratic officeholders who are trying to cripple Administration efforts to expose evidence of mismanagement, bribery, and corruption in connection with government operations. It is vital that there be a public Presidential statement, verbal or written, reaffirming the right of access to tax information by the White House for the following reasons:

1. To examine the qualifications of potential appointees as well as of persons holding office.

2. To make inquiries into allegations of corruption and of mismanagement by government officials and others where there is a federal jurisdiction.

3. To make inquiries to assure the integrity and the fairness of the federal tax collecting system itself.

Past access to federal tax returns has been under proper authority, on a sharply limited number of tax matters, and the information has been kept confidential as required by law. In brief, there has been no abuse by me of the authority to obtain tax information. Each request has been in writing on a form approved by Commissioner Thrower and under a system he established and he approved. Each request has been for the purpose of obtaining information on the integrity of an Administration appointee, or for the purpose of following up allegations of corruption or mismanagement in government. Up to the present time there has been no request for the tax returns of United States Senators or United States Representatives. This has represented the ultimate in restraint for there are a number of cases in which inquiry was probably merited but was delayed because of the sensitivity of making requests for such tax information.

There is a fine line between this restraint and negligence in not taking proper steps to obtain information. I have been concerned that my lack of inquiry in some instances might be interpreted as negligence in not following through on evidence of financial irregularities.

With the exception of the information obtained in connection with Judge Haynsworth's much criticized gift of a house to Furman University, I have not disclosed any information from the tax returns to any news reporter, nor have I made tax return information available to anyone in the White House. I did notify the personnel office of a possible serious problem in connection with one potential appointee. Also, I have submitted one document to the Office of the President.

At the present time there is pending a problem involving a Maryland political figure and it would appear there is a real need for access to his tax returns for a two or three year period. This case is more than a simple rumor and involves evidence indicating irregularities in the AID program in recent years, as well as possible tax law violation and other violations. I feel that we might be negligent in not assuring ourselves that this matter is being properly pursued by officials of all federal agencies. It is only realistic to assume that there might be some reluctance on the part of lower level career employees to pursue this as they would any other taxpayer because of the position the official holds.

I would appreciate the opportunity to discuss these or any other related matters.

HRH139

APRIL 15, 1970

TO: **Mr. Chapin**

FROM: **L. Higby**

The President would like to keep available, for use on occasion as gifts, a stock of the "police hats" that were used with the dress uniform for only a short time.

The hats are being purchased by the President, and all have been given to the Secret Service and locked up in a vault in the EOB. I have informed Alex of the President's desire and he is obtaining a quantity to keep on hand for the President. You may want to get in touch with Alex, or have Steve Bull get in touch with him, and decide on a suitable location to store a small supply.

As you know, these hats are a very valuable item and tight inventory control needs to be exercised over them. Alex probably should be the point of control since he has overall responsibility for contact with the Secret Service and is familiar with the background of what the President wants done in this regard.

cc: Mr. Butterfield

HRH59, 60

APRIL 21, 1970

TO: **Bob Haldeman**

FROM: **The President**

Just a reminder, whenever you can discreetly do so, I want you to call
Rogers and Laird with any directive to them from me rather than leaving
it to Henry. This will increase Henry's viability with them and will reduce
the number of times that he must call them on the nit-picking matters.

PPF2; HRH138, 229

APRIL 21, 1970

TO: **Bob Haldeman**

FROM: **RmWoods**

Quite a few of the attached memoranda might well be classified "BURN
AFTER—if not BEFORE—READING."
    Until we are able to stop the leaks of our confidential memoranda
it seems rather dangerous to have some of these floating around. I think
conversations in person or on the telephone would be safer on several of
the attached.

PPF2

APRIL 22, 1970

TO: **Bob Haldeman**

FROM: **The President**

In talking to J. Edgar Hoover I found that he was enthusiastic about the
Vietnam speech but he said that the picture did not come out as well as
it should have. He said it had a yellowish rather washed-out look rather
than the healthy appearance that he thought I projected in person last
night. It is possible that we are not looking at these objectively enough.
Check a few other places and if you reach the same conclusion maybe we
should do something about lighting or makeup or both before the next
television appearance. (Hoover, incidentally, said that Clyde Tolson who
was at a different television set had exactly the same impression.) I have
not heard this from others but it may be that they are too polite or
unobjective to say so.

PPF2; HRH138, 229

APRIL 22, 1970

TO: **Rose Mary Woods**

FROM: **The President**

Would you see if you could find one of the pins with the diamonds in it like I gave to Mrs. Eisenhower at Christmas and have it gift wrapped and delivered to the Chinese Embassy for transmittal to Madame Chiang Kai-shek. As you know, she has been quite ill and I think this would be a great lift for her. I told him that Mrs. Nixon and I wanted to send along a small gift to her with him. This will mean a great deal to her and in view of her support through the years is the right gesture for us to make even though the gift is on the expensive side.

PPF2

APRIL 22, 1970

TO: **The President**

FROM: **Randolph W. Thrower**
Commissioner of Internal Revenue

RE: **Disclosure of Information from IRS Files**

In the recent spate of publicity over the disclosure of information from returns and other files of the IRS, one matter appeared in the press to which I feel compelled to call your personal attention. It involves an apparent "leak" of highly confidential tax information to columnist Jack Anderson on a current tax investigation involving Gerald Wallace of Alabama, brother of the former Governor.

A brief memorandum summarizing the status of our current income tax investigation of Gerald Wallace was sent by me to Mr. Clark Mollenhoff on April 2, 1970. Eleven days thereafter a portion of this information was reflected in Jack Anderson's column in a manner which indicated the probability of my memorandum as his source.

I am satisfied by Mr. Mollenhoff that this memorandum was handled by him in the greatest confidence. This is consistent with our general arrangements for providing information on your behalf.

I recognize that the unauthorized release of the information, if it came from the memorandum, could have occurred within the IRS even though the memorandum was tightly controlled here and hand carried between a very few individuals. I have directed our Inspection Service to make this the subject of a formal investigation. I felt, however, that you should know of the possibility that, despite precautions, this may have happened in some way after the memorandum reached the White House.

HRH139

TALKING PAPER—JEB MAGRUDER*

1. Put someone on the *Washington Post* to needle Kay Graham. Set up calls or letters every day from the viewpoint of I hate Nixon but you're hurting our cause in being so childish, ridiculous and over-board in your constant criticism, and thus destroying your credibility.

2. Nofziger should work out with someone in the House a round robin letter to the *Post* that says we live in Washington, D.C., read the D.C. papers, but fortunately we also have the opportunity to read the papers from our home districts and are appalled at the biased coverage the people of Washington receive of the news, compared to that in the rest of the country, etc.

3. Follow up on the yacht story—get something in Monday, etc. so that we can get some mileage out of that. Also, see if you can think of any other things to do to follow up on it.

4. Get some letters to the Kopechne case judge, congratulating him on his courage in pointing out the discrepancies in the case.

*[Magruder's memo of 5/6/70 to Haldeman implies that Haldeman drafted this memorandum during the week of 4/27/70.]

SENATE COMMITTEE
FINAL REPORT 292

1970

MAY–AUGUST

Kent State Documents Being Shipped to Yale

COLUMBUS, OHIO—Victims of the Kent State University shootings say they don't trust the state of Ohio, so records of the 1970 incident are moving to Yale University, where they will be open to the public.

No new information is expected on the May 4, 1970, shootings by Ohio National Guardsmen that killed four people and wounded nine during a campus protest of the Vietnam War, said lawyer Steven Keller.

Ten boxes of documents and photographs, the first shipment of about 110 crates, are scheduled to arrive at Yale, in New Haven, Conn., in the next few weeks. The documents are leaving Ohio at the request of those wounded and the families of those who died.

"Some of the people involved in all this, a lot of them, don't trust the state of Ohio. . . . Ohio might take some of this stuff and destroy it to destroy some of its unpleasant history," said Dean Kahler, 38, one of the wounded students who is now a county commissioner in Athens, Ohio.

—WASHINGTON TIMES, JUNE 22, 1988

MAY 1, 1970

TO: **Chuck Colson**

FROM: **Murray Chotiner**

John Lindsay of *Newsweek* did a spot check and finds that it is the opinion of a number of key people in Massachusetts that Senator Kennedy is in trouble and that the man who can defeat him is Henry Cabot Lodge.

cwc95

123

MAY 4, 1970

TO: **Rose Woods**

FROM: **J. V. Brennan**

On the day following the President's historic speech in which he announced his decision to send military forces into Cambodia, I had the privilege of being in his company for most of the afternoon. I was so moved by the spirit, determination, dedication and patriotism which he conveyed that I feel obliged to record the mood for history. May I humbly submit this:

Memorandum for the President's Files

May 1st, 1970, was a warm clear spring day in Washington as the motorcade carrying the President, Mrs. Nixon, Mr. and Mrs. David Eisenhower, and Mr. C. G. Rebozo departed the White House en route to the Washington Navy Yard. The group of tourists outside the southwest gate was much larger than usual, although no notice was given of the President's imminent departure from the White House.

At the Washington Navy Yard, we boarded the Presidential yacht, *Sequoia.* It was then that I noticed how very tired the President was. I had never seen him appear so physically exhausted. Yet, contrary to his normally pensive mood when he is tired, today he seemed to feel exuberant inside and made special efforts to chat with the commanding officer of the yacht and to the crew members.

At about 2:30 P.M., the family and Mr. Rebozo were seated in the stateroom awaiting lunch when the President sent for me. He then gave me instructions regarding the honors to be played when passing George Washington's tomb at Mount Vernon.

Now, the President knows that it is mandatory for all Naval vessels to render honors when passing Mount Vernon, and he has participated in this ceremony several times. Yet, on this day, he was very emphatically emphasizing the importance of this ceremony, and was specific about how it should be done with feeling. He told me he wanted the National Anthem "blasted out." He wanted it to be heard! He emphasized this point by punching the air with his closed fist. (He, of course, was not staging this ceremony for the benefit of the public because honors are rendered while in the channel, and could not be heard from shore under any circumstances.)

Following these instructions, I excused myself and turned away. He then called me back in a manner which he has not done before. In a deliberately gruff voice, he said, "Hey!" I returned and the President, in a tough-sounding voice, and with very serious facial expression, said, "As a Marine, do you approve of what I said last night?" After I told him that listening to his speech was one of the proudest moments of my life, he said, facetiously, "Don't you think that I took too hard a line for the Marines?"

My aghast facial expression was part of my answer and I said, "I only wish I were over there to help carry out what you've ordered." The President said, "I do too. I think I'll resign and we'll go together."

My feeling during this brief conversation was that the President was very proud and pleased with the action he had taken; but that it was a lonely time for him. It was his decision alone; he knew he was right, and wanted other people to agree. He certainly knew my feelings before he asked the questions.

Later he asked to be called ten minutes prior to arrival at Mount Vernon and, consequently, the time for rendering honors.

As the time neared, the President was quite anxious. He was standing in position at the bow of the yacht well in advance of the prescribed time for the ceremony. He stood at rigid attention during the ceremony; Mrs. Nixon to his right, then David, Julie and Mr. Rebozo. As the ceremony ended, the President turned to the men of the crew with a wide smile and "thumbs-up" gesture.

This spirit of pride prevailed throughout the day.

PPF11

MAY 11, 1970

TO: **H. R. Haldeman**

FROM: **The President**

I would like for you to have a talk with Klein and Ziegler with regard to some very strict instructions on the handling of the *New York Times* and the *Washington Post*. I will make these instructions precise and I want them carried out precisely for the next sixty days.

With regard to the *New York Times, no one* from the White House staff under any circumstances is to answer any call or see anybody from the *New York Times* except for Semple. Try also in a quiet way to get this word carried out wherever you can in the departments without getting in a position where somebody is going to report it back to the *Times.* I just want it done. The only exception with the *Times* staff will be, of course, as far as the social stuff is concerned which Connie Stuart can continue to handle on the same basis, and with regard to economic matters where Ed Dale can be talked to. I want you to tell McCracken that under no circumstances is he or anybody else on his staff to talk to anybody on the *New York Times* about anything and are to answer no calls whatever on the economy except calls from Ed Dale, unless he gets my specific permission.

With regard to the *Washington Post* I reaffirm the directive I gave two weeks ago but which has not been carried out. Ziegler under no circumstances is to see anybody from the *Washington Post* and no one on the White House staff is to see anybody from the *Washington Post* or return any calls to them. They are to be handled as part of the general press corps. This includes Kilpatrick, Oberdorfer, and everybody else. I realize the argument that has often been made that Oberdorfer one time out of ten gives us a good story. I [am] now reiterating the policy that I want followed out—just treat the *Post* absolutely coldly—all of their people are to be treated in this manner. Of course the same exception with regard to the social reporters who will be handled by Connie Stuart along the lines she best determines. If there is any exception to this directive you are to raise it directly with me and I will determine on a case by case basis, but under no circumstances will any individual on our staff, on his own, move in other directions. At the same time I want a policy in which the *Washington Star,* the *Washington Daily News,* the *New York Daily News,* the *Chicago Tribune* and, for the time being, the *Los Angeles Times* and others who may be competitive with the *New York Times* and *Washington Post* continue to receive special treatment when Ziegler and Klein may determine it is in our interest. They will not agree with this policy but it is one I have decided upon after long consideration and I want it carried out.

HRH140, 164, 229
W/RN from HRH138

MAY 11, 1970

TO: **H. R. Haldeman**

FROM: **The President**

After reading the stories in Henry's backgrounder I have reluctantly concluded that we must take him off this assignment and find another way to get out our news in cases like this. You were right in your appraisal that Henry goes into so much detail about the philosophy and the procedures, etc., that the main thrust doesn't come through. I say this particularly because Ziegler thought this was the best of his backgrounders.

HRH138, 164, 229
W/RN from HRH140

MAY 11, 1970

TO: **H. R. Haldeman**

FROM: **The President**

Will you make a careful check of the arrangements for the Japanese trip and give me your best judgment as to where we move from here. I know that several have raised questions about the advisability of the trip because of the possibility of student demonstrations when they are there. On the other hand, if we cancel it now it might reflect on what we are doing in Cambodia. This is going to be a very close judgment call but we must make a decision soon so that it doesn't appear that whatever we did was done under pressure just before the trip was scheduled.

HRH138, 164, 229

MAY 13, 1970

TO: **Bob Haldeman**

FROM: **The President**

Attached is a memorandum covering my recollections of my visit to the Lincoln Memorial. When you read the full memorandum, and incidentally after you read it you can distribute it on a very limited basis to possibly Ehrlichman and anybody else who may have raised questions with regard to what was discussed so that they may have it for background information.*

[Name missing] suggested that Sidey would like to do a piece for *Time* on it. I doubt if we ought to give it to him because he is likely to chop it up in any event. Maybe you can find somebody else who would do a better piece.

*[Mr. Nixon describes his visit to the Lincoln Memorial in his *Memoirs*, pp. 459–466.]

HRH229
W/RN from PPF2

MAY 13, 1970

TO: **Bob Haldeman**

FROM: **The President**

The attached is a memorandum of what actually took place at the Lincoln Memorial.

After you read it, I think you will share my complete frustration with regard to coverage of my activities. I realize we didn't have Ziegler at my elbow every minute or Krogh making notes. If they had been, it would have spoiled the whole thing. On the other hand, while Krogh could not hear it all—apparently his recollection was only of those matters that this memorandum clearly indicates I told the students were *not* important rather than those matters of the spirit that were important. Ziegler, of course, in his questions wanted to know what time I got up, how long I had been there, what I had for breakfast, etc., all of which were essential to the story but which were completely irrelevant as far as getting across the whole spirit and thrust of the story.

I can understand why John Ehrlichman got the idea from the news reports that I was tired and all I talked about was surfing and nonsensical things. This, of course, reflects on two points—even when I am tired I do not talk about nonsensical things and also more fundamentally, I am afraid that most of the members of our staff, to their credit, are enormously interested in material things and what we accomplish in our record, etc. etc. but that very few seem to have any interest and, therefore, have no ability to communicate on those matters that are infinitely more important—qualities of spirit, emotion, of the depth and mystery of life which this whole visit really was all about.

Perhaps it might be well for you, Ehrlichman, Moynihan—maybe Garment, Price, Keogh, Safire and Buchanan—to read this. Most of them will not really understand what I am talking about and most of them will disagree with the approach. I realize it would have made more news from the standpoint of the students for me to engage in a spirited "dialogue" with them about why we were in Cambodia, why we haven't ended the war sooner, morality of the war, etc. This kind of conversation would have been infinitely more easy for me. It would have made more news but as I evaluated the situation this was the one time this group of students—most of whom perhaps were middle class or lower middle class—most of whom were about as poor as I was when I was in college and who had driven all this long distance to Washington—this was the only time they had ever talked to a President of the United States. They will see me many times discuss these heated, angry subjects that they would hear later at the Monument and that they hear in their classrooms. Perhaps the major contribution I could make to them was to try to lift them a bit out of the miserable intellectual wasteland in which they now wander aimlessly around.

I do not write this memorandum to you critically of our staff because I think it is the best staff any President has had by far in terms of loyalty, willingness to work, etc. The only problem is that we seem to lack on the staff any one individual who really understands or appreciates what I am trying to get across in terms of what a President should mean to the people—not news, not gimmicks like rushing out to the Negro Junior College with a covey of newsreels following. All of this seems to be big stuff and I realize makes big news—perhaps it is. But on the other hand I really wonder in the long run if this is all the legacy we want to leave. If it is—then perhaps we should do our job as easily as we can—as expeditiously as we can and get out and leave the responsibilities of the government to the true materialists--the socialists, the totalitarians who talk idealism but rule ruthlessly without any regard to the individual considerations—the respect for personality that I tried to emphasize in my dialogue with the students.

As you recall, the press conference was at 10 o'clock Friday night. After the press conference I had approximately 20 calls from VIPs in addition to hundreds from others which I, of course, could not take. I completed returning my calls at approximately 2:15 in the morning. I then went to bed, slept soundly until shortly after four o'clock. When I woke up I got up and went into the Lincoln Sitting Room and was listening to an Ormandy recording with Entremont (?) at the piano playing a Rachmaninoff album for piano and orchestra. Manuel [Manolo] apparently heard and came down to the Lincoln Sitting Room and asked if he could get me some coffee or hot chocolate or something else. I told him no but then as I looked out of the window and saw the small knots of students begin to gather on the grounds of the Washington Monument I asked him if he had ever been to the Lincoln Memorial at night.

He said he had not. I said, get your clothes on and we will go down to the Lincoln Memorial. I got dressed and at approximately 4:35 we left the White House and drove to the Lincoln Memorial. I have never seen the Secret Service quite so petrified with apprehension. I insisted, however, that no press be informed and that nobody in our office be informed. Apparently, they disobeyed my instructions on the latter point because Bud Krogh, I understand, and Ron Ziegler showed up toward the end of my meeting with the students.

Manuel and I got out of the car at approximately 4:40 and walked up the steps to the Lincoln statue. I showed him the great inscription above the statue and told him that that, along with the inscription over the Tomb of the Unknown Soldier, was, in my opinion, the most moving sight in Washington, and then showed him the Gettysburg Address on the left and Lincoln's Second Inaugural on the right. Manuel was quite familiar with both. While he is a new citizen he is deeply interested in American history and reads it at every opportunity.

By this time a few small groups of students had begun to congregate in the rotunda of the Memorial. I walked over to a group of them and walked up to them and shook hands. They were not unfriendly. As a matter of fact, they seemed somewhat overawed, and, of course, quite surprised. When I first started to speak to the group there were approximately 8 in it. I asked each of them where they were from and found that over half were from upper New York State. At this point, all of them were men. There were no women. To get the conversation going I asked them how old they were, what they were studying, the usual questions. I asked how many of them had been to Washington before and found that over half the group had never been to Washington before. I told them that it was a beautiful city, that I hoped they enjoyed their visit there, that I wanted them, of course, to attend the anti-war demonstration, to listen to all the speakers; that I hoped they had the time to take a tour of the city and see some of the historical monuments.

I told them that my favorite spot in all of Washington was right where we were standing—the Lincoln Memorial at night—that I had not been here at night for ten years, that I had come down here because I had awakened early after my press conference and wanted Manuel to see this wonderful sight.

Two or three of them volunteered that they had not been able to hear the press conference because they had been driving all night in order to get here. I said I was sorry they had missed it because I had tried to explain in the press conference that my goals in Vietnam were the same as theirs—to stop the killing and end the war to bring peace. Our goal was not to get into Cambodia by what we were doing but to get out of Vietnam.

They did not respond and so I took it from there by saying that I realized that most of them would not agree with my position but I hoped that they would not allow their disagreement on this issue to lead them to fail to give us a hearing on some other issues where we might agree. And also particularly I hoped that their hatred of the war, which I could well understand, would not turn into a bitter hatred of our whole system, our country and everything that it stood for. I said, I know that probably most of you think I'm an S.O.B. but I want you to know that I understand just how you feel. I recall that when I was just a little older than you, right out of law school and ready to get married, how excited I was when Chamberlain came home from Munich and made his famous statement about peace in our time. I had heard it on the radio. I had so little in those days that the prospect of going into the service was almost unbearable and I felt that the United States staying out of any kind of a conflict was worth paying any price whatever. As I pointed out too the fact that I came from a Quaker background I was as close to being a pacifist as anybody could be in those times and as a result I thought at that time that Chamberlain was the greatest man alive, and when I read Churchill's all-out criticism of Chamberlain I thought Churchill was a madman. In retrospect, I now realize I was wrong. I think now that Chamberlain was a good man but that Churchill was a wiser man and that we in the world are better off than we would be because Churchill had not only the wisdom but the courage to carry out the policies that he believed were right even though there was a time when both in England and all over the world he was extremely unpopular because of his "anti-peace" stand.

I then tried to move the conversation into areas where I could draw them out. I said that since some of them had come to Washington for the first time I hoped that while they were young that they would never miss an opportunity to travel. One of them said that he didn't know whether he could afford it, and I said I didn't think I could afford it either when I was young but my wife and I borrowed the money for a trip we took to Mexico and then one to Central America. The fact is, you must travel when you are young. If you wait until you can afford it you will be too old to enjoy it. When you're young you can enjoy it. I urged them to start with the United States. I said there was so much to see in this country. I told them that as they went West, that I particularly thought they should go to places like Santa Fe, New Mexico, and see American Indians. I pointed out that I knew that on their campuses that the major subject of concern was the Negro problem. I said this was altogether as it should be because of the degradation of slavery that had been imposed upon the Negroes and it would be impossible for us to do everything that we should do to right that wrong, but I pointed out that what we have done with the American Indians was in its way just as bad. We had taken a proud and independent race and virtually destroyed them, and that we had to find ways to bring them back into decent lives in this country.

I said along the same lines that they would find in California that the Mexican-Americans were even from an economic standpoint worse off than the Negroes. I said that in both cases we needed to open channels of communication to Indians, to Mexicans as well as to Negroes, and I hoped that they would do so.

At that time a girl joined the group and since I had been discussing California I asked if anybody there was from California. She spoke up and said she was from Los Altos and I said that was one of my favorite towns in Northern California and I hoped it was as beautiful as I remembered it. She did not respond.

In trying to draw her out, I told the rest of the group that when they went to California that they would see there what massive strides we could take to deal with the problem of the environment which I knew they were all interested in. I said that right below where I live in California there was the greatest surfing beach in the world, that it was completely denied to the public due to the fact that it was Marine Corps property, and that I had taken steps to release some of this property to the public for a public beach so that the terribly overcrowded beaches further north could be unburdened, and so that the people could have a chance to enjoy the natural beauty which was there. I said that one of the thrusts of our whole quality of life environmental program was to take our Government property and put it to better uses and not simply to continue to use it for military or other purposes because it had been used for that way from time immemorial.

Most of them seemed to nod in agreement when I made this point.

I then spoke of how I hoped that they would have the opportunity to know not only the United States but the whole world. I said most people will tell you to go to Europe. I said Europe was fine, but it's really an older version of America. It is worth seeing but the place that I felt they would particularly enjoy visiting would be Asia. I told them my great hopes that during my Administration, and certainly during their lifetime, that the great mainland of China would be opened up so that we could know the 700 million people who live in China who are one of the most remarkable people on earth.

Most of them seemed to nod in agreement when I made this point.

I then went on to say, however, that they should not overlook when they were in Asia the people of India. I said the people in India are terribly poor, but they have a history and philosophical background and a mystique which they should try to understand.

I also touched lightly on places like Malaysia. One of them mentioned that we had a Peace Corps in Malaysia and I said, that's right, we have them in several of these countries wherever they will allow it.

I then moved on to the Soviet Union. Then one of them asked me what Moscow was like, and I said gray. It's very important if you go to

Russia, of course, to see it because of the historical and governmental operations that are there, but if you really want to know Russia, its exciting variety and history, you must go to Leningrad. I said that in Russia Leningrad was really a more interesting place to visit, that the people were really more outgoing there since they were not so much under control and domination of the central government.

I also said that in terms of beautiful cities they would find Prague and Warsaw of much more architectural beauty than Moscow. I made this point because I was speaking directly to one of the students who said he was a student of architecture. In fact, there were two who said they were studying architecture and I thought that they would be interested in knowing about [words missing] but the most important point I made about Russia was that as you went across the country, that they should go to places like Novosibirsk, a raw, new city in the heart of Siberia, and Samarkand in Asian Russia where the people were Asians rather than Russians.

One of them asked whether it would be possible to get a visa to such cities, and I said I was sure they could and if any of them took a trip to Russia and wanted to contact my office I would help out.

This seemed to get a little chuckle from them.

I then moved back to the problem and my thrust then of what really mattered in the world was people rather than cities and air and water and all the other things that were material. I said, for example, Haiti of all the countries I have visited in Latin America is probably the poorest with Bolivia slightly poorer, but that the Haitians, as I recalled from 1955, while they were poor had a dignity and a grace which was very moving, that I always had wanted to return, not because there was anything in Haiti worth seeing in terms of cities or good food, etc., but because the people had such character.

I then made this same point again with regard to the people I had seen in Asia and India and returned again to the United States where I again emphasized the importance of their not becoming alienated from the people of this country, its great variety.

I expressed distress that on the college campuses the blacks and whites, while they now go to school together, have less contact with each other than they had when they weren't going to school together on some of our major campuses. This seemed to get through, although none of them had much to say and none of them responded specifically.

By this time the group around me had begun to get considerably larger. I would say that the original group of approximately 8 to 10 had now become perhaps 30 and some of those who seemed to be more leader types and older began to take part in the conversation.

One spoke up and said, "I hope you realize that we are willing to die for what we believe in."

I said I certainly realize that. Do you realize that many of us when we were your age were also willing to die for what we believed in and were willing to do so today. The point is that we were trying to build a world in which you will not have to die for what you believe in, in which you are able to live for. I put in one brief comment with regard to the point I had made in the press conference that while we had great differences with the Russians we had to find a way to limit nuclear arms and I had hoped that we could make some progress in that direction. They seemed to have very little interest in that subject. Perhaps it was because we moved through so fast and perhaps because they were overawed by the whole incident.

Then another spoke up and said, we are not interested in what Prague looks like. We are interested in what kind of life we build in the United States.

I said the whole purpose of my discussing Prague and other places was not to discuss the city but the people. For the next 25 years the world is going to get much smaller. We are going to be living in all parts of the world and it is vitally important that you know and appreciate and understand people everyplace, wherever they are, and particularly understand the people in your own country.

I said I know that the great emphasis that is currently being put on the environment—the necessity to have clean air, clean water, clean streets—that, as you know, we have a very bold program going further than any program has ever gone before to deal with some of these subjects, but I want to leave just one thought with you, that cleaning up the air and the water and the streets is not going to solve the deepest problems that concern us all. Those are material problems. They must be solved. They are terribly important. We must have clean air and clean water. We must make the country more beautiful and remove the ugly blotches that our modern society has put on the face of the earth. But you must remember that something that is completely clean can also be completely sterile and without spirit. What we all must think about is why we are here. What are those elements of the spirit which really matter. And, here again, I returned to my theme of thinking about people rather than about places and about things. I said candidly and honestly that I didn't have the answer, but I knew that young people today were searching as I was searching 40 years ago for an answer to this problem. I just wanted to be sure that all of them realized that ending the war and cleaning up the streets and the air and the water was not going to solve spiritual hunger which all of us have and which, of course, has been the great mystery of life from the beginning of time.

The last 20 minutes of the conversation Manuel made mention to me a couple of times that I had a telephone call in the car. I, of course, smiled and said, let it wait. I realized that the Secret Service were becoming more and more concerned as they saw the crowd begin to mount and probably feared that some of the more active leaders would get word of my visit and descend upon us. By this time the dawn was upon us, the first rays of the sun began to show and they began to climb up over the Washington Monument and I said I had to go and shook hands with those nearest to me and walked down the steps.

A bearded fellow from Detroit was taking a picture as I began to get in the car. I asked him if he wouldn't like to get in the picture. He stepped over with me and I said, look, I'll have the President's doctor take the picture, and Tkach took the picture. He seemed to be quite delighted—it was, in fact, the broadest smile that I saw on the entire visit. As I left him I said, I came back to the theme I had made up above, and I knew he had come a long way for this event and I knew, too, that he and his colleagues were terribly frustrated and angry about our policy and opposed to it. I said, I just hope your opposition doesn't turn into a blind hatred of the country. But remember this is a great country with all of its faults. I said, if you have any doubt about it go down to the passport office and you won't see many people lining up to get out of the country. Abroad, you will see a number lining up to get in.

He smiled and took it all in good humor. We shook hands, I got into the car and drove away. From there I asked the driver to take us up to the Capitol. Manuel had never been in the Capitol before—I took him for a tour of the House side, the Senate side, the Rotunda where I told him the services for President Eisenhower and Senator Dirksen had been conducted.

Finally, we found a fellow by the name of Frazer (Fraser) who said he had come to the Congress the same year I did in 1947 as a page boy for Charlie Halleck. Frazer had the morning shift and opened the House Chamber to us. We walked in with the Secret Service men, Tkach—I had Manuel go up and sit in the Speaker's Chair. We all clapped as he got into the chair.

When we left we tried to find some place to see if we could have breakfast down there and, of course, nothing was available. Several of the Negro women who do the cleaning came up to speak to me. Three of them had known me when I was there as Vice President. One of them asked me to sign her Bible. I told her that it made me very proud to sign her Bible and I was glad to see that she carried it with her but that the trouble is that most of us these days didn't read it enough. She said, I read it all the time. After I signed her Bible she went down and brought up two or three others who were working on the cleaning detail for signing of pictures and other odds and ends that they had for their children, grandchildren, etc.

We then left the Capitol and went down to the Mayflower restaurant. I hadn't been in a public restaurant in Washington since becoming President except, of course, on official functions. They were all delighted to see us and I had corned beef hash and poached egg for the first time in five years, and at the conclusion signed autographs for everybody in the restaurant. I found, incidentally, almost without exception, individually the waitresses were for what I had said, what we were doing in Cambodia. As we drove away from the restaurant, eight to ten of the waitresses all stood at the door, outside on the street, and waved goodbye.

PPF2, 11; HRH229

First five paragraphs W/RN
from PPF2 and PPF11

RN TAPE 2

MAY 13, 1970

TO: **Haldeman**

In talking to Sidey with regard to his upcoming story I think you might give him a few shots on a subject that I have without success gotten our PR people to get carried in some of the columns and that is that to the extent the President has any support whatever on Cambodia, this is a devastating indication of the lack of credibility of the national media, particularly the two news magazines, the *Washington Post* and the *New York Times,* and the three networks. Point out that all of them have opposed RN violently on this issue. Point out also that this is not something new, that RN is the first President in this century who came into the Presidency with the opposition of all of these major communications powers, that since he has been in the Presidency with only very few exceptions he has been heavily opposed, not just editorially but primarily by the slant of the news coverage due to the attitude of reporters and that the fact that he now survives all this with even 57 percent approval by the people indicates not so much something about RN as it does something about the news media. Point out that this 57 percent, incidentally, is a rather remarkable figure in view of the fact that it is in a period of economic slowdown, that Eisenhower in the whole year of 1958, when he had Lebanon and other foreign policy successes had a Gallup rating which dropped into the 50s. You might say that this is really a time for soul-searching on the part of the press to see whether it is they who are out of tune with the people rather than the President. Also point out that the President has taken all this with good grace. He has never during his period of office called a publisher, commentator, editor, etc. for purposes of criticizing him and that the real meaning of it is that the President himself has finally reached the conclusion which should be one which should cause the media some concern. He realizes that he does not have to have their support. He realizes that they are going to write from a biased viewpoint and he just doesn't pay any attention to their views although he, of course, reads many columns, particularly Sidey's!

  This is a subtle point to get across but I think it is one that can have considerable effect on the press and news media if they finally realize that they are losing their most important listener, viewer, and reader—the President of the United States—not because he personally objects to what they say about him because he doesn't, but because they have consistently opposed everything he stands for regardless of what the merits were with an occasional exception like the postal strike where nobody could be on the other side, because he knows that their influence in the country is not what the people in Washington think it is. Finally, make the point that the President wouldn't be where he was if he had had to depend upon [words missing] in spite of what they did and said rather than because of him.

  (That's the end of the memorandum—a copy of it goes to Haldeman.)

TO: **Haldeman**

I might again suggest that this would make a very good column for one of our friends if Herb could bring himself to get it out. I think it could be extremely helpful in certain quarters if it were gotten out. Perhaps another way to get it out would be to have some very important person—maybe a major advertiser—write a letter to the news media, the *Times*, the *Post* and *Time* and *Newsweek*, simply laying it on the line like this and asking them some searching questions. I would write the letter in each instance to the publisher.

TO: **Haldeman**

Another item I would like for you to follow through on—on this one I have not developed a considered opinion but I would like for you to give great weight to my views within the staff—is with regard to Agnew. I believe that the next Agnew attack—one that would come with great responsibility and could have enormous effect—would be one on the three turncoats, Clifford, Harriman and Vance, or call them the three Monday-morning quarterbacks or what have you. Talk to Henry about this with regard to the facts but here they are in summary.

These three men were all architects of the policy that got us into Vietnam and that escalated the fighting so that our casualties in 1968 were the highest in five years (put in the number here) so that we had 525,000 Americans there at that time. All that they have ever been able to accomplish during this entire period so far as the move toward peace was the stopping of the bombing on November 1 in which they gave away America's hole card in the negotiations and got nothing whatever in return for it. During this entire period when they were in charge of our policy RN while he was critical of the conduct of the war strongly supported our effort in Vietnam, both at home and abroad, and always supported the decisions of the Commander-in-Chief to defend our fighting [words missing] any of the actions by Johnson with regard to negotiations because he said (you can get a quote here) we have only one Commander-in-Chief, only one man can bring peace. I will do nothing which might destroy that chance although it may be a slim chance. Get the exact quote. There is a very simple line. I have asked for this before and nobody has dug it up but I am sure Buchanan can find it. Now come these three, at a time when we have withdrawn 115,000 men, when casualties have been reduced in the first quarter to the lowest in five years, when we actually have a plan for peace and have laid a concrete proposal for negotiation on the conference table in Paris—now come these three and not only publicly oppose the President but privately cut him up at every possible opportunity. Contrast their conduct with that of President Johnson and Dean Rusk.

This I think would make an excellent speech by Agnew. It should be built up in advance and it would bring a howl of outrage from the other side, but it needs to be said and it will have repercussions in a few other quarters as well. While he is talking along this line Agnew might drop in, and this would be the time to do it, the fact that the likes of Fulbright who voted for the Tonkin Gulf Resolution and many Democratic Senators were completely silent when Johnson was escalating American participation in the war and now are jumping to criticism. You should pick them name by name in this instance. [Words missing] to work on it.

HRH138, 164

W/RN from HRH229

RN TAPE 3

MAY 13, 1970

TO: **Haldeman**

I would like for you, in this instance work through Kissinger's shop but don't get Henry involved in it himself, to get me the information with regard to the distribution of DOD research funds to major colleges and universities. Two hundred million dollars, I think is the total package. I would like a list of all colleges and universities that receive such funds with the amounts indicated. I would like this by noon today. My approach here, which I would like for you to discuss on a very closely held basis with anybody you consider knowledgeable on the subject is that DOD funds would continue to be provided to universities even though they play games with ROTC ———. On the other hand, I believe that no DOD funds for research should be provided to any university unless the faculty by a majority vote approves receipt and use of the funds for those purposes. Do not put it to the students—they are not around—you couldn't get a vote. But from now on no funds should go to any university if a majority of the faculty opposes the receipt of such funds. Put the faculties, not the university presidents, on the spot. Give me a report on this.

HRH164

W/RN from HRH138,
HRH229, and PPF2

MAY 14, 1970

TO: **Bob Haldeman**

FROM: **The President**

I found to my amazement that Halperin was still a consultant to the NSC staff even though Kissinger said he had fired him. Now Halperin is going to make a big thing out of resigning as a consultant during this period. I want Flanigan or Flemming or whoever you can put on this job to find out who consultants are around the government and let's do a little house-cleaning and sanitizing in this respect.

HRH229

MAY 14, 1970

TO: **Dr. Kissinger**

FROM: **H. R. Haldeman**

The President would like you to follow up with regard to Turner Shelton in making sure that we get Shelton's list of who our friends and opponents are in the Foreign Service.

He also would like you to consider the possibility of getting Shelton back in the department in some position. We know that he is loyal and would undoubtedly give us information on what is going on there.

Obviously this needs to be handled discreetly, but he would like your report as to what your plan is.

HRH140

MAY 14, 1970

Attached* is a memorandum regarding the authority of the President to permit incursion into Communist sanctuaries in the Cambodia-Vietnam border area.

William H. Rehnquist
Assistant Attorney General
Office of Legal Counsel

*[Letter to Charles W. Colson, special counsel to the President]

MAY 14, 1970

RE: **Authority of the President**
to Permit Incursion into Communist Sanctuaries
in the Cambodia-Vietnam Border Area

Although the authority to declare war is vested in the Congress, the President as Commander-in-Chief and sole organ of foreign affairs has constitutional authority to engage U.S. forces in limited conflict. International law has long recognized a distinction between formal declared wars and undeclared armed conflicts. While the precise division of constitutional authority between President and Congress in conflicts short of all-out war has never been formally delimited, there is no doubt that the President with the affirmance of Congress may engage in such conflicts.

Congress has clearly affirmed the President's authority to take all necessary measures to protect U.S. troops in Southeast Asia. Having determined that the incursion into the Cambodian border area is such a necessary measure, the President has clear authority to order it.

cwc102

SECRET

MAY 18, 1970

TO: **General Hughes**

FROM: **Charles W. Colson**

James Gavin is Chairman of the Board of Arthur D. Little. He has been an outspoken critic of the President and our Southeast Asia policies. His company does substantial business with the Government.

There is no reason that he should not be free as any other citizen is to speak his mind. There is also no reason why we should continue to favor him at the same time. I have discussed this with Bob Haldeman and I think it is something that requires a very confidential discussion between us. Would you please call me at your convenience.

cwc14

MAY 20, 1970

TO: **Harry Dent**

FROM: **Charles W. Colson**

Let's see if our Republican organization in South Dakota can get a constitutional amendment on the ballot this fall to provide for a recall. In fact, it should provide for petition and recall which means that as soon as it became law a petition campaign could be started to recall McGovern.

I don't know how difficult it is to get things on the ballot in South Dakota but in most states it is fairly easy even at this point in time.

cwc99

MAY 25, 1970

TO: **Bob Haldeman**

FROM: **The President**

In talking to Billy Graham and also to Bill Middendorf independently both commented on the fact that CBS in its coverage of the construction workers march gave approximately a minute of time to the 150,000 who demonstrated in New York and two or three minutes to the 1,000 left-wing lawyers who came to Washington. The purpose of this memo is simply to be sure that you jog our watch-dog group to see whether they needle CBS a bit for unbalanced coverage. When I talked to the construction workers by phone they also were complaining about the fact that TV didn't give them nearly the coverage that it did to the left-wing opponents.

HANDWRITTEN HALDEMAN NOTE: "Memo to Magruder."

PPF2; HRH140, 229
W/RN from HRH138

MAY 25, 1970

TO: **Bob Haldeman**

FROM: **The President**

As I am sure you have noted, Martha Mitchell gave an exclusive interview to Myra McLaughlin [McPherson] of the *Washington Post* and got chopped up again. Would you have a talk with Dick Moore and see if he can exert any influence on her press advisor to keep her from sticking her neck out. Perhaps a way you can accomplish it is simply to tell her that this is part of the game plan of not talking to the *Post* or the *New York Times.* If we can keep her from those two sources perhaps we will have mitigated the damage she can do to an extent.

PPF2; HRH138, 229

[JUNE 3 OR 4, 1970]

TO: **Bud Evans**

FROM: **Chuck Colson**

Please look up the following facts as soon as possible so they can be included in my speech which is now being prepared. I would think that most of the information could be obtained from the Bureau of the Budget Library:

1. Was it President Madison who sent American troops into Tripoli?
2. Was it in 1801?
3. What country is Tripoli in?
4. Was this done because of piracy in the Mediterranean?
5. What was the purchase price of Alaska?
6. Re: the draft law of 1940—what was the exact name of the statute?

7. When was it passed—exact date?

8. What was the vote in the House on the draft law?

cwc126

JUNE 8, 1970

TO: **H. R. Haldeman**

FROM: **Tom Charles Huston**

One of the problems which the President mentioned on Friday was the manner in which information from various intelligence agencies dribbled in piece by piece. I think we will begin to solve some of this problem by virtue of the study we have underway. However, I think part of the problem could be solved within the White House if we implemented the understanding which we reached in our meeting some weeks ago.

If you have not done so, it might be helpful if you were to advise Dr. Kissinger that in the future intelligence information from CIA, NSA, DIA, and the military services relating to the foreign activities of American revolutionary leaders (i.e., anything which relates essentially to the domestic intelligence problem) should come to me for coordination with similar information from the FBI and other strictly domestic collection sources.

The activities of Stokely Carmichael in the Caribbean, for example, are only one part of a broader intelligence picture which requires more input than is available from CIA. Under current practice, the CIA input goes to Henry, while the FBI contribution comes to me—and never do the twain meet.

Could you discuss this with Dr. Kissinger?

HRH70

JUNE 11, 1970

TO: **H. R. Haldeman**

FROM: **John R. Brown III**

One of the observations set forth in the memorandum from the staff members who visited the college campuses was that "many students feel that the President's early morning visit to the Lincoln Memorial on May 9 confirmed what the students feel is the President's disdain for student opinion because, according to press reports of interviews with demonstrators, he concentrated on topics they considered irrelevant." It was noted that this is our PR failure.

ss84

JUNE 19, 1970

TO: **H. R. Haldeman**

FROM: **Larry Higby**

Herb Kalmbach has forwarded a list of people who are our financial angels. He has placed checks in pencil by the ones that may be considered new. The desire you had for ten new financial angels does not seem to have been fulfilled. Herb feels this is a project he can't take on right now while he's trying to nail these other areas down.

    Do you wish me to give this to Herb as a long range project or handle it now in some other manner?

W. Clement Stone
John King
John Rollins
Sam Wyly and Charles Wyly
H. R. Perot

Walter Annenberg
Richard Scaife
David Parr
William Liedtke
Henry Ford*

Vincent de Roulet
Mrs. Blanche Seaver
Henry Salvatori
Fred Russell
Shelby Davis

Arthur K. Watson
Kenneth Franzheim
J. Howard Pew
Max Fisher
Kent H. Smith

Robert H. Abplanalp
Walter Davis
Howard Newman
Kingdon Gould
James Crosby

Thomas J. Morrison
John P. Humes
Guilford Dudley
J. William Middendorf
Robert Hill

Mrs. Helen Clay Frick
Willard W. Keith

Richard Pistell
Robert O. Anderson
Willard F. Rockwell, Jr.

Dudley Swim
Edgar W. Brown, Jr.
Thomas Pappas
Loren Berry
Clement Hirsch*

Wayne Hoffman
Albert H. Gordon
Roscoe Pickett
Arthur Lipper
David K. Wilson

Ned Gerritty
William Casey
DeWitt Wallace
Robert McCulloch
Charles Luckman

Frank K. Greenwall
Benson Ford
Claude Wilde
Jack Mills
John M. Shaheen

Foster McGaw
Bernard Johnson
F. K. Weyerhaeuser
A. C. Nielsen
John and Spencer Olin

Charles Payson
John Hay Whitney
Elmer Bobst
William Lasdon

*[check marks]

HRH3

142   FROM: THE PRESIDENT

JUNE 25, 1970

TO: **H. R. Haldeman**

FROM: **Tom Charles Huston**

RE: **Coordination of Domestic Intelligence Information**

Attached is a cover letter from Dick Helms for a CIA report on revolutionary youth activities world-wide. You will note that it is addressed to Dr.
Kissinger, with copies to Bob Finch and me.

This points up the type of problem which I believe ought to be
rectified. There are now three copies of this report in the building. I
suspect that no one knows exactly what to do with it since they don't know
what the others will do. Any one of us may decide that the President
should see a summary of this report, or all of us may decide to file it on
the assumption someone else is going to make use of it.

I suggest that all incoming intelligence relating to revolutionary
youth affairs come to me. I can then route copies to others having need
for them and indicate who should take action on the material. In this way,
we won't have to worry about too much or too little being done.

This is the practice with all information coming from the FBI, and
I believe it should be the same with CIA, DIA, NSA, and the military
services.

HRH70

JULY 6, 1970

TO: **The President**

FROM: **Clark Mollenhoff**

I'm attaching copies of letters purported to be signed by a number of State
Department and AID employees protesting the Administration's position
on Cambodia.

Contrary to some published reports, there were no efforts to compile a dossier on these individuals. My action to obtain copies of letters
signed by these individuals came following a number of requests from
various individuals in the Administration who urged that they be obtained
simply for purposes of safeguarding as well as for possible use by the White
House.

My action was limited to acquiring the list and obtaining a brief
identification of those whose signatures were affixed to the letters.

I had been informed by usually reliable sources that the State Department was engaged in making some arrangement to destroy the letters
as a part of some deal made through the personnel office. This destruction
of letters seemed inconsistent with proper functioning of government. It

is my understanding that some of the letters were destroyed and that those I obtained represent only a part of the whole picture. I have no way of knowing whether this is or is not a fact.

I had assumed it was possible that the Secretary of State had made the whole list available to you directly, but had no way of checking to determine the accuracy of that assumption.

The information attached is self-explanatory. As you can see, it was only an effort to make certain that this information would not be destroyed and that there would be an identification of those who had expressed their views on Cambodia.

I have made no requests for the FBI or any other intelligence agency to provide secret intelligence information on those involved.

The information is submitted for your use in any manner in which you see fit.

HRH59

JULY 10, 1970

TO: **The President**

FROM: **Charles W. Colson**

RE: **AEI Financing**

Following your meeting with John Swearingen, there have been a number of significant developments.

The Scaife-Mellon Foundation has agreed to increase its level of support of AEI to $1 million per year—three times the amount that it has ever given. This is on a one-year trial basis, but if we are satisfied with their work, Scaife-Mellon will continue.

The Pew Family Foundation has now agreed to release a $1 million commitment—$250,000 a year over a four-year period.

Swearingen is spending his time presently meeting with individuals and foundations with substantial resources. He will do a broad based canvass of industry starting in September.

HANDWRITTEN HALDEMAN NOTE: "[Richard Mellon] Scaife will be at the *Sequoia* dinner & should be thanked for AEI support."

HRH61, 139

JULY 10, 1970

TO: **H. R. Haldeman**

FROM: **Tom Charles Huston**

RE: **Bombing and Arson Attacks in the United States**

I am disturbed at the fuss that is being made over the visits by IRS agents to two public libraries to inquire about those requesting books dealing with explosives.

It appears the standard pattern is developing: the *Washington Post* drums up a story, Sam Ervin gets outraged, and the Administration acts like a kid caught with his hand in the cookie jar. Ziegler's response to press inquiries implied: (1) some local, zealous agents were operating on their own; (2) we didn't know anything about it; and (3) it is being stopped, implying we shouldn't have been doing it to start with.

My concern about this incident is limited to one fact: it is another example of inadequate coordination within the intelligence community. As a matter of operating procedure, I think it is perfectly legitimate (if effective) and certainly justified by the facts of life in a country which has witnessed 776 bombing and arson attacks in the past 18 months.

I think we make a mistake to tremble every time the same muckraking journal "exposes" another example of incipient "repression." After the fact, for whatever value it may be, I am attaching a brief fact sheet which suggests that the Government is not only justified in taking reasonable measures to counteract the terroristic use of explosives, but would be derelict in its duty if it failed to do so.

Having heard the President's expression of concern about the internal security threat, I am more than a little puzzled by some of the subsequent actions of the Administration which suggest that the prevailing attitude is directly contrary to that which the President expressed so clearly.

HRH70

JULY 11, 1970

TO: **Mr. Ehrlichman**

FROM: **H. R. Haldeman**

The President wants to be sure now that you follow up on your plan for defense funds to the universities and that it be done immediately with no delay.

Starting right away, he'd like a daily report on the progress on this from you.

ss83

JULY 13, 1970

TO: **The President (Per HRH)**

FROM: **Patrick J. Buchanan**

John Gardner is being pushed by a number of fat-cat types, reportedly led by Andre Meyer, of Lazare Freres on the East Coast, and Norton Simon on the West, to run for President in 1972. That is reportedly the purpose behind his committee of concerned citizens about the problems of the cities or whatever it is. The group, essentially financial types, has raised some $200,000 for Gardner, to build his national image by having him speak out against the current Administration and on the nation's problems—then proper distribution of these speeches, etc. What is interesting is that the people backing the effort are among the Lindsayites in New York and would be expected to be pushing Lindsay in this type of operation. Apparently, the Fund for the Republic, that tax-exempt little off-shoot of the Ford Foundation, is involved. Gardner is reportedly in a "tell me more" state—as these moneyed types keep telling him he is the man to save America.

I have encouraged the people who gave me this information to give it to Bob Novak to see Gardner's reaction if and when he is smoked out—and to also put the taint of "politics" on his future criticisms of the President.

HRH139

EYES ONLY

JULY 14, 1970

TO: **Mr. Huston**

FROM: **L. Higby**

Bob asked that I pass the following along to you:

It is reported that a growing number of New Left Congressional Staffers are associating themselves more and more closely with the activist, peace-loving groups on the Hill. These staffers are becoming a more effective group through the intellectual guidance of the new weekly seminars conducted by Brookings and by the Institute for Foreign Policy Studies. The seminar structure includes the rank-and-file "Government in Exile" and serves members of the Departments of State and Defense. Other instructors like Noam Chomsky and Richard Barnet are occasional visitors to Hanoi.

With regard to the above you should go after Brookings and the Institute for Policy Studies. You should have the Internal Revenue make some discreet inquiries *if* it is political.

What do we have to work on the House and Senate staffers for our line through staff?

JULY 16, 1970

TO: **Mr. Ehrlichman**

FROM: **H. R. Haldeman**

The President asked again today about the follow up on the plan for cutting campus funds for research projects.

He wants a regular, continual report on what is being done on this, and apparently doesn't feel he's gotten it.

ss83

JULY 16, 1970

TO: **H. R. Haldeman**

FROM: **Tom Charles Huston**

I have the following observations on the problems posed by Brookings, Institute for Foreign Policy Studies, etc.

1. Making sensitive political inquiries at the IRS is about as safe a procedure as trusting a whore. With the bark on, the truth is we don't have any reliable political friends at IRS whom we can trust and, as I suggested nearly a year ago, we won't be in control of the Government and in a position of effective leverage until such time as we have complete and total control of the top three slots at IRS. Since we don't appear to have any disposition to move against Thrower, et al., I think the risks of leakage from making inquiries about major tax exempt foundations is greater than any benefits which might accrue. Over a year ago, I requested, at the direction of the President, that IRS conduct an examination of several radical tax exempt organizations which were clearly operating in violation of existing IRS regulations. To date, nothing has come of this request, although Dr. Burns and I twice met personally with Thrower. This is too typical of the type of non-cooperation we get in those quarters.

2. To the positive side, I think it would be both very valuable and quite feasible to set up an operation which would enable us to get our point of view across to the Congressional staff members whose principles are generally sympathetic to the Administration. In this respect, I would think we could, perhaps, make use of the Georgetown Foreign Policy Institute. My idea would be to get some qualified fellow (Dick Whalen comes to mind) to establish and administer a program in which we make

1970: MAY–AUGUST   **147**

available our staff people to participate in seminars for Congressional staff. Although the format would have to be in seminar form with a full exchange of views, these sessions could be programmed to enable us to get our policy line across and to furnish our friends with the facts they need to help us on the Hill. John Lehman would be an excellent guy to handle it on this end.

The best and most effective Congressional relations are those conducted on a staff to staff basis. Members of Congress rely heavily on their staff, and if their staffs are well informed, the Members will be well informed.

In essence, what I am suggesting is to play the Brookings game ourselves. One able guy on the outside with a little money and some real help from here could handle this task with ease.

3. Pat Buchanan has been researching the activities of Ford, Brookings, and other tax-exempt organizations for some time in anticipation of preparing a series of broadsides for the Veep to launch. These attacks would be on higher and less vulnerable ground than an attack based merely on their anti-Administration foreign policy briefings, and would thus be more effective. In short, the material is available to blast the hell out of these outfits and to scare the living hell out of them, assuming Thrower is willing to cooperate even passively. I suggest that Pat be asked to crank these speeches out and that the Veep unload at the earliest possible time.

4. There is also the low road which should not be passed by. We can gather a great deal of material about the pro-Hanoi and anti-American activities of some of these outfits which would arouse the wrath of the Unenlightened folks west of the Appalachians. I think John Lehman and I could pull this material together and put together a hefty package which could be turned over to some people on the Hill and some friendly columnists to soften up the enemy in anticipation of the Veep's more gentlemanly attacks. I would have only one caveat, however. It doesn't do a damn bit of good for some Senator to read this type of material into the Record. He should go out into the heartland and deliver a speech which the local wire service representative will pick up. I don't know why these experienced politicians don't realize that they can get better press nationwide from a speech out where Senators are news than they can here in Washington where a Senatorial speech is just another non-event.

5. If we reach the point that we really want to start playing the game tough, you might wish to consider my suggestion of some months ago that we consider going into Brookings after the classified material which they have stashed over there. There are a number of ways we could handle this. There are risks in all of them, of course; but there are also risks in allowing this government-in-exile to grow increasingly arrogant and powerful as each day goes by.

HRH70

JULY 17, 1970

TO: **Mr. Chapin**

FROM: **H. R. Haldeman**

The noon meeting in the President's office today pointed up once again
the need for some kind of planning regarding the use of the South Lawn
for Rock Band rehearsals. It was awfully hard to hear anything in the Oval
Office.

Perhaps we can figure out some way of coordinating the timing on
this kind of thing so that these rehearsals could be held when the President
is in the EOB.

DLC18; HRH61

JULY 23, 1970

TO: **Mr. Colson**

FROM: **L. Higby**

In checking back on things, it is my understanding that you turned off
Gleason from getting the necessary funds to get Paul Simpson's television
project at Vanderbilt off the ground.

This is a project that we do want going, and I have indicated to
Magruder and Buchanan that it is to be turned on and moved forward. I
am not sure just what the conflicting problems are here, but apparently
everybody is giving Gleason instructions without any coordination.

In an attempt to resolve this matter, if you feel that we should not
be doing this project I would appreciate your getting in touch with me.
Buchanan has been working on it for about 6 months now and, as you can
see by the attachment, Haldeman and the President are interested in
seeing that it goes forward.

Please advise.

CWC118; HRH61

JULY 27, 1970

TO: **The President**

FROM: **Brigadier General James D. Hughes**

RE: **King Timahoe**

Mr. Eldridge would like to keep King Timahoe until Friday. He has reported that the skin problem is caused by improper diet and is not serious.
He is going to put him on a special diet and the condition should be
substantially improved by Friday.

Mr. Eldridge's veterinarian said that the dog's ears are in bad condition. They have taken a culture and will have the results by Friday. He said King Timahoe is receiving proper treatment for his ears at Walter Reed, but not often enough, and that these treatments can be given at the Residence. Mr. Bryant will pick up the dog on Friday at which time he will be instructed by Mr. Eldridge as to medication for his ears, proper diet and better grooming.

Mr. Eldridge has given the dog all of his required shots.

HRH139

AUGUST 4, 1970

TO: **Bob Haldeman**

FROM: **Bill Safire**

According to *Newsweek*, Larry O'Brien (along with Cliff White) will be on the board of directors of an "international consulting firm." Lobbying for foreign governments without the appearance of lobbying, I guess.

Can't we raise a big fuss about this? Insist that he register as a foreign agent, demand to know what fees he will be getting for what work and "to what extent the Democratic National Committee is available for sale to foreign governments"?

We could have a little fun with this and keep O'Brien on the defensive.

HRH70;
21 SENATE HEARINGS 9738,
23 SENATE HEARINGS 11114

AUGUST 6, 1970

TO: **Larry Higby**

FROM: **Charles W. Colson**

In response to your memorandum of July 23rd, I have no problem whatsoever in Gleason raising funds to finance Paul Simpson's television project at Vanderbilt. I did tell Jack some months back that I did not think it would be *necessary* for him to do so.

I'm sure Bob will remember that we discussed some time ago trying to get the same results through the FCC. We both felt it would be preferable for us to do so, rather than again hitting our backers for money when we need them so badly in other areas.

Dean Burch assured me that he would have the FCC require the networks to put tapes of their news and public service broadcasts in a Federal Depository of some sort. He thought he could handle this administratively and would not have to ask for legislation. In fact, he proposed doing it at the time that he commented on the Baker Bill.

I realize that there has been a slippage of some months. I keep talking to Burch and he keeps assuring me that he's going to do it but to date there has been little action. Burch has spoken on the subject, but as yet has not gotten the FCC to require it.

I frankly think that out of the Pastore hearings and in the light of all of the cases pending at the FCC, someone is going to require at the Federal level that the networks keep in a central depository these tapes. As I understand it, that's all that Simpson is doing.

My feeling remains that while this is a very worthwhile project, it's one that we ought not to have to get funding for from our small band of loyal contributors. We are hitting so hard for campaign funds, Hatfield-McGovern money, ABM money, AEI money, etc., that this is one burden that I'd like to pass off onto a public agency if possible.

I never told anyone *not* to fund Simpson. I merely said I thought we could get it done other ways. My feeling in this respect is that it is just a matter of priorities and the use of limited resources. Anytime anyone wants to move ahead on funding for Simpson, it is fine as far as I'm concerned. I do think, however, it can be done in other ways very soon.

cwc118

EYES ONLY

AUGUST 10, 1970

TO: **Mr. Dean**

FROM: **L. Higby**

RE: **Reiners [sic] vs. IRS Court Case**

This is a trial that is taking place in Los Angeles and apparently the lawyer for IRS is anti-Administration and could be interested more in damaging us than in seeking an equitable solution.

Apparently Reiner had received $140,000 settlement from Howard Hughes involving a loan problem that Hughes had.

The question is whether or not the settlement was taxable. This, of course, depends on whether or not it was considered a settlement or a payoff. As you probably remember there was a Hughes/Don Nixon loan controversy several years ago, and the prosecution of this case could re-open that entire issue which could be very damaging politically.

The real question here is whether or not the government lawyer is really the lawyer we would want involved in this case. Sorry I cannot provide you with any more information, but hopefully this will give you enough to at least begin checking it out.

HRH70

AUGUST 11, 1970

TO: **Mr. Dean**

FROM: **H. R. Haldeman**

I reviewed your memorandum of August 3 regarding Presidential salary and pension with the President. He agrees that alternative No. 1 is preferable.

He would like, however, to tie the retirement allowance of former Presidents to the current salary of the President. In other words, to be sure that Truman and Johnson are covered now, the retirement allowance should be raised from $25,000 to $100,000, but it should be specified that after the President's salary reduction from $200,000 to $100,000 is accomplished, the retirement allowance for former Presidents should be based on the current salary for the Presidents. So, as Presidential salaries are increased in the future, the retirement allowance for former Presidents will go up at the same rate.

As to the question of making soundings on the Hill, this would seem to make sense and I think you should check with John Ehrlichman and Bill Timmons as to whether it is a good idea and, if so, who should carry it out.

HRH70

AUGUST 14, 1970

TO: **Larry Higby**

FROM: **Charles W. Colson**

Reference our exchange of memoranda on the Simpson project. You will be pleased to know that our friends in the Scaife/Mellon Foundation have stepped up to bat once more for us and will fund Mr. Simpson. If the FCC later steps up to this, the private funding can be turned off if that is the wise thing to do at that point.

HRH61; CWC118

AUGUST 17, 1970

TO: **H. R. Haldeman**

FROM: **John R. Brown III**

The August 17 News Summary reported that Roger Mudd said Sunday that RN used to say "Let me make this clear" until his advisers suggested that he quit it. The President noted that this is a silly thing for our "advisers" to talk to the press about.

Thank you.

SS84; HRH61

AUGUST 17, 1970

Dear Professor Bork:*

The President has asked me to reply to your good telegram of July 31st. I am sure that you read the press reports with respect to the President's comment on the Heard report. In the event that you have not seen a copy, I am enclosing that portion of the transcript in which he replied to a question involving the report.

We are glad that there are some who recognize that the responsibility for maintaining order on the college campuses cannot and should not be placed on the shoulders of the President. We must do our part, of course, but basically it is the administrators on each campus who must be responsible for preserving order and the rule of reason.

Thanks again for wiring.

With the President's best wishes,

Sincerely,

Charles W. Colson
Special Counsel
to the President

*[Letter to Robert H. Bork, professor, Yale University]

cwc127

AUGUST 18, 1970

TO: **Larry Higby**

FROM: **Charles W. Colson**

You might for the fun of it like to show the attached to Bob. I am sure he would enjoy a lighter moment in his day.

As you will see from the attached, we go to great extremes in this office to get support for the President. Providing Mr. Garcia's lawn mower does not break down on the New Jersey Turnpike, he will be at the White House gate to present us with a million signatures in support of the President. My suggestion is that we receive him when he arrives on Sunday, September 6, and then invite him to cut the South Lawn of the White House. We could always have him stay over the seventh and give the President a ride on his lawn mower.

We have prevailed upon him to ride down the median strip of the New Jersey Turnpike which will be both safer from his standpoint and will serve the second purpose of cutting the lawn along the way.

P.S. By the way, Mr. Garcia tells George Bell that he has chosen Sunday of Labor Day Weekend because there will be less traffic on the road and he is less likely to be run over. Would you like me to send him out to your house afterwards; perhaps he could trim your lawn as well. You might also be interested to know that, when he leaves the White House, Mr. Garcia is departing for Vietnam. I believe, however, that he is not going by lawn mower but rather flying.

bcc: Lyn Nofziger

AUGUST 12, 1970

The Honorable Richard M. Nixon
President of the United States
The White House
1600 Pennsylvania Avenue
Washington, D.C.

Dear Mr. Bell [sic],*
    At this time, it gives me great pleasure to inform you that as of last weekend I have passed the 500,000 point. I am sure that I will surpass the 1,000,000 figure by our deadline September 6, 1970.
    My plans are as follows: After a 9 A.M. Mass at St. Patrick's Cathedral I will board my rideable lawnmower, proceed down Fifth Avenue and through the Holland Tunnel for my first stop in Jersey City at 11 A.M. My next stop is Newark at 12 P.M., New Brunswick at 2 P.M., Trenton at 5 P.M., Camden at 8 P.M. and my last stop for the day Philadelphia at 9 P.M. The following day I will arrive in Wilmington at 8 A.M., Baltimore at 12 P.M. and on to the White House at 3 P.M. I expect about 10 vehicles in my entourage and 100 invited guests to be present during my presentation.
    At your earliest convenience, Mr. Bell, I would like very much to discuss with you, in detail, this event and our participation during the ceremony.

Very truly yours,
[s/Benjamin M. Garcia]

*[Letter from Benjamin M. Garcia, of the Ben Garcia "One Million" Crusade, East Brunswick, N.J. The motto on the letterhead reads, "Supporting Our Men in Vietnam."]

AUGUST 19, 1970

TO: **Chuck Colson**

FROM: **Lyn Nofziger**

    1. I see that Mr. Garcia will be "clipping" along at a good pace with a number of friends. Oh well, the mow the merrier, as we say in East Brunswick.
    2. It will be a sod thing if this doesn't pan out.

TO: **Lyn**

FROM: **Chuck**

Thanks—We'll be coming a lawn way (you forgot that one).

cwc122

AUGUST 27, 1970

TO: **Mr. Brown**

FROM: **L. Higby**

Bob feels that the idea of having the RNC fund our advertising operations is basically bad. By getting this money from the RNC we identify it almost directly with the White House. The ideal solution is to set up a group of independent outside sources and coordinate their donations. If there are other reasons that are not properly presented in either your memo or Magruder's please forward them for reconsideration. Talk to Colson about this.

cwc97

1970

SEPTEMBER 1, 1970

TO: **General Hughes**

FROM: **H. R. Haldeman**

The President mentioned today that the portions of meat (specifically the huge steaks) served regularly on the *Sequoia,* at Camp David, etc. are too large and he would like the size cut down substantially.

    This came to his mind because of the size of the meat portions at the luncheon given by us at Porta [sic] Vallarta. As you will recall they were quite large and most people eat only a very small fraction of the piece of meat served them. I've already asked Connie Stuart to make sure that the portions at the San Diego dinner are cut down substantially, but I would appreciate your following up with the White House Mess people to be sure that they are also reduced at Camp David and on the boat and I presume also at Key Biscayne when the mess stewards do this service.

ss85

EYES ONLY

SEPTEMBER 8, 1970

TO: **Mr. Ehrlichman**
    Mr. Finch
    Mr. Haldeman

FROM: **John R. Brown III**

The September 5 News Summary reported that despite the passionate political minorities on the right and the left, the majority of people in the West between the Alleghenies and the Rockies believe most of the following: the Vietnam war is a mess we never should have gotten into—"but after all, it is coming to an end." The rebellious kids are both wrong and a menace. More cops and tougher penalties are needed to stop crime—not slum clearance. The Supreme Court has assumed too much "legislative" power. "Taxes are too damn high." The poor are poor, mainly though not entirely because they don't work and have too many kids. Education is a trouble because "they" teach everything but what counts, i.e., reading and writing. The Communists are still a menace and at the very least cutting the defense budget is dangerous. Negroes have rights but forced integration will leave everybody worse off. One of our main national problems is permissive parents. Private enterprise can do anything better than government, so government should be reduced to a minimum. Growth is not only inevitable but good—thus big business is good and bigger business is better. But big government is terrible and bigger government is dangerous.

The President asked that you take note of this. He feels that we'd better shape up and quit trimming the *wrong* way. It is very late—but we still have time to move away from the line of our well-intentioned liberals on our own staff. It is dynamite politically and wrong usually on the merits.

The President went on to say that he can't emphasize too strongly his concern that our Administration team—including White House staff—has been affected too much by the unreal atmosphere of the D.C. press, social and intellectual set. Perhaps Cambodia and Kent State led to an overreaction by our own people to prove that we were pro students, blacks, left. We must get turned around on this before it is too late—emphasize anti-crime, anti-demonstrations, anti-drugs, anti-obscenity. We must get with the mood of the country which is fed up with the liberals.

ss83, 84

SEPTEMBER 8, 1970

TO: **Mr. Colson**

FROM: **H. R. Haldeman**

The President wants you to take on the responsibility for working on developing our strength with the labor unions and union leadership.

He feels this must be done by picking them off one by one. The general approach that Hodgson and Shultz take is to work with Labor leadership on an overall basis, whereas politically we have to pick them off as individuals.

He strongly urges that you work closely with Curtis Counts in this regard, since he is more attuned politically to what our needs are than most of the other Labor Department people. For example, Counts brought Fitzsimmons of the Teamsters Union up to talk with the President and the President found that he is extremely friendly and that we should move ahead to cultivate him politically in any way that we can.

You should, of course, also check with Hodgson and, perhaps more importantly, with Bill Usery who can be very valuable in helping you to identify those Labor leaders who tend to lean our way and are worthy of nurturing.

The President has specifically in mind the Teamsters, the Firefighters, the Marine Union, the Carpenters, etc. There is a great deal of gold there to be mined.

As another step, the President would like you to check with all of our people from the White House and the Labor Department who were at the dinner and ask each of them to give you an evaluation of the Labor leaders who were seated at their table, and with whom they had a chance to converse during the evening. What you want is an evaluation of which of these are worth cultivating.

Usery again can be a great deal of help to you in this regard— identifying those whom we can win.

Another good point of contact is Suffridge of the Retail Clerks who is a long-time, good friend of the President and would probably be very happy to help.

As a bit of further guidance, I notice the President has checked on his guest list for the dinner the names of Peter Brennan, J. M. Calhoun, Joseph Curran, Frank Fitzsimmons, James Housewright, M. A. Hutcheson, Joseph D. Keenan, Jay Lovestone, John H. Lyons, Thomas Murphy, James Suffridge. I am not sure what the significance of those names might be but they might be a good starting point for you.

Another point, the President would like each of the table hosts (and you will have to check on who that would be, preferably a White House or a Cabinet Member) to write a personal letter to all of the Labor men seated at his table at the dinner with an enclosure of the Message to Congress we are sending up at the end of the week, saying that since it wraps up in pretty comprehensive form the Administration's entire program now before the Congress, we thought it would be nice for them to have it. This should be a personal letter.

For your information the President is also sending a personal letter to everyone who was at the dinner outlining his position on unemployment, since that seems to be a question bothering these people and grossly misunderstood by them.

The President would like to have Bill Usery brief him at some point on how to deal with Labor leaders, and he very much wants to be sure that he briefs the Vice President. This should probably be set up before the Vice President leaves on his campaign tour if you can work it out with Harlow.

Also, the President would like to bring Suffridge in with a small group of Labor leaders who are friendly to discuss with them what the best way might be to continue the dialogue that has now been set up with Labor leadership.

As you can see from all of the above, he is most anxious to move hard, fast and extensively in this whole area, and he is counting on you to see that this is done.

CWC77

(Copy of a handwritten letter)

TUESDAY, SEPTEMBER 14, 1970

Dear Mr. President:

I was very touched to receive your warm and sympathetic letter about my Mother's death. Many thanks both for your thoughts and for your generosity of spirit in writing.

I hope some day—at your convenience—you will consider doing an editorial lunch with *Post* and *Newsweek* editors. I am not unmindful of how you might feel about this idea. It would of course be a great honor. I also believe strongly that free and frank exchange is helpful.

Again my profound thanks.

Sincerely,

[s/Kay Graham]

PPF188:
MATERIAL REMOVED
FROM PRESIDENT'S DESK

SEPTEMBER 16, 1970

TO: **John Brown**

FROM: **L. Higby**

Ron Ziegler informs me that while the President took the tour of Pennsylvania Avenue last week with Moynihan he mentioned some items that he wanted taken care of. Among these were the signs that currently marked government buildings taken down and replaced with more attractive signs. He felt that the aluminum sterile signs that we now have up weren't very good. They should be made with more strength and have more dignity to them.

He also mentioned that he wanted the lower portion of the Capitol sandblasted, but Ziegler said this probably can't be done.

cc: H. R. Haldeman

SS86

SEPTEMBER 21, 1970

TO: Bob Haldeman

FROM: The President

I would like for you to talk with Kalmbach with regard to how Mulcahy was developed into a major contributor and tell him that I think we ought to check on three or four people of this type across the country who might be worth my time—new people who are not yet on our list—and see if we can't bring them along for 1972. We have Mulcahy and Clem Stone in this category and my guess is we could pick up three or four others if we just know how to go at them. Here you will not find the candidates on a list of chief executive officers. Most of them are unable to make significant contributions, but among people who have developed their own businesses and built large fortunes. In fact, what ought to happen here is that Flanigan or somebody in his shop should look over the list of the top 10 to 15 who have significant fortunes and see what, if anything, can be done to bring them along. Of course, Mulcahy is not in that category and there may be people like him who would welcome the opportunity to move heavily into political activities if they knew that Presidential attention would be one of the results.

PPF2; HRH138, 229

SEPTEMBER 21, 1970

TO: Bob Haldeman

FROM: The President

I have been greatly impressed, as you know, with the performance of Colson and Morgan on the assignments I have given them. I think we need to look for four or five more people of this caliber who might be moved into our top-flight of operators with direct access to me and with specific assignments. We probably have them right within our own group. It is just a case of determining which ones have the ability to take tough assignments and carry them out and then continue following through on it. Colson and Morgan certainly are a good start and once Morgan completes this school operation I think we should use him on another assignment of similar importance.

PPF2; HRH138, 229

SEPTEMBER 21, 1970

TO: **John Ehrlichman**

FROM: **John R. Brown III**

The September 21 News Summary reported that Martha Mitchell telephoned a UPI reporter at home, irate over the published report of her
husband's statement at a women's press club cocktail party on Wednesday.
Upon reviewing this, the following was noted: "Again."

cc: H. R. Haldeman
    A. Butterfield

ss83

PERSONAL AND CONFIDENTIAL

SEPTEMBER 21, 1970

Dear Pat:*
     This is just a reminder that as soon as Mulcahy is back in New York,
it is high priority for you, Pete Brennan, Mike Maye and myself to meet
with him. There is some political chicanery that we should get going on
as fast as possible.
     Best personal regards.

                                        Sincerely,

                                        Charles W. Colson
                                        Special Counsel
                                        to the President

*[Letter to William J. O'Hara, New York, New York]

cwc77

OCTOBER 2, 1970

TO: **Lyn Nofziger**

FROM: **Charles W. Colson**

You may recall that I talked to you about a friend of mine who wants to
dispose of several television stations. He was down a few weeks ago and
left with me a lot of information about these stations, which I am enclosing.
If you know anyone who is interested, who is a friend of ours, let's put

them together with Norman Knight. I have no interest in this other than it would always be nice to have these kinds of stations in the hands of friends.

Knight is apparently desperate for cash and a hard deal could presumably be made.

Let me know if you have any interest in pursuing this further and if so, I will have Knight come in and see you.

cwc127

OCTOBER 6, 1970

TO: **John Dean**

FROM: **Charles W. Colson**

I hope this is one that we can get under control before it is too late. Let's be absolutely certain that nothing happens in this area until we have had an opportunity to review it and no formal action should be taken unless we know of it in advance.

The Longshoremen are among our most vigorous hard hat supporters and this well could be a potential catastrophe. Let's get it under control ahead of time.

cwc73
w/RN from cwc127

OCTOBER 6, 1970

TO: **Henry Cashen**

FROM: **Charles W. Colson**

As a follow-up to the development of some pro-labor legislation, we should be thinking about federal legislation that would obviate the need for major strikes, some form of "voluntary" compulsory arbitration. This is something Meany is very interested in and would have broad general appeal as well as being strong in the labor area.

cwc127

OCTOBER 7, 1970

TO: **H. R. Haldeman**

FROM: **John R. Brown III**

The October 6 News Summary reported that Duffey, the Democratic candidate for Senate in Connecticut, holds a narrow lead over Lowell

Weicker. Duffey got 29% of the vote while Weicker got 25%.

It was requested that we go all out in support of Weicker. We should arrange for him to receive an additional $200,000 in campaign contributions.

Thank you.

ss84

OCTOBER 7, 1970

TO: **H. R. Haldeman**

FROM: **Charles W. Colson**

Nick Thimmesch is going to do a piece for us on the phoniness of the Harris polls. He will hit hard on the "only fair" question and the timing of the releases.

Interestingly enough as he has checked around with other pollsters, he has found that Roper, Gallup and John Kraft all believe that Harris is dishonest and slanted, a point he will be able to make in his story.

This should help Dan Lufkin in his efforts to christianize Harris.

cwc69

OCTOBER 7, 1970

TO: **Tom Huston**

FROM: **Charles W. Colson**

Can we get a quick name check through the FBI files on any of the people on the attached. They are all in and around Boston. All of them were in attendance at a secret fund raising party in Cambridge for Phil Hoff. It's perfectly obvious, as you can see from the list, who some of them are, and I would have grave suspicions about the others.

cwc127

OCTOBER 13, 1970

TO: **H. R. Haldeman**

FROM: **Charles W. Colson**

"Duster" Miller, who heads the Southern Region for the Teamsters, is actively backing George Bush with money and political support.

cc: Harry Dent
    George Bell—Be certain this guy is in our Labor book and rewarded appropriately.

cwc127

W/RN from CWC1

OCTOBER 13, 1970

TO: **Ken Cole**

FROM: **Charles W. Colson**

In response to your "Who's on First?" memo of October 9th, let me give you a short answer by enclosing a copy of the new, new, new, revised position of the Department of Justice. What it does for me is to thoroughly shake my confidence in the Justice Department to the same degree that yours has already been apparently shaken. I talked with Ruckelshaus on the telephone and his attitude was quite different than that reflected in the attached. He further told me that John Mitchell felt very strongly, which may mean that Mitchell and Kleindienst aren't talking to one another these days.

Despite all the confusion, they have raised a very interesting point. The legislation could be amended so as to confer jurisdiction on the Court of Claims in a way that would allow the Court of Claims to make judicious factual determinations that might or might not give rise to government liability. One advantage of this, of course, is that the Court of Claims takes about 8 years to handle a case, so that the Budget impact of any cyclamate indemnification would come in the next Administration, or maybe not until David Eisenhower's term. There is a precedent for this approach. A lot of private bills are handled this way. It puts us in a motherhood position. We can't really be criticized by anyone. And finally, it provides a lot of lucrative business for Washington Court of Claims Lawyers.

In all seriousness, I think there is the germ here of a very equitable, politically salvable solution.

cwc127

OCTOBER 20, 1970

TO: **The President**

FROM: **Murray M. Chotiner**

Your suggestion that our people use the line "It's time for the Silent Majority to stand up and be counted" works.

Last night I spoke in Hershey, Pennsylvania, at a meeting of the Governor's Club, consisting of 100 businessmen. After pointing out the type of opposition we are combating and giving them a graphic picture of the demonstrations, I wound up that phase with your suggestion:

"The President says, let's not answer them with rocks and obscenities. It's time for the Silent Majority to stand up and be counted."

Believe it or not, 100 businessmen stood up and applauded.

And just as important, I understand they put up $50,000 to $60,000 by the time the meeting ended.

Bob Mooma and Reeves Bunting who were in charge of the meeting and Governor Shafer sent their regards to you.

HRH139

OCTOBER 23, 1970

TO: **H. R. Haldeman**

FROM: **Charles W. Colson**

Attached is a memo from Mort Allin on Network Coverage. As you can see, ABC continues to play it straight and CBS is doing much better; NBC remains a thorn in our side.

I've had the feeling, watching the news, that CBS is trying hard to do better. I believe that this is because of the court case and the other pressures.

I asked for this report because on Monday, Julian Goodman is coming in to see me. He had offered to do this when I saw him in New York; I suggested the Monday date only when I learned that he was invited to the Romanian dinner. (He shouldn't have been because he certainly doesn't deserve any recognition from us.) I decided to, therefore, use the occasion of his being here to continue our dialogue; so that he doesn't get the impression we are getting soft and inviting him to a dinner as a "reward."

If you have any particular points you would like me to make with him, let me know.

cc: Ziegler, Klein

CWC1, 93

NOVEMBER 2, 1970

Dear Rose:*
    Will you please see that the President gets this.
    Thanks, and best wishes

[s/Don]

*[Letter to Rose Mary Woods from F. Donald Nixon, the President's brother and vice president of the Marriott Corporation. This note refers to the following memo.]

HANDWRITTEN RN NOTE: "H[aldeman] Let's see that Brady gets a promotion."

MADRID, SPAIN
13 OCTOBER 1970

Memorandum for Mr. F. Donald Nixon

This is in response to your request for a brief note on a comment I made to you today concerning the visit of President Nixon to Spain.

One of my friends in the Spanish Foreign Service told me that the warm feelings of the Spanish people towards the President, and the great success of the visit here, were not based solely on recent actions of the President or on the excellent state of current relations between Spain and the United States. He told me that a characteristic of the Spaniard is that he never forgets a favor or a friendly act. He then referred to the United Nations Conference in San Francisco in 1945 when Alger Hiss was a vociferous and unrelenting opponent to the admission of Spain to the United Nations. Hiss was very influential within the American delegation which in turn was influential with other delegations. Spain was of course denied admittance.

When Hiss's Communist ideology and treasonable actions were exposed a few years later by your brother, the exposure served to put a new light on the reasons behind Hiss's opposition to Spain. The Spanish feel that President Nixon did Spain a favor by his effort against Hiss and that is one additional reason why the visit to Madrid was such an outstanding success.

> Thomas A. Brady, Attaché
> Embassy of the United States of America

PPF188:
MATERIAL REMOVED
FROM PRESIDENT'S DESK

NOVEMBER 6, 1970

TO: **The President**

FROM: **Charles W. Colson**

RE: **1970 Congressional Campaign**

Neither the failures nor the successes of this campaign can be attributed to any one factor. Indeed, there were significant regional and local factors which weighed heavily in the final outcome. As an illustration, one half of our total national House losses occurred in four contiguous Congressional districts located in North Dakota, South Dakota and Minnesota. Obviously, the farm issue was critical and nothing else in the national campaign could overcome it.

We must also remember the inherent difficulty of translating Presidential popularity into support for individual candidates. We lost many states that you would have carried handily had this been a Presidential election. We just couldn't succeed in making *your* supporters feel that they had to vote for *your* candidates. Nor historically, has this ever been easy to do.

Your campaigning was vital in terms of arousing our own troops and eliminating the apathy, which contrary to the normal historical pattern would have this year worked against us. Finally, by campaigning you demonstrated your loyalty to the candidates and to the party. The results, had you not campaigned, would have been far worse and you would have taken the full blame which would have hurt in 1972.

Beyond these general observations, I think some specific points can be made:

1. *Law and order is a national issue but it affects voting patterns differently in different areas.* The issue helped us in the liberal urban, suburban Northeast but, ironically, did very little for us in the conservative, rural Midwest and Far West. The reason, I think, is that the issue is meaningless where there is no crime and violence problem. If the people in North Dakota are not really concerned about crime or the safety of their homes, they can't get very worked up about their own Senator just because of his poor record on that issue. In the urban areas of the East, where fear of crime and violence is widespread, our stand on law and order (and that of our candidates) was *the* key issue (except where the economic issue surpassed it).

2. *Except in the urban Northeast, we did not succeed in making the public believe that Democrat, Liberal permissiveness was the cause of violence and crime.* There are a combination of reasons for this. As noted above, people in the more conservative states, while they are all for law and order, don't blame their own liberal Senator for a problem that they don't personally confront. Secondly, the Democrats in many cases recaptured safe ground on the issue: Stevenson is a classic example. Thirdly, our campaign pitch didn't really come across in a way to lay the responsibility onto the Democrats. In this sense we were, perhaps, too negative. Everyone knew that we were against permissiveness and violence but we didn't sell the point that violence and disorder in our society are caused directly by the rhetoric, softness, and catering to the dissidents which the Democrats have engaged in. We just didn't make the connection in the mind of the average voter.

3. *The war issue became neutralized in the campaign.* People are generally very satisfied with your handling of the war. Because they are and because it, therefore, has become something of a non-issue, they weren't motivated to vote *against* those who have opposed you on the war. In short, the issue would have been an enormous plus had you been the candidate but it didn't significantly benefit our supporters or hurt our opponents. Evidence of this was in Massachusetts which has been the most "dovish" state in the union. There was a war referendum on the ballot— 440,000 supported immediate withdrawal, 190,000 supported an all-out military victory and 711,000 supported the President's peace plan. At the same time doves won big margins. Your success with the peace issue probably helped us generally, but it didn't hurt our opponents.

4. *The economic issue hurt badly.* The pocketbook issue is always the gut issue in any campaign. It was this year a question of fear more than fact; concern over whether the country is heading into another recession or, perhaps even depression coupled with continued inflation, was a potent factor in a number of areas. As Scammon has pointed out in his book, the social issue is dominant only if there is no pocketbook issue. This one obviously hurt us in California. (Also, however, was the problem of Murphy's image, age and the Technicolor retainer.) It hurt in a number of Congressional races particularly in the Midwest and in certain areas of particularly heavy unemployment (the vote in Seattle is an example). The economic issue was compounded by the GM strike which unquestionably cost us the Indiana race—if we have lost it—and made the Taft race closer than it should have been. The general economic issue was further compounded by the farm problem. Republicans did badly in those states in which high parity price support has always been *the* issue (Nebraska, the Dakotas, Kansas, for example); witness the four contiguous House seats in which the farm issue beat us and a number of districts that we should have won, but for the farm issue. We had been warned of discontent in the Farm Belt but it was too late to counter it.

5. *In general, we probably peaked too early.* The Vice President peaked in late September, his line became very predictable and with many voters "old hat." Once committed to it, there was, of course, no way to turn around; perhaps, the tempo and approach could have been varied. Clearly, the Vice President had a very healthy impact in arousing our troops, raising money and generating campaign activity. (His Goodell strategy was a key to New York.) Once he had peaked, however, his line became increasingly ineffective in winning either Democrats or Independents.

In this general regard the Democrats scored against us, by engendering sympathy. They charged us with dirty campaigning and excess spending, which tended to make us appear to be "overkilling." They were clever in making this more of an issue than it should have been. The press continually reported that we were outspending the Democrats 5 to 1 but failed to report that approximately $3 million was being spent on Democratic campaigns by the Council for a Livable World, the McGovern Fund ($1 million alone), COPE and the National Committee for an Effective Congress. I am told this issue killed Burton even though Moss outspent Burton 2 to 1. Winthrop Rockefeller was a case in point, as was the sympathy for Lawton Chiles's "poor boy" campaign.

People became tired of the campaign ten days to 2 weeks before it was over.* We took the blame for excessive spending in campaigning. This hurt us as people became sick of politics and the usual charges and counter charges which they then tended to dismiss.

6. *We made significant inroads with the blue collar, white ethnic vote, George Gallup's comments to the contrary notwithstanding.* This vote elected Beall, defeated Duffey, elected Buckley and put Prouty over big. We are scoring in this area because of law and order and patriotism.

(We are conducting an analysis of selected blue collar districts to test this conclusion.) Prouty, who was a colorless, ineffective campaigner, carried Democratic blue collar wards in Burlington because of their antipathy toward his excessively liberal opponent. The same happened in Baltimore. Dodd took the blue collars away from Duffey. Buckley swept the white ethnic, blue collar vote. Significantly we did well in areas where unions we have begun to win over are strong (construction workers); badly, where we haven't made progress (the UAW, steelworkers).

7. *As in every campaign, there were mistakes made in individual states which hurt us.*

Texas: For weeks prior to the election, George Bush was convinced that he had the election won provided no one rocked the boat. He refused to allow us to use some very derogatory information about Bentsen. He resisted any ads—positive or negative—and refused to attack Bentsen. We probably should have forced him to do more. Dick Scammon thinks that Bush lost it for this reason and because he ignored the social issue and tried to be more liberal than Bentsen.**

Maryland: In the case of Beall, he similarly refused to attack. We ended up doing it for him in a variety of ways and the political situation in Maryland reversed itself dramatically in the last week of the campaign.

Florida: Clearly the split in the party cost us the state.

Illinois: There was no way ever to elect Smith but his campaign grew excessively negative and, I am told, turned the liberal moderates in the Chicago suburbs sour. Also Ogilvie has serious splits in the party (there are some serious warnings here for 1972).

Ohio: The state ticket scandal cost us the Governorship.

Maine: With just a little help from the national level we might have elected a Governor (Irwin was hurt by the feeling the state was written off).

Pennsylvania: Shafer was so disliked, no Republican could succeed him. Scott won, which indicates the Governorship was purely a state issue.

New Jersey: Our candidate made classic mistakes, shifting positions and creating distrust.

Michigan: There was no hope without a candidate.

8. *Negativism.* Rightly or wrongly, the Democrats and the press made us (the Vice President in particular) appear to be too negative. As indicated in my memo on the Broder articles, we need to stress more and more the positive theme of accomplishment; that we are not only against unlawfulness and disorder but that we are doing things to control it and that we are reforming Government. We need to promote our record of accomplishment as we have done so well in foreign policy.

Conclusion: We made maximum use of national media. Our analysis shows that your campaign resulted in giving us twice the coverage the Democrats got. Without this, I am convinced the result would have been much worse because, especially in the closing days, the effect of your campaign was to take the economic issue out of the news.

As indicated above, in hindsight, I think we could have won a few more, particularly in the Senate, and with stronger party machinery could have done better with our Governorships.

On balance, we did better than the press and the pundits credit us with doing. If you accept the premise that it is inherently difficult for Presidential popularity to rub off on local candidates, then we did very well, particularly in the House.

Finally, I do not think the elections reflect any loss of support for you. To the contrary, I am convinced that had this been our election, we would have won big.

*HANDWRITTEN RN NOTE: "True"
**HANDWRITTEN RN NOTE: "probably true"

PPF6; CWC14, 88
W/RN from CWC127

EYES ONLY

NOVEMBER 6, 1970

TO: **H. R. Haldeman**

FROM: **Charles W. Colson**

I have reviewed with Dean Burch the election night coverage. He is as incensed about it as we are and has agreed to call the three network presidents in for a meeting on the subject. He intends to tell them that unless they take steps on their own to correct the problem, he will consider regulatory action or legislative recommendations.

This, following on the heels of our request of each of the three networks for transcripts of their election night coverage will, I am convinced, have a real impact the next time around and will undoubtedly be salutary, generally speaking.

CWC127

EYES ONLY

NOVEMBER 16, 1970

TO: **H. R. Haldeman**

FROM: **Charles W. Colson**

In connection with the general housecleaning discussed last weekend, even though the State Department is exempt, it would sure be nice to get at least one Nixon man into a sensitive spot over there.

You have doubtless read the Saturday article of the "exoneration" of Senator Tydings. I talked to Macomber who says naturally that the press completely misplayed it. The fact is that in many respects, the State Department has grossly mishandled this. I have not yet read the report but I can simply say that the way it was handled was incredible, particularly in the light of what John Mitchell told me last weekend.

By whitewashing a number of aspects of the Tydings matter at State, the Department has made the whole thing look political—exactly what we did not want. I suppose this is academic since Tydings has been beaten but I think it makes the Administration look very bad in the eyes of other members of Congress.

I knew they were going to do this; the problem is we have no one over there we can deal with on sensitive political questions.

CWC127

W/RN from CWC118

NOVEMBER 17, 1970

TO: **H. R. Haldeman**

FROM: **Charles W. Colson**

Our analysis of the election night coverage on NBC confirms just what we thought; it was terrifically slanted toward the Democrats.

Dean Burch has agreed to convene a meeting with the three network presidents together. He will call them to task on their coverage and advise them that steps have to be taken on their own to deal with this problem or the FCC may have to consider regulatory remedies. Burch is in the process of trying to arrange the conference and is aiming for the 23rd or 24th in New York. I will let you know the outcome.

I don't believe that we should have any direct contact with the networks on this particular subject until we get a report from Burch. I also think it would be very inadvisable to make any public statement at this time about election night coverage inasmuch as the networks would have a perfect answer, that is, we outscored the Democrats better than 2 to 1 during the two months prior to the campaign.

I have reviewed Pat Buchanan's memo to the President of November 4th, which interestingly enough confirms my own offhand judgment that overall we did very well on the networks during the campaign. ABC and CBS have improved considerably over the past couple of months since my visit with them. Mort Allin's reports and opinions also substantiate this.

NBC on the other hand, if it has changed at all, has gotten worse since my meeting. While Stanton has become uncharacteristically silent— no major speeches, no more crusading for equal time, etc.—Goodman has gone just the other way and has now made three speeches warning of the dangers of government interference and political pressure on the networks. Goodman has decided to test us and, in effect, to call our bluff. In addition to Goodman's own attitude, NBC news coverage has become increasingly bad. We enjoyed much more coverage during the campaign on NBC as with the other two; on the other hand, they really stuck it into us on the economy and during the President's European trip with very slanted negative reports.

Pat makes the point in his memo that we should stop romancing Goodman. Believe me, nobody is romancing him. I have had two very tough sessions. He was invited to the Romanian Dinner by mistake. Bob Dole suggested it to Timmons, who passed it along to Rose Woods who put him on the list without consulting anyone. This was a serious mistake. As arrogant as he is, he interpreted this as a sign of appeasement, I am sure.

I do not believe that we should make a public blast at the networks or specifically at NBC at this time. To attack one of the three will cause them all to close ranks, which we do not want in view of the progress we are making with CBS and ABC through the quiet pressure technique. I also think it would look bad coming on the heels of what the public is being made to believe was a rancorous political campaign.

With respect to NBC, we should perhaps consider an approach to the management of RCA, the parent corporation. Secondly, the Republican National Committee could file a fairness complaint against NBC on the issue of biased news coverage. I intend to explore this latter possibility with Burch; it is a treacherous course because we could only win on a partisan vote which might have more negatives than positives.

I would like to explore the second option only after I have had a run on the RCA management which, in my opinion, is the next step to be taken.

How we handle the network problem in the next two years is a very critical subject which I would like to discuss with you when we have time to talk it through thoroughly. There are, in my opinion, five strategy considerations:

1. Continued quiet but firm pressure from here. For example, when I asked Al Snyder the day after the election to request from all 3 networks a transcript of their election night coverage, the reverberations were felt throughout the organizations. CBS very quickly volunteered us a "Face the Nation" guest spot. Al believes this was strictly because of the request for the transcripts. Morton went on, as you know.

2. We need a better system for briefing and backgrounding friendly or neutral network commentators in getting our line out to them regularly, personally and directly. This should be the positive side of our activity. We spend a lot of time cultivating newspaper columnists but we do none of this with TV analysts and commentators. It probably would be only marginally effective, but still worth the effort, in my judgment.

3. At a modest cost (at least compared with buying a network), we can establish a TV news service here in Washington, a private entity that will feed out TV news spots directly to licensees for use on non-network news programs. Lyn Nofziger has prepared an excellent plan which I will review with you.

4. Through Dean Burch we should keep heavy regulatory pressures building. The networks are fully aware that we can influence the FCC in policy matters and this is a cause of *great* concern to them.

5. See to it that individual stations stay in friendly hands and try to get our friends to pick up stations that are presently hostile.

CWC88
_____
W/RN from CWC127

NOVEMBER 18, 1970

Things to Do

1. CWC job outline
2. CWC staff analysis and requirements
3. Creation of political control group—Rumsfeld, Garment, Dent, Ehrlichman, Colson—memo to HRH
4. New memo to President regarding phone call contact program
5. Memo to HRH regarding Justice Department
6. Complete update on how we are using contact program
7. Youth activities
8. Memo on LeTendre
9. Nofziger role
10. Write up on media plan
11. Write up on Becker plan—blue collar analysis
12. Memo to HRH re Malek
13. Nofziger TV plan
14. Memo to HRH re Dick Moore
15. Memo re Defense contracts
16. Memo re internal political group
17. Suffridge memo
18. Memo to President on meeting with network executives

_____
CWC127

NOVEMBER 20, 1970

TO: **Mrs. Winchester**

FROM: **H. R. Haldeman**

I hate to come in with a negative approach, and perhaps you've already gotten these comments anyway, but, for the record, here goes.

I had the feeling last night, and, after a little checking, found that others concurred, that the dinner served to the Ash Council group was not up to our usual quality standards.

For one thing, there was a very large dose of crab shells mixed in to the crab aspic, and I noticed that everyone was busy trying to figure out how best to remove these bits of shell from one's mouth daintily and still look like one possessed the proper savoir faire for a White House dinner.

The main course was rather barren, with only a piece of meat and some stringbeans. Don't we usually have two vegetables or a potato?

The Bel Paese cheese was served very hard and chilled. It should be at least at room temperature, and soft enough so that it is easily sliced.

The apple strudel–type dessert is pretty unfancy, and not very tasty for White House fare. I commend to your attention the apple crisp served in the White House Mess as a point of comparison.

Most of our dinners have been outstanding, with minor failures here and there. This one did not seem to be up to the usual standards.

cc: Mr. Butterfield

ss86

NOVEMBER 21, 1970

TO: **Lyn Nofziger**

FROM: **Charles W. Colson**

Al Capp has been one of our truly great supporters. He has asked a personal favor. He wants to get Frank Sinatra to Boston for a big POW rally on December 6. Can you pull this off through Reagan? It would really be a big one for us and Capp is a guy we want to cultivate hard.

cwc127

EYES ONLY

NOVEMBER 22, 1970

TO: **Henry Kissinger**

FROM: **The President**

On a very confidential basis, I would like for you to have prepared in your staff—without any notice to people who might leak—a study of where we are to go with regard to the admission of Red China to the UN. It seems to me that the time is approaching sooner than we might think when we will not have the votes to block admission.

The question we really need an answer to is how we can develop a position in which we can keep our commitments to Taiwan and yet will not be rolled by those who favor admission of Red China.

There is no hurry on this study but within two or three months I would like to see what you come up with.

PPF2; HRH229

NOVEMBER 22, 1970

TO: **Pat Buchanan**

FROM: **The President**

It occurred to me that you might want to respond to Reston's piece of November 6 in the *New York Times*—but in better temper, naturally, than in the way you very appropriately handled Childs. When he compares Nixon with Johnson on the political front he, of course, misses one fundamental point—Johnson did nothing in 1966 to campaign in behalf of his candidates because none of them wanted his help whereas RN's activities were the direct result of requests from all over the country in this respect.

Also, you might needle him a little on his comment with regard to the governorships of Pennsylvania and Ohio. Point out that in 1960 we won the two big states where we did not have governors (Ohio and California)—and lost the two big ones where we did have them (New York and Illinois).

I am not sure this is a good idea, but if you think well of it go ahead with a personal note to him—particularly pointing up to him what the consequences would be if we had lost two in the Senate rather than gaining two in terms of how it would have affected RN's ability to carry on the foreign policies which Reston admittedly agrees are in the nation's best interests.

PPF2; HRH229

NOVEMBER 23, 1970

TO: **Bob Haldeman**

FROM: **The President**

I have a delicate matter which I would like for you to work out with regard to John Mitchell. When I offered our Florida place to them I did not realize that Julie and David plan to go down there for the week before Christmas which is the first time he will have off after his intensive indoctrination at Newport. Under the circumstances, I would like for you to get ahold of Bebe and see if he can arrange for them to have a really good villa at Key

Biscayne. I know that is where Martha wants to go and she is always bugging us because she says they never give them a good villa. Bebe should use all the weight he possibly can to get this villa for them. Once that is done then you can call John and tell him of the mix-up and express our regrets.

You can also tell him that if they are there before Julie and David arrive or are there after they leave we want them to use our beach facilities—something Bebe will always be ready to arrange.

HRH229

NOVEMBER 24, 1970

TO: **Larry Higby**

FROM: **Charles W. Colson**

If you decide to give this to Bob, I fully expect to be fired—or assassinated by Kleindienst. I don't know any way, however, to make the problem go away; hence, I find myself in the continuing and uncomfortable position of being the House Bastard.*

*[Attachment follows.]

CWC39, 127

NOVEMBER 24, 1970

TO: **H. R. Haldeman**

FROM: **Charles W. Colson**

Have you been read in on the Clem Stone judgeship situation?

According to Dave Bradshaw, Kleindienst met Stone at the airport when he came to Washington last week and advised him that the ABA would not approve Epton. Clem had earlier been advised the same day by a member of the ABA Committee that a new and highly favorable ABA report had been prepared on Epton and sent to Justice. Clem did not tell Kleindienst.

I don't know who is right or wrong nor is it really relevant. Clem feels that he is being thrown a curve. What he thinks, not what the facts are, is what is important.

He has told Bradshaw that he is very disappointed with us. Clem obviously doesn't understand the intricacies of the ABA clearance process (nor do I). He does remember, however, that we told him six months ago that everything would be worked out.

???

CWC127
W/RN from CWC39

NOVEMBER 24, 1970

TO: **The Attorney General**

FROM: **Director, FBI**

RE: **Dunes Hotel**
Las Vegas, Nevada—
Anti-Racketeering

The purpose of this letter is to advise you of information received which indicates that Howard Hughes has renewed his efforts to purchase the Dunes Hotel in Las Vegas, Nevada.

It has been reported that Robert Maheu, chief executive of Hughes' Nevada operations; E. Parry Thomas, Chairman of the Board, Valley National Bank, Las Vegas, Nevada; and Edward P. Morgan, Washington, D.C., attorney contacted the Securities and Exchange Commission, Washington, D.C., to determine if that agency would interpose any objection to a cash purchase of the Dunes Hotel by Hughes. It was reported that the Securities and Exchange Commission advised no objection will be interposed.

It was reported that Morgan has strongly implied that there will be no objection from the Antitrust Division of the Department of Justice concerning Hughes' efforts to purchase another Las Vegas casino.

As you will recall the Antitrust Division objected to Hughes' attempt to purchase the Stardust Hotel-Casino in Las Vegas in 1968.

Although no definite price has been set it is believed that Hughes will offer in the neighborhood of 80 to 81 million dollars for the purchase of the Dunes Hotel.

You will be kept advised of any further information received in connection with this proposed transaction.

1—The Deputy Attorney General
1—Assistant Attorney General, Antitrust Division

26 SENATE HEARINGS 12879

NOVEMBER 30, 1970

TO: **H. R. Haldeman**

FROM: **The President**

What became of our investigation of NET. Is there anything we can do to get better control in that area—at least where government assistance is involved.

HRH229

NOVEMBER 30, 1970

TO: Mr. Colson

FROM: H. R. Haldeman

What became of our investigation of NET. Is there something we can do
to get better control in that area—at least where government assistance
is involved?

HRH71

w/RN from CWC1

NOVEMBER 30, 1970

TO: H. R. Haldeman

FROM: The President

Before Moynihan leaves would you try to get him pinned down on that
list of intellectuals he believes we should be talking to. As a matter of fact,
once he is gone he can cultivate a few of these people and come in with
them on some occasion in the future.

HRH138, 164

NOVEMBER 30, 1970

TO: H. R. Haldeman

FROM: The President

With regard to the celebrity list, despite the fact that we must, of course,
go for all the new stars, when we look at some of those who might go with
us now, it is a pretty imposing list: Ruby Keeler, Gloria Swanson, Joan
Crawford, Ginger Rogers, Bette Davis. Consequently, let's be sure they
are in our '72 list and that we get some of them lined up as well as the new
ones.

HRH138, 164, 229

NOVEMBER 30, 1970

TO: H. R. Haldeman

FROM: The President

What became of the project with regard to a rerun of *Friendly Persuasion*?

HRH229

NOVEMBER 30, 1970

TO: **Mr. Ehrlichman**

FROM: **The President**

Just a reminder for you to discuss with George Shultz the necessity for expanding the Productivity Council's staff and for the need to get an Executive Director of the staff who can put a little imagination and verve into the meetings of the Council and into its reports. You must talk quite frankly with George as to the weakness of Paul McCracken and also George's staff. In getting such an Executive Director we, of course, might borrow trouble if we got one who is so much of a go-go guy that he went off on his own. But the present situation is most unsatisfactory and there needs to be urgent reappraisal of our staff needs for the Council.

HRH229

W/RN from HRH138, 64, and 229 [correct]

NOVEMBER 30, 1970

TO: **Dr. Kissinger**

FROM: **The President**

While I believe your recommendation that we keep Helms should be accepted, I will do so only on [the] condition that there be a thorough housecleaning at other levels at CIA. I want you to get him in and tell him the people you want changed and work out the situation. Also I want a good thinning down of the whole CIA personnel situation, as well as our intelligence activities generally.

HRH138, 164, 229

NOVEMBER 30, 1970

TO: **Dr. Moynihan**

FROM: **The President**

I would like to see your recommendations of the ten best political biographies and histories. As you know, I do quite a bit of late evening reading, and I want to be sure that I am reading the best!

HRH164, 229

NOVEMBER 30, 1970

TO: Mr. Butterfield

FROM: The President

I have noted that in choosing the domestic California wine they have had the Beaulieu Vineyard Cabernet Sauvignon, rather than the Louis Martini Cabernet Sauvignon. It may be that Beaulieu Vineyard has purchased Louis Martini since I made the original choice. If so, I understand. If that is not the case, however, I prefer Louis Martini. Beaulieu Vineyard is a very big commercial winery and once they take over a small winery like Louis Martini the quality goes sharply down.

HRH164, 229

DECEMBER 1, 1970

TO: John Brown

FROM: Charles W. Colson

RE: White House Office Papers

We really haven't had time in this office to give much thought at all to how official White House papers might be preserved. I suppose whenever we leave we could simply go through our files and pull out those things which we believe should be kept for posterity and for the President's own possible future use. Another thought would be to keep copies of anything which, in our judgment, would have any permanent significance from a historic standpoint, or from the President's own standpoint. We could start doing this with relative ease from this point forward.

I don't think you want to create one central point for the collection of all papers which every staff member thinks might be appropriate. There are many things in this office I would not want kept in any other part of the building. Additionally, it would be a tremendously burdensome task. I suspect that almost everything of any importance, as a matter of fact, at one time or another passes through your office, so to that extent you do have a certain amount of control.

In any event, whatever system you do develop let us know and we will try to comply.

cwc127

DECEMBER 1, 1970

Dear Brad:*

Thanks a million for the fabulous suspenders. I don't need suspenders often. Because of my bulging gut, I actually need nothing to hold my pants up. These I will wear, however; they are marvelous.

They match perfectly my Marine Corps tie clip, the American flag in my lapel, my Nixon cuff links, and my red, white and blue underwear.

See you soon.

Best personal regards.

Sincerely,

Charles W. Colson
Special Counsel
to the President

*[Letter addressed to Representative F. Bradford Morse]

CWC127

DECEMBER 4, 1970

TO: **Mr. Haldeman**

FROM: **The President**

Rumsfeld has the feeling that Bob Dole may be losing some of his effectiveness because he is a "knee-jerk" defender of the Administration. I am inclined to think that Rumsfeld may be overreacting on this point but, of course, it is important that we not let Dole destroy his usefulness by having him step up to every fast, hard one. Consider this matter, but consider it in the context of the fact that many people who are jealous of Dole's publicity may be trying to knock him down. This may be one way to get at him.

On another subject, one very important PR theme which we should now start to play up is the underdog role. We have not made enough of this in the past—the fact for example that, for the last two years on national defense, on Vietnam, on Cambodia, on standing up against radical students, on fighting for law and order, etc., RN has stood alone—opposed, for example, on Cambodia by most of the White House staff, most of the Cabinet, most of the Congress, including members of his own Party, and 90% of the press. Elaborating on this theme, I have asked previously for a column to be written, and now I suppose the one to have to write it is going to be Lasky, on the fact that never has a President in this century had more opposition and less friends among the press than RN, and that it is a miracle that he has been able to withstand it. If our Gallup rating were to depend upon how the press was covering this, we would stand at about 15%.

But the general theme of RN as standing up alone, against his Cabinet, against the White House staff, against the Congress, and against the press is one that people like and should be developed and followed through on.

Another point that Rumsfeld makes quite effectively is that we are "too busy selling something new each week." What we have to do is to pound, and pound, and pound on three or four major themes and let the other themes be handled in a subsidiary way. These themes, of course, on the domestic front are items like revenue sharing, where we have allowed the ball to get completely away from us, reform, and, of course, our old theme of RN's strong position on law and order.

In regard with our relations with the Congress I think it is important that you get the whole staff together and particularly emphasize, with those who handle our relations on the Hill, as well as with our top White House staff, these points [sic]:

1. We have people like Ed Brooke and Cliff Case and Chuck Percy who are coming up this year, and, regardless of what they may do to us, our primary goal is to avoid any action or words which may be harmful to them in terms of their re-election.

But expanding to a larger question, I think there is a tendency for us not to recognize that people like Brooke, Case, Schweiker, Saxbe, Cooper, Percy, even Javits et al., have their constituencies, or at least believe they are playing to their constituencies, but try to be with us when they can, and when they are against us do not try to make a virtue out of being against us, which of course was Goodell's major fault.

I want you to emphasize with our staff that with all the Republicans that may be against us, I want even-handed treatment and once we have lost a battle in getting their votes, we forget that battle and try to win the next one. This does not mean that we do not give some special attention to our friends, but it does mean that you don't read people out of the Party at this point when we're going to need every one of them with us in 1972.

HRH164

W/RN from HRH138, 139, 229, and 164

DECEMBER 4, 1970

TO: **Mr. Flanigan**

FROM: **The President**

I want to be sure, to the extent this office has anything whatever to do with it, and I assume that, because of the Independent Agency program, we probably have very little to do with it, that IDS gets its lumps for the shocking way it handled that stock transaction in which they sold stock after getting inside information about the decline in profits.

IDS, which, of course, is in Pittsburgh, is not a very admirable group. I say this as one who was on the Board of Investors which, of course, is independent. We were always fighting IDS and found them to be engaging in sharp practices. Loeffler is the bad guy in the whole outfit and I want to be sure, to the extent you can properly do so, that IDS be given absolutely no redress whatever from this charge.

HRH229

W/RN from HRH138

DECEMBER 4, 1970

Dear Mr. President:

In view of the news stories about possible plots of kidnapping, I would like to state my position in the extraordinary event that this should occur.

If such an attempt should succeed, I would like to ask you to meet no demands of the kidnappers, however trivial. I would assume that any demand that is met would establish a precedent which is against the national interest.

If you should receive any communication from me to the contrary, you should assume that it was made under duress.

Respectfully,

Henry A. Kissinger

The President
The White House

PPF10

DECEMBER 5, 1970

TO: **Jim Keogh**

FROM: **Chuck Colson**

RE: **Your Memo of November 30th re Charles Kaman**

Do you think my letter causes any problems? If so, I can call them and ask them not to publish it in their anniversary brochure. I don't think we should do anything with the Secretary of Defense because of their defense business.

The fact is that Kaman has been a fanatic Nixon man. His is an unorganized non-union plant and like the good old tycoon of 100 years ago, he marches his people to the polls to vote straight Republican. He is also mad as a hornet on a very bad deal he got on a contract recently—at least he thinks he got a bad deal. I, therefore, felt there should be a little extra massage.

Please advise.

CWC127

DECEMBER 9, 1970

TO: **H. R. Haldeman**

FROM: **John Dean**

RE: **IRS**

In response to your memorandum of December 2, 1970, regarding my activities on reorganization and infusing new personnel at IRS, I want to advise you that after conversations with persons knowledgeable in this area both within government (Tax Division—Justice) and outside government, I have concluded that a major reorganization is neither necessary nor wise. There is a serious problem in politicizing IRS or taking action that would give the appearance of politicizing IRS. A reorganization which infused a large number of politically appointed people into IRS would undoubtedly have such an effect or give such an appearance. This is not to say that we cannot vastly improve upon the existing situation, where we have a 60,000 man agency vital to the government, with *one* political appointee.

Accordingly, I have been working with Fred Malek, who has devised the overall game plan for IRS (see attached Malek memo of December 4, 1970). More specifically, I have given Jamie McLane my thoughts and had him attend a meeting in my office with Assistant Attorney General Johnnie Walters (Tax Division) to discuss how IRS might be organizationally improved.

I concur fully in Malek's game plan and I anticipate further discussion with Malek and McLane this week regarding what *can* be done to improve the organization of IRS.

HRH70

DECEMBER 9, 1970

TO: **Ken Cole**

FROM: **Charles W. Colson**

I hope that someone on the White House staff is giving some serious thought to the form of campaign spending limitation bill which we might be willing to accept or propose. Recognizing that the most desirable outcome for us is no bill at all, the best way to accomplish this is to have a plan of our own that we are willing to fight for. The Congress will hardly accept our plan but we would then be in a position to veto theirs on the grounds that ours was superior. Having our own plan also puts us in a more comfortable position insofar as knowing what we can and cannot live with. In addition our proposal will help muddy the waters and slow down the legislation process.

This requires some real thought and analysis. I would be glad to contribute my two cents worth, but someone should be working on it. Simply because we beat the political broadcasting bill does not mean the issue is going to go away.

cwc127

DECEMBER 10, 1970

TO: **Mr. Chapin**

FROM: **H. R. Haldeman**

For your background guidance, there is a strong feeling that the gimmick suggestions for Presidential participation are not acceptable when they are obvious. They are good when they are spontaneous.

In other words, an unannounced drop-by at the Home for the Incurables is a good thing to do. A planned visit to the Childrens' Conference to look at exhibits is a bad thing to do. The point is to do these things without announcement and then let the word get out afterwards.

This would also apply to stops in a motorcade. We shouldn't set up an obvious stop and heavy-handedly do it there—we should work out where the stop is and do it spontaneously.

HRH70

DECEMBER 11, 1970

TO: **Jeb Magruder**

FROM: **Charles Colson**

RE: **Pat Moynihan**

Pursuant to our discussions this morning, I reached Pat Moynihan. He is very charged up and will talk to as many of his liberal columnist friends as he can get to.

He expressed, in his own inimitable way, his view that the entire Washington press corps is corrupt as well as the entire editorial staff of the *New York Times,* which he told them to their faces—this morning in a meeting in New York. (I would have loved to have been a fly on the wall.)

bcc: H. R. Haldeman—Pat asked me to pass on to you the fact that he met with the *New York Times* this morning and, as he described it, gave John Oakes hell.

cwc127

DECEMBER 12, 1970

TO: **Dwight Chapin**

FROM: **Charles W. Colson**

Apropos our conversation the other day concerning Howard Hughes—his retainer with Larry O'Brien was cancelled as a result of the latest escapades. Bob Bennett, presently Director of Legislative Liaison for DOT and the son of the Senator from Utah, has signed a contract with Hughes and will be their representative in Washington. He is a good friend of ours and has volunteered to do anything we want at any time with the Hughes people.

cc: Larry Higby

cwc14, 127

DECEMBER 14, 1970

TO: **Larry Higby**

FROM: **Charles W. Colson**

RE: **Polling Organization**

Political polls as such have very little credibility unless they are released by political organizations. It just isn't logical that AEI or any of the Scaife operations or the Chamber for example would release a poll that was obviously political; more importantly, a tax exempt organization could not spend their funds for such a poll.

Issue polls are something else again. For example, a poll on whom the public blames for inflation (one I would hate to see done) could be put out by AEI or the Chamber with ease.

The best solution to this dilemma is to use a nationally known polling firm that will publish the results in their own name. They will say, if questioned, that the poll was commissioned for a private client and they don't generally disclose the client without the client's approval. What is needed, of course, is a pollster who has a national reputation and who generally makes a practice of releasing polls. ORC is a perfect illustration. While the POW poll did not get picked up around Washington their polls are generally released and used around the country. There are a number of other regional polling firms like Becker in New England that are very well established. They, of course, will do the same thing that ORC will do.

This overcomes the credibility problem almost entirely. Everyone knows that ORC and Becker would not slant a poll. Moreover these firms customarily release Political Polls.

A further point, of course, is that if it is a poll that we commission we can decide whether to release it or not—depending on whether it is to our advantage.

My recommendation, therefore, is that we use Chilton, which I gather we prefer to do because it is fast and cheap, in those instances when we know we will not want to publicize the poll results; but that we use ORC or other known, credible organizations when we think we may want the results published.

cwc127

W/RN from cwc102

DECEMBER 15, 1970

TO: **Murray Chotiner**

FROM: **Chapman's Friend**

This is by way of being the first in progress or assessment reports and memoranda about Senator Muskie.

As of the moment, the media have been carrying stories to the effect that Muskie is beginning his race for the Democratic nomination quite early. When I asked him why this morning, he replied: "It's the old story. I'd be left at the post if I didn't get going."

Yesterday and today, I also spoke to some people in the Teddy Kennedy entourage and to Jay Lovestone and Andy Biemiller of the AFL-CIO. The Kennedy people (in his Senate office) seem rather amused by the Muskie preparations and publicity-seeking. They convey the clear impression—and I have noted this impression for some time now—that Kennedy may well go for the nomination. Their (the Kennedy crowd) presentation of Muskie is calculated and somewhat amused contempt.

This attitude may well be contrived. The AFL-CIO higher-ups with whom I have had several discussions, openly sneer at Muskie. His dovish image is what Meany obviously detests and Jay Lovestone and Andy Biemiller reflect this. Meany would love to see Senator Scoop Jackson try for the nomination. Jay Lovestone and Biemiller told me today that labor would go "all-out for Scoop." They admit, though, his chances are very slim indeed.

Back directly to Muskie: His offices—outside the Senate and for his bid—are presently in Suite 1040 at 1660 "L" Street, N.W. There is as yet no name on the legend plate of the office building. And, the suite door remains unmarked.

All of that will be changed very shortly, Don Nicholl, his A.A., told me. Nicholl is still on the Senate payroll although he has hardly in months devoted himself to any Senate business. Muskie says that Nicholl very soon will be politicking for him—sort of an overseer—full time. Will Nicholl then be transferred to another payroll?

Nicholl has been with Muskie a long time, going back to the time he was Governor of Maine. Small in size physically, with ferret-type features and a much pocked face, Nicholl can be extremely unpleasant. He

1970: SEPTEMBER–DECEMBER **187**

has earned the displeasure of most reporters already. Muskie's executive assistant in the Senate, Jock Whitehead, is infinitely more affable and tries assiduously to take the sting out of any encounters people have with Nicholl.

As I mentioned earlier, the Muskie office—known loosely now as the "Muskie Election Committee"—is basically run by Nicholl. There are plans afoot to appoint all types. The present office, incidentally, is one floor beneath that of Harry McPherson, who was counsel to LBJ. In the Muskie office proper, rooms are carved into cubicles. It has the appearance of quiet disorder; so far, terribly unprofessional. The behavior pattern may be one deliberately cultivated for Muskie; the rumpled, reflective, instant late 20th-century Lincoln.

When I was in the office the other day, R. W. (Johnny) Apple, of the *New York Times* was on hand. He subsequently wrote a story that appeared, which added little. Apple seemed annoyed, as an ambitious young man (he covered Humphrey among others from start to finish in 1968). He told me that the *Times* was about to put him on the "Muskie Trail" as an assignment from here on in through the conventions.

While Apple and I were conversing, the young girl at the modest switchboard took a call and couldn't grasp the name. I took it, and it was Bill Haddad, whom I've known for years.

Haddad is known in the trade as a professional loser—with a big bankroll, that of his father-in-law, Jock Whitney. I doubt that he can tap Jock for any mammoth sums. But his wife, the daughter of Betsy Cushing Whitney (she was adopted by Jock and her first name is Kate—ex-Roosevelt), managed when necessary to get goodly sums from her mother.

In any case, when I took the Haddad call at the Muskie office, he wanted to know where and how he could render assistance to Muskie. I noted that offer for the switchboard girl. It was somewhat surprising because Haddad always tried in the past to link closely with the Kennedys. He tries, however, to be an agile rabbit. His political ambitions remain great, if utterly unfulfilled.

Some of the people coming in to "assist" Muskie—besides names like those of McPherson, Clark Clifford, Jack Valenti, etc.—are led by a bankroller whose name I have so far as Alexander (Sandy) Greenberg. He is said to be 29 years old, who already has made millions in the computer business. He also is supposed to be handling the Israeli phase of the Muskie trip, scheduled for January or February of 1971, that will also take in Europe.*

Stew Alsop took up my suggestion to interview Muskie. He came away quite annoyed with him. For the first time, Alsop reported, Muskie had a stenographer in the room, noting down the conversation. "He is trying to be extra-careful," said Alsop. "For a politician running for the cigar, his attitude as expressed to me isn't very astute."

Alsop also told me that his impression of Muskie now added up to:

"He just didn't seem to have the visceral quality to follow up and be a fighter for what he says he wants."

In addition, Alsop said that in his view, Muskie has aligned himself too inextricably with the doves. "All these guys are still fighting Lyndon Johnson and his policies about Vietnam. They just don't seem to realize it is a very different ball game now."

On the economy, Alsop said that Muskie seemed "very fuzzy and always drifted back to ecology. I wonder if he knows anything about ecology or if he has assimilated some terms and jargon."

I'd suggest checking on this Alexander (Sandy) Greenberg to see if the name is right and the background too; I will check further myself. In addition, I wonder where the line divides on Don Nicholl being on the Senate payroll for all his recent past while working on the Muskie for President nomination program.

*[After this paragraph, a paragraph of approximately eight lines was withheld by NARA because it is considered to be national security classified information.]

HRH342

DECEMBER 15, 1970

TO: **H. R. Haldeman**

FROM: **Charles Colson**

RE: **Nick Thimmesch Article**

I think we have a potential in Nick Thimmesch of another "house columnist," with probably more credibility than Lasky.

He is not widely circulated but we can use him for reprints and his circulation can be expanded.

I merely made a suggestion to Thimmesch some weeks ago when the Gallup Poll came out that he do something like this and without any further encouragement, this is what he came up with—which is an excellent piece. He also told me during the conversation that he really is our friend, wants to help us but that no one here gives him any cooperation or support. He is dying to write some favorable magazine articles since he needs extra money but, obviously, we would have to give him some sort of inside help.

In any event I think he could be cultivated and someone should be assigned the job.

CWC84

W/RN from CWC127

DECEMBER 16, 1970

TO: **Chuck Colson**

FROM: **John Dean**

RE: **Student Travel to North Vietnam—Passports**

Pursuant to your recent inquiry, I asked Tom Huston to review the case law in this area and discuss the matter with the Department of Justice. As you can see, there is a glimmer of a hope that passports could be revoked although, from a prior review of this area of the law, I can tell you it is anything but clear as to the prospects for successfully accomplishing such a revocation. Accordingly, that is why I agree with Haig's analysis that it cannot be done and that it often creates a greater issue in attempting to revoke the passport than merely letting the individuals travel.

CWC122

DECEMBER 17, 1970

TO: **H. R. Haldeman**

FROM: **Charles W. Colson**

RE: **NET**

In response to your memo of November 30th re NET, unhappily, I have to report that there is very little, if anything, we can do to get control of it. Under the statute the federal funds go directly to the Corporation for Public Broadcasting. Budget information and funding data are attached as Tab A.

The only member of the board (see Tab B) that I would dare even to talk to is Al Cole. The corporation is run by John Macy, who was chairman of the Civil Rights Commission and Johnson's personnel man—no friend.

I will have a talk with Al Cole but I suspect, looking at the board, that he would not be able to do very much for us. Frank Pace, a Democrat, is Chairman and also no particular friend.

The only point of attack might be through OMB cutting the budget request. This would be a little heavy handed and could cause an adverse reaction.* Alternatively, some of our friends on the Hill could attack the budget item. All they would do would be to put a little scare into the corporation.

Whoever dreamed this one up created a monster. The one thing we should be certain to do at this point is to clear very carefully the one vacancy on the board to which we can make an appointment.

*HANDWRITTEN COLSON NOTE: "It appears to be contract authority & hence, out of our control."

HRH71
W/RN from CWC1, 127

DECEMBER 18, 1970

TO: **H. R. Haldeman**

FROM: **The President**

With regard to the musical entertainment, I do not want to take the time to make suggestions with regard to numbers that would appeal to the audience. On the other hand, if somebody else doesn't assume this responsibility who has more sensitivity with regard to what an audience will respond to, I shall have to do it.

Last night we had a really first class performer. He had just won the Chopin International competition. The Poles were rioting in Warsaw and in other cities. His selections were three numbers which probably the critics will rave about because they were not familiar to most people except for possibly one of them and were somewhat off-beat and "different."

I am sure Heath probably liked it because he is far above the average listener we have at these dinners. I am somewhat above average because I know something about music and frankly, I was pretty bored because I realized he could have selected numbers that would have communicated far more effectively with that entire audience.

In the future I do not want you to have anybody from Garment's shop or Connie's, who obviously liked this esoteric music, have anything to do with the selection of the numbers. I realize this may have been a rather difficult one to handle because he was expected to play Chopin, but Chopin generally is pretty dull, except, of course, for one number which relates to the earlier point that I was making—the Polonaise. Of course, everybody plays the Polonaise and great pianists usually disdain to play it because it is so "common." But at least audiences understand it and it would have ended the evening on a really high climax. I suppose part of the problem here is that I do not find much of Chopin's music of particular interest to an unsophisticated audience, except for that one number, and I would have suggested to the pianist that he do the Polonaise at the conclusion and then show his versatility by doing some other numbers that would at least have some faint recognition factor for the audience.

HRH229

w/RN from HRH164

DECEMBER 18, 1970

TO: **H. R. Haldeman**

FROM: **The President**

If it is not too jammed, I would like to include the Chief Justice for the evening tonight at the White House. Just call him informally and ask him to drop over for a family party. Also (and neither of these is a must), the

Freemans could be invited because Frost is staying with them. The Freemans are not really necessary, although it would be a nice gesture since they are leaving Washington right after Christmas for London. The Chief Justice would be a very good one to include because our other guests would be impressed by seeing him there.

HRH138, 164

W/RN from HRH138 [correct]

DECEMBER 19, 1970

TO: **Colonel Redman**

FROM: **L. Higby**

Thank you very much for your memorandum regarding the handling of magnetic tape. In addition would you please prepare for Mr. Haldeman an explanation of the process involved with magnetic tape, in other words, what makes a recording on a magnetic tape and what things can affect that recording, i.e. is it OK to have tapes x-rayed; do abnormal temperatures affect tapes; what other things can erase tapes, etc.

Thank you.

HRH70

DECEMBER 21, 1970

TO: **Mr. H. R. Haldeman**

FROM: **Dwight L. Chapin**

RE: **Elvis Presley**

Attached you will find a letter to the President from Elvis Presley. As you are aware, Presley showed up here this morning and has requested an appointment with the President. He states that he knows the President is very busy, but he would just like to say hello and present the President with a gift.

As you are well aware, Presley was voted one of the ten outstanding young men for next year and this was based upon his work in the field of drugs. The thrust of Presley's letter is that he wants to become a "Federal agent at large" to work against the drug problem by communicating with people of all ages. He says that he is not a member of the establishment and that drug culture types, the hippie elements, the SDS, and the Black Panthers are people with whom he can communicate since he is not part of the establishment.

I suggest that we do the following:

This morning Bud Krogh will have Mr. Presley in and talk to him about drugs and about what Presley can do. Bud will also check to see if there is some kind of an honorary agent at large or credential of some sort that we can provide for Presley. After Bud has met with Presley, it is recommended that we have Bud bring Presley in during the Open Hour to meet briefly with the President. You know that several people have mentioned over the past few months that Presley is very pro the President. He wants to keep everything private and I think we should honor his request.

I have talked to Bud Krogh about this whole matter, and we both think that it would be wrong to push Presley off on the Vice President since it will take very little of the President's time and it can be extremely beneficial for the President to build some rapport with Presley.

In addition, if the President wants to meet with some bright young people outside of the Government, Presley might be a perfect one to start with.*

Approve Presley coming in at end of Open Hour **_____

Disapprove _____

*HANDWRITTEN HALDEMAN NOTE: "you must be kidding"
**HANDWRITTEN "H" SIGNIFYING APPROVAL

Dear Mr. President:
First, I would like to introduce myself. I am Elvis Presley and admire you and have great respect for your office. I talked to Vice President Agnew in Palm Springs three weeks ago and expressed my concern for our country. The drug culture, the hippie elements, the SDS, Black Panthers, etc. do *not* consider me as their enemy or as they call it the establishment. I call it American and I love it. Sir, I can and will be of any service that I can to help the country out. I have no concerns or motives other than helping the country out. So I wish not to be given a title or an appointed position. I can and will do more good if I were made a Federal Agent at Large and I will help out by doing it my way through my communications with people of all ages. First and foremost, I am an entertainer, but all I need is the Federal credentials. I am on this plane with Senator George Murphy and we have been discussing the problems that our country is faced with.
Sir, I am staying at the Washington Hotel, Room 505–506–507. I have two men who work with me by the name of Jerry Schilling and Sonny West. I am registered under the name of Jon Burrows. I will be here for as long as it takes to get the credentials of a Federal Agent. I have done an in-depth study of drug abuse and Communist brainwashing techniques and I am right in the middle of the whole thing where I can and will do the most good.
I am glad to help just so long as it is kept very private. You can have your staff or whomever call me anytime today, tonight, or tomorrow. I was nominated this coming year one of America's Ten Most Outstanding Young Men. That will be in January 18 in my home town of Memphis, Tennessee. I am sending you the short autobiography about myself so you

can better understand this approach. I would love to meet you just to say hello if you're not too busy.

Respectfully,

[s/Elvis Presley]

P.S. I believe that you, Sir, were one of the Top Ten Outstanding Men of America also.

I have a personal gift for you which I would like to present to you and you can accept it or I will keep it for you until you can take it.

WHCF:HE 5-1:20

DECEMBER 21, 1970

TO: **The President's File**

FROM: **Bud Krogh**

RE: **Meeting with Elvis Presley,**
Monday, December 21, 1970, 12:30 P.M.

The meeting opened with pictures taken of the President and Elvis Presley.

Presley immediately began showing the President his law enforcement paraphernalia including badges from police departments in California, Colorado and Tennessee. Presley indicated that he had been playing Las Vegas and the President indicated that he was aware of how difficult it is to perform in Las Vegas.

The President mentioned that he thought Presley could reach young people, and that it was important for Presley to retain his credibility. Presley responded that he did his thing by "just singing." He said that he could not get to the kids if he made a speech on the stage, that he had to reach them in his own way. The President nodded in agreement.

Presley indicated that he thought the Beatles had been a real force for anti-American spirit. He said that the Beatles came to this country, made their money, and then returned to England where they promoted an anti-American theme. The President nodded in agreement and expressed some surprise. The President then indicated that those who use drugs are also those in the vanguard of anti-American protest. Violence, drug usage, dissent, protest all seem to merge in generally the same group of young people.

Presley indicated to the President in a very emotional manner that he was "on your side." Presley kept repeating that he wanted to be helpful, that he wanted to restore some respect for the flag which was being lost. He mentioned that he was just a poor boy from Tennessee who had gotten a lot from his country, which in some way he wanted to repay. He also mentioned that he is studying Communist brainwashing and the drug culture for over ten years. He mentioned that he knew a lot about this and was accepted by the hippies. He said he could go right into a group of young people or hippies and be accepted which he felt could be helpful to him in his drug drive. The President indicated again his concern that Presley retain his credibility.

At the conclusion of the meeting, Presley again told the President how much he supported him, and then, in a surprising, spontaneous gesture, put his left arm around the President and hugged him.

In going out, Presley asked the President if he would see his two associates. The President agreed and they came over and shook hands with the President briefly. At this meeting, the President thanked them for their efforts and again mentioned his concern for Presley's credibility.

WHCF:HE5-1:20

DECEMBER 23, 1970   7.00 P.M.

TO: Ron Ziegler

FROM: Charles Colson

RE: Press Calls

I have taken no press calls since yesterday afternoon's flap with the exception of Don Larrabee, who is an old personal friend and who I was able to turn off by telling him, simply as a friend, it was a bad story.*

I also talked to Marty Schram inasmuch as I thought he could do the same thing with him—but more importantly, hoped I would get some leads as to where the story came from. I did.

*[Attached to a copy of article in *Washington Star* of December 23, 1970, by Paul Hope saying the White House has declined to comment on reports that Colson is being considered for chairman of Republican National Committee.]

CWC77
W/RN from CWC127

DECEMBER 23, 1970

TO: Dwight Chapin

FROM: Patrick J. Buchanan

I talked with Paul Hope about the column on Colson—he would not give the source, of course, but from what he said it could have either been White House, but more likely I think there was White House verification of what he got elsewhere—thus the use of "Republican sources" rather than "WH sources." He said that the headline that Colson was at the top of the list was far stronger than the tip he got which was only that Colson was one of those under consideration. He would not identify whom he spoke with—and given the nature of his story, I would think that he is going to be extremely alert about any attempts to get it out of him. We talked off the record, of course; he said he had picked up serious opposition to Colson; he doesn't know whether or not this would dissolve if Colson were named. He said Colson has a lot of enemies.

HRH70

DECEMBER 28, 1970

TO: **Mr. Colson**

FROM: **L. Higby**

Simply for your peace of mind. You recall that tape you gave me the other day has been completely erased and then cut up into very, very small pieces. I doubt if anybody will find it useable again.

HRH70

DECEMBER 29, 1970

TO: **George Shultz**

FROM: **Charles Colson**

RE: **OFDI***

Off and on over the past year I have been involved with the various aspects of our Foreign Direct Investment Program. Some months ago John Ehrlichman and I met with Harold Geneen of ITT and as a consequence of that meeting I assumed the responsibility of preparing a brief for liberalizing controls, which brief John asked me to submit to the new Foreign Economic and Trade operation that was to be set up under you.

The fact that the office has not been formally established has provided a most convenient excuse for me to postpone preparing the memo that John wanted. I do understand, however, that the OFDI 1971 program is before you for review. If it would be at all useful, I would be glad to prepare some material based on all of the data that has been supplied to me by a number of the larger companies which have had particular hardships with the program. There have, in fact, been a number of constructive suggestions to Maury Stans and to several people here in the White House. The proponents of liberalization have, thus far, made no progress with Arthur Burns who I gather is unequivocally opposed to any modifications, even those of a technical nature.

There are some changes—some quite modest—that would facilitate both better administration of the program and relieve severe burdens on some of the major companies, which have been very good friends of ours.

If you would like me to put this together and get it to you, I will; or, if you have someone working on this on your staff, I would be glad to talk to whoever it is.

cc: John Ehrlichman

*[Office of Foreign Direct Investment]

cwc38, 127

1971

The first months of 1971 were the lowest point of my first term as President. The problems we confronted were so overwhelming and so apparently impervious to anything we could do to change them that it seemed possible that I might not even be nominated for re-election in 1972. Early in January it was announced that unemployment had reached 6 percent—the highest point since 1961. In February we became involved in the Laotian operation, which turned out to be a military success but a public relations disaster. In May 200,000 antiwar demonstrators converged on Washington and, led by hard-core agitators who had been openly encouraged by the North Vietnamese, mounted a violent but unsuccessful attempt to close down the government for a day. In June the publication of the Pentagon Papers assaulted the principle of government control over classified documents. The economy was in bad shape and did not look like it was going to get better very soon. On the foreign exchange markets the dollar hit its lowest point since 1949. As the opinion polls registered my losses, they marked Muskie's gains. The Soviets had set back détente by their adventurism in Cuba and the Middle East, and the likelihood of a breakthrough in SALT or the other outstanding issues between us seemed remote. Similarly our tentative approaches to Communist China appeared to have fallen on deaf ears. Without these levers to bring pressure to bear on Hanoi it looked as if the war could drag on indefinitely, although the increasing strength and confidence of the antiwar forces in Congress might mean a sudden termination vote or cutoff of funds at almost any time.

—RICHARD NIXON MEMOIRS, 1978

ADMINISTRATIVELY RESTRICTED

JANUARY 3, 1971

TO: **Gordon Strachan**

FROM: **John Dean**

RE: **Use of the Presidential Seal—
Committee for the Re-Election of the President**

In response to your inquiry, I concur completely with Gordon Liddy's
advice that the Presidential Seal should not be used on posters of the
Committee.

Such a use would not only be contrary to the letter and spirit of
Public Law 91-651 which restricts the use of the Presidential Seal for
nongovernment purposes, but also would be inconsistent with this Administration's policy and the President's strong feelings that the Seal should
not be used in connection with unofficial or political activities.

cc: Gordon Liddy
 Jeb Magruder

JFB2

JANUARY 6, 1971

TO: **H. R. Haldeman**

FROM: **Charles W. Colson**

RE: **Attached Article**

I have reason to suspect that the attached comes from the same source as
the previous hatchet jobs. My skin is thick and I am getting used to this
although I have to admit that every now and then it is a little demoralizing.
It seems to me we all have enough to do here without backbiting.

I didn't come in here to win a popularity contest. I came here to
do a job for the President. I am also not paranoid as you think I am; there
is some justification in my concluding that someone is working very hard
to do me in.

I further realize that little can be done about it, unless someone is
prepared to get rough.

cwc128

JANUARY 11, 1971

TO: The Staff Secretary

FROM: Patrick J. Buchanan

RE: Log no. P1257H, Evans-Novak Column

I talked with Dick Garbett of New Jersey, a Nixon friend, who was at the Elly Peterson party. He denies that such was the mood. As for the individual statements, they are next to impossible to run down, if you don't get the source directly, it seems to me. However, in my explorations I have found a considerable degree of real hostility on the right—about which I memoed the President and Bob. That hostility is rising—I am getting inklings of a Reagan for President move which may be centered in the ACU—their board meets February 5th, the day after the Conservative Awards Dinner. I have my people looking into all this right now—but we have serious problems on the right. Also, from talks, there are some troubles on the left; but my lines there are simply not that good.

PJB1

JANUARY 11, 1971

TO: Mr. Tom Huston

FROM: H. R. Haldeman

Find out as much as you can about the Conservative Spring Offensive you mentioned in your memo of December 31. Also, if there is a meeting to be held, let's make sure that one of our people is in attendance if at all possible.
        Thank you.

HRH70

JANUARY 12, 1971

TO: George Bell

FROM: Charles W. Colson

        1. Would you please put in for Gil Hahn and his wife to be invited to a White House dinner. I think as Chairman of the D.C. Council and as former National Committeeman this should be done. Mayor Washington apparently has been invited on many occasions. Hahn should be considered a co-equal but, as a Republican, he has never been invited—a little bit of reverse discrimination.

        2. Put in a request immediately for Mr. and Mrs. Howard Hunt, Witches Island, Potomac, to be afterdinner guests at the dinner for Juan Carlos. Hunt was the head of all of our intelligence operations in Spain.

His wife is presently the Spanish Ambassador's secretary. Howard is a staunch Republican who is now in PR business on the outside and is beginning to take on a number of special assignments for us of a very sensitive nature. It is very important politically that we let him know he is in the family and this happens to be a unique occasion as far as he and his wife are concerned.

cwc86

JANUARY 14, 1971
ABOARD AIR FORCE ONE

TO: **H. R. Haldeman**

FROM: **The President**

It would seem that the time is approaching when Larry O'Brien is held accountable for his retainer with Hughes. Bebe has some information on this although it is, of course, not solid but there is no question that one of Hughes' people did have O'Brien on a very heavy retainer for "services rendered" in the past. Perhaps Colson should make a check on this.

HANDWRITTEN NOTE BY HALDEMAN: "Nof[ziger], Dean . . . Let's try Dean . . ."

HRH140

JANUARY 14, 1971
ABOARD AIR FORCE ONE

TO: **H. R. Haldeman**

FROM: **The President**

I think it is important that Buchanan take on the responsibility for preparing a briefing paper for Dole periodically. As a matter of fact, he will find that what he prepares for me about every thirty days can be easily used as a basis for briefing for Dole as well. Dole has good intuition but on the other hand Buchanan could feed him a lot of facts that could be very effective and also could give him some material that would not fit for me but that would be very appropriate for Dole to use.

PPF3; HRH140, 230

JANUARY 15, 1971

TO: **Roy Goodearle**

FROM: **Charles W. Colson**

Bob Bennett, son of Senator Wallace Bennett of Utah, has just left the Department of Transportation to take over the Mullen Public Relations firm here in Washington. Bob is a trusted loyalist and a good friend. We intend to use him on a variety of outside projects.

One of Bob's new clients is Howard Hughes. I'm sure I need not explain the political implications of having Hughes' affairs handled here in Washington by a close friend. As you know, Larry O'Brien has been the principal Hughes man in Washington. This move could signal quite a shift in terms of the politics and money that Hughes represents.

Bennett tells me that one of the yardsticks by which Hughes measures the effectiveness of his Washington lobbyist is the important people he knows; that's how O'Brien got on board. Bob Bennett tells me that he has never met the Vice President and that it would enhance his position greatly if we could find an appropriate occasion for him to come in and spend a little time talking with the Vice President. Maybe you can think of a better way to do this than a meeting in the office; maybe there is a social occasion that Bennett could be included in on. The important thing from our standpoint is to enhance Bennett's position with Hughes because Bennett gives us real access to a source of power that can be valuable, and it's in our interest to build him up. Could I have your thoughts on this please?

CWC14, 128;
21 SENATE HEARINGS 9747,
23 SENATE HEARINGS 11123

JANUARY 15, 1971

TO: **Dwight Chapin**

FROM: **Patrick J. Buchanan**

To commemorate the fourth anniversary of the Romney tour from Alaska to Pocatello, Edmund Muskie is leaving for a five day swing in California. Bruce Biossat, to whom I talked last night, has his schedule. Perhaps we can get it down tighter—and perhaps plan a demonstration or two in his behalf. If you want to talk about this—let me know.

PJB3

W/RN from PJB1

JANUARY 18, 1971

TO: **H. R. Haldeman**

FROM: **The President**

One weakness in our research shop is on the humor side. I do not want to employ somebody who will be known as a gag man, but until we do get somebody who has a little more imagination in this area, perhaps we should give Moore this assignment. As time goes on, you or Ray may find somebody else who could be useful in this respect.

This, of course, is a very difficult area for the people we presently have on our research staff because basically they are pretty serious-minded. It would be helpful, however, if I could get a few suggestions from time to time for either humor or just warm color which might trigger an extemporaneous comment or two. Possibly this assignment could be given to Moore as I have suggested, and then he might find someone to take it on more or less full-time, not only for me but for others who must make appearances.

PPF3; HRH140, 230

JANUARY 20, 1971

TO: **Larry Higby**

FROM: **Bill Safire**

RE: **Superlatives**

Somebody is using your name to circulate a supposedly high-priority memo that is an hilarious satire on our public relations efforts.

It is a clever put-on—calling for a "list of superlatives"—but I think you will want to track down and burn the copies in case some historian a century from now sees it and does not realize it was intended to be tongue-in-cheek.

cc: Morgan, Magruder

HRH70

JANUARY 22, 1971

TO: **H. R. Haldeman**

FROM: **Dwight L. Chapin**

Secretary Rogers called to report that he had called Katharine Graham after reading the *Newsweek* "Midpassage" article. He called on a personal basis and told her that the article was inexcusable and a deliberate hatchet job.

This is the first time that the Secretary has called to complain about a *Newsweek* article since he has been in office. He feels it will have some effect.

Kay Graham stated that she had felt that the piece was out of the ball park and she had known that the White House was disturbed by it. She indicated to the Secretary that they were making space available for Elliot Richardson to respond.

It is Secretary Rogers' suggestion that Herb Klein get Stewart Alsop and have him write a response to the article.

The Secretary indicated that he would appreciate my passing on to the President that he called Kay Graham.

HRH71

JANUARY 22, 1971

TO: **H. R. Haldeman**

FROM: **Chuck Colson**

Jay Lovestone has an intelligence network worldwide, which is second only to, and perhaps superior to, CIA's. I talked with Al Haig about this and he confirmed that Jay's intelligence sources are excellent. Al feels that we should be able to put enough credence into the following:

1. Muskie was briefed by Dobrynin before he left the United States, a lengthy, several-hour long session.

2. Kosygin's reaction to him was that he was a nice, pleasant, but "politically naive man." Throughout their meetings Kosygin repeatedly made the point that Americans are too rigid and inflexible. To this, it was reported, Muskie agreed.

3. The general feeling in the Soviet Union is that Muskie would be a "pushover" President. They would be delighted to see him in office.

4. Golda Meir was distinctly unimpressed—felt that Muskie was not well informed and his convictions about the situation in the Mideast very weak. As it was described to me, she was "in no way fooled by him."

5. Lovestone said that the entire trip was a disaster in many respects—and that his information comes from high sources in both governments.

cc: General Haig

cwc128

JANUARY 22, 1971

TO: **Larry Higby**

FROM: **Chuck Colson**

Per our telephone conversation yesterday, enclosed is the information with regard to Time, Inc.

Effective control is exercised by the Luce Foundation, Henry Luce, III, and Roy Larsen. As you will see, they control about 20%, which is more than enough to maintain control.

The advertisers are very significant—all but IBM and Kaiser would be regarded as good friends.

TIME, INCORPORATED

1. As of April 16, 1970, there were 7¼ million shares outstanding.
2. As of April 1, 1969, the Henry Luce Foundation, Incorporated, a charitable corporation, owned 876,069 shares of common stock—12.1% of the company.

Directors of the Foundation

1. Henry Luce III (Director)
2. Peter Paul Luce
3. Mrs. Elizabeth Luce Moore
4. Morris T. Moore
5. Roy E. Larsen
6. Charles L. Stillman

Directors of the Corporation

1. Andrew Heiskell—33,500 common stock
2. Roy Larsen—270,051 common stock (84,612 by Mrs. Larsen)
3. David Brumbaugh—35,000 common stock
4. Hedley Donovan—41,200 common stock
5. James A. Linen—33,000 common stock
6. Henry Luce III—115,000 common stock—(a) Indirect 246,093 owned by various trusts, wife, minor children—(b) 23,283 residuary trust—Total 284,376
7. Charles Stillman—14,000 (1,000 wife)

LIFE MAGAZINE

1. Distillers Incorporated Corporation (Seagrams, etc.)
2. General Motors
3. Philip Morris
4. American Brands (principally tobacco)
5. Ford Motor Company

Note: The automobile companies were off because of strike

TIME

1. Distillers Incorporated Corporation
2. General Motors
3. Magazine network
4. IBM
5. Philip Morris

FORTUNE

1. Kaiser
2. General Motors
3. First National City Bank of New York
4. RCA
5. Dow Chemical

SPORTS ILLUSTRATED

1. General Motors
2. Distillers Incorporated Corporation
3. Rapid America Corporation
4. Ford Company

OVERALL

1. Distillers Incorporated Corporation
2. General Motors
3. Philip Morris
4. Ford
5. Toss-up

cwc14

EYES ONLY

JANUARY 22, 1971

TO: **Chief Justice Warren**

FROM: **Pat Buchanan**

Attached is the full record of the first sitting on the High Bench—we must get together to discuss the transfer of cases.

PJB1

JANUARY 25, 1971

TO: **George Bell**

FROM: **Tom Huston**

Attached is a list of some groups and individuals that may be categorized as unfriendly. I am not sure how much detail you want since to compile a complete list would require volumes—it would be easier to list our friends and assume those not listed were otherwise.

Quite obviously there may be some dispute as to my characterization of Father Baroni's organization.

1. *Think Tanks*

    a. Brookings Institution—Halperin, Gelb
    b. IPS—Barnet, Raskin
    c. Ford Foundation—Bundy, Howe
    d. Potomac Associates—Watts, Cantril

2. *Academics*

    a. Establishment types—Kingman Brewster, Seymour Martin Lipset, Derek Bok
    b. JFK Crowd—Schlesinger, Galbraith, Weisner, et al.
    c. New Left—Noam Chomsky, et al.

3. *Congressional Lobbyists*

    a. Clarence Mitchell—NAACP
    b. Andy Biemiller—AFL-CIO

4. *Organizations*

    a. Common Cause—John Gardner/McCarthy/Goodell/Hickel/Stein
    b. National Welfare Rights Organization
    c. Calumet Community Congress/Baroni operation
    d. Council for a Livable World
    e. National Committee for an Effective Congress

cwc38

JANUARY 26, 1971

TO: **H. R. Haldeman**

FROM: **John Dean**

RE: **Hughes' Retainer of Larry O'Brien**

Pursuant to your memorandum of January 18, 1971, I have conducted an inquiry into the relationship between Larry O'Brien and Howard Hughes. My preliminary findings are set forth below.

First, Lyn Nofziger, who you thought had been doing some work in this area, reported that he had no knowledge of specifics, but had hearsay information of the relationship.

Second, I discussed the matter with Bebe Rebozo who indicated that his information regarding the retainer had come from Robert Maheu, the recently released head of Hughes' Nevada operation. Bebe said that this information had come to his attention at a time when Maheu was professing considerable friendliness towards the Administration, but that it was not documented information. Bebe indicated that he felt that Maheu had possibly retained O'Brien for his services without any direct knowledge by Hughes himself. Bebe is under the impression that Maheu had a good bit of freedom with Hughes' money when running the Nevada operation. Bebe further indicated that he felt he could acquire some documentation of this fact if given a little time and that he would proceed to try to get any information he could. He also requested that if any action be taken with regard to Hughes that he be notified because of his familiarity with the delicacy of the relationships as a result of his own dealings with the Hughes people.

Third, I have also been informed by a source of Jack Caulfield's that O'Brien and Maheu are long time friends from the Boston area, a friendship which dates back to early or pre-Kennedy days. During the Kennedy Administration, there apparently was a continuous liaison between O'Brien and Maheu. When O'Brien left the White House prior to becoming Postmaster General, it is alleged that Maheu offered O'Brien a piece of the Hughes action in Las Vegas (believed to be about a $100,000 arrangement).

O'Brien apparently did not accept the offer. After leaving the government, O'Brien formed a Washington–New York based public relations firm and brought into the firm a man by the name of Claude Desaultels, who had been O'Brien's Executive Assistant while he was Postmaster General. There is some basis to believe that the Hughes-O'Brien financial retainer transactions have been handled by Desaultels and Maheu, with O'Brien one step removed.

Caulfield's source further indicated that Maheu, apparently, was the man who forwarded all Hughes' political contributions, personally, to both parties over the last ten years. It is asserted that he dealt with a man by the name of Vic Johnson (now deceased) who he believed was one of the Nixon fund raisers over the years. I assume this is the Vic Johnson who was with the Congressional Campaign Committee. It is also noted that former Republican Congressman Pat Hillings, who is a friend of Murray Chotiner's, has been retained by Maheu in connection with the Hughes interests for several years. It is further alleged that former FBI Agent Dick Danner has served as an aide to Maheu and Danner is an associate of former Senator Smathers and Danner professes a friendship with Bebe Rebozo. I have not confirmed this latter fact with Bebe. The Clark Clifford law firm has been the Washington representative of the Hughes legal interests in Washington for a number of years.

Fourth, Bob Bennett, son of Senator Wallace Bennett of Utah, has recently left the Department of Transportation to take over the Mullen Public Relations firm here in Washington. Chuck Colson informs me that Bob Bennett is a trusted and good friend of the Administration. One of

Bob's new clients is Howard Hughes. Bennett informs me that there is no doubt about the fact that Larry O'Brien was retained by Howard Hughes and the contract is still in existence. The arrangements were made by Maheu and Bennett believes that O'Brien, through his associate Desaultels, is going to seek to have Hughes follow through on the alleged retainer contract even though Maheu has been removed. Bennett believes that Larry O'Brien has removed himself from the operation in a visible way, but for all practical purposes, is still involved with the former Larry O'Brien Associates which is now run by Desaultels. Bennett believes that Desaultels is collecting on the Hughes contract and placing funds in a reserve account for O'Brien when O'Brien returns to the firm. Bennett also indicates that he will be going to the West Coast to talk about the specifics of his Hughes relationship with Mr. Gay (the man who is responsible for releasing Maheu). Bennett also indicated that he felt confident that if it was necessary to document the retainer with O'Brien that he could get the necessary information through the Hughes people, but it would be with the understanding that the documentation would not be used in a manner that might embarrass Hughes.

As I am sure you are aware, information in this area is somewhat difficult to come by. Bob Bennett appears to be the best source readily available. I have requested that he get back in touch with me when he returns from California. I will report further at that time and shall continue to explore other sources in the interim.

Any other instructions?——

HRH70;
8 SENATE HEARINGS 3370,
21 SENATE HEARINGS 9751,
23 SENATE HEARINGS 11127

JANUARY 28, 1971

TO: **John Dean**

FROM: **H. R. Haldeman**

RE: **Hughes Retainer of Larry O'Brien**

You should continue to keep in contact with Bob Bennett, as well as looking for other sources of information on this subject. Once Bennett gets back to you with his final report, you and Chuck Colson should get together and come up with a way to leak the appropriate information. Frankly, I can't see any way to handle this without involving Hughes so the problem of "embarrassing" him seems to be a matter of degree. However, we should keep Bob Bennett and Bebe out of it at all costs. Please keep me advised of your progress on this and any plans you decide on.

HRH70;
8 SENATE HEARINGS 120, 3369,
21 SENATE HEARINGS 9754,
23 SENATE HEARINGS 11130

FEBRUARY 1, 1971

TO: **H. R. Haldeman**

FROM: **Charles W. Colson**

RE: **Celebrity Program Follow-up**

Going down to the Apollo 14 launch yesterday, I had a chance to talk with the Vice President about Frank Sinatra. The V. P. invited Frank's 82-year-old mother to accompany him, which she did. Both the Vice President and Mrs. Sinatra talked to Frank from the plane—a very nice touch.

Pete Malatesta of the Vice President's staff (Bob Hope's nephew and close friend of Sinatra) told me that Sinatra is "ready" to be invited aboard with us—politically, that is.

We really need to make a basic decision. Our celebrities experts are unanimous in their opinion that Sinatra is the most powerful person in the Hollywood entertainment community—that he has the muscle to bring along a lot of the younger lights. If we are going to cultivate him, as I believe we should (I also recognize the negatives), then he should very shortly be invited to the White House to entertain. Apparently the Vice President's office recommended that he and Hope provide the entertainment for the Governors' Dinner, but I am told that Sinatra's role was vetoed. Perhaps he could be considered for the Colombo Dinner?

Just about everyone that Cashen talked to, including Paul Keyes, believes that Sinatra is the single most important person for us to cultivate in the entertainment community (I believe there are also important ethnic arguments as well).

What we need at this point is a decision. If it is in the affirmative then we need a White House invitation.

cwc128

FEBRUARY 1, 1971

TO: **H. R. Haldeman**

FROM: **Pat Buchanan**

There is a report that Alain Enthoven is to be named head of the Federal Government–Ford Foundation $6 million program, or rather institute, here in Washington on the Environment. If there is one way to destroy all the good work the President has done in two weeks with the conservatives and the Hill, appointment of this Democrat, McNamara Democrat at that, would do it. Understand this is close to fruition. If it is possible to stop it, we should do it. He is not a friend of the President's and will give us trouble until we leave. One of the top McNamara "Whiz Kids," he is anathema to the President's friends on the Hill.

PJB3

FEBRUARY 2, 1971

TO: H. R. Haldeman

FROM: John R. Brown III

RE: Jack Anderson Comments

The January 29 News Summary reported that Jack Anderson, appearing on the Cavett Show, said that he gets a lot of his information from intelligence digests made available to him; also he has RN memos, and private transcripts of White House meetings provided.

On reviewing the above it was noted that we should believe him and a question was raised as to what we are going to do about it.

ss84

FEBRUARY 3, 1971

TO: John W. Dean

FROM: Jack Caulfield

RE: Hughes-Mahew [sic]

I am sure you will find it interesting if you view the last half of CBS's "Sixty Minutes" show last night.* It dealt with the ongoing Hughes controversy, including an in depth interview of Mahew. Also an indication of Intertel's activity in Nevada.

*[Transcript is at 21 Senate Hearings 9915.]

21 SENATE HEARINGS 9756,
23 SENATE HEARINGS 11132

RE: Hazard Posed by White House Staff with Security Officials in Howard Hughes Corporation Interests in Las Vegas

Information has been received from a source believed to be reliable indicating that the Howard Hughes operation in Las Vegas is in serious financial difficulty. Source states that former FBI agent Mayhew, longtime associate of the Hughes operation, had been placed in complete charge of the Hughes hotel and gambling interests in Las Vegas. Source advises that Mayhew has gone completely sour in that close and ominous relationships have been established between Mayhew and well known Mafia figures. Further, that Mayhew and these figures have been criminally skimming huge profits from casino operations for their own benefit. Assertedly, only now are the Hughes corporate officials becoming aware of the extent of the monies being stolen. It is feared that substantial millions are involved.

Source advises that Mayhew is a consummate namedropper and has convinced Hughes corporate officials that he has close, influential contacts at the White House. Assertedly, only now are these officials becoming aware that Mayhew has no influence in this area.

It is alleged that representatives of Mayhew may have picked up hotel and bar tabs for the Presidential advance party in connection with the October 31st visit to Las Vegas. Further, that the same activity may have been involved with the V.P.'s trip there during the campaign.

23 SENATE HEARINGS 11134

FEBRUARY 8, 1971

TO: **Bob Haldeman**

FROM: **The President**

Some time ago I pointed up the importance of unmasking Muskie's moderate image and I urged that this particularly be done in the South.

In talking to Billy Graham Sunday he came at this point very strongly and said that Muskie was becoming increasingly acceptable in the South because most southerners thought that he was a moderate, both domestically and in the field of foreign policy.

The purpose of this memorandum is two-fold:

What happened to the suggestion that I made with regard to getting the true facts across in the South?

And, second, can we put somebody on this project now who will follow through on it effectively?

Dent, of course, can be helpful, but I was thinking of somebody on the PR side like Buchanan. And, of course, everything should be worked through Nofziger and Dole. The Muskie record, for example, voting against both Haynsworth and Carswell; his record of opposition on Cambodia and supporting peace groups generally; and anything else that might be helpful in getting the true picture across in the South should be developed as effectively as possible.

HRH140

W/RN from PPF3

FEBRUARY 8, 1971

TO: **Bob Haldeman**

FROM: **The President**

A good column—which Buchanan's shop might be able to do some research on—is the subject I have come back to on several occasions—the best quotes writing off RN over the years. You could go back to the aftermath of the '62 election and get some real gems by some of the top commentators, columnists, as well as the news magazines on this subject.

In any event, whether a column is written or not, I want the study made for my own purposes because I am going to include this in some material I am preparing for another purpose.

Give somebody the assignment and ask them to report back in about 6o days.

PPF3; HRH140, 230

FEBRUARY 8, 1971

TO: **John Ehrlichman**

FROM: **The President**

In talking to Whitney Young on the telephone, on the call you suggested the other day, he hit me with regard to the appointment of a Black Judge in the South. Apparently, no Black Judge has ever been appointed from the South. He pushes strongly for Ortiz or Ortig (I don't know which name it is) for the Eastern District of Louisiana. He says that Russell Long and our friend the publisher of the *New Orleans Times-Picayune,* Healy, would both support him, and even suggests that Eastland would not oppose him. I haven't the slightest idea as to whether his information has any foundation in fact but it would be well for you discreetly to check this with Kleindienst. I would not run it through the Garment operation.

He also suggests that when Hasty retires we ought to put in Ferguson who is Dean of Law at Howard (or was Dean of Law at Howard). Again, this should be checked with Kleindienst. I understand in that connection that Case has been pushing someone by the name of Ferguson for a judicial appointment. It may well be the same individual. My recollection is that this is the same man who went to Biafra for us last year.

Kleindienst, of course, will understand that we do need some appointments of this type and if we could make one that happened to be suggested by Young and who also was qualified, this would kill two birds with one stone.

HRH140

W/RN from PPF3 and HRH230

FEBRUARY 8, 1971

TO: **John Ehrlichman**

FROM: **The President**

If the busing decision in the Supreme Court goes in the wrong direction, I think we should have a game plan prepared for a Constitutional Amendment. Put some of your boys on this.

PPF3; HRH140, 230

FEBRUARY 9, 1971

TO: Alex Butterfield

FROM: H. R. Haldeman

In seating at State Dinners, the President feels that Henry should not always be put next to the most glamorous woman present. He should be put by an intelligent and interesting dinner partner and we should shift from the practice of putting him by the best looking one. It's starting to cause unfavorable talk that serves no useful purpose.

HRH196

FEBRUARY 11, 1971

TO: H. R. Haldeman

FROM: Jack Caulfield

RE: Anderson Leaks and Alleged Access to Presidential Memoranda

During his recent appearance on the "Dick Cavett Show," Jack Anderson made the following comments:

I have access to intelligence digests because people show them to us.

. . . some of the President's private memos, some of the transcripts of confidential minutes.

Two thirds of the State of the Union Message two or three days before it was delivered.

I can assure you that if the President knew who was leaking these memos, he would be fired tomorrow.

Writer has analyzed the Anderson columns for the three month period preceding the State of the Union leak, as well as discreetly conferring with selected White House staff members. Resultingly, the following observations are offered:

1. Anderson does, indeed, have access to intelligence digests, and he proves it on a daily basis. It also appears his reference to private Presidential memoranda is valid, but most likely when such material leaves the White House and is circulated on an agency level. On more than one occasion, examination of a Presidential quote in context indicates strongly that the leak came not from within the White House, but from the agency concerned with the subject matter.

2. Anderson's comment regarding "some of the transcripts of confidential minutes" possibly refers to verbatim quotes of comments made at White House leadership meetings.

Two of the White House staff members interviewed independently expressed the view that Senator Hugh Scott or a member of Scott's staff is suspect. If you were not aware of this possibility and wish the names of the staff members, they will be furnished to Larry Higby upon request.

Examination of the Anderson columns of January 21, 22 and 23, all of which are concerned with the reorganization of the federal government, apparently refers to his State of the Union comment indicated above.

In this connection, it has been determined that *all of the above information* contained in those three articles appeared in one black bound, working looseleaf booklet. Further, that twelve late copies of such booklet were prepared and forwarded to the Office of Management and Budget from the Domestic Council under strict security conditions in advance of the Anderson leak.

An examination of the subject document, along with a studied review of the subject Anderson columns, indicates that the book was made available to Anderson, most likely in its entirety.

Domestic Council members interviewed make a valid case for the leak to be pinned on OMB, Human Resources Section. I, personally, wish to reserve judgment until more evidence is at hand. It has been brought to my attention that George Shultz has been apprised of these suspicions, and has taken the position that a "smoking out" type investigation would be inadvisable.

Resultingly, I do not feel it proper to proceed with this aspect of the inquiry, unless or until you so advise.

Having looked at this matter with all its serious implications for the future, I feel it advisable to immediately suggest that all of the section chiefs on the White House staff be briefed by your office with a view towards a minimization of leaked material and comment. I also suggest that an overt firing of a person directly connected with a leak would go a long way towards making the ability of the Andersons of the world to gain White House information both difficult and hazardous.

Please advise.

3 SENATE HEARINGS 1101

FEBRUARY 11, 1971

TO: **Dwight Chapin**

FROM: **Charles W. Colson**

I note that the CBS executives are tentatively planned for Friday the 19th. You will recall the little problem we had before and I suspect it will arise again. Of all the networks it is probably more important that I be present on CBS. For one reason, I have developed a good personal relationship with Paley which has been very helpful to us on a number of occasions. Secondly, Stanton is the guy with the most far-out ideas.

The President would have been caught on a couple of technical questions in the ABC meeting if I had not been present; a danger which is even greater with CBS.

I am simply anticipating a possible problem.

cwc128

FEBRUARY 12, 1971

TO: The President

FROM: **Patrick J. Buchanan**

RE: **J. Edgar Hoover**

While this may appear unorthodox coming from me, I think the President should give serious consideration to replacing Mr. Hoover as soon as possible—for his good, for our good, for the country's good. First, Mr. Hoover has already passed the peak of his national esteem. At one point I would guess that ninety-five percent of the nation felt he was doing a phenomenal job, he has had nowhere to go but down; and he is going down steadily. He cannot possibly reverse the trend in my view; the attacks on him are mounting and mounting and the deterioration in his standing with the country are necessarily going to diminish in face of these attacks. His own place in history is secure; but, with each of these new picayune battles in which he involves himself, his place is being sullied. It would be a crime if these battles at the end of his career brought his end of office at a time when it was widely desired that he go.

Mr. Hoover stands today with the American people as an almost unvarnished symbol of what is right with American law enforcement. He must retire in a matter of a few years anyhow—and now in my view will be better for that symbol, for his place in history, than anything hanging on a handful of years could help accomplish.

Secondly, Hoover is under terrific heat; and instead of his former practice of ignoring his critics, he is responding, which is what they want. On more and more of these quarrels, Mr. Hoover is not totally right—and comes off as something of a reactionary. Among young people, especially, who do not have anything near the esteem for him as do their parents, he is increasingly becoming a villain; and he is tied totally to us. McGovern is making him a focal point of attack—this is certain to continue; and on one of these issues one of these days soon, one can guess that the public is going to think Mr. Hoover wrong and McGovern right.

Finally, if Hoover goes now, he can be retired in full glory, at a time of his own choosing. If we wait, it will be something like the departure of General Hershey which had all the appearances of a forced departure.

Again, I would think we would want Hoover's replacement—the President's man—in that job, before the choice of such a man becomes an issue in 1972—as Fortas became an issue because of the timing of his replacement.

There is the possibility—although looking down that roster on the other side I don't see any of them even in our league—that we may not win in 1972. God forbid that we should then have a Ramsey Clark or some politically oriented Democrat placed in that job for the next fourteen years.

My strong recommendation would be to retire Hoover now in all the glory and esteem he has merited and deserved; and not let him—for his own sake and ours—wind up his career a dead lion being chewed over by the jackals of the Left.

PJB4

W/RN from PJB1

FEBRUARY 15, 1971

TO: **Lyn Nofziger**

FROM: **Dwight L. Chapin**

I noticed in the President's News Summary this morning that in Senator Dole's criticism of the television coverage given Republicans he states, "Walter Cronkite can't even pronounce Republican."

This is strictly my own feeling. However, taking on Walter Cronkite cannot do us any good whatsoever. It is like attacking the Lord himself.

I can see the merit in keeping the heat on the networks, but I think to take on an individual such as Cronkite may be a mistake. You might want to check around to see how some others feel about this and then once you've reached a consensus of opinion, pass it on to the Chairman. Anyway, I would like to add my comment for what it is worth.

cc: Mr. Colson

CWC82

FEBRUARY 18, 1971

TO: **H. R. Haldeman**

FROM: **Charles W. Colson**

RE: **Jim Suffridge**

On November 24 I sent you a memo regarding the possibility of bringing Jim Suffridge in here as a consultant on Labor matters, copy attached. It is my thought that he would be principally valuable as a political activist in recruiting friendly labor leaders.

You quite correctly told me to clear it with Shultz, Hodgson and

Usery. I talked with Shultz who said he thought highly of Suffridge, but that I should clear it with Hodgson and Usery. I have talked with Hodgson several times. Personally, he thought it was a great idea, but said he would have to "sell" it to Usery. As you will see from the attached memo of February 13 from Hodgson he still hasn't succeeded.

In my opinion, this is all getting a little silly. This was Suffridge's idea—he wants to help get the President reelected. He would be working strictly in a political area and not in any way cutting into anyone's jurisdiction. Bill Usery has been in ten meetings with the President at which I have been present and the President consistently builds him up to the skies. I do the same thing at every opportunity, as does Hodgson. He has no reason to be insecure about anything. He is probably the most influential Assistant Secretary in government. The fact is, however, he just cannot be a political operator for us and doesn't want to.

We parade business leaders through here daily and no one at Commerce gets sensitive about it. We have farm groups in all the time and Hardin thinks it is fine. I realize that Usery's role is unique, but I don't think it should be so unique that we don't do the things vitally necessary from a political standpoint.

In short, if the Suffridge proposition makes no sense on its merits, we shouldn't do it; if it is a good idea as part of our effort to mobilize groups for political support, then we should simply make the decision and not let personal sensitivities get in the way. Usery has gotten over completely his insecurity concerning me, which at one point was very serious. I am positive the same thing would happen with Suffridge, who is a much nicer guy to get along with than I am. Maybe this can be settled in the meeting that you have indicated you wanted on labor, but if you want to wait for that please let's get the meeting held. I think Suffridge will soon give up on us.

cwc77

W/RN from cwc128

FEBRUARY 19, 1971

TO: **Pat Buchanan**

FROM: **H. R. Haldeman**

We've obviously got a good thing going in the law and order field in that article in *The New Yorker* this week regarding the *Black Panthers.* I assume you've read it.

Is there something we can do to get some more mileage out of the author? Shouldn't he get a Pulitzer Prize for reporting and for his diligent research into the failure of the press to accurately handle this story in the beginning?

I'm sure many other things will occur to you, but this is one point where we were getting a pretty bad working over a couple of years ago and now the tables have been totally turned. Let's see if we can get the working over reversed also.

CWC84

ACTION MEMORANDUM

FEBRUARY 22, 1971

We need to get a petition started in McCloskey's district demanding his resignation on the basis of his calling for the impeachment of the President.

The petition should read that "we condemn Congressman McCloskey for the highly irresponsible and ill-advised action that he has taken and the statements that he has made. He has cruelly betrayed the trust of those who elected him," etc.

HRH

cwc13

FEBRUARY 24, 1971

TO: **H. R. Haldeman**

FROM: **Charles W. Colson**

RE: **Section 315 / Campaign Spending Bill**

In response to your memo of February 19, I can only say that everything we do has risks. The risk of trying to defeat repeal of 315 and getting caught is to me much less serious than having section 315 repealed.

One way we might get a little bad publicity—the other way the Democrats get out from under their debt. To me, the choice is rather clear.

cwc128

FEBRUARY 24, 1971

TO: **Ray Price**

FROM: **Jon M. Huntsman**

RE: **Future Anecdote**

The recent letter to the President that quoted a story has been recommended as a good anecdote for future use.

The statement goes as follows—I am reminded of the Quaker lady awakened in the dead of night by a thief in her house. She took her husband's shotgun and sneaking downstairs surprised friend thief. "Sir," she said, "I wish thee no bodily harm but thee is standing right where I am going to shoot."

cc: Mr. Haldeman
Mr. Butterfield

ss85

FEBRUARY 24, 1971

TO: **Mr. Butterfield**

FROM: **H. R. Haldeman**

You should know that one of the guests at the Governors' Dinner last night was seen to complain bitterly about the condition of the food which he was served. Mr. Ehrlichman has notified me that every single bit of his dinner was cold (I presume that his complaint doesn't extend to the ice cream which I assume he would accept in a cold state without objection).

Perhaps we have a problem here in the preparation or serving of the food and then again, perhaps we simply have a problem of Mr. Ehrlichman not eating fast enough, or being seated in a distant part of the room. In any event I'm sure you'll want to be aware of this situation.

cc: Mr. Ehrlichman

HRH196

FEBRUARY 24, 1971

Dear Dean Abel:*

As an alumnus of Columbia School of Journalism, I wanted to drop this strong recommendation that the next issue of the *Journalism Review* re-run the splendid piece on the Panthers, done by Edward Epstein for *The New Yorker*. Many papers have already confessed their sins on this one; and the kind of research that Epstein did, destroying one of the pervasive and pernicious myths about this Administration, did a genuine service I think to journalism and the country.

Best regards.

Sincerely,

Patrick J. Buchanan
Special Assistant
to the President

*[Letter to Elie Abel, dean of the Graduate School of Journalism, Columbia University]

PJB1

FEBRUARY 25, 1971

Dear Fred:*

Pursuant to our conversation this morning, I have prepared a rough draft expressing some of the thoughts we discussed. It is marked Draft #2. Draft #1, also enclosed, was prepared by one of our speechwriters, but I don't think it quite hits the mark.

I am sending you both drafts, however, because I am sure that you will want to put all of this in your own words and can write it better than I or the speechwriter have done. Also enclosed is a mailing list which I would suggest, although once again you may have ideas of your own. This list is drawn from our records of prominent business leaders, NAM Directors and the Business Council.

I am sure that you have all the facilities to get this out but if you need help let us know. Of course, it would be best if the letters are individually signed and maybe you will want to personalize them in some way—probably with some reference to your position as former Chairman of the Business Council. In any event, this will give you something to start with and we can discuss this by phone tomorrow at your convenience.

Your help is deeply appreciated.

Sincerely,

Charles W. Colson
Special Counsel
to the President

*[Letter to Fred Borsch, chairman of the board, General Electric Company]

cwc128

FEBRUARY 26, 1971

TO: **The President**

FROM: **Charles W. Colson**

In accordance with your request, Fred Borsch, former Chairman of the Business Council, is sending a personal letter to about 400 top business leaders, pointing out the courage that it took for you to support Davis/Bacon, asking for their support of your action and urging them to help fight rising prices. The letter is being mailed this weekend and Borsch is releasing it to the *New York Times.*

For your information, Harry Van Arsdale of New York called to express his support for your decision, saying that if he had been Chairman of the Democratic National Committee, nothing would have delighted him more than for you to have imposed a freeze on construction wages. In short, he believes that your action was right and politically sound.

cwc128

FEBRUARY 26, 1971

Dear Kay,*

Just a note to thank you sincerely for a most worthwhile day yesterday.

Your dinner party was delightful and the lunch was most helpful to me.

I asked our news summary people to go back in the old *Post*s and find me the Lou Harris poll story on the President and Senator Muskie. They report to me this morning that they are unable to locate it.

Would it be too much trouble for someone on your staff to give my office a call and provide us with the date and page where that Harris poll ran?

Thanks again for a very good time.

Yours sincerely,

John D. Ehrlichman
Assistant to the President
for Domestic Affairs

*[Letter to Katharine Graham, publisher, the *Washington Post*]

cwc69

MARCH 1, 1971

Dear John:

Thank you for your nice note and for calling us again on the Harris poll, which our guys thought we had run. You were right, as I'm sure Gene Patterson has told you. This is recent enough so we can still easily run it, and we will.

The question of the use and play of polls has been somewhat of a problem, and this example will make us take another look at the procedure. It was a goof, as the poll is a good one. It was not a plot, I hope you know.

This sort of thing is another good reason for keeping the channels open. Another is that I enjoyed seeing you and Jean.

Sincerely,

Katharine Graham, President

cwc69

MARCH 1, 1971

Dear John:*

When you were here for lunch some of us thought you were wrong in your impression that the *Post* had omitted a Harris poll of Feb. 22 that showed President Nixon leading Senator Muskie in his positions on 10 major issues. We were wrong and you were right. (The Feb. 22 poll we printed was the Harris finding of the previous week which showed them fairly even in personality traits.)

You may be sure the Nixon lead on issues will appear right away in the *Washington Post,* and that steps have been taken to assure that Harris and Gallup findings will be handled with care here by editors newly designated to keep track and guarantee balance.

I wish you would accept my invitation to call more such things to my attention. It really is wrong for you to be doing a slow burn about something that I would want to give a quick fix plus a permanent repair if I could know about it.

Sincerely,

[s/Gene]

cc: Mrs. Graham

*[Letter to John Ehrlichman from Eugene C. Patterson, managing editor, the *Washington Post*]

cwc69

MARCH 1, 1971

TO: **Len Garment**

FROM: **Charles. W. Colson**

It has come to my attention that you have been involved with Sandy Trowbridge in setting up a Foundation-type operation for long-range studies. This, I gather, would be under the auspices of the NICB.

This might create some problems inasmuch as we have been trying to expand and build up the operations of AEI. In a sense, while they might not be competitive substantially, we would be drawing money from many of the same sources.

I don't know if the rumor I have heard is true or not, but if this is something that you have been involved in, you and I need to talk about the coordination of our efforts in this area. I don't think it is a problem but I think it is something that should be focused upon.

cwc14

w/rn from cwc128

TELEPHONE CALL RECOMMENDATION

MARCH 2, 1971

Name: Frank Sinatra
Recommended by: Charles W. Colson, Henry C. Cashen, and the Vice President's Office

Background

A. Sinatra has the makings of another Al Capp; he is thoroughly disenchanted with liberals, as evidenced by his support of Reagan and his current friendship with the Vice President. Most of our Hollywood friends believe that Sinatra is the most influential celebrity in the country because if he goes, so go many other prominent figures, particularly new young stars.

B. On Friday it was announced that Sinatra would receive the Jean Hersholt Humanitarian Award. Bob Hope was the first recipient of this award. It is a prestigious award within the celebrity circle.

Talking Points

A. Congratulate Sinatra on the award.
B. Tell him not to play golf with the Vice President.

cwc128

MARCH 4, 1971

TO: **Henry Cashen**

FROM: **Charles W. Colson**

Pearl Bailey performed at the Radio & TV Correspondents' dinner last night. A good half of her performance was to tell the stories of her visits with the President, describing how she got the pin that she was wearing, telling about her role as Ambassador of Love, etc. It was one of the most pro-Nixon performances I have seen anyone put on.

Come up with some gimmicks like getting her a special passport or a new Presidential pin that is solid gold which the President could send her with a note, since the last one is probably worn out. This pin might have her name on it.

This thing has got to be kept alive and fueled—it is too good to let go.

cwc128

MARCH 5, 1971

TO: **H. R. Haldeman**

FROM: **Jon M. Huntsman**

RE: **RN in Iowa**

The March 3 News Summary stated that RN feels his one-day trip to the Midwest to sell his "New American Revolution" went well, even if it did

draw a strange coalition of demonstrators who, in RN's view, were ama-
teurs. He seemed undaunted by the pickets and the snowballs they threw
at him. But *some of his Aides were a little concerned about the construction workers and farmers among the ranks of obscenity shouting anti-war
forces.*

With regard to the [italic] portion of the above paragraph, it has
been stated that the staff should never show concern in situations such as
these.

Thank you.

cc: Mr. Butterfield

ss84

MARCH 6, 1971

TO: **Dwight Chapin**

FROM: **Charles W. Colson**

I recommend a brief, private meeting between the President and Gerry
Ford; probably only Timmons should be present. The President has told
me that he thinks Ford can become a more articulate spokesman for us.
For some reason Ford, himself, is reluctant to do this. We had a terrible
debacle yesterday when we sent camera crews up to his office and he
refused to issue the statement that he had earlier told Timmons he would
issue.

I think all it would take would be ten minutes alone. If he felt the
President wanted him to carry the ball publicly on some of our key issues,
Ford would do it. He is a good soldier but he, I think, needs just a little
inspiration from the President.

For example, as a matter of practice, he will not call networks in to
his office. He doesn't mind giving a blistering speech, but he just won't try
to publicize it. I am afraid only the President will be able to get this
message across to him and it is my strong feeling that we should be
building Jerry up for a spokesman for these kinds of things.

cc: Bill Timmons

cwc128

DRAFT

MARCH 8, 1971

TO: **H. R. Haldeman**

FROM: **The President**

When I saw Arthur Burns at the Church Service today he said that he
wanted to see me. I want you to drag your feet on this and to have a good
talk with Shultz before arranging it. When the meeting is to be held, I
want plenty of lead time on it. In fact, you ought to talk to Shultz and
Connally and possibly with McCracken as well, and let them determine
when the meeting with Arthur should be held. Under no circumstances
will I see him alone. You should be present. I have begun taking a hard
line with him and I'm not going to let him come in with some of his
'doomsday' predictions and force me off of it.

HRH140
_____
W/RN from HRH140
[correct], 230

MARCH 8, 1971

TO: **Dr. Kissinger**

FROM: **The President**

One project I want to put great emphasis on is the completion of the Pan
American Highway all the way from the United States to the tip of South
America. I want a report as to where the project presently stands and what
we are going to do to carry it out.

     You will find that the bureaucracy is like molasses as far as this
project is concerned. First of all, they do not like highways and dams etc.
They prefer programs that provide, as they say, for the "needs of the
poor," i.e., education, health, etc. For example, only by my pressure were
we able to get through the Pan American Highway down through Central
America. It was going to take twenty-five years when I took my trip
there in 1955 and I came back and got Eisenhower's support in pushing
it through in five years. It actually finally took ten, but at least that was
some improvement. I want to have a similar sense of urgency in getting
this highway finished and I want no nonsense from the bureaucracy on this
point. We will transfer funds from other projects to this one and get this
done so that this will be one part of the Nixon legacy (and a very vital
project where the country is involved) which we will get accomplished
while we are here.

HRH140, 230

MARCH 10, 1971

RE: **William J. Casey Nomination**

Aside from Senator Proxmire's rumored postmortem vow to take this nomination to a Floor fight, there is another development which demands our attention. Eileen Shanahan has returned to her old haunts at the SEC, and today reportedly stated that Casey "is a crook and I want to stop him" and said she was preparing an article for possible publication on Sunday. It appears that she is still working on a connection with the Re case.

In order to insure we have not overlooked something and so that we may be able to anticipate a possible additional charge, answers to the following should be obtained as soon as possible:

1. The gravamen of the Re case was that the Res, as specialists on the American stock exchange, would seek to have a security listed and then, as its specialists, manipulate the price. Therefore, it seems imperative that we determine whether Casey or his firm or any company with which he was associated was ever handled on the American exchange by the Res. Likewise, it should be determined whether there is any connection between Thornton and/or Rothchild [sic] & Co. and the Res.

2. There may be an attempt to draw an analogy between the Re case and the handling of the securities of one of the corporations in which Casey was involved. In this regard, the testimony in yesterday's hearing indicated that the Kalvar market price was extremely high in relation to its book value. Since Mr. Casey has made a great deal of money on his Kalvar stock, we must ascertain whether Thornton and/or Rothchild acted as a specialist in the trading of Kalvar stock at any time.

3. Although the preceding relates to the Kalvar stock, it should also be ascertained whether Thornton and/or Rothchild ever acted as a specialist in the stock of any company with which Mr. Casey was involved, and also whether Thornton or Rothchild ever was instrumental in attempting to have any such stock listed on any exchange.

4. At the hearings Proxmire asked Casey whether it was not true that he and Thornton had discussed the Re case in a recent telephone conversation. Mr. Casey replied in the negative. It should be ascertained what Thornton said to Proxmire and what Thornton said to Casey in his recent conversations.

5. Is there any past or present relationship between Mr. Casey or his firm and Milton Gould, Esq.?

_____
                                                                        JWD2

MARCH 12, 1971

TO: Henry Kissinger
      H. R. Haldeman

FROM: Patrick J. Buchanan

RE: "Full generation of peace"

Repeatedly in recent weeks, the President has been hitting the theme of
a "full generation of peace," which now seems to be moving from a vague
hope to a near commitment, with RN's "our last war" statement to Sulzberger. While this has some appeal, surely, to a war-weary people, there
are serious dangers in this.

     The first is for the President's place in history. The United States
has only partial control over whether we are going to war again—the
other half of the debate belongs to those who may desire to test our
commitments. By making these statements—especially the "our last" war
statement—the President is leaving it to some dictator, or Communist
government, to make a fool of him, by limited aggression against one of
our treaty allies. What is the impact of this kind of statement on those who
are our allies, and those who may be our potential adversaries[?]

     Secondly, while a remote fear, I am concerned that the President's
"last war" statement may turn out to be as foolish as Chamberlain's "peace
for our time." We are promising something which we alone cannot deliver.

     Finally, this repeated talk of "a full generation of peace" and again
"our last war" tends to induce a sense of serenity and calm and even
complacency among the American people which (a) hardly seems justified
by the situation and (b) is certain to undercut our own arguments for more
dollars for strategic defense. We ourselves seem to be contributing to the
ongoing psychological disarmament of the American people, which itself
is the major obstacle to our getting the dollars needed for maintaining
parity and preventing Soviet superiority.

PJB3

W/RN from PJB1

MARCH 12, 1971

TO: Larry Higby

FROM: Charles W. Colson

The enclosed memo to my file has been written to protect my skin.* Don't
bother Bob with this—it is relatively minor unless the President wants to
know why I didn't do what he told me to do.

     It is typical of the problem I have, but I can live with it. As we get
operating down the road I will simply do these things without informing

Herb because it is obvious what will happen. At this point I do not want to risk a confrontation.

Do you agree that I am handling this correctly? Do you think I should go ahead anyway? Do you think I should mention it to Bob? It all seems damn trivial and I *don't want* to escalate a Klein controversy at this time.

*[The memo to which Colson refers is in CWC128.]

CWC128

MARCH 15, 1971

TO: **The President's File**

FROM: **Charles W. Colson**

RE: **Meeting with CBS Executives,* March 9, 1971, 4:00 P.M.**

At the outset of the meeting the President asked that no notes be taken. He told the CBS Executives that this would be a completely informal, candid discussion of anything they wanted to bring up and problems, of course, relating to the broadcasting industry.

The President said at the beginning that he appreciated CBS running the Colombo Dinner on "60 Minutes," that he thought it had gone very well and hoped that the public found it informative and useful. The CBS officials seemed very pleased that the President was aware of this— they said they thought it was an excellent program which was well received by their audience.

The CBS officials seemed somewhat reluctant to begin the discussion. They said they would like to hear from the President whatever he might have on his mind. There followed a general discussion of business problems and particularly general broadcast industry problems. The President explained the purpose of the meeting again—explained that he had met with ABC and that he would subsequently be meeting with NBC.

There was then a discussion of a possible one-on-one program. The President said that he would be glad to have anyone that CBS wanted to do the interview, that he was soon going to do Howard K. Smith and that would be followed whenever it seemed appropriate by a similar one-on-one interview with CBS. There was no response from the CBS Executives.

The President then talked somewhat about press conferences and the fact that he did not want to use prime time all the time because he felt that this would be an unfair burden on the networks. He did say that at his next office press conference he would have a camera so that the networks could use it for news program purposes.

*[Participants included William Paley, Chairman of the Board; Frank Stanton, President; John Schneider, Executive Vice President; Richard W. Jencks, President of the Broadcast Group (all owned and operated stations); Bob Wood, President, CBS-TV; Richard Salant, President, CBS News.]

There followed a brief discussion of Fairness Doctrine problems—the President said, as he did to the ABC Executives, "All I ask is that you are as fair to them (the Democrats) as you were to us when we were on the outside." He made reference to the fact that any change in policies ought to be prospective and not retroactive—that if we lived on the outside with certain rules, those rules shouldn't be changed now because we happen to be on the inside (this was an obvious reference to Stanton and his attempt to start a loyal opposition series). The President looked directly at Stanton during this part of the meeting but Stanton said nothing.

There was a discussion regarding environmentalists. The President said he thought they had gone too far in many instances—that they were challenging everything, that we do live in a civilized society, that some people want to go back in time when men lived primitively and that was really a very unhappy existence for people. He said he had no sympathy with the environmentalists who were demanding equal time on the air for every reply to every issue. This led to some discussions of the present concern that the Fairness Doctrine will be applied to advertising. The President asked what could be done about this, and I explained that with the exception of Nicholas Johnson the FCC seemed to be very solidly on the side of the broadcasting industry on this issue. Herb Klein explained the status of the case which is presently in the courts in California. The President said that he would be very conservative in his view here, would agree with the industry completely and would, of course, do whatever he could to help. Paley said he wished the President could represent CBS as their lawyer.

The President then talked at some length about the need for a healthy industry, the dangers of over-regulation, the proliferation of stations (citing L.A.), the need for the industry to be fair itself in its treatment of all issues. He used a very effective analogy saying that he always feels with respect to government employees that he must bend over backwards to be certain that he is being fair, inasmuch as government employees are denied the right to strike. He made the point that the broadcast industry itself should be extremely concerned that it is being fair so that government regulation is not imposed on it. He pointed out that the industry had a special duty in view of its somewhat privileged position.

The political broadcasting bill came up early in the discussion with the CBS Executives asking the President where he stood on the issue. The President talked at some length on why he vetoed last year's bill—that it was discriminatory, that it did not apply to any elements of the media other than TV, and that it was largely a very unenforceable bill. The President said that Colson was working on the subject—that they should stay in close touch with him and that he expected that there would be an Administration position. I talked for a few moments about the present status of the bill, some of the problems with it and restated Bob Dole's position that if section 315 is to be repealed that the repeal should apply to all political candidates—not just to the Presidency. Stanton said that

CBS, of course, agreed with this position (Stanton's testimony in the Congress, however, referred only to removing the equal opportunities doctrine of section 315 for Presidential elections). Both Stanton and Paley seemed to be pressing the President on the point of 315 as to how he personally felt. The President said that this was, of course, a political issue and that he doubted that any legislation would come out inasmuch as the Democrats would always press for something that was for their advantage and the Republicans, of course, would want something to their advantage. He said this was an extremely difficult area in which to legislate and that he doubted that the parties could get together in view of the conflicting political positions. I once again talked about the difficulty of enforcement, particularly with respect to labor unions and also the difficulties that the FCC would have in administering section 315 if it were repealed. The President picked this point up and followed it through. We never really gave an answer to their question regarding our views on 315; eventually they dropped the issue.

The President asked the CBS Executives how they had found their relationships with Dean Burch. They were highly complimentary saying that he was one of the best chairmen that they had ever dealt with—that he knew his job thoroughly—that he was very fair and always took all viewpoints into account. Stanton said he had heard that Burch was leaving. The President asked me whether this was so and I said there had been such a rumor but that I did not think Burch would leave. The President said he thought Burch had been an excellent chairman, that he wanted him to stay on and then asked me to arrange to bring Burch in for a meeting with him (this had a very significant impact on the CBS Executives). The President said that he had never really met with the FCC; he had them in once for a brief discussion but that he wanted to have a more extensive discussion of broadcasting industry problems with Burch.

Stanton raised the question of the satellite issue which is now before the FCC. He said that CBS had wanted its own satellite, but really now was only concerned that satellite service would be available; they would prefer it however not connected with AT&T because they would be back in the same monopoly situation and have the same difficulties which they now have in dealing with simply one source for transmitting their signal. The President asked that I look into this problem and do what I could to be helpful.

There was considerable discussion about the effectiveness of Tom Whitehead's office. The President asked whether Whitehead was thoroughly staffed, whether he had good people and whether he was doing what he should be doing. I indicated that I thought he was doing an excellent job—that he was studying the overall communications problems, the impact of executive branch policies on the future of communications. Both Stanton and Paley stated that they had good relationships with Whitehead—that they had met with him frequently; they did not comment on whether he was adequately staffed or doing the things that needed to be done. The President asked that I check into this, and also at that point told the CBS Executives that I was his "expert" in this field and that I was a lawyer. Paley had earlier made reference to my meetings with him in New York. The significance of the President's reference was not at all lost on the CBS Executives. Stanton looked visibly taken aback by this comment and I am sure he fully understood its implication.

The President asked whether CBS, like ABC, was concerned with the cable question. Paley replied that they were really not in the same way, that they were endeavoring to spin off their subsidiary which was in the cable business but they had thus far been held up by the FCC and prevented from doing so. They expressed the hope that the Viacom (the subsidiary) spinoff would soon be approved because if it were not there would be a chaotic impact on CBS (the President and I had a subsequent discussion about this point).

The President also raised the license renewal problem saying that he understood the difficulties which many stations had and that he came down on a conservative side of this issue; he thought it was important that there be continuity of ownership in order to provide the necessary capital investment to provide service to the public (CBS has had its problems in this regard, but made no comments).

On a number of occasions during the meeting the President made the point that he was on "their side" on the business policy and economic issues. He said that we may often differ on coverage and we may often take issue with what CBS reports—that is understandable and that has always been the case—but "I want you to know that I come down on your side on these issues because I believe that a strong and healthy industry is important for the country."

There was a discussion about the Frazier/Ali fight. CBS said they had no objection—they could understand why something like this would be done closed-circuit, because there was so much more return to the promoters. They expressed apprehension that the Super Bowl contract when it is up for renewal will go the same route and the public will be denied the benefit of seeing it.

The President impressed Bill Paley very much by recalling golf games which he had played with Paley at the Links. The President said he remembered the outstanding food and turned to Paley and said "Will you please tell the chefs at the Links that I do recall what marvelous food they served and give them my best. Tell them that I miss it." Paley was very flattered by the President's recollection and the personal comments that were directed to him both on this occasion and at other times during the meeting.

As the meeting was about to adjourn the President said he wanted to take just a few minutes to talk about some general philosophical concerns. He then talked at great length about the need for the U.S. to maintain its role in the world—why it is so important to our future security, why the wave of neo-isolationism is wrong. He used the SST as an example, pointing out that a great nation must continue to forge ahead, even taking many risks and even using resources that people would argue should be used in other ways—for example, in improving the ghettos and life here at home. He said that a great country, however, cannot falter. It must make explorations in space; it must build new, technologically difficult aircraft; it must continue in a posture of a world power, which in our case is a power for the forces of peace not for the purpose of aggression. He spelled out in some depth the arguments of the isolationists and then took issue with each of them, pointing out why he felt they were misguided, albeit honestly misguided.

Throughout the meeting the CBS Executives, with the exception of pressing for an answer on section 315, really skirted all of the difficult issues. It seemed that the President was having difficulty in drawing them into conversation. They really raised very few points on their own—seemed reluctant to engage in a real "give and take" like that which occurred during the ABC meeting. This left the President in the difficult position of having to keep the conversation going for the entire period of the meeting. They were very restrained in their attitude; obviously very pleased with the President's comments on the business side of the broadcasting industry and equally impressed with several points during the meeting when the President took a very firm line on what have been controversial issues between the Administration and CBS. They never at any point attempted to take issue with him. Overall they seemed very weak in their presentation, making it difficult to maintain a good discussion.

cwc128

EYES ONLY

MARCH 16, 1971

TO: **John Ehrlichman**

FROM: **Charles W. Colson**

I have just been informed that the Justice Department has under serious consideration an antitrust action against the three major networks. Apparently this has been under study by the Antitrust Division staff for several years, but there is some indication that it is being prepared for prosecution. My source was not very precise as to the imminence or even the probabilities.

In view of the problems we have had with the networks I wonder if we want to launch a major antitrust action. It would be viewed as merely an extension of the Vice President's charges and further repression.

I happen to be an advocate of hitting these guys and hitting them hard whenever their excesses become obvious, but I think we should, on this one, think through very carefully whether it is a wise strategic move.

Is there any way we can get a handle on this? I emphasize that I do not know how reliable my information is.

cc: John Dean

cwc82, 128

MARCH 23, 1971

TO: **John Dean**

FROM: **Charles W. Colson**

I would like to check out the tax-free status of the attached organization. It seems to me that there is a real question, based on their literature, as to whether this is a tax-free educational operation or a lobbying group.

bcc: George Bell   *GB:* In connection with blacklists that we, from time to time, compile this group should definitely be included. You can see what a group of bomb throwers it is. Would you also find out from Bill Marriott how the Marriott Foundation ever got included as a sponsor in this. I don't think that Bill would mind a call. Would you simply inquire— just say you are curious because of the composition of the group—that is, the rest of the sponsors.

cwc128

MARCH 24, 1971

TO: **H. R. Haldeman**

FROM: **Charles W. Colson**

RE: **Senator Jackson**

FYI. My intelligence (Lovestone) is that Senator Jackson and LBJ met recently. Ironically, the President tried to call Jackson while Jackson was meeting with LBJ. I understand that the call was completed.

I am told that LBJ promised Jackson his support for the Democratic nomination and, in fact, told Jackson that he was the only candidate that he, LBJ, could support against the President.

I passed this on to the President by phone today.

cwc128

MARCH 24, 1971

TO: **John Dean**

FROM: **Charles W. Colson**

A person by the name of Lenny Davis is in charge of the youth section of the Muskie headquarters. I am told that he has a long record of involvement with Communist Party affairs in New Haven. Would you please have an FBI check run on him. Be certain that they do a thorough one and let me know as soon as we have the result.

Tickler—April 24

cwc128

MARCH 26, 1971

Dear Lou:*

    I hope you will treat the attached with the utmost confidence. As you will see, apparently the evaluation board picked Opinion Research both on technical and cost grounds.

    I send the enclosed to you because I would like you to have the full story, but we don't like to get the White House into these things, as you know, so please treat it accordingly.

    This is a subject that you and I should discuss when we have the meeting that we've talked about.

    Best personal regards.

Sincerely,

Charles W. Colson
Special Counsel
to the President

*[Letter to Louis Harris, of Louis Harris and Associates, Inc.]

cwc69

APRIL 5, 1971

Dear Mr. President:

    Your thought of me in sending me *The Turning Point* was most kind indeed. I was most appreciative and grateful. The story of those two campaigns before the Eleventh Amendment is a gripping one, which I have read again with great interest. Jefferson is to me a baffling figure. The

Louisiana Purchase was a great and bold act. He had enormous talents—a real eighteenth century man, even more gifted than Franklin. But he has always seemed to me as much interested in words as in the reality behind them. The more solid, less glittering qualities of General Washington are what it took to get the country started.

What a treat you gave me in an escape from pollution and home rule—perhaps, the same thing—to battles long ago and a romance in the press. Why don't you promote the same tender feelings between one of your press secretaries (or are they all married?) and Mrs. Graham as Mr. Smith inspired in Miss Bayard?

Most respectfully,

[s/Dean Acheson]

The President
The White House

PPF188:
MATERIAL REMOVED
FROM PRESIDENT'S DESK

(Handwritten letter)

APRIL 7, 1971

Dear Mr. President—

Before you go on tonight I want you to have this note to tell you that—no matter what the result—free peoples everywhere will be forever in your debt. Your serenity during crisis, your steadfastness under pressure have been all that has prevented the triumph of mass hysteria. It has been an inspiration to serve.

As always

[s/H(enry Kissinger)]

PPF10

APRIL 8, 1971

TO: **Chuck Colson**

FROM: **H. R. Haldeman**

RE: **"Natural Enemies"**

While many of our "natural enemies" are individuals or groups, there is also a lot of mileage to be made out of attacking general issues which the public is well aware of such as the bureaucracy, taxes, organized crime, drugs, left-wing radicals, etc. These are problems that many of our Domestic programs are trying to solve, yet this fight is not directly related to the President in people's minds.

There is a great opportunity to position the President as a strong opponent of these problems with a concerted effort on our part. Please get a reading as to which of the issues mentioned above and any others you wish to add can be attacked with the best results from the public relations standpoint. Then let's come up with a plan and implement it to really "lay into them."

Due April 17

cwc128

APRIL 12, 1971

TO: **John Dean**

FROM: **Pat Buchanan**

Can you tell me offhand the status of the Director of the FBI—is he now an appointive figure, who can be shifted out by the party in power? In other words, were we to replace Hoover now—could the Democrats waltz in and throw our guy out and put their guy in—in 19 months?

PJB1

APRIL 16, 1971

TO: **H. R. Haldeman**

FROM: **John Dean**

RE: **Candidate Protection—'72**

In response to your recent request for information regarding the status of candidate protection, I would say that virtually nothing of moment has occurred since my memo of January 13, 1971. Set forth below are the only informational matters of significance regarding candidate protection.

I. *McGovern Incident.* In February the Secret Service received a telephone call from Gary Hart, identifying himself as Senator McGovern's campaign manager. Hart reported that while the Senator was driving his automobile from his residence to the Capitol his front car windshield was struck and shattered by an undetermined object. Hart requested that the Secret Service investigate the incident. The Secret Service was reluctant to do so, advising that this was a matter for the Metropolitan Police or the FBI. However, upon prodding by Hart, the Service did examine the vehicle and conducted an investigation. At one point Hart stated to the Secret Service that he desired a ballistics examination to determine if the object which struck the windshield was a bullet. He further said that if it was determined that the object was a bullet, definite steps should be taken by the Secret Service to provide McGovern with protection. The Secret Service brought the car to the FBI laboratory and the FBI and Secret Service concluded that the object was not a bullet and most likely a rock. This information was conveyed by the Secret Service to Hart and no further requests have been made.

II. *Secretary Connally meeting with Secret Service on March 29.* The Secret Service has provided Secretary Connally a full briefing on the matter of major candidate protection. I understand they discussed budgetary aspects and manpower requirements. I further understand that the Secretary indicated that he has had informal discussions with the four members of the Advisory Committee (which has not yet been formally convened), namely, Congressmen Albert and Ford and Senators Mansfield and Scott. The Secretary also indicated that he was reluctant to formally convene the Advisory Committee too early, fearing that they would grant protection to their colleagues as they were requested. The Secretary also indicated that it was his feeling that protection might start earlier than the Secret Service had anticipated. The Secret Service has planned to provide such protection about March of 1972.

III. *Preparations for Advisory Committee Meeting.* As soon as the Secretary directs, Treasury officials are prepared to present the four committee members with appropriate briefing documents indicating the legislative history of the statute and setting up procedures for what should subsequently occur, such as the appointment of a fifth member. The White House has also suggested some names to Treasury as candidates for the fifth member of the Advisory Committee.

I have requested the Treasury Department to keep me fully advised on this matter and notify me of any activity or planned action.

JWD2

APRIL 19, 1971

TO: **H. R. Haldeman**

FROM: **Patrick J. Buchanan**

RE: **Political Memorandum, 1972**

Congressman McCloskey is now traveling at times in the company of Jerry Cooke and Charles U. Daly. Have uncovered nothing about the former, but the latter is an old New Frontiersman, a John F. Kennedy man, a Bobby Kennedy man—and a protégé and close friend of Larry O'Brien. This raises up interesting possibilities. Is the Democratic Party providing staff assistance and/or financial assistance to the McCloskey Campaign[?] If so, we can discredit McCloskey as not a man of principle, but as a party traitor, who is trafficking with New Frontiersmen to defeat a Republican President. Good stuff can be made out of this—damaging to McCloskey's budding effort.

If we could find out where the money is coming from, to McCloskey, we might build a case that he is simply a pawn. Anyhow, we should have some of our political people looking out for this sort of thing.

PJB3

W/RN from PJB3

APRIL 21, 1971

TO: **H. R. Haldeman**

FROM: **Patrick J. Buchanan**

RE: **Vietnam Veterans**

I understand that the Vietnam Veterans, opposed to the war, have been given until four-thirty to vacate the Mall, where they are camped. I trust we are not going to use force to throw them out, if they refuse to go. They are getting tremendous publicity; they have an articulate spokesman; they are being received in a far more sympathetic fashion than other demonstrators.

I know we have Burger's go-ahead—but my understanding is that these guys are leaving Friday the 23rd, anyway—they are *not* the guys we want the confrontation with. Those guys are coming in Friday and staying until May. My recommendation is that we have a top Justice guy go over to the Mall, and tell them we have an order for them to vacate, but that we will do a deal. If they agree to demonstrate peacefully, and leave on Friday, after the rally, then they can stay there.

Seriously, the "crazies" will be in town soon enough; the whole public is antipathetic toward their violence; and if we want a confrontation, let's have it with them—not with the new Bonus Army. This is not a recommendation that we not be tough—but that we pick the most advantageous enemy from our point of view.

PJB3

W/RN from PJB1

APRIL 21, 1971

TO: **Dick Howard**

FROM: **John Andrews**

RE: **RN Human Interest Story Program**

I thought you might be interested to see the kind of thing I am gleaning in my staff interviews. The attached package includes all stories I have collected so far. The effort is proceeding rather slowly because I keep getting other assignments that take priority.

Leadership, Courage

RN's take-charge instinct runs deep. One night Chuck Colson was in RN's car as they drove home from the Broad Street law office. Traffic halted abruptly and they could see that there had been a car-truck collision up ahead. The two drivers had gotten out and were fighting in the street. Turning to comment on the scene, Colson found RN's seat empty—he was already striding up to the front of the line of stalled cars. He physically pulled the combatants apart, talked to them until both calmed down somewhat, and coaxed them back into their vehicles. When Colson expressed mild amazement as the car got moving again, RN's attitude was, "What did I do that was unusual?" (COLSON)

Principles

RN attributes much of his own success to self-discipline—a quality he also assesses carefully in taking the measure of other men. Recently when the name of a certain prominent politician, with obvious Presidential aspirations, came up in conversation, RN commented, "He just doesn't have the self-discipline to make the grade as a Presidential candidate. He is the kind of man who can't turn down that third drink on the night before an important meeting." The reference, of course, was not to any weakness for alcohol, but simply to the man's inability, as the President judged, to sharpen himself and "point for the big ones"—to marshal all his actions toward a chosen goal. (COLSON)

Work Habits, Sports

The President has said that he derives most enjoyment these days from activities that relate directly to the Presidency, and there is evidence of this in a sort of finite relaxation span—just the reverse of an attention span—which close associates observe in him. Roger Johnson remarked that even during the Nixons' January 1971 stay in the Virgin Islands, RN could only swim, relax, and chat on the beach for limited periods—then he would abruptly turn to the telephone or papers for a "work break." The same pattern appears when the President is watching televised sports. Johnson says only the closest contests really rivet him to the action; in most he will continually move away from the set for snatches of business.

(JOHNSON)

Humor, Sports, Staff Members

How hard it can be to say what the boss likes to hear . . . RN walked up to a group of staffers one day at Camp David and remarked with some pleasure that he had just shot a hundred and twenty. "Ah, your golf game is improving, Mr. President," Henry Kissinger ventured diplomatically. The President rejoined, "I was bowling." (SAFIRE)

Personal Contacts, Minorities

Walking on Fifth Avenue or Park during trips to New York as Vice President, RN would sometimes stop to have his shoes shined by one of the Negro teenagers along the Avenue—less for the shine's sake than for the boy's. He liked to question them offhandedly about their interests and aspirations and always tried to encourage them to keep after their schooling and self-improvement. When a boy impressed him as particularly industrious and sincere, he signalled quietly to Roger Johnson who knew by custom that the Vice President wanted a $5 bill slipped to the boy. It was RN's way of offering a little extra help without grandstanding or embarrassing the shine boy. Johnson adds that RN always repaid him the five later, without reminder. (JOHNSON)

GENERAL PR MEMOS, CWC 13

APRIL 27, 1971

TO: **John Ehrlichman**

FROM: **The President**

Wiley Mayne, the Congressman from Iowa, has introduced a bill to change the name of National Airport to Eisenhower Airport. I think this is an excellent idea. See whether we can do it without doing it through legislation. If not, see if we can give a little push to the legislation.

PPF3; HRH140, 230

APRIL 27, 1971

TO: **John Ehrlichman**

FROM: **The President**

Could you get me the number of people who were in the OPA* at the peak period during World War II?

*[Office of Price Administration]

PPF3; HRH140, 230

APRIL 27, 1971

TO: **Henry Kissinger**

FROM: **The President**

What progress have we made in getting the Peace Corps out of the Marianas?

HRH140, 230

APRIL 27, 1971

TO: **Henry Kissinger**

FROM: **The President**

Moynihan's idea of buying the entire Turkish opium crowd is one that seems intriguing. I realize there are problems here, but would you have a check made to see what, if anything, could be done. Connally seems to like the idea, provided it does not have other foreign policy implications which would militate against it.

HRH230

EYES ONLY

APRIL 27, 1971

TO: **Patrick J. Buchanan**

FROM: **Jon M. Huntsman**

RE.   **Right Wing Leader**

The weekend News Summary stated that *Kransnaya Zvezda,* the Soviet military's paper, has mentioned Patrick J. Buchanan as one of several "prominent right-wing leaders" whose appointment to the White House staff favors the "growth and consolidation" of the Ku Klux Klan.

The President read this with interest and stated "Shame!—you didn't tell me!"

Thank you.

ss81

EYES ONLY—NOT FOR DISTRIBUTION

APRIL 28, 1971

TO: **John Ehrlichman**

FROM: **The President**

When we were meeting with Elmer Bobst I was not doing so simply for his benefit. I am convinced that we are falling here into what is too often the major failing of our Administration—doing things well but not packaging them in a way that will get us major credit.

And in this instance, I am not sure that Elmer is far from the mark when he says that the plan we have adopted for putting the whole thing in NIH, which has from my personal experience over twenty-five years been usually a hopeless boondoggle, is the wrong approach to take on cancer research. I realize that the professionals like David, Shultz, et al., will come down hard for doing it the traditional way.

I think we should re-examine the whole subject on two grounds. One, on the merits. I seriously doubt if a man with a—It's the old story that those that can do, and those that can't teach. George Shultz is one of the few notable exceptions to this very sound rule. I am inclined to think that what is needed here is a good, well-organized layman in charge of the whole business. This is not meant to be at all critical of Ken Cole who must be expected to come up with the usual, routine way of handling problems within the government, and ordinarily his approach is the right one. In this case, however, I really think we need a new approach, not only in appearance, which I will discuss in the next paragraph, but in fact. As far as appearance is concerned, the arguments are overwhelming for setting up a special organization for cancer research alone. In fact, you may recall that HEW and NIH fought our hundred million dollar cancer research right down to the last minute before we put it in the State of the Union. The reason they fought it is that they want free funds to throw around any place they think is appropriate at a particular time. In other words, they simply want to continue to fund the bureaucracy to go along its merry way to do as it damn pleases. Ted Kennedy is on a sure-fire public relations and political wicket here when he comes out for a special approach with a special agency. If we are going to spend the money, the least we can do is to get some credit for having a new approach. We will not get it if we simply put another hundred million dollars out in the bowels of NIH, and have the program lost forever as far as public view is concerned, under the management of a good, routine research scientist from Stanford who won't have the slightest idea as to how to get anything across from a public relations standpoint.

What we must realize is that this is primarily a public relations problem. We knew this when we put it in the State of the Union, and now we must follow through with the approach, and I want you to follow through and reopen the whole subject, having in mind some of the principles I have discussed in this memo, and that I mentioned in our conversation with Elmer.

As far as Kaplan is concerned, give him a job in the Bureau of the Budget if he still wants to come to Washington, or put him over in NIH where they have plenty of slots for a man of his capabilities. But don't put him in charge of something like this where we need a manager, a public relations expert and a good, tough political man all wrapped into one.

HRH230

W/RN from HRH140

APRIL 29, 1971

TO: **H. R. Haldeman**

FROM: **Charles W. Colson**

RE: **Selling of the Pentagon**

You might enjoy reading the Commission's decision on the Selling of the Pentagon case. As Dean Burch indicated to the President, there was no basis to find "deliberate distortion" as defined in the law. But the mere laying out of the facts, as he has done, clearly shows the deplorable editing techniques which CBS used. This should be considered as a serious black eye for them, although they will play it as if they were cleared.

cwc128

EYES ONLY—HIGH PRIORITY

APRIL 29, 1971

TO: **Van Shumway**

FROM: **Charles W. Colson**

The attached is a fascinating decision which the FCC reached yesterday. While they do not find "deliberate distortion" as defined by the law (they really couldn't do so, because they have to rely on extrinsic evidence and must show malice), they nonetheless give CBS a real rap on the knuckles by showing that they did indeed fudge in editing the tape. I don't know whether this has moved on the wires or not, but it is a good story and should be gotten out. If you get it out, be sure not to have it in any way traceable back to the White House, and be sure whoever writes the story really sticks it in to CBS as they deserve. Note also Dean Burch's separate opinion in which for the first time he publicly takes on Nicholas Johnson.

You can really have some fun with this one.

cwc128

MAY 4, 1971   1:30 P.M.

TO: **The President**

FROM: **John Dean**

RE: **Demonstration Status Report—May 4, 1971.**

Description of Current Activity: Demonstrators complied with traffic regulations, and marched four abreast in an orderly manner down the sidewalks to the Department of Justice; currently assembling peacefully on sidewalks at 10th Street at the Department of Justice. MPD in area in large numbers. Large number of spectators.

Estimated Number of Demonstrators: Four thousand on the route of march from Franklin Park and/or on the sidewalks of 10th Street at DOJ.

Total Arrests: 685 arrests (majority: disorderly conduct and misdemeanors, i.e., jaywalking and failure to move).

Anticipated Activity: Demonstrators have requested permission to proceed to Reflecting Pool area with contingent of SCLC. Department of Justice has refused to grant such permit. Demonstrators will be permitted to remain on sidewalks at DOJ as long as crowd remains peaceful.

Information of Note: Live bomb found suspended underneath Taft Street Bridge; deactivated by military bomb squad.

JFB1

MAY 4, 1971   5:00 P.M.

TO: The President

FROM: John Dean

RE: Demonstration Status Report—May 4.

Description of Current Activity: Arrests of demonstrators at DOJ continue; offenders are dancing and singing and offering no resistance to arrest, and the situation in the area is calm. No significant activities in any other part of the city.

N.B. The activities at DOJ have been covered extensively by news and the media.

Estimated Number of Demonstrators: It is estimated that there are 600–800 demonstrators yet to be arrested at DOJ.

Total Arrests: An estimated 1,785 demonstrators have thus far been arrested and processed.

Anticipated Activity: Meetings of two demonstrator groups are scheduled for 7 P.M. this evening in local churches (St. Stevens; Dumbarton), to discuss future plans.

Information of Note: All federal agencies report attendance levels as normal or above normal for this date.

Military troops from posts outside of the Washington area are scheduled to be returned to regular duty stations in phases, until the total of such troops remaining in this area is reduced to 3,000 by 6 P.M., Wednesday, May 5. Troops on alert that are normally stationed in the Washington area (approximately 4,400) will be used as necessary until the cessation of current demonstrations in the city.

FBI and MPD now indicate that the "live bomb" previously reported to have been found at the Taft Street Bridge was a bogus, harmless device.

JFB1

MAY 6, 1971

TO: Bill Timmons

FROM: Charles Colson

Enclosed is the draft resolution which we really need to have one of our tougher guys in the House submit. If the House is not going to be in, this would still be worth a press release enclosing the resolution and saying that it would be filed next week. Obviously, it should be a joint resolution and should include Members of the House like Ronald Dellums, Bella

Abzug, Father Drinan, Parren Mitchell and, to keep everything bipartisan, Paul McCloskey (?).

If this is put out as a press release a day in advance, for example, put out this afternoon with tomorrow's release date, I will guarantee extensive coverage.

Let's for a change be demagogues.

[MAY 6, 1971]

Joint Resolution

Whereas, the capital of the United States has been the focus of disruptive protest, and

Whereas, the protesters have attempted unlawfully to prevent employees of the United States Government from carrying out their appointed duties, and

Whereas, same disruptions have sought to prevent the lawful workings of the Congress of the United States, and

Whereas, the protest leaders maintain that they will continue their disruptive activities until the United States has signed a dishonorable treaty with the enemy in North Vietnam, and

Whereas, continued activities would be contrary to the orderly Constitutional procedures of this government, and

Whereas, the Congress of the United States has solemn responsibilities of governance as the central legislative body in our Nation, and

Whereas, because of Congressional responsibilities, it is the symbolic center for our democracy,

Now therefore be it resolved that in order to maintain decorum, order and proper procedural process within the capital of the United States a Select Committee of the Senate shall be appointed to ensure that further contravention of the law be halted, and

Be it further resolved that because of their great ability to communicate with young people and because of their continued support, encouragement and rapport with those who dissent against our Nation's policies, Messrs. Bayh, Hughes, Humphrey, McGovern and Muskie are hereby appointed and directed to serve on said Select Committee of the Senate.

cwc14

MAY 6, 1971

TO: **Ron Ziegler**
      (Attention: Diane Sawyer)

FROM: **John Dean**

RE: **The President's Taxes**

Because of the recent media coverage of Governor Reagan's personal tax
situation, it is likely that you may get an inquiry regarding the President's
taxes. While I personally feel this is none of the press's "g.d." business, you
may feel some response is necessary. Accordingly, I have set forth below
the necessary information for you to frame your response.

Federal Taxes

—The President pays federal income taxes just as any other citizen.

—The President's salary, established by Congress, is fully taxable as income. The President's salary is the sole source of his income, with the
exception of a small amount of interest he receives on bonds and savings
accounts.

—Any discussion of the specifics of the President's tax returns (e.g., deduc-
tions, etc.) is unwise and unnecessary.

State Taxes

—The President pays property taxes in both California and Florida, where
he owns homes.

—The President is legally domiciled in California, where he votes, but he
is not required under California law to pay state income tax in that he
receives no income from California sources.

—The President, while in office, is in a position similar to that of a man
in the military; he is not required to pay California income taxes while he
is temporarily not living as a full time resident in California, and not
receiving any income from a source in the state.

                                                                    JWD2
                                                   _____

MAY 7, 1971

TO: **Peter Flanigan**

FROM: **Charles Colson**

Just a reminder with respect to your recruiting this weekend of top-level
business people for the Accuracy-In-Media operation. I think Mahoney
would be an outstanding Chairman. We should also be looking for people

who are both big advertisers and sufficiently well-heeled to put a little money in, which we are going to need.

If you pick up the recruits on the business end and advise me next week, I will then attempt to get Milton Friedman, Smith Hempstone and perhaps Pat Moynihan. Please let me know.

CWC14

W/RN from CWC129

MAY 8, 1971

TO: **Chuck Colson**

FROM: **Jon M. Huntsman**

RE: **The Left Also Plays Games at the State Level**

The May 8 News Summary stated that California's Attorney General was asked to investigate how Governor Reagan's income tax return was "leaked." The student radio announcer who broke the story invoked her "journalistic privilege" and refused to divulge her sources. What still is not known—and Reagan says he has no intention of telling—is what kind of "investment losses" he suffered to result in his owing no state income tax for 1970. Confronted by a mounting controversy that threatened his political popularity, Reagan reluctantly summoned newsmen to read a statement. Reagan left hurriedly after reading the statement and refused to answer questions.

The statement was made—"that even at the *State* level there are those who will play the left's game."

Thank you.

cc: H. R. Haldeman
    A. Butterfield
    J. Ehrlichman

CWC14; ss83

SUNDAY, MAY 9, 1971

TO: **H. R. Haldeman**

FROM: **The President**

RE: **White House Correspondents' Dinner**

Before you get reports from some of the naive members of our staff who were present, let me give you a hard-nosed appraisal of the White House Correspondents' Dinner, the mistakes our staff made in scheduling me at the dinner, and some lessons for the future.

You will recall that I noted that the reporters receiving the awards were way out left-wingers. Obviously, anybody could have done a little checking to find out why they were being honored at this dinner. Every one of the recipients was receiving an award for a vicious attack on the Administration—Carswell, wire tapping, Army surveillance, etc. I had to sit there for 20 minutes while the drunken audience laughed in derision as the award citations were read.

I'm not a bit thin-skinned, but I do have the responsibility and everybody on my staff has the responsibility to protect the office of the Presidency from such insulting incidents. I'm sure that Ziegler, Klein, and possibly Scali and Price approved this charade because it would demonstrate that the President was a "good sport." I do not have to demonstrate that. I have done so many times over the past 24 years. As one of the few friendly reporters told me after the dinner, he had been attending Gridirons, White House Correspondents' and other dinners for 24 years and that this was by far the worst, but that he had never seen one in which the audience was friendly or the program, as far as the press participation was concerned, was not directly or indirectly aimed at embarrassing me.

In this instance there simply was no excuse for my arriving until after the awards had been given. I at least had the satisfaction of rising and shaking the hands of the award winners as they went by my table, but I could have arrived as I told you and Ron in the office at the time that Jack Southerland was being introduced and have been there for enough of the boring 3-hour program as it was. As far as this part of the memorandum is concerned, I simply want our staff to do a better job of checking out such occasions and clearly apart from my own personal feelings which are very deep, indeed, on this subject, just assume that it is your responsibility to defend the Presidency from such barbed insults.

The dinner, as a whole, was probably the worst of this type I have attended. The audience was drunk, crude and terribly cruel to Jack Southerland when he followed Lisagor's very clever speech with the kind of plotting [sic] attempt to humor which you would attempt from him. The only note in it that was gratifying from our standpoint was when John Mitchell needled Lisagor into introducing Police Chief Wilson when he mentioned him in a speech. Wilson got a good hand—not of course from the reporters—I looked around and saw several of them deliberately turning up their noses when he was introduced, but from some of their guests who were present. Typical of the attitude of the audience was that when the comic Arte Johnson had any joke aimed at the Democrats, they pretty much sat on their hands. On the other hand, they completely broke up even when Lisagor got off one of his less effective lines and most of them were very effective. Also typical of the attitude was when the country music girl singer opened with "On the Fighting Side of Me"—from then on she was dead before this audience. I was the only one at the head table who cheered except for a couple of Cabinet Officers.

My remarks, thankfully, were brief and were accepted as well before this disgusting group, as you might expect. However, I don't want any of our naive staff members to give you any impression that as a result of my going there and sitting through three hours of pure boredom and insults, I thereby proved I was the "good sport" and therefore may have softened some of the press attitude toward the President. On the contrary, the type of people who are in the press corps have nothing but contempt for those who get down to their level and who accept such treatment without striking back. That's one of the reasons they have some respect for Agnew. Incidentally, I think Agnew is right in not going to such events and I do not want any pressure put on him to do any such events in the future. I will get to this subject in greater detail a little later in this memorandum.

What I want everybody to realize is that as we approach the election we are in a fight to the death for the big prize. Ninety-five percent of the members of the Washington press corps are unalterably opposed to us because of their intellectual and philosophical background. Some of them will smirk and pander to us for the purpose of getting a story but we must remember that they are just waiting for the chance to stick the knife in deep and to twist it. I just feel that Ziegler and his people and even more, of course, a newcomer like Scali, haven't the slightest idea of what we are up against. Like Ray Price, Len Garment and Herb Klein, they always bemuse themselves by thinking that "Well, if we just keep trying we may win some of them or at least soften them." Forget it. They will neither be won nor softened by giving them the opportunity to insult the President and more important the opportunity to insult his office as they did so at the White House Correspondents' dinner.

David put his finger on the situation pretty well when he pointed out the difference in reaction now from what it was two years ago shortly after we were in office. Then, with no election coming up, they had no choice but to get along with us. Now, they are out to get us and we simply have to start growing up and being just as tough, ruthless and unfeeling as they are or otherwise they will sink us without a trace. David also answered completely the argument that I get from Klein, Ziegler and even Moore, that by going before these groups and making a pleasant little speech at the end—"We always win." David pointed out that there will never be anything to surpass the piano duet act that Agnew and I put on at the Gridiron last year, and yet, he said, "Within 24 hours after you did that, the press was more vicious than ever and there was hardly anything said about the effectiveness of the act, except five or six paragraphs down in stories when some reporter would lamely admit that it had been an impressive performance." Also, Agnew's excellent performance at the Gridiron this year did him no good whatever with the members of the Gridiron who were present, or, for that matter, with their guests—most of whom were part of the intellectual elite—who, like a bunch of sheep, go along with what seems to be fashionable at the moment. This brings me to several conclusions:

1. Under absolutely no circumstances will I attend any more dinners of this type in the future. I will not go to the Gridiron, the White House Correspondents', or the Radio and Television Correspondents' Dinners next year. I want you to inform Ziegler of this now because I know they make their plans well in advance. We need no excuses for my not going. I simply do not care to go and also I do not want any pressure whatever put on Agnew to go. He is to go only if he wants to go.

2. Next year I will attend the Photographers' Dinner for personal reasons of which you are aware. Also, I will attend the Alfalfa because I want to attend once during the four-year period in case I don't have an opportunity to do so at a later time.

3. Beyond the Alfalfa and the Photographers, I will do no dinners of this type *whatever*. This, of course, includes the lesser varieties of such events—Women's National Press Club, the National Press Club, the Negro National Press Club, etc. etc.

I realize that you will get some strong arguments to the effect that in an election year, we might just gain something by doing all these dinners, or at least relenting on one or two of them. This, of course, is sheer sentimental nonsense and has no relation whatever to the hard facts of political life. When I am not there these clowns are going to have a lot harder time getting top-flight entertainment. Also, they're going to have a hard time to run their dinners with just the Democratic candidates there. Let's let them be shown for what they truly are—a third house supporting the Democratic candidates. Now I realize that an argument can be made that we do have some friends in the press and that we hurt them as well as our implacable enemies by following the line that I am suggesting. The way to handle that problem is from now on for us to deliberately invite our friends to events where it will be a compliment for them to come. For example, in the future for White House Dinners, White House Receptions, Church Services or any other event in which I participate, I want *no one whatever invited* from the press or radio unless he is a friend of ours or, at the very worst, neutral (i.e., a wire service reporter). By friend, of course, I do not mean someone who writes positively all the time. I do mean someone who is not in the other corner. Perhaps the best thing to do here is to simply submit the list to me because I'm afraid that even though our press boys have been around for almost 2½ years, I should not expect them to know as much about these people as I have learned in 24 years. And of course, hope springs eternal among people who have been in the press corps or are associated with it as is the case with Ziegler, Klein, Moore, Scali, Price, et al.

Applying this same reasoning to a broader area, I want my schedule arranged so that as far as Congressmen, Senators and other officials are concerned, only those who are friends or who might become friends or supporters should be put on the schedule. This is exactly the way Johnson and Kennedy both played it and we're going to play it the same way. I don't want any more suggestions made to me that we have to invite some left-wing Democrat down in order to prove that we are "fair." The press is going to charge us with being unfair even if we had the whole Democratic National Committee in for a reception! Let's give them good reason to make that charge if they're going to make it anyway.

In other words, you and I both know that the President can't see everybody. All of those I really ought to see among the group that could be considered friends or potential supporters before the elections in 1972 I would only scratch the surface [sic]. From now on we are going to play the game my way in this respect. I have gone all out in seeing the elite of the Business Council most of whom are not our friends and the various other way-out groups like that miserable collection of volunteers I saw in the Dining Room a couple of weeks ago. Unless it is an event like the Negro Congressmen, which I, of course, can well understand has to be put on for very practical purposes, I simply am not going to have time taken and the Office of the Presidency degraded by events or appointments which can only have the effect of giving our opponents an opportunity to go out and laugh behind our backs and talk about how really naive and stupid we are. As far as the press is concerned, you can reassure Ron, and of course Scali and others who may raise the point, that the way I will handle the press is through the medium of the press conference which will be an arms-length proposition, and we shall have more, of course, as we go along if our interests will be served thereby.

Incidentally, with regard to the press, I want to cut down very sharply on the number of occasions when press people come into the office for "photographic opportunities." From now on there will be *one a day only.* The other times it will be a photographic opportunity for photographers only or for Ollie Atkins only in case the writing press insists on coming in with their own photographers. I want this handled ruthlessly, exactly as I have laid it out here. There is no appeal from this decision— I've thought it through and have concluded.

HRH164

W/RN from HRH140

MAY 10, 1971

Dear Mr. President:

I was tempted to phone you Saturday night after the dinner but feared I might disturb your household. Your fortitude and forbearance in the face of gross rudeness by your hosts will always have my unbounded admiration. In my many personal observations of the press corps over the past 18 years this was one of their worst performances. To respond as you did with dignity and charity is a mark of your qualities and I suspect it was not lost on all those present.

It is no comfort but it is perhaps instructive to remember how the press treated your predecessors, and particularly Washington and Lincoln. Having been reading closely some of the events from 1789 to 1800, fairness to the present day press corps compels acknowledgment that they are now slightly less savage, less sadistic and less cruel than 150 to 200 years ago. So viewed, this is progress of sorts.

I repeat that Saturday night marked a new measure of your capacities that will in time be recognized, and enlarged my respect and esteem.

Sincerely,

[s/Warren E. Burger]
Chief Justice
Supreme Court of the United States

PPF6

MAY 11, 1971

TO: **John Dean**

FROM: **Fred Fielding**

RE: **J. Edgar Hoover**

Jack Anderson's column indicates that Mr. Hoover has collected more than $250,000 in royalties from three books researched and ghostwritten for him by FBI employees on government time. The column indicates that royalty checks were made out to Hoover personally, not to charities, but noted that the J. Edgar Hoover Foundation records indicate no royalty payments or cash donations were received from Mr. Hoover. The column further reports that Mr. Hoover received $50,000 from Warner Brothers for the movie rights to his book, which was never produced into a movie, and suggests that the payment was intended so that he would permit Warner Brothers to film the TV series "The FBI." If these facts are accurate, the following points should be noted:

1. 28 CFR 45.735-12(b) provides that "no employee shall receive compensation . . . for any . . . writing . . . the subject matter of which is devoted substantially to the responsibilities, programs or operations of the department. . . ."

2. 28 CFR 45.735-10 prohibits an employee from using for financial gain for himself or any other person, information which comes to him by reason of his status as a DOJ employee and which has not become part of the body of public information. In this regard, I don't know whether any of the material used in Mr. Hoover's books is deemed to be "part of the body of public information." Likewise, 28 CFR 45.735-12(c) prohibits an employee from engaging in writing, with or without compensation, that is dependent on information obtained as a result of his employment except

when that information has been made available to the general public or when the Deputy Attorney General gives written authorization for the use of non-public information on the basis that the use is in the public interest.

3. It is not clear whether Warner Brothers has made any payments for the TV rights to "The FBI." The article intimates that such payments were made to Mr. Hoover. If so, the above cited provisions would appear applicable.

4. In view of the reported fact that Warner Brothers paid Mr. Hoover $50,000 for movie rights for his book, it would appear, depending on the circumstances and the timing, that Mr. Hoover may have been disqualified from participating in any negotiations for the TV rights to "The FBI" unless a 208(b) disclosure and determination had been made. 28 CFR 45.735-5(a).

5. It is not known whether Mr. Hoover has reported on a periodic basis his outside interests in these royalties, etc., as required. I would assume that Bill Rehnquist, as the designated Department Counsellor, would be the party to whom Mr. Hoover's reports would be sent.

6. It might be argued that much of this activity took place prior to the promulgation of existing standards of conduct law and regulations; this would have to be checked, but in any event would not be a credible defense for past activities and any current activities.

7. The use of government employees to ghostwrite, research or otherwise assist in the writing of a book for which Mr. Hoover received personal gain would also be an abuse of his position.

As noted above, the foregoing presupposes the validity of Anderson's comments, which may be far from accurate or maybe significantly incomplete. Also, Mr. Hoover's activities may have been subject to discussion and prior clearance at DOJ. However, I think we must anticipate further criticism of Mr. Hoover on the basis of this article.

In a related news story, the board chairman of TWA yesterday advised the press that Mr. Hoover wrote him personally to reveal a TWA pilot's prior "difficulties" with the Air Force, after that pilot had strongly criticized the Bureau's handling of an airplane hijacking incident. McGovern has jumped all over this, alleging that a release of information from the pilot's service record is violative of the Civil Rights Act, the Constitution and Air Force Regulations governing disclosure of information about personnel.

JFB1

MAY 12, 1971

Dear Warren:*

Your note of May 10 could not have been more thoughtful. I recall another period which was, of course, far more difficult just after my Cambodian speech when you came over to the White House to see me.

It is certainly true that anyone who reads history will realize that particularly during the Washington and Lincoln periods the press, if anything, was more vitriolic than it is today. I suppose the major difference is that now we have the added factor of television coverage which reaches masses of people within a matter of minutes. It has been my observation that TV news is probably in its way considerably less objective than news reports which appear in papers due in part to the need for each network to try to keep one step ahead of the other in sensationalism.

The President, on the other hand, has an enormous advantage when he can go on before 50 to 60 million people in a news conference or with a speech. If this device is not overused—my guess is about once a month is the maximum the market will bear—anyone in office always has a fighting chance to survive.

In any event, the days are never dull!

Sincerely,

[Richard M. Nixon]

P.S. I appreciated your note with regard to the toast to IIST. Your suggestion provided a good bridge in the serious part of my remarks.

*[Letter to Warren E. Burger, the chief justice of the United States]

PPF6

MAY 12, 1971

TO: H. R. Haldeman

FROM: Charles Colson

RE: Dick Scaife

As you will see from the attached, Dick Scaife is feeling very down on the Administration at the moment. Inasmuch as Scaife has been one of our biggest financial backers, I think we need to consider perhaps some unusual steps to rebuild relationships. No one seems to know what really has him bothered; I gather it is a combination of things. He doesn't like revenue sharing and some of our other domestic programs.

This memo is simply to advise you that we will keep in touch with Kalmbach on the situation, arrange an early social invitation and also propose that on his next trip here he get a briefing from Ehrlichman on the domestic front.

CWC129

MAY 14, 1971

TO: **Mr. Haldeman**

FROM: **Charles W. Colson**

RE: **Public Broadcasting System**

There are several things in the works to give us additional leverage with the Public Broadcasting operation.

The Corporation for Public Broadcasting, which funds the Public Broadcasting System, has a total of 15 members, three of whom were appointed by this Administration. Another member, Zellman George of Cleveland, is to be appointed by the President. Members of the Board (total of 15 of which no more than 8 shall be of the same party) serve from 2 to 6 year terms, and cannot be removed. Tom Whitehead has a regular pipeline to our people on the Board, and he and Al Snyder have worked out an arrangement where our specific complaints about programming will be transmitted in this manner.

The Corporation is pushing for permanent government funding. Under the interim setup they are funded year-by-year. Whitehead's people are working on legislation that would set up long term financing for 5 years, which would be subject to review each year. In addition, the legislation would funnel a greater proportion of this money to local stations to make them more self-sufficient and independent of the network. (If we really want to put the screws on PBS, we can kill the legislation??)

We are also going to attack this problem by getting to local stations which carry PBS programs. These stations depend on local and regional contributors for a good chunk of their money. If contributors made known their displeasure over specific network programs, this could have some impact on up the line.

We have a list of educational TV stations in key states where we will begin to funnel letters after we see a biased program. I have asked Ron Baukol to get a list of contributors to each of these stations, to determine whether we have any contacts here, and in general to get them on our mailing list.

Finally, the Public Broadcasting Service has nine members on its Board of Directors who are responsible for determining which programs are placed on the Network. Five of the nine are local station managers. We are putting together a list of Board members to hit them along with the rest.

We are being discreet with PBS President Hartford Gunn since the Public Broadcasting Act of 1967 forbids outside "interference" in connection with "program content."

cwc129

MAY 21, 1971

TO: **Alex Butterfield**

FROM: **John Dean**

RE: **Recommended Presidential Telephone Call**

I recommend that the President call Miss Marty Taylor, a 25-year-old Bank of America employee in San Francisco who, on May 5, observed anti-war demonstrators burning an American flag and rushed into the crowd, grabbed the flag, and extinguished it with her bare hands.

_____ JFB1

MAY 24, 1971

TO: **H. R. Haldeman**

FROM: **Charles Colson** .

RE: **John Connally**

In response to the attached, I agree we are overworking Connally. All I was trying to do was carry out a Haldeman action memo—and by the way, avoid some embarrassment in the process.

If John Connally prefers to be called "Mr. Secretary" he is the first ex-Governor I know who is either a Senator or Cabinet Member who prefers to be called by his new title. Even George Aiken, who was a Governor 30 years ago, is quick to correct you if you call him Senator. Obviously, Texans are a different breed.

_____ CWC129

EYES ONLY

MAY 25, 1971

TO: **Charles Colson**

FROM: **Al Haig**

RE: **Lou Harris**

Both Henry and I met with Lou Harris today and followed the scenario in your May 25 memorandum. Lou left highly charged and confident he was performing an important mission. Henry asked him to pass on to us any intelligence he picked up on the Soviets either via McGeorge Bundy or directly.

_____ CWC69

MAY 27, 1971

TO: **H. R. Haldeman**

FROM: **Charles Colson**

RE: **Teamsters Situation**

Pursuant to our conversation this afternoon with respect to the Teamsters situation, I recommend:

    1. The appointment of Fitzsimmons to a prestigious Presidential Commission as soon as possible after his election as President.

    2. A private discussion between Fitzsimmons and myself as to his support in the 1972 campaign and the formal support of the Teamsters. Fitzsimmons invited this discussion, told me that if elected he would like to discuss this with me and that it was his intention to try to deliver the Teamsters to us next year. Maybe someone else should have the discussion but I have at least started it and have an open invitation from him. Also, he and I have hit it off very well personally.

    There is some urgency to Point 2. If Fitzsimmons is elected, steps will begin immediately to bring the Teamsters back into the AFL/CIO. What I would like to do is to get their commitment before that happens.

cwc129

EYES ONLY

MAY 27, 1971

TO: **Dwight Chapin**

FROM: **Charles Colson**

Whatever happened to the ad that you were having secretly run? Could you let me know?

cwc129

JUNE 1, 1971

TO: **John Ehrlichman**

FROM: **The President**

I would like to have a study made by some outside business group (on a very confidential basis) as to where we go now as far as SST is concerned.

    I do not think it is necessary to give up simply because one track has been closed to us. Maybe we have to think in terms of a venture in which an American company has the planes made in some other country (a joint American-Japanese venture). In any event, I think it is vitally important that the United States not drop out of this field and I want to see what option, if any, is left open to us. Perhaps Magruder can give me something on this. The main thing is that he must forget the whole Boeing enterprise and start fresh on a new canvass and see what we can come up with.

PPF3; HRH140, 230

JUNE 1, 1971

TO: **John Dean**

FROM: **Charles Colson**

The attached is absolutely fascinating. Jay Lovestone gave me this. It is a report from a friend of his who was in Monte Carlo. As you will see, he had a long conversation with Stewart Udall. As Jay puts it, Udall sounds more like he is a visiting businessman from the Soviet Union than from the United States. Somebody should certainly keep an eye on this guy.

CWC129

JUNE 2, 1971

TO: **Bob Haldeman**

FROM: **The President**

I hope you will note the next time you are talking to Ziegler, Scali and Klein that in this first press conference after the appearance at the White House Correspondents' Dinner where I played the "good sport" role the reporters were considerably more bad-mannered and vicious than usual. This bears out my theory that treating them with considerably more contempt is in the long run a more productive policy.

PPF3; HRH140, 230

JUNE 2, 1971

TO: **Al Haig**

FROM: **The President**

It occurred to me that as far as the memorial to the dead who fought on the Southern side in the Civil War is concerned, that perhaps a good way to handle it would be to have a memorial to Lee and Grant. Both were graduates of West Point; both were the outstanding generals on their side during the war; and both handled themselves in the best tradition of opposing generals at the conclusion of the war.

It may not be possible to get any kind of a memorial of this type at West Point, but I have a strong feeling that erecting something either to Lee or to other West Point graduates who fought and died on the Southern side could have a dramatic effect in healing some of the wounds in the South that still exist a hundred years after the war has been completed.

PPF3; HRH140, 230

JUNE 4, 1971

TO: **Henry Hyde**

FROM: **Patrick J. Buchanan**

Thanks for the note on the discretionary money. When you put people into office who have no interest in Richard Nixon, then Richard Nixon's interests are not going to be computed into their decisions. What's going on is our own damn fault.

PJB1

JUNE 4, 1971

TO: **Fred Fielding**

FROM: **John Dean**

Attached are several classified documents regarding expenditures and funding relating to the new left and the April 19–May 6, 1971 demonstrations in Washington. Please prepare a concise memorandum that can be sent to Ehrlichman, Haldeman and possibly the President, showing the available information we have regarding the funding of these groups. This question has been posed several times and I have been asked where do these people get their money. This is the best information we have been able to come up with to date.

JWD2

JUNE 8, 1971

TO: **Chuck Colson**

FROM: **John Dean**

RE: **Jane Fonda**

Attached is the chronology of the case against Jane Fonda. You will note (Attachment 4) that the charges were dismissed because Justice did not feel it had a good case and did not want to provide a forum for Fonda in the federal courtroom.

cc: John Ehrlichman
    H. R. Haldeman
    A. Butterfield

JWD2

EYES ONLY

JUNE 8, 1971

TO: **Herb Klein**

FROM: **Charles Colson**

RE: **Jack Kemp**

Bob Haldeman has asked that we get Jack Kemp operating as the "truth squad" to refute McCloskey.

It is my thought which I suggested to MacGregor that a luncheon be set up for you, me, Clark and Jack Kemp so that we can explore how such a system would operate and the extent to which Kemp could handle this for us. Do you concur in this?

cwc129

TO: **The President's File***

RE: **NBC Executives' Meeting, June 9, 1971**

During the first hour of the meeting, the general discussion centered around economic issues facing the broadcasting industry, advertising problems raised by the FTC investigation, the Chevron case in California, the cable question (which NBC somewhat waffled on, first saying they had very little interest in it but later expressing considerable interest that CATV not be expanded at the expense of the broadcast industry), the prime time access rule and the same general gamut of issues touched upon in the ABC and CBS meetings. Julian Goodman did address the question of attacks on the media and the networks. He didn't specifically point at the Government but he talked about how everyone found it fashionable to criticize the media. He did make the point that the media credibility was challenged severely when there were loud public attacks, particularly by Government officials. The President answered by saying that, of course, people are always talking about the credibility of the Administration and therefore that [it] is "fair game" to talk about network credibility. He did not apologize for any of the attacks on the networks; he simply used the credibility analogy. Goodman really backed down very quickly on the topic and went back to discuss economic issues.

The President was very articulate in his convictions about being "pro-industry" as far as economic issues are concerned affecting the broadcasting industry. After the first hour of the meeting and when it appeared about to break up, the President buzzed for coffee and said he had one more question he wished the NBC officials would address themselves to and to feel free to be perfectly frank and candid. He raised the repression question and said "why don't you fellows address this, give me your views, we might as well have it out on the table." Goodman went into a more pointed speech about attacks on the media by Vice President Agnew, Dole; he even mentioned Hansen and Simpson. He said that they, of course, tried very hard to be fair and objective in their reporting, that it was not really a question of not being objective; it was just how people perceived it. He said he wished the President would watch television and make his own judgments. The President had earlier talked about reading news summaries of TV rather than watching because he thought he got a more dispassionate view of what was said and reported. The President had made the point in the discussion also that oftentimes a commentator by an expression, a wink or the inflection of his voice could put a very different meaning on a story. He also pointed out that a lot of time they had conclusions in advance and then simply cited facts to support those conclusions rather than just reporting facts. He also made the point that reporting in the printed media and reporting in the television area were quite different, the impact was quite different and that there was a higher responsibility as a result of a higher duty upon the networks. After Goodman explained his concerns over the attacks on the media the President, very quietly smiling and looking very calm, explained that he understood fully that most of the commentators and the reporters were biased, that their bias was quite obvious, but that this didn't bother him a bit; he understood it fully; he had come to accept it and live with it and so long as he had the opportunity to go directly to the American people from time to time, he didn't mind reporters being biased in their presentation of the news. He said, "I know, of course, that most of the reporters here disagree with my views on the war and our policies with respect to the war; they disagree with most of our foreign policy and, of course, they always are against most Presidents, probably particularly with respect to me because of my background and because of my own philosophical views." This seemed to stun Goodman. The President then went on to relate a story of an editor that he had talked with at one time who was very conservative in his viewpoint and who told of all the problems he had in hiring reporters. He would tell them what to write and tried to slant the news his way, but they went on doing what they wanted to. The President then made the point that, of course, the network executives had no control over their reporters. They couldn't possibly change this and they shouldn't be at all concerned about it and he understood they were powerless to do anything about it. Goodman was at a loss for words but one of the other executives spoke up and said he had had many conversations with Frank Shakespeare about this, that newsmen after all were professional, disciplined in being objective, and that it was the responsibility of the networks to insure that its reporters were "objective professionals." The President answered by saying, "Oh, well, I don't agree with that at all. I don't expect people not to be biased; I'm biased, everyone is biased in their own ways and it's perfectly understandable that most of your commentators are biased against me and I fully understand that you can't do anything about it." He said, "most of my staff have come to me from time to time and said why don't you call Stanton or Paley or Sarnoff or Goldenson" and the President said, "I told my staff that it won't do any good. They only own the networks but they can't control what the newsmen or commentators do and they can't change their bias." Goodman with his hand visibly trembling said, "I'm very sorry you feel that way, Mr. President; we try very hard to be objective and professional and I would wish you would watch the news once in a while and you might understand that we just report facts the way we see them."

The President laughed very loudly when Goodman used the word repression. The President said, "Well, I occasionally do see these fellows and when you look at Brinkley, Chancellor and others, they hardly look like they are repressed." He said, "You don't feel repressed, do you, Julian?" And he said, "if those are repressed fellows, I'd hate to see them when they weren't repressed."

The President went on to say that "We have never used the economic power of government to gain any leverage over the networks and we don't intend to do so. I agree with you on the business side of the issues and I am very sympathetic and understanding of the fact that you can't do anything about biased news coverage." He then made the point once more about direct access to television. He said, "If I didn't have direct access to the people through television I would be dead. I would have been dead long ago," citing the 1952 "Checkers" speech, 1956 and, of course, 1968. He said, "So long as I have an opportunity to take my views directly to the American people, I won't complain." There was numbed silence on the part of Scott and the others. Ruben [sic] Frank looked stunned. There was really nothing any of them could say at this point and the President, as the conversation progressed, became increasingly cheerful, friendly, and almost patronizing. The President broke the meeting up, offered them all cuff links, golf balls, made a great number of light jokes and then reminded Julian Goodman of a lunch he had had with Lou Nichols and Goodman 6 or 7 years ago. Goodman looked very startled that the President remembered it and the President said at that point, "I never thought that I would be here in this office at that time" and Goodman almost childishly said, "I knew you would be."

They were very cordial leaving the meeting. Herb Klein advises me that after the meeting, going back to the EOB, Goodman several times raised the point with Herb, "perhaps I shouldn't have gotten into the question of attacks on the media. I guess I shouldn't have raised that subject."

*[Written by Charles Colson on July 28, 1971]

CWC88, CWC129

JUNE 9, 1971

TO: **H. R. Haldeman**

FROM: **John Dean**

RE: **Shenandoah Tribe—Proposed Demonstration During Wedding on June 12**

As you may be aware, pursuant to a plan we worked out with Interior, Justice, and U.S. Attorney's Office, the Shenandoah Tribe was offered two alternative sites for their proposed demonstration during Tricia Nixon's wedding (West Potomac Park and the Reflecting Pool area), and after they declined these proposals we went into court for a restraining order against the demonstration. Judge Hart granted the government's request for an order which did not include any alternative site. It does not appear that the Shenandoah Tribe will file an appeal. As an aside, Hart told the government attorneys that he expected them to carry out his restraining order even if it "necessitated using armed forces."

Unless an appeal is filed in this matter and is successful, the only demonstration planned for that date will be five members of the Quaker Peace Movement who will be permitted in Lafayette Park. There is no anticipated problem in this regard.

I will keep you advised of any further development in this matter.

cc: R. Ziegler

JFB1; JWD2

JUNE 10, 1971

TO: **Jon Huntsman**

FROM: **Chuck Colson**

RE: **Your Memo of June 5 re Jane Fonda**

The Justice Department dropped its charges against Jane Fonda because it did not feel it had a good case; did not want to provide a forum for Fonda in Federal Court.

After reviewing the file, however, there may be information here that can be leaked out to friendly reporters. We are exploring the feasibility of doing so.

cwc129

JUNE 10, 1971

TO: **John Dean**

FROM: **Chuck Colson**

RE: **Jane Fonda**

Thanks for your reply on the Jane Fonda case. I would assume but I see no markings to indicate that it is confidential? We might be able to have some real fun with this in the press if we can use it.

cc: Dick Howard: When Dean's answer comes back, give it to Shumway to use as he wants depending on how good he feels it is.

cwc129

JUNE 11, 1971

TO: **Mr. Haldeman**

FROM: **Charles W. Colson**

Attached is the Letters to the Editors Report for the period of June 1–4. Nine letters were published out of a total of 28.

cwc129

JUNE 14, 1971

TO: **Jon Huntsman**

FROM: **Charles Colson**

RE: **McCloskey, Kemp and Cavett**

In response to Action Memorandum P1741 I think it is true that McCloskey held something of an edge over Jack Kemp on the Cavett show. On the other hand, Kemp did a very effective job, particularly in view of the stacked audience and Cavett's obvious bias. In a fair one-on-one debate Kemp would hold his own well with McCloskey.

We have set up a procedure for using Jack Kemp to rebut McCloskey in as many forums as we can arrange. Kemp is a fresh new face, very articulate and attractive, totally loyal to the President and perhaps the best balance we have for McCloskey. McCloskey is very good on TV. All we can hope for is to neutralize him and at least answer him on the spot which is better than giving him a free run at it. I think Kemp is the best we have in this area and as we coach him and as he gets more experience, he will do better.

We are hoping to use him whenever McCloskey is invited on national TV. We also plan to send him into areas where McCloskey is holding rallies so that Kemp can perform the old truth squad function, hold press conferences, speak at different forums and hopefully engage McCloskey in debate.

cwc14, 129

JUNE 14, 1971

TO: **Jon Huntsman**

FROM: **Chuck Colson**

Could you please obtain for me a copy of the book *Bridge at Chappaquidick* by Jack Olsen. I understand it is available in paperback, which will serve my purpose, at the Saville Bookstore in Georgetown [address]. Thank you.

cwc14

JUNE 14, 1971

TO: **Alex Butterfield**

FROM: **John Dean**

RE: **White House Office Papers**

The recent release of documents by former government employees to the *New York Times* should certainly set the climate for instituting our proposed regulations to govern the White House staff in disposition and handling of White House Office papers. I would like to urge that we take advantage of this situation and have that memorandum staffed and ready for release by the end of this week. If I can be of further assistance, please advise.

JWD2

JUNE 14, 1971

TO: **Chuck Colson**

FROM: **John Dean**

RE: **Tax Exempt Status—National Education Association**

Contrary to Van Shumway's memorandum, it appears that the NEA quali-
fies for tax exempt status by virtue of Section 501(c)(6) of the Internal
Revenue Code, rather than 501(c)(3). Pursuant to this Section, NEA is
classified as a "business league" rather than a charitable operation, and as
such is not specifically prohibited from attempting to influence legislation
and similar activities. This change in characterization has been, however,
the basis for denying donors a deduction for charitable contributions.

The IRS has taken the position that a "business league" is permitted
to engage in germane legislative activities without the threat of loss of tax
exemption for the organization. Therefore, it would appear that the only
attack that could be made to this classification would be a challenge that
NEA was not a business league. However, since the Service is the arbiter
of such classifications, and a cursory reading of case notes indicates that a
variety of organizations qualify under such a definition, I would not recommend pursuing an inquiry which in effect would be a direct challenge to
the IRS determination.

We might consider calling for Congressional hearings to review the
records of NEA affiliates to determine whether any of those still qualifying
as charitable organizations are in fact funneling deductible contributions
to the treasury of the mother organization. If this activity could be established, the funding affiliate would then be subject to lose its charitable
status. The IRS has indicated that in passing on future applications from
affiliates for charitable status it would require sufficient record keeping to
assure that funds were not passed to NEA. However, it is not clear whether
the IRS is also going to require this a *quid pro quo* for continuation of
charitable status of those organizations formally granted exemptions. The
call for a complete review might be justified by the fact that NEA, as the
parent company, had its charitable status terminated and was reclassified
in April 1970.

However, before bringing this matter up or calling for Congressional hearings, I think it imperative that we ascertain whether there is any
evidence or probable basis for finding any wrongdoing. Even if such facts
do exist, I think we should consider calling for Congressional hearings only
if the evidence is strong and if Treasury cannot be convinced of the need
for an investigation of the matter.

I would appreciate your advice as to whether you are currently
aware of any such additional facts in this regard.

JFB1; JWD2

TO: **Fred Malek**

FROM: **Chuck Colson**

The attached caught my eye from today's News Summary. You will notice that J. Edgar Hoover says that the Polaroid Corporation has funded the Black United Front.

Dr. Edwin Land is head of the Polaroid Corporation, runs it with an iron hand and if Polaroid put money into the Black United Front you can be sure Land would be the force behind it. I have known him over the years. He is an extreme liberal although obviously brilliant.

What distresses me is that he is a member of the Foreign Intelligence Advisory Board. I would assume he would have to have the highest security classification. Maybe he is all right on national security matters but I can assure you he is way off to the left fringes on every issue I have seen him involved in.

I raise this only because, particularly apropos of this morning's conversation and the weekend leak of documents, I think we have to be super cautious. This guy has always worried me and this may be reason to check him out a little more carefully. He is a Democrat but we appointed him to the FIAB.

cwc129

EYES ONLY

JUNE 15, 1971

TO: **Bob Haldeman**

FROM: **The President**

In view of the *New York Times'* irresponsibility and recklessness in deliberately printing classified documents without regard to the national interest I have decided that we must take action within the White House to deal with the problem.

Until further notice under *no circumstances* is anyone connected with the White House to give any interview to a member of the staff of the *New York Times* without my express permission. I want you to enforce this without, of course, showing them this memorandum. I want you particularly to bring this to the attention of Kissinger, Peterson, Rumsfeld, Finch, Safire, Ehrlichman, Ziegler, Klein and anyone else on the White House staff who might be approached by the *New York Times* for information or for a special story.

Under absolutely no circumstances is anyone on the White House staff on *any subject* to respond to an inquiry from the *New York Times* unless and until I give express permission (and I do not expect to give such permission in the foreseeable future).

This is a delicate matter for you to handle and all the orders, of course, must be given orally. It is vital, however, that there be absolutely no deviations within the White House staff because if there is the message will not get through.

I realize that you will have a number of objections raised that we are hurting ourselves by this policy. However, I have made the decision because of the national interest and the decision is not subject to appeal or further discussion unless I bring it up myself.

PPF3; HRH230

JUNE 15, 1971

TO: **Mr. Haldeman**

FROM: **Charles W. Colson**

Attached is the Letters to the Editors report for the week of June 7–11. As you can see, five were published out of a total of thirty-eight.

CWC129

ACTION PAPER

JUNE 15, 1971

RE: *New York Times* **Papers**

We need someone to handle this whole situation on an overall basis to develop a basic position. Perhaps Safire should take the project of pulling it together or ask Ray Price who would be best to take it over. The main thing is to put together a team to determine strategy and launch an attack.

We need to explain why this injures national security and why secret documents must be secure. This point needs to be thought through.

These should be referred to as the Kennedy/Johnson papers on the war.

The point is that they are washing their dirty linen in public and we will not get into it, but we do believe in the security of secret documents.

We need to get across the feeling of disloyalty on the part of those that publish these papers. We need some hard-hitting speeches in Congress—that the *Times* is putting the press interest above the national interest.

We have nothing to hide. This is a family quarrel in the previous

Administration regarding the Kennedy/Johnson conduct of the war. We, on the other hand, have developed a new policy and it's working.

One real question here is how this sorts out around the country. We should get Cliff Miller to get a reading on the reaction overall.

Also, Tom Johnson should get LBJ's people to speak out—Acheson, Rusk and McNamara.

Kissinger should mobilize some of the old establishment to hit the *Times.*

HRH

HRH112

DRAFT

[JUNE 15, 1971]

TO: **The President**

FROM: **John Ehrlichman**

Outline for Remarks Re: *New York Times*

I. The government has sued the *Times* because top secret documents have been stolen and published, in violation of Federal law.

A. Congress has prohibited one in possession of (any) classified documents from publishing them.
   1. It is our job to enforce the law.
   2. Beyond that, such a law is needed and should be enforced:
      (a) We must classify some documents, *not* to deny information to those who have a need or right to know, but to permit government business to be successfully conducted, *e.g.,* negotiations at SALT, Berlin, textile trade quotas, etc.
      (b) Advisors must be able to rely on the confidentiality of their advice for a free flow of ideas.

B. The Constitution does not *oblige* a paper like the *Times* to print everything it can lay its hands on.
   1. The First Amendment *protects* certain *rights*—it imposes no such obligations.
   2. The rights protected are *not absolute*—paramount national interests supersede and preclude publication of secrets vital to national security.
   3. Under our system the Congress (elected) and the Executive (elected) decide on the classification system and its application; owners of newspapers cannot be permitted to decide which documents will be declassified-by-publication.

(a) A declassification procedure exists and could have been followed. The national interest would be weighed against the public's conditional right to know. No request for declassification was made by the *Times* when it got the documents. It resorted to vigilante tactics, on the theory that the *Times* nourishes some "higher sense of morality" which transcends mere national security laws.

4. On the face of it a law has, apparently, been intentionally violated. It's the government's job to enforce such laws. Whether the law technically applies to this case will be decided by the courts, of course.

   (a) At the same time, assuming disclosure of more secret documents will be harmful

   (1) because what they contain might help unfriendly countries; or

   (2) because the mere fact of their theft and publication weakens the confidence of friendly countries in our ability to maintain the privacy of our dealings with them,

   the government must attempt to mitigate such harm by trying to get an injunction against further unlawful disclosures.

   (b) Is this "censorship," as some are writing? The process of classification, long established by Congress, does sequester information and, I believe, properly so if its release could harm our national interests.

II. What I have said to explain our legal response to the *Times'* very irresponsible actions is not a comment on what the Kennedy-Johnson documents contain or the subject to which they refer.

A. The classification law either applies or it doesn't. This obtains whether the *subject* is Vietnam, Iceland or atomic bombs. The law is the law whether the documents were prepared by people working for President Eisenhower or President Kennedy or President Johnson.

   1. The fact that the *Times* obviously disapproves of the Johnson Administration and the Vietnam war does not remove the application of the secret documents law from its editors.

B. The documents are critical of the Kennedy-Johnson policies and conduct of the war. Recall, I was critical of these policies and conduct in the last three elections. Our action against the *Times* has nothing to do with agreement or disagreement with the actions of past Presidents. The *Times* violated a very important law. It's that simple.

PJB3; JDE22

JUNE 15, 1971

TO: **H. R. Haldeman**

FROM: **Charles Colson**

RE: **TV Ratings on Wedding**

The total ratings for the wedding shows last weekend equal 59 million viewers. 15 million additionally viewed the CBS Friday night preview—details attached.

cc: Dwight Chapin

cwc129

EYES ONLY!!

JUNE 15, 1971

TO: **Dick Howard**

FROM: **Charles Colson**

Please pass the word within the staff, to everyone for whom we are in any way accountable, that no one is to communicate in any way, shape or form with anyone from the *New York Times* until further notice. Don't make a big thing out of it and don't let anyone indicate that they can't talk because it is the *New York Times.* Simply be sure that phone calls are left unanswered, that *New York Times* people are not included in any briefings (be certain on the drug issue, the briefing is scheduled for tomorrow).

We want no cooperation, no inquiries answered, nothing with respect to the *Times,* no contact, social or otherwise. Do not circulate a memo, do this by word of mouth. Urge discretion, we do not want this to become an issue. Simply ignore the *Times.*

cwc129

JUNE 15, 1971

TO: **Van Shumway**

FROM: **Charles Colson**

Did we inspire this article or is it an accident? If we had anything to do with it please return this to me and let me know.

cwc129

JUNE 15, 1971

TO: Van Shumway

FROM: Charles Colson

I have read a copy of your memo to Al Snyder regarding the UPI request
for a Kerry/O'Neill debate. This is fine but the major story that should be
pushed here is that Kerry has avoided every invitation for a debate: the
Frost show, the Cavett show, "Face the Nation," it is now a consistent
pattern. I think we have Kerry on the run, he is beginning to take a
tremendous beating in the press, but let's not let him up, let's destroy this
young demagogue before he becomes another Ralph Nader. Let's try to
move through as many sources as we can the fact that he has refused to
meet in debate, even though he agreed to do so and announced to the
press he would.

cwc129

EYES ONLY

JUNE 16, 1971

TO: Lyn Nofziger

FROM: The Spectator

Be absolutely certain not to use this. I just thought you would like to have
it for your information. Be very careful; do not dare let it get any distribution.

Hubert Humphrey and the Secret Pentagon Report

Many people are finding it hard to believe that Senator Hubert Humphrey
as Vice President of the United States was not aware of the various behind-
the-scenes events leading to the escalation of the Vietnam War. Humphrey has denied any knowledge of the very damaging disclosures by the
New York Times this week obtained from a top secret Pentagon report
dealing with the early stages of the war. Suspicions surrounding Humphrey's "shock" and "surprise" are especially widespread among those
who view his public innocence in the light of his unannounced bid for a
second try at the Presidency. Said Humphrey when interviewed this week
on the CBS Morning News, "I was as shocked and surprised as any other
citizen; it makes you wonder how those decisions were made."

There is little doubt in the minds of most Humphrey-watchers that
Senator Humphrey in his public pronouncements of this week is engaging
in more of the very same public evasiveness and deception revealed by

the report about the Johnson-Humphrey Administration. His innocence is unconvincing and few Americans accept his explanation. To believe that the Vice President of the United States, a man just a heartbeat away from the Presidency, was unaware of the behind-the-scenes evolution of the most important single preoccupation of the Johnson-Humphrey Administration is more than most people can imagine. If Mr. Humphrey is leveling in this instance, and most believe that he isn't, then he must be, by implication, criticizing Lyndon Johnson for failing to discharge one of the most basic responsibilities of the Office of the President. In either event his statements are distressing to most Americans.

Senator Humphrey has been running hard for the Presidency and obviously sees nothing but bad news in the series of articles run by the *New York Times*. Humphrey's disclaimers come at a time when the entire nation and the world await judicial determination as to future publication of articles by the *Times*. Perhaps he knows something that the public doesn't. There just might be some indication of Humphrey's behind-the-scenes role in getting America involved in the Vietnam conflict in the unpublished articles.

Unconvincingly Senator Humphrey remarked "you sort of wonder if we're getting all the information." It is clear that the Senator either knew that he was supposed to hush up the escalation of the War in 1965, or was incredibly naive in not asking his boss for a briefing in the matter. 1965 was the year that America's troop strength in South Vietnam jumped from a mere 17,000 to 185,000 men. Senator Humphrey fails to state publicly whether or not he ever bothered to ask President Johnson what his policy was in Southeast Asia and what his basis was for that policy. It is clear that Humphrey is still refusing to stand foursquare before the American people with the truth.

Furthermore, one wonders about Humphrey's failure to publicly discuss the issue in its most basic terms during his unsuccessful bid for the Presidency in 1968. Instead of presenting the Johnson-Humphrey Administration's true basis for escalating the action in Southeast Asia, the Vice President chose instead to evade the War issue and to publicly support Lyndon Johnson. He never complained that he was not being informed of the policy decisions during the crucial years from 1964–68, nor that he was not fully aware of his Administration's justification for proceeding the way it did.

Certainly it is not too much for the American people to expect that their Vice President should insist on keeping fully abreast of matters involving grave issues of war and peace. The cost of the Vietnam War in lives and treasure should have been sufficient justification for Mr. Humphrey to act more responsibly. Perhaps if he had taken the time and insisted on full access to matters relating to the War, America might not have made so many of the tragic errors that it did during the Johnson-Humphrey years. For Senator Humphrey to state before the American people, particularly those who have lost fathers, sons and brothers in the war, that he wasn't aware of the behind-the-scenes activities preceding each escalation of the war is a travesty indeed. The American people no longer will tolerate such deception, and it is apparent that Mr. Humphrey will be called upon to fully explain himself as a result of the *New York Times* disclosures.

It would behoove the American people to challenge Senator Humphrey on this issue. He is actively seeking his party's nomination for the Presidency. If he earns that nomination, then he should be called upon to state his role in escalating America's involvement in the Vietnam War, and to explain his utterly unbelievable assertions of this week that he was unaware of what was going on around him. The Democratic Party has much soul-searching to do in this matter. The Office of the Presidency is no longer a place for secretive and deceptive conduct. The War in Vietnam bears witness to the tragic results flowing from such practices.

Senator Humphrey owes an obligation to the American people to publicly explain himself. The people have entrusted him with serious responsibilities as Vice President and United States Senator. They deserve more than misleading innocence and deception.

CWC96

JUNE 17, 1971

TO: **Fred Fielding**

FROM: **John Dean**

A group called "Accuracy in Media" is seeking incorporation in the District of Columbia and has made a request to Chuck Colson for assistance in expediting their incorporation. They are aware of the fact that Honor America Day was incorporated in less than 24 hours and thought that we might be able to give some assistance. The incorporators are: Reed Irvine, Abe Kalish and John McLain.

Would you please check with Don Santarelli to see how we might be able to give some assistance although I do not want the White House involved in anything that would result in an extraordinary procedure for this group. Nonetheless, if we can expedite it with propriety let us do so.

JWD2

EYES ONLY

JUNE 17, 1971

TO: **Al Snyder**

FROM: **Charles Colson**

How about getting Charlie Rhyne onto one of the talk shows like Carson. Also explore whether we could get Reagan on the Griffin program or perhaps David Frost. If you could get either one of them placed, I think

I could program them to kick hell out of the *New York Times* and pick up our line as to why it is we have taken the action we have against the *Times*.

CWC129

JUNE 22, 1971

Thoughts on the *New York Times* Strategy

The key now is to poison the Democratic well.

The problem here is that we left the New York case to a Liberal lawyer and a Liberal judge and then basically lost the case; we failed to move on to the PR stage. We should have been able to make the PR case, at least, even though we couldn't carry the legal case.

Kissinger still raises grave doubts regarding the declassification process and the precedents it sets.

Haig and his team must go to work on the papers to determine which ones are important and, therefore, not to be declassified.

Also, we have to follow up on the call the President has had from the *Chicago Tribune* to declassify World War II, Korea, Bay of Pigs, and Cuban confrontation papers. Everything in these papers that is not involved in current security is to be declassified. We need a team of pros in here to handle this. All those not affecting national security should be released. We need an answer from Moore and Ehrlichman on whether we go on to the Supreme Court. The question here is whether it appears we quit if we don't and whether we lose our friends that way. We need a strong offense. The question is—can we sell it—that is, can we sell not going to court? We can make the point that it will require too much delay, etc., but we need this problem thought about.

The poll needs to be analyzed in terms of the one or two points that we can sell and the points that we cannot sell and then zero in only on those where we can get somewhere.

We need to get Huston back; get a small team going under Ehrlichman. This is an order to Haig—start going through all the secret documents, especially the Cuban Missile Crisis as well as Korea, etc., and follow up on the demand that these be released.

All this must be handled in a way that does not hit LBJ too directly or too hard.

Our whole concern now must be the public aspects of this. The morality issue is moot because the papers are already out. We must, however, get off the wicket of appearing to cover up for Johnson.

HRH

HRH112

JUNE 22, 1971

TO: H. R. Haldeman

FROM: Charles Colson

RE: Letters to Editors

Attached is the Letters to Editors report for June 14–18. Out of the 37 sent,
13 were regarding the McNamara papers.
    As you can see, seven letters were published this week.

cwc129

JUNE 23, 1971

TO: George Bell

FROM: Chuck Colson

RE: Social Invitation for Lou Harris

Please be sure that Lou Harris is invited to the next social function—a
dinner type affair—at the White House. This is a REAL MUST.

cwc129

JUNE 25, 1971

TO: H. R. Haldeman*

FROM: Charles W. Colson

RE: *New York Times* Article

Because I think that the *New York Times* / Kennedy-Johnson papers controversy is and will continue to be a very major issue with very important
political ramifications, I think we should at each stage of the game very
carefully assess where we stand, what our strategy is, short and long term,
and we must be exceedingly careful not to overreact or to worry about the
particular daily turn of events. This issue, in my opinion, has profound
implications which could easily be extremely important, if not even deci-
sive in the next election. Therefore, what happens tomorrow or even next
week is of less consequence than how we play it over the long pull.
    I think you know that I am very impulsive by nature. I tend to
plunge hard into the issue of the moment and like to join battle on every
hot topic that comes along. In this case, however, because I feel that the
issues are so profound I am in effect advocating what is for me a very
uncharacteristic caution.
    Attached is a summary of where I think we stand at the moment,

how I think the issues may develop and what some of their longer term implications are.

A. WHERE WE STAND TODAY

As Opinion Research has pointed out, this issue has not had the enormous impact on the public that one would expect from the intensive press coverage. To the extent that the public is aware of it, they do not understand the issues very well. I believe there are two perceptions:

1. We are against the press;

2. The government lies—more specifically LBJ and the Democrats lied us into Vietnam.

The heartland isn't really aroused over this issue. There is nothing like the Calley case here. People know there is a controversy; but they're not entirely clear as to what it is all about. Partisan Republicans don't quite understand why we are suppressing information that could be damaging to the Democrats; some people, I am sure, think that we are covering up our own failures and most importantly, no one is really excited about what they regard as the leak of "ancient" documents. They do not understand the security issue (if on the other hand we prosecute Ellsberg and it becomes a notorious trial, this could spark a major readily understandable issue and a strong public reaction with our natural constituency rallying behind us).

The Democrats are horribly divided on this issue. They are split, confused, angry and scrambling to get away from it. As of today, they are delighted that the issue is focusing on Nixon vs. the *New York Times* but most of them are very well aware that the major thrust of the controversy will eventually become the Kennedy-Johnson mishandling of the war as to which every possible Democratic candidate except McGovern, McCarthy, Bayh and Hughes stand to lose badly.

B. NIXON VS. THE PRESS ISSUE

Over the short term, this will remain a hot issue, but it will pass. After the court decision (regardless of the outcome) the vast majority of the people will forget it. The liberal press will keep bringing it up and will keep trying to knife us with it, but it is not the kind of an issue that will last. People just don't give a damn that we beat the *New York Times* in the Supreme Court or the *New York Times* beat us.

Those who believe we are anti-press will simply have their views confirmed even further, but most of those who believe we are anti-press aren't with us anyway. Those who believe the press is biased and irresponsible will continue to think so.

The prosecution of Ellsberg could have some positive benefits for us in that if he is really painted as a villain, the fact that he conspired with the press and the press printed the documents that he stole is bound to have a bad ruboff on the press. Once again, however, the issue is going to tend simply to confirm beliefs people already have; it is not likely to switch very many people.

As for the working press, as a result of this controversy, they will like us even less and that is the case whether we win or lose in the Supreme Court. The vast majority of the press are hostile to us; that is a fact, not just our paranoia. Yet we somehow manage to continue to maintain a solid base of popular support; hence we will survive the continued—yes, even aggravated—hostility of the working press.

On balance, therefore, I don't see any real gain or loss out of the press issue. The only way in which it hurts us is that for the moment, it obscures what are the real issues; that is, the Democrats' mishandling of the government during the Kennedy-Johnson years and the theft of classified documents. Hence, it is clearly in our interest to let this issue fade. The longer it remains around the longer it will take to get into the public's mind what we want to be the continuing issues that emerge from this controversy.

For these reasons, I would not recommend that we use the Vice President; that would only escalate the press issue. I would not recommend that we attack the press or that any Administration spokesmen attack the press. I would not even recommend that our supporters on the Hill start attacking the press because to do so would only keep the press issue *itself* alive. Let me qualify this by saying that I would prosecute any newsmen if it can be demonstrated (as in the case of Neil Sheehan perhaps) that they were conspirators in the theft of these documents or that they conspired in having them reproduced. It is worthwhile to paint an individual bad if it is part of the prosecution of a natural enemy like Ellsberg.

There are two points that we must make with respect to the whole press issue. We must make them through our most effective spokesmen and make them often enough so that we're sure that they are reasonably clear in the public's mind. We can then let the rest of the issue go away.

1. *This Administration cannot allow stolen documents to be distributed, printed in the press, etc.* Classified documents are classified for a good reason. *Admittedly the government may overclassify.* But we cannot risk having anyone take the law into his own hands to make that individual judgment, in effect to put himself above the law because one document could endanger lives—many lives.

2. *The Government has a duty to enforce the law.* When once the press was warned not to publish and then said that notwithstanding that warning it was going to publish, the Attorney General had no recourse but to bring the action he brought.

These two points need to be articulated very clearly, very crisply, very simply, very nonlegalistically. Several of our spokesmen can make the point. Klein does it very effectively when he goes around the country; Rogers is an excellent person to make the point (and we might get him to once the issue quiets down); the Attorney General can make this point as well. We should endeavor to get responsible lawyers around the country making the point. Professor Freund's argument in today's *New York Times* is very helpful. *Finally the President should make these two points and just these two points,* either in an address to the nation or in his next press conference. At the moment, I am very much inclined to think that an address to the nation would over-escalate the press issue and involve us much too deeply in the whole controversy. I think a press conference will probably be a far more desirable opportunity.

Over the long haul, we might well consider recommendations like Scali's that the President meet with a selective group of newsmen, perhaps the leaders of Sigma Delta Chi and the American Society of Newspaper Editors. These are things that can be done once the issue is quiet. They should not be done while the issue is hot because they will only escalate it and give the appearance that we are dealing from a position of weakness. In [due] course this can be done, both to get a better understanding, face to face, with journalists and also to demonstrate that we are not "anti-press."

Further we can continue to push declassification and declassification practices and procedures. For example, at the right time an executive order or a clarifying memorandum pointing out the documents should not be classified unless there is a real national security reason will help make the point with the public that we do believe in the "right to know." Once again these should not be done now; they would only escalate the issue and [we] would only appear to be reacting. We should over a period of time prove that we believe in the right to know by *what we do. It is more important than what we say.*

C. CREDIBILITY OF GOVERNMENT (AND THE DEMOCRATS IN PARTICULAR)

In my opinion, most people do in fact associate the Kennedy-Johnson papers with the Democrats. It is true that the issue is blurred; it is true that people believe that we are covering something up; partisan Republicans complain repeatedly that they can't understand why we are covering up Democratic papers and, of course, finally this has an impact on the office of the Presidency, its credibility and the credibility of government, generally.

As for the credibility of government, a case can be made that it has already reached its low point. This incident simply confirms what many people think anyway. According to Lou Harris' theory (and Howard Smith's interestingly enough) at least 50% of the American people at least will always believe what any President tells them because they want to believe what any President tells them. If the President goes on television and makes a flat-out statement, people tend to want to believe it. They will still answer questions in polls that the government is not telling them all that it should or all that it knows, but they nonetheless will believe the President. I question, therefore, whether this incident has caused any further serious erosion of Presidential credibility—maybe some but not a great deal—and there are ways we can rebuild President Nixon's credibility. Indeed this incident may offer us an opportunity to do so by deed rather than by words.

For example, if we were to release authentic documents that demonstrate how the President arrived at his change in Vietnam policy (for example, a study of decisions leading up to the November 3 speech) we would not have to say that we are being candid, that we are not covering up, we would prove that we are not. The more we talk about the fact that we are telling the truth, that there is no "credibility gap," that we are not misleading the people, the more people tend to be suspicious. In other words, talking about the fact that we are telling the truth may in actual fact be counterproductive. But doing things that demonstrate that we are telling the truth and that we have been telling the truth can be very powerful. The Kennedy-Johnson papers give us a real opportunity in this regard in that it permits us to do things that will be in vivid, sharp public contrast with the whole Kennedy-Johnson affair.

Further, we must make every effort to keep ourselves out of the controversy over the Kennedy-Johnson era. We must not attack LBJ; we must not defend LBJ; we must subtly, but very effectively, encourage and fuel the division within the Democratic ranks *without* getting caught, because that simply would inject us back into it.

If we keep ourselves out of the fight over the Kennedy-Johnson papers and the issues they raise and at the same time demonstrate, not by words but by deeds, our own candor and credibility, then it is my opinion that the President's credibility and indeed the government's credibility can be enhanced by this entire episode, rather than hurt by it. We can be the ones that restored credibility, honesty and candor to government and the contrast with the prior Administration is very dramatic and effective.

D. THE ELLSBERG PROSECUTION

There is another opportunity in this whole episode, that is the prosecution of Ellsberg. It could indeed arouse the heartland which is at present not very excited over the whole issue.

First of all, he is a natural villain to the extent that he can be painted evil. We can very effectively make the point of why we had to do what we did with the *New York Times;* we can discredit the peace movement and we have the Democrats on a marvelous hook because thus far most of them have defended the release of the documents. If we can change the issue from one of *release* of the documents to one of the *theft* of the documents we will have something going for us.

Second, a prosecution of Ellsberg can help taint the press (to the extent that that in fact helps us). If he indeed conspired with members of the press and he is painted black, they too will be painted black.

Third, this is a clear, clean, understandable issue. People can relate to it.

Fourth, the prosecution of Ellsberg protects the credibility of our case against the *New York Times.* It will dramatize why we had to go to court, it will make the case clear to the public that the release of classified information can be harmful.

Fifth, it helps keep the whole Kennedy-Johnson papers issue very much alive and on the front pages.

Finally, this is a motivational issue, particularly if the Democrats are foolish enough to defend him.

E. KEEP THE DEMOCRATS DIVIDED AND FIGHTING

This should happen anyway but we would be foolish to simply lie back and assume it. We should ensure in subtle ways that it happens. This needs to be planned out with great thoroughness and executed with utmost care. The greatest risk would be to get caught in what we are doing or to have our efforts become obvious. I have not yet thought through all of the subtle ways in which we can keep the Democratic party in a constant state of civil warfare, but I am convinced that with some imaginative and creative thought it can be done.

Some examples do come to mind. The continued release of documents will keep the issue very much alive. We might of course orchestrate carefully and quietly a defense of LBJ; to the extent that his stock rises those who have now disowned him lose a valuable constituency. We could of course plant and try to prove the thesis that Bobby Kennedy was behind the preparation of these papers because he planned to use them to overthrow Lyndon Johnson (I suspect that there may be more truth than fantasy to this).

The Ellsberg case, if pressed hard by us, will of course keep the issue alive. Developing the case factually of why the President changed the policies will continually bring the papers themselves back into the public spotlight.

We should encourage, *not* discourage, the Hill from carrying on intensive hearings and well publicized hearings over the Kennedy-Johnson papers and over how we got into Vietnam. If the Hill during the Fall makes a major production out of an investigation of why we got into Vietnam at the same time the President is winding the war down in Vietnam the contrast is once again very vivid. We don't need to spell it out; the public is smart enough to see on the one hand the horrors of how we got in and on the other hand, the skill with which the President is managing to get us out. I realize that Kissinger and others in the establishment at State and Defense will fight hard against these hearings. In my view, it can be in our political interest that they go on and be well publicized.

We can, of course, play up the Humphrey and Muskie comments of recent weeks which as time passes are going to look more and more stupid.

We can encourage through our political operation resolutions in various Democratic state conventions, damning the Johnson-Humphrey Administration and denouncing the Humphrey-Muskie ticket which ran in 1968—defending the Johnson Administration.

In short, there is a wide open political field which we can exploit if we play it right and keep ourselves out of it.

F. CONCLUSION

In recent days, an interesting collection of people whose political judgment I respect have separately stated that they believe this incident *has* re-elected the President. While this is an obvious overstatement it does show how strongly people believe the politics of this issue will cut. People who have said this range from Lou Harris on one end of the spectrum to Bill White on the other, with Dave Bradshaw and a few of my liberal congressional friends tossed in the middle. (Bradshaw by the way is a very shrewd politician with excellent political instincts, whose judgment I have always found to be very close to the mark.)

In short, I think it is very clear that there are profound political implications, that this offers us opportunities in ways we perhaps did not initially appreciate, that we can turn what appeared to be an issue that would impair Presidential credibility into one that we can use by effective contrast to improve the credibility of this Administration; and further, that it is a tailor-made issue for causing deep and lasting divisions within the Democratic ranks.

For this reason, I feel that we must not move precipitously or worry about tomorrow's headlines. We must keep our eye on the real target: to discredit the Democrats, to keep them fighting and to keep ourselves above it so that we do not appear to be either covering up or exploiting.

The foregoing thoughts need a lot of refinement, need to be sifted carefully through the staff, need a lot of creative input added and then our strategy needs to be very carefully executed. While I detest the term, this is one issue that calls for a full fledged, carefully thought out "game plan" that we pursue to the hilt.

*HANDWRITTEN HALDEMAN NOTE: "President's Folder"

cwc14, 18, 129

(From Charles Colson's handwritten notes of a meeting with the President)

8 A.M. 6/29/71

Most important cabinet meeting

Check Tell it to Hanoi money

Pentagon Papers—best advise—Talking about now.

Watch out for enemies in civil service

HRH [Haldeman] is lord high executioner

P [President] must have best advice "with the bark off"—but not in press—

Press don't want to live—what [word indistinct]
   1. needs
   2. screw RN—

P [President decisions]—I want discipline—when he calls—I want action—

Bogus comments—Talking in the press

What matters is whether P [President] is right or wrong—

the advisor can [indistinct] both ways; P [President] cannot—

You are free to express your views if you support the P [President]

only one thing worse than being wrong—that's being "not sure"

—Pick your scapegoats—everyone is sniping at you—

Fed is the problem—

no wage/price control

Steel will be in—

Depreciation allowance—

Tax deferral—

must show confidence that we know what we are doing—

going forward with Ellsberg & hang the son of a bitch—

Don't talk to Press until it is decided—

   P [President] has right to advise without pressure

HRH [Haldeman] has worst job—he's my "Pratt Boy"—

HRH [Haldeman] to cabinet officers on every specific point—

Burden of Proof is on agency—

We have to do staff work for HRH [Haldeman]

cc's to JDE [Ehrlichman]

any extracurricular acts of disloyalty

JULY 1, 1971

TO: The President

FROM: Alexander P. Butterfield

RE: Senator George McGovern's Military Record

We have checked the full military record of Senator George McGovern. According to Colson, there is nothing in the folder that would be of interest to us or to anyone else. The information is routine and clean. McGovern flew 35 combat missions as an Army Air Corps pilot in World War II. He earned several Air Medals and the Distinguished Flying Cross.

ss82

EYES ONLY

JULY 1, 1971

TO: Van Shumway

FROM: Charles Colson

There is a school of thought which is gaining momentum that the Pentagon papers were initiated by Bobby Kennedy forces to be used in the '68 campaign to throw over LBJ. More and more evidence of this mounts, particularly note the attached story in today's News Summary.

cwc129

JULY 2, 1971

TO: The President

FROM: Patrick J. Buchanan

Jack Kemp phoned. He was delighted with the briefing, had half the audience with him this time—feels he scored much more strongly this time. And one indication is that McCloskey was a bit peeved after the show was over. The show will run the 16th of July; we will monitor it. But Kemp feels elated, and enthusiastic about more engagements.

PJB1

JULY 7, 1971

TO: **Al Snyder**

FROM: **Charles Colson**

I have just talked to Ev Ehrlich at ABC regarding the Cavett show. He told me very confidentially that management had now insisted that the Cavett show adhere to the requirements of the Fairness Doctrine. As you know, in the past it had been considered an entertainment program and the general Fairness Doctrine requirements had not been applied by ABC management.

Ehrlich said that he had reviewed the various appearances, particularly in March and April, and had concluded that our earlier complaint was absolutely justified. Cavett is now under strict orders to review *in advance* his proposed guest list with the General Counsel's office. Ehrlich assures me that they will religiously follow the "Today Show" procedures and that if an anti-Administration spokesman is interviewed, they will call us and invite us to suggest an Administration spokesman. For example, this week Ehrlich insisted that someone answer Lindsay, and Goldwater will appear on the Cavett show to respond.

In light of this, I think you can safely push the Cavett show producers to take some of our spokesmen and if you run into any complications, let me know and I will work through Ehrlich to see that they cooperate.

Ehrlich was very strong in his view that our position has been correct in this. He did ask that we keep this completely confidential, which I assured him we would.

cwc129

EYES ONLY

JULY 8, 1971

TO: **Mr. H. R. Haldeman**

FROM: **Alexander P. Butterfield**

RE: **Opponents**

In late June I received a copy of the very sensitive Eyes Only "Opponents List" put together by Messrs. Colson and Bell. I do not see in the media section of that list the names of Candy Stroud, Judith Martin or Maxine Chesire who, according to my understanding, are on the current "Freeze List." At the same time, I do note the names of others on the "Freeze List"—namely, Senators Nelson, Kennedy and Muskie, Congressman Kastenmeier and Sandy Vanocur.

Am I wrong to assume that the "Freeze List" is something over and above the "Opponents List"—that it is a list of those opponents who are absolutely frozen from attendance at any White House events . . . be they social, ceremonial, etc.? And if I am not wrong thus far, the "Opponents List" *should* include Stroud, Martin and Cheshire (see attachment).

If you will straighten me out on this matter, I will pass the word to Colson, Bell, Rose Mary Woods, Lucy Winchester and others who have a need to know.

Thank you.

ss82

JULY 8, 1971

TO: **William H. Rehnquist**
      Assistant Attorney General

FROM: **John W. Dean, III**
      Counsel to the President

RE: **Contempt of Congress—CBS**

We are advised that early next week the House is expected to vote on whether to hold CBS President Frank Stanton in contempt for his refusal to provide the House Interstate and Foreign Commerce Committee with portions of unused film from "The Selling of the Pentagon." As I am sure you are aware, Stanton has taken the position that the forced disclosure would be violative of the First Amendment Freedom of the Press.

In anticipation of this vote, I would appreciate your office preparing a memorandum detailing the legal authority upon which the House would be acting and setting forth the expected scenario of events and the various ways that the Executive Branch could become involved in the event that the House does vote to hold Stanton in contempt.

Because House action on this matter is expected in the immediate future, I would like to receive your response as soon as possible.

Thank you.

JFB1; JWD3

EYES ONLY

JULY 8, 1971

TO: **John Ehrlichman**

FROM: **Charles Colson**

RE: **Luncheon with Howard Smith**

I called Smith back today to be sure to record precisely what he said. You might find the conversation interesting. Yesterday at lunch he said the same thing but went on to say that he couldn't understand why Gill was begged not to do this. You will notice that on Page 2 of the attached, the word "begged" comes in again. It was said with considerable feeling.

I don't understand this but we are trying to put the pieces of the puzzle together. I would suggest you would want to keep the attached very secure.

cwc129

EYES ONLY

JULY 9, 1971

TO: H. R. Haldeman

FROM: Charles Colson

RE: Public TV

Peter Flanigan, Al Snyder, Tom Whitehead and I met today to discuss our future strategy with respect to public TV. For your information we agreed on four essential points:

1. Funds for the Corporation for Public Broadcasting should be cut significantly on the theory that it need no longer give extensive support to local stations and instructional programming thanks to direct Federal Assistance. Funds to these outlets would be increased to bolster local programming, thereby making stations less dependent on the network product. In addition, new legislation would require the Public Broadcasting Service to sell programs to local stations, which currently receive them free of charge. This would put the screws on PBS to provide programming acceptable to grassroots stations, which generally are more conservative in outlook. Local stations, therefore, would have a stronger voice as to what comes down the network line. The net result would still be an increase in overall Federal support for public broadcasting. This will be a plus for us on the Hill where there is bi-partisan support for educational TV, and among segments of the public which consider PTV a sacred cow.

2. Remove Macy as head of CPB, and cut funding of NET, the largest of the production centers, to near zero. Flanigan will meet with Cole and Rather of CPB to sell them on this, in exchange for Administration support of the new bill.

3. There should be a change of top management at the Public Broadcasting Service. Macy hired the President of PBS, Hartford Gunn. Gunn and his General Manager, who is Friendly's protégé from the Ford Foundation, should be replaced with professionals who reflect our thinking. PBS is the distributor of network programs, and has overall authority as to what goes out to local stations.

4. As funding for NET is cut, money should be directed to another production center that would be created to reflect objectively on subjects relating to the Administration. This would replace NET as a major producer and would create an important alternate source of network programming. The other major production centers in Boston, Los Angeles, San Francisco and Pittsburgh are equally as biased as NET. New PBS management would help remedy this, and a new program source would be a major factor in the overall network product.

cwc129

JULY 9, 1971

TO: **Stephanie Wilson**

FROM: **Fred Fielding**

RE: **"Pat Nixon" Camellia**

> *considering the camellia caper*
> *quiescent . . .*
> *. . . at present,*
> *with a grateful staffer's smile*
> *it's taking root in flora file*
> *(First Family variety)*
> *until further plea*
> *from thee . . .*
> *. . . to me.*

JFB1

JULY 13, 1971

TO: **Doug Hallett**

FROM: **Charles W. Colson**

I was fascinated to read the attached. You can note some of my marginal comments that I made as I went through it.

I'm afraid you have become too good a Republican. We Republicans always like to play things fair and square, we worry about how well we govern, we don't demagogue, we are terribly concerned about good government and we are miserable politicians.

The best evidence of this is the fact that we have been in power approximately 10½ of the last 40 years and it is precisely because we are lousy politicians and we don't understand how to exploit political issues. We spend most of our time doing precisely what you recommend, trying to govern well.

Maybe in the long run, history will reward us for this, but in the meantime, we will probably spend a larger part of our time out of power than in unless we learn how to connive, promise and exploit opportunities the way the Democrats have.

CWC129

JULY 14, 1971

TO: H. R. Haldeman

FROM: Charles Colson

RE: **CBS Contempt Citation**

For your information attached is a transcript of my phone conversation with Sandy Lankler, a lawyer here in Washington whom I have known for many years. He also happens to be the Republican State Chairman in Maryland. He has persuaded CBS that we were instrumental in helping them. MacGregor on the other hand is convinced, as am I, that whether we had lifted a finger or not the contempt citation would have been defeated. So I believe we are getting credit for nothing. I do not really believe they needed us. In any event, I am going to play it for all it's worth as you will see in the attached.

Paley called me this morning and was profuse in his thanks. He asked me to be sure to pass it on to the President. He said that it really meant a great deal to him.

Stanton, as you will see from the enclosed, has asked to see me. I am going to take with him exactly the line which I took on the phone with Lankler. They propositioned us, we didn't proposition them. We are not asking for anything other than fairness and a decent break. I intend to be very rough, however. I do not expect a repeat of the Ehrlichman situation because I have several witnesses to the fact that CBS offered the deal, we didn't.

This may get us nothing. On the other hand it just might.

[Marking indicates President was verbally briefed on the contents of this memorandum.]

CWC15

JULY 15, 1971

TO: H. R. Haldeman

FROM: Charles Colson

RE: **Lou Harris**

Lou Harris just called me in a fit of rage over the fact that the *Washington Post* did not carry the very negative poll today on Kennedy, the lead of which was to the effect that 51% of the American people do not believe that Kennedy is qualified to be President.

Poor old liberal Lou Harris is suddenly discovering what his liberal friends are like.

cwc129

JULY 16, 1971

TO: John Ehrlichman

FROM: Charles Colson

RE: Rand Corp/FBI/Ellsberg

Frank Stanton, who was on the board of the Rand Corporation, told me yesterday that at a recent executive committee meeting it was disclosed that the FBI had made an extensive investigation at Rand in April of 1970. The investigation centered about an alleged leak of documents by Ellsberg. I am sure this is the incident you told me about over the phone.

According to the report given to the Rand executive committee, the FBI had a solid case but did nothing with it. Stanton suggested that it should be a matter of great concern to us especially if there is any truth to Rand's assertion that there was a solid case and the FBI elected not to act.

In view of the fact that Rand obviously used this as a way of protecting themselves and shifting responsibility back on us, I would think that the file should be very carefully examined and we should be certain of precisely what happened internally that caused the case to be turned off.

cwc129

JULY 16, 1971

TO: John Dean

FROM: Charles Colson

RE: Hughes Aircraft

Bob Bennett saw me yesterday with respect to a matter I understand he had already discussed with you. That is, the tax status of the principal stockholder of Hughes Aircraft Co., a private medical research foundation.

I am sure you are familiar with the facts of the case. Treasury is attempting to impose regulations requiring medical research foundations to spend at least 4% of their endowment value per year. The entire endowment of the Hughes medical research foundation is the common stock of Hughes Aircraft. Hence, Hughes Aircraft must produce dividends of at least 8 percent a year which is a pretty tall order for any private corporation.

I can fully understand why the Treasury is taking the attitude it is. Obviously the Congress deliberately left a loophole in the law. Nonetheless a loophole that many private foundations might try to use. On the other hand, I could see no good argument for not including a grandfather clause that would not virtually put out of business the Hughes medical research foundation.

Yesterday the general manager of Hughes Aircraft met with Charlie Walker. Walker seemed interested in a grandfather clause approach but his tax experts indicated that might put into question the validity of the entire regulation and I can't conceive of why that would be the case.

Because of some possibilities that we have been working on with respect to Hughes, this is a matter of some considerable importance and I wonder if you could pursue it to see if there isn't some possible way to work a resolution. Could you advise me, please?

cwc129

JULY 19, 1971

TO: **Henry Kissinger**

FROM: **The President**

One effective line you could use in your talks with the press is how RN is uniquely prepared for this meeting and how ironically in many ways he has similar character characteristics and background to Chou. I am just listing a few of the items that might be emphasized.

1. Strong convictions.

2. Came up through adversity.

3. At his best in a crisis. Cool. Unflappable.

4. A tough bold strong leader. Willing to take chances where necessary.

5. A man who takes the long view, never being concerned about tomorrow's headlines but about how the policy will look years from now.

6. A man with a philosophical turn of mind.

7. A man who works without notes—in meetings with 73 heads of state and heads of government RN has had hours of conversation without any notes. When he met with Khrushchev in 1959 in the seven-hour luncheon at the dacha, neither he nor Khrushchev had a note and yet discussed matters of the greatest consequences in covering many areas.

8. A man who knows Asia and has made a particular point of traveling in Asia and studying Asia.

9. A man who in terms of his personal style is very strong and very tough where necessary—steely but who is subtle and appears almost gentle. The tougher his position, usually, the lower his voice.

You could point out that most of these attributes are ones that you also saw in Chou En-Lai.

As a matter of fact, one of the ways that you could subtly get this across is to describe Chou En-Lai and to go into how RN's personal characteristics are somewhat similar.

HRH140

JULY 20, 1971

TO: **H. R. Haldeman**

FROM: **Charles Colson**

RE: **Meeting with Frank Stanton, July 15, 1971**

This is to report on my meeting last week with Frank Stanton. He was accompanied by his new counsel here in Washington, a long time Republican, Alexander Lankler (now State Chairman in Maryland). After disposing of the initial pleasantries, Lankler introduced the subject at hand. He pointed out that he had solicited our assistance in helping Dr. Stanton avoid the contempt citation and that in return Stanton had asked to come in and see us to discuss the coverage which CBS provides the Administration. At the first opportunity, I made the point that we were asking for nothing; that this had not been our proposal nor had it been our idea; that it was CBS's proposition that we were here to discuss and that all the Administration sought was "occasional fairness." Stanton agreed that we had not made any overtures, that this was CBS's initiative and that he personally was taking steps to try to correct the situation with respect to CBS's coverage of the President and the Administration.

I proceeded to point out to Stanton some recent illustrations of CBS "screwing us." I expected Stanton to take issue with some. In most cases, he said that he had seen the clip in question and agreed fully that we were justified in our criticism. He said that the POW report was indeed bad journalism as was Roger Mudd's reporting the Gallup Poll and not reporting the Harris Poll, drawing the conclusion that the President was slipping in public popularity to new lows. I described this as dishonest journalism and then decided my term was a little harsh and began to back off at which point Stanton said it was "dishonest journalism." We talked about the Pierpoint coverage of the economy. Stanton said that he had seen that himself and had been outraged and had already taken steps to correct it. We went through comparative coverage over the past several weeks of NBC, ABC and CBS, pointing out that in at least 10 separate instances ABC and NBC had given extensive film coverage to an important Administra-

1971: MAY–AUGUST   **295**

tion event; CBS had given it, if anything, only a verbal note. I had complete documentation, times, issues, etc. Stanton took elaborate notes. I also referred to the way in which CBS and the other networks had covered unemployment increases as against unemployment decreases. On all of these points Stanton acknowledged that we have been very badly treated. I couldn't get him to argue on a single point.

His attitude was markedly different than it ever had been in the past; he was contrite, apologetic, almost obsequious. There was none of the typical explosive arrogance and I tried very hard by being rough to draw him out because I thought I could achieve the best results by pressing him to the wall.

At one point he said he was taking several steps to correct the "situation." He said that he did not wish to elaborate at that point on what they were until he had them accomplished but when they were accomplished he would be in touch with me. He said, "I will see that this is corrected. You have my assurance."

I happened to mention that the President had expressed his feelings to NBC to the effect that corporate management really is concerned with the economics of the network operation and can't get involved in the judgment of the news department. Stanton interrupted to say that he had had a long talk with Julian Goodman and that Goodman had told him in depth of the President's conversation. It was obvious to me from the way Stanton said it that Goodman was very disturbed and concerned over the President's attitude, precisely the effect the President was trying to create.

Stanton, as I expected he would, rose to the bait when I said I was sure he really couldn't do much about these things and said, "you're damn right I can do something about them and will!" I told him that I couldn't imagine him calling Roger Mudd to complain about a report and he said, "No, I wouldn't call Roger Mudd, but I would certainly call the President of CBS News and raise hell."

The upshot of the hour and a half discussion was that Stanton has promised that he is taking steps to try to straighten out the acknowledged CBS news bias against the Administration; that he will report to me on the steps he has taken when they are completed and that in the future I should feel perfectly free on any instance where CBS gives us a bad time to call Stanton and tell him that. He will then attempt to correct it and further that anytime we have a major news event as to which we would like any kind of extra coverage, I am to call Stanton and alert him in advance. This, by the way, was his offer. He said sometimes "our people won't sense what is to you a very important story and if you will simply let me know in advance I will see that our people are aware of its importance."

I have rather complete notes of the meeting and of the statements made. There is no way, based on what was said in the meeting, that Stanton can use this against us. Quite to the contrary, it is clear that he is the one who made the proposition. His acknowledgments were rather extraordinary and if he follows up his offer it could be very helpful to us in the future. The fact that he even made it is a remarkable concession.

I don't expect great things. Anything we will gain will be a plus. It is interesting that in the last few nights, CBS has given us perhaps a little better and stronger treatment than the other networks. This is typical of the pattern if you remember my meeting with him last August. We got a rash of very good coverage for a few weeks thereafter before they fell back into their old ways. We shall see, however.

[Marking indicates President was verbally briefed on the contents of this memorandum.]

cwc15, 129

JULY 21, 1971

TO: **H. R. Haldeman**

FROM: **John Dean**

RE: **Memorandum to White House Staff Re Xerox Machine Carelessness**

Pursuant to your earlier instruction I have been checking on a daily basis the Xerox machines and to my amazement finding incredible documents being left there. I have been calling offices on a daily basis to inform them of the carelessness being exercised at the Xerox machines but I think that the problem is widespread enough to alert all members of the staff to this problem. Accordingly I would like to forward the attached memorandum.

Agree _____
Disagree _____
Comment _____

JULY 21, 1971

TO: **The White House Staff**

FROM: **John Dean**

RE: **Documents Left at the Xerox Machine**

It has come to our attention that many members of the staff are leaving very sensitive documents at the Xerox machines after copying. Before your office is embarrassed by leaving such documents at the Xerox machine, you are urged to exercise greater care.

JWD3

CONFIDENTIAL/EYES ONLY

JULY 21, 1971

TO: **Leonard Garment**

FROM: **John Dean**

Attached are excerpts of an intelligence report indicating that Leonard Bernstein has been commissioned by the Kennedy Center for the Performing Arts to compose music for the dedication ceremony for the Kennedy Center and that Bernstein's secret intention is to compose a Latin Choral program that will be sung at the dedication ceremony and it will really be an anti-war theme in Latin. It is anticipated that high government officials will attend the dedication ceremony, perhaps even the President, and will applaud the composition without recognizing the true meaning and later be embarrassed by the situation when it will be reported in the press that the true meaning of the score is of an anti-war nature.

    I would like to request that you take a close look at this problem and monitor it and make sure that none of our officials are embarrassed by such a program if this is an accurate report.

    Would you also advise me when the proposed dedication ceremony is scheduled and what information is available at this time regarding the dedication ceremony.

    Thank you, Leonard.

cc: Dwight Chapin

JWD3

EYES ONLY

JULY 22, 1971

TO: **H. R. Haldeman**

FROM: **Charles Colson**

RE: **CBS**

There are some pretty good initial indications that Frank Stanton is in fact delivering on his commitment last week.

    You probably noted in the press (*New York Times* article attached) the beginnings of a rather major personnel shakeup in CBS. My information is that it will lead to Salant's removal which I am positive is what Stanton was talking about when he said significant changes would be made. Hopefully we will get some people in place who are a little more objective than CBS news management is at present.

More concrete evidence, however, comes from CBS's coverage over the past week. As you observed, they have been playing our China initiative more heavily and more favorably than the other networks. They haven't missed an Administration news event and yesterday we had perhaps the most significant indication of all. In an effort to try to fill in some Administration news on a dull news day when nothing was flowing out of the White House, we programmed Don Johnson to have a press conference at the VA in which he would talk about the success of the VA drug program, but more importantly the success of the Jobs for Veterans program, with particular emphasis on the declining unemployment rate among Vietnam veterans. Al Snyder called the three networks Tuesday night to inform them of the press conference.

CBS was the only one to show up. Pierpoint was there himself, asked a number of questions and Cronkite carried almost a full minute of this last night, a very positive account of the declining unemployment rate. There was no news in the press conference; it was a pure "puff" job. Cronkite's report was a pure "puff" job. Neither of the other networks carried it and it was not really that much of a news story.

I conclude from this one instance plus the general coverage that Stanton has clearly passed the word on. How long it will stick is another question, but at the moment CBS is being most responsive.

[Marking indicates President was verbally briefed on the contents of this memorandum.]

CWC15
_____
W/RN from CWC129

EYES ONLY

JULY 22, 1971

TO: **John Ehrlichman**

FROM: **Charles Colson**

RE: **Further on Pentagon Papers**

As we discussed earlier this week I met today with Bud Krogh and reviewed with him what he has done to date and what his immediate plans are.

We both agreed that the major task at hand is to pull together all of the information that is available in Justice, Defense, CIA, State and outside. We must determine whether we have a case that can be made public with respect to Ellsberg and any conspiracy with his colleagues.

At the moment I think Bud has a good investigative mechanism (although he thinks he will need the full time services of Jack Caulfield, a matter I would like to discuss with you). Leddy [sic] is an excellent man. Hunt can be very useful.

Within a week or ten days I would think we should be in a position to evaluate the case. We must then decide where the focus of action is to be on the Hill, i.e., the Armed Services Committee, the Ichord Committee or both. Ichord is now showing signs of interest if we can demonstrate to him that we have a case. Mardian has already worked a deal of sorts with Hebert, but both Krogh and I feel that the Armed Services Committee may not be the right forum nor are the personalities the kind of tigers we need.

Whether we can make the case publicly is one question; a second question is where the political punch line is even if we can make the case. To paint Ellsberg black is probably a good thing; to link him into a conspiracy which suggests treasonous conduct is also a good thing, but the real political payoff will come only if we can establish that there is what the *National Review* has called a "counter government" which is deliberately trying to undermine U.S. foreign policy and the U.S. position in the world and that it is the President who stands against this "counter government," who conquers them and who rescues the nation from the subversion of these unsavory characters. We must be certain we can direct this effort in a way that gives us the political positions we need and ties our political opposition into the enemy camp.

There is a second objective, however, as to which I think the political payoff is even more significant. Congressional hearings will begin this fall in both the Senate and the House on the revelations of the Kennedy/ Johnson papers. It is in this forum that we can clearly nail our prospective Democratic opponents, thoroughly discredit the Kennedy power elite which masterminded our foreign policy during the Kennedy Administration and which LBJ unfortunately inherited. There is considerable research which must be done into the events and personalities of the entire era. We need to know the vulnerable points like the Diem coup, build our case from what is in the public record and what we can dig out ourselves and see that it is adequately fed to the people on the Hill who will be on our side during the hearings. Bud had not focused on the second objective. In my opinion, it is politically more promising to us, although I am clearly in favor of doing both.

As to the first effort (i.e., Ellsburg) [sic] Bud and Dave Young are working in tandem. I question, however, whether Dave should be involved at this stage in the second effort.

I have assigned Howard Hunt the job of going through the Pentagon Papers, picking out those areas where we might be able to expose the Harrimans, the Warnkes, the Cliffords, the Vances, the McGeorge Bundys and McNamaras, etc. He will begin an independent investigation of the facts surrounding each of these key targets as he has done with the coup episode. Each of the prospective Democratic opponents next year can be vulnerable if we can tie them or their advisers into gross misjudgments committed during this period.

There is some considerable internal delicacy to this second phase. My thought is that Howard should do a complete evaluation both substantively and politically over the next few weeks. When that is completed we will have to make a decision as to the points that we can and want to make and the modus operandi.

It seems to me that at this point you and I need to spend a few minutes to be sure that we are tracking correctly on this and to cover one or two administrative points that have been raised.

[Marking indicates President was verbally briefed on the contents of this memorandum.]

cwc15

EYES ONLY

JULY 23, 1971

TO: **H. R. Haldeman**

FROM: **Charles Colson**

RE: **CBS**

I don't know that I can stand it. CBS Morning News yesterday gave us a sickeningly favorable report on the casualty situation. Last night Cronkite was the only one of the 3 networks to take note of the fact that during Kerry's POW press conference yesterday he was harassed by angry pro-Administration wives who accused Kerry of using the POWs for political profit.

I don't know what's next, but at the rate they are going they might even start having Cronkite praise the Vice President. I'll bet this is really paining these guys.

cwc129

JULY 23, 1971

Dear Lou:*

The Air Force survey that you wrote me about has already been awarded unfortunately to the Retail Credit Corp. [address]. That's all I've been able to find out, but I'm checking further as to why you didn't get an opportunity to bid.

One thing you should clearly do is to write to all contracting agencies asking to be included on a bidders list. Sometimes when these come in for clearance as in the case with the present VA poll, the contractor has already been selected and hence every now and then, like this instance, it will be too late when we learn of it.

I think a general letter from you asking to be on the list would be very useful.

Sincerely,

Charles W. Colson
Special Counsel
to the President

*[Letter to Louis Harris, of Louis Harris and Associates]

cwc129

JULY 24, 1971

TO: **Pat O'Donnell**

FROM: **Charles Colson**

We should always consider using George Bush more often as a good speaking resource. He is very good on his feet, he generally can get media attention, he does have Cabinet rank and he takes our line beautifully. I would make more of an effort to get him into things as you find good forums than we have done in the past.

cwc129

EYES ONLY

JULY 26, 1971

TO: **H. R. Haldeman**
        John Ehrlichman

FROM: **John Dean**

RE: **Nixon Library**

Attached at Tab A is a report which I requested GSA prepare on the potential utilization of the land which you inspected at Camp Pendleton as a site for the Nixon Library. I have been assured by Casselman that knowledge of the project was restricted to completely loyal and trusted persons.

There would appear to be several essential and immediate steps necessary to obtain the property for a library site:

First, the restrictive language placed in the Military Construction Authorization Act of 1972 must be deleted by the Senate. Clark MacGregor is working on this in the context of the general question of turning over Pendleton property to California (see Tab A).

Second, agreement should be reached on the precise parcel(s) of land we are interested in. I had DeMarco visit the site with the GSA people and he believes that the 132 acres designated in the rough survey and contained in the GSA report are ample. Apparently other potential sites have been smaller and the architect has indicated that 100 acres would be ideal.

Third, the potential library site property must be excluded from that portion of the property to be leased to California. We can make a strong argument that it must be set aside for security reasons. The Secret Service feels that it will create serious security problems if the lands become a public park. Accordingly, this land should be excluded on security grounds, which will keep it available for later acquisition.

After the land has been quietly set aside for security reasons, I do not think anything should be done until after the election. Obviously, acquiring this land for a Presidential library is going to be *very* controversial. Accordingly, we should take no action until immediately after the election. In the interim, we should carefully plan each step necessary to make the acquisition.

I will await your guidance.

JWD3

W/RN from JFB4

JULY 28, 1971

TO: **H. R. Haldeman**

FROM: **Pat Buchanan**

Clark Mollenhoff called—he is very concerned about two things.

One is the impending release of Hoffa at the end of August when he comes up for Parole.* Mollenhoff feels this would be a disastrous mistake, that Hoffa is a crook, and that Fitz jumps when Hoffa whistles. Also, it is true that we are getting some flack from columnists on this one—they are writing about a "deal" with the Nixon Administration. Mollenhoff says he is writing a book about organized crime—and that we can be the beneficiary of this in 1972, if we don't go and free Hoffa.

Secondly, he strongly urges that we put a stop to the Hirschhorn Museum project on the Mall.** Hirschhorn is a convicted crook, who paid fines in Canada, a sleazy wheeler-dealer of the old school, and Mollenhoff says that the Administration should stop proceedings on the Hirschhorn Museum pending determination of what has been uncovered by the McClellan Committee. Dillon Ripley of the Smithsonian, who is pushing this thing, is no friend of ours.

*HANDWRITTEN NOTE FROM HALDEMAN: "Buchanan—Remind Mollenhoff it is the *Parole Board* that frees Hoffa—not us—if anyone does."
**HANDWRITTEN NOTE FROM HALDEMAN: "I agree."

PJB3

W/RN from PJB1

JULY 28, 1971

TO: **H. R. Haldeman**

FROM: **Pat Buchanan**

Edith Efron's book on the networks (which Roche mentions)—a devastating indictment of anti-Nixon bias in the 1968 campaign—you have in hand. As it makes its way to the book stands, we should do our best to see that it gets broad circulation, as one can be sure the major book clubs and reviews will either skewer or ignore it. And it is published by a very small company, so columns should be encouraged.

Thus far, I have:

a. Provided a jacket endorsement, and sought one from Mollenhoff as well—which should prove highly controversial in content.

b. Talked with a foundation about mailing it to editors and campus editors around the country—*if we can pony up the cash for the books and the mailing.*

Further, this might be something which the Vice President can mention in the course of a speech, or simply hold up and recommend it—to give it maximum publicity. Once it becomes public, there will be no question but that it will become a focus of public national debate. (Behind Miss Efron is a foundation on which W. F. Buckley and others are situated. They are the ones who tracked me to it.) One word of caution—there will be a massive attempt to discredit her sources, and her research—and a national quarrel of sorts over the book itself.

But the broader circulation it gets, the better for us.

HRH71; PJB3

W/RN from PJB1

JULY 29, 1971

TO: **Larry Higby**

FROM: **Charles Colson**

RE: **Herb Klein**

The attached speaks for itself.

In recent weeks I have been running into increasing Herb Klein problems. I have not wanted to raise them with Bob because I'm a big boy and I've got to straighten it out myself. Herb is reorganizing his office parallel to mine. Malek and Horton would be able to give you the gory details. It's too agonizing for me to get into. I now see the problem, however, from looking at the enclosed.

Herb has decided to stop traveling so that he can stay here and protect his staff and his role. What he is doing is getting in the way of everything. His assignment, as I understood it, was to get on the road and recruit editors. Obviously he is not doing that.

Do you think this should be raised with Bob so that Bob might ask Herb how he is doing on his principal assignment, i.e., getting editors, which might encourage Herb to get back out on the road? Honestly, I'm not being picayune about this—he does us much more good away from here than here.

At this point I would just like your personal reaction. It is obvious to me that he is staying close to home for protective reasons.

cwc129

JULY 31, 1971

TO: **Charles W. Colson**

FROM: **Doug Hallett**

In case you haven't heard about it, Monday's Kevin Phillips column is going to be a steam-roller job on Father McLaughlin, portraying him as an overly sexed left-winger, and blasting the administration for lousy personnel policies.

cwc99

AUGUST 2, 1971

TO: **Mr. H. R. Haldeman**

FROM: **Alexander P. Butterfield**

RE: **Tennis Court on the South Lawn**

The subject of the tennis court on the South Lawn has come up again—and, in short, the President believes the facility to be an eyesore and would like a plan for better use of that particular area.

The purpose of this note—in addition to making you aware of this current displeasure—is to tell you that I have asked Rex Scouten to come up with some alternatives. I will keep both you and the President informed of developments; but in the meantime I should think that we would want to discourage the President's following through with his present intention to have the court removed. As you will recall, we just completed some fairly fancy construction work out there—enlarging the court to the standard size and resurfacing it. Moreover, it *does* get its share of use by our tennis buffs. I suppose what I am saying here is that we may want to "delay" until late fall, then take another reading of the President's mood and inclination.

ss82

AUGUST 2, 1971

TO: **Brig. General James D. Hughes**
Military Assistant to the President
Brig. General Alexander M. Haig
Deputy Assistant to the President for National Security Affairs

FROM: **Alexander P. Butterfield**

RE: **Governor Reagan's Forthcoming Trip to the Far East**

Having discussed with the President this afternoon the matter of Governor Reagan's forthcoming trip to the Far East, I can now confirm his desire and intention to:

—Send the Governor as his personal emissary;

—Provide an aircraft from the Special Air Mission fleet, preferably a VC-137 or a VC-135.

ss82

AUGUST 2, 1971

TO: **Charles Colson**

FROM: **Howard Hunt**

RE: **Kennedy Holdovers in the Nixon Administration**

My taped interview with Clifton DeMotte yields the following:

—Teresa Krause, a member of JFK's campaign team, is now secretary to a high GSA official, probably in Washington.

—Jack McNally, also a Kennedy aide, is Administrative Assistant to the Regional Director of the Small Business Administration in Boston.

HANDWRITTEN NOTE FROM COLSON TO GEORGE BELL: "G B—Check these out, please—and advise me CWC"

cwc5

AUGUST 3, 1971

TO: **H. R. Haldeman**

FROM: **Charles Colson**

RE: **Conservative Support**

Is someone around here working on suggestions for what we might do to bring the conservatives back into line? I've talked several times to Buchanan about it who does not offer any positive suggestions; I have the feeling that Pat feels hurt that we have not heeded his advice before.

I will be glad to convene a little task force to see if we can come up with ideas in this area. It seems to me that we need to make some significant gesture—not immediately and not too obviously—to the conservatives. That is what they are playing for and if we give them no signal back, they can become intractable and vindictive. I know them well as you do and the longer they stay out in their isolated position, the tougher it's going to be to bring them back onto the team.

Van Shumway has come up with the idea of Ronald Reagan speaking at the National Press Club here supporting the President's China initiative. I think this is an excellent idea and the timing would be very good to show that the top elected conservative leader is strongly with us. There may be a whole series of things like this that we can develop which are cosmetic and I would suspect that we could do some substantive things in the domestic area.

Do you agree as to the need? If you indicate no one else is thinking about this, we will get started immediately.

cwc129

AUGUST 4, 1971

TO: **Mr. Haldeman**

FROM: **Charles W. Colson**

RE: **FYI—Mailing of Editorial on the Pentagon Papers**

The Martin S. Hayden editorial, "Our Colleagues Err on War Issue," which criticized the publication of the Pentagon Papers in the *New York Times* and other involved papers, was mailed on July 30th to:

> Editorial writers
>
> Radio and TV editorial personnel
>
> Republican Senators and Congressmen
>
> Democratic Senators and Congressmen
>
> Political Magazine writers
>
> Total mailing: 1675

The editorial, which appeared in the *Detroit News,* was accompanied by a letter from Peter B. Clark, publisher and president of the Evening News Association.

The *Reader's Digest* will publish the editorial in its September issue.

cwc129

AUGUST 4, 1971

TO: H. R. Haldeman

FROM: John Dean

RE: Nixon Papers and Memorabilia—Status Report

This project, which has turned out to be somewhat larger than I first anticipated, has been divided into four areas.

First, I am focusing on precisely which papers generated by the Administration are Presidential papers. While there is no law on the matter per se, there is a good deal of precedent and a few related statutes that peripherally deal with the matter.

Second, I am developing options for controlling the ultimate disposition of these papers.

Third, I am examining the estate and tax problems that should be considered in the President's disposition and handling of his papers.

Fourth, I am examining the related problems that should be of concern to the key staff members with regard to their own papers.

I am hopeful of completing the project by the end of next week.

JWD3

AUGUST 4, 1971

TO: Charls Walker
        Under Secretary of Treasury

FROM: John W. Dean, III
        Counsel to the President

RE: Hughes Medical Institute

Attached is a letter I recently received from Bob Bennett, who I understand represents Howard Hughes in some of his Washington concerns. Could you please advise me of the status of this matter and provide an appropriate draft response to Mr. Bennett.

Thank you for your assistance.

JWD3

AUGUST 4, 1971

TO: Al Haig

FROM: Charles Colson

RE: Lou Harris

Lou Harris was in today. He will soon be visiting the Soviet Union at their invitation. He has asked whether he should ask for a meeting with Brezhnev and if so what the appropriate channels are, do we approve of his doing so and does our ambassador render any assistance.

Lou also suggested that it would help his stature enormously if there could be even a small reception for him at the American Embassy. He says that the Russians are very conscious of these kinds of things and that this would improve his stature during his visit. He is, of course, eager to give us a complete debriefing on his meetings.

He told me that since the China initiative in particular, the Russians have been calling him with all sorts of invitations and entreaties that he visit the Soviet Union. They are intensely interested in American public opinion and are very anxious to learn more about Harris' polling system which they "claim" that they want to duplicate in Russia.

I don't know whether the reception idea is feasible. It would be a very good stroke from our standpoint if it is. In any event I would hope someone would send a message to the Ambassador urging that he extend all possible courtesies.

cwc129

w/RN from cwc69

AUGUST 6, FRIDAY

TO: **CWC**

FROM: **GTB**

Per the attached:

    1. Kingsley's ofc advises they are working on McNally.

    2. GSA has no record of a Krause working for them.

cwc5

AUGUST 10, 1971

TO: **George Bell**

FROM: **Charles Colson**

I am very sorry that we missed [William] Eberle's appointment earlier. I raised it with Haldeman this morning. He has been offered it and has accepted. It is, therefore, too late to do anything. We simply have to chalk this one up as a missed bet. We never should have let the guy through here anyway. By the way, did you ever find out whether we were consulted on this one?

cwc5

w/RN from cwc129

AUGUST 12, 1971

TO: **The President**

FROM: **Pat Buchanan**

Clearly, the approach to John Lindsay, on the part of Republicans, should be mockery and ridicule and humor in answer to his candidacy or his attacks.

Here is an individual who has presided over the utter collapse of America's greatest city—now presuming to offer us the same for the greatest nation in the world.

New York's problems should be tied to Lindsay in all "deep backgrounders" by Presidential aides; we should laugh about the ridiculousness of his position; we should portray him as the candidate of charisma and incompetence.

Lindsay is getting out of New York before it's taken into receivership. Rockefeller should use this line, Reagan, our people on the Hill (like Buckley), and others, in interviews, to attempt to make a laughingstock out of him. Paul Keys might well have some first-rate joke ideas about the Lindsay candidacy—connecting it always with the horrible mess that exists in New York. As one writer put it, in the pick-up softball games in Central Park, you can't get anybody to play center field for fear of getting mugged.

He is the Candidate of Broadway—taking the Lindsay Show on the road; Mr. Swinger; we should portray him as the utter antithesis of the Common Man. Hopefully, however, his candidacy will polarize the Democrats and produce some drive for a Fourth Party.

Interesting to note, however, is that if Lindsay is a hardnosed realist—rather than a softhead—he might well stay in his party and fight for the Democratic candidate to assure his own station in the Democratic party for a statewide run in 1974. At present he cannot, in my view, conceivably win his party's nomination, but he may be able to derail Muskie in the late primaries; he creates a real problem for Edward M. Kennedy, who has now a credible challenger for the leftwing banner in the Democratic party, and he offers some attractions as a Vice Presidential candidate.

PJB4

W/RN from PJB1

AUGUST 16, 1971

TO: **H. R. Haldeman**

FROM: **Charles Colson**

The attached is the Letters to the Editors report for the week of August 9. Fifty-one letters were sent and six were published.

CWC129

AUGUST 20, 1971

TO: **Miss Gertrude Brown,** Security Assistant

FROM: **Alex Butterfield**

RE: **Mr. Daniel Lewis Schorr**

The purpose of this memorandum is to confirm word passed to you earlier in the day via telephone—that you should instruct the FBI to proceed with the full field background investigation of Mr. Daniel Lewis Schorr, CBS Correspondent.

(I have talked to Mr. Higby about this matter and henceforth he will inform me as soon as requests of this nature are generated.)

ss82

AUGUST 26, 1971

TO: **The President**

FROM: **Patrick J. Buchanan**

The attached article in *Atlantic,* plus two reviews of it in *Time* and *Newsweek,* is a seminal piece of major significance for U.S. society—in where its conclusions lead. Basically, it demonstrates that heredity, rather than environment, determines intelligence—and that the more we proceed to provide everyone with a "good environment," surely the more heredity will become the dominant factor—in their intelligence, and thus in their success and social standing. It is almost the iron law of intelligence that is being propounded here—based on heredity. This fellow is for sure to get the Jensen-Shockley treatment for this thesis. But the importance of this article is difficult to understate [sic]. If correct, then all our efforts and expenditures not only for "compensatory education" but to provide an "equal chance at the starting line" are guaranteeing that we wind up with the intelligent ones coming in first. And every study we have shows blacks 15 I.Q. points below whites on the average. This is a powerful and seminal article—would suggest that the President write Irving Kristol and Pat Moynihan, among others, for possible refutation.

If there is no refutation, then it seems to me that a lot of what we are doing in terms of integration of blacks and whites—but, even more so, poor and well-to-do—is less likely to result in accommodation than it is in perpetual friction—as the incapable are played consciously by government side by side with the capable.

This piece could serve, frankly, as an intellectual basis for political decisions either "realistic" or rather frightful.

PJB4

AUGUST 28, 1971

My dear Mr. President:

I just heard with deep regret that you and Mrs. Nixon could not be present at the official opening of the John F. Kennedy Center for the Performing Arts. While I am most appreciative of your thoughtfulness in turning over the center to the Kennedy family, I personally feel it will be a most disappointing evening for me and all the guests if you and Mrs. Nixon cannot share this inaugural performance. Your presence will add a glowing tribute to my son, the late President, and will add dignity and lustre to this opening night.

Dear Mr. President, let us all show that our hearts as well as our minds are united in making this Center truly a mecca where Americans can join together, and through their participation in its programs spread knowledge of the arts, and inspiration to pursue them, among all the people of our country.

My best personal remembrances,

Very sincerely,

[s/Rose Kennedy]

PPF188:
MATERIAL REMOVED
FROM PRESIDENT'S DESK

ACTION PAPER

AUGUST 30, 1971

The President is very much interested in Milton Friedman's suggestion that we make it legal for Americans to own gold.

Friedman's point was that this is a move that would very much please the Conservatives, would be a very big marker with them and would have no appreciable significant effect otherwise.

The point is that FDR took away the right for Americans to own gold and Richard Nixon could get the credit for getting it back.

Friedman suggested this to Shultz. The President would like the research done on it and a proposal in to him as quickly as possible.

HRH

HRH112

SEPTEMBER–DECEMBER

SEPTEMBER 7, 1971

TO: **Chuck Colson**

FROM: **Pat Buchanan**

The "Statue of Responsibility" does not sound like something I would like to visit, and the use of Alcatraz for the Statue of Freedom does not appeal to me. Something uniquely West Coast—in San Francisco Harbor—might be a good idea, but it does not seem to me something that could be in the works or useful prior to a Second Term. Do not like the idea of "copying" the Statue of Liberty, which is unique and should remain so. Perhaps some other use of Alcatraz can be found—if we can get the Redskins off.

PJB3
_____
W/RN from PJB1

SEPTEMBER 9, 1971

TO: **H. R. Haldeman**

FROM: **Charles Colson**

RE: **Senator Bob Dole**

As you know we have a continuing problem with Bob Dole attacking many of the Democratic Presidential candidates who are senators. Senators don't do these things and never refer to one another on the floor of the Senate in other than a complimentary fashion.

What Bob has to do is attack hard in speeches when he is not on the Senate floor. We gave him two speeches in the last two days attacking Muskie. They were good Buchanan hardliners. Dole watered them both down considerably, taking out most of the personal references.

I intend to meet with him to talk about this. He seems generally receptive whenever we talk to him personally but he needs to be constantly reminded of his role as the principal partisan defender of the President.

The only purpose of this memo is to suggest that if and when you are talking to Dole, you lay the point on him very hard.

CWC57

W/RN from CWC130

SEPTEMBER 9, 1971

TO: **H. R. Haldeman**

FROM: **Pat Buchanan**

Need immediate action on this, or issue will be moot.

John Sears, as counsel, represents a number of Japanese clients. Am sure he would be interested in attending that dinner for the Japanese Cabinet members and trade officials. Would be most helpful to him— however, it could be helpful to us also. Recognize that Sears is not on the best of terms with the Attorney General [and] a few White House Staff, but from the President's standpoint, he can be valuable. First, his contacts with press are excellent. Secondly, he is highly regarded as a source of political analysis by media. Third, most all the right-wingers who are bitter with the Administration are high on Sears, and value his judgment and advice. Fourth, despite the fact that, as Sears contends, "I have a short but impressive list of political enemies," he remains loyal to the President personally, and at a word from the President would be helpful with some of our political problems—acting as an independent free agent. All the President would have to do in my personal judgment is say, "How are you, John, I might be calling on you for some political services or analyses, from time to time, in the future."

My view is that despite personal feelings, in 1972, we are going to have to become more inclusive; we are going to need every hand on an oar. If this can be arranged, all concerned would benefit.

bc: Dick Allen

PJB3

W/RN from PJB1

SEPTEMBER 10, 1971

TO: **Henry A. Kissinger**
    H. R. Haldeman

FROM: **Patrick J. Buchanan**

That invitation for me to join a group of young political leaders, under the auspices of the American Council of Young Political Leaders, has been formalized. The invitation runs from October 28 to November 14. Am getting the itinerary, etc., in a few days.

As for the reservations, they seem exaggerated. First, it would be the simplest of things for me to respond to any queries on SALT, Mideast, China, etc., with the standard response that "there are foreign policy issues outside my area of expertise and responsibility; negotiations are underway with which I am not conversant; and because I am a member of the President's staff, I would prefer to hold off any comment, lest the wrong impression be given."

Secondly, my own views and position—to the right of the President—are not unknown to the Soviets; they have been noted in Soviet publications, and surely those three years of contacts with their KGB man at the UN did not leave them in the dark as to whom they were dealing with. In short, the Russians already know from their own experience with me, and surely with the Administration, that my personal views are not those of the President.

Third, there would be no problem on my part simply to opt out of any discussion—from my side—of foreign policy questions, if that were required. On the other hand, if there is any message that is desired to be transmitted—this could be done as well. .

Fourth, a simple expedient to guarantee no wrong signal could be a phone call to Dobrynin, telling him that Buchanan was a conservative who maintains our contact with the American Right, and his views of course are not the views of the Administration.

In short, I don't see any danger—and if there is one, that could be easily removed.

Finally, this is a golden opportunity to get a first-hand look at the Soviet Union, for me to get some fixed impressions—and I hate to be denied the opportunity simply because my views about Soviet intentions and trustworthiness do not correspond with those of Uncle Ave.

If I am not to be allowed to go, then I would like to have that decision made by the President, and to have him see this memorandum.

Thanks.

PJB3

W/RN from PJF1

ACTION

SEPTEMBER 11, 1971

TO: **The President**

FROM: **John Ehrlichman**

RE: **Antitrust Action Against Television Networks**

In my recent conversation with John Mitchell he raised the question of proceeding with the antitrust action against the television networks.

You will recall that at the time of the Pentagon Papers–*New York Times* controversy I felt strongly that such an action would be misconstrued as a part of a concerted campaign against the media.

I think that undoubtedly the climate is now changed and I would have no objection to the Justice Department going forward with the proposed lawsuits.

If you concur, we will advise the Attorney General to proceed immediately after preparation of a p.r. game plan which will make our motives and the merits of the case as clear as possible. We have to anticipate that the television media will counter-attack vigorously and it is necessary for us to have mobilized the film industry, the print media and others to clearly set forth our side of the case.*

Concur in the recommendation that the Justice
Department proceed immediately with the antitrust
actions against the television networks _____

Delay the institution of the suits further _____

See me _____

I will talk to the Attorney General about this personally _____

*HANDWRITTEN RN NOTE: "vitally important to plan the P.R. aspects. Get Coulson [sic] in on this phase of it."

POF13

_____

SENSITIVE/EYES ONLY

SEPTEMBER 17, 1971

TO: **The Honorable John B. Connally**
       Secretary of the Treasury

FROM: **Jon M. Huntsman**
       Special Assistant to the President

RE: **Outline of Proposal for Interim International Monetary Arrangements Proposed by David Rockefeller**

The President read Dr. McCracken's memorandum of September 13, 1971, which included a brief outline of the discussion held with David Rockefeller about international economic developments and their implications for policy. (A copy is attached.)

It was stated that the President totally disagreed with the direction proposed by Mr. Rockefeller and requested that you advise those on the staff who are concerned with this matter. It was pointed out that Mr. Rockefeller wants to go back to the patched-up old system supported by all other international bankers. It was also noted that this kind of a system may be right for international bankers, but is totally wrong for the country.

Thank you.

ss83, 86

SEPTEMBER 17, 1971

TO: **The President**

FROM: **Patrick J. Buchanan**

Understand thought is being given to televising nationally the RN appearance before the Detroit Economic Club. Don't think we should do that—for the following reasons:

1. An hour's show with Richard Nixon answering the concerns of some Detroit Fat Cats does not seem to me particularly good television; it will lack the adversary setting of a press conference and the sharpness of questions RN can expect from editors and writers.

2. An hour is simply too long—to sustain the interest of Middle America.

3. We have nothing really new to say, from my knowledge; the President has already covered the "news" in Thursday's conference.

4. The President's greatest political asset is the Presidency—part of the power of that asset adheres in the *distance* between the Presidency and the people. Harry Truman as Harry Truman is a clown—as President, he fills the shoes of Lincoln, Wilson, etc. The more we show of RN the individual in front of a camera, the more in my judgment we diminish some of the mystery, aloofness that surrounds the office. We make the President too "familiar" a figure—and not in the best sense of that word.

5. What makes China such an interesting, important country and De Gaulle such an interesting man—is the aloofness, the distance, from the hoi polloi. Every time we put the President on the camera in a conventional setting—answering Q and A—we tend, I think, to bring him down closer to the average man—and I don't believe that is to our political advantage—partly for the next reason.

6. I have never been convinced that Richard Nixon, Good Guy, is our long suit; to me we are simply not going to charm the American people; we are not going to win it on "style" and we ought to forget playing ball in the Kennedys' Court.

This new emphasis of running the President on the tube at more and more opportunities is a corollary of the theorem that the more people who see the President, the more who will become enthusiastic about him. We are selling personality; but we know from our experience with television shows how even the most attractive and energetic and charming personalities don't last very long.

7. As I wrote the President long ago, in 1967, we watched Rocky rise twenty points in the national polls in a year in which he was probably not once on national television. When Rocky took to the airwaves in 1968, running around the country—he dropped in the polls as he did in 1964. In short, what is said and written around Nelson Rockefeller's accomplishments—compared with the accomplishments of others—is invariably better received than the presence of Rocky himself in a competitive situation.

8. The President is going to be on with Phase II in October, and with the Vietnam announcements in November. My judgment is that we ought not to put him on the air without serious thought, and usually only in context with some significant pronouncement.

9. Finally, am not at all against some of the more imaginative ideas for presenting the President—but they should come out of a Media Strategy, which I don't know we have right now—or I don't see how this fits into it.

PJB4

w/RN from PJB1

SEPTEMBER 17, 1971

TO: **Bruce Kehrli**

FROM: **Pat Buchanan**

Your approach here is wrong and unrealistic. First, you are dealing here with some real intellectual heavy-weights, among the more brilliant thinkers in American academic life. What they and the average White House staff person would talk about is beyond me. Secondly, on au courant issues, we are more likely to be up to date, and more sophisticated than they— such as the political impact of Presidential decisions, etc. These fellows with few exceptions are Governor Wallace's "pointy-heads." Their ideas are available to us in better form, written than spoken. For example, Glazer's piece in *Commentary* this weekend is going in to the Old Man; Banfield's book should be must reading for the Nixon Domestic. As contacts—used in the manner of country chairmen—they would be of little value to us; since there is no "functional" purpose in doing this, simply therapeutic, the use would not be regular and thus the benefit none.

What we would like from these fellows is not verbal reports; they are probably less useful in something like that than calling a sharp political mind (with the exception of Buckley). Rather what their advantage to the President would be is identification with the President, association with him. We can get their ideas out of their publications. But their presence at White House functions, Kristol-type dinners, with Moynihan and Kissinger present, discussions (the practical value of which I would not say is great) would reflect well on the President, which is what we want.

Between you and me, I don't think the President places a high priority on association with these types; he enjoys it; but he has more important things to do in his own mind; and other ways to exercise intellectually.

Here is the problem in a nutshell. The advantage of these academicians to the President is not verbal communication of their ideas (their ideas are better presented in the tight brilliant articles they write, not the conversation they have) but rather in the burnishing of the President's image as a Man of Thought by public association and intellectual ease in company with these cerebral power-houses.

We cannot get the latter by WH aides calling up Glazer or Trilling and asking them what they think of the "freeze" or RN's speech. To get the benefits that I have in mind, and likely what Moynihan may have in mind, RN must be seen in the company of such men himself. The problem is that the President himself, I don't believe, feels this is such a high priority with all the other "requirements" that he has to get his work done. That is not unnatural. None of us is really "taking advantage" of the intellectual stimulus and interesting associations available to a White House Assistant—we tend to be less the intellectual aristocrat or man of ease, than the hard-working drones of the President.

Moynihan, similarly Kissinger, are the type of fellows who enjoy spending an hour or so in intellectual swordplay with the names included here. Most of the President's appointments, and what they have to say, is of immediate utilitarian value to RN. Most of the fellows on this list, with some few exceptions, are not of that type. Lionel Trilling in a room with the Old Man, the AG, Connally, H & E would be about as much in place as the President amidst Sly and the Family Stone.

PJB4

W/RN from PJB1

HIGH PRIORITY

SEPTEMBER 20, 1971

TO: **Dwight Chapin**

FROM: **H. R. Haldeman**

RE: **Racing Plan**

Lest you think you have fulfilled your commitment with regard to a plan to identify the President with auto racing as a result of the event scheduled next week, let me assure you that is not the case.

I therefore am asking once again for a comprehensive plan to identify the President with auto racing.

What you have given me so far is a brief celebrity stint. Please try again and have the results in by Wednesday.

HRH197

BRIEFING PAPER

SEPTEMBER 20, 1971

TO: **H. R. Haldeman**

FROM: **Patrick J. Buchanan**

We will be making a serious mistake if we attempt to brief in depth or program Julie in any way. Among her most attractive features is her ebullience and spontaneity and freshness; we don't want to lose that. Further, in working for some years around the shop, don't recall any occasion when she has seriously muffed the ball, or when she has not been a tremendous asset to the President. She should act her natural self. However, some thoughts on issues where she will be pressed, and where the "outlines" of a position might be helpful.

Hostile press will attempt to draw her into (a) controversial social issues, (b) generational conflicts, and (c) sex-related issues. Much of the back-page emphasis these days, as one may tell from reading the *Washington Post,* is upon cultural issues, as well as political—it is in this sensitive, controversial area where Julie is more likely to step on land mines and more likely to get quoted on one or another side of one of these conflicts.

Examples:

Civil Rights Issue: On this question Julie should have herself thoroughly briefed in what the Administration has done for the blacks, with some focus upon the records (in terms of "spending") and the "firsts" in terms of appointments (Admirals, etc.). Will provide some of these from my briefing book; and have Bob Brown's shop send over its condensed summaries.

(Note: Materials that I recommend will either be attached to this memo by my secretary or forwarded to Julie through you, when we get it into this office.)

Her general posture in this area should be one of deep sympathy for the aspirations of blacks, pride in her father's record, and disagreement with the conventional wisdom, which is false, that her father and his Administration are anti-black.

The more personal anecdotes she can use in discussing issues, the more effective, more interesting, more newsworthy her responses.

Marijuana: A down-the-line generational issue, where reporters will attempt to posture her in a position of being a "square" guilty of generational treason. PJB suggestion for posture. (1) Believes marijuana use wrong and stupid; don't need artificial stimulants to be "turned on to what is good for the world." (2) Believes it should *not* be legalized. (3) Believes, however, that those who use it may be stupid or foolish; but they are not felons or criminals. Especially when millions of college kids have tried it; they are foolish but not criminal.

Sex: The morality of the new generation versus that of the old is another "generational" issue. Framework of her position should be (a) Sex is a thing for individuals to determine (b) Her own personal standards might be considered somewhat strict and prudish and (c) Much of this "sexual revolution" is overblown prose produced by individuals who are far away from the present generation. Again, however, it is best if Julie answers something like this in her own way.

Her Father & Youth: Will send across some Q and A prepared for past press conferences, on why the President is not strong with young people. Grist for the mill here. Also, Julie in answering this should not hesitate to point up those areas, environment, volunteer army, ending the war, where the President has moved farther than any of his predecessors. Think perhaps on this one, an answer we worked up some time ago for the President might be useful.

Environment: Will provide from my past briefing books a list of the Nixon Administration accomplishments on the environment, which Julie should become acquainted with—as this is a clear youth-oriented issue, likely to come up.

Women's Lib: The Butch Brigade will be after Julie to come off one hundred percent for the movement; and strongly recommend that she not do so. Again, I think that the best approach is the one drafted in the President's own briefing book of last August, which puts RN on record of "Equal Pay for Equal Work," but which emphasizes the dignity in the role of housewife, the necessity of "freedom of choice" and the President's opposition to having women in social roles such as bearing arms in the nation's defense. She will probably have to finesse the women's rights amendment. Some in here think RN ought to push it—my view is that it is not good for the country; although we have endorsed it in the past; and our position should be to finesse it, i.e., the President has supported it in the past; but he is opposed to the drafting of girls and women to bear arms.

As for the extremists in the movement, they are a target of opportunity so far as I am concerned. A defense of femininity and the woman's role in American life would be well-received. Female militants are more of an object of ridicule and a pain in the butt than the black chauvinists.

Abortion: My personal judgment is that Julie should be opposed to abortion on the same grounds as her father used—she could do, politically, a world of good, with a spirited defense of the rights of the unborn. If she so believes, and needs more material than is provided in her father's statement, then she can come here for it. And we will find something for it.

Population Control: These are not her father's people; and Julie should steer clear of any endorsements of population control in my judgment. On the question of birth control information and services, she should say of course this is a matter of individual choice, based on individual standards, and those who want such information and help and cannot afford it should be helped—but does not believe in coercion or compulsion in this area. Again, the scare-mongers are not her father's friends and recent statistics show their predictions to be drastically over-stated.

Again, however, this issue will move at once to abortion. My view, again, is that Julie would personally be against abortion, as contravening her personal standards—in the case where the life of the mother is at stake, of course the choice is between the life of one and the life of the other—that choice is best left to the individual. But she believes that "abortion" is an unacceptable social policy in a country with our Judeo-Christian heritage, etc.

The above issues, cultural-political, are the kinds of issues that will be pressed on Julie by those looking for the "news" story.

Going beyond this, if Julie, on conversations with press, runs into repeated questions—where she wants some guidance—will be happy to provide some. Also, could put her at once on the President's News Summary List.

Again, however, Julie is not "expected" to be precise on the issues; what the interviewer and nation want to know is what kind of daughters Richard Nixon has raised. The girls are among the President's strongest assets—particularly in current times when it appears so many of the young from the best of families have "freaked out."

If Julie's personal views are inconsistent with those of many of her peers, in sharp disagreement, she should not hesitate to express them. The vast majority of the country I am sure prefer the "life style" of Julie and Tricia to the "Haight-Ashbury" style of the more lionized young. A ready sense of humor, of course, also is an indispensable commodity, in dealing with the ultra-seriousness of the probes that come of movement politics— whether Right, Left, Young versus Old, Women's Lib versus Male Chauvinism.

Finally, one brief suggestion. Why not have Julie call up Miss America, invite her to the White House for lunch, drop in on her father and then march her over to the Press Gallery for a light press conference—the newsies would enjoy it.

PJB4

W/RN from PJB3 and RJB1

VERY SENSITIVE

SEPTEMBER 24, 1971

TO: **The President**

FROM: **John Ehrlichman**

RE: **For Your Information—FBI Director Hoover and the Bureau's**
        Internal Problems

Talks with John Mitchell and Bob Mardian this week have emphasized the
strong possibility that two of the top four or five people under Hoover may
quit before October 1. (The head of the organized crime division of the
Bureau has retired.)

John and Bob say that one has been demoted and the other has been
asked to retire, by the Director. Both have large and devoted followings
within the Bureau. Both possess very derogatory information about the
Director.

You will recall that I told you of a similar potential situation about
two months ago. You had John Mitchell step in to prevent Brennan from
being summarily fired. The Director has now removed him from his position and demoted him.

John and Bob are fearful that the efficiency of the Bureau is suffer-
ing materially. The Ellsberg–Pentagon Papers work is lagging. The Berrigan investigation is going very well. Mardian explains that Hoover's direct
involvement in the Berrigan charges accounts for the difference.

The threat of a Congressional focus on Hoover has apparently
evaporated. However, press attacks have resumed and the Attorney General expects them to increase in the near future.

A "research project" at Princeton on the FBI will be published
soon. John expects it to be very rough on Hoover.

POF13

SEPTEMBER 24, 1971

TO: **Henry A. Kissinger**

FROM: **Pat Buchanan**

RE: **Buchanan Trip to the Soviet Union**

Thank you for withdrawing your objections to my trip to the Soviet Union.
You have my assurances that the visit will involve as little publicity as
possible.

PJB1

SEPTEMBER 25, 1971

TO: **The President**

FROM: **Patrick J. Buchanan**

Our operations contra Muskie have met, with Muskie's assistance, with considerable success. His slippage is considerable; there is a possibility Wallace could take him in the second major primary; Proxmire in the third (Wisconsin); perhaps even Jackson in Oregon—and EMK is running two-to-one ahead of him in California. We are doing a major analysis of the "gauntlet" Muskie must now run to the nomination for First Tuesday.

However, a problem has arisen and we need a decision:

a. Should we continue to focus upon Edmund Muskie, and do all we can to damage him; or should we turn to Edward M. Kennedy—whom some consider (Nofziger among them) the most difficult candidate the President could face.

b. We think the time has come to do a major *Monday* piece throwing Jackson into the same basket with all the rest of the Democrats—and unless we hear otherwise, shall do so.

c. Bob Finch feels very strongly the time has come to lay the groundwork for the "Do Nothing" Congress charge. He recommends a Cabinet meeting, clear of aides, in which RN calls on each member of the Cabinet to begin a round of speeches, taking on the Congress for its failures to push the Nixon Programs—and following which each member of the Cabinet goes about the country, both hitting the general Congressional failings—and the specific Congressional failings in their own area.

After making the initial pitch, the President might depart, leaving Bob Finch to fill in the details.

There should be produced for these Cabinet officers a set-piece speech, in which each Cabinet officer could insert materials in his own area of expertise.

Purpose—To lay the groundwork now, to leave open the President's option in 1972 to put the Democrats on the defensive as negativist Do-Nothing Congress. The schedules should be coordinated through our Cabinet speakers bureau; and a major speech drafted which would stand up for a month or so—in order that individual Cabinet officers could make variations on theme.

bcc: Bob Finch
Ken Khachigian

PJB4

W/RN from PJB1

SEPTEMBER 27, 1971

TO: **H. R. Haldeman**

FROM: **Charles Colson**

RE: **Upcoming Harris Poll**

I called Harris today who as I indicated to you has just returned from the Soviet Union. He was very distressed at the text of his column coming up on Thursday. It was not the way he had originally written it; it was edited while he was abroad.

He immediately phoned the *Chicago Tribune* syndicate which has sent a telegram to all major subscribers deleting the entire first paragraph. The column has therefore been amended as per the attached.

As you will see, this changes it from a negative to a positive lead from our standpoint. I am convinced from Harris' startled sound on the telephone that he was genuinely surprised at what someone had done to his piece.

Caution: The telegram may not catch up with columns in all instances.

[Marking indicates that the President was verbally briefed on the contents of this memorandum.]

cwc69, 130

OCTOBER 1, 1971

TO: **The President (Per HRH)**

FROM: **Patrick J. Buchanan**

RE: **China Trip**

When the list is made up [for] the trip to China, I would hope that my name, as the writer aboard, will not be ruled out because of my doubts as to the advisability of having made it. The following are the arguments for taking Buchanan along:

1. In terms of service Buchanan has longer consecutive than any other writer (just under six years).

2. Buchanan is the only writer who has yet to make a foreign trip with the President: (Safire and Huebner made the two European trips; Price went around the world—Buchanan only got a ride home from Romania).

3. Just as Buchanan's presence in San Clemente invariably leads to speculation about a "tough line," so my presence on the trip would not hurt from the standpoint of the Conservatives where we are hurting. Indeed, it might reassure some. Further, it would provide me with the

credentials to defend what the President has done among Conservatives, to answer any written attacks.

4. When this Administration is over, and diplomatic passports are withdrawn, if there is one writer who has not a chance whatsoever of being allowed in the People's Republic, it is Buchanan.

5. With the possible, but not certain exception of Safire, Buchanan is the best briefer, and backgrounder on issues among the writers.

6. Buchanan has worked on the majority of major foreign policy drafts with the President since Cambodia; and Buchanan is responsible for the foreign Briefing Book re-write.

7. Buchanan works okay with Marshal Kissinger.

8. Buchanan's long-term goals are foreign-policy-oriented and coupled with the visit to the Soviet Union, this will give me the credentials I need to make the requests I intend to make of the President in the second term.

PJB4

W/RN from PJB1

OCTOBER 1, 1971

TO: **H. R. Haldeman**

FROM: **Pat Buchanan**

We are taking a public relations beating on this woman on the Court thing. First was the near unavoidable controversy; then came the raising of hopes by the President and Mrs. Nixon and other top officials saying they were considered. Some of this came by accident and necessity, i.e., in response to a question; thus unavoidable.

But last night, some cluck obviously told Dan Rather on background to knock down the report, that we were backing away from a woman. That exercise was only damaging to the President, as Rather went on the air to "tell" the Nation's women we were backing down, and then to "tell" them that this would adversely affect the President at the polls. Clearly, Rather used the opportunity to impress upon women that they were being ignored by the President and the thing to do is retaliate at the polls. What should have been done, it seems to me, once the women thing was raised, was say nothing—until the appointments—when the new names, if not women, would be the "lead" on the story—while the fact that a woman was not chosen was buried. If hopes had to be dashed, they should have been submerged in the news of the appointment itself—not as was done.

PJB3

ACTION PAPER—Ehrlichman

OCTOBER 4, 1971

About November 15 and shortly after the second trip announcement, we should announce the plan to form the Whittier Institute for International Understanding and World Peace.

We should not worry about the legal problems, etc., or the details but just announce it is going to be done. This is the right timing for it. We can say at the same time that the Library will be in another location to be determined later. It should not be the Whittier Institute of Public Affairs or Politics but should very definitely be slanted to international understanding and world peace playing off the Quaker interest, etc.

HRH

HRH112

OCTOBER 11, 1971

TO: **Mr. John D. Ehrlichman**

FROM: **Alexander P. Butterfield**

RE: *Life* **Magazine Poll** (FYI Only)

The President could scarcely have been more astounded by a piece of news than he was this morning when he read of the *Life* magazine poll of 65 "academic experts" who ranked Earl Warren among the 12 great Justices of the total of 98 in the Supreme Court's history. He was equally taken aback by the report that Justice Brennan had been placed in the "near great" category.

His comments of surprise and bewilderment were directed to you.

ss82

OCTOBER 14, 1971

TO: **H. R. Haldeman**

FROM: **Pat Buchanan**

Clearly the President should be in line this year as one of the top two or three nominees for *Time*'s Man of the Year. With China, the Economy and Moscow—the recovery from the 1970 elections low point—the liberal media has to credit this—even as the conservatives do not.

We ought to ascertain—perhaps from Jim Keogh who worked at the top echelons of *Time*—as to how they go about selecting the top man. (Jimmy the Greek says it will be John B. Connally.) When we find out, we can touch those levers, and begin a gradual letter campaign, etc. as we attempted in 1966. This might be something that we should give some serious thought to—if and when we can come up with the necessary information on how the selection is done.

PJB3
_____
W/RN from PJB1, 3 [correct]

EYES ONLY

OCTOBER 14, 1971

TO: **Pat Buchanan**

FROM: **Charles Colson**

RE: **Attached Kennedy Speech**

You might enjoy reading through the attached; that is, if you can get all the way through it without throwing up. It's really disgusting. It is a subtle attempt to incite riot and revolution while appearing to say just the opposite. It seems to me that you might pass this around selectively to see if those who mold opinion have the same reaction that I did.

cc: Van Shumway

cwc130

OCTOBER 15, 1971

TO: **Bruce Kehrli**

FROM: **Pat Buchanan**

RE: **Your Memo on the "Bookstores"**

Assume this is to be used as a way to get Edith Efron's book on the bestseller list. This is the long way around Robin Hood's Barn. If we have to buy thousands of books simply to get tenth on a list—then I think the money can better be spent elsewhere. In a meeting with Neal Freeman and Chuck Colson, we covered this ground—suggested and agreed on a course of action to get publicity for Edith and her book. She is, incidentally, getting excellent press coverage already—in syndicated columns and front page stories in some papers (Boston, St. Louis). Freeman has her a good speaking schedule on the tube. She will appear now before Sam Ervin's committee in January, which will be good timing.

As for the bookstores—Neal Freeman says there are three bookstores in New York, which one should buy at prodigiously, which are always called by "listers" which we should focus on—if we want to go that route, which he does not recommend. My view is that—even if our idea is to get the maximum publicity and purchases for Vic Lasky's book—there are other and better ways to do it.

PJB4

W/RN from PJB4

OCTOBER 18, 1971

TO: **Jay Lovestone**

FROM: **Charles W. Colson**

As you will notice from the attached, the SDS is moving into the labor movement. Note Page 5A.

cwc130

OCTOBER 19, 1971

TO: **Larry Higby**

FROM: **John Dean**

The attached document which was found at a Xerox machine would indicate that someone on the staff is in the process of preparing his personal memoirs.

Do you have any suggestions as to who this might be before I pursue my own investigation of the matter?

JWD3

EYES ONLY

OCTOBER 20, 1971

TO: **H. R. Haldeman**

FROM: **Charles Colson**

RE: **CBS**

We have been putting some very intense pressure on CBS through their affiliate board. I just obtained a copy of a memo from Salant to one of his assistants which would indicate that perhaps the pressures are doing some good. As you will see Salant is really putting the heat on Marvin Kalb.

I don't know whether this proves anything but it's clear that continuous pressure does at least penetrate the news organizations to some

extent. The attached has been retyped because the copy was not very
legible.

cwc130

OCTOBER 20, 1971

TO: **Gordon Strachan**

FROM: **John Dean**

I am forwarding the attached material regarding the distribution of the
film *Millhouse* for your information. I will keep you advised as we monitor
the situation and try to do anything we can to deal with it.

JWD3

OCTOBER 21, 1971

TO: **Peter Flanigan**

FROM: **Charles Colson**

RE: **Corporation for Public Broadcasting**

I have reviewed once again all of our options with respect to the Corporation for Public Broadcasting. I agree with you that none of them offer an
immediate solution to the problem and none of them *guarantees* us the
immediate control that we would like.

It's clear that we cannot get control of the Board until Spring, *if
then.* It's also clear that the 1972 appropriation has been either spent or
committed and we, therefore, cannot curb funds during the present fiscal
year.

The options we have discussed involving legislation to prevent net-
work-type news programming probably have a slim chance particularly in
an election year *unless* we are able to get the support of other commercial
broadcasters and networks, something which I believe we should now
begin to explore. Even if the prospects aren't good, I think we would still
be well advised to seek legislation if for no other reason than to focus on
the issue and to get people in the Congress debating the activities of CPB.

All of the options we have discussed involve the "carrot" approach
rather than the "stick"—for example, if we make more money available
to local stations perhaps they will support us in cutting back on CPB. Since
none of these "carrot" approaches offer any immediate prospects for a
solution, it's time to try the stick. For example, we could cut the 1973
authorization and budget request from this year's $35 million to $20
million. Obviously the proponents of public television will scream and
I recognize that this includes our friends on the Board. Conceivably we
will be rolled in the Congress although once again, in this instance if we

get the support of the broadcasters and the networks we just might pull it off.

The principal reason for making these two overt moves, i.e., seeking corrective legislation and cutting funds, would be to precipitate a confrontation with the Board. At that point one of us should have a heart-to-heart talk with Frank Pace who might be persuaded to get rid of Macy. In the final analysis, if the Board members feel that getting rid of Macy is the price they have to pay to get our support they just might do it. If we could put our man in in place of Macy, he could, of course, replace the operating officials at the Public Broadcasting Service as well as bring the programming under some semblance of control.

In short, I am suggesting that we create a head-on confrontation and then make it quite clear to the Board, specifically Pace, that unless Macy goes, we intend to fight CPB all the way.

The case that we must make with Pace and the Board is *not* that we are trying to get control of CPB, but rather that CPB has violated its mandate from the Congress, has been mismanaged and has on a number of occasions strained the fairness doctrine to the limits. This case can be made solidly as you will see from Al Snyder's excellent memorandum to me, copy attached. The April 20 "Advocates" show is a flat-out violation of the fairness doctrine. The Agronsky program last Friday night not only violates the fairness doctrine but is in extremely bad taste and totally partisan. Newspapers and commercial TV and radio stations have refused to run ads for the movie, *Millhouse;* yet Agronsky gave him 20 minutes on a supposedly non-political government and foundation funded network. The job that was done on the FBI is another typical example of programming abuse. Under the heading of mismanagement, it is apparent that network "rejects" are being hired at very high salaries with extensive fringe benefits, once again paid from public and foundation funds.

While the statute prohibits government officials from interfering with CPB programming activities, it by no means exempts CPB from other Communication Act requirements. The Carnegie report also clearly warned CPB not to interfere with local broadcasting. This is, of course, precisely what they are doing by creating a fourth network. Moreover, I think what they are doing is a gross perversion of the enabling legislation.

In conclusion, I believe that we must join the issue head on and simply make it clear to the Board that we are not going to tolerate the present CPB activities. If we do this right, we can put the onus on them. They are the ones who are allowing CPB broadcasting to become political. We should not be defensive; we are not the ones seeking to take political control. We are on the side of the angels; we are simply attempting to see that CPB fulfills a non-political public service as it was originally established to do. We might find there is much more support for this point of view than we presently think.

cc: Malek & HRH

cwc130

OCTOBER 26, 1971

TO: **The Staff Secretary**

FROM: **John D. Ehrlichman**

RE: **P-1903—Mills Attack on President**

The reason no one has taken Wilbur Mills on is because it is our understanding that it is the President's desire that there be no counter attacks on Wilbur Mills.

If this is not a correct signal, then we'd better all get together and set our line differently.

cwc130

OCTOBER 26, 1971

Dear Mr. Gollob:*

I am flattered by your letter of October 15th but at the moment writing a book is the furthest thing from my mind.

As you perhaps surmised from the *Wall Street Journal,* which I assume prompted your letter, what I would like to write would be entirely unprintable—at least by any publishing concern that wished to maintain its standing among professional journalists in America.

Assuming that we are able to continue to successfully run the Government, the press notwithstanding, and assuming that I leave here in one piece, perhaps after a year of recuperation I will give it some thought and I will, of course, remember that you were the first to write to me.

Best regards.

Sincerely,

Charles W. Colson
Special Counsel
to the President

*[Letter to Herman Gollob, editor-in-chief, Atheneum Publishers]

cwc130

OCTOBER 27, 1971

TO: **John Scali**

FROM: **Charles Colson**

The attached is terribly bad. We are walking a very fine line and the domestic political reaction to the expulsion of Taiwan could, as you know, be exceedingly harmful, especially if people think that that's really the way we wanted it to turn out. You know and I know that the attached is absolutely untrue and I think Reasoner owes us a correction tonight. I wouldn't even care if he made a news story out of the fact that the White House called him in anger to say that that was not true.

Also, would you take a check, please, today on how the briefings are being set up for Bush when he comes down here? We really need him to help sell the case that we did everything we possibly could.

cwc130

NOVEMBER 5, 1971

TO: John Scali

FROM: Charles Colson

Just so my nice note earlier doesn't go to your head, I am sending this nasty note.

When I suggested you call the networks today regarding the unemployment story, you told me this was one we could rely on to give us a fair break. Chancellor's performance you should rerun. It's scandalous, yellow, shabby journalism (which as you know is pretty scandalous, yellow and shabby). We should not bother to call him, we should break his goddamned nose. But, it's our fault because we rely upon the integrity of news broadcasters of which there isn't any.

cwc130

EYES ONLY

NOVEMBER 10, 1971

TO: Larry Higby

FROM: Charles Colson

RE: Public Broadcasting Memo

I have reviewed Whitehead's memo to the President on public broadcasting. I have a few minor word changes, as you will see from the Xerox copy attached. My major points are these:

1. The President shouldn't meet with anybody from Corporation for Public Broadcasting under any circumstances. The fight is going to get dirty (see this morning's *Washington Post*), and it's, therefore, imperative to keep the President out. Nothing in this memo, by the way, should talk about the President's desire or goal for changing CPB because Whitehead and his office are as leaky as the *Titanic*.

2. Nobody suggests in this memo how we get rid of Macy and Pace. The controversy is now out in the open, ergo, there is a problem. Macy and Pace can't now step down gracefully so they must be removed. My suggestion is that Flanigan meet with Pace and document the case of mismanagement and bias, a case which I think can be made very effectively. If Pace has any self-respect he will offer to resign, but I wouldn't accept it. I would trade Macy's removal for Pace's offer or maybe if we were lucky, we could get rid of both in one fell swoop. Flanigan knows how to do this and I have given him the case (see my memo to Flanigan attached and my supplement).

3. We have to make a public case against CPB. Whitehead can start doing it in his speeches, friends on the Hill can raise hell and we can start planting some columns. CPB has apparently brought the fight out in the open so all's fair at this point. We can put together a very effective attack here. Note for example this morning that the *Post* says that Vanocur's salary will not be disclosed. Step number one might be to disclose it. Seventy thousand dollars a year plus extensive fringes. This in and of itself would be a good opening blast considering that we are paying a large part of that salary.

In short, I think the memo to the President needs to avoid anything that could ultimately suggest that he was responsible for this. Secondly, it needs to be toughened up. Thirdly, it needs to be a little more explicit as to how these things will be accomplished and when. As you will note, I have scaled down the dollar proposals. We don't need to give them $50 million in FY '73. We should only have a proposal of $40 million.

cc: Al Snyder
    Peter Flanigan

cwc130

NOVEMBER 12, 1971

TO: **Bob Haldeman**

FROM: **The President**

Pat Boone spoke to me about Goldwater's appearance in Atlanta and told me how effective it was. He urged strongly that Goldwater be used more all across the country.

I want a special effort made to follow up to see that Goldwater is scheduled in as many events as possible throughout the country, and particularly television events. I don't want this handled by the National Committee or in the usual routine way.

PPF3; HRH140, 230

NOVEMBER 12, 1971

TO: **Alexander Butterfield**

FROM: **The President**

I would like to make another purchase for long-range plans of the 1966 French Bordeaux, Chateau Margaux, Chateau Lafite-Rothschild and Haut Brion. Both the large bottles, the regular size bottles and the splits are acceptable. Would you have a check made both in New York stores and Washington stores as to what we can purchase.

Check with Rose Woods as to how we can handle this through my personal account.

I am thinking in terms of the equivalent of as many as 30 or 40 cases of the regular size bottles.

PPF3; HRH140, 230

NOVEMBER 12, 1971

TO: **Henry Kissinger**

FROM: **The President**

I think we ought to find an occasion where we can get [Admiral] Moorer in alone with me without [Defense Secretary] Laird to talk about national defense matters. Try to arrange this at some time in the near future.

HRH140, 230

W/RN from PPF3

NOVEMBER 12, 1971

TO: **Henry Kissinger**

FROM: **The President**

Before Connally returns it might be well for you to go over and have a talk with Volcker if he is in town and if not with Walker, and if both are here with both of them, to get them programmed for some of the problems we will have to discuss with Connally when he returns. It is important that Volcker and Walker not set up a cabal against the White House as we make these very important decisions.

HRH140, 230

W/RN from PPF3

NOVEMBER 15, 1971

TO: **The President**

FROM: **Clay T. Whitehead**

RE: **Public Broadcasting**

You have expressed serious concern over our failure to reform the Corporation for Public Broadcasting (CPB) and over CPB's continued sponsorship of slanted public affairs programming. (See Tab A for details of the current situation.) I have conducted a thorough review of the problem, including discussions with key senators and congressmen, various segments of the public broadcasting industry, and our friends on the CPB Board. This memorandum sets forth my analysis of the problem and recommendations for its solution.

The immediate goal is to eliminate slanted public affairs programming on public television as thoroughly and quickly as possible. The longer range and more fundamental goal is to reverse the current trend of CPB toward becoming a BBC-like fourth network supported by public funds, which inevitably would reflect the taste, politics, and morality of the national artistic and intellectual elite. Unfortunately, neither of these goals can be achieved easily. (See Tab B for background.)

Elimination of Slanted Programming

There are two approaches to achieving the immediate goal insofar as the use of Federal funds is involved: (a) a drastic cutback of funds for CPB, and (b) a redirection of CPB's expenditures. It is an unpleasant fact that neither of these approaches can succeed this fiscal year. OMB advises that we have no authority to withhold any funds appropriated to CPB; in any event, almost all of the $35 million appropriated for FY72 has been disbursed to CPB and has been irreversibly committed by CPB to programming organizations. There are, however, several steps we can take to correct this situation over the next year:

1. Induce the programmers themselves to keep some balance, under pressure of criticism from our friends on the CPB Board and among the general public. Peter Flanigan and I will meet soon with our loyal Board members to emphasize the serious concern.

2. Replace Frank Pace and John Macy. We would try to do this immediately by telling them they have lost the confidence of the Administration and thereby have become obstacles to the progress of public television; our loyal friends on the CPB Board can help in this appeal. If this is not successful, we would have them voted out next year after getting firm control of the Board. Fred Malek will begin recruiting for their replacements as soon as your approval for this move is gained.

3. Take more effective control of the CPB Board. Although we have now appointed eight of the fifteen members, because of political pressures

at the time of appointment, only four or five can be counted on to help us. We can take more effective control over the Board next April when you have five appointments to make. This will enable us to reduce drastically the CPB funding of the offensive commentators effective next summer.

4. Build more actively the public case against CPB programming bias through speeches by friends in the Congress, selected columns, and my speeches.

Redirection of Public Broadcasting

Even with a loyal Board and top management at CPB, there are limits to the change that is possible within the current structure of the Public Broadcasting Act. No matter how firm our control of CPB management, public television at the national level will always attract liberal and far-left producers, writers, and commentators. We cannot get the Congress to eliminate CPB, to reduce funds for public television, or to exclude CPB from public affairs programming. But we can reform the *structure* of public broadcasting to eliminate its worst features.

There is, and has always been, a deep division within public broadcasting over the extent of national control versus local station control. Many local stations resent the dominance of CPB and NET. This provides an opportunity to further our philosophical and political objectives for public broadcasting without appearing to be politically motivated.

We stand to gain substantially from an increase in the relative power of the local stations. They are generally less liberal, and more concerned with education than with controversial national affairs. Further, a decentralized system would have far less influence and be far less attractive to social activists.

Therefore, we should immediately seek legislation to: (a) remove CPB from the business of networking; (b) make a drastic cut in CPB's budget; and (c) initiate direct Federal operating support for local stations on a matching basis.

Senators Magnuson and Pastore have introduced a bill to extend CPB's authorization for one year at the current level of $35 million. We think it likely that this is intended to set the stage for a major effort next summer to increase CPB funding significantly on a permanent basis. Supporters of CPB are unhappy with our delay in proposing long-term financing and are certain to press for this long-sought goal during the election year. The Democrats are sure to seize any opportunity to cast you as the politically motivated opponent of public television. They will have the case they need if we combine a vigorous takeover of CPB management with a failure to deliver the improved financing we have promised.

We will be in a far better posture if we take the initiative away from the Democrats with legislative proposals based on the nonpolitical principle of localism—and do so as soon as possible before the election. The key to the success of this approach is to provide more Federal funding to the local stations than they can get from CPB. We estimate that CPB could be cut back to $20 million and that local station support for our proposals could be bought for about $30 million. Thus Federal funding would increase in total from $35 million currently to about $50 million.

This approach meets both our long and short-term objectives. It means a fight, but the fight will be conducted on solid grounds of principle, and there is a good chance of success. Even if our legislation does not pass next year, we will be in a better posture than if we had not introduced it.

Recommendations

1. Take control of the CPB Board in April with five new tough-minded Directors. Replace Macy, Pace, and other top management with our people now.

Approve ——————— Disapprove ———————

2. Seek legislation now to establish a basic new structure for public broadcasting—(a) removing CPB from the business of networking; (b) making a drastic cut in CPB's budget; and (c) initiating direct Federal operating support for local stations.

Approve ——————— Disapprove ———————

NOTE FROM BUTTERFIELD QUOTING THE PRESIDENT: "Proposed funding in new legis[lation] should not exceed $30 million."

TAB A

Current Public Broadcasting Activities in Public Affairs and "Commentary" Programming

According to the Public Broadcasting Service (PBS)—the network arm of CPB—40 percent of its current network schedule is devoted to public affairs and "commentary-type" programming. These programs include the Bill Moyers news series—"This Week"; "Black Journal," a half-hour commentary and analysis series; and six special documentaries, which are all produced by NET in New York. PBS will also be distributing the Vanocur and MacNeil "news" programs produced by the new National Public Affairs Center for Television (NPACT), which is funded by CPB and Ford Foundation and is headed by Jim Karayn, the ex-chief of NET's Washington Bureau. NPACT will also produce the Liz Drew interview show—"30 Minutes With . . . ." Agronsky's "commentary" program is not done by NPACT, but is produced by the Washington ETV station, which receives $500,000 of CPB support.

PBS also feeds two other public affairs programs to its network of stations—Bill Buckley's "Firing Line," produced by South Carolina ETV, and "The Advocates," produced by the Boston and Los Angeles stations. These two programs always present juxtaposed viewpoints on public issues and thereby achieve some balance and objectivity. But the PBS schedule includes no program in which the moderate to conservative viewpoints are featured to balance the Moyers/Vanocur/MacNeil/Drew/NET type of programming.

NET continues to dominate the national affairs programming of PBS despite the fact that it has been "merged" with the New York City ETV stations. Its current operating budget of $10 million is far and away the largest of all the public broadcast production centers. While only $4 million of its budget comes from CPB, it also receives substantial funding from Ford Foundation and other foundations. As a result of this large program budget, roughly half of all programs distributed nationally by PBS are funded and produced by NET. Other national program production is spread among seven ETV station centers—which all compete for CPB program funds and some Ford grants. The $4 million to NET is the largest single programming grant CPB makes, indeed twice the next largest, and it represents 25 percent of CPB's total budget for programming. CPB claims to be encouraging the growth of national program production centers other than NET in order to decrease NET's dominance. But it seems clear by now that they have no intention of reducing the NET support in the near future. Jack Wrather has established a committee of the CPB to set program standards including objectivity in public affairs, but there is no evidence that this is very effective.

1. OMB believes it has no legal authority to withhold money from CPB this fiscal year. Even if it did, it has already delivered $30 million of the $35 million appropriation. CPB has in turn already funded or committed itself to fund the organizations supporting the offensive commentators. The Public Broadcasting Act is now structured to minimize Executive Branch control over CPB and its activities. We cannot target cuts in funds to hit selectively at public affairs.

2. "Public television" has become something of a sacred cow because most people associate it with educational programs like "Sesame Street" for children, quality TV drama and the like, rather than with the public affairs commentary we find so offensive.

3. There is considerable Congressional support for public television, since there are local stations in 223 Congressional districts. Senators Magnuson and Pastore regard themselves as the fathers of CPB and chair the appropriations and authorizations subcommittees, respectively. CPB and the Hill are thinking of ultimate federal funding levels over $100 million annually. There continues to be support for "permanent" financing, and your last budget promised "improved" financing arrangements would be introduced this year.

4. This Administration has consistently increased the CPB budget ($5 million in FY 69 to $35 million in FY 72), emphasizing the educational

side. CPB, however, has emphasized popular programming and public affairs. They have increased NET funding from $1 million in FY 69 to $4 million in FY 72 in spite of your explicit wishes to the contrary. Our friends on the Board are supportive of most CPB activities and growth, and want only to try to bring more balance to CPB programming.

5. While the local stations are unhappy with the domination of public television programming by CPB and NET, they are hard pressed for funds and will support CPB against any efforts to reduce federal funds for public television. CPB emphasizes public affairs programming on national issues and is advertising extensively to build an audience for its prime time programming. The local stations, on the other hand, are more attuned to local needs and are heavily oriented towards non-controversial educational and instructional programming. A national public television programming organization such as CPB will *always* attract management and talent of a liberal and far-left persuasion. Unless some reforms are made in the Public Broadcasting Act, CPB will always have the potential to be and will slowly (or not so slowly) grow into a U.S. version of the BBC under the constant nurturing of the Democrats.

POF15
W/RN from SS85

NOVEMBER 18, 1971

TO: **The President**

FROM: **Patrick J. Buchanan** (As Requested)

RE: **President Lincoln's Positions on Rebels/Deserters**

On December 8, 1863, President Lincoln granted a "full pardon" to those "who have directly or by implication, participated in the existing rebellion" (i.e., Confederate soldiers and sympathizers) on "condition" that they take an oath of allegiance. He excepted from this group—high officers in the Confederacy, former Congressmen, former U.S. Judicial officials, those who had given up commissions in the U.S. Army to join the Rebels, and others.

As Lincoln died within a few days of the War's end, we find no record of a general Presidential amnesty declared for all Rebels.

On the questions of Deserters, Lincoln on March 11th of 1865 directed that all "deserters" who within 60 [days of] their desertion returned to their regiments "shall be pardoned."

However, the Congressional Act, on which this Proclamation was based, stated explicitly:

that, in addition to the other lawful penalties of the crime of desertion from the military or naval service, all persons who have deserted the military or naval service of the United States who shall not return to said service or report them-selves to a provost-marshal within sixty days after the proclamation hereinafter mentioned shall be deemed and taken to have voluntarily relinquished and for-feited their rights of citizenship and their rights to become citizens, and such deserters shall be forever incapable of holding any office of trust or profit under the United States or of exercising any rights of citizens thereof. . . .

In a letter to Erastus Corning and others, June 12, 1863, Lincoln wrote among other things:

And yet again, he who dissuades one man from volunteering or induces one soldier to desert, weakens the Union cause as much as he who kills a union soldier in battle.

In the same letter:

Long experience has shown that armies cannot be maintained unless desertion shall be punished by the severe penalty of death. The case requires, and the law and the Constitution sanction this punishment. Must I shoot a simple-minded boy who deserts, while I must not touch a hair of the wily agitator who induces him to desert.

One further notes that when riots took place in New York City against the National Conscription Act, which Mr. Lincoln had signed on March 3, 1863 (which provided that a draftee could pay $300 to find a substitute, or find a replacement), the poor called it a "Rich Man's War, a Poor Man's Fight" and rioted. Federal troops came in, and put it down with an estimated 500 dead and 1,000 wounded.

PJB1, 4

NOVEMBER 23, 1971

TO: **Pat Buchanan**

FROM: **Charles W. Colson**

I have obtained a copy of the DNC confidential analysis of the President which you might find useful.

PJB3

NOVEMBER 30, 1971

TO: **H. R. Haldeman**

FROM: **Pat Buchanan**

In the course of a conversation with Jerry Schecter, a most interesting thought came up on the check-off plan for political parties. We might have the lawyers here or the Attorney General's people look into this. Here is the idea.

If the President has to okay that tax bill with the political provision, we face the certainty of a Wallace candidacy (as I understand it he gets six million for his effort last time) and the high likelihood of a Fourth Party on the Left, and the possibility of a National Conservative Party. Given the current mood among conservatives, that could well happen.

However, suppose we cut a deal with the Conservatives:

a. The Republican Party, like the Democratic Party, takes the $20 million, and no private contributions to run its campaign.

b. A National Conservative Party is formed and nominates Richard M. Nixon, and becomes the beneficiary of any amount of private funds up to the twenty million limit. It chooses identical electors as the GOP; it places its resources in those States where the Republicans are a minority party, and where Democrats are reluctant to pull a Republican label. I.e., the Deep South, and New York State and perhaps Michigan.

c. What the conservatives get out of the deal is of course a National Party; what we would get would be the re-election of the President.

Indeed, in a four-way race—Muskie, McCarthy, Nixon, Wallace—with the President on two lines having been nominated by *two* national parties—we might win in a walk.

What would Mr. O'Brien say if he knew there was going to be a Fourth Party all right, the National Conservatives; and they, too, were going to nominate Richard Nixon; and they would be uninhibited in the amount they spent, right up to the top figure.

Our contributors could pour their dough into the Conservative effort to re-elect the President, while the Government funded the Republican effort to re-elect the President.

What we need to check on is whether the Democrats have been wise enough to say that the third, fourth and fifth parties cannot nominate the same candidate as the GOP, or the Democratic Party; or whether they put any top limit on the amount that could be spent for a candidate, or whether they merely zeroed in on PARTY expenditures. If they left that baby wide open, methinks we could cut a deal with the Conservatives nationally, with commitment to fund their national campaign, and make them a force on the national scene. If that happened, we can be sure, the Democrats would be quick to repeal their legislation.

This option should be checked out before the President vetoes that tax cut proposal. If we can make O'Brien's Treasury rip-off work to the President's advantage, there would be a measure of poetic justice involved.

Another reason this should be checked is that not only are branches of the American Conservative Union being established on a state-wide basis now, but Conservative parties are shaping up in both Michigan and Massachusetts on the Buckley example in New York. There is further a meeting of the Manhattan Twelve today, which my guess is would make a final break with the President—and may perhaps move more openly to get some Conservative to challenge him in a primary.

——————————————
PJB3

W/RN from PJB1

DECEMBER 1, 1971

TO: **H. R. Haldeman**

FROM: **Pat Buchanan**

Would be happy to put together The Conservative Case for Richard Nixon—but the time to do that is not now. Definitely not.

First, The Conservative Case for Richard Nixon, if it is to be effective, would have to be comprehensive. What Nixon has done for Conservatives in three years. Thus, we would throw the book at them (Four Justices of the Supreme Court, the unleashing of the Vice President, ABM, Vietnam, Cambodia, Middle East crisis, Law and Order, etc., etc., etc.).

Methinks a very convincing case could be made—but once made, the job can't be done again, with the same dramatic impact. And we don't need it done so much now—as we are going to need it done later. The reasons are these:

Coming up are the trade with the Soviets decision, which is going to outrage them further, the Budget which they will look at extremely closely in the defense area, the trips to China and the Soviet Union, about which they are deeply apprehensive, the decision on FAP, and the outcome of SALT. These are the Big Rocks.

The time to make the case for the President is after these are *behind* us.

If we shoot our wad now, many conservatives will say, "Well, that's a powerful argument; I think we have to be for Nixon." But then comes some supertrade deal with Moscow, and FAP—and any gains we made go right out the window—and The Conservative Case for Richard Nixon cannot be made again; and *then* is when it will be most needed.

We ought to compile all the materials for The Conservative Case for Richard Nixon, but go with a piece for massive mailing—only when the crunch comes and we need it. Not a year before the election.

Right now, the Manhattan Twelve have decided upon a course of action, I know not what. And if they go the primary route, which I suspect they desire, then, when the primary date approaches, we will have to go with it.

But there are yet more arguments to be heard, with months to go before the convention, before the time for a summation of The Conservative Case for Richard Nixon. We will lose some of those battles in the interim, with conservatives; we will win some. Let's wait until the conservative case for the prosecution of Richard Nixon has completed its closing arguments, before we make our pitch in his defense.

PJB3

W/RN from PJB1

DECEMBER 6, 1971

TO: **Henry A. Kissinger**

FROM: **Jon M. Huntsman**

RE: **Gandhi & India/Pakistan Conflict**

It was reported in the December 3, 1971 News Summary that Mrs. Gandhi told the world's major powers to mind their own business and let India find its own solution to the crisis. She continued, "The times have passed when any nation sitting 3 or 4 thousand miles away could give orders to Indians on the basis of their *color superiority* to do as they wished."

It was requested that you note this report and especially the [italicized] section above. It was noted that this is the heart of her anti-Americanism. She doesn't seem to mind the color of our aid dollars.

Thank you.

cc: H. R. Haldeman
    Alexander P. Butterfield

ss85

DECEMBER 8, 1971

TO: **Patrick J. Buchanan**

FROM: **Ken Khachigian**

Muskie is going to announce on January 4 from news accounts. I recommend that we ask John Ehrlichman and Bob Haldeman to give some consideration to an "important" administration announcement on the same day.

It would be nice to blow Muskie off the front page or at least prevent him from grabbing headlines and maybe even push him back a little bit on the network shows.

Do we have anything ready to go that we can cut loose on January 4th?

PJB3

DECEMBER 10, 1971

TO: John D. Ehrlichman

FROM: Jon M. Huntsman

RE: J. Edgar Hoover

It was reported in the December 10, 1971 News Summary that the President is actively studying whether J. Edgar Hoover should *step down at the end of the month* or after the election. Carl Stern reported that the President wants to make his decision now. He said that the President and his advisers fear Hoover will make a mistake which could embarrass the Administration in an election year. It was further reported *that the Administration would also like to avoid a bitter Senate confirmation fight over the FBI successor during the election year.*

It was noted that this report is embarrassingly close to the President's own plan and suggested that we should quit informing White House Staff members of the President's private plans.

Thank you.

cc: H. R. Haldeman
    Alexander P. Butterfield

ss84

DECEMBER 10, 1971

TO: H. R. Haldeman

FROM: Pat Buchanan

My understanding is that Mr. "James Earl Jones" who attended the White House dinner the other night, some two years ago made reference to the incredibly wretched leadership we had here in the United States. We can't quite dig up the quote right now, but our recollection is that the implication was the existing Administration (i.e., us) was somehow fascist-tinged. The purpose of this memo is not to bemoan the past, but to suggest that some of the "entertainment" types, or "artistic" types invited to the White House be simply run by Mort Allin for a review; Mr. Allin has a veritable warehouse of knowledge of just who has ever uttered a public political obscenity about the President—and as important, is aware of those who, in obscure publications, have said an occasional nice thing about the President. Would it be impolite to suggest that he be asked for recommendations on artsy-craftsy types to come to dinner, and be shown a list of those who are to be invited, for ideological and political laundering?

bcc: Allin

PJB3

DECEMBER 13, 1971

TO: John Ehrlichman
       Bud Krogh

FROM: Pat Buchanan

On page 21 of the weekend news summary, one learns that Ossie Davis, the old fellow traveler, has landed the drug office's contract to produce the anti-drug film. This, it seems to me, could well be filed under "More Horrendous Examples of Administration Subsidies To Its Political Enemies." Is there not something we can do to take this considerable patronage away from a fellow, one of whose characteristics is 100 percent opposition to Richard Nixon and the political goals which he pursues?

bcc: Agnes Waldron

PJB3, 4

w/RN from PJB1

DECEMBER 15, 1971

TO: The Attorney General
       H. R. Haldeman

FROM: Patrick J. Buchanan

Following are Ken Khachigian's and my brief ideas on the outlines of an anti-McCloskey campaign in New Hampshire.

Our best hope for a tiny McCloskey turnout lies in an open, active, hard-fought, interesting, increasingly evenly matched battle on the other side of the ballot—in the Democratic Primary. If McGovern appears to have a chance; if Muskie is forced to go all-out; if Yorty-cum-Loeb are pulling upward in the polls, all national and New Hampshire media will focus on this crucial race—and McCloskey's seemingly ineffectual run against the President will be relegated to back pages.

Thus, to advance our dual purpose—to diminish both the size of the Muskie victory and the size of the McCloskey vote—our interests dictate that George McGovern and Sam Yorty be given as much assistance, publicity-wise and other-wise, as we can muster. Statements by RN people, on background and off the record, that McGovern's organization may surprise everyone, that Muskie may be in trouble, etc.—in addition to heated in-fighting among Democrats—are to be encouraged, in any way possible.

Our public posture from this theory would be to a) Set a hurdle publicly so high that Muskie can't possibly reach it, and b) Put out the word that a hell-for-leather run by McGovern and Yorty seems on the verge of denying Muskie the margin he needs to impress the polls, and press and nation.

Specific Posture Toward McCloskey Candidacy:

1. Publicly, it should be ignored, by all top Administration officials, WH officials, and no statements should be made which would enter us into media debates with the Congressman himself. In our official view, he has a "right" to run in the Republican primary—and we are content to leave it to the New Hampshire voters to assess both the wisdom and efficacy of that kind of approach by a Republican politician.

The worst thing we could do would be to go after him in such a fashion as to enable him to don the garb of the "martyr for principle," the David of the Republican Party, fighting the Goliath of the White House and all the Philistine host of media experts and advance men.

2. An intelligence operation should be conducted to determine a) all the Democrats supporting him publicly and privately, b) all the Democratic money he is receiving, c) all the connections he has with the peace wing of the Democratic Party, i.e., Lowenstein & Co., d) the party affiliation of all his workers, and e) where his dough comes from.

If McCloskey's campaign can be portrayed—with any legitimacy, as the covert effort of Democrats, attempting to use a Republican to damage or destroy the Republican President in a Republican Primary—then we have a tremendous case to use with every Republican who leans to McCloskey.

If every speaker we have programmed for New Hampshire can lead off his speech thus:

I know Pete McCloskey; he is a nice guy; but he is being used as a cat's paw by the big money of the Democratic Party; he is simply being exploited to do the dirty work of Larry O'Brien, he is getting secret big money from left-wing Democrats who don't give a damn about our party, only about destroying our Republican President. . . .

A simple listing of all the big names back of the peace money, New York Jewish money, and California fat cat money—in a lead piece in the *Union-Leader*—might throw McCloskey on the defensive for much of the campaign: Example:

Now, if you folks here in Nashua think that Mister Howard Stein, the left-wing Democratic fat cat who runs the Manhattan Dreyfus Fund, has done so much for the people of New Hampshire that he has a right to buy Mr. McCloskey some votes in the Republican Primary here—why then you vote for Mr. McCloskey. But if you folks think Richard Nixon is doing his best for peace and prosperity—and that New York Democratic fat cats ought to keep their fat wallets out of our Republican Primaries—why then you give the President the same kind of landslide you gave him in 1968, and maybe this country can have that generation of peace it hasn't had in our lifetimes.

The Purpose: To paint McCloskey as a Democratic tool, and destroy his credibility as a legitimate Republican.

3. Rule out at this point face-to-face debates with McCloskey by such as Jack Kemp. McCloskey is unknown, attractive, articulate—and the greater exposure he gets, the more likely his vote is to rise at least to a presentable figure.

4. Have RNC/Khachigian gather the *Most Extreme* and least popular of McCloskey positions—say, ten of them—and then provide pro-President rebuttal material for each of these points; provide this ten-page Briefing Book to every Republican who goes to New Hampshire on behalf of the President, every Republican working in New Hampshire for the President.

Likely, all McCloskey's unpopular views on issues of importance to students should be provided to our students for his campaign appearances at the schools and universities—where surely, he will focus attention.

All his extreme statements should be gathered as well for Mr. Loeb of the *Union-Leader*—and perhaps run in an advertisement in that paper. Our people should publicize and comment upon these, but really, more in sorrow than anger, "Poor Pete, he's gone off the deep end, etc. . . ."

5. Have a brief study done of which national columnists have the widest circulation in N.H. (In 1968, Drew Pearson was in all papers but Loeb's, and big columnists were the *Times* boys, Reston, Wicker, et al.) and feed from Washington to *these* columnists the materials which paint McCloskey as the dupe of the left-wing Svengalis of the Democratic Party.

6. Perhaps the Gay Liberation and/or Black Panthers and/or Students for a Democratic Society at Dartmouth could be prevailed upon to contribute a grand or so to the McCloskey campaign. And when the check was cashed that fact brought to the attention of the voters of New Hampshire—by the *Union-Leader*—who might be skeptical of the source of the funds.

7. The three New Hampshire Congressmen, who are Republicans, should be programmed for an early Enthusiastic Endorsement of the President. When asked about Pete McCloskey, the "Pete's a nice guy, but he's just being used by the Democratic Party; he hasn't a snowball's chance in hell; they're just exploiting and using a naive nice guy . . ." might be an approach that could be taken.

8. A Congressional Truth Squad should be hand-picked, and briefed with background on [the] McCloskey position, and readied—but not sent, until the need for heavier artillery becomes clearer than it is today. These Congressmen should be briefed on our line; they should be young, articulate, attractive, the Buckleys and Brocks and the moderate, articulate Republicans in the House. Perhaps a group of us can get together and pick these fellows out. Youth, attractive[ness], articulateness should be the criteria—as no one is going to know their ideology.

9. We should be exceedingly wary of any kind of slick, commercialized approach to this campaign—as am sure that McCloskey is waiting to use the charge that the President's PR men and media experts and ad-

vance crew are not substitutes for simple honesty and truth, "Pay no attention to their slick commercials, etc."

10. If Ashbrook can be prevailed upon to stand down, contact should be made with the *Union-Leader* management so that a working relationship can be constructed—for the campaign against McCloskey. Buchanan can undertake this, if desired. Mr. Loeb controls perhaps the most powerful political weapon in the State and he has no hesitancy or qualms about wheeling it out at every biennial juncture.

11. The RNC, working with Ken Khachigian, should go over the McCloskey record, and find those issues where McCloskey has taken positions unpopular with the GOP centrist-conservative philosophy of the New Hampshire Republican Party—and literature should be prepared for speakers, and voters with this material contained. Brochures might be prepared and tailored for the various audiences in New Hampshire, students, regular Republicans, Catholics, etc.

12. If McCloskey does get Guggenheim, as is being bruited about, we should turn this to our advantage by charging that Mr. McCloskey has gotten the biggest merchandiser of Democratic candidates to sell to the people of New Hampshire, by slick commercial, a McCloskey candidacy, which could not get a vote on its own merits. In short, if they go in for slick advertising, we should charge them first with what they are surely going to charge us. Pictures of Guggenheim—the Master Merchant of Image—should be prominent throughout the State, and in its media, should he get aboard.

13. Questions should be drawn up by analysts of the McCloskey record, and provided, as stated, for press and students—whenever McCloskey's schedules allow for a Q and A environment. Again, Khachigian/RNC to handle.

14. As McCloskey is zeroing in on Truth in Government, anything to catch him waffling, or hiding something—whether on issues or about support in his campaign—should be publicized and the "Truth in McCloskey" charge hurled back at him.

15. On the four issues where McCloskey is running, i.e., Truth in Government, Judicial Respect, Vietnam, Civil Rights—a short, strong briefing of the RN record—taking the offensive—should be provided our New Hampshire organization and all our speakers, with other abovementioned materials.

16. Lastly, let's keep our options open. If McCloskey begins to move in the polls, the President may *have* to go in. If we are going to use television, my idea would be to put in the can something straight from the President, and straight from the Heart. Thus:

People of New Hampshire, and especially my Republican friends in New Hampshire. We have known each other many years. Your support in 1952, twenty years ago, helped me to become Vice President. In 1956, your tremendous help in the write-in for Vice President stopped in its tracks the old Dump Nixon movement of those years. In 1960, in the Primary and General Election, you stood behind me in defeat. In 1968, in the Republican Primary especially, and in the General election, you gave me the greatest measure of support any Republican candidate has ever received. Without the votes of the people of New Hampshire, I would very probably not be President of the United States today. Few men who have not grown up in New Hampshire know its people and its places as well as I, from Dixville Notch to Manchester, from Nashua to Concord, from Berlin to the White Mountains. I have just come home from Communist China; I am trying to build a more peaceful world for your children and mine—I am asking you, once again at a critical juncture in my lifetime, voters of New Hampshire—to give me the support on Tuesday you have given me for twenty years, etc. etc. . . .

PJB3

W/RN from PJB1

DECEMBER 15, 1971

Dear John:*

Patty and I enjoyed greatly Barbara's and your hospitality. It was a delightful evening from start to finish (we were almost finished trying to find our way home) and we look forward to the chance to reciprocate once we are a little better settled in our new house.

The only thing which marred an otherwise perfect evening was being "one-upped" by Rollie Evans. It is going to take a long time for my ego to recover.

In any event, I am sending you my copy of *Nixon in the White House*. I have carefully erased all of the underlining and very naughty words that were written in the margins.

Thanks again for a delightful time.

Best personal regards.

Sincerely,

Charles W. Colson
Special Counsel
to the President

*[Letter to John Chancellor]

cwc130

DECEMBER 16, 1971

TO: **Chuck Colson**

FROM: **Mort Allin**

If Francis Plimpton isn't on our opposition list as of now, this piece should seal his fate.

PJB1

DECEMBER 20, 1971

TO: **H. R. Haldeman**

FROM: **Charles Colson**

RE: **La Raza Unida**

I think there is a very fertile political opportunity in giving some sub rosa financial and/or organizational support to La Raza Unida. The attached memo from Doug Hallett illustrates very vividly what impact they can have in critical areas. There was also a local election in Tucson, Arizona, that was decided our way by the normal Democratic vote being split.

La Raza Unida, as you know, is the far left Chicano militant party which would draw almost exclusively from the Democrats.

Imagine what they might do if they were on the ballot in California or in Texas as a splinter party in the Presidential election?

In my judgment, money spent this way can be as effective, if not more so, than money spent for our own advertising or promotion.

We have a mechanism for working through La Raza Unida, if you or the Attorney General make a policy decision at some point that it is worth doing. Obviously this has to be fit into the priority scale somewhere and if you think the idea has promise, we will staff it out thoroughly.

If it is worth doing, it has to be started fairly quickly because it will take time to infiltrate and get them organized in California and/or Texas.

_____ cwc130

EYES ONLY

DECEMBER 23, 1971

TO: **H. R. Haldeman**

FROM: **Charles Colson**

The President this afternoon asked that I discuss with you a project that he would like undertaken in New Hampshire which will require some money. May I see you about this at your convenience?

_____ cwc130; hrh278

1972

Watergate was a breach of trust. I think to keep it in perspective . . . that 1972, as you know, was a very big year. A lot of things were going on. Winston Churchill once wrote that strong leaders usually do the big things well, but they foul up on small things, and then the small things become big. I should have read that before Watergate happened. In 1972 we went to China. We went to Russia. We ended the Vietnam War effectively by the end of that year. Those were the big things. And here was a small thing, and we fouled it up beyond belief. It was a great mistake. It was wrong, as I've pointed out over and over again. But under the circumstances now, people as they judge that period have to see what we accomplished and what we did wrong. And for the future, I would advise all those that follow me in the position of president: do the big things as well as you can, but when a small thing is there, deal with it, and deal with it fast; get it out of the way. Because if you don't, it's going to become big, and then it may destroy you.

—RICHARD M. NIXON ON NBC'S "MEET THE PRESS," APRIL 10, 1988

JANUARY 3, 1972

TO: **Mr. Charles W. Colson**

FROM: **Jeb S. Magruder***

RE: **Dan Rather**

We generated approximately fifty telegrams to Dan Rather this morning complaining about his treatment of the President last evening. These telegrams were sent by area residents as well as some of our people from throughout the country. Samples are attached.

In addition, we have programmed telephone calls throughout the day to Rather's Washington office.

*[Memorandum written on Committee for the Re-election of the President letterhead]

HANDWRITTEN COLSON NOTE: "Eyes *ONLY* file *CAREFULLY*"

CWC17

JANUARY 10, 1972

TO: **Bob Haldeman**

FROM: **The President**

I think there is a very good column or feature article in the Presidential telephone calls. There has been, of course, a great deal of attention paid to those that get publicity like the ones to Don Shula and George Allen. I do not think it is a good idea, however, to allow the impression to get abroad that these are the only calls the President makes. For example, the fact that I made a call to Mrs. Willis Smith when her son was killed in an airplane accident—to Mrs. Acheson and Mrs. Win Prouty when their husbands died—to the football players who were seriously injured and to the parents of one who died after an accident on the football field—to the mothers of boys who are killed in Vietnam—to an old friend like Mac Faries who has had a heart attack—to the 18-year-old boy who wrote me a very touching letter about his brother who had committed suicide with LSD—and, of course, the expected ones to Congressmen and Senators, be they Democrats or Republicans, who have birthdays, when time permits me to do so—to Cabinet officers and others when they make good speeches—to Herb Kaplow's wife when his mother-in-law died.

I think Rose should be able to work with Ray Price's office and the telephone operators to get up a pretty good chapter and verse that could be given, possibly to Hugh Sidey or to Helen Thomas, or maybe even to both. Dick Moore might be the conveyer belt for the story, but I think that the individual who writes it should talk to Rose since she is very familiar with all these calls that I make and suggests many of them herself. Sidey might be the best candidate since he tends to blow hot and cold on the President's private life, etc. This kind of a story should impress him and I think it would be picked up by others if he writes it. If, however, he shows no interest, Helen Thomas I think would be a good candidate.

HRH162

W/RN from PPF3

JANUARY 10, 1972

TO: **Ken Cole**

FROM: **Chuck Colson**

As I indicated to you, Lou Harris did not use our poll. He cited an ATT poll and got their permission first. He would obviously check with us first if he wanted to use any part of our poll. He was, by the way, very distraught that we would think he would release any of our data.

cc: Ed Harper

cwc131

JANUARY 12, 1972

TO: **Charles W. Colson**

FROM: **Doug Hallett**

I talked to a friend of mine at Stanford today. He said he had never before been a supporter of the President, but had watched the "Day in the Presidency" (for which, as I told you earlier, I've gotten very mixed reviews), the Christmas Eve Special because he's been so impressed with the first, and, finally, the Rather conversation, and had now decided that the President was a real, live human being and not "a wind-up doll." He told me he can't understand the President's "platitudinous speeches which cover up what he's really all about," but liked what he saw of the more casual Nixon and said we ought to do a lot more to get that across.

P.S. Now, I wouldn't be passing this along to you because my friend agrees with me, now would I?

P.P.S. For whatever it's worth, I thought the First Lady did a terrific job on her African trip. If we can't improve the President's public image in the next 120 days, what do you say we drop him and run Mrs. Nixon instead???

CWC1

JANUARY 15, 1972

Dear Bob:*

I thought you might be interested in the attached. This is what these liberal bastards (in this case, the correct word is bitch) love to seize upon—any kind of rift between Republicans.

I note in here that Nancy says she talked with you. She didn't talk to me and I frankly can't believe that you said to her what she's used here. But, as I say, these kinds of reporters will pick at anything.

Hope to see you soon now that Congress is back.

Best personal regards.

Sincerely,

Charles W. Colson
Special Counsel
to the President

*[Letter to Senator Robert Dole]

Inside Washington —NANCY DICKERSON

TAPE DATE: 1/4/72
AIR DATE: 1/7–1/13
PROGRAM # 242

SUGGESTED LEAD-IN: *Hostility is growing between President Nixon's staff at the White House and the Republicans on Capitol Hill. For an* Inside Washington *story about that, here is our reporter in the Capital, Nancy Dickerson. Nancy . . .*

NANCY: *Relations between the Nixon staff and the Republicans in Congress are bad. Consider this: Republican Senator Robert Dole of Kansas is President Nixon's own handpicked Chairman of the GOP National Committee—yet the Nixon staff recently tried to do a hatchet job on him. When Dole was telling me about congressional relations, he sounded more like the Chairman of the Democratic National Committee rather than the Republican. Dole is particularly irked at Charles Colson, the presidential aide who is called the Nixon hatchet man. Dole tells me that it is Colson who causes trouble back home for those Republican Senators who don't vote the Nixon way.*

For months there have been growing complaints about the Berlin wall, meaning Robert Haldeman and John Ehrlichman—the two Nixon aides who so often say "no" to Congressmen who want to see the President. Since neither Haldeman or Ehrlichman have ever run for political office, there is a good deal of contempt for them by Congressmen who have and therefore consider themselves more sensitive to issues that can mean defeat or reelection.

Probably the best congressional friend of the White House staff is Barry Goldwater, who refers to them as "my kids" since they once worked for him.

The growing animosity between the White House and the congressional Republicans means trouble for the President this year. In a Congress controlled by the Democrats, President Nixon cannot sustain many defections in his own party and still get congressional approval to do the things he has promised he would.

This is Nancy Dickerson in Washington.

cwc57

JANUARY 17, 1972

TO: **Robert Finch**

FROM: **John Dean**

RE: **Derogatory Film about the President**

During a recent trip to Los Angeles, we received information that the Smothers Brothers were producing a derogatory film about the President. A pretext inquiry at the offices of SmoBro International Productions, Inc., Los Angeles, revealed that that company had just completed production of a film entitled *Another Nice Mess.* It is scheduled for nationwide distribution beginning in March.

The film is described by SmoBro's press agent as a satirical spoof. The President and Vice President are portrayed as Laurel and Hardy.

I would appreciate any thoughts you might have on how we could develop further information about this film, its proposed distribution, and its backers, in order that we may be in a better position to assess its potential impact.

cc: H. R. Haldeman
    Chuck Colson

JFB2; JWD4;
21 SENATE HEARINGS 9874

JANUARY 18, 1972

TO: **H. R. Haldeman**

FROM: **Bruce Kehrli**

RE: **Howard Hughes**

Please note the attached comment from the January 18th, News Summary.

cc: Alexander P. Butterfield

CBS said it learned "new details" on the loan granted Don Nixon by Howard Hughes. On film former Hughes aide Dietrich said that not Clark Clifford, but Hughes-lobbyist Frank Waters negotiated the loan for DN. *Dietrich noted that Hughes loved to have political influence and he was probably aware that DN was VP Nixon's brother. Asked if there was any favoritism shown to Hughes after the loan was granted he said that Hughes had been refused a routine IRS exemption on a medical foundation he'd begun. Not too long after he made the loan, he got the exemption. Dietrich said that it could have been pure coincidence but one has to draw his own conclusions. Cronkite said that neither DN nor Waters were available for comment but wires show DN comments that the loan was secured by his mother's lot in Whittier. He also said he never asked his brother to do anything for him or anyone else. A gas station was built on the lot; it was worth $228,000 when it was finally given in payment for the loan.**

A low-key but effective Tom Whitehead was interviewed on CBS AM News. He refuted accusations that he capitulated on CATV saying that the goal is for CATV to grow without tearing down over-the-air TV. He stated that FCC will continue to be necessary and that TV will have to be regulated where newsprint is not because of its access to the public air waves. He said that political judgments would not be a danger in regulating PBS as neither Congress nor the Exec per se will have a hand in it.

The WH confirmed that a computer firm controlled by Ross Perot received without competitive bidding a $62,000 contract for work for RN's Domestic Council. *The company was said to have unique qualifications to carry out the pact.*

*HANDWRITTEN RN NOTE PERTAINING TO THE ENTIRE LOAN STORY: "H—not bad!"

ss84

JANUARY 18, 1972

BY MESSENGER

Dear Bob:*

As you know from our conversation this morning, the President specifically asked that you read two books. One is Lord D. Cecil's *Melbourne* and the other is Robert Blake's *Disraeli*.

You might tell him at dinner Thursday night that you have the books and you understand the point. I think he would appreciate it.

Best personal regards.

Sincerely,

Charles W. Colson
Special Counsel
to the President

*[Letter to Senator Robert Dole]

cwc13, 107, 131

JANUARY 19, 1972

TO: **Shelley Buchanan**

FROM: **Joan Hall,** Secretary to Charles Colson

Enclosed is the key for the refrigerator—sorry I forgot to remind Chuck to bring it back sooner.

Chuck had a comment to make this morning when he returned it: He thinks it is ridiculous to have a medallion of JFK on the key to President Nixon's box furnishings. He believes a RMN medallion or seal should be on the keys. (No charge for that comment.)

cwc131

JANUARY 24, 1972

Dear Stephen:*

I was most pleased to hear from you again, and I appreciated receiving your suggestion of Executive Clemency for Alger Hiss.

At this time, I am not in a position to speculate on what action the President might take were this matter to come before him. Such speculation would also be inappropriate since under present policy and regulations, only the person seeking Executive Clemency can initiate the action by the filing of a formal petition addressed to the President and filed in the first instance with the Department of Justice. The Department of Justice investigates and reviews the petition and the Attorney General then forwards it, along with his recommendations, to the President for final action. Thus, the President can consider granting Mr. Hiss a pardon only after he has filed such a petition, which he is entitled to do at any time, and the Attorney General has made his recommendation.

I hope you will understand my position in this matter, but I certainly appreciate your interest and concern.

Whenever you are again in Washington, please do not hesitate to call.

Sincerely,

John W. Dean, III
Counsel to the President

*[Letter to Stephen Jones, Enid, Oklahoma]

JWD4

JANUARY 28, 1972

TO: Bob Haldeman

FROM: The President

On further reflection I think your idea of having Tricia and Julie, and for very major events Pat, go to political affairs around the country is an excellent one.

What you should do is to always have a Cabinet officer or other good speaker on the program. The presence of Tricia, Julie or Pat there will simply hypo the publicity in an enormous degree. Julie has worked out a very good formula where she does a TV interview in each case, but I am sure Pat and Tricia will follow suit—Tricia, of course, a little more quickly than Pat because Pat doesn't like interviews. In Pat's case the big receptions are probably a good idea in the country because they really mean a great deal to people who are not in Washington.

I again urge, however, the necessity for beefing up the staff work in getting better scheduled events for Julie, Tricia and Pat in the country.

I consider this top priority.

HRH162

JANUARY 28, 1972

Dear John:*

Perhaps you have noticed the statue of Nathan Hale in front of the Justice Department on Constitution Avenue. Some of my associates who enjoy a sense of historical perspective have suggested that we link the Agency with one of the nation's first intelligence operatives by placing the statue in front of our Headquarters building. Attached are their notes which give a few facts about the statue and a rationale for the move.

Before pursuing this idea further, I should appreciate knowing whether you foresee any problems or any reluctance on the part of the Department of Interior to approve the relocation of this statue. Should the move take place, I would arrange that it be done without ceremony or publicity, although it might well come to public notice.

Sincerely,

Richard Helms
Director

*[Letter to John D. Ehrlichman from Richard Helms, director of the Central Intelligence Agency]

WHCF/PA4

JANUARY 31, 1972

TO: **H. R. Haldeman**
John Ehrlichman

FROM: **John Dean**

RE: **Hughes Loan to Don Nixon**

I learned today that Jack Anderson has his leg man, Les Whitten, looking for information on the Hughes loan to Don Nixon.

I have been collecting additional information on the matter to anticipate any new allegations which might be forthcoming.

I will keep you posted.

cc: Chuck Colson

(Blind Note: Ed Cohen, Treas. Dept., called to inform me that a Mr. Olscher—former staff man with Putnam—had been contacted by Whitten. It appeared like a fishing expedition.)

JWD4

JANUARY 31, 1972

TO: **H. R. Haldeman**

FROM: **John Dean**

RE: **Potential Disruption at the Republican National Convention**

Plans for demonstrations at the 1972 Republican National Convention in San Diego are now being formulated by a number of organizations. The principal focal point for these plans is the People's Coalition for Peace and Justice (PCPJ). During their noticeably unsuccessful "Fall Offensive" in October 1971, the PCPJ began a long-range campaign aimed at disrupting the Republican Convention. In meetings since that time, this organization has developed serious splits with one faction urging that PCPJ engage in violent disruptive activities at both national conventions and another faction arguing that such tactics would cause loss of support from various religious and pacifist organizations. As of this moment, the split has not been resolved and no definite strategy adopted.

Other national new-left organizations have also indicated their intentions to take part in demonstrations at San Diego. The Youth International Party, commonly known as the Yippies, recently met in Madison, Wisconsin to discuss their plans. These include a "Grapes of Wrath" caravan to be held in San Diego during August 1–20, 1972, which will be followed by demonstrations during the convention. The Worker-Student Alliance faction of the Students for a Democratic Society (SDS) and a new organization called the New American Movement have similarly announced plans to participate in disruptive activities at San Diego.

A number of new-left leaders have also publicly stated their intentions to play a role in demonstrations at the Republican National Convention. These include figures prominent in past demonstrations such as Jerry Rubin, Thomas Hayden, John Froines, Rennie Davis, and Father James Groppi. Significantly, though, the National Peace Action Coalition (NPAC)—the group which has staged the largest and most successful demonstrations in Washington—has made no definite plans for San Diego. The extent of their possible participation in whatever activities are formulated for the convention remains unclear.

Locally in San Diego, a group known as the San Diego Convention Coalition (SDCC) has been formed to plan disruptions at the convention. This organization consists of such protest groups as the Young Socialist Alliance, Venceremos Brigade, Non-Violent Action, and assorted hippie communes, underground newspapers and draft resistance groups. Meetings of the SDCC have been occurring regularly since October 1971 and a loose organizational structure has been established. The political objectives of SDCC are to bring about an immediate end to the war in Indochina, to struggle against the alleged domestic police state and to expose the Republican party as the party of the ruling class and thereby strip it of its legitimacy as a leader.

SDCC plans include the circulation of petitions in the San Diego area protesting the presence of the convention in the city, formation of a "people's platform" which will state their goals, massive demonstrations at the San Diego Sports Arena during the convention, and "Expose '72" which will be held during the convention and include exhibits and presentations on war, repression, minority groups, etc.

The SDCC has been in contact with many of the national protest groups and leaders concerning the planned demonstrations. However, they have made it very clear that they will vigorously oppose any attempt by the national protest leaders to take control of the local movement or to direct the demonstrations in San Diego. Due to the youth and relative inexperience of SDCC leaders in coordinating major demonstrations, it is doubtful if they could retain control of the demonstrations should such leaders as Rennie Davis or David Dellinger decide to take charge.

In light of these facts, a general task force has been established to coordinate the activities of all interested local, state and Federal law enforcement agencies. Inspector J. W. Connole of the San Diego Police Department heads this task force which includes representatives of all neighboring police departments, San Diego Sheriff's Office, California Highway Patrol, District Attorney's Office, FBI, Secret Service, and the Alcohol, Tobacco, and Tax Division of IRS. Contingency plans are now being drafted by separate committees of this task force.

The picture presented at this time is still too undefined to draw sound conclusions. Although we can be certain to have demonstrations at the Republican National Convention, it is too early to predict their size and nature. From past experience, it can be expected that the convention will serve as a magnet to attract numerous "street people" and veterans of past demonstrations. The militancy of the protest activity will undoubtedly be affected by national and foreign developments between now and the time of the convention. Though most of the leaders are now stressing non-violent tactics, the inherent momentum of these demonstrations has proven time and time again that such activity can rapidly escalate into violence.

I shall be in close touch with this situation as it develops and shall keep you informed as a clearer picture of the magnitude and proportions of this problem emerge.

My recent visit to San Diego indicates that the San Diego city government is well aware of the problems that face them and are taking all steps necessary to be prepared. Mayor Wilson is involving himself personally in this problem and is cooperating fully with us.

JWD4

FEBRUARY 1, 1972

TO: **The President**

FROM: **Ron Ziegler**
Charles Colson

RE: **One Photo Opportunity Per Day**

We have been advised that you have decided that there should be only one press photo opportunity per day. While there is merit to this as a general proposition, there are instances when it is to our advantage to have more than one.

A morning photo will often make the P.M. papers and during the same day an afternoon photo will be picked up by the A.M. papers of the next day. If there is only one photo opportunity per day it will likely favor the A.M. papers and we will tend to lose photo coverage in the P.M.s. The A.M. and P.M. cycle should be considered very carefully, particularly since a number of cities have a larger P.M. circulation than A.M..

Secondly, when we are dealing with different subjects they are not necessarily in competition with one another. For example, the appointment of Mrs. Whitman would have in no way conflicted with our drug announcement. They are two entirely different stories. Today is an example of when 3 pictures can play: the Nebraska football photo would be on the sports pages; the Prayer Breakfast in the news section (P.M.s) and Governors Evans and Reagan will play primarily on the West Coast regardless of what other photos move. When the subjects are the same or the types of groups or photo opportunities are similar, then it is obviously wasteful to do two in one day. When the subjects are totally different we do have the opportunity of getting two photos into print instead of one. The same holds true for TV which often uses footage of two Administration events, providing the subjects are both important and newsworthy.

As a final consideration, some photos are important regionally (as with Evans and Reagan) and we shouldn't miss these simply because another news event takes precedence on a particular day.

In short, we should judge the news events on each day for their intrinsic value and with some consideration given to the A.M. and P.M. news cycles. Moreover, it should be remembered that the networks do not have a monopoly on TV news. By network feed, many local stations will run one story with footage of the President while the network picks up another. All three networks now feed footage to their local stations for local newscasts; hence, even if one story dominates the networks, another might well be welcomed by local TV news shows so they are not forced to repeat an event already covered by the networks.

The two objectives for limiting photo opportunities to one per day are, as we understand it: (1) conserving the President's time, and (2) not scooping ourselves. As much as possible we try to plan only one major news story a day, but when on occasions there are two, we should not lose the coverage by operation of this rule.

cwc131

FEBRUARY 1, 1972

TO: **Henry Kissinger**

FROM: **Chuck Colson**

This is in response to a call from your office requesting my opinion of an invitation you received from the National Women's Political Caucus. Your asking me on this is like the Pope seeking religious guidance from the Vicar of my local Protestant church. Who am I to tell you what to do about women?

The National Women's Political Caucus are the bomb throwers—the Gloria Steinems of this world and a lot of your *other* girl friends. I wouldn't be caught dead in the place—but then, I am not the Administration's "swinger."

Under the circumstances, I don't see how you can possibly avoid it; your absence would be conspicuous but then so would your presence. Whatever you do, don't go halfway. They want you to buy 4 tickets and bring 3 girls. Do them one better. Buy 8 tickets and take 7 girls.

You might be interested in the sponsorship of the caucus—everybody (including several Cabinet wives) is behind it—God knows why. It is going to be one of those Washington "happenings."

On balance, in view of your widespread fame with the fairer sex, I think you have had it—you simply have to go and run the terrible risk that you will not be attacked physically. It is simply the price you pay.

P.S. If you go, you will be the butt of all the humorous barbs of the evening along with some of the serious ones. If you don't go, you will be the butt of all the humorous barbs of the evening along with some of the serious ones.

cwc13, 131

FEBRUARY 3, 1972

TO: **John Ehrlichman**

FROM: **John Dean**

RE: **Hughes Loan**

The following is a chronology of certain events coinciding with the Hughes loan.

On June 1, 1955, the Howard Hughes Medical Institute of Miami Beach, Florida (Institute), filed for tax exempt status with the IRS.

On November 29, 1955, IRS denied the exemption on the basis that the Institute was merely a mechanism contrived to siphon off otherwise taxable income into a tax exempt organization which would accumulate that income.

On March 26, 1956, the Institute formally protested the IRS ruling.

On March 1, 1957, the IRS reversed its ruling and gave the Institute tax exempt status. It should be noted that this tax exempt status was made retroactive back to the date of the Institute's formation (1954), which meant no taxes were owed by it for the years 1954 and 1955 ($482,697 in taxes would have been owed by the Institute for those 2 years). It should also be noted that the IRS ruling came some three months *after* the date of record of the Hughes loan, which was December 10, 1956.

The attorneys of record in the exemption matter were Milton West, Jr. of Houston, Texas, and Seymour Mintz of Washington, D.C.

Other events relating to Hughes which might have coincided with the date of the loan are being checked into, and I will report to you on whatever is found as soon as possible.

JWD4

FEBRUARY 3, 1972

TO: **Dick Howard**

FROM: **John Dean**

RE: **McGovern's Campaign Soliciting Activities**

Under 18 U.S.C. 602, Senators, Representatives, Federal employees, and other persons receiving salary or compensation for services from Treasury funds are prohibited from directly or indirectly soliciting or receiving contributions for any political purpose from any other such officer, employee, or person. Under 18 U.S.C. 603, solicitation of contributions for political purposes in any room or building occupied by any of the aforementioned persons while engaged in the discharge of their official duties is prohibited. A violation of either provision is punishable by up to 3 years imprisonment, a fine not exceeding $5,000, or both.

Senator McGovern's campaign solicitation letter addressed to "Dear Friend" at the Department of Interior's Bureau of Outdoor Recreation seemingly contravenes both of these statutory prohibitions. Although the letter was not addressed to any specific person, the fact that it was addressed and directed to the Bureau of Outdoor Recreation raises a clear implication that it was intended for employees of that agency in an effort to induce them to contribute to McGovern's campaign fund. Thus, from the facts, it appears that McGovern's solicitation letter is of the type prohibited by 18 U.S.C. 602.

As to the second violation, solicitation by letter or circular, addressed to and delivered by mail or otherwise to a Federal employee at the office or building in which he is employed in the discharge of his official duties, is a solicitation "in a room or building" in violation of 18 U.S.C. 603.

Although the facts seem to establish violations of the Federal Corrupt Practices Act, absent other more flagrant violations, I seriously doubt whether this is the type of case the Department of Justice would prosecute. I pass this information along to you for any unofficial use you might wish to make of these technical violations of the law.

JWD4

FEBRUARY 4, 1972

TO: **Jeb Magruder**

FROM: **Charles Colson**

RE: **Attached Speech**

I don't know who you have writing political material for people going into key states, but I have just read Rog Morton's speech for tonight in New Hampshire. It's awful. It wouldn't get a single line of press anywhere except in the *Concord Monitor* which I suppose would have to cover the speech because he is speaking in Concord. The basic trouble is that it is pure fluff. It says nothing except a lot of political platitudes that could be written in any campaign about anyone at any time.

The particular speech tonight has been rescued by a speech insert dealing with Muskie's upsetting of our peace negotiations which conceivably will make it newsworthy. What bothers me is if the first draft is an example of what we're giving to people who go into states, we aren't going to make political points and we aren't going to make news. Maybe the problem here is Morton who I know has to be pushed hard and cranked up hard.

On major speeches like Morton's we would be glad to help and now have some writers who have been producing some good substantive material. This is not intended as criticism but rather as a constructive suggestion. I think if you yourself read the original Morton speech you will see that it is a total zero.

Also, it is going to be very important, and I know Van Shumway understands this, that major speeches like this be released here in Washington as well as in Concord, New Hampshire, and at the top of the release the contact should not only be the New Hampshire press person, but the Washington press person as well. A Rogers attack on Muskie moving out of Washington news bureaus will get a hell of a lot more play around the country than if it moves only on the wires out of New Hampshire.

cwc131

W/RN from CWC48

EYES ONLY

FEBRUARY 9, 1972

TO: **Larry Higby**

FROM: **Charles Colson**

RE: **Your Memo of February 8**

My hat is off to you after reading your memo to me, attached. I knew you were a superb staff man but I didn't realize how good you really are. The fact that you were able to attach a copy of my memo to Pat Buchanan to Buchanan's memo to Haldeman and me before I had sent Pat my memo and, in fact, before I had sent you the copy of it is as brilliant a piece of staff work as I have ever seen. The fact is that I had just signed the memo to Buchanan when the memo of Buchanan's with Haldeman's comment on it was returned to my office. So, all I can do is congratulate you for a spectacular clairvoyance and/or a good spy system and/or both.

Putting my old trial lawyer's hat back on and re-reading the Buchanan memo to Haldeman and Colson, there are several points made by Buchanan:

1. Smith and Goldwater are irritated by the nature of statements sent down to them from the White House.

2. The frequency of the demands made upon them.

3. The fact that we end-run the Senator.

4. We have a long way to go in the campaign and Muskie attacks are going to get worse so we should not react to each of them in a tough fashion.

5. Buchanan agrees with the foregoing.

6. It is wrong to hammer him continually from the right.

7. We need more attacks from Republican moderates.

To all of this Haldeman says, "I agree." On a witness stand, I would ask him which of the foregoing seven points he agrees with.

You will be interested to know that Tony Smith notwithstanding, Goldwater is unloading with all barrels today on the Democrats for their hypocrisy, getting us into the war, demanding Republican bipartisan support as they got us in and then not practicing what they preach as we're getting them out, etc. etc. Hence, proverb, "All's well that ends well." Finally, old trial lawyers' proverb, "Always be sure of your facts and/or take the Fifth Amendment."

cwc131

FEBRUARY 15, 1972

TO: H. R. Haldeman

FROM: Charles Colson

RE: Attached Letter

As I mentioned to you, my father called me the first night of your TV debut and now I have just received the attached from him. I thought you would like to know that there are some out in the provinces who continue to cheer you on.

By the way, you are the Ying [sic]—John Holdridge tells me that is the dark, furtive, sinister character of the two. The Yang is described as being the bright, warm, sunshiny type—that's Kissinger?

cwc131

FEBRUARY 16, 1972

TO: **Chuck Colson**

FROM: **Pat Buchanan**

As you are aware, the movies in recent years have carried a greater and greater ideological baggage. What has become different, however, is that the right—as opposed to the left—is being favorably portrayed in such films as *Dirty Harry* and *The French Connection,* where the police come off as honorable, hard-working, principled, tough and unrewarded, while the hippies and the left are portrayed in an unfavorable light.

The President would make something of a splash if at the next dinner, Gene Hackman, who played "Popeye" in *The French Connection* and Clint Eastwood, who played Dirty Harry, were in attendance.

PJB5; CWC5, 86

FEBRUARY 17, 1972

TO: **Pat Buchanan**

FROM: **Charles Colson**

If in any movie recently you have detected the right being portrayed as a hero, you are, in my opinion, in great danger of becoming a left-winger. Have you seen *Nicholas and Alexandra*? It obviously deifies the Bolshevik revolution, Lenin and Co. and draws some insidious parallels with what is happening in this country.

I have not seen either *Dirty Harry* or *The French Connection.* I should point out to you that I have not seen *The French Connection* because my wife, who is Catholic, claims that it is on the non-approved list. All of which probably also proves that your theology is getting as liberal as your opinions about movies. Therefore, I can't make any assessment of inviting Gene Hackman to a dinner, but I think Clint Eastwood absolutely should be; whether he was a good guy or a bad guy in the flicks, he's a good guy in the flesh and a leading member of your Youth for Nixon operation. I will put this in the works.

cc: Dwight Chapin
    George Bell

cwc5, 86, 131

FEBRUARY 18, 1972

TO: **Roland Elliott**

FROM: **Charles Colson**

RE: **Presidential Letter for Louis Harris**

Lou Harris has been most helpful in providing us with poll data beyond that which he normally publishes. He also has been very helpful in giving us data in advance. Wednesday of this week Harris turned his whole organization upside down to run through his computers the latest field survey conducted in early February. He did it Wednesday so that he could call me by midnight and I could give the results to the President before he left for China, which, in fact, I did. The President, I think, was most appreciative and I would like to have a "Dear Lou" letter prepared that the President could sign on his return, thanking Harris for going to such extraordinary lengths to make his current polling data available to us. It could make reference to the fact that "Colson got the data to me just before I left for China and I was most appreciative of the efforts that I know you went to . . ."; something along those lines. Would you prepare this and I'll have it run through to be signed when the President returns. Thanks.

cwc131

FEBRUARY 24, 1972

TO: **George Shultz**

FROM: **Charles Colson**

RE: **Bell Memo/Roche Column**

Per our conversation on the plane going to Florida, I am enclosing a full copy of the file concerning the so-called George Bell memorandum which George Meany read on "60 Minutes." I think you will see that on the face of it, the memorandum is a phony. It was not on White House paper. We've checked with Roche and he said it was on plain "oversized government" paper. If you will also look through the entire file of all the memos and correspondence leading up to the President's speech to the AFL-CIO, you will see that there is absolutely nothing of a similar nature in the file. In fact, the alleged memo is very inconsistent with everything else that Bell was writing prior to the President's trip. If we had had any hint that there would be a confrontation, I think you would have discovered it in one of the other memos.

The thrust of the alleged memo was that we would come out smashingly well as a result of the confrontation, but as you will see, we never expected it. I'm sure it was in the back of our minds that we might run into a raucous demonstration and that was one of the things, if you will recall, that really concerned us. Had we thought that Meany would treat the President the way he did, I for one would have recommended against the trip. While we are Machiavellian around here at times (I am; Bell never is), I don't think we could possibly have anticipated the way it turned out and, as you will see, every memo indicates that we expected the President to be treated politely and courteously. My one concern was that Gorman might put on something of a demonstration; we were assured that wouldn't happen. In fact, the reason we were calling people was to assure that the President would be well received. A cool audience, yes; but Meany's rudeness and affronts, no. That we never expected, as is obvious from this file.

If George Meany wants more reassurance, George Bell's secretary would be glad to produce an affidavit, as would George, that such a memo was never typed or prepared in this office and that indeed we had never seen it until it appeared in Roche's column and Roche subsequently sent us a copy.

I do think this should be cleared up with Meany, if indeed he thinks it is real, because it simply is not. I'm not too concerned about what kind of a public issue is made of this, but I think that Meany should be aware that we are not, as he fears, out to "get him."

cwc131

FEBRUARY 25, 1972

TO: **John Dean**

FROM: **Charles Colson**

RE: **Attached Letter**

Tom Casey is an old personal friend of mine. I've known him for ten years. We have a social as well as at times business relationship, since Tom is one of the IT&T people here. He invited me to use his boat while in Florida which I did. We went out on it for one day; box lunch and booze were provided.

Casey had originally extended the invitation when he thought he and his wife would be there. Then his plans changed and he was not so we used the boat anyway.

I understand that it is an IT&T chartered vessel, that they use it for visiting VIPs and their own executives.

I assume there is no problem in view of the fact that Casey is a personal friend and I have had nothing to do with IT&T affairs for over a year. Cashen was on board with me; he has been doing some things with IT&T.

Do you see anything objectionable or any problem with respect to the trip? I suppose I can offer to pay the expenses of the day which I of course would have no objection in doing.

cwc131

FEBRUARY 25, 1972

Dear Tom:*

I want you to know how very much we appreciated the opportunity to use your boat while we were in Miami this week. It was really one of the highlights of the first vacation I've had in two and a half years and probably the only one I'll have, at least until November.

I am not ever content sitting still and by Wednesday I had just about had it with the pool so that being able to get out on the water was really marvelous. Henry Cashen and Leslie and another friend of ours, Jim Low, all made the trip. I mention the last point in particular because if you discover that the liquor supply was badly depleted, I want you to know that it was Cashen's doings and not mine (although I must say I helped them a bit)!

Please thank Bill McHale also for his courtesies in bringing lunch and supplies on board. You were very kind of think of us and we do appreciate it.

Best personal regards.

Sincerely,

Charles W. Colson
Special Counsel
to the President

*[Letter to Thomas Casey, International Telephone and Telegraph, Washington, D.C.]

cwc131

FEBRUARY 28, 1972

TO: **The Attorney General**

FROM: **Charles Colson**

I assume you already know about the attached. It is an advance copy of a Jack Anderson stiletto which I have just obtained.*

*[Colson sent similar memoranda plus copies of the Anderson column to Haldeman, Ehrlichman, Ziegler, and Dean. Attached to all were copies of a Jack Anderson column which at the time was being distributed to subscribers for publication in early March. The article discussed lobbying efforts by ITT prior to the settlement on July 3, 1971, of three Justice Department suits against the conglomerate. It cites in particular a memorandum allegedly

written by Mrs. Dita Beard, an ITT lobbyist, which indicated the settlement favorable to ITT had come in return for a pledge by ITT of up to $400,000 for the 1972 Republican convention in San Diego. Reporter Brit Hume, an associate of Anderson, quoted her as saying that ITT security officers had put most of her files through a document shredder to prevent their being subpoenaed. However, she confirmed the authenticity of a memorandum she had written to the head of ITT's Washington office in June 1971, after she had met John Mitchell at a reception given by Kentucky Governor Louis Nunn at the time of the Kentucky Derby. "Mitchell is definitely helping us, but cannot let it be known," Anderson quoted the memorandum as saying. A Justice Department spokesman was quoted as confirming the meeting between Mrs. Beard and the Attorney General in Kentucky while denying that there was any truth to the rest of her story.]

cwc131

MARCH 1, 1972

TO: H. R. Haldeman

FROM: Charles Colson

RE: Press Functions

I assume that the President is planning this year to attend none of the Washington press ordeals, including the Gridiron Dinner.

After last year's debacle with the White House Correspondents Dinner, I would think he would be more than justified simply summarily dismissing them all. You might want to think about one interesting political twist, however. All of the Democratic candidates are boycotting the Gridiron because of its policy on women even though this year for the first time some women are invited. It might look very non-political and rather gutsy for the President to go in view of the fact that the Democrats have made such a sharp issue of it. Don't misunderstand me; we will not convert any of the snakes of the Washington press corps, but it might be a little bit of public political one-upmanship if the President were to show that he didn't give a damn about what all the Democrats consider the negative political implications of attending the dinner. That is a line which we could move, I am quite sure.

cwc131

MARCH 2, 1972

TO: Doug Hallett

FROM: Charles Colson

I need to talk to you about getting in touch with your friends in the McGovern camp for a secret suicide mission—theirs, not yours, that is.

cwc131

MARCH 3, 1972

TO: **H. R. Haldeman**

FROM: **Charles Colson**

RE: **Attached Tidbit**

I expect this happy little tidbit was a hand-out from some junior zealot at 1701 [the Committee for the Re-election of the President]. I am certain John Mitchell had nothing to do with it and I am also certain that it is characteristic of the kind of back-biting that we can expect as time goes on of the campaign jealousies [sic].

What makes me furious, however, is the discussion of half-million special party fund. Goddamn few people know about that!

cwc131

MARCH 3, 1972

TO: **Charles W. Colson**

FROM: **Steve Karalekas**

It has been suggested to me that the appropriate office in this Administration should commence an investigation into the background and circumstances surrounding the leasing arrangement of the Department of Transportation headquarters building in Washington.

According to my source, it seems that Larry O'Brien, present Democratic National Chairman, and two cohorts were involved in very shady dealings with LBJ. These dealings resulted in an extremely lucrative leasing arrangement with O'Brien and company as the lessors and the U.S. Government as the lessee.

I am unable at this time to be more specific, but according to my source, it is well worth checking. His suggestion was triggered by the current ITT–Jack Anderson revelation.

21 SENATE HEARINGS 9883;
23 SENATE HEARINGS 11136

ACTION MEMO

MARCH 6, 1972

Mitchell and Stans have got to know that the President cannot talk to any potential contributors. The Kleindienst case bears out the wisdom of this approach.

HRH

HRH112

MARCH 6, 1972

TO: John Ehrlichman

FROM: Bruce Kehrli

RE: ITT

The Weekend News Review of March 6 contained the following paragraph:

On Wash. Week in Review, Corddry of the Balt. Sun *said the ITT/Kleindienst hearings offer potential for a political "blow-up" which could affect the election. If the truth of Dita Beard's memo is established, it would be a "fantastic scandal"—perhaps the worst in 100 years. Corddry cautioned, however, that it's well known in DC that lobbyists are self-serving in their memos to the boss, so that seeing Mitchell in a restaurant suddenly becomes having had lunch with Mitchell. He noted that Nader and the press are out "beating the bushes" in search of evidence. Corddry said the case wasn't a parallel of the Sherman Adams scandal, as the Adams case didn't involve a public trust. If a link to Mitchell is proven, it will amount to a bribe, Corddry said. He noted that while Scott has taken the GOP lead to drop the matter, there are "some Republicans" who are "very disturbed." On the Dem side, Eastland seems to want to drop it, said Corddry, and Hart shows sympathy to Mitchell. Only EMK and Bayh are pushing.*

Referring to the [roman text of lines 9–10] of the above, the question of whether the Attorney General benefitted personally was raised.

It was also noted that this was certainly putting the story in its worst light.

You may want to raise both of these points, if you haven't already, in any future meetings on this issue.

cc: Charles Colson
    H. R. Haldeman
    Alexander P. Butterfield

POF39; ss84

MARCH 6, 1972

TO: Chuck Colson

FROM: Bruce Kehrli

RE: Sammy Davis

It was requested that you note the following from the March 6 Weekend News Review:

Sammy Davis, Jr. and others have raised $38,000 for Angela Davis' trial fund at a benefit in Los Angeles.

cc: H. R. Haldeman
     Alexander P. Butterfield

HANDWRITTEN NOTE BY PRESIDENT TO HALDEMAN: "and Garment thinks we should embrace him?!"

POF39; CWC1, 17, 131; SS83

ACTION MEMO

MARCH 7, 1972

Have someone do some thorough investigation on where the Democratic Convention support for Miami is coming from. In other words, what contributions are being made to support the Democratic Convention in the sense that the Sheraton contribution is being made to San Diego to support the Republican Convention.

HRH

IIIIII112

MARCH 7, 1972

TO: **Henry Kissinger**

FROM: **Bruce Kehrli**

RE: **State Department**

It was requested that you note the following from the March 7 News Summary:

Time *also notes State's morale—"lower than at any other time" since McCarthy.*

cc: H. R. Haldeman
     Alexander P. Butterfield

SS85

MARCH 7, 1972

TO: **The President**

FROM: **Charles Colson**

RE: **The Stock Market**

You asked me to call Don Reagan [sic] of Merrill-Lynch to get his current opinion of what is happening in the market. Reagan made the following points to me today in a conversation:

1. He believes the prediction he made the end of November that the market would turn around and experience a very strong recovery is proving correct, and the recovery is now taking place right on schedule. As he said to me, "Whatever other problems the President has, forget the stock market. This is not going to be one of his problems."

2. He believes the public has started back into the market, not the odd-lot or small speculative investor, but the sophisticated individual— lawyers, doctors and business executives.

3. Contrary to what institutions expected, the individual investor has in fact caused the current uptrend. Hence institutions are now encouraged and are beginning to draw upon their reserves. Hence in the next few weeks, there will be combined public and institutional volume which should cause the current rise to continue.

4. Reagan believes there will be a sustained increase in the market between now and June. The market always has to correct itself so there will be ups and downs but a general upward course is indicated; it will not take much more to put the Dow over 1000.

5. One of the major influences on the market at the moment is good economic news coming out of Washington. Reagan says if this continues the market should really move in a very healthy way.

6. The Federal Reserve Board's decision to cut the margin requirement back to 55% in December has proven very effective. Coupled with the drop in interest rates (brokers are now loaning at 5% on margins) it has brought in the sophisticated small investor and Europeans as well. Reagan said in the last two weeks there has begun a reverse flow of dollars coming back into the stock market from abroad.

7. The really small investor (those whom Reagan describes as having a few thousand extra in their savings accounts) will start to come in in the next 3 or 4 weeks. He believes that with savings accounts now at a very high level, this could provide a very important additional stimulus to the market.

8. Reagan thinks the Dow Jones is not truly representative of the market. He believes that the New York Stock Exchange index, the Standard and Poor index or the *New York Times* index are much better barometers and they have all reached new all-time highs.*

9. In short, Reagan is very much a bull.

*RN HAS UNDERLINED THE SECOND SENTENCE OF #8 AND HAS WRITTEN: *"very important."*

POF16; CWC1, 17, 131

ACTION PAPER

MARCH 8, 1972

RE: **IT&T**

We should consider several alternatives on things that can be done at this point. Perhaps, for example, we should ask the Host Committee to give the money back to IT&T, along with a real blast by the Mayor of San Diego saying this is a smear job and so forth. We could also, in the process, make the point that we've always refused the $400,000, that Dick Herman issued such instructions last November, and we could knock down the point that the President had any knowledge of this at all, which of course he didn't.

In any event, we need a counterattack. We must not let them get away with the only attack on this. We've got to build up the Miami story and anything else that we can.

Why is there no statement from Mitchell or Kleindienst at this point?

We've got to find a way to turn around the PR on this. We're getting taken unfairly and we should be taking some initiative ourselves.

HRH

HRH112

MARCH 8, 1972

TO: **Noel Koch**

FROM: **Charles Colson**

How about putting together today a couple of quick, hard blasts at the Democratic National Committee. All the hoopla that has gone on about ITT helping San Diego finance the Republican National Convention and here is ATT giving $1½ million to help finance the Democratic Convention. ITT has been all over the front pages for 10 days for a paltry $100,000. Here's ATT bailing out the Democrats to the tune of $1½ million and it is back with the corset ads. In whatever speech you put together, do not spell out American Telephone and Telegraph or International Telephone and Telegraph.

cwc131

MARCH 8, 1972

Dear Tom:*

Per your conversation with Henry Cashen, enclosed is what I understand to be the expenses for the boat in Florida. This is all too ridiculous for words but in view of all the turmoil of recent days, what started out as a friendly invitation from an old friend is best handled, I am sure, in this manner.

Best personal regards.

Sincerely,

Charles W. Colson
Special Counsel
to the President

*[Letter to Thomas Casey, International Telephone and Telegraph, Washington, D.C.]

cwc131

MARCH 9, 1972

TO: **Chuck Colson**

FROM: **Bruce Kehrli**

RE: **Muskie**

The March 9 News Summary contained the following paragraph:

In a lengthy, detailed review of press coverage—or the lack thereof—of Muskie's crying episode, the National Observer's *Jim Perry gives a good number of his* colleagues low marks for the way they played down, *sometimes virtually ignoring, Big Ed's tears.*

Referring to the [roman portion of line 3] of the above, it was requested that you note how Senator Muskie was protected by the press during this period.

cc: H. R. Haldeman
Alexander P. Butterfield
Ron Ziegler

POF39

EYES ONLY

MARCH 11, 1972

TO: **Henry Kissinger**

FROM: **The President**

Looking ahead on Vietnam we must take several political factors into consideration as we draw near to the Democratic Convention in early July.

I would not be surprised if the Democrats might lie low a bit on Vietnam insofar as troop withdrawals are concerned with the idea that they would like to have a pretty large residual force in Vietnam at the time of the Convention so that they could make an issue of the fact that after three years we still have not ended the American involvement. In other words, we should not take any particular comfort in the fact that Vietnam at the moment is not an issue. It is not an issue only because they are not making it an issue and may not even want to do so on a massive scale at this point. We can be sure, however, that once their Convention meets with the anti-war crowd constituting a majority of the delegates they will have a platform plank and an acceptance speech on the part of their candidate which will take us on hard on this issue unless we have defused substantially by that time.

I do not want to do anything in the April announcement that will in any way reduce the chances for some success on the negotiating front in the meeting you have in Paris at that time. As you know, I have very little confidence in what such a meeting may accomplish and I do not believe that they are going to negotiate until after the election. But in any event, we have to play the negotiating string out but we must not let that string hang us in the fall by failing to do what we can to present the very best possible case for our position on the assumption that no negotiated settlement will have been reached.

As far as the troop announcement in April is concerned, whether it is for one month or two months or three months is irrelevant. What is vital, however, is that a final announcement of some kind must be made before the Democratic Convention in July. Either in April or in June when we return from Moscow our announcement must be one which indicates that all American combat forces have left, that the residual force will be retained there until we get our POWs, that the residual force will be a solely volunteer force, and whatever else we can develop along those lines.

What I am emphasizing is that for over three years and through 12 fruitless meetings in Paris we have pursued the negotiating front. I think we must continue to do so throughout May and June for reasons that we are both aware [of]. But before the Democratic Convention we must make a final announcement of some type or we will be in very serious trouble.

HRH230

[MARCH 11, 1972]

Senator Dole Statement Released Sunday 6 P.M.

Republican National Chairman Robert Dole said today that upcoming "action or inaction" by the Democratic controlled Congress may shed a telling light on why *the giant public utility, AT&T, was so willing to indefinitely postpone payment of $1.5 million owed by the Democratic National Committee.*

Dole pointed out that on Tuesday, March 14, Dean Burch, chairman of the Federal Communications Commission, will appear before a House appropriations subcommittee, to urge approval of $800,000 in carryover funds for fiscal year 1973 in order to continue its ongoing investigation [of] AT&T, a regulated corporation.

Burch will make a similar appearance on April 20 before Sen. John Pastore's Senate appropriations subcommittee. In both instances, the ability of the FCC to conduct its ongoing probe of AT&T will be tied directly [to] decisions made by those subcommittees and ultimately by the full Congress, "which to our dismay is controlled by the party that AT&T is treating so generously."

"Within the next few weeks, the people of this nation may obtain an insight into the real difference between public pronouncements and meaningful action or inaction," Dole said. "We will see the people are informed on whether their Democratic representatives in the Senate and the House really want to match their words with deeds by approving the necessary funds to maintain an ongoing investigation of their party's convention benefactor."

Dole pointed out that when the FCC voted on Dec. 23, 1971, to suspend its probe of AT&T for lack of funds, Democratic senators and congressmen loudly proclaimed a "sell-out" by the regulatory agency. Since that time, he added, FCC in cooperation with the Office of Management and Budget has obtained waivers of budgetary restrictions, rearranged some of its internal priorities and taken funds from other projects to reinstitute the AT&T investigation.

"But the real key to that resumption lies in FCC being able to carry over $800,000 from the current fiscal year," said Dole.

"And that permission must be obtained from the Democrat majority in Congress."

Dole said that when Democrats, notably Senator Fred Harris of Oklahoma, first charged that the FCC was backing off its investigation of the big public utility, AT&T hadn't yet agreed to postpone its demand for a back debt of $1.5 million from the Democratic party, an act which may have violated a federal law barring corporate contributions to political parties.

"It will be interesting to analyze how these Democratic senators and congressmen act toward an AT&T investigation now that the utility, in effect, has permitted them to hold a convention," Dole said.

cwc131

_____

From President's News Summary of March 11, 1972:

EMK refused to yield to Hruska who then walked out. Phil Hart wrapped up NBC by saying on film that public believes something is wrong in this case and those responsible must be discovered or the whole incident will lead to further undermining of confidence in gov't. Philosopher Hart's views also concluded CBS report from Hill as his view was verbally noted that if public financing of campaigns was in operation, this incident wouldn't have occurred.

After note of Mrs. Beard denials and her desire to testify, Dan Schorr told us she's not remembered on Hill as an irrational drunk but as a hard-driving, tough woman—a GOP Abzug—who pushed hard but was reasonable and never drank excessively. She's a real sentimentalist and very warm toward her kids who she has taken great pride in raising, said Schorr.

Anderson and Hume voluntarily turned over Hume's notes of the Beard interview. Hume said he had given the notes to EMK last week but "forgot" to tell the Comm. about it when he refused GOP demands to turn them over . . . Hume also testified that Mrs. Beard told him she struck a bargain with Mitchell at Nunn's Derby Day dinner.

Kleindienst charged two Dem. Admins. refused to touch the ITT anti-trust case and said its settlement was one of the "great achievements" of the RN era. He said McLaren stopped ITT's headlong rush of conglomerate acquisitions and that McLaren had "to pinch" himself to believe it necessary to defend the action.

ITT said Sheraton had pledged $100,000 to the San Diego tourist bureau to attract the convention. A possible $100,000 additional was pledged with the condition it be matched by other local contributions. ITT said the $400,000 figure was erroneous.

Tho not noted by the nets, the Star features on p. 1 a Walters story that "the law firm headed by RN's personal attorney in Calif. (Kalmbach) sought [in an unusual request] and received Justice's legal sanction for the arrangement which allowed ITT to contribute up to $400,000 to the GOP Convention."

Kempton, on CBS Spectrum, pointing up the historical political role of Justice, said most lib Dem. Senators weren't upset by Kleindienst's "alacrity" on phone tapping, but became aroused when he started to do business like a Senator. Kleindienst is a partisan Republican, said Kempton, but that doesn't come up because both parties, by consent, use Justice as the primary tool for rewarding friends and punishing enemies of the party in power. Partisanship is the real corruption Kleindienst represents, but his opponents don't mention this as (the principle) has served them well before and they trust it will again.

NBC note that Dole said AT&T seems to be forgiving and forgetting the $1.5M debt in agreeing to provide phone service at the Miami Conv. On CBS film the Sen. said ATT's very substantial contribution was far more than ITT offered to San Diego; he emphasized it was not offered to RNC. . . . Note on both nets of O'Brien's "smokescreen" retort and ATT statement that Dems will pay all and on a cash basis.

Dole didn't say who was to conduct the hearings, but presumably it would be the FCC. Dole blasted the furor made over the ITT arrangement, saying it was being done for obvious political advantages. Dole said the ATT arrangement must be considered "at the very least a loan, if not an outright gift." . . . Dole said the unpaid phone bill was "old news," but insisted it wasn't relevant that he'd waited until now to urge investigation. Asked if he wanted to take the opportunity to deny that any other corp. has made a "substantial contribution" to the GOP, directly or indirectly, Dole said "no."

POF39

TO: The President's File*

RE: Meeting with Charles Colson and Ken Clawson, March 13, 1972

Informal discussion of the role of the typewriter in the Alger Hiss espionage case; relating this experience to current events insofar as the technique used in the Hiss case appears to be applicable in a given set of circumstances. General discussion of ITT case.

Some personal discussion of Clawson's newspaper career, including fact that Clawson was the recipient of Nieman Fellowship at Harvard University and had covered White House for *Washington Post* before coming to work for the President.

The President specifically related to Clawson some of the problems in dealing with the press as White House spokesman and encouraged him to remain current on all information in areas where he would be a spokesman.

*[Written by Mr. Colson July 11, 1972]

cwc1, 88, 132

MARCH 13, 1972

TO: Bob Haldeman

FROM: The President

Pat has decided that the Pandas must go to the Washington Zoo. She said that in talking to Chou En-lai he indicated that since they came from Peking she had indicated in response that perhaps they should go to the National Zoo here. Since she feels so strongly about it, I think that is what we should do.

One project that I would like to be undertaken discreetly is setting up the display of the State gifts from China for tourists to see. Pat had not yet heard from Chapin at all as to what had happened to the gifts. I think it is very important that the gift from Mao Tse-tung, Chou En-lai and other mementos of the trip be set up on a much more elaborate basis than has been the case for previous state visits. I think, for example, that Ollie's pictures are very good but they are wasted simply showing them in the West Wing where nobody sees them except members of our staff and occasional visitors. Perhaps a picture display from Ollie's collection in the whole area [near] the place that the state gifts are displayed might be in order. Also, along these same lines, as you know I have instructed in each case that wherever there is a dinner—state or otherwise—a member of the staff, particularly the military staff, has the obligation to pick up the menu and place card. I assume that that was being done in Peking, Hang-chow and Shanghai. If it was not done, I would like for you to check other members of the staff to see if they happen to have them because we need them for our historical records. What I would like done, however, at the present time is that a menu for each of the dinners and the place cards when they are available should be put on display in this general area that I have spoken about. Also, since there will be duplicate menus, I would like for you to see that duplicate menus and duplicate pictures that are appropriate be given to Tricia and Julie for display in areas that they are planning to use in Jacksonville and Cambridge to commemorate the trip. Tricia, for example, is going to put out the cloisonné vases that Pat bought for her in Peking. If some appropriate pictures and the menus for each dinner could be added to the display it could be quite meaningful and, of course, anything else that we may have collected that could be of interest. Julie, in Jacksonville, is going to do the same with something that Pat brought back from China for her—a tea set I think it was. Ollie's pictures plus a collection of the menus might be very much in order here.

In addition, I would put out chopsticks that were ostensibly used for the two dinners in Peking. I realize that some member of the press said he picked them up but that doesn't make any difference. We undoubtedly have some chopsticks—ivory or otherwise. As a matter of fact, Chou En-lai insisted on using wood ones and on occasions I accommodated him in that respect. Just indicate that these were the chopsticks used by the President on the occasion of the dinner of ———.

I realize that none of these things seem particularly important, and they aren't in terms of the overall impression, but I consider them impor tant from a personal standpoint and I want some follow-through and a report made directly to me as to what has been done first with regard to the display for White House visitors to see as they come in the East Wing—and, second, what has been made available to Tricia and Julie for the displays that they are presenting or loaning to the art museums or whatever it is in their respective localities.

I realize that none of these things may seem important to us who have been in China and for whom they have become routine. On the other hand, there will be an enormous amount of interest from the people who happen to see them in the areas concerned. I would like for you to put Chapin or Ron Walker or someone else who has the time and the energy to follow through on this and give me a complete report.

Along these same lines, in talking to Henry today I gathered that he was feeling some disappointment that with only two weeks gone since the China trip was completed, the press interest has substantially evaporated. This, of course, is no surprise to me though it is a surprise to him. You may recall that I reminded him and you prior to the visit that it took the press only two days to forget the SALT announcement and they desperately did their best to forget the Peking announcement when we made it on July 15th and managed to sink it within the matter of a week. Where Kennedy was concerned with regard to the test ban or another affirmative event they would keep the story alive for five to six weeks to two or three months afterward. In our case, they deliberately try to sink any story that they think might be of help to us.

This brings me to the point. It is very much in our interest, of course, to keep the China story alive in terms of the enormous public impact that it has had. That is why the Kissinger broadcast is probably a good idea. Also, in that connection, I trust that we are putting every effort that we can behind building up sales for the pocketbook on China. This should be a best seller at various party events that occur over the next few months.

In any event, I would like for you to put somebody to work on seeing what can be done to follow up on the China visit so that the press does not succeed in its obvious effort to bury it as quickly as possible due to the fact that they know it is a plus for us. We are going to confront the same situation with regard to the Soviet visit so we may as well get in practice right now. This may mean that a few more appearances and speeches, etc., by people who were on the visit might well be considered despite the obvious risk of having something said that might disturb Henry's sensitivities. Give some thought to this and give me a recommendation on it. The main point for us to recognize is that it is very much in our interest to keep the China visit in the minds of people across the country and not to allow the press to succeed in its efforts to submerge it completely by concentrating on other issues. As a matter of fact, the IT&T case I think was deliberately surfaced at this time for the purpose of knocking down public interest and coverage of the China visit. In that connection, it was a brilliant success although not a total success due to the fact that we had a few announcements to make after the IT&T story broke. But make no mistake about it. This is exactly why Kennedy et al. broke that story at this point. They have had it for a long time and they saved it up for right now so that they could torpedo the China visit. I am sure that Henry and others concerned would not understand that this is what the deal was all about, but I could see it the moment that I saw the stories begin to surface on Friday after we had returned from China on Monday.

PPF3; HRH162

All text after "mean" in line 6
of last paragraph W/RN from
PPF3.

MARCH 13, 1972

TO: **Bob Haldeman**

FROM: **The President**

I believe the best way to get across to Henry some of the points that you think he might make in his backgrounders and in the event he does a television broadcast some areas to emphasize, would be for you to write a memorandum to him along the lines that I will touch upon very generally in this memorandum to you. This memorandum is only for your information. It should not go to him or to anybody else. It should simply be your observations with regard to points you think he might well make in order to strengthen the RN image in the whole field of foreign affairs.

As far as the China trip is concerned, television at least got across the points of dignity, Presidential presence, etc., which are, of course, very important in the long term.

On the other hand, insofar as substance is concerned there is still a great deal of mystery. Not about the communique which has been discussed at such great length that the average person is probably tired of hearing about it but about how the meeting between RN and Chou-En-lai and also Mao Tse-tung really went.

Among points that Henry is best qualified to emphasize are the following:

1. RN goes into such meetings better prepared than anyone who has ever held this office. He takes voluminous briefing materials that are prepared by the NSC staff and by the State Department, reads them all and also reads a lot of other materials and talks to a great number of people and then sits down and makes up his own mind as to what his approach should be. He does not memorize, he does not follow a predictable pattern and as a result he is able to handle any question that comes up on the spot without being frozen into a position which may prove to be untenable.

2. He has the great advantage of an exceptional knowledge of world problems gained in eight years in the Vice Presidency, eight years of travel while he was out of office and then, of course, his three years in office. In other words, he has been up against big league pitching for a longer period of time than any world leader. He has had extended conversations with the best of them—DeGaulle, DeGasperi, Adenauer, Khrushchev, Nehru, Yoshida, Sukarno—not to mention the current batch of leaders from both large and small countries whom he has met as President.

3. One mark of his style is that he treats all leaders, whether from large or small countries, with equal dignity and respect.

4. As far as tactics are concerned, he never gives an inch on principle. As a matter of fact, he is perhaps more rigid on principle than his advisors would want him to be.

5. He never quibbles over debating points. He always keeps his eye on the main goal and constantly finds ways to bring the subject back to that goal rather than being diverted into argumentative discussions that would have no effect whatever insofar as achieving our main purposes is concerned.

6. The qualities of subtlety, humor—never being belligerent but being very tough, of speaking most quietly when he is making the strongest points.

7. The quality of knowing the other man and all of his positions as well as he knows his own. Something, incidentally, which also characterized Chou-En-lai and which made the meeting between the two such a fascinating discussion.

8. The quality of absolute discipline going clear back to the time when he had the seven-hour luncheon with Khrushchev and through all the many summits as well as the meetings with the Chinese. He never takes a drink during the course of the meetings or prior to any important conversation and he even carries it to the extent of resisting the temptation which was so obviously presented to him, particularly with the Chinese, of eating nuts and other goodies that were put before him during the course of the discussion. RN has the theory that either drinking or eating tends to dull the reaction time as far as he is concerned although he, of course, would not apply this same test to others for whom either eating or drinking may help their reactions, as was the case presumably with Churchill and others.

9. The quality of candor but candor not for the purpose of embarrassing his opposite number but for the purpose of establishing a degree of mutual trust and confidence so essential for any meaningful discussion.

In your memorandum, I think you should go on to suggest that Henry review his recollections and his notes to see how any personal tidbits without revealing the substance of conversations could be used to bear out these points. This does not have to be limited to his discussions with Chou-En-lai. For example, he can go back to the discussions with DeGaulle, Wilson, Pompidou et al., as well as Ceausescu, Tito, to make the point. Wherever it is appropriate to do so, he could make the point that RN has acquired a great deal of respect from world leaders because of his conduct of these sessions without resorting to staff, notes, etc.

Finally, the quality of stamina. The ability to be at his best regardless of the length of the session.

I do not know whether you can get some of these points across to Henry but it seems to me that these are things that he has often mentioned to others in his own conversations on a private basis and if some of this can get into the public domain it would, of course, be extremely helpful.

It is very important that you suggest this on your own as being your ideas based on what you have heard from me and from him, etc., and then see if he picks it up.

HRH162

W/RN from HRH230

ACTION MEMO

MARCH 13, 1972

We need a statement developed for Stans to use regarding contributor lists and it should be supplied to other people who have to answer questions on this subject also.

The point we should make is that we will report everything as required according to law.

The statement should say that we have absolutely nothing to hide and that we are setting up the machinery now to provide a reporting facility as the law requires.

In the meantime we should point out the President is not doing any campaigning in the primary campaigns.

HRH

HRH112

EYES ONLY

MARCH 14, 1972

TO: **Bob Haldeman**

FROM: **The President**

I want you to get me a report today on how much IT&T grew during the three Kennedy years and the five Johnson years. My guess is that the growth was very substantial, particularly during the latter period. The figure may mean nothing, but I would like to have it in the event we want to make a case on the point that the Johnson Administration, as well as the Kennedy Administration, failed to bring action to stop the growth of IT&T whereas this Administration did so.

Also, you should follow up with Colson's office to see whether any lawyer from the Anti-Trust Division at IT&T would be loyal enough to say that prosecution was recommended during the Johnson years and nothing happened. If it is not possible to make hay this way, an avenue which would be just as effective almost would be to have Geneen cover this in his testimony.

PPF3; HRH162, 230

MARCH 14, 1972

TO: **Bob Haldeman**

FROM: **The President**

Another item I need today, which you can get from Mort Allin's shop as a result of a quick check, is whether any editorials whatever or columns have been written criticizing the Judiciary Committee for taking libelous testimony against the President of the United States on hearsay fourth removed.

Also, at a later point, because it will probably take them a matter of several days to get this, I would like for some bright young person to go back in the files during the days of the Hiss case and the Un-American Activities Committee and get a ringing editorial from the *New York Times* or the *Washington Post* condemning [them] for using hearsay once removed in such cases. It may be that our theory doesn't hold up, but at least I would like our researchers to see what the facts are.

PPF3; HRH162

MARCH 14, 1972

TO: **Bob Haldeman**

FROM: **The President**

I assume that the meeting with Billy Graham's religious leaders is going forward. Would you please check and if it is not being done this week be sure it is done the week after Henry gets back from his vacation. I do not believe the problem is potentially too great a one, but it could become one in the event that the extremists get to them before Henry has a chance to put the record straight.

In that same connection, by giving Henry groups that are important to us politically it will take the pressure off of him to do some of the columnists and others who inevitably are going to be pressing to see him. Obviously, he is going to fill his schedule and it is better that he fill his schedule with people who will be of interest to us politically rather than the international set type who almost inevitably would otherwise get to him.

With further regard to Graham, would you be sure to place a call to him about once every two weeks to discuss the political situation. I would prefer not to get into these matters as directly with him, but I do want a continuing contact kept with him so that he doesn't feel that we are not interested in the support of his group in those key states where they can be helpful.

HRH162

W/RN from PPF3

MARCH 14, 1972

TO: **Bob Haldeman**

FROM: **The President**

For the Gridiron church I would like to have the Army Chorus. It is the best of the three choruses and since the Gridiron is devoid of speeches ostensibly and full of music, why not have a half-hour church service with scripture reading, prayer and the Army Chorus without trying to have any remarks. Anyone we get to speak will fall flat before that group of cynics. At least, whatever we do on the speaker's side make it short and let's have the Army Chorus for a number of good religious numbers, including a Negro spiritual which they are very good at with that big baritone who is a member.

HRH162

___

ACTION PAPER

MARCH 15, 1972

RE: **Follow-up with Chuck Colson**

With regard to the coverage we've been getting on ITT, and particularly the *New York Times*'s picture this morning, we should call the publisher of the *Times* and make sure that an appropriate retraction is printed.

Mitchell should make sure he tries to get this on television this evening. If not, we should call the nets and send 100 letters to the *Times*.

Also, somebody should be attacking Kennedy, both personally and in the Committee.

LH
HRH112

___

MARCH 15, 1972

TO: **Secretary John Volpe**
      Chuck Colson
      Jeb S. Magruder
      W. Richard Howard

FROM: **Clark MacGregor**

RE: **Jeno F. Paulucci**

According to the *New York Times* of Wednesday, March 15th, Jeno F. Paulucci has contributed $42,000 to the Presidential campaign of Hubert H. Humphrey.

CWC98

___

MARCH 15, 1972

TO: **Dick Howard**

FROM: **Charles Colson**

Where do we stand on a meeting for the President with Jeno Paulucci? Right now, noticing that Paulucci is one of Humphrey's biggest contributors, I suspect that the meeting should be put into a suspense status at least until I can have Volpe talk to Paulucci. Paulucci has indicated he wants to get aboard our campaign, as you know, but I think when he made the offer he thought Humphrey was down the drain. This morning he may think otherwise.

cwc131

MARCH 15, 1972

TO: **The Honorable John N. Mitchell**

FROM: **G. Gordon Liddy***

RE: **Democratic National Convention Finance Investigation**

Below is a summary of the results to date of the investigation, which began March 12, 1972.

Howard Hunt reported on March 13, 1972:

The following individuals are members of the Tourist Development Authority and in addition to donating funds themselves to the DNC they have served as conduits for other funds.

1. Jesse Weiss—owner of Joe's Stone Crabs Restaurant

2. Bob Olin—Seville Hotel

3. H. Bant—Seville Hotel

4. Jack Gordon (Chairman of the Authority)

5. Hans Marcuse—Algiers Hotel

6. Herbert Rolbin—Carillion Hotel

7. William Leonard (not further identified)

8. Ben Grenold (owner of a number of drug stores)

Information indicates that the exposition areas will be located in two places: the Fontainebleau Hotel and Convention Hall. The Mancraft Agency, a national organization specializing in such expositions, is the agent for booking space. However, all space bookings must go through, and have the approval of, James Teague, an employee of the Democratic National Committee, whose business telephone number for Miami is [number].

Mancraft has an agent, one Barry Block, at the Fontainebleau, but he can do nothing without Teague's approval.

Hunt advised further that the Spanish language (Cuban) radio in Miami is carrying a news item to the effect that the Republicans are "looking around town" to "get something on the Democrats," in connection with the convention.

A pretext attempt was made to book exposition space in the Fontainebleau. The reply was that all Fontainebleau space has been booked and that the only space remaining is in Convention Hall.

On March 14, 1972, T-1, described as an experienced political correspondent for major news media in the Miami area, but who has not reported previously and whose reliability is, therefore, untested, advised as follows:

The GFC (Florida-Askew) raised one million dollars. He advised further that the Democratic National Committee is receiving a 25 percent kickback from the funds raised through the exposition to be held at the Fontainebleau Hotel and Convention Hall during the Democratic National Convention to be held in Miami Beach in July 1972.*

A transcription of the tape-recorded interview of T-1 is attached at Tab A.

ADMINISTRATIVE

Investigation at Miami and Miami Beach continues.

*[Memorandum on Committee for the Re-Election of the President letterhead]

HANDWRITTEN COMMENT BY MR. MITCHELL OPPOSITE NEXT-TO-LAST PARAGRAPH: "Need more info"

3 SENATE HEARINGS 1152

ACTION PAPER

MARCH 17, 1972

Some columnists should be interested in an editorial or column blasting the double standard that applies to Congressional hearings as far as they are covered by the press. For example, during the Nixon/Hiss era, and then later in the McCarthy era, when Communists were being investigated by the House Un-American Activities Committee, the Committee was constantly being attacked because they weren't following the rules of court in conducting their investigation and it's curious to note what's happened to those attacks now when the President of the United States is being slandered, or the Attorney General, or an outstanding business leader—no one raises his voice—even when the Committee allows fourth removed hearsay evidence.

The double standard here is rather obvious and might be worth pointing out.

HRH

HANDWRITTEN NOTE BY MR. HIGBY: "See if Buchanan could peddle this one—"

HRH112

MARCH 22, 1972

TO: **Bob Haldeman**

FROM: **The President**

In talking to Senator Bentsen and his wife last night they spoke glowingly of Julie's performance at the dedication of the Eisenhower bust by the Texas Society at the Kennedy Center. As Bentsen put it, appearing on the program were Connally, Tower, Bentsen and two or three other very effective old pros. But Julie came in and with her freshness and charm stole the show.

I think that our scheduling staff is under-estimating her effectiveness. I know you have a good man checking over the invitations that she gets and working on her schedule. But I want a study made at the highest level, under your direction, of appearances that she can make in key states between now and the election. She is willing to do anything and I note in several cases she has taken invitations that I thought frankly weren't worth her time. The fact that she is willing to do this should not be a reason for us to have her take the invitations, but steps should be taken immediately to get her into New York, Ohio, Illinois, Texas and, of course, again in California as well as Pennsylvania. They should be non-political appearances preferably, with a political appearance being made only if there is a television dividend. Once the particular engagements are agreed to she will be sure that the scheduler puts in the right events because she is very good at insisting on television, news conferences, etc.

What I am concerned about is that she is still accepting engagements on the basis of going through invitations we receive rather than creating the opportunities in those areas where with the same amount of effort she could do a lot more good for us.

Tricia also is willing to make appearances, although she cannot go out for any length of time. She should handle the New England area, New York, New Jersey, and Pennsylvania where she would not have to be away for an evening, but she is willing to do so provided we work up the proper events.

Pat, too, will do events, but again in her case they must really be worthwhile and should be only in key states.

I am not suggesting that Julie and Tricia should not do anything in other than key states because I realize we have to make some appearances there. What I am suggesting is that more emphasis must be put on the key states and that we must take charge of the schedule in a very effective, planned way.

There is no complaint with regard to the way the events are handled by the staff once they are accepted. Andrews is doing a very good job in preparing talking points and the advance men are doing very well. The problem really is in the decision at the higher level in the first instance as to what appearances really ought to be taken and which ones will be most useful.

As I have said on several other occasions, I want the appearances by Julie, Tricia and Pat to receive the same considered appraisal that appearances I make receive. In many instances they can be more effective than I can be, particularly in the time before the convention.

HRH162

W/RN from PPF3 and HRH230

MARCH 22, 1972

TO: **Henry E. Petersen**
Asst. Attorney General, Criminal Division

FROM: **John W. Dean, III**
Counsel to the President

RE: **William Baranek**

Pursuant to our conversation of this date, I am attaching the statements prepared by members of my staff in regard to telephone conversations they have had with Mr. Baranek. I have not personally talked to the man.

I now understand he is also calling John Ehrlichman's office, but know no further details in this regard.

MARCH 22, 1972

FROM: **Fred F. Fielding**
Associate Counsel to the President

On March 21, 1972, at approximately 8:15 A.M., I took a phone call on White House line 446. The caller asked for John Dean and identified himself as Bill Baranek. I advised Mr. Baranek that Mr. Dean was not available at the moment and asked if I could take a message or have him return the call.

Mr. Baranek told me that his position with the Post Office had been "taken away" unfairly sometime ago and generally described the circumstances, the details of which I did not note. He further advised that he has been in court on this matter, and made several allegations of judicial impropriety.

Mr. Baranek then told me that he had overheard and observed a meeting, "down at the Watergate" between the Attorney General, a woman he later identified as Dita Beard, and a judge (apparently McLaren) when they made the ITT "deal." He said that he had brought this information to the attention of Senator Hugh Scott last Tuesday, and Scott therefore had lied when he went before the cameras on Friday, and announced that the memo was false.

Baranek said that he wanted us to get his job back in exchange for this information. I advised him that he was making what sounded to me

1972: JANUARY–APRIL   393

to be a solicitation to bribery and I did not want to hear any more of the details since what he was proposing would constitute a violation of federal law. I told him that if he wanted to leave his phone number I would leave a message for Mr. Dean that he had called, but that I did not wish to discuss this with him further. He said that he knew how these things worked and he did want to pursue this with John Dean, and that if he did not give this information to Dean he would have to give it to the networks. I took his phone number and terminated the conversation.

At no time did I identify myself, to the best of my recollection.

I immediately brought this matter to John Dean's attention.

At approximately noon I returned to my office and was advised by Miss Jane Thomas, John Dean's secretary, that Mr. Baranek had called and said we could disregard his call.

Later in the afternoon my secretary, Miss Barbara Ann Vidler, advised me that Mr. Baranek had again called and discussed the subject of his call with her, and requested that someone call him back.

MARCH 22, 1972

FROM: **Barbara A. Vidler**

Mr. Baranek called yesterday afternoon (3-21-72) and asked to speak with John Dean. I informed him that Mr. Dean was out of the office and could I help him. He proceeded to tell his story of being ousted out of a job at the Post Office because of his political involvements and attending a political rally. He said that political power and Administration-swayed judges removed him from his job. He has repeatedly been unsuccessful at attempts to gain back his old position.

He stated that what he really wanted was his old position back in return for not disclosing information that he knew regarding ITT. He stated that he heard and saw Mr. Mitchell, Dita Beard and Judge McLaren at the Watergate last year discussing ITT cases. I asked him if he was positive it was the ITT cases and he assured me that he was certain. He would not disclose exactly what was said.

For not disclosing this information to NBC or the Democrats he would like in turn to have his old job back at the Post Office. He said that he has learned to play our game. He also stated that he has spoken with Senator Scott and had given him this same information. He accused Sen. Scott of lying at his news conference when Scott denounced Mitchell's involvement with Beard at that conference.

He would not leave a number or address where he could be reached, fearing involvement for the party (a woman) where he was staying. He insisted on speaking with John and stated that he would call back.

JFB2

W/RN from JWD4

MARCH 23, 1972

TO: **H. R. Haldeman**

FROM: **John Dean**

RE: **Potential Disruptions at the**
1972 Democratic National Convention

After a slow start, interest in organizing demonstrations at the Democratic National Convention scheduled for July 10–13, 1972 at Miami Beach—appears to be picking up but is not yet as strong as that centered on San Diego. Several national radical figures and organizations have already announced their intent to demonstrate at the convention, and are now formulating plans. Unlike the situation in San Diego, however, there is little interest in such activities on the part of the local Miami activists.

The principal organization that has committed itself to organizing demonstrations at the Democratic National Convention is the Youth International Party (YIPPIES). This group, at a meeting in Chicago in late January 1972, formed a political wing known as the ZIPPIES, which is to coordinate planning for demonstrations at the national political conventions. The ZIPPIES tentatively have scheduled activities for the July 4th weekend in Washington to be followed by the travelling of participants to Miami for a "Freak Circus" during the Democratic convention.

YIPPIE leaders Jerry Rubin and Stu Alpert are talking in terms of 15,000 persons journeying to Miami for the demonstrations. Tactics under discussion include marijuana smoke-ins, guerrilla theaters, and "selective trashing" of specific targets. Between now and July, several other activities aimed at attracting attention are also planned to interest followers in coming to Miami before proceeding to San Diego.

The other national New Left groups which have indicated a desire to disrupt the Democratic National Convention are the People's Coalition for Peace and Justice (PCPJ), the Vietnam Veterans Against the War (VVAW), the Red Balloon Collective, a recently formed organization, and the Congress of African Peoples, a black separatist group. The VVAW has already voted to demonstrate in Miami. Sentiments are more mixed at the PCPJ. Rennie Davis, the former PCPJ leader who is very influential in movement circles, expressed one faction's opinion when he recently suggested that it would be best for the New Left if the Democratic convention were to be relatively peaceful. As for the two remaining organizations which have expressed their intent, the Red Balloon Collective has been losing air ever since its formation while the Congress of African Peoples is a relatively unknown group.

So far, there has been little planning by activist groups in the Miami area. One organization, the "Miami Snow Plow Company" which was created to coordinate local activities, is already in financial difficulty. Another group, the Florida People's Platform Coalition, is also supposed to sponsor two days of nonviolent protest during the convention, but this coalition appears to be of little significance.

Law enforcement planning in Miami is not as well organized and extensive as that currently in progress in San Diego. Important federal agencies such as the Immigration and Naturalization Service, Alcohol, Tobacco, and Firearms Division and the U.S. military services are not involved in the planning. In addition to being able to develop pertinent information regarding possible disruptions at the convention, these agencies would also be in a position to furnish either logistical support or manpower to assist in assuring convention security.

As in the case of the Republican National Convention, the planning of the organizers of demonstrations at Miami is in constant flux with the outlook changing from day to day. I shall, however, provide you regular situation reports as this planning takes shape.

_____ JWD4

EYES ONLY

MARCH 23, 1972

TO: **John Dean**

FROM: **Charles Colson**

If the Internal Revenue Service even considers McGovern's complaint against the VFW, I will personally detonate the dynamite that will blow the IRS building off the map. Please be damn sure that this doesn't get out of control.

_____ cwc131

MARCH 27, 1972

TO: **Bob Haldeman**

FROM: **The President**

Four weeks after our return from Peking—I believe we can look back over this period and derive some good guidance for the future.

Our positive activities could probably be summarized as follows: there were a number of messages on domestic issues which received some notice in the newspapers, but very little on television. The two primaries, New Hampshire, and Florida, both came out positively as far as we were concerned, but due to the fact that most of the action was on the Democratic side and due to the media's desire not to play up anything too much which helps us, we got very little lasting benefit from the primaries. What benefit we got was the fact that the Democrats had their troubles. The busing television speech on the 16th, the trip to New York on the 20th, the

Meany statement on the 23rd, were the only occasions when we were able to get anything across on television. The office press conference on the 24th had limited television coverage, as you have already pointed out.

In this same four-week period there was hardly any activity by the Cabinet or Republicans in Congress which made positive news as far as the Administration was concerned, except, of course, for Connally's Today Show appearance. It might be well to see if we were in error in not having the news vacuum in this period filled more by our spokesmen at a time when I was not as active as I might usually be.

On the negative side, we have been on the defensive on ITT for three weeks, and on the economic side, while the economic news has generally been fairly good, the news on food prices has far overwhelmed any positive good we got from the other indices.

As anticipated, we have been taking a beating on busing due to the bent of the media and we must give them credit that they have handled it very cleverly by so confusing the issue that many people are not aware of where we really stand—that we are really against busing. The only thing that saves this situation for us at all is that I made the television appearance on the 16th rather than simply going with the written message on the 17th as we had originally planned.

Perhaps our biggest disappointment has been in failure to follow up on the China trip. As we should have anticipated, the press—even those who travelled with us—were for the most part so anxious not to let us have a positive bounce that they either dropped the subject from their news accounts, except when forced to bring something in like the panda story, or when they could bring up a negative point like the Rogers-Kissinger dispute.

On the other hand, on the foreign side, we were fortunate in March in having very little negative news on Vietnam.

Certain conclusions from this rundown would seem to be in order:

1. When I allow a news vacuum as far as my own activities are concerned, as was the case from the 28th until the 16th of March, we cannot assume that the Cabinet or Republicans in Congress will fill it. Or putting it more fairly, even when they try to fill it they don't get a play which meets the need.

2. As the election approaches the media are going to step up their attempts to cut us down, particularly as they see the Democrats having such troubles in their primaries.

3. We cannot assume that there is significant lasting effect of even such a great event as the China trip. There are two reasons for this. First, people are so surfeited with media spectaculars that after a week or so they are looking for something new and forget what went before. The second reason is perhaps even more fundamental. The media simply aren't going to give us any breaks whatever in keeping alive a story which they know might help us.

The other conclusion is that we must assume that we are going to be cut up unless we keep the initiative. That brings me to what kind of a program we have to adopt to meet that goal.

As far as the activities of others are concerned, we have to recognize that messages on domestic issues, while necessary, do us very little good except as a defensive maneuver, unless I find a way to tie into one of them personally, as in the case of the drug bill signing.

Recognizing that our strength is in the foreign policy area, we should go forward with the plans on regional appearances which I have already discussed with you for Kissinger, Scali and Rogers to the extent he is willing to do so. Here the important thing to do is to get them on television so that their effect is not limited to their media audiences and the writing press.

On the domestic side, I think we have to get a better plan for Connally to make regional appearances and be sure that when he makes his appearances he gets on TV locally. Particularly with the cost of living issue now surfacing again, he is the man who must take the lead to fight it out. Klein has been effective in these regional appearances and to the extent other Cabinet officers or top Administration officials can get a hearing on TV in a regional appearance we should use them also. Building up our other Cabinet officers seems to be an almost impossible task, but we have to continue to try because as the campaign gets further along they are going to have to carry more of the load. Agnew, of course, has his own special role to play, but it might be well for us to do some long-range planning with regard to how he could be used more effectively, particularly on the attack where we believe one should be made.

As far as my own activities are concerned, I believe we should aim for an average of one televised press conference every three weeks. The Moscow trip and the Republican Convention, of course, will be counted as a substitute for one of those conferences. In addition to the televised press conference, I believe we should try to have one event each week aimed at hard news, such as the drug trip to New York. For example, as I look at the schedule for this coming week, beginning the 26th, it is just like the first two weeks of March—useless as far as any impact on the general public is concerned. I think what we should do is to cut the frills down even more than we have. For example, I can see why we would include another session on the cancer crusade, but I do not see why we would include the retarded children's poster child. These should generally be done by PN, Julie or Tricia from now on unless there is a very special reason for me to undertake one.

When I speak of a hard news lead I think this fills the vacuum which Connally constantly refers to with regard to the country wanting leadership, particularly in a period when the Democratic candidates are hammering night after night on the news shows on lack of leadership from Washington.

Supplemental to the television appearances which, of course, are by far the most important, might be three or four radio talks. I still think these are probably a good idea, particularly because we can get a pretty good play with minimum effort on my part.

For the immediate future these four issues should be emphasized: man of peace, cost of living, drugs, and anti-busing. It would be particularly helpful if our other speakers could zero in on these issues with lines that eventually might get through to the people generally.

You will note that I have not mentioned any of the soft news items with which we have been so heavily concerned in the past. My feeling is now that we probably aren't going to be able to get much of that through the media blackout and that at this point we had better concentrate our fire on hard news events which they have to carry because they will be basically issue-oriented rather than person-oriented. We can only hope that the way we hit the hard news stories in press conferences, on our trip abroad, and in other appearances we can get some of the personal dividends as was the case in the China trip.

I have already sent a memo with regard to Julie's schedule and I particularly want to emphasize those same points with regard to PN's schedule, as well as Tricia's. We have covered North Carolina, Georgia and Florida pretty well, but except for Pat's trip to California we have not had the appearances in the major states which we so very much need. I would like to see a plan laid out which will indicate what we are going to do in Pennsylvania, New York, Ohio, Illinois and Texas, with possibly Indiana and New Jersey added and Michigan and Wisconsin at a later point if we decide an effort there is worthwhile. Of course, the same analysis should apply in scheduling Connally and the major Administration speakers. I do not mean to suggest that no appearances whatever should be made in other than the key states because that would be too obvious a ploy and we have to buy insurance in the smaller states to cover some of the deficiencies we may run into in failing to come through in the big states. But up to this point our big state emphasis has not been adequate and from now until November we have to get a game plan worked out and then stick to it.

I would suggest that in about ten days, around April the 8th, when I will be going to Florida we might go over some tentative plans on the items I have touched on in this memo.

HRH162
W/RN from PPF3

MARCH 28, 1972

TO: **W. Richard Howard**

FROM: **John Dean**

RE: **Flag Code Violation**

In reference to your recent memorandum concerning a possible violation of the flag laws by NBC, 36 U.S.C. 176(g) provides:

The flag should never have placed upon it, nor on any part of it, nor attached to it any mark, insignia, letter, word, figure, design, picture, or drawing of any nature.

In view of the foregoing, it would appear that NBC has violated the provisions of this section by using the flag to form part of the numeral "7" in the "Decision '72" sign introducing campaign coverage. However, the law provides no civil or criminal penalties for violation of this section, and it further does not appear that NBC's use of the flag would fall within the criminal sanctions of Title 18 prohibiting flag desecration, defiling, or destruction.

This information is furnished to you for whatever unofficial use you wish to make of it. However, before taking any action, it would be advisable to contact John Nidecker to ascertain what uses the Committee for the Re-election of the President and the Republican National Committee have been making of the flag in their activities.

cc: Bill Timmons

JWD4

MARCH 29, 1972

TO: **Henry Kissinger**

FROM: **The President**

At the dinner for King Hussein one of the guests was Bob Amory. Amory, as you may recall, used to be an assistant to Allen Dulles. He reminded me of an incident that I had forgotten. Back in 1954 or '55 Bill Bundy came under very severe attack by Joe McCarthy because he had contributed $500 to the Alger Hiss defense fund. Allen Dulles was unable to get anybody on the White House staff to come to his defense. Allen spoke to me about it personally, told me that he felt Bill contributed to the fund only because of his Harvard connection, and that he was a completely loyal and hard-working government official. He asked me if I would try to speak to McCarthy about it and thereby save Bundy's job. I went up to see McCarthy, told him about the case, and because of my personal intervention he laid off of his investigation of Bundy.

As you can imagine, the Bundys never gave me any credit for this, but Amory remembers it vividly because he said without me there was no one in the White House, including President Eisenhower, who would handle this very sensitive personal problem.

The footnote to the story is that in 1968, when George Ball made his vicious attack on me during the campaign, Bob Amory wrote a letter to the *New York Times,* which they reprinted after cutting most of the laudatory phrases out, and recounted this incident.

The purpose of this memorandum is to point out that Amory is one of the few of the Eastern establishment crowd who for this personal reason is in our corner, even though I had not seen him for 15 years.

It occurred to me that in trying to find somebody to serve on the Arms Control or other boards that this name might be considered. There is no urgency on this, but I just thought you might want to have it in mind in case an opportunity arose.

HRH162

MARCH 29, 1972

TO: **The President** (Per HRH)

FROM: **Patrick J. Buchanan**

McGovern's Deputy Campaign Manager, a friend from my Soviet trip, a level-headed fellow, called me today to say that McGovern will win in Wisconsin. He gave me the following polls:

McGovern's Private Polls		*AFL-CIO Quayle Poll*	
Humphrey	23	McGovern	24
McGovern	19	Humphrey	18
Muskie	14	Muskie	15
Jackson	13	Jackson	13
Wallace	9	Wallace	10
Lindsay	4	Lindsay	1
Other	3	Undecided	19
Undecided	14		

My friend tells me that in the McGovern Poll, McGovern is carried much lower than normal—*since it does not include the Second District (Madison)* where McGovern is conceded to be immensely strong, compared with the other Democrats. Further, he says that those polled were those who intended to vote in the Democratic Primary, including Republicans.

This is hard to believe. Seems to me, even if these figures are accurate, however, that George Wallace will pick up some of the undecided—he surely did in Florida.

But the McGovern fellow contends that Muskie could come in fourth or even fifth in the race—which would be a climactic disaster for Big Ed.

Again, if these figures are accurate—McGovern would be greatly enhanced; the liberal press would fall all over him for the next two weeks. Humphrey would be set back. Muskie would sustain a near fatal blow. Big John Lindsay would be finished. The situation would be more confused than ever. The likelihood of a first ballot nomination for the Democrats would be increasingly remote. In short, if this is the outcome, it would seem that the pressures on Kennedy would be substantial to move.

NOTE: If we have some hard poll information, and this is a possibility, then we should have Republicans cross over and vote for George McGovern. Word should go forth today.

CWC17

MARCH 29, 1972

TO: **Dick Howard**

FROM: **Chuck Colson**

I asked you to have John Dean check out that ad in last Sunday's *Post.* If there is no such book, then, of course, a great case of postal fraud. What I didn't think about, however, is that this is a marvelous opportunity for nailing the *Washington Post.* They do have a responsibility for their ads and it is, appearing on the face of that ad, apparent that the book has not been published. Therefore, there could be a false advertising and fraud charge of which the *Post* could be a conspirator. It has been a long time since I have studied this section of the law but be sure that Dean probes this very hard because maybe we finally have something to nail the *Washington Post* with. It would obviously contribute to the story that they were delighted to run a fraudulent ad because it was embarrassing to the President.

CWC131

MARCH 31, 1972   8:15 A.M.

TO: **H. R. Haldeman**

FROM: **Charles Colson**

RE: **My Weekend Plans**

As we talked last night, I have decided to stay home; three days will do me more good, both Patty and I agree, than anything else. Please tell the President that I appreciate his wanting to help get me away somewhere but I know I can relax best working around my grounds, reading and taking walks and being away from people. When I am tired I am basically a misanthrope.

You were nice enough to say last night that you would tell the President not to bother me this weekend. When I get to the point where the President of the United States calling me is a bother—that's time for me to quit everything. Please tell him that I am just going to be reading and taking it easy and while I will cut off the other phones, I am flattered anytime he wants to call me.

Many thanks—I do need a breather.

Dictated from home by Mr. Colson, transcribed and delivered in his absence.   JH

CWC131

APRIL 3, 1972

TO: **Chuck Colson**

FROM: **Bruce Kehrli**

RE: **ITT**

The April 3 Weekend News Review contained the following note:

Times *lead edit calls ITT affair a scandal and says it must be resolved.* . . .

Referring to the above, it was requested that a strong letter to the editor be sent answering the charge. The letter should be signed by a prominent person.

Please follow up on this request and submit a report on actions taken to the Office of the Staff Secretary by April 10.

cc: H. R. Haldeman
Alexander P. Butterfield

POF40

APRIL 6, 1972

TO: **The Honorable Charles W. Colson**

FROM: **Tom Evans***

I agree that we need a meeting as soon as possible and will contact you for a mutually convenient time. In the interim, your memorandum of April 3 does require some comment on my part.

It came as a surprise, to say the least, to read that you were "horrified" at my "reluctance to defend the Administration on the ITT matter." We always have been and continue to be ready to defend the Administration in every way. You must have missed the excerpts from the address I made several weeks ago on this subject in which I attempted to put the

ITT matter into proper perspective. You must also have missed page 22 of the current *First Monday*, which contains a story headlined "Media Distorts ITT Matter."

There will be more in next week's *Monday*.

My memorandum of March 31 only questioned the method to be used in this extremely sensitive case. I believe strongly that we should not damage the credibility of an effective, hard-hitting publication by making statements that we have not had time to evaluate fully. The matter is of such importance, and—as I stated in my previous communication to you— there have been enough inconsistencies, that those of us who share the same objectives should be sure that we are working in concert and with the same set of facts before doing anything further.

As you say, there is probably very little that we can accomplish by exchanging memos. I look forward to meeting with you soon, and will be calling to agree upon a time that suits all concerned.

*[Thomas B. Evans was co-chairman of the Republican National Committee.]

cwc107

APRIL 6, 1972

TO: **Chuck Colson**

FROM: **John Dean**

Per your suggestion, I have looked into the possibility that Larry O'Brien and others were involved in some highly questionable leasing arrangements with the United States Government during the Johnson Administration. Specifically, I reviewed the subject of lease arrangements with GSA for the DOT Headquarters Building, but apparently his activities were even more widespread.

As a result of my investigation and discussions, it appears that it would be extremely difficult to establish the direct tie-in between O'Brien and GSA. Even if this could be done, however, it is the consensus of all with whom I have discussed this that raising the issue might open a Pandora's Box that we would later regret opening. It is not that this Administration or prior Republican Administrations have been as culpable as it is obvious the Democrats were; rather charges of alleged impropriety could be leveled against the current GSA Administration, and our point would be lost in the smoke.

This is not to say that I think we should forget the whole matter. For your information, Senator Proxmire has had GAO people investigating the GSA leasing policy for some time now. If it appears that the Senator will attempt to make this another of his "causes" during the election year, which I currently think is not a realistic possibility, we should be prepared to show that we are at worst guilty of bad judgment whereas the Democrats were actually guilty of criminal conversion, etc.

21 SENATE HEARINGS 9884;
23 SENATE HEARINGS 11137

APRIL 6, 1972

TO: **John Dean**

FROM: **Fred Fielding**

Today's Anderson column talks about a memo "from the confidential files of President Nixon's Campaign Finance Committee" listing major donors. The confidential list is reported to have been drawn from "known major donors" to "Republican Senatorial Campaigns in 1970."

Presupposing that Anderson really has such a memo, two obvious implications may be drawn.

First, we have a leak at 1701 and/or the Republican National Finance Committee. It should be relatively easy to determine the origin of the memo, and those having access to it. I would think it imperative that this be determined immediately, since we may have to minimize a very serious situation.

The other possibility is that this information was supplied by Jack Gleason. It relates to Republican Senatorial Campaigns in 1970 and Gleason was certainly intimately familiar with that race.

JFB2

W/RN from JWD4

APRIL 8, 1972

TO: **H. R. Haldeman**

FROM: **The President**

RE: **Advance Preparations for RN Appearances**

I believe it is necessary to shake up our advance men somewhat so that they are sharper than they have been on two or three recent events.

For example, in Philadelphia it was extremely well advanced from a technical standpoint. However, there was not an adequate description of the makeup of the audience. I gathered from the remarks that had been prepared that the entire audience was to be delegates to the convention, whereas, as you will recall, there were several hundred high school students and others in the balcony. In the future, be sure that before all appearances I have a pretty good rundown in a sentence or two as to the type of people who will make up the audience. This is as you know a standard requirement for an advance and should be strictly adhered to because it will help me in any opening remarks I will make—also in preparing the general speech.

Along the same line, but at a different level of magnitude, was the appearance with the two customs agents. It was only by interrogating them when they dropped in to see me for 10 minutes before going out to have their picture taken, that I found that the younger one had been in the customs service for only five months and that he was totally dedicated to the work he was doing because, just after he entered the service, his 23-year-old brother was found dead of an overdose of heroin on the streets of New York. The older man was a Marine veteran who served on Guadalcanal.

These are small items but particularly the first one is one that could have been picked up by whoever was handling the event and passed on to me. I think the problem here is in leaving too much of this to the Military Aide who does not have that kind of responsibility or that kind of sense of news, or even for that matter leaving it to a substantive man who does not recognize the possibilities in getting some color like that for my use. I doubt even if Ron sees such opportunities, or, putting it perhaps more fairly, he probably doesn't assume it's his responsibility to try to find out facts of this sort which can be helpful in whatever statement I make.

In the future I think it would be well to see that our advance man is always one who is aware of these factors and who does his best to provide some color information that might be useful in any remarks I might decide to make.

PPF3; HRH162

APRIL 8, 1972

TO: **John D. Ehrlichman**

FROM: **The President**

Over the past weekend I have had some opportunity to evaluate the activities we will be engaging in for the next seven months before the election. I have concluded that, at this point, your assignment should be substantially changed in substance while remaining the same insofar as title and format are concerned. In essence, I want you to concentrate on selling our domestic programs and answering attacks on them, rather than developing those programs, and riding herd on them within the Administration to see that everybody follows the line in executing them.

You have handled the development of the programs with superb organizational ability and substantively have seen to it that they have come out along the lines of my own thinking. This task, however, is now completed and what remains to be done—modification, implementation, etc.—can be done by others whom I will mention in a moment in this memorandum. They may not be able to do the job you have been doing quite as well as you are doing it, but that will not matter too much. What is important is that you will be released to do something that they either cannot do at all or which you can do far better—selling the programs personally and working and planning with others in that respect.

What I would have in mind would be for you to delegate to Ken Cole the responsibilities that you now undertake for overseeing the domestic programs, insofar as substance is concerned. In addition, I think it would be well for you to talk to George Shultz and have him undertake the responsibility that he perhaps should have been given long before now—that of bringing to life the management side of OMB which has been somewhat dormant. In other words, where conflicts arise between the various Cabinet officers on programs, let George have the responsibility for working them out and, to the extent you can, you stay out of them so that you can be free to undertake the other assignment that I am going to describe.

In any event, the players who will take your old assignments will be a matter for you to decide. I am simply suggesting the line of my thinking and will abide by any recommendations you make and any decisions you make which further the objective I am trying to reach.

What has really led me to this conclusion is the fact that we have a number of programs which, from a substantive standpoint, deserve broad public approval. On the other hand, we have been singularly ineffective either in selling those programs to the public or, more often, in identifying the Administration and the President with those programs. The confusion with regard to busing is a case in point. The fact that the property tax issue has now been picked up by our Democratic friends is another example. The fact that, despite a great deal of effort, only 20% of the people think the President has an effective program in the drug abuse area is another item. The fact that we have lost the initiative in many areas with regard to fighting the battle of the high cost of living must also cause us concern.

As I run down these items, I know that the automatic reaction of the White House staff will be—"why doesn't the President go on television and make a fireside chat,"—or "why doesn't he engage in some kind of a gimmick which will spotlight the particular issue,"—or "selling isn't our job, we have others to do that." I am perfectly willing to do anything or say anything that will help us get across our points in these areas. However, as I look back over the past three years, our great failing, particularly in the domestic area, has been that once the President shoots the big gun the infantry doesn't follow in adequately to clean up and to hold the territory. Perhaps the best example of a case where we did do so was in selling revenue sharing and government reorganization, but I am afraid those are pretty tepid issues as we get into the fall campaign. As I see it now the gut issues are cost of living, busing, drug abuse, and possibly tax reform as it relates to the property tax. There are of course other subsidiary issues like the environment, revenue sharing, etc., where we can make some points. And then of course there are always the issues where the opposition is on the attack. The Administration's closeness to big business, its support of the big man as against the little man, etc.

The ideal way, of course, to handle all these issues is to leave them to the Cabinet officers involved to do so. But we have to face the fact that in the domestic area, except for Connally in those cases where he wants to go to bat, we do not have powerful enough spokesmen. For example, the failure of Richardson, Shultz, et al. with the Leaders in the meeting on the busing issue is a case in point. I do not mean to suggest that there may not be occasions when we can get Morton out on a positive issue where he will be effective, or that Peterson may not be able to develop into an effective spokesman, or that the other members of the Cabinet in certain spot cases may not be able to do an effective job. Also, we have to take into account the fact that in certain cases we can use Agnew and, of course, there are Rumsfeld, Klein, and Finch, who can be brought into play where the issue happens to fit them.

But one of the conclusions which has come home to me very strongly as I have thought about this over the past weekend is that you are the best all-round spokesman for the Administration's domestic programs. You have an orderly mind, you are convincing, you are tough and you are very effective on television. I know that you have been reluctant to be a public spokesman for the reason that sensitivities of Cabinet officers might be irritated—bruised. As a matter of fact, up until this time, I might tend to agree with the proposition that our relations with the Cabinet are more important than putting you out front as a salesman of some of our programs. But from now until the election, we can't be concerned about whether Cabinet officers have bruised feelings. I think that where we find that you are the most effective spokesman for a particular program, we should have you go out and do the job.

Your personal participation, however, is only half of the assignment I want you to undertake. The other half is for you to work directly with Haldeman and Colson in planning the appearances by others. That means members of the Cabinet, key Congressmen and Senators, now and then a Governor, etc.

In this respect, I emphasize again that what is needed is not someone who will be thinking constantly as to how I can go to bat more often and more effectively—everybody in the White House staff and the Cabinet and in the National Committee will be spending plenty of time on that project. What we need is an operation that will plan for the troops to follow up once the President makes a statement or to counterattack when the enemy levels with an attack against us.

In the foreign policy field, I pretty much have to do this job myself. The impossible relationship between Rogers and Kissinger is such that we find it very difficult of course to get follow-up of my foreign policy initiatives by Rogers unless he feels it is a pretty sure thing insofar as public approval is concerned. Since I have to devote so much of my time to the planning of our foreign policy public relations as well as substance, since we have no one else to do it, I want you to do what I would do in the domestic front if I had the time to spend on that as well.

I have discussed this with Bob and perhaps you would like to sit down with him and see how the suggestions I have made can be implemented.

I would simply close this memorandum by saying that the way that I look at most of our domestic programs is that we have done an excellent job of conceiving them and a poor job of selling them. I realize that much of the reason for our doing a poor job of selling them is that we don't have a very good cast of characters, and also that we have an almost impossible situation with the media; but that means that all we have to do is to try harder. Great ideas that are conceived and not sold are like babies that are stillborn. We need some deliveries within the next few months, even if they have to be cesarean. I will approve any programs you have to bring about those deliveries, provided of course you recognize my total opposition to any abortions.

cc: H. R. Haldeman

HRH162

W/RN from PPF3

FOR RELEASE: 12:00 P.M. MST   SATURDAY, APRIL 8, 1972

NEWS *FROM THE REPUBLICAN NATIONAL COMMITTEE*

Dole Asks for Fair Treatment from ATT, Suggests Solution

PHOENIX, ARIZ.—Senator Bob Dole, Chairman of the Republican National Committee, today suggested that the "average American . . . pay your telephone bill into an escrow account" to say to the American Telephone and Telegraph Company "that you want to be treated fairly."

Citing AT&T's failure to collect from the Democratic National Committee "a half or two million or three or whatever it is" that is owed from the 1968 campaign, Dole continued, "It's legal—we have a right to be treated without discrimination, and the right to a remedy when we are discriminated against—as we are now. And believe you me, it will be effective."

In remarks prepared for delivery at noon before the Republican Women's Regional Conference here, the Kansas Senator also said that Senator Edward Kennedy ought to declare himself a presidential candidate. "Kennedy is a candidate with a deliberate, thoroughly worked out game plan for winning the Democrat nomination—for whatever that nomination is worth."

Kennedy's plan, Dole asserted, "calls for the present candidates to exhaust each other's resources in an inconclusive series of primary battles. . . . So they'll turn to the man who wouldn't get his feet wet. . . . I think it is time for Kennedy to declare himself.

"In short, I think what we want to see is a little less profile, and a little more courage . . . ," Dole concluded. "I ask Senator Kennedy to please come out and join the struggle; to come out and try to earn what he wants."

(A text of Senator Dole's remarks is attached.)

[Marking indicates President was orally briefed on this release.]

CWC17

APRIL 9, 1972

TO: **John D. Ehrlichman**

FROM: **The President**

With further reference to the memo I wrote you with regard to the need to sell our domestic programs, it might be well to put it in the context of domestic policy compared with foreign policy.

In the case of foreign policy, selling the policy is very important just like making the policy is important. Without selling the policy, public support for it which is so essential to get the approval of funds where necessary in Congress, is not generated. On the other hand, substance in the case of foreign policy is infinitely more important than substance is in the case of domestic policy, insofar as long-range consequences are concerned. For example, I could easily have rejected the Cambodian and Laotian operations and not ordered a response by air to the current North Vietnamese offensive. This would have been an easy policy to sell. It would have been disastrous from the standpoint of substance, however, because while it would have received short-range approval, in the long term it would have left the United States with no credible foreign policy position not only in Southeast Asia but in any other part of the world. In other words, while selling foreign policy is important, substance is indispensable. The classic example, of course, is Chamberlain coming back from Munich receiving an 85% approval in the British gallup poll because he had brought "peace in our time." Within a year the fact that he had made such a grievous error on substance resulted also in his losing his public support.

The situation with regard to domestic policy is quite different. I do not mean by that that it is [not] important to make the right decision on matters like busing, the environment, welfare reform, revenue sharing, etc. And also I would have to admit that making the wrong decision will sometimes result in the nation starting down a road from which there will be no turning away. But generally it can be said that the substance of domestic policy is not as critically important as the substance of foreign policy. Mistakes in domestic policy can be rectified. Very seldom is that the case where a major foreign policy mistake is made.

Putting all this in a political context, and looking at the programs which we have before the Congress, we would have to agree that what is now infinitely more important than dotting the *i*'s and crossing the *t*'s on the substance of each one of our programs is trying to sell them to the voters. Our ability to rectify mistakes of the past, to develop new programs, and most important the survival of our philosophy of government is involved in the outcome of the election. Therefore, fighting, bleeding and dying over some domestic policy is not only wrong politically but wrong for the country in the long term. This again is the reason why I want you to delegate all of the operational activities and the development of any future domestic programs we may have to have between now and the election to Shultz, Cole, or others you think are competent to handle them. Your responsibility will simply be to come in on the big plays to give me your advice. Your primary responsibility, however, will be to try to sell our programs to the country, not only by your personal appearances and activities, but also by working with Colson and Haldeman in planning the activities of others.

In my other memorandum I indicated the domestic issues I thought had political bite. You may not agree with my list, and so I would like to have recommendations for additions or deletions. What is important is to pick three or four positive issues that we want to hammer home—issues which we would like to have in the voters' minds rather than the issues which our Democratic opponents are going to be talking about. For example, they do not want to talk about the crime issue, the marijuana issue, the hard-line welfare issue (work requirement, etc.), and we should force them to talk on those issues, but, even more important, have the voters thinking of those issues, rather than be constantly dragged into answering them on "is the Administration pro big business?" etc.

I have only scratched the surface insofar as what the issues should be, and I am not going to try to prejudice your thinking with regard to how the selling program should be developed. I would urge, however, that you get a program together as soon as possible so that, when I complete this swing to Canada and my appearance before the editors next Thursday, we can have a game-plan ready to put into action.

On a substantive matter which you will probably want to pass to Krogh or, probably better, to Shultz to implement, in talking to the customs agents who picked up the $5 million heroin haul here in Miami, I found that there are only 500 customs agents in the country. We have apparently requested two or three hundred more. I asked Ambrose how many he could really use without wasting personnel if he were to do an adequate job of search of vessels, automobiles and airplanes. He said 2,000. This may be an exaggeration, but here is an area where I believe in using the maximum force possible to try to cut down on this traffic. Have one of our technicians look into the matter and if that many agents can be used effectively and can be trained, let's get going on it.

HRH162

W/RN from PPF3

APRIL 9, 1972

TO: H. R. Haldeman

FROM: The President

This is just a reminder to you of McCrary's advice with regard to always having a Sunday morning story from this time on. In consultation with Ehrlichman, I would like to see this recommendation carried out over the next seven months. I see no reason whatsoever for our not being able to have a major Sunday morning story every Sunday in that period. Now and then, of course, you can move over to Kissinger's shop and pick something up in the foreign policy area. But generally they should be domestic policy oriented.

HRH162

APRIL 11, 1972

TO: John Nidecker

FROM: Charles Colson

Knowing how jealous people around here are regarding their jurisdictions, the last thought that would ever cross my mind is taking away your role as either Santa Claus or the Easter Bunny—and even more remote is the thought, as you suggest in your memo, that I would like to be the Easter Bunny. I would like it to be a matter of record that I have none of the qualifications required. I might like to have some of the proclivities of a rabbit, but I don't have time; that, in itself is a rather sad commentary.

Nor have I ever even discussed someone else taking over this unique honor that you have enjoyed over the past three years. I hope that you stay in the job for another five years and after that time, I would be more than happy to recommend you for the Macy's Parade or the Woodward and Lothrop Santa Claus. I wish you a long and prosperous career as both Santa and Bunny and the last thing I would ever do is encroach upon your domain either in seriousness or in jest. I am a great believer in the W. C. Fields axiom that "a man who hates kids and dogs can't be all bad"!

NOTE: The only temptation I have is if you will let me use your costume, I would be delighted to kick Maxine Cheshire in her cottontail!

cwc131

APRIL 11, 1972

TO: **Bob Haldeman**

FROM: **The President**

As a general outline for some of the matters you will want to consider in developing with Ehrlichman et al. the program on the PR side for the next several months, I would like for you to have in mind the following considerations.

1. *Players*—here I would like for three or four of you to sit down and make up a list of the 10 best players we have. Obviously, the Vice President, some members of the Cabinet, a few members of Congress, a couple of Governors, some members of the White House staff including, of course, people like Finch and Klein, political people like Dole and perhaps truth squad people who may be developed.

In another category you have, of course, the members of the family for the so-called soft news and then, of course, at a secondary level you have the sub-Cabinet and non-political types in labor, veterans and other organizations which are on file in the Colson office.

By having this list in front of you it will serve two purposes—one, when a story has to be told you will be able to look over the list and pick the ideal man or woman to tell it. Two, you will have the small group who can be pulled together for briefing when the story is important enough to require that kind of treatment.

2. *Tactics*—there should obviously be one major story a day including particular emphasis on a major Sunday story. Have in mind the fact that our plans should be built around the assumption that I will have one hard news story each week in which television will be involved.

What is most important about the tactics, however, is not the number of stories but *repetition* and *follow-up*. Once I start on a line, for example, in a news conference or a speech there should be sustained follow-up day after day until we finally hammer the point home. Don't be concerned about the fact that each story is not carried. The important thing is to follow up and not to scatter our shots, so that we get some sustained themes through one way or another.

In this discussion of tactics I am referring only to our positive stories. Obviously, the counterattack or answer desk operation should be supplemental to these positive stories and on some occasions they will naturally override the positive stories, because we may feel that it is more important to get out answers to an opposition attack than simply our own positive story. But on many days both should run because we never can tell how the media will play them.

3. *Theme*—here, getting across the basics about the man—strong, courageous, intelligent, patriotic, country first politics second particularly in view of the recent Vietnam development.

4. *Issues*—I have already discussed this matter on several occasions but will list the issues in order of priority as I see them at this time.

a. Peace and foreign policy generally still have to be at the top of the list. Temporarily, the emphasis will not be on the generation of peace—that will come back when we go to Moscow and when we return—temporarily the issue must obviously be the strong, experienced foreign policy leader who is at his best in a crisis.

b. Cost of living with particular emphasis on the cost of food.

c. Crime with particular emphasis on drugs.

d. Property tax—of course, in those areas where people are interested hit hard on tax relief for non-public schools.

e. Jobs.

f. Busing—where our major effort should be to put our Democratic friends strongly on record in favor of busing and us on record against it and getting this across in areas where it is an issue.

g. "For all of the people"—this is a tough one to handle but it is the only way that we can answer the charges that we are solely interested in big business, etc. This will require some real PR effort.

h. Reform—here I have mixed feelings as to which direction we should follow. We have an excellent program of reform—welfare, revenue sharing, reorganization, health, environment, etc.—on the other hand, the question is whether it is wise to stir up the voters on the basis of reform and change and excitement or to use that theme as a subsidiary issue before audiences of special interest and emphasize more of the stability and a return to some kind of confidence in government after so many years of crises and upheaval. Of course, both themes can be played at the same time, but at least this should be a matter for discussion within the political group to see which way we should move. If we decide to go all out on the reform issue this means going all out on an attack on the Congress. The latter, incidentally, is probably a good idea in any event, and should occur immediately after the Democratic Convention with the groundwork being laid before. This will tend to deflect some of the fire which is directed against the Administration to the Congress for failing to carry out the recommendations the Administration has made.

I am not suggesting that this list of issues is exclusive or that it will not change as time goes on. For example, we may want to hit the environment and other issues if they appear to be lively. Connally, of course, feels strongly we should hit foreign competition and the need to build America's competitive position, but in any event this memorandum will give you an idea as to my own thinking, and I would like for you to use it as a framework at least for discussion with the political group.

HRH162

W/RN from HRH230 and PPF3

APRIL 13, 1972

TO: The President's File

FROM: John Andrews

RE: Color Report on the President's Meeting with Youth Conference Follow-up Delegation

Woodstock it wasn't—but still, in its own square way, a heavy trip.

Opening chitchat during the picture-taking and formal presentation of the reports was ominously bland. While the cameras rolled, the President shrewdly positioned himself next to the most scenic of his visitors, 22-year-old Chris Garcia from UC Santa Barbara, and made animated conversation. Here was a perfect setup for the "politically sensitized small talk test." Obvious topics for RN to broach with this young woman were: (a) Too bad about Isla Vista; (b) too bad about the oil spills; (c) viva la raza; (d) power to the sisters; or (e) the Whittier/UCSB football rivalry in the Thirties. You guessed it. Gridiron nostalgia reached out across the generation gap.

For the Young Ear, it evoked uncomfortable echoes of the pre-dawn football talk that left Cambodia/Kent State student protesters so cold at the Lincoln Memorial two years ago. At the same time, though, it reminded the Ear again just how much this man is *not* the chameleon he is so often painted to be. There has always been and still remains just one Nixon, not the succession of new ones voyeurs think they see, and he is a man true to himself, as he described that self at a private dinner last January: "We in this Cabinet, and this Cabinet family, have been charged with being a group of gray men and women, pragmatic, practical, and non-idealistic. So be it. . . . What we lack is demagoguery. What we believe in is not the show of idealism, but getting it done, doing something, making progress in areas where it has never been made before."

All of which was demonstrated emphatically by what came after the photos and formalities at this particular meeting. Steve Bull, gliding in to whisk the delegation away now that the scheduled event was supposedly complete, was waved aside. "I want to talk with them a little longer," RN said, motioning the group over to the sofas by the fireplace.

There the talk quickly got around to the substance of the conference recommendations. Mike Dively, the 33-year-old Michigan State Assemblyman who has chaired the WHCY follow-up committee, explained the seven implementation grants being awarded, including one for lower age of majority studies at the University of Michigan. The President indicated familiarity with Dively's and Governor Milliken's efforts on this issue, and suggested that testimony on it be offered before both party platform committees this summer.

He paused a moment, then broadened his advice: why not a major effort to get many of the best WHCY recommendations into the GOP and Dem platforms? He directed Steve Hess and Ken Cole to work with Republican platform chairman John Rhodes on assuring the young people a hearing at San Diego, and to pass on a similar "bipartisan request from the White House" to DNC convention officials.

So there it was. No beads, no bellbottoms, just no-nonsense counsel about how to achieve an objective, from the mouth of a consummate political professional. The next step for young people, RN had said in his letter transmitting the Federal response to the WHCY, must be effective political involvement; now he was telling them how. The simple but potent suggestion had Dively, himself a young pro in politics, shaking his head after the meeting: "The platform committees—of course. It's so obvious. Why didn't we think of that?"

As the session closed, RN restated his commitment to action for young goals: "The important thing is to see that the work you've done doesn't just get buried in some report. There are reports like this by the thousands gathering dust on shelves all over Washington. We have to do better with this one." Then it trailed off into pleasantries. "I hope you travel . . . perhaps China . . . these dwarf trees came from . . ." See the world—another theme familiar from the Lincoln Memorial incursion.

But the resolute Dively bore in one more time: "We have been gratified by the follow-up so far; we'll hope for your continued support." Looking him in the eye, RN pronounced a telling judgment: "You are responsible leaders. We'll do all we can." Then, gesturing at the Ear and other staff present, "These people, look how young they all are, they'll make us follow through."

The young, it seems to the Ear, could do worse than cast in their lot with this 59-year-old Republican patriot who is too focused on being a great President to bother pretending he's with it. One thinks of the tribute paid Bill Buckley by Dick Gregory across all kinds of political and cultural differences: "a beautiful cat."

POF88

APRIL 13, 1972

TO: **Fred Malek**

FROM: **Charles Colson**

RE: **Hobart Rowen Article**

The only way in which we can soften the attached is to send the Army in to take over the *Washington Post*—something I've been advocating for the past two years. Obviously immediately after the Army took over, we would have Hobart Rowen beheaded. We do not play this theme any more. Rowen loves to stick the knife into us any place he can. We do emphasize "head of household" or "breadwinner" categories on the unemployment rates because that makes us look very good and I realize that some people think that is male chauvinism. It isn't, it's just good politics, but we are no longer saying that the fact women are unemployed is not unhealthy to the economy. We've stopped that, but there's no way you can stop Rowen printing his nasty little jabs at us. Short of the suggestion I have proposed, of course.

CWC131

APRIL 14, 1972

TO: **Bob Haldeman**
       Ron Ziegler

FROM: **RMW**

The instruction at the beginning of the tape said that RmW was to deliver this memorandum to each of you personally.

Bob—you are to discuss the memorandum with Buchanan and Mort Allin but you are not to leave copies with them as the President does not want anyone but the two of you to have a copy. The only other copy will be in his personal file.

PPF3
W/RN from HRH230

EYES ONLY

APRIL 14, 1972

TO: **Bob Haldeman and Ron Ziegler**

FROM: **The President**

As all of you know, I believe the news summary is one of the best things we do on the White House staff. As we enter the six months before the campaign, however, there needs to be some modification in it and I want the following directions carried out without deviation.

I know that the news summary people and Ziegler feel that it is important always to include John Osborne and Hugh Sidey—not because they agree with them but because they believe they have "influence" with other members of the press. But, deep down, what we have to realize is that the reason that everybody on the White House staff is obsessed with Sidey and Osborne is not only because they have influence but because they are considered to be President watchers and, consequently, we subconsciously tend to over-react to their criticisms of Presidential conduct. What we have to realize is the cold fact that both Sidey and Osborne are totally against us. They are not honest reporters. They are out to defeat us. I recognize the point that Haldeman and Ziegler often make that Sidey will write one column in four which leans in our direction—but that column would be written in any event because he has to do so in order to retain his appearance of objectivity. But both have spoken in the most vicious derogatory terms of RN in the place where you really find out what the people think—the Georgetown cocktail parties. The evidence on this is absolutely conclusive. You do not need to ask me where I got it.

What this brings me to is that what they will be writing—particularly as the election draws near—is not anything which in any way represents their views as to how the President is conducting himself. They will be less and less concerned about maintaining some objectivity. What they will be doing is to try to write those things which will get under our skin and by their criticism force us to do things that we should not do, or to quit doing things we are doing—not because they are right or wrong but because they are being effective.

Under these circumstances, I have no objection of course to whatever anybody on the White House staff wants to read in his free time—but from now through the election neither Sidey nor Osborne is to be included in the news summary regardless of what they write, positive or negative.

I do not include, for example, in this group others who are just as strong in their criticism as Sidey and Osborne are because we need to know what our critics are saying. But, I include these two because I know they have an inordinate influence on the White House staff and we simply have to keep our busy people from reacting to such an obvious ploy on the part of those who are dedicated enemies in a political sense. In other words, they should be treated exactly as we treat Reston. We learned early in the Administration that Reston was exactly like Sidey—as we get closer to the election he will become more and more vicious even though at times he will throw in something that is favorable.

This also brings me to the other point. I know this will be hard for Ron and other members of the staff to understand but I am now ordering that, to the extent possible, the fifteen people on Ron's list of friendly columnists and reporters be given priority attention in terms of interviews and that Osborne and Sidey be cut off in as effective a way as possible. This means that their calls simply don't get returned, etc.

I do not suggest that they be kept off trips because that would be too obvious a ploy but there are other ways for us to see that we do not fall into the pattern that we have been following for so long, up to this time—where Osborne, for example, has had more time with senior White House officials than Ron's group of fifteen friendly columnists had altogether. This is the same mistake Hagerty made for Eisenhower and since we only have six months until the election just as a personal matter I do not want to continue making that mistake at this time since I should benefit from that experience.

I am not suggesting that critics be kept out of the news summary. I prefer that we see just as much criticism, and preferably more, as the election draws near than we have in the past. I am simply suggesting that for Sidey and Osborne to substitute another editorial or column from the *New York Post* or *Tass* or some other admitted critic who makes no bones about the fact that he is out to get us.

I shall expect Haldeman to enforce this order in a discreet way with no memorandum being written.

As far as the news summary is concerned, obviously Mort Allin and Pat Buchanan will follow my directions.

As far as the interviews by staff are concerned, I realize you have a problem with some of our prima donnas—but Haldeman should do his best and Ziegler should follow up where he can and see that we balance the precious time that we have to give out between now and the election. The way you should explain it to the senior staff officials—particularly those who have a compulsion to spend most of their time with the Sideys and the Osbornes—is to tell them very simply that from now until the election we absolutely have to concentrate on our friends and that we should see only those enemies in the press who can serve a very useful purpose. I realize they will try to use their own judgment as to which enemy will serve a useful purpose. I am over-riding their judgment on these two men because I have followed them long enough to know better than any member of the staff what they are up to and my decision on how they are to be handled in the future is final. There is no appeal whatever— I do not want it discussed with me any further.

PPF3

W/RN from HRH230

APRIL 14, 1972

TO: **Gordon Strachan**

FROM: **Charles Colson**

RE: **Pandas**

My own advice is simply let this thing rest. Clem has promised to get the pandas to Chicago. Let's not say anything that either encourages or discourages him. Unless you hear further from someone, I think I would leave the matter just where it is.

CWC13

APRIL 17, 1972

TO: **Bob Haldeman**

FROM: **The President**

One procedure that might be changed with regard to our advance group is that of anybody riding in the jump seat where the jump seats are not set up in such a way that they leave adequate leg room for me. The situation in Canada was intolerable. Taylor insisted on sitting on the jump seat where he could have just as easily sat in the front seat because there were only two in the front seat. The jump seats were constructed in such a way that they bent completely back on both Pat and me so that in her case she had to put her legs over on the other side and I, of course, was totally uncomfortable all the way.

We simply have to get Taylor and the other Secret Service people to understand that their presence is not all that necessary, particularly where the Soviet Union is concerned. Perhaps in Canada some excuse could be found, but in the Soviet Union if we do not have a Secret Service man in the car it won't bother me a bit. I simply am not going to have the discomfort of having somebody ride with me when I know that they are not really necessary to the exercise.

This brings me to the matter of interpreters. I do not want to have in the Soviet Union two interpreters if that is going to mean crowding the car. What we should work out is an alternate procedure whereby the Russian interpreter will be used on one occasion and our interpreter on another. What we have to realize is that room must be left for me to sit comfortably in the car without some interpreter or some Secret Service man sitting on my lap. I want you to work the situation out so that it can be handled properly in the future.

At the dinner for the OAS on Saturday night Pat was informed that the Strolling Strings were not available because they were busy that night. This is probably a matter you should discuss with Butterfield, but in any event, of course, there should never be an occasion where any service organization is not available whenever we have a function where we have invited them. The Marine Corps chamber music was a disaster. It was perfectly adequate providing it was done in the proper atmosphere but under the circumstances somebody should have checked with me or with Mrs. Nixon before scheduling it in place of the Strolling Strings.

I realize that Garment et al. will say that we are sort of routine and deadly because we always have the Strolling Strings. Don't worry about that. The main thing is to either have the Strolling Strings or the Army Chorus or some other upbeat group in the room with great drama and presence rather than the situation that we had on Saturday night.

The fault, of course, was not of the Marine Corps group. It was excellent for the type of function that it normally plays for. But that kind of music simply doesn't fit unless those at the dinner can see it and in these circumstances it was a very bad call on the part of whoever on our staff made the call.

You will recall that in Canada I asked for a report on whether or not any of the members of the press caught the favorable reaction to the toast that I gave in Canada. There is no urgency on this but I would like a report one way or the other as to whether or not any members of the press handled this matter in the way that it should have been handled.

I am not a bit concerned about the fact that they may not have noted it. What, however, this will teach us is that we should not bother with the so-called "color" background material that we are constantly trying to feed to the press.

Speaking of background material, I think one area of failure, except for an article that appeared in the *New York Times* in a rather condescending way about two or three months ago, is in pointing up the quality of the entertainment we have brought to the White House.

Jackie Kennedy received bravos for years because she brought Pablo Casals to the White House to play his cello 40 years after his prime. When we look over the list of people that we have had at the White House they make the Johnson years appear almost barbaric and the Kennedy years very thin indeed.

I realize that Garment and Hanks don't approve of the kind of entertainment we have because they would prefer some offbeat modern ballet such as that utterly disgusting group we had from New York for one of our dinners.

On the other hand, when we have had people like Birgit Nilsson and [Dorothy] Kirsten the great majority of Americans recognize that they are really super stars. Perhaps you might give this to one of the "squares" on our staff if you can find one to get out the fact that never has the White House had a greater variety and more quality in terms of its entertainment than during the three years that we have been here.

HRH162

W/RN from HRH230

APRIL 17, 1972

TO: **Alex Butterfield**

FROM: **The President**

For the Retiring Members of Congress dinner, I want the Army Chorus for the entertainment. One of the numbers they do should be "Stout-hearted Men."

cc: Lucy Winchester

PPF3; HRH162

APRIL 17, 1972

TO: **Charles Colson**

FROM: **Pat Buchanan**

Harris made some interesting points when you spoke with him. The primary one with which I agree fully is that the President at all costs should avoid "stridency" and crass partisanship, and any manner of attack upon his opposition which is seen as inconsistent with his position as leader of all the people. As for the bland campaign, too early to call that one. There may be an issue on which the President can win, by elevating it in the public focus, as he did in November 1969. And should we appear bland and unemotional—while the Democratic Party has whipped up an emotional anti-establishment campaign—we could be writing our own death. The stridency point should be kept before us at all times—but to lock in to a bland campaign now would be unwise—there are issues which transcend party, on which we are on the majority side—and heating up these issues could turn to our advantage.

A final note—I would not trust Harris so far as one could throw him. He has long been, in Teddy White's phrase, a "Kennedy fanatic," and I would not be surprised if Kennedy were not getting carbons of what he sends to you.

PJB5

APRIL 17, 1972

TO: **Doug Hallett**

FROM: **Charles Colson**

Take another reading early this week and then late in the week with your stooge in McGovern's camp to see what feed-back you get from Massachusetts. Everything I hear is that Muskie is on a fast down-curve, but your man has usually been pretty good in his reports. Let me know.

cwc131

[*Markings indicate the President read his news summary of April 18, 1972, from which the following is an excerpt.*]

McGovern said US won't bomb NVN to peace table. Rather, it will unite them "in the same way as continued Nazi raids over England united the British in WW II."

EMK called decision to bomb, "senseless, unjustifiable, and reckless" and added it was "a dangerous and extravagant exercise in brinkmanship to which RN would never have succumbed."

Case said the bombing points up the essential importance of ending US involvement in SE Asia. "We must renew our effort to get Congress to fix a firm date . . . subject to POW release." . . . Findley said he was concerned over what if any Constitutional authority RN had for the raids. . . . Hughes called the bombing a "reckless gamble" and said Admin. was playing a game of "nuclear roulette."

House Dem. Whip O'Neil said bombings risk WW III. . . . Cranston questioned, "After 3 years of RN, is LBJ back in the WH?" . . . Long-time dove Rosenthal warned RN was "risking a total nuclear confrontation."

Albert said, "I've supported Vietnamization and the program and the withdrawing of troops responsibly. I've never supported brinkmanship and I hope that isn't what this is." He added "I still have no information as to the reasons behind what appears to be a change in policy. I hope RN will explain to the people what effect this bombing will have on Vietnamization. . . ." Despite his new, questioning attitude, Albert said it was unlikely that he would support previously scheduled effort to rally Dems behind antiwar legislation.

Rep. Anderson said he hoped the Admin. would take up the NVN proposal, halt the bombing and get back to the peace table.

Tunney said "there is despair in the country and it's increasing and it's deepening and it's real and it's legitimate."

Mrs. Vinson of the Natl. League of Families of POWs and MIAs, emphasizing she was speaking personally, said she was "heartsick" and filled with "moral outrage" over the escalation. (DOD said US bombers avoided areas where POWs are held.)

The NVN communist party paper *Nhan Dan* said RN "like a grievously wounded bear . . . is striking out madly and doesn't stop at the worst crimes." RN's involved the US in new and most serious military adventures "to save the disintegrating Saigon puppets," the paper said.

POF53

[*From Mr. Colson's notes of his meeting with the President on April 18, 1972*]

OVAL OFFICE

Be dirty and hard and tough like to see Muskie, HHH and EMK pushed hard

———

Connally 11:00
We will do
Politics be damned—RN will do what is right risking Moscow summit, generation of peace
Can't earn real Peace by Submission

P[resident] spends time thanking cabinet officers for doing what they ought to do

P[resident] is doing what is right

P[resident] Eisenhower shouldn't have to commend people for doing their duty

Use lines that come close to treason (such as) defending Enemy, instead of U.S.

Trying to humiliate the U.S.

Speech lines

Brave Americans

Communist aggressors and enemy—

Bloodbath

Blatant Communist aggression

V.P.

only way to get by the Press is to be tough

rhetoric has to be tough and have calling

Use Clawson to write tough lines

Get Rizzo to speak out on the war

Vicites say "want enemy to win and the U.S. to lose—

cwc17

APRIL 19, 1972

TO: **John Ehrlichman**

FROM: **Charles Colson**

RE: **Attached DNC** *Fact*

Attached is the handbook of the Democratic National Committee which as you will see is a very detailed, comprehensive attack on the Nixon Administration's record. After reading through it, one can only appreciate the wisdom of Herb Stein's quip that according to Larry O'Brien there is no such thing as good news. It occurs to me that perhaps a member of your staff, working in conjunction with the people at 1701, should do a detailed rebuttal of this. Not that we will want to publish it, but rather so that we can be prepared to answer the Democratic attack. Most of their candidates for office presumably will be drawing upon this book.

Beyond that there is an opportunity here, it seems to me, to use some of the Democrats' arguments to our advantage. Where, for example, they argue that our air pollution standards are too weak, I would think that their point would be of considerable interest to the UAW and the automobile industry. Where they call for more spending in a particular area, we could use that against them in an anti-inflation argument. Where they talk about not doing enough in terms of integrating the building trades, we can really use that to our advantage with the building trades leaders who are not terribly eager to integrate their unions. What I am suggesting is that if someone really studies this with a political eye, we will find areas here we can turn their attack on us to our advantage with specific groups and perhaps even generally speaking.

cwc131

20 APRIL 1972

TO: **Charles W. Colson**

FROM: **Doug Hallett**

My McGovern man called to thank us for the bombings. He says they're now confident of a very big win in Massachusetts and a decent showing in Pennsylvania. He says they took a poll of steelworkers in Pittsburgh and it showed McGovern a point ahead of Humphrey—thus McGovern took a trip down to Pittsburgh. They're planning to concentrate heavily on the blue-collar types from now on—one reason for going into Ohio. According to my friend, McGovern thinks only the labor bosses can keep the nomination from him, but they can be prevented from doing so if McGovern continues to show strong support among the rank-and-file.*

*[Marking indicates that Mr. Colson verbally briefed the President on this document.]

cwc18

APRIL 20, 1972

Dear Mr. Bell:*

    Mr. and Mrs. Charles Colson accept with pleasure your kind invitation to attend the preview of *The Burglars* on Monday, May 15, 1972.

Sincerely,

Joan C. Hall
Secretary to Charles Colson

*[Letter to J. Raymond Bell, New York, N.Y.]

cwc131

APRIL 21, 1972

Dear President and Mrs. Jaworski:*

 Mr. and Mrs. Charles Colson regret that they will be unable to accept your kind invitation for cocktails and buffet on Thursday, the eighteenth of May, due to a prior commitment.

Sincerely,

Joan C. Hall
Secretary to Charles W. Colson
Special Counsel
to the President

*[Letter to Leon Jaworski, president of the American Bar Association]

cwc131

ACTION MEMO

APRIL 24, 1972

We should start immediate contingency planning for post-November staffing on the basis of resignations of all present holders of Cabinet and top agency posts. For restaffing, we should start on the basis of bringing in people with total loyalty. Youth should be emphasized with men in their 30s and 40s, and we should look for people with complete selflessness who don't need to be babied, and who are set up on a new kind of basis.

 The point here will be to develop the building of the new establishment.

HRH

HRH112

EYES ONLY

APRIL 24, 1972

TO: **John Mitchell**

FROM: **Charles Colson**

Clem Stone's son-in-law was in to see me last week and during the course of the conversation he mentioned that Clem very much wants to be our Ambassador to Great Britain after the election. I told Bradshaw that obviously Clem should make his desires known to you and Maury Stans. Dave informed me that Clem doesn't operate this way, that he feels that one should not ask for positions of this kind, that he assumes that everyone knows he wants the job and that he will not seek it. This is a rather unusual attitude, but very characteristic of Clem. I gather he simply expects that he will be picked as the best man available in the country and therefore he needn't ask. I am, therefore, simply advising you that he very much wants it and expects it but will not ask for it.

CWC48

[Marking indicates that the President read the following news summaries.]

APRIL 25, 1972

News Summary (nets, wires and mags)

The Major Stories of the Day:

All nets led with what NBC called the "nasty turn" taken by the NVA offensive as the Communists opened up a 3rd front dealing what CBS called "a telling blow" to SVN's tender midsection. Kontum's fate called "up in the air" by one source; "catastrophic" by another. . . . B52's again hit 80 miles from Hanoi. . . . Mme. Binh's letter to MCs is called "presumptuous folly" by WH and "stupid" by Sevareid who says it can only help strengthen RN's currently threatened domestic position. Letter raised "uproar" on Hill. . . . Lengthy CBS/ABC film of Lt. Col. Iceal Hamilton who is recovering after being rescued from 11 days behind NVA lines during which he never gave up hope. . . . *Time, U.S. News, Newsweek* all lead with VN story, featuring RN's decision to bomb deep in NVN as a move needed to maintain a strong, credible foreign policy.

  Politics again a big story with familiar ground covered in lengthy reports: Muskie's effort in heavily-jobless Mass. verges on disaster and HHH's likely win in Penn. means a double header setback for Big Ed—approaches fatality, said NBC. . . . And GOP prepares to go to Miami Beach with ITT called an underlying reason. (Re: ITT, EMK claims Flanigan contradicts Kleindienst testimony in letter and both men should be recalled.) [. . .]

POF53

APRIL 26, 1972

News Summary (Tuesday nets, wires, columns)

The Major Stories of a Busy News Day:

Henry Kissinger returns from another secret trip—his 14th—and the WH shortly thereafter announces RN will speak Wed. nite on VN troop *levels,* not withdrawals, thus leaving option open to freeze pullouts. Lead on all nets where WH admission of "lying" to cover HAK's presence was noted. ABC said some sort of understanding was apparently reached on the "human hotline's" mission to "salvage" the summit and WH now says the Moscow visit is absolutely certain. . . . Following RN's speech, the Paris talks will be resumed Thursday. (Came too late for nets.)

Mike Gravel on all nets questioned how RN could embark upon Vietnamization when NSSM 1 said it would take 8–13 years for ARVN to reach point of self-defense. "Gloomy assessment" on ARVN and value of bombing partly printed in *Post* but Gravel blocked from getting this new Pentagon Paper into Record by Griffin and Saxbe who warned of possible censure. Note by 2 nets that Admin says study dealt with guerrilla warfare and today's bombings are countering conventional warfare.

NVA is moving methodically toward Kontum having seized 2 more ARVN bases—that's 28 since the offense started, said ABC. . . . 10 GIs killed in copter crash near Tam Cahn. Films of tough time US and ARVN air is having in rain and fog. Film also of the continuing siege of An Loc. . . . On ABC John Vann sees NVA seeking to build US domestic criticism so as to squeeze RN into forcing GVN to negotiate surrender—Vann believes offensive to be a strategic blunder.

Prosecution allowed to introduce as evidence two of Angela "love letters" to Soledad Brother George Jackson but an especially powerful one was disallowed by judge. Film on 2 nets.

2 Iowa families finally get thru federal gov't red tape and are reimbursed for damages done by Air National Guard crashes. Film on 2 nets. . . . And Brinkley with another of his anti-Establishment blasts also let the federal government have it.

Film of Apollo 16 spacewalk on all nets—splashdown is Thursday afternoon.

McGovern sweeps Mass.—nearing 50% of vote—and is engaged in close battle for 2nd with Muskie in Pennsylvania—each with 22%—where HHH has finally won a primary with around 35%. Wallace, 3 days campaigning in Pa., with surprising 18%.

Indochina

FROM THE WH

HKS led ABC saying the WH, following "dramatic disclosure" of another HAK trip, announced the RN speech—the 1st time since offensive that he'll have spoken out. . . . In his lead, Rather focused on RN speech, noting troops will be down to 69,000 by Monday. Recently they've declined on ground but are up in naval and air forces, observed Dan who, along with Jarriel, pointed to RZ's use of term "troop levels" rather than "withdrawals" in describing RN speech. Thus, speculation, said Rather, of slowdown, even freeze, in ground troop pullouts. . . . Following HAK and Gravel reports, Chancellor noted RN speech, saying RZ wouldn't tie it to HAK's return even tho RN decided—said Chancellor—to go on after HAK was back. It will be RN's 1st official statement on war since offensive began Easter weekend.

In announcing Paris talks for Thurs., Ziegler said the NVA invasion will be the main topic and as long as it continues, there'll be no meaningful talks. Moreover, the U.S. will take all steps necessary to stymie the invasion, including bombing military targets in the North.

With a report on HAK's secret trip, Jarriel, over silent HAK/RZ footage, stated that RZ admits "having deliberately lied when he said HAK was at Camp David." [. . .]

POF53

APRIL 27, 1972

TO: **Ken Clawson**

FROM: **Charles Colson**

Please congratulate your friends at your alma mater, the *Washington Post*, on their now unblemished record with respect to Harris polls. Interestingly, all Harris polls since the last trial heats have been prominently published in the *Washington Post*, those dealing with public attitudes on the media, the birthrate of monkeys, the migration trends of blacks, support for endangered species legislation and other politically sensitive subjects. Once again, however, by some odd happenstance, the trial heats showing the President way ahead of all the Democratic contenders have somehow been missed. Obviously it is simply coincidence, but your friends might like to know that we have noted that they have a perfect batting average—a 100% blackout of pro-Nixon polls.

I am sending a copy of my memo to all those who regularly accept Kay Graham's dinner invitations so that perhaps they can take note of this curious phenomenon while enjoying Mrs. Graham's hospitality. I will not have the opportunity since the last time I was invited, I told Ben Bradley [sic], across the table, that I thought the editors of the *Post* should be tried as war criminals for publishing the Pentagon Papers. For some reason I have never understood, half the guests had to excuse themselves right in the middle of their duck under glass.

cc: Peter Flanigan
    Henry Kissinger
    John Ehrlichman
    Don Rumsfeld
    et al.

CWC131

[APRIL 28, 1972]

TO: **H. R. Haldeman**

RE: **Times of TV News Items, Thursday, April 27, 1972**

A. *Administration News*

  1. RN Speech*

  ABC   :10
  NBC   :40
  CBS   —

B. *Other Major Stories*

  1. Apollo 16 Splashdown

  ABC   2:15
  NBC   3:15
  CBS   2:40 (lead)

  2. Muskie Withdrawal*

  ABC   6:25 (lead)
  NBC   4:00 (lead)
  CBS   10:05

  3. Paris Peace Talks

  ABC   3:00
  NBC   :50
  CBS   2:00

  4. Indochina

  ABC   :40 (+1:45 commentary)
  NBC   2:20
  CBS   3:30

  5. McCabe Antibusing March

  ABC   1:10
  NBC   1:00
  CBS   2:15

cc: Chuck Colson
    Ron Ziegler

*HANDWRITTEN NOTATION FROM MR. COLSON TO MR. HALDEMAN ON MR. COLSON'S COPY
OF MEMORANDUM (LINES ARE DRAWN TO BOTH OF THE INDICATED PARAGRAPHS, WHICH
ARE ALSO CIRCLED.): "Bob—unbelievable! Shouldn't we [word indistinct] bitch? An incredible comparison."

cwc13

APRIL 29, 1972

TO: **H. R. Haldeman**

FROM: **The President**

I think it is important that you meet with the political group including, of course, Mitchell and try to develop a strategy with regard to McGovern, Humphrey, and Teddy Kennedy. I want to be sure that we don't go off in all directions. By the end of next week I think we should pretty well have in mind what we expect is going to develop, and by that time, we should synchronize our own efforts to attempt to contribute to the kind of result we want. I would like to see a report on this by the end of next week.

PPF3; HRH162, HRH164, 230

PERSONAL

APRIL 29, 1972

Dear Jay:*
   Since you are normally in New York on Friday, you may have missed the attached article yesterday. I bring to your attention especially the last paragraph.
   It certainly sounds like a reasonable trade to me that McGovern could now say that he is opposed to Right to Work Laws, provided George Meany says that for 20 years he has been wrong on foreign policy. I am sure your boss will have no trouble swallowing this one. This arrogant son of a bitch, in my opinion, is a traitor. Instead of running for President, he should be running from the gallows. I really would like to see you next week.
   Best personal regards.

Sincerely,

Charles W. Colson
Special Counsel
to the President

*[Letter to Jay Lovestone, director, International Division, AFL/CIO]

cwc78

TELEPHONE CALL RECOMMENDATION*

4/30/72**

TO: **Former President Lyndon B. Johnson**

Background

Former President Johnson suffered a heart attack during the pre-dawn hours on Friday, April 7. He and Mrs. Johnson had come from Governor Buford Ellington's funeral in Tennessee the previous day and were staying with their daughter and son-in-law, Lynda and Chuck Robb, at their home in Charlottesville, Virginia. He was taken to the University of Virginia Medical Center on April 7th where he remained for one week.

After his condition had improved sufficiently, he was taken to Brooke Army Medical Center at Fort Sam Houston, Texas. He was released on Wednesday, April 26, and flew to the LBJ Ranch where he is now resting comfortably.

Former President and Mrs. Johnson had been invited to the Connally Dinner on Sunday, April 30, but will not be able to attend because of the former President's condition.

Talking Points

1. I just wanted to let you know how happy I am that you're at home and feeling better.

2. Most other men would still be in the hospital, but it's clear that you were just too much for the illness.

3. I think that must be a trait of Southern statesmen. I remember a story I read about Thomas Hart Benton. One day a constituent asked Benton his age and the Senator replied, "According to the calendar my age is seventy-four, but when anything is to be done I am thirty-five years old, sir."

4. Neither of us is thirty-five anymore, but as someone who appreciates your wise counsel, I'm glad you're as tenacious as you were when you were thirty-five.

*[Marking indicates the President made the recommended telephone call.]
**[The President called President Johnson from Picosa Ranch, the residence of Treasury Secretary John Connally in Floresville, Texas. They talked from 7:17 to 7:28 P.M. Nixon phoned Johnson again on May 2 to inform him of the death of J. Edgar Hoover.]

POF17

APRIL 30, 1972

TO: **H. R. Haldeman**

FROM: **The President**

It is vitally important that you follow up on the Colson group to see that they continue, particularly at this time, a strong assault on the press, on the Democratic candidates, and our opponents generally in the Congress and in the country on the Vietnam issue. Don't let our people let up on this issue because of their concern over the ups and downs of the news from the war front. All of this will pass one way or another, but either way, we have to make the case very strongly on these points.

First, they have failed to criticize the Communist and the enemy that is invading Vietnam and have been relentless at criticism of their own government and of the President.

Second, without attacking our motives, it is very clear that their actions and words put them on the side of the Communist and the enemy and against the American men who are fighting to help a small country defend itself against a Communist invasion.

Third, they who got us into war are sabotaging the efforts of the President to get us out.

Fourth, they are undercutting the President on negotiation at a time when there is the best chance for negotiation there has been since the war began. Get some quotes from Hanoi or some intelligence reports indicating how the leaders there are bragging about the support they have from the American people and particularly from various leaders here and the press. If negotiations now fail, they must assume a major share of the responsibility for their failing by encouraging the enemy to wait until after the election to negotiate the peace that everybody wants so much. They must also assume the responsibility for not getting our POWs home sooner, which would be the case if their encouragement to the enemy were not a factor.

It is necessary that this attack go forward at the very highest level for three reasons:

1. Because our negotiating position will actually be injured if attacks by leading Democratic opponents get too much off the ground and are not effectively answered;

2. Because we can attack now with far more effect than we will be able to later. They are out on a limb and believe they have a good issue. The thing to do is hang it on them hard while we can, rather than to wait when they will all jump back on board and get away with it with the willingness as to the press;

3. If the attack is made effectively and successfully now, it will have an enormously great impact on the primaries and on the Democratic Convention and will set in in such a way that if we finally do get a negotiation or success on the military front, we can constantly come back to this thing in the months ahead.

I would like you to personally follow up with the Colson group to see that an adequate program is maintained in all of these areas. I realize that some of the more faint-hearted types or even some of those who are pretty tough may have some doubts because of how the war news runs day by day. But, if you will recall, this is exactly what I warned in my speech— that there would be some battles lost and some battles won—but that in the end Abrams's view was that the South Vietnamese would hold. This is still my view, but even assuming I'm wrong, this is the only way to play it. As Ehrlichman has said to Buchanan, "Tough it through." Colson and some of the others in his office understandably are emphasizing the need to hold out the hope for negotiations, etc. This would buy us a little public support at the moment, but it would be exactly the wrong thing to do from the standpoint of helping to get negotiations, and that allows our opponents off the hook. Keep the heat on all the way.

HRH162, 230

APRIL 30[?], 1972

TO: **Charles Colson**

FROM: **Pat Buchanan**

Most of the questions we set up for ORC* are so ludicrous as to be laughable; some of them are platitudinous; some are so slanted as not to be believable even to the most gullible. If we push some of that crap out—all it will accomplish is to destroy the credibility of ORC for the future. I have based this "release" on the three questions, which I think we can probably get away with—although I have my doubts about the believability of the last one. Anyway, the way it is written, is brief and tight and makes the specific points we want without trying to put over the less believable parts of the hoax.

     Question: The ruthless Communist regime in Hanoi says it will hurl the filthy American imperialists and their Saigon puppets and running dogs into the East China Sea. Do you agree or disagree with President Nixon's courageous resistance of the Hanoi Communists?

*[Opinion Research Corporation, Princeton, New Jersey]

PJB5

1972

<hr>

MAY–AUGUST

MAY 1, 1972

TO: **John Dean**

FROM: **Charles Colson**

I think the attached from the *New York Times* is absolutely horrifying. I cannot believe that the IRS would make a computer analysis from actual tax returns available to Brookings, of all people in the world.

Of course, what Brookings did was turn it into a major anti-Administration study which will undoubtedly be the basis for more of the Democrats' arguments for tax reform. To me this is preposterous especially when we seem unable to get any data at all out of the IRS.

cwc131

<hr style="width:30%; margin-right:0;">

MAY 1, 1972

TO: **Jeb Magruder**

FROM: **Charles Colson**

Attached is an announcement of a rally upcoming this week at which I am sure our friends who would like to send more SAMs to North Vietnam to shoot down U.S. pilots will be present. Now that we have a little warning, let's orchestrate this one perfectly. I think without any doubt we can get a couple of Viet Cong flags, several posters and perhaps one or two scalps. Would you put your troops* into this and let me know how it is set up in advance so that we can perhaps turn the publicity our way for a change.

435

*[The "troops" apparently were the Cuban exiles who later participated in the Watergate break-in.]

cwc48

MAY 1, 1972

TO: **Ken Clawson**

FROM: **Chuck Colson**

There is a fascinating project at Vanderbilt University that has gotten virtually no press. Vanderbilt has set up a TV monitoring system whereby they record faithfully to the second every TV news segment from each of the three networks. This is put on video tape, filed in a library and available for recall by the public. Tapes can be purchased of any news segment from the University Library and a monthly index is published.

As you know, every major newspaper is kept in libraries for years. The print journalists can be held accountable for what they write almost forever. This is the first time, however, that TV journalists can be held accountable for what they have said or shown on every newscast. It is, of course, invaluable for researchers and not of insignificant interest to those that feel that the news coverage is slanted.

The existence of this project has had a shock impact on the networks. Network executives have decried it as horrendous censorship. They have obviously enjoyed the luxury of saying and showing what they wanted with no one ever able to question them after the fact.

Strangely, this has not received the press attention that it should have. It is really a very significant project. Of course, if the public is unaware of it, then it really constitutes a very insignificant deterrent against bias because even though the record is being kept, if people don't seek it out then who cares?

You ought to take on as a major project getting publicity for this Vanderbilt operation. We really need to get people talking about it and thinking about it. I would think it would have general press interest but particular interest in journalism publications.

Also this might be a marvelous subject for a speech by Herb before the next journalism or news group he speaks to.

CWC131

MAY 2, 1972

TO: **John Ehrlichman**

FROM: **Charles Colson**

You might have the occasion on Sunday to comment on the Pulitzer Prize. This is probably the first time in history that the award hasn't been given for excellence in journalism, but rather for skill in grand larceny. The two top winners were those who demonstrated that they were more adept at theft than at original writing or reporting. The "award for grand larceny" line would be a very neat way to make the point that journalism standards today are at a new low.

CWC131

ACTION MEMO

MAY 8, 1972

Investigate the possibility of installing a swimming pool at Blair House in the courtyard—an outdoor, heated pool.

The question is whether it is feasible and if so, what degree of privacy it would have, etc.

If such a project is at all possible, Walter Annenberg would be interested in contributing the pool as he has done in England to the Prime Minister.

HRH

HRH112

ACTION MEMO—EHRLICHMAN

MAY 8, 1972

The President's family were concerned about several questions you apparently got on "Meet the Press" regarding the President making decisions in an emotional, rash way. He feels it is very important that we get across the idea that decisions are always made on a very cold and deliberate basis, and that we must pound this point home to the staff and externally.

HRH

HRH112

MAY 9, 1972

TO: **Bob Haldeman**

FROM: **RmW**

The President asked me to remind you that he feels very strongly about someone taking Teddy on—After all, the President (as a candidate for Governor) was immediately on the air (he says he was first) backing JFK at the time of the Cuban missile confrontation even though he knew it probably meant defeat for him.

HRH48

[The following is a note to Mr. Colson from his secretary.]

MAY 9, 1972

Howard Hunt says:

McGovern is going to re-introduce the End the War Amendment this afternoon.

cwc122

MAY 12, 1972

TO: **Bruce Kehrli**

FROM: **Charles Colson**

RE: **Xerox Machine**

The attached is something I don't want to happen. Since the last time we requested some kind of Xerox machine, I have personally been watching the amount of time people spend out of my office waiting for a Xerox machine or trying to find one that either works or isn't locked up. It has really gotten ridiculous. The amount of wasted time that is spent and with the extreme pressures my entire office is under, I can certainly understand their frustration.

I can't believe a desk top copier is so expensive that we couldn't justify one if I added up the costs of wasted personnel time.

Please let me know what the problem is and why we can't get our own copier. I would also like some costs information for the various copiers available because if for some reason I can't convince you of the need here, I'm going to have to find another way to solve my problem.

Thanks.

cwc131

MAY 12, 1972

TO: **Bill Rhatican**

FROM: **Charles Colson**

I don't give a damn how many telegrams we receive at this point. If somebody sometime can give a respectable number, please keep track of the letters and telegrams next week. However, by Monday they should be all sorted and we will then be able to get a complete count. Just keep me advised. Western Union tells me this afternoon they have in fact delivered 52,000 telegrams to the White House. Kehrli reports 29,000 because he doesn't count any until they have been physically sorted. Also, stay very close to Dick Moore on the whole operation because Dick is looking for good telegrams that can be fed to the press and we have also come up with a marvelous scheme for shipping all telegrams from each state to the Senators from those states. We will have to find out whether Clark Mac-Gregor wants to do it, but I think we could use the telegrams and letters to really put the screws to the Congress and get more press.

cwc122, 131

MAY 12, 1972

TO: **Ken Clawson**

FROM: **Charles Colson**

I think for the next several weeks that Vic Riesel should be quarantined. He has written a column yesterday that is absolutely catastrophic to us politically and has been on television. The son of a bitch has done this to us now too many times. Just do not take his phone calls, nor will I and I would like to pass the word around to others that he calls from time to time that we're just not available for Riesel. Period.

cwc131

MAY 12, 1972

TO: **Chuck Colson**

FROM: **Des Barker**

It has come to my attention that a former secret service agent, Jim Golden, who was assigned to the President at the time he was Vice President and who was part of his protective force through the 1968 campaign, is now a Vice President of Intertel and assigned to the Hughes operations.

He is reported to be a name dropper and within the past few days has said to some of the Hughes people that Henry Kissinger called him and said "We need to have all of the information you may have on the Hughes-Nixon Loan."

CWC5

EYES ONLY

MAY 12, 1972

TO: **Fred Fielding**

FROM: **W. Richard Howard**

Henry Kimelman is Campaign Treasurer/Fund Raiser for McGovern. He was nearly indicted last year because he is a liquor importer in the Virgin Islands and apparently he really rakes off the profits. While Udall was Secretary of Interior he wheeled and dealed because the Virgin Islands was under Interior. We believe there must be material at Justice and Interior on this sleezy character that we would like to obtain through your fantastic sources. We could, of course, control the release of this material but need your help in getting what apparently is some pretty good stuff.
      Thanks.

21 SENATE HEARINGS 9885

MAY 15, 1972

TO: **Bob Haldeman**

FROM: **The President**

On further consideration and after discussion with Henry, I believe we should invite the leaders for the briefing before the Moscow trip on Tuesday morning before the Senate meets for its vote on the Byrd Amendment. Work out a time with MacGregor that is suitable, but one that fits my schedule and not theirs. I am not concerned that some of the leaders may not be able to attend on Friday afternoon. It should be around four o'clock as far as my schedule is concerned.

I would prefer to work something out so that we didn't have to include Ellender. This would only mean knocking out the Appropriations Committee which I don't think is particularly a problem at this point. You might check with Henry and see whether he thinks we might include the representatives from the Agricultural Committees and the Commerce Committees due to the fact that we are going to be talking about some trade with the Soviet Union. I think making the group larger this time is probably useful since there isn't much we want to talk about except to inform them as to what we are going to be doing. On the other hand, expanding the group to include the other Committees probably makes it more difficult to exclude Appropriations, so work out something with MacGregor that is satisfactory to all concerned. If in the final analysis we have to include Appropriations we will have to do so. But, of course, Ellender will cause us considerable problems and will bore the other Senators even more than he will us in the course of the meeting.

PPF4, HRH102

W/RN from HRH230

MAY 15, 1972

TO: **Chuck Colson**

FROM: **The President**

I believe that you should have your staff check over the TV commentators, as well as the editorials and comments in the news magazines, which went out on a limb and predicted that the mining of Haiphong would lead from everything to World War III to cancellation of the Summit. Have them dig out from the commentaries, as well as the columns and editorials, the specific sentences that put them most out on a limb. And then on Friday, just before the take-off for Moscow begins, develop some sort of an effective way to demand that the commentators, columnists and editorial writers have the good grace to admit that they were wrong. Along the same line, you might have a check made of the statements made by Presidential candidates and Senators which also took this line. Some of our people up in the Senate might have a little fun taking them to task for their over-emotional reaction and then suggesting that they have the good grace to retract.

PPF4; HRH162

MAY 15, 1972

TO: **Henry Kissinger**

FROM: **The President**

I have decided that funds for the ILO should now be shut off.
    Please carry out this instruction immediately.
    I do not want to hear any further appeals from the State Department or any other Departments on this issue.

cc: Caspar Weinberger
    John Ehrlichman

HRH162

MAY 15, 1972

TO: **Dwight Chapin**

FROM: **H. R. Haldeman**

RE: **Car Gift for Brezhnev**

Will you please work with Henry regarding the idea of a car gift for
Brezhnev. Since the French gave him a car, the President feels that there
is nothing wrong with our getting an American company like Ford to
follow suit. While it will be a new precedent for us, it really doesn't make
any difference. For Ford, of course, it would be a pure business deal, since
they are negotiating with the Russians for putting in a plant.

HRH199

MAY 15, 1972

TO: **Larry Higby**
   Gordon Strachan

FROM: **John Dean**

Attached is a report on protest activity which occurred during the past
weekend.

REPORT NO. 1

11:00 A.M., May 15 [1972]

Protest Activity During Weekend of May 13–14

Protest activity this past weekend fell dramatically short of what had been
promised by many antiwar activists and was in sharp contrast to the level
of activity that occurred from Tuesday through Thursday. Numerous regional demonstrations, largely sponsored by the National Peace Action
Coalition, were held across the country on Saturday, but none drew more
than several thousand participants. There were also few civil disturbances
and not many arrests. On Sunday, there was virtually no protest activity.
Listed below are the demonstrations which occurred on Saturday, May 13.

WASHINGTON, D.C.—Between 10 and 11:00 A.M., a crowd of 500–700
persons assembled at the Ellipse for a march to the Capitol as part of
a demonstration sponsored by the Washington Area Peace Action Coalition. By the time the group reached the Capitol, the crowd had reached
a peak of 1,000–1,200 demonstrators. Jerry Gordon, National Coordinator
of NPAC, I. F. Stone, and several other noted antiwar speakers addressed the crowd. The rally dispersed in the middle of the afternoon
with no incidents.

The Ukrainian Congress Committee of America demonstration against the Russians attracted approximately 300–400 protesters on Saturday afternoon. This group marched from Lafayette Park to the Soviet Embassy where they were prevented by the police from approaching the Embassy itself. Angered by this police action, the demonstrators returned to Lafayette Park and crossed Pennsylvania Avenue to the White House sidewalk where shouts were exchanged with the Quaker Action Group. When the Ukranians refused police orders to disperse and proceeded to block traffic on Pennsylvania Avenue, approximately 30 demonstrators were arrested.

NEW YORK CITY, N.Y.—Approximately 2–3,000 demonstrators attended a rally in Central Park. Speakers including Bella Abzug urged participants to attend the demonstration in Washington on May 21. No incidents or arrests occurred.

CHICAGO, ILL.—Approximately 2,900 demonstrators rallied in Grant Park, where again speakers urged attendance at the May 21st Washington demonstration and circulated petitions calling for the impeachment of the President.

DENVER, COLORADO—Approximately 2,000 persons attended a rally, but no violence or civil disobedience occurred.

SAN FRANCISCO, CALIF.—Near the Embarcadero about 1,200 persons assembled and then paraded through the downtown to the steps of City Hall. The rally dispersed without incident.

ST. PAUL, MINN.—Approximately 5,000 individuals, primarily consisting of students from the University of Minnesota, marched to St. Paul for a rally. No incidents or arrests occurred.

SANTA BARBARA, CALIF.—About 1,000 students from the University of California at Santa Barbara staged a rally and picketed Government buildings and Republican Headquarters.

DEL MAR, CALIF.—Approximately 300 protesters interfered with railroad operations in protest of the Vietnam War. Police arrested 35 persons.

KEY BISCAYNE, FLA.—Six boats with approximately 40 demonstrators attempted a "Blockade for Peace." The boats approached within 2½ miles of the President's Key Biscayne residence and floated balloons to represent the mining in North Vietnam harbors. Ten citations were issued for littering. A counter-demonstration in support of the President was held by Cubans in another boat who pelted the protesters with eggs.

BOSTON, MASS.—Approximately 1,500 demonstrators attended a rally at the Boston Common and then marched to the Charleston section of Boston. There were no incidents or arrests.

CHICOPEE, MASS.—In a continuing demonstration, approximately 350 demonstrators again attempted to block the entrance to Westover Air Force Base. 125 individuals were arrested after failing to disperse.

ALBUQUERQUE, NEW MEXICO—On the University of New Mexico campus approximately 1,000 persons held a peaceful march and rally.

ITHACA, N.Y.—Students and townspeople organizing a "Block Party" refused to disperse upon police orders. The crowd which grew to about 1,000 persons was finally scattered with tear gas. About 20 individuals were arrested for disorderly conduct.

PORTLAND, OREGON—Approximately 300 demonstrators assembled and held a peaceful rally and a march.

PHILADELPHIA, PA.—A march for peace attracted about 500 participants and ended with a rally at Rittenhouse Square. The speakers urged participation in the demonstration scheduled for Washington on May 21.

SEATTLE, WASHINGTON—About 500–700 individuals assembled at the Federal Court House for a rally. The demonstration was peaceful.

MILWAUKEE, WISCONSIN—A demonstration to protest the appearance of Admiral Zumwalt attracted approximately 300 persons. No incidents or arrests occurred.

JWD5

MAY 15, 1972

TO: **Chuck Colson**

FROM: **Al Haig**

Thanks for sending us Des Baker's memo on Jim Golden. Henry has, of course, not been involved in any way with the Hughes business.

cwc5

MAY 15, 1972

TO: **John Dean**

FROM: **Charles Colson**

John Ehrlichman has received the attached. It is, of course, a shocking violation of the statute for Senator McGovern to be sending letters to the White House soliciting campaign funds.

Secondly, he is continuing to use a U.S. Senate return address on his outside envelope. Obviously the inside envelope is addressed back to his political committee. By virtue of having the return address on the outside envelope the United States Senate, his mailing list is kept constantly up to date at the public's expense. As we discussed once before, the Postal Service will track down the addresses of any people who have moved and report new addresses free to the sender if the sender is a Member of

Congress. This is a service for which they charge commercial mailers. It is obviously the only reason that McGovern uses the Senate envelope.

McGovern has the image of being really straight-arrow, but he is bilking the taxpayers and violating the law to boot. I want to make a major issue of this. We tried it before, but it fell through the cracks.

Before I do I need to know from you exactly what is going on inside the Postal Service. If you recall the previous exercise in this area, we asked the Postal Service to conduct an investigation but I have no idea what if anything has come of it. If they have been doing this for him for a period of time, they should send a bill or stop doing it. In any event, we should make a major public blast at him for it. Can you get me the facts quickly so I can proceed?

cwc131

EYES ONLY

MAY 16, 1972

TO: The File

FROM: Charles W. Colson

RE: Wallace Shooting, May 15

I first talked with Mark Felt at approximately 7:30 P.M., May 15, from the President's EOB office. He told me that he had now taken full charge of the case, that agents were assigned to assure the personal security of Mr. Bremer (a point I emphasized to be of highest priority to the President), that the psychiatrist was questioning him and that FBI agents had not yet been allowed to question. I told him we had heard rumors that there were political motivations in the killing, to wit: Bremer had ties with Kennedy or McGovern political operatives, that obviously there could be a conspiracy and an immediate danger to others and it was therefore absolutely imperative that the Bureau begin questioning as soon as possible. Felt assured me he would do this. He gave me essential details about Bremer.

At 8:15 P.M., Felt talked with the President. I was not present, but I called Felt back immediately: he told me the FBI was at that point interviewing, that the psychiatrist considered the man dangerous to himself as well as to others and possibly very disturbed. He told me of a previous arrest on November 18, 1971. He further told me that the FBI was interviewing friends and family in Milwaukee and that the Secret Service had entered the apartment and obtained documents. One of them was a hand-written document on "How to Become Notable." Another was a paper on how to survive in long periods of confinement. Felt told me that the Bureau was obtaining these documents, that they were being flown in by the Secret Service. At 9:30 P.M., Felt phoned me to say that he had obtained a further report from the Milwaukee police that Bremer had been arrested last November on a country road where he was parked in a car under mysterious circumstances. The police noticed ammunition on the seat of the car, searched him and found a concealed weapon. He was charged and convicted. Further, Felt said that Bremer has refused to talk without his attorney and has been taken to a local magistrate and will be formally arraigned and confined in the Baltimore county jail. Felt cautioned that no information should leak out with respect to the psychiatrist's diagnosis or the documents found for fear a defense counsel could use it in pleading insanity. Felt said that the Bureau would not go into the apartment until they had obtained a search warrant. I suggested to Felt that he consider the use of informants in the jail in order to engage Bremer in conversation to try to determine motives. I explained that it was terribly important in a case of this kind to know what was behind the attempted assassination because it might have other implications but that obviously nothing should be done that would prejudice an ultimate prosecution. I suggested that his men be instructed to obtain information as soon as possible and under whatever circumstances they could.

Pat Gray called at 10:45 to say that he was now in charge of the case, that when Bremer was being fingerprinted, he asked the FBI agents if they could give him help publishing his autobiography. He said, "I have come from nowhere and I am going nowhere." Gray said he had instructed agents to engage in conversation. Gray further said the record revealed that he was a dues-paying member of the Young Democrats, politically active but that his brother, Theodore, reported that he, Bremer, was a Wallace supporter. Gray told me of his education and his part-time employment. I advised Gray that he should be aware of the need to determine the political motives as quickly as possible. He said he understood fully and was pursuing that avenue very aggressively.

He gave me a full report on the measures being taken for Bremer's security and for further immediate investigation, search warrants, etc.

cwc18

MAY 17, 1972

TO: **Charles Colson**

FROM: **John Dean**

RE: **Senator McGovern's Campaign Solicitation Activities**

In response to your recent inquiry concerning Senator McGovern's campaign solicitation activities, I am advised that the U.S. Postal Service has reviewed its policy of providing address correction services to members of Congress at Postal Service expense and has decided to bill Congress for the costs incurred in providing these services. In a letter of May 11, 1972, the Postal Service advised each member of Congress that henceforth, charges for address corrections will be included in the Service's annual billing to the Congress for the cost of handling franked mail. The charges will be at the same rate available to the general public—5¢ per name on a list submitted in advance or 10¢ per name on individual pieces of mail.

Charges for requested address corrections, however, will not be billed by the Service directly to individual Senators and Congressmen. The Service is treating the address correction in the same manner as the franking privilege—Congress created the franking privilege for the use of its members with respect to correspondence on official business, and therefore Congress alone has the responsibility to assure the proper and lawful exercise of the privilege.

The Service does not currently determine what is or is not official Congressional business, and I am advised that the Service will not determine what is or is not a proper use of the address correction service. Such determinations will be deferred to Congress.

In the case of Senator McGovern's prior requests for address corrections on campaign solicitation mail, I am advised that the Postal Service billed McGovern for those address corrections and that the bill has been paid in full. The Postal Service has no evidence that McGovern is continuing his prior improper practices with respect to address correction requests on campaign solicitation mail. The letter to John Ehrlichman is properly stamped and does not bear any request for address correction. Thus, it would appear, in this regard at least, that McGovern is staying within the bounds of law and ethics.

However, Senator McGovern's campaign solicitation letter addressed to "Mr. John Ehrlichman, Assistant to the President, White House" seemingly contravenes 18 U.S.C. 602 and 603.

Under section 602, Senators, Representatives, Federal employees, and other persons receiving salary or compensation for services from Treasury funds are prohibited from directly or indirectly soliciting or receiving contributions for any political purpose from any other such officer, employee, or person. In the instant case, Senator McGovern is soliciting campaign money from a Presidential Assistant, whose salary is payable out of Treasury funds, and thus is in violation of section 602 of Title 18.

Under section 603 of Title 18, solicitation of contributions for political purposes in any room or building occupied by any of the aforementioned persons while engaged in the discharge of their official duties is prohibited. A solicitation by letter or circular addressed to and delivered by mail or otherwise to a Federal employee at the office or building in which he is employed in the discharge of his official duties is a solicitation "in a room or building" for purposes of establishing violations of section 603. Thus, in the instant case, the letter to John Ehrlichman at the White House appears to be clearly violative of section 603 as well as section 602.

It has also been brought to my attention that Bob Haldeman and

Pat Buchanan also received solicitation letters from McGovern addressed to them at the White House. It appears that McGovern has purchased or gained access to various mailing lists and has not bothered to screen the names and purge the lists of Federal employees' names and office addresses. I would imagine that he is using computerized lists which are probably difficult to screen. For example, earlier in the year one of his "Dear Friends" letters was sent to the Department of Interior's Bureau of Outdoor Recreation.

As more and more letters are received by Federal employees at their office addresses, we seem to be building a prosecutable case for the Department of Justice under 18 U.S.C. 602 and 603. However, before making any move in this regard, I think we have to consider the feasibility of screening and purging our own mailing lists to avoid the same pitfall McGovern and others have encountered. If we proceed against McGovern only to find that we are doing the same thing he is, it will put us in a rather compromising and embarrassing position.

If you have further questions or need additional assistance on this, please so advise.

JWD5

MAY 18, 1972

TO: **Bob Haldeman**

FROM: **The President**

One department which particularly needs a housecleaning is the CIA. The [first] problem in the CIA is muscle-bound bureaucracy which has completely paralyzed its brain and the other is the fact that its personnel, just like the personnel in State, is primarily Ivy League and the Georgetown set rather than the type of people that we get into the services and the FBI.

I want a study made immediately as to how many people in CIA could be removed by Presidential action. I assume that they have themselves frozen in just as is the case with State. If that is the case I want action begun immediately, through Weinberger, for a reduction in force of all positions in the CIA in the executive groups of 50 percent. This reduction in force should be accomplished by the end of the year so that we can then move to get in some better people. Of course, the reduction in force should be accomplished solely on the ground of its being necessary for budget reasons, but you will both know the real reason and I want some action to deal with the problem.

In another area of recruiting I want you to quit recruiting from any of the Ivy League schools or any other universities where either the university president or the university faculties have taken action condemning our efforts to bring the war in Vietnam to an end. We are totally justified in doing this anyway because the government simply has too many Ivy League people in relationship to the percentage of Ivy League graduates compared with the total number of college graduates in the country.

In filling our needs I want you to give first priority to those schools who have presidents or faculty members who have wired us or written us their support of what we have done in Vietnam. Have the mail checked very carefully to see which ones these are. After you get past those you can then go to other schools in the Midwest, in the South, and even possibly some in the far West (not, of course, including Stanford or Cal) where we would have a better chance to come up with people who would be on our side. Retired military people are also good for this purpose.

cc: Fred Malek

HRH162

MAY 18, 1972

TO: **H. R. Haldeman**

FROM: **The President**

I was distressed to learn from Don Kendall that in his trying to get Business Chairmen for us in the various States, he had struck out in city after city after going down the list of names that he received from people on the White House staff, the Campaign Committee, and from other sources. He said that he had to date called 12 business leaders in San Francisco and not one of them would agree to serve as the Nixon Chairman. He said that he had also had some difficulty in Los Angeles although he had finally come up with a name. Only through Connally's intervention was he able to get Clement to take the job in Texas.

As I have already told you, Kendall's reaction of course was that, immediately after the election, we had to spend more time romancing the business community and developing a group of them to support us. I told him that, if I looked back over my calendar for the last three years, businessmen probably took two-thirds of my time when we figured my appearances before Chambers of Commerce, NAB, the Business Council, and the terribly boring series of meetings I have had with business advisors and consultants on a number of issues.

I told Don that we have to realize that the old establishment just like the old establishment in the university community and in the media simply weren't going to be with us and that we had to build a new establishment. I told him that we needed people like himself, Bob Abplanalp, Mulcahy and others who, though they don't fit socially with the business elite, have real character. There are simply bound to be a number of people around the country who will fit this category. Stans probably knows some of them because he had to build a whole new group of contributors when he went through the last campaign. I would also imagine that the wire and letter response to the May 8 speech might prove very useful in getting some names for Kendall to approach.

What I am sure of is that what we have been doing to date with the business community is altogether wrong. When I think that we have had the likes of Irwin Miller in to Blair House meetings and when I look over the lists as I sometimes do of those who are invited to such meetings, I find that even our most conservative people on the White House staff inevitably go to the so-called business elite when they want to get support for some of our policies.

I want you to have a really tough talk with Flanigan and Ehrlichman on this subject and eventually, as a result of your discussions, perhaps we can give Kendall some help in attempting to develop this new group on the business side. Malek, of course, could be helpful in such a discussion and Stans, also, from time to time.

In sum, what I am trying to say in this memo is that we have been striking out over and over again in attempting to enlist business support for our policies due to the fact that we have been talking to the wrong audience. The business elite, if anything, has less guts than the labor elite or the farm elite. What we have to do is to find those few people in the business community who have some reputation as being successful in business but who haven't been taken in by the idea that they must only attach themselves to "fashionable" causes.

PPF4; HRH230

W/RN from HRH162

MAY 19, 1972

TO: **John Ehrlichman**

FROM: **The President**

I have been doing a lot of thinking about the way our busing legislation is bogged down in the Congress. I know that the responsible position is the one that we have taken. On the other hand, the very worst thing that can happen is to be responsible and also impotent at the same time. We are rapidly getting ourselves into that position. I don't think anybody on our staff really believes that we are going to get the moratorium in the form that will be useful and the chances of getting the second half of the package are even less.

Under the circumstances, I believe we are going to have to come to a Constitutional Amendment. My view is that we should come out with a Constitutional Amendment about the first of September. I want you to put your staff to work on the very best possible form of a Constitutional Amendment so that I can be prepared to do so at that time.

This has the added advantage of drawing the line with whatever Democratic candidate they finally select. We must make no mistake about the fact that after the results in Michigan our Democratic friends will try to fuzz up the issue and even say some things which would indicate that they were not so pro-busing as they seem to be. We are not going to gain any brownie points whatever by being so responsible that we appear to be totally ineffective.

It may be that we want to move on the Constitutional Amendment route further, but in any event I have now reached the conclusion that we have to move in that route by the first of September at the very latest. As a matter of fact, it may be that we will have to move in this route before the Republican Convention, although having a platform fight on it isn't too good an idea. In any event, get the troops working on what we want to come up with and have in mind that this is the direction in which we are going to move. In the meantime, all hands should do everything they possibly can to try to point out what our present proposal really is and try to sell it all over the country. I am inclined to think that it is too complex to sell effectively, but in any event let's do the best we can at this point with an unsatisfactory situation and then hit the issue hard, clear and clean two months before the election.

PPF4; HRH162, 230

MAY 19, 1972

TO: **Chuck Colson**

FROM: **The President**

I have the impression that the way we work on members of the Senate and House may not be as effective as it can be. It is quite clear that the opposition, the peaceniks, the radicals, etc., primarily concentrate not on mail and telephone calls but on sending delegations in who insist on seeing the victim and then proceed to work him over and get a commitment from him. Having been in this spot myself on many occasions I know how hard it is to turn one of these groups off without saying something that is favorable to their cause.

I think you ought to have a discussion in your own shop and also with MacGregor as to how we can get delegations to insist on calling on Senators and Congressmen so that they can hammer home what we want and get commitments from them. You have to remember that there are very, very few people with any backbone in the Senate or House anymore, and that they are really patsies for a group that comes in and puts it to them hard on an issue. What we need are some strong, vigorous people who will act just as effectively as our opponents do in going from office to office in groups and trying to get commitments for our point of view.

PPF4; HRH162, 230

TO BE CABLED

MAY 23, 1972

TO: **The President**

FROM: **Charles Colson**

RE: **Items Missed in our Phone Conversation**

Because of the lack of security of the telephone, I felt I could only allude
to the Haig backgrounder in very guarded terms last night. Haig briefed
selected newsmen yesterday afternoon and the wires and those in attendance have been playing it extremely well (page one of today's *Star*). The
major point made has been the serious strains on North Vietnam in terms
of materiel, morale and political structure as a result of U.S. actions. The
story has run extensively on the wires and in the press. Also a 7th Fleet
Commander reinforced the point that no vessels have come through the
mine fields. This was in response to another report, this time from a UPI
story, that one Soviet ship had gone through the mine field.

   In addition to being a good story for us to get out it has really hit
the *New York Times* hard. They were not invited to the backgrounder and
complained vigorously afterwards. In fact their management contacted
Clawson to appeal the exclusion. The story was good enough, however,
that they had to give it prominent play today (under AP by-line) and had
to use Clawson's report that the *New York Daily News* had been invited
which seemed to Clawson to cover New York adequately. As a result of
this and the earlier efforts (including attacks by Scott and Goldwater)
Anthony Lewis's front page story in the *Times* this morning is headed
"Closing of Ports Conceded in Hanoi," (also carried in the *Star* today and
on the wires). Lewis reports that foreign observers now believe the mining
by the U.S. has effectively blocked all ship movements. Hence Lewis has
come full circle. The *Times* is desperately seeking our assurance that they
will not be excluded in the future; we are giving no such assurance. For
the first time I think we have really gotten through to them. [. . .]

   As for the reporting from Moscow and reactions here, you have set
exactly the right tone as I indicated to you on the phone last night. The
impression is of a serious, determined, hard-negotiating President. There
is a good businesslike atmosphere and the reactions from the soundings I
have taken are very positive. This trip will not inspire the same excitement
as the China trip which had something of exploring the unknown but it
will build, in my judgment, if the press continues as they have started, an
impression of a strong, knowledgeable world leader accomplishing a very
historic undertaking between the world's two super powers. In short, the
reactions will be very different but this may possibly have an even more
significant political impact because of visible evidence of the accomplishment.

   A point which I did not want to make on the phone is that Harris
thinks this trip will have a major political impact and he is going into the

field next week; the only downside risk he sees is if the press plays the line that all of these agreements were pre-determined and pre-scheduled for announcement this week and that the Summit is really a signing cere-mony. He feels that the public reaction would be very cynical to this and the Summit would look to them like showmanship. He feels, therefore, it is critically important that the point be made from Moscow that very hard negotiations are going on, really substantive issues are being hammered out by the President and Brezhnev and that nothing was really settled firmly in advance of the trip. The important impression must be that the President is personally doing the hard, tough, negotiations on the big issues. So far he feels that we have handled it very well and thought that the Kissinger statement from Austria was very helpful in this respect. He urges more on it if possible, i.e., preserving something of an air of uncer-tainty and making clear that there are big issues that the President is personally handling. Harris feels that if you come out of this as the man who really personally brought about very historic agreements and a new era in super-power relations that this will so enhance your leadership image as to be a very powerful issue in the election. [. . .]

One other item which I forgot to mention last night which may be of interest to you: WTTG here ran daily ads in the *Post* and the *Star* last week with coupons to be clipped expressing support or disapproval of the mining action. The report announced Friday night was fantastic: 82% of the 6,000 coupons sent in were in support of your decision. This poll is being widely circulated.

Also, as I mentioned on the phone last night, the McGovern cam-paign is moving in high gear. Both the Gallup and Harris polls showing McGovern stronger than Humphrey in trial heats have given him a lift; his agents are continuing to wreak havoc with the Democratic Party. In Vermont his delegates adopted resolutions favoring unqualified amnesty, totally legalized marijuana and abortion on demand. The whole Irish-Catholic-Democratic establishment in Vermont has just signed on with us. McGovern took 9 of the 12 delegates so the trend is continuing.

cwc131
w/rn from cwc85

DRAFT CABLE—SECRET/EYES ONLY

MAY 23, 1972

TO: **Honorable John Warner,** Secretary of the Navy [in] Moscow

FROM: **Charles W. Colson**

Per our telephone conversation, Ed Brooke and I met yesterday. Brooke is solidly supporting the President and will not, contrary to some press reports, disavow him in the campaign. This has been a concern to some people and it has been considerably speculated because Brooke's opponent, Professor Galbraith, has already announced he will make a big issue in the campaign against Brooke [of] Brooke's support of the President. Clearly Ed would be better off selfishly by running totally independent in the campaign in the style that Keating for example did in 1964 when he was on the ticket with Goldwater. Clearly also this would be terribly damaging to us, not in Massachusetts which we have little chance of carrying but very damaging around the country with blacks who might otherwise be persuaded to vote for the President. If Brooke were to discreetly disavow us it would have harmful national implications. In my conversation with Brooke yesterday, however, he made the point that he is indeed vulnerable to the charge that while he supports the President and has remained close to the President, Massachusetts has been very badly treated by this Administration. Unemployment is high; there have been huge layoffs in defense contracts and there are very few things Brooke can point to that he has done for the State. Hence he is being asked, even by his own supporters, what he can point to as something he is getting as a result of his support for the President at some political peril to himself.

He is terribly concerned over the Quincy Shipyard which is a General Dynamics yard. Apparently General Dynamics intends to announce its closing in early June if it does not win one present Navy contract. Ed said it has a bid in in competition with Litton for a submarine tender, but that the decision may not be made by Navy until July at which point the Quincy yard may be out of business.

Those of us in the White House have assiduously stayed out of trying to get into any Government contract problems. I have talked this over with Weinberger who believes as I do that the Brooke situation has sufficient national implications that it would be most helpful to us if you could take a look at it simply from a political viewpoint. Obviously we do not want to do anything for political purposes but if all other things were equal or it looks like some encouragement could be legitimately given, it could be very helpful in our relationships with Brooke. Be assured we are not trying to influence anything or effect the outcome in any way. If, however, the prospects have any promise, then perhaps the procedure could be speeded up enough for us to advise Brooke and for him to in turn advise General Dynamics to forestall their announcement. I should emphasize also that Brooke is not suggesting this as a price of his support. He does, on the other hand, on the merits make a very good argument that it would be helpful to him to have something to show for his continued support.

As you can understand, I do not want to talk to Frank Sanders about this and with the time so short, it is my hope if you can look into this that perhaps only you will know the reasons for our concern.

cwc48

W/RN from cwc85

MAY 23, 1972

TO: **John Dean**

FROM: **Charles Colson**

RE: **Contact with Demonstrators**

I have just reviewed the Haldeman memo attached dated May 19 regarding contact with demonstrators.

According to Haldeman's memo I am to clear all contacts well in advance with you. This is to advise you that I am planning tomorrow night to drive my Pontiac Station Wagon up onto the curb of Pennsylvania Avenue in front of the White House and run over all of the hippies who are lying there. My plan is to do this while they are asleep sometime between 2 and 3 A.M. Would you please let me know what coordination you would like to arrange?

cc: H. R. Haldeman

JWD5; CWC131

MAY 23, 1972

TO: **Al Haig**

FROM: **Charles Colson**

Note the attached wire service story quoting John Ashbrook. This is what we have to guard against. Reagan is absolutely indispensable to us. In fact, we are in big trouble without him. Please coordinate this with the Vice President's office as soon as possible. Send someone of high stature out—I hope tonight. The Vice President's ready to arrange it and in view of Ashbrook's statement it becomes critically important from a domestic political standpoint as well as getting a successful end result.

HANDWRITTEN REPLY BY HAIG: "Reagan is on board—briefing in detail on Friday & agrees w/our psn [position]."

CWC85, 131

MAY 24, 1972

TO: **Mike Balzano**

FROM: **Charles Colson**

In connection with your speech before the Italian-American gathering in Central Park in New York, I want you to know that whatever happens, we all think you have been doing a superb job. I told the President of your planned speaking engagement and even though he has not had a chance to have you in as he plans to do, he wanted to be sure before you go that I tell you how much he appreciates what you are doing. I pass this on to you simply in the event anything should happen that would make it impossible for him to talk to you personally after the speech.

Do not get the wrong impression from this memo. The President simply wants you to know that he really has taken note of what you are doing and in the event of any untoward incident, he did want you to have the satisfaction in your mind of knowing that he recognizes how valuable you had been.

By the way, don't for a moment miss the theatrical opportunity that this could present. If you are going down for the count anyway, you should go down in a blaze of glory. Regardless of where the bullet enters, you should always clutch your left side over your heart. That makes a much more dramatic photograph. Be sure also that reporters are within earshot so you can say "long live Richard Nixon, the greatest President in history." Remember that down through the years, dying words have always been those the longest remembered.

cwc5, 131

MAY 26, 1972

Dear Jay:*

Per our conversation, I think you will find the attached to be all the research that you will need. It is quite a story and I hope you can put it to good use.

Personally I am sure that George Meany will endorse McGovern. I would like you to invite me to be present when he does because I would love to see him admit how wrong he has been all these years on the cold war and foreign policy.

Best personal regards.

Sincerely,

Charles W. Colson
Special Counsel
to the President

*[Letter to Jay Lovestone, director, International Division, AFL/CIO]

PRESIDENT RICHARD NIXON'S DAILY DIARY
(See Travel Record for Travel Activity)

PLACE DAY BEGAN				DATE (Mo., Day, Yr.)
KREMLIN PALACE ANNEX				MAY 28, 1972
MOSCOW, U.S.S.R.				TIME DAY
				8:25 A.M. SUNDAY

TIME		PHONE P=Placed R=Received		ACTIVITY
In	Out	Lo	LD	
8:25				The President had breakfast.
8:42	8:48			The President and the First Lady motored from the Kremlin Palace annex to the Moscow Baptist Church.
				The President and the First Lady were greeted by: Rev. Ilya Ivanov, Chairman of the All-Union Council of Evangelical Christian-Baptists
				White House photographer, in/out
8:48	9:26			The President and the First Lady attended worship services conducted by: Rev. Ivanov; Rev. Alexei M. Bichokov, General Secretary of the Soviet Baptist Church Council; Rev. Michael Y. Zhidkov, Pastor of the Moscow Baptist Church
				Seated with the President and the First Lady were Director of Communications Herbert G. Klein and a Soviet Interpreter.
9:26	9:35			The President and the First Lady motored from the Moscow Baptist Church to the Kremlin Palace annex.
9:35				The President and the First Lady returned to their suite.
9:50	9:55			The President met with his Press Secretary, Ronald L. Ziegler.
9:55	10:00			The President met with his Assistant, Henry A. Kissinger.
10:21	10:22	P		The President talked with Mr. Kissinger.
10:25	10:35	P		The President met with Mr. Kissinger.
11:11		P		The President requested that his Personal Secretary, Rose Mary Woods, join him.
11:19		P		The President requested that his Assistant, H. R. Haldeman, join him.
				The President met with:
11:30	12:20			Mr. Haldeman
12:15	12:35			Miss Woods
12:22		P		The President telephoned Mr. Kissinger. The call was not completed.
12:42	12:43	P		The President talked with Mr. Kissinger.
12:49	12:50	R		The President talked with Mr. Kissinger.
12:58	1:00	P		The President talked with Mr. Haldeman.
1:10	1:13	P		The President talked with Mr. Haldeman.
1:20				The President had lunch.
4:07		P		The President telephoned Mr. Haldeman. The call was not completed.
4:09	4:10	P		The President talked with Miss Woods.
4:16	4:31		P	The President talked long distance with Secretary of Commerce Peter G. Peterson in Washington, D.C.
4:31	4:40			The President met with Miss Woods.

PLACE DAY BEGAN				DATE (Mo., Day, Yr.) MAY 28, 1972
KREMLIN PALACE ANNEX MOSCOW, U.S.S.R.				TIME DAY 4:41 P.M. SUNDAY

TIME		PHONE P = Placed R = Received		ACTIVITY
In	Out	Lo	LD	
4:41		P		The President telephoned Mr. Ziegler. The call was not completed.
5:33	5:36	R		The President talked with Mr. Ziegler.
6:02	6:04	P		The President talked with Miss Woods.
6:30		P		The President requested that Mr. Haldeman join him.
				The President met with:
6:36	7:19			Mr. Kissinger
6:36	7:40			Mr. Haldeman
7:53		P		The President telephoned Mr. Haldeman. The call was not completed.
8:19		P		The President telephoned Mr. Haldeman. The call was not completed.
8:20				The President went to the Green Room in the Grand Kremlin Palace.
8:30				The President addressed the people of the U.S.S.R. and the U.S. The remarks were broadcast live on radio and television in the Soviet Union and simultaneously, via satellite, in the United States. Immediately following the broadcast a photo opportunity was held for members of the press.
8:54				The President returned to the Kremlin Palace annex.
8:55			R	The President was telephoned by his Assistant, Peter M. Flanigan. Miss Woods took the call.
8:58	8:59	R		The President talked with Mr. Haldeman.
9:03		P		The President requested that Miss Woods join him.
9:05		R		The President was telephoned by his Special Assistant, William L. Safire. Miss Woods took the call.
				The President met with:
9:10	10:20			Mr. Haldeman
9:20	9:40			Miss Woods
10:12	10:16	P		The President talked with his Special Assistant, Raymond K. Price, Jr.
10:19	10:21	P		The President talked with Mr. Haldeman.
10:27		P		The President requested that Mr. Haldeman join him.
10:30	10:58			The President met with Mr. Haldeman.
11:01	11:04		P	The President talked long distance with his Special Counsel, Charles W. Colson, in Dover, Massachusetts.
11:07	11:08	P		The President talked with Mr. Haldeman.
11:12			P	The President telephoned long distance to Mrs. Jane G. Thompson, widow of Llewellyn E. Thompson, Jr., former Ambassador from the U.S. to the U.S.S.R., in Washington, D.C. The call was not completed.

cwc78, 131

[*Address by President Richard M. Nixon of the United States delivered at the Great Kremlin Palace, Moscow, and telecast live to the people of the Union of Soviet Socialist Republics on May 28, 1972 (partial text)*]

Dobry vecher (Good evening) [. . .]

Most of you know our country only through what you read in your newspapers and what you hear and see on radio and television and in motion pictures. This is only a part of the real America.

I would like to take this opportunity to try to convey to you something of what America is really like—not in terms of its scenic beauty, its great cities, its factories, its farms or its highways, but in terms of its people.

In many ways, the people of our two countries are very much alike. Like the Soviet Union, ours is a large and diverse nation. Our people, like yours, are hardworking. Like you, we Americans have a strong spirit of competition.

But we also have a great love of music and poetry, of sports and of humor.

Above all, we, like you, are an open, natural and friendly people. We love our country. We love our children.

And we want for you, and for your children, the same peace and abundance that we want for ourselves and for our children.

We Americans are idealists, we believe deeply in our system of government. We cherish our personal liberty. We would fight to defend it if necessary, as we have done before.

We also believe deeply in the right of each nation to choose its own system.

Therefore, however much we like our own system for ourselves, we have no desire to impose it on anyone else. [. . .]

Through all the pages of history, through all the centuries, the world's people have struggled to be free from fear. Whether fear of the elements, or hunger, or fear of their own rulers, or fear of their neighbors in other countries.

And yet time and again people have vanquished the source of one fear only to fall prey to another. Let our goal now be a world free of fear. [. . .]

Spasibo i do svidaniya (Thank you and good-bye).

MAY 30, 1972

TO: **The President**

FROM: **John Ehrlichman**

RE: **CIA vs. Marchetti**

You will recall that Dick Helms asked you for help in connection with a former CIA agent who threatened to publish secrets obtained during his tenure.

At your instance we got Helms the necessary help to file an action against Marchetti and the District Court has entered a comprehensive injunction against Marchetti disclosing any secrets.

Attached is a letter from Helms expressing his gratitude for White House assistance. The case is on appeal but we are optimistic about its ultimate outcome.*

*PRESIDENT'S COMMENT IN MARGIN: "Good"

POF17

MAY 30, 1972

Dear Mr. Bell:*

Incredible though it seems, I was unable to attend the informal preview of "The Burglars." Maybe we are just jinxed. I have been anxious to meet you for many months but each time there is an informal preview something happens to prevent me from attending. I had to work with the President the evening that "The Burglars" was being shown leaving my wife sitting at home dressed for the evening and unable to even give you advance notice that I would not be present. Please accept my apologies and I hope to try again on Monday, June 19th, for the showing of "Butterflies are Free"—barring any recurrence of problems. I look forward to meeting you then.

Best regards.

Sincerely,

Charles W. Colson
Special Counsel
to the President

*[Letter to J. Raymond Bell, New York, N.Y.]

CWC131

MAY 31, 1972

TO: **John Dean**

FROM: **Charles Colson**

RE: **Attached Ad**

Enclosed is a copy of the ad in today's *New York Times* calling for the impeachment of the President. I assume you have already seen it and I would hope that you have in process a thorough investigation of the people behind this. Thus far, the investigative processes of the United States Government have left me distinctly unimpressed. I have yet to see anything worth a damn come out of any of our inquiries. My most recent disappointment was on the McGovern fund-raising operation and some of the unsavory characters associated with it. I would hope on this one we could somehow get someone interested in it enough to do a half decent job. I am sure I need not emphasize the imperative need to discredit these guys. All we have to do is find one of them a Communist and we can discredit the entire operation.

I want to see the FBI reports on every name associated with this ad, especially Vern Countryman.

Furthermore, it seems to me that this ad clearly violates the new campaign contribution statute. In an election year to call for the impeachment of the President is clearly to work against his re-election. This ad contains no disclaimer. The greatest thing we could obviously do is to hang this on the Democrats and McGovern in particular.

For once let's do this professionally. Get the goods on these guys and then be in a position to launch a devastating counter attack.

JFB5; CWC5, 95, 131

JUNE 1, 1972

TO: **H. R. Haldeman**

FROM: **David C. Hoopes**

RE: **Memorandum for the President's File**

It has been discovered that a request for a Memorandum for the President's File was not made for his meeting with Former Attorney General John N. Mitchell on Wednesday, April 12, 1972 at 3:29 P.M.

Our records show that you were present during this meeting. Since the President desires that this important file be as complete as possible, I would like to ask you to prepare a summary of what transpired, what commitments were made (if any) and what kind of mood or atmosphere prevailed.

Your Memorandum for the President's File need not be lengthy, but you should keep in mind the historical significance of your report and understand that its significance will increase greatly with time.

We hope you will be able to write and return such a Memorandum to this office within five (5) days.

Thank you.

POF88

JUNE 5, 1972

TO: **Dick Howard**

FROM: **John Dean**

RE: **Henry Kimelman**

Per our conversations, to date we have been unable to come up with any material on Kimelman that might be used to illustrate the true nature of the money man in McGovern's life.

Last September we did receive information alleging the possibility that Kimelman's corporate activities might be violative of the anti-trust laws, and also allegations of organized crime involvement. At that time the information was reviewed by the Department of Justice and we were advised that there was no sufficient basis to verify such charges.

I am still seeking further data on Kimelman from Interior and other sources, and will keep you advised of the results of these inquiries as soon as they are available.

21 SENATE HEARINGS 9887

JUNE 6, 1972

TO: **John Mitchell**

FROM: **The President**

One of the factors that brought Goldwater down to such a shattering defeat in 1964 was the success of the media in tying him to ultra-right-wing supporters like H. L. Hunt, the John Birch Society, etc. While we will not have the media cooperation in a similar effort directed against McGovern, at least we can try to develop a tactic to the extent that it will sail. For example, the fact that Abby Hoffman, Jerry Rubin, Angela Davis, among others, support McGovern should be widely publicized and used at every point. Here an ad or a piece of literature from a veterans' group might be in order. This must be carefully done but nailing him to his left-wing supporters and forcing him either to repudiate them or to accept their support is essential. In fact, one effective way to operate here is to have a prominent Democrat or Independent, or a veterans' leader or a labor leader, demand by letter or otherwise that McGovern repudiate the support of Abby Hoffman and Jerry Rubin and any others who are well known of this type that you can find. Keep calling on him to repudiate them daily until you finally break through the media blackout into the clear. I consider this a top priority objective.

cc: Bob Haldeman
    Chuck Colson

PPF4; CWC19; HRH230

JUNE 6, 1972

TO: **John Mitchell**

FROM: **The President**

[The text of this memorandum dealing with "sensitive political matters" has been withdrawn from PPF4 at President Nixon's request.]

JUNE 6, 1972

TO: **H. R. Haldeman**

FROM: **John Dean**

Attached is a copy of the official program for the Democrats' National Convention, which I am forwarding for your perusal. After you have perused, I would appreciate having it back so that I can analyze the ads, etc., for my own purposes. I then plan to forward it to Colson.

JWD5

JUNE 8, 1972

FROM: **Buchanan/Khachigian**

Assault Strategy

Herewith the Assault Book on which Ken Khachigian and I have been working the past week. Within are enough McGovern statements, positions, votes, not only to defeat the South Dakota Radical—but to have him indicted by a Grand Jury. *If* we can get these positions before the public; and *if* the election hinges upon issues—only with enormous effort could we boot this election away.

However, in addition to the statements, issues and positions of George McGovern there are "perceptions" which we must address as well—"perceptions" that, unless dramatically altered, could give us considerable difficulty in the fall.

1. In a country where the "politician" is in increasing disrepute, George McGovern is perceived as a candid, honest, straightforward citizen non-politician.

2. In a nation where the "Establishment" is viewed with a mixture of frustration and contempt by left, right and the angry Wallace center—George McGovern is perceived by many as an anti–status quo, anti-Establishment figure—the candidate of the common man.

3. In a political year when the mood, we are told, is "throw the rascals out," we are the "ins" and Mr. McGovern is perceived clearly as one of the "outs." He is outside the power elite of the Democratic Party; he is perceived as outside the power elite of the American Government.

4. George McGovern has been and remains the "underdog" in a nation that has always had a warm spot for the "underdog."

5. In an era when the public yearns constantly for a "new face," George McGovern is the newest, freshest face on the national scene, and the face of Richard Nixon is the most familiar of any political figure in the United States.

Before addressing how I feel we should deal generally with each of these "perceptions," and specifically with the assault materials provided let me add these concerns:

1. The Republican Party is sleek and fat and incumbent. Our Conservative foot soldiers who out-marched the Democrat's union troops in 1968 are sullen, bitchy, angry. Our little old ladies in tennis shoes are not all enamoured of H.R. 1, wage and price controls, and $100 billion in deficits—while George McGovern has an organization the likes of which the U.S. has not seen since the Goldwater Legions.

He has tens of thousands of True Believers, working night and day for him—spurred on by unanticipated triumphs and the anticipation of running the "Old Politics" right out of the White House.

As of now, in a seat of the pants judgment, I would say that if we are running 50–50 with George McGovern in the polls election day—he could conceivably beat us by four to six points, on the basis of his first-rate get-out-the-vote machinery.

2. The hard-fought Democratic primaries have resulted sharply in increased registration—especially by McGovern types—and any lopsided registration figures will be lopsided anti-Nixon votes in the fall.

3. While McGovern's positions are woolly-headed, he is an ambitious and pragmatic politician—who will not hesitate to move crab-wise to the center to win this election. Some of the more garish of his positions will surely be shed by the fall. Further, my understanding is that his campaign film biography is an excellent piece of work—designed to portray him as the antithesis of the "radical," indeed, as the bomber pilot who won the war against Nazi Germany. We can anticipate that his commercials will be equally designed to hit the Democratic center.

Clearly, in addition to the problems listed, we have tremendous advantages—the Presidency, the view of millions that McGovern is some sort of wild radical, the split within the Democratic Party, the tendency of McGovern's red hots to "stick it" to the Daleys and Meanys when the opportunity arises, etc. But this memorandum is directed toward both general and specific suggestions to resolve our problems, to get the radical record of McGovern into the public record, to change the national perceptions of the two.

General Recommendations

1. We should move to re-capture the anti-Establishment tradition or theme in American politics. Incumbent Presidents *can* do this; RN did it in November 1969, when, as President of U.S., he called on the common man to stand with him against the elitist-backed mobs in the streets. That, coupled with the Vice President's standing up to the Establishment media, and slugging it out, raised RN to the highest point of his Presidency—69 percent approval. Why did we reach that level? Because, even though *Newsweek* led "Nixon in Trouble," even though Broder was writing of the "Breaking of the President"—RN held both the Presidency position and the anti-Establishment position. How do we enhance our anti-Establishment credentials—and take Mr. McGovern's away—without surrendering the political asset of Incumbent President?

a. We need to shed the "in bed with Big Business" image. PJB believes we should seek out the opportunity to "take on" some egregious, giant, preferably, but not necessarily Democratic, corporation publicly—as Kennedy did with Big Steel in 1962. Business will be with us in 1972—but one of our problems is a too close identification in the public mind with Corporate Power. ITT reinforced that. Public presidential anger at the price-gouging of some Big Business firm would be, in my judgment, a good thing.

b. If we have abandoned the idea of introducing or supporting "tax reform"—I trust we have not—I would recommend RN publicly veto one, two or three huge spending bills—on national television. Two minutes would be sufficient. The focus of the veto is that the taxpayer is already burdened enough by massive liberal spending programs that accomplish nothing, but break the back of the taxpayer. And RN believes the time has come in this country, for less massive federal spending, not more; for lower taxes, not new inflation, and not new taxes. Most likely, McGovern will be voting for all these spending bills.

Our objective: Move him visibly into the posture of more and more government spending—and get ourselves on the "tax cut," working-man side of the issue. In my political judgment—what the nation wants is not more spending or the taxes or inflation required to pay for it—but less spending and lower taxes. Government takes too damn much of the earnings dollar in everyone's view, and we should be anti-tax in 1972.

(Indeed, in my opinion, this would apply to the so-called added value tax as well—since the average fellow is not likely to make the distinction between good and bad taxes.) One recalls that some years back, the President, in a quite effective television piece, vetoed, with a sweep of the pen, a major spending bill. Suppose we knocked off three in a row—calling for holding the line on spending and holding the line on taxes.

c. As the campaign progresses, we should increasingly portray McGovern as the pet radical of Eastern Liberalism, the darling of the *New York Times*, the hero of the Berkeley Hill Jet Set; Mr. Radical Chic. The liberal elitist are his—we have to get back the working people; and the better we portray McGovern as an elitist radical, the smaller his political base. By November, he should be postured as the Establishment's fair-haired boy, and RN postured as the Candidate of the Common Man, the working man.

(How about RN going to Cadillac Square on Labor Day this year!!)

Just as Goldwater ended up 1964 portrayed *both* as a 100% Conservative—and a radical; so George McGovern must end up in 1972 portrayed *both* as an extremist and as the pet of the national liberal Establishment. Both are, after all, true.

d. The individual nationally who has done the best job on the above is Kevin Phillips—who writes of George hobnobbing with Schlesinger, Ford Foundation liberals, the radical chic, prancing around his $100,000 Japanese palace in $15 Pucci ties. My recommendation is that PJB—using our Radical Chic materials, as well as the Assault Book materials, write, not a full-length book but a 5000-word piece, using full color, good paper, like *First Monday*, with pictures of Hiss and Hoffman and other endorsees, and that this be printed and distributed by the millions. A quality, brightly written, colorful, picture biography of McGovern of 5000 words would be infinitely superior to those old full-length hatchet biographies that are never read.

e. "The clammy hand of consistency should never rest for long upon the shoulder of a statesman."—Senator Ashurst.

In addition to portraying McGovern as radical—we should, at the same time, never let the public forget he was part and parcel of the Democratic liberal establishment that passed all the huge spending programs of the fifties and sixties that failed. McGovern's high spending, high tax proposals have been tried. They failed to help the poor; they bankrupted the workingman; they are taxing to death the middle class.

2. We cannot allow McGovern to succeed in this fraudulent effort to portray himself as Mr. Honest Citizen—rather than Mr. Politician. He can and should be nailed as a waffling, deceptive, crafty politician. In this, I disagree with the President. We should not only nail him with his radical positions, *but also* hold up a mirror to his shifts of position—which are certain to come. There are any number of sticks to beat him with—including that of the waffler who doesn't know where he stands. *The use of one does not exclude use of the other as well.*

Further, though a bit outrageous, McGovern can be charged, among Democrats, with "packing" caucuses, with "stealing" the nomination from the more popular candidate, with not representing the average man in the Democratic Party—but rather the left-wing organizers. As stated in an earlier memo, we should also wait until his people take delegates from Wallace—and then charge him with "stealing" delegates from a man in a hospital bed—discrediting his "reforms" and his "new politics," as no more than the old Gut Politics of the past. Also, anything that shows the McGovern people, making deals, softening positions, backing off, waffling—should be spotlighted—not downplayed.

3. To reverse the "underdog" image of Mr. McGovern—we should, upon his nomination, cease speaking of an easy win. We should, in public, both to rally our troops and to remove this "underdog George" label—argue that the Democrats have the largest party. We should leak polls showing us worse off than we are. We should attempt as well and often as possible, again, to show McGovern as the Candidate of the *New York Times,* the Ford Foundation, Harvard, elitist left-wing professors, snot-nosed demonstrators, black radicals, and the whole elitist gang. This contest must wind up not as they envision with McGovern, Honest Man from South Dakota against Tricky Dick and his advertising budget—it should be Richard Nixon, candidate of Middle America, against the radical darling of the Liberal Establishment.

When Harriman and Clifford, and the old gang assemble around him—that will be the moment to strike.

4. About the "new face" thing—little we can do. Except to use the attack materials herein to fill in all the blanks in the McGovern image, fill them in with some of these materials, in working-class neighborhoods, and we cannot but turn them off of George McGovern. The man has not been known well at all nationally—except for two weeks or two months at most. Impressions of McGovern may be favorable, but they are not fixed. They can be changed. And we should be moving this material into the public record. How?

a. Not bitterly or stridently. To do so gives the appearance of arrogance and power which we want desperately to avoid. Thus, when our "heavies," if you will—the Vice President, Bob Dole, etc.—use this material they should for the present be scrupulously exact and precise, and avoid for the present—the blistering attack. There will be "time enough."

b. The material should be targeted—not shot-gun. For example, abortion, amnesty, pot, the removal of the personal tax exemption (a killer for large Catholic families), these should be targeted for speakers, and for pamphlets and for ads in Catholic and ethnic areas, Catholic and ethnic papers, Catholic and ethnic forums.

c. We should focus *at once* on the welfare schemes here—and on the military budget. They hurt George in California. McGovern is clearly moving on these proposals; even his friends, at the *Post* and *Times,* are signaling him to get off them; and he is indicating that he might. They ought to be hung permanently around his neck as the first order of business.

d. We must not blow all of this assault material out of the cannon now; in 1970, we shot our wad in two weeks. There are five months between now and the election, and we should hang these one at a time around McGovern for the rest of the year.

Specific Recommendations

CATHOLICS

1. The abortion, ZPG statements, aid to parochial schools, and marijuana statements—as well as the removal of the personal tax exemption, which would be devastating to large Catholic and ethnic families—should be used in a campaign flyer (contrasted with McGovern positions) to be distributed at Catholic churches in key states on Sundays—and should be used as the basis of targeted ads in the Catholic and ethnic press. (Once after the Convention—and last 2 Sundays of campaign.)

2. Volpe could take up McGovern propositions and before a national Knights of Columbus group—indicate that unintentionally, some are "anti-Catholic" in character, which Catholics concerned about Catholic values and the preservation of the Catholic family should fight. (If we could get Volpe to do this—PJB could write the two-page speech insert, for release, all media.)

JEWISH VOTERS

3. No reason why, with McGovern, we cannot make strong inroads here. Suggest that Secretary Laird devote a single speech to the impact of McGovern's Navy cuts on the American Sixth Fleet—with the conclu-

sion, not unjustified, that the future of Israel, the survival of Israel—with McGovern's naval cuts—would be the decision of the Soviet Politburo. Again, the lead should be that—with George's defense cuts, without building the F-14 and F-15 to combat the MIG-23, "U.S. Navy could not intervene to save Israel."

4. The gist of the attack materials here on Israel—the HHH, the Jackson quotes about Israel being endangered by McGovern's position included and McGovern's voting record—should be used in speeches before Jewish groups, in soliciting funds of Jewish groups. (Needless to say, above should be surfaced on television stations in N.Y.C., Chicago, Los Angeles.)

SPACE

5. Again, targeted material here. Florida, Texas, Southern California. We should get a list of the top ten defense plants in the country, the top ten aerospace plants, as well as the five NASA centers. And leaflets should be prepared and distributed at each of these entrances—at least twice this coming fall.

Lines: *If McGovern wins, Los Angeles will have an unemployment rate that will match Seattle's and Southern California will be the West Virginia of the seventies.*

The SST votes, as well as Jackson's quotes, should be used in media ads all over the State of Washington. (We lost it in 1960.) McGovern should be blamed for not only threatening future unemployment in Seattle—but for the existing unemployment in aerospace. But, again, the pamphlets should be targeted—and the statements should be made on regional television, primarily.

DEFENSE

6. As stated, Laird is doing an excellent political job. But we ought to go down this list of military cutbacks of McGovern—determine what firms (such as McDonnell in St. Louis) build these various weapons. And all these firms and their employees should be notified by campaign workers, by ads and the like—*just what plants will have to be shut down.*

7. We have Defense already busy at work on a major speech or statement by Laird which will name all the bases that will have to be shut down, by McGovern's defense cuts. This information should be also provided to both Democratic or Republican Congressmen in that district, and to the local press there. And the Democrats should be called upon to support or repudiate McGovern's cuts.

8. In every "conservative" district—our people should be provided with the McGovern book; and Republican candidates should be encouraged to call upon their Democrats to repudiate this or that particular stand of their national candidate. This will require distribution, eventually of hundreds of copies of our completed book.

9. We believe sections of this attack book should be sent out, piece-meal, to all pro-Nixon columnists and newspapers in the country. We can have it printed in sections by the Republican National Committee—condensed even further than it is in a tight handy book for newsmen and editorial writers. But this should be done—only after the specifics in each section have been used to make front-page attacks.

10. All military publications, Navy League, etc., including the conservative publications (NR, ACU, HE, YAF, ASC) should be induced to run in brief, but full, the McGovern Defense Programs, ASAP.

11. We yet believe that the focus of attack on defense should be—at the national level—scare the hell out of the public first; and then follow on and say, that incidentally, this would also mean a loss of X million jobs. McGovern will want us to focus on jobs first—but we should not lose the Defense Argument—we are stronger here, frankly, than on the jobs argument. (For if we don't need those planes and ships and missiles, hell, everyone would want to switch over, as at the end of WWII.)

WELFARE

12. McGovern has two proposals. He has tried to get away from the $6500 per family one—but he can be hung with both. Our speakers, our people on the tube should be conversant with each.

One good line: *"Under George McGovern, two dozen and one hippies could get together and set up a commune in Taos, New Mexico, and not do a lick of work all year—and McGovern would send them every year a check for $25,000. No wonder Jerry Rubin and Abby Hoffman enthusiastically support his candidacy."*

PROGRAM FOR BUSINESS

13. Again, these two pages should be double-checked, then used for fund-raising, and for possible ads in the WSJ, and for scaring the living hell out of the business community.

14. At appropriate time, Shultz and/or John Connally should give a hair-raising speech on what the McGovern proposals would mean to American society, and the American economy and the stock market.

15. From the way the market is reacting, it is apparent that McGovern's nomination should bring about a sharp drop. We should do nothing to prevent this from happening. Indeed, if Shultz or Connally or one of them can predict that McGovern's election would mean a depression or panic on Wall Street, and do it credibly, then they might well do so.

16. Specific business groups—such as real estate firms and brokers and the like—should be the target of *direct mail,* with a brief outline for each of what the McGovern proposals mean to them. To other business groups—direct mail, in this case, is the best means of alerting the business-

man, without alerting the liberals—the mailings might well be done (these and others) by independent groups. (Needless to say, the McGovern plan to phase out the oil depletion allowance should not go unnoticed in the Lone Star State.)

INTEGRATION & RACE

17. This has to be handled gingerly—but on digging up that Ribicoff proposal, we find it legitimate to charge McGovern with wanting to use federal coercion to integrate the suburbs, with favoring "racial balance" in the nation's public schools, with believing that bussing is an "essential" tool to accomplish the job.

On this, our speakers should say, we know George is sincere, but we think that compulsory integration of neighborhoods and schools would lead to racial tensions and disorders, not racial peace and harmony: we oppose him on all three.

18. Southern Senators and Congressmen should be shown the specifics of the Black Caucus program which McGovern has endorsed "in toto"—even before we use these publicly. The Southerners will have to repudiate McGovern or force McGovern to repudiate these proposals—or take hemlock. Our candidates in the South—Senate and House—should be provided all this material by Harry Dent. As should our State Chairmen in the South. We can put it into form.

19. When McGovern backs off some of these Black radical schemes, as back off he must—we should continue to hang them around his neck—and then mail his recantation to the black media.

20. In Forest Hill, Missouri, and Warren, Michigan—and in blue collar neighborhoods, frankly, speakers should argue against the McGovern integration proposals—and in favor of retaining the integrity and value of ethnic neighborhoods.

CHICAGO AND DEMONSTRATORS

21. McGovern has said that the May Day demonstrators would not be on the streets but "having dinner at the White House" if he were elected. In this section—we have an idea for a commercial—juxtaposing RN and McGovern on the May Day demonstrators and indicating a vote for McGovern is a vote to have Rubin and Hoffman ("Guess Who's Coming to Dinner") at the White House.

22. McGovern's comments about the Chicago police ("those sons of bitches . . . those bastards") should be used—not prudishly, not condemning him for bad language. He can be excused for that—but condemned for the attitude his statement represents, a lynch mob attitude toward the nation's peace officers, a knee-jerk tendency to exonerate hell-raisers and condemn the policy. This should be done also in letters to the editor to all Chicago papers.

(Indeed, our letters operation—as well as speakers—should be using these materials to target in on sections of the country.)

23. Resurrecting McGovern's comments on Hoover would be most effectively done by the ex-AG and Pat Gray and the Vice President.

24. *Monday* can do an effective job for us—by back-paging each week one of a numbered series of effectively written and documented attacks on McGovern—giving readers materials for use themselves, in the boonies. (For example, suppose *Monday* one week simply ran the McGovern Defense Program as outlined in our package for the locals.)

ELLSBURG [sic]

25. McGovern's personal encouragement of Ellsburg [sic] to violate Federal law is a matter which we should wait to exploit . . . say two months after the Democratic Convention—it should serve as a centerpiece of a national speech—perhaps by the Vice President. (Again, our concern is that we not "mix up" our attack.) One specific area per speech, rather than the Scott, "Three A's—abortion, amnesty, and acid" approach. This last is so "cute" as to make it appear we are simply political, not serious, in our disagreement with McGovern.

VIETNAM

26. Two points should be hammered here: (a) McGovern has been constantly wrong in his predictions about what Hanoi would do; he has even been duped by Xuan Thuy and (b) the SOB would leave our prisoners in Hanoi—and count on the good will of that barbarous regime to get them back. Any attack on his Vietnam position should be prefaced by saying "We do not question his patriotism."

27. McGovern's Right from the Start can be countered—but this is a defensive maneuver for us since presumably we think his position wrong now and wrong then. Rather, the approach to be taken here is to charge that he is (a) Old Sour Grapes harassing and stabbing in the back the President who is ending a war his President could not win or end and (b) McGovern waffled all over the lot on the War, like every other Democratic politician and we have the quotes here to prove it.

RHETORIC

28. We have dug up a 1964 quote where McGovern called Goldwater the most "unstable radical and extremist" ever to run for the Presidency, which can be used against him. Also, his rhetoric, which we have documented, should be used to make either a pre-emptive or retaliatory strike for his certain charge that we are "polarizing" while he is attempting to "bring us together."

29. In terming McGovern as an extremist—we should begin by quoting Democrats like Carter, Yorty, Humphrey and Jackson, of course—

just as the Rockefeller quotes were more devastating against Goldwater than the LBJ attacks.

MCGOVERN'S FRIENDS

30. This fellow Mott, who bankrolls McGovern, is, I understand, a screaming fairy who makes $800,000 a year and pays no taxes—we are trying to interest *Monday* in doing a take-out on him in the near future.

SPEAKERS

31. To make the case against McGovern most credible, we not only need our heavy hitters—but we need the Democrats mentioned—and especially our liberals. Neal Freeman suggests the following be commissioned to do some of the rough work on "George McGovern extremism."

1. Rockefeller   4. J. S. Cooper
2. Javits   5. Douglas Dillon
3. Aiken   6. Scranton

If, of course, we could get Meany, Wallace or Jackson—that would be outstanding.

32. Ken Khachigian and I will monitor McGovern's appearances and hopefully be mailing and phoning questions to any panels or interviewers. If we have an advance man traveling ahead of the McGovern campaign—he should be providing the questions, which we can provide him.

33. Some on the media are slobbering all over George; they may have to be charged publicly with being pro-McGovern—to force them to back off a bit. In this light, Godfrey Sperling had an excellent piece today, we understand, which perhaps our people should be quoting. (Incidentally, given his performance the other night, Vanocur is a positive disaster for us—and McGovern's most effective campaigner. He may have to be fired or discredited—if we are to get anything approaching an even shake out of that left-wing taxpayer subsidized network.)

34. Again, we have to be on guard against any too harsh or strident an attack. With a hostile media out there—they will pounce on the first allegation of "Tricky Dick," or "smear" campaign. Perhaps an early address—attacking some of the smear leaks around already about the President, and some of McGovern's comments might be used to pre-empt or mitigate this certainty.

35. Mr. Dent can make the argument that George McGovern "said he would be delighted to run with a black man, but not George Wallace."

36. We need to dig up film of McGovern at some of these demonstrations with the VC flag in the background, and with demonstrators chanting and shouting, etc.

37. From McGovern's statements, it is fair to say he would cut off all assistance to our NATO ally Greece, but consider giving military aid to the black guerrillas in Southern Africa.

38. McGovern favors giving away (Black Caucus) 1% of U.S. GNP to foreign aid, with priority on Africa—which amounts to $11 billion— about a 400 percent increase in foreign aid.

39. McGovern's old statements about Henry Wallace, about the U.S. starting the Cold War, etc., should be moved into all the ethnic language publications. And all his far left background should be disseminated to the far right in the U.S. for them to publish as it is too complicated for us to handle.

NIXON'S THRU IN '72

40. This is a slogan we can turn to our own advantage. For example, if Daley is booted out of the Democratic convention—on his arrival at his Mayor's office in Chicago—some bearded types can be out front with signs—"Daley's Thru in '72—Vote McGovern—or some such. Other combinations—about Meany, for an example, come to mind. Or at Defense Plants—"The MIC is Thru in '72" (Military Industrial Complex) Vote McGovern."

We have some other thoughts and ideas—but we are sending these along for immediate consideration.

HRH 137

JUNE 10, 1972

TO: **Pat Buchanan**

FROM: **The President**

In talking with Chuck Colson after the press covering McGovern came back to Washington from California, I think there are two lines of attack that might be developed through a well-done column, a TV broadcast by one of the political commentators, or, if neither of the first two are possible, by a mailing which might get into the hands of opinion makers. Of course, a column in *Monday* is also a possibility.

The first thing should be a column on the press coverage of the McGovern campaign to date. It might be entitled, "The McGovern Protective Society." The takeoff for such a column could well be Godfrey Sperling's piece in the *Christian Science Monitor* where he speaks about the love affair between McGovern and the press. He specifically makes the point that it isn't what the press says about McGovern so much as it is what it leaves out. Colson's discussion with a top news magazine reporter interestingly enough hits this very same theme. What we have here is a situation where the working press, because they really believe in their hearts exactly what McGovern believes in, are frantically doing everything they can to clean him up and make him a respectable candidate for the nomination. My guess is that if you were to interview the working press traveling with McGovern, you would find that 90% of them were agreed with his stand on amnesty, abortion, pot, surrender in Vietnam, confiscation of wealth, the $1000 baby bonus for welfare recipients, etc. As realists they know that these positions, however, may sink him in the election. And typical of the left wing they are willing to use any means whatever to get their man nominated, even if it means covering up his real views during the period of the campaign so that he can win the election and then have the opportunity to put his views in practice through the power he acquired.

Here we see the fundamental difference between the right wing extremists and the left wing extremists. The right wingers would rather lose than give up one iota as far as principle is concerned. The left wing's primary motivation is power. They are always willing to compromise their principles in order to get power because they know that without power they cannot put their principles into effect.

In any event, I think this theme could be extremely interesting if picked up by columnists, commentators and political experts across the country. It is very important in terms of the final campaign that the media be effectively discredited. In this instance, they are asking for it and when their own colleagues, like Sperling and Colson's contact, complain about their biased coverage of the McGovern campaign, it provides an opening which should be exploited.

Of course, one of the very best ways for this opening to be exploited would be to have one of the Democratic candidates like Humphrey or Muskie pick it up. Perhaps getting this theme into their camps might be an idea. In any event, if Buchanan could write out a good quotable piece on this, Colson and his group, with Buchanan's advice, could probably find a way to get it broadly circulated.

The second column, which I think could prove useful in the longer term, is somewhat similar in theme to the first one but broader in scope. What we have here is a situation where the Eastern Establishment media finally has a candidate who almost totally shares their views. Here again, if you consider the real ideological bent of the *New York Times,* the *Washington Post, Time, Newsweek* and the three television networks, you will find overwhelmingly that their editorial bias comes down on the side of amnesty, pot, abortion, confiscation of wealth (unless it is theirs), massive increases in welfare, unilateral disarmament, reduction of their defenses, and surrender in Vietnam. Now they have a candidate within sight of the nomination who shares all these views. Now the country will find out whether what the media has been standing for during these last five years really represents the majority thinking of the country or is, in fact, a minority view. Incidentally, that piece by Father Greeley in the *Wash-*

ington Star recently may be somewhat prophetic in this respect. As you may recall, he entitled it, "The Movement Has Had It." I would put it somewhat broader: The Liberal Establishment Media May Have Had It.

I do not mean to suggest that the battle ahead will not be a vicious, brutal one because the left wing media will fight much more cleverly than the right wingers have fought. As I pointed out above, they will clean up their candidate, they will lie, distort and do anything that is necessary to get into power. They never allow their piously held principles to get in the way of their overriding drive to gain and wield power.

In any event, I think these are two things which Buchanan has been writing on eloquently over the past ten years and he should be able to do justice to them in developing these themes now. It will then be up to the operating staff to find ways to get Buchanan's effort appropriately distributed.

cc: Chuck Colson

PRESIDENT RICHARD NIXON'S DAILY DIARY

(See Travel Record for Travel Activity)

PLACE DAY BEGAN	DATE (Mo., Day, Yr.)
	JUNE 12, 1972
THE WHITE HOUSE	TIME DAY
WASHINGTON, D.C.	8:33 A.M. MONDAY

TIME		PHONE P=Placed R=Received		ACTIVITY
In	Out	Lo	LD	
8:33				The President had breakfast.
8:45				The President went to the Oval Office.
9:05	9:07			The President met with Marjorie P. Acker, Secretary to Rose Mary Woods.
9:09	10:57	P		The President met with his Assistant, H. R. Haldeman.
9:56	9:58			The President talked with his Personal Physician, Dr. William M. Lukash.
11:10	11:15			The President met with his Deputy Assistant, Alexander P. Butterfield.
11:21				The President went to the Red Room in the Residence.
11:21	11:26			The President met with:
				The First Lady
				Warren E. Burger, Chief Justice of the U.S. Supreme Court
				Richard G. Kleindienst, Acting Attorney General
				Mrs. Richard G. Kleindienst
				George P. Shultz, Director of the OMB and Secretary of the Treasury–designate
				Mrs. George P. Shultz
				Caspar W. Weinberger, Deputy Director of the OMB and Director of the OMB–designate
				Mrs. Caspar W. Weinberger
				The President was briefed by his Special Assistant, Mark I. Goode.
11:26				The President and the First Lady, accompanied by Chief Justice Burger, went to the East Room.
11:26	11:41			The President participated in the swearing-in ceremonies of Mr. Kleindienst as Attorney General, of Mr. Shultz as Secretary of the Treasury, and of Mr. Weinberger as Director of the OMB. Chief Justice Burger administered the oaths of office. For a list of attendees, see *APPENDIX "A."*
				Members of the press, in/out
				White House photographer, in/out
11:41				The President and the First Lady went to the Blue Room.
11:41	12:13			The President and the First Lady hosted a reception in honor of Attorney General Kleindienst, Secretary Shultz, and Mr. Weinberger. For a list of guests, see *APPENDIX "A."*
				White House photographer, in/out
12:13				The President returned to the Oval Office.
12:19	1:31			The President met with Mr. Haldeman.
1:33				The President went to his office in the EOB.

PRESIDENT RICHARD NIXON'S DAILY DIARY

(See Travel Record for Travel Activity)

PLACE DAY BEGAN	DATE (Mo., Day, Yr.)
	JUNE 12, 1972
THE WHITE HOUSE	TIME DAY
WASHINGTON, D.C.	2:32 P.M. MONDAY

TIME		PHONE P=Placed R=Received		ACTIVITY
In	Out	Lo	LD	
2:32		P		The President telephoned Senator James L. Buckley (Conservative–New York). The President talked with Patricia A. Gleason, Secretary to Senator Buckley.
2:35		P		The President telephoned CBS News Correspondent Dan Rather. The call was not completed.
2:43	2:45	P		The President talked with Mr. Rather.
2:52	2:56		P	The President talked long distance with Senator Jacob K. Javits (R–New York) in New Haven, Connecticut.
3:02				The President returned to the Oval Office.
3:03	3:24			The President met with: Bui Diem, departing Ambassador from the Republic of Vietnam to the U.S. Maj. Gen. Alexander M. Haig, Jr., Deputy Assistant Members of the press, in/out White House photographer, in/out
3:30	4:09			The President met and was photographed with: Donald F. Rodgers, Consultant Michael P. Balzano, Staff Assistant Charles W. Colson, Special Counsel White House photographer, in/out The President met with:
4:09	5:40			John N. Mitchell, Campaign Director for the Committee for the Reelection of the President
4:40	5:40			Mr. Haldeman
5:39	6:07			Henry A. Kissinger, Assistant
6:05	6:09			Mr. Butterfield
6:09				The President went to the South Grounds of the White House.
6:11	6:19			The President and the First Lady motored from the South Grounds of the White House to Pier 1, Washington Navy Yard with Mr. and Mrs. Edward F. Cox.
6:24	8:25			The Presidential party went boating on the *Sequoia*.
7:00	7:45			The Presidential party had dinner on board.
8:25				The Presidential party boarded the *Rockfish*.
8:34				The *Rockfish* docked at the Mt. Vernon pier.
8:39	8:47			The Presidential party flew by helicopter from Mt. Vernon, Virginia, to the South Grounds of the White House. For a list of passengers, see *APPENDIX "B."*
8:50				The Presidential party returned to the second-floor Residence.
8:56	9:05	P		The President talked with Mr. Colson.

PPF4, HRH162

[The following is an excerpt from the President's News Summary of June 12, 1972, with a marking by Alex Butterfield indicating that Mr. Nixon had read the document.]

Politics

RN holds his widest leads over McG and HHH in latest Gallup Poll taken while RN was in USSR: RN—43%; McG—30%; Wallace—19%. RN—43%; HHH—26%; Wallace—22% with Wallace out, RN margin increases: RN— 53%; McG—34%; RN—52%; HHH—32%. Gallup noted 22% for Wallace was highest ever.

Mullaney in *NY Times,* writes that most Wall Streeters believe RN could defeat McGovern.

2,500 blacks gathered in DC to support RN and to enrich GOP by more than $200,000 at a fund-raising dinner. Reelection aide Jones said RN "has delivered on black capitalism. We are doing better." McKissick, former Dir. of CORE said "the reason we've got problems with the economy and with civil rights is because the labor unions aren't responsive to our needs."

Pollster Field says if Wallace decides to campaign for RN he would almost cinch his reelection. He said Wallace could deliver 147 electoral votes from the South.

Noting $10 million contributions to RN's reelection, Common Cause said: "The sad fact is that the refusal of the President . . . to reveal where $10 million has come from can only lead the people to conclude that the office of the Presidency already has been sold to the highest bidders."

Replying to the group's statement, Mitchell said: "anyone from Common Cause or anywhere else should be severely chastised verbally and I am doing so here." "There is no possibility of anyone contributing to the reelection of the President having any influence on the operations of this government as long as RN is Pres," Mitchell said.

O'Brien said GOP has a "moral obligation to release those names. I think RN should personally instruct John Mitchell to make those names public."

AP leads a dispatch: "The first full-scale financial reports required under the new Fed elections law trickled in today and they showed—as expected—that GOP war chests are bulging while Democrats are reeling from multimillion-dollar primary spending."

POF40

JUNE 12, 1972

TO: **Bob Haldeman**

FROM: **The President**

You might discuss with John Mitchell sometime the possibility of setting up a rather broad advisory group of maybe a dozen people or twenty, supplementing the hard-core small group which we already have. This gets more players into the act and it also may get us some ideas that we otherwise might fail to get on our own.

PPF4; HRH162

JUNE 12, 1972

TO: **Bob Haldeman**

FROM: **The President**

Would it not be well for Mitchell to have a two-day strategy session, including not just the top four but perhaps expanding it to include various work groups like Price, Garment, etc.[?] I think it might be well over this next weekend to have a strategy session so that recommendations could be made which I could look over as to what we do between now and the Convention and thereafter. The Buchanan memorandum is a very good document from which to start and then we could make some decisions as to where we go from here.

PPF4; HRH162, 230

JUNE 12, 1972

TO: **John Mitchell**

FROM: **The President**

In reading Buchanan's analysis, you will note he is highly critical of our organization compared to what we had in 1968. I am inclined to think that some of his criticism may be justified and that some of it may miss the mark, but at least we should have it in mind as we build the organization for the future.

In 1968 when we were the outs we naturally had more volunteers and more zeal and determination than we perhaps have in 1972. On the other hand, there is no reason why we cannot have in 1972 a considerable degree of fire and enthusiasm if we can only charge up the troops effectively. I think one danger that must be guarded against is to over-pay people or to have staffs that are too large. It is certainly true that too large a paid staff means a staff that is somewhat fat and lazy. I am not suggesting that ours is either at this point, but the Buchanan criticism is something that must be examined.

I am not, incidentally, so impressed with his argument that our conservative foot soldiers were the ones who beat the union troops in 1968. As a matter of fact, the conservatives weren't all that enthusiastic about us in 1968 as Pat probably will remember if he examines the situation pretty carefully and objectively. Nevertheless, there is a need for having a lean, hard-hitting, enthusiastic organization to combat the McGovern organization. I think the way we can do it is to have people who not only are *for* us but also by having people in our organization who are really stirred up about the great danger of McGovern becoming President and who will get out and work their heads off in order to beat him. People can get far more excited working against a candidate than they can working for one.

On another subject, I think it is important to keep the Republican organization and the Citizens for Nixon or Democrats for Nixon, or whatever we are going to call it, separated wherever possible. We should give them each separate tasks and then have them work both sides of the street.

cc: Bob Haldeman
    Chuck Colson

CWC19; HRH162, 230

JUNE 12, 1972

TO: **Charles Colson**

FROM: **The President**

Just a reminder that I would like somebody in your office to identify to the extent possible those members of the press travelling with McGovern who are having the so-called "love affair" with McGovern to which Godfrey Sperling, Lindsay of *Newsweek* and others have referred. It may not be possible to identify them completely but I would imagine a few names would come to mind immediately—for example, Paul Hope of the *Star*, Apple of the *Times* and I would assume some television people. At least, I think getting that list together would be worthwhile and then seeing that it gets in the hands of Ziegler and others so that we know whom to watch in the future.

PPF4

JUNE 12, 1972

TO: **Henry Kissinger**

FROM: **The President**

Would you go over the record of all of our conversations with the Soviet leaders and get the best anecdotes and colorful phrases which they used during the course of our meetings. You will recall that I had this done from the record of your meetings with Brezhnev. I would like the record of both meetings to be looked over again with this in mind so that I can have a good compilation of anecdotes and of the most colorful language that any of the three used during the course of our meetings. I am not interested here in substance but only in anecdote and phrase-making material.

PPF4; HRH162

POLITICAL STRATEGY PAPER

JUNE 12, 1972

We should probably have a strategy meeting, or retreat, going for a couple of days to get down to some basic decisions, both from the standpoint of therapy and ideas.

There should be a bigger advisory group putting in some thinking time such as the Committee of 100 and the Committee of 9, who thought they were running the Campaign, and were actually helpful for ideas and in enlisting loyalty.

We may be missing some smart people, such as some key Senators and Congressmen, or some Governors.

We are overlooking some of the old hands on our staff such as Price, Garment, Safire, Finch, Dent, Buchanan, Chotiner, Rumsfeld and Weinberger.

The great danger is for two or three people to think that they are the fount of all wisdom. Of course, the other side of this coin is also worse, which is to try and run a campaign with a dozen or a hundred people. We need to get better organized on the process of touching bases, however.

We must avoid getting too ingrown in terms of political strategy decisions. We should follow the pattern at the retreat of the August 15 Camp David meeting with sub-groups working on specific areas and then reporting to a small executive group of two or three.

HRH

HRH179

POLITICAL STRATEGY PAPER

JUNE 12, 1972

One weakness of the Buchanan memorandum is that it fails to recognize the necessity to keep *our* strength up front and center. In other words, all of our attack lines on the opposition should end up also emphasizing our strength.

Wc must not gct trapped into McGovern's bog of peddling himself as a new face. If people want new ideas and so forth, this Administration has had the bold[est] initiatives in history.

Buchanan deals almost entirely with domestic matters and totally misses our big issues which are in foreign policy. Who is the bold leader? Who is the fresh leader? Who is the dramatic leader in foreign policy?

We should attack McGovern in a way that surfaces our point, not just hitting his points. We should not get trapped into putting out the enemy line.

We have to build the foreign policy issue in terms of the question of changing horses in mid-stream. In other words, President Nixon has launched some very major, far-reaching, foreign policy initiatives. We can't afford to let an inexperienced novice come in and pick up the reins at this point. We cannot afford to have McGovern in the White House in terms of foreign policy. His inexperience and naivete in the foreign policy field would be disastrous. Do we really want "White Flag McGovern" in the White House?

We need an addendum written to the Buchanan memorandum that takes up the point of how we attack McGovern in a way that builds the President's foreign policy image.

In other words, Buchanan overlooks our strong point in foreign policy. One reason for this is because he doesn't agree with the major foreign policy initiatives.

Someone needs to develop a battle plan as to what the holes are in the Buchanan piece. What are the four things that *we* want to have come out?

HRH

HRH179

JUNE 12, 1972

TO: **Mr. H. R. Haldeman**

FROM: **Bruce Kehrli**

RE: **McGovern**

Please note the attached comments from the June 12 Weekend News Review.

Magruder and John Mitchell are aware of this comment from Lyn Nofziger and will reprimand him for it.

cc: Alexander P. Butterfield

Semple, in *NY Times*, writes that "the men who are running RN's re-election campaign seem to worry about the prospect of a McG candidacy the closer they get to McG himself." While nat'l aides are confident they can pin "radical" tag on George, Semple says others in primary states are cautious. One Calif. RN worker said: "Contrived or real, McG is projecting an impression of freshness, seriousness of purpose and candor, building himself for a direct confrontation with the old politics in Nov."*

Semple, in earlier piece, says "the suspicion is that RN is richly enjoying the commotion" caused by his refusal to specify VP. He adds that new Connally mission, tho, has prompted some to ask if they aren't being conned "by a Pres whose taste for little surprises and grand theatre is beginning to make even the great Lyndon look like an amateur." Semple says WH staff feel VP Agnew will be on the ticket, but writer feels that the VP's ambiguity about whether he really wants the top job may affect RN's choice.

Furguson writes that primary results "say clearly that moods and personalities matter far more to the voter in 1972 than issues and events." Thus RN, who's doing all he can to influence issues and events, may still face problems. RN "will be open to just the same kind of damaging contrast with McG" as HHH was in Calif., says Ernest.

NY Times magazine has article by Rice on Sen. Smith of Maine. She faces a tough primary and/or reelection campaign, says author, as many feel she's old or hasn't done enough for Maine.

C.S. Monitor's Strout writes that the "much-criticized U.S. presidential primary system seems once more to have vindicated itself." Its cruel but effective ordeal by publicity has cut down the supposed front-runner, and brought another from obscurity into lead. And further, primaries have delineated the "major issue of the campaign—the depth of the current of unrest and dissatisfaction running through U.S." "Many criticize Presidential primaries but it's hard to find an alternative," he concludes. [. . .]

NBC's Brokaw reported from Calif., where McGovern's delegates are "more than one-half women: 40% under age 30; 19% black, and 19% Mexican-American." Many delegates are so poor, said Brokaw, that McG's people will pay their way to MB. Brokaw said that "this kind" of slate has a problem: So many interests are represented and so many feel so strongly on speaking out, few things will be settled quickly. . . . UPI reports Tunney was booed and hissed when his name was put before McG delegates at Calif. Dem meeting.

Mankiewicz claims McG is about 150 short of 1,509 needed for nomination.

Lyle Denniston, in full-pg article headed: "Just What *Would* McGovern Do?" attempts to answer the question. He says McGovern platform "is one of exceptional detail," and he goes on to detail, point by point, McG's platform. . . . McGrory says McG offers hope of a "second Camelot"—a hope that gov't "might become rational and human again, as it was in JFK's day." JFK was "responsive and civil and . . . those qualities seemed irrevocably lost during the LBJ–RN years."

Wash *Star* edit headlined "Defense Could Be *the* Campaign Issue" says McG's pledge to cut $30 billion from defense "is a most essential feature of the McG program and one which'll be certain to stir bitter controversy." *Star* says McG defense proposals "are all highly dubious" and "they would certainly reduce the capacity of U.S. to defend itself and its allies abroad." Also, "they'd have a devastating effect on the military-political balance of world power."

Braden writes that McG "has made up his mind to offer VP spot to EMK, but McG's younger aides are strongly opposed to it.

Peirce, of *National Journal,* writes in Wash *Post* that McGovern's rise "marks a portentous turn in U.S. politics," and he adds that in Nov. RN "will bear the burden of virtually symbolizing the politics of stalemate and rhetoric that has frustrated the country. Fairly or not, McG seems fresh and direct by contrast."**

*HANDWRITTEN NOTE FROM THE PRESIDENT TO HALDEMAN IN MARGIN: "It is good to run scared—*but* it is *stupid* to put out *their* line." (Emphasis in original)
**HANDWRITTEN COMMENT BY THE PRESIDENT: "here is where our people should be talking about our bold foreign policy initiative never undertaken by JFK et al."

POF40

W/RN from ss84

JUNE 12, 1972

TO: **Mr. Chuck Colson**

FROM: **Bruce Kehrli**

RE: **Hanoi Comments**

It was requested that you note the following from the June 12 Weekend News Review:

Hanoi paper Nhan Dan *said "the repeated successes" of McGovern in Dem primaries "manifests the great intensity and scope of anti-war feelings" in U.S. . . .*

cc: H. R. Haldeman
   Alexander P. Butterfield
   Ron Ziegler
   Henry Kissinger

POF40

EYES ONLY

JUNE 12, 1972

TO: **John Mitchell**

FROM: **Charles Colson**

Thus far our apparatus here in the White House has failed to deliver any information about Mr. Kimelman (see attached article).* I have been told by very reliable sources that several agencies investigated Mr. Kimelman's affairs. Among other things he apparently profited through his father-in-law from the deal in which Udall tried to convert public lands in St. Croix for airport use. This was publicized at the time quite widely. I am further told that as part of our efforts to get Postal Reform through, Moe Udall requested that we suppress the information that we had. Since Kimelman is McGovern's chief fund raiser, I think we are unwise not to be pursuing this with real vigor. Maybe you can do better talking to Kleindienst than John Dean has thus far been able to do. If we have McGovern on one here, we should not let it drop.

cc: John Dean

*["The Money Man for McGovern" from *Newsweek*.]

CWC5, 48, 131

EYES ONLY

JUNE 12, 1972

TO: **John Dean**

FROM: **Charles Colson**

I have received a well-informed tip that there are income tax discrepancies involving the returns of Harold J. Gibbons, a Vice President of the

Teamsters Union in St. Louis. This has come to me on very, very good authority.

Gibbons, you should know, is an all-out enemy, a McGovernite, ardently anti-Nixon. He is one of the 3 labor leaders who were recently invited to Hanoi.

Please see if this one can be started on at once and if there is an informer's fee, let me know. There is a good cause at which it can be donated.

4 SENATE HEARINGS 1686

JUNE 12, 1972

TO: **Al Haig**

FROM: **Chuck Colson**

I received the following information last week from Lou Harris who was visited by Vladimer L. Rykov:

"He said they can't sell the North Vietnamese on that. First he gave me all that crap about—you know, they really have to back up Hanoi and all this stuff and I said, Look, I've been through all this parallels and crap, and I said, get to the heart of it, you're giving them the supplies and the weaponry and they can't stand up without you, right? And I can understand you're worried about the Chinese coming in if you double cross Hanoi so they can understand your delicate position, but what we're talking about is we've got some very definite peace terms and all you have to say is these are good peace terms and we see no reason why you don't take them. I said it's as simple as that. I said the one point you'll never get the American people to agree to is the coalition government and I got out my column for Monday and showed it to them—gave them a copy and I know enough with them to know they think that's a great coup. So I said here—I went through the prisoner thing and the coalition government thing and came last to the neutral government and said, now I'm speaking just for myself here, not anybody else, but I said the American people are willing to go this far. It's not that they have great faith in the Thieu government, in fact they are willing to see a neutralist government, but they can't take having Communists in the government in Saigon. He said, and he really surprised me, he said, I think Hanoi would take that neutralist government, they will not take cease-fire because he said they are afraid that as long as Thieu is in that a cease-fire that two forces [sic] will go on forays and take over land and all this kind of thing, so their home Vietnam, South Vietnam, would make quite a difference, that's why they didn't like the cease fire. But he said, this solution you'd have peace, prisoners back and everything. He said, this is my personal view, I don't know what went on between Mr. Brezhnev and Mr. Nixon but on the other hand, they know a guy this new here doesn't come unless . . . He did see Dobrynin yesterday when he got back, so I don't think he would say anything he didn't think was official, do you?"

cwc13

JUNE 12, 1972

TO: **Doug Hallett**

FROM: **Chuck Colson**

Please dig out for me the last two or three campaign speeches given by Prime Minister Macmillan in 1959. Dick Scammon at lunch last week quoted at length and from memory on what he regarded as very important passages from one of these speeches. He recalls it as the last campaign speech. In any event, it is one which eloquently called upon the British people to give Macmillan their trust and confidence.

cwc131

JUNE 12, 1972

TO: **Ken Khachigian**

FROM: **Charles Colson**

Could you assemble a collection of photographs of McGovern that show him with his raunchiest-looking supporters? I vividly recall the one on the eve of the Wisconsin Primary when he was surrounded by long-haired, shaggy-looking bomb-throwers. What we would like are perhaps 20 or 25 of the best photographs which show McGovern really with the kookiest kind of people. This is necessary for a research project which has to be completed by mid-week, so I would appreciate whatever you can put together by Tuesday night. Of course stills can be made from TV shots, which probably means that you will need to review some of the tapes as well.

cwc13, 131

JUNE 12, 1972

TO: **Ken Khachigian**

FROM: **Charles Colson**

Can we get the proceedings of the 1948 Wallace Convention? Specifically McGovern's speech to the Convention? Do you have any research in this area that we could use? I need this immediately because some of our labor friends would like to distribute it.

cwc13, 131

JUNE 12, 1972

TO: **Bruce Kehrli**

FROM: **Chuck Colson**

RE: **Your memo of June 7th (attached)**

I am staggered by your memo of June 7th. It is completely inapplicable to anyone in the Colson operation in any way, shape or form and I would hope that it would be equally inapplicable to other parts of the White House. I can't believe that you are really encouraging any vacations this summer. There are 148 days between now and election!

cwc131

JUNE 12, 1972

TO: **Ken Khachigian**

FROM: **Fred Fielding**

RE: **McGovern**

Following up our conversations regarding Senator McGovern's activity while at Northwestern during the Wallace era, you may wish to check further on the following items:

1. 1947 "open letter" by several Northwestern faculty members urging Wallace to run for the Presidency.

2. It is reported that McGovern prepared leaflets for Wallace espousing anti–cold war causes (including the defeat of the Mundt-Nixon bill).

3. McGovern's activities in the campaign of Curtis MacDougal (Northwestern journalism professor) running against Senator Paul Douglas in 1948.

4. McGovern letter to the editor of the *Mitchell Daily Republic* endorsing Wallace (1947–48).

5. McGovern letter to *Mitchell Daily Republic* regarding a speech on Wallace's behalf he made before the local Kiwanis club.

6. Any recorded votes, speeches, etc., by McGovern at the time he was a member of the Illinois delegation to the Progressive Party Convention in Philadelphia.

7. The subject and content of McGovern's graduate dissertation.

I am sure that you have already checked out McGovern's early campaigns, but I understand that his race against Harold Lovre for Congress in 1956 was a most bitter contest.

cc: Dick Howard

JFB2; CWC78

JUNE 13, 1972

TO: **Pat Buchanan**

FROM: **Charles Colson**

At a meeting with Haldeman today, it was decided that all requests for information with respect to opposition candidates should come through you. Hence for your information, enclosed is a series of requests I have been making of John Dean for information on a Mr. Kimelman. I have also now asked Mitchell to get in the act. Maybe you have sources beyond Dean's. I have a reporter ready to go with this if we can give him anything.

CWC5, 131

JUNE 14, 1972

Send a copy of the Irving Kristol book to Governor Reagan with a cover note from the President saying:

Dear Ron:

I came across a new book that I found extremely perceptive in its analysis of some of our political, social, and educational institutions.

I thought you might find Chapter VII on restructuring the universities especially interesting and I commend it to you.

Cordially,

RN

HRH112

JUNE 14, 1972

TO: **The President**

FROM: **Ray Price**

RE: **The McGovern Eclipse**

A fascinating fact that my staff just brought to my attention: On the day the Democratic convention opens in Miami, July 10, there will be a total eclipse of the sun. The eclipse will be full in Alaska and Northern Canada and partial in the rest of North America and Western Europe.

At 4:42 P.M. EDT, the sun will be 80 percent covered in New York City.

They even made the sun not to shine . . . !

HANDWRITTEN NOTE FROM THE PRESIDENT TO COLSON: "Your people should be able to do something about this—"

POF17; CWC5, 79; SS83

JUNE 14, 1972

Mitchell Folder

Notes for Discussion with Mitchell:

1. Hint at Secretary of Defense.—Jackson

2. Jackson told Kissinger he wanted to help in the campaign against McGovern.

CWC48

JUNE 16, 1972

TO: **The President's File**

FROM: **John Andrews**

RE: **Color Report on Vann, Medal of Freedom Ceremony**

The authoritative account of the President's private remarks to the Vann family prior to press pool's arrival in the office will no doubt surface in the column of Joe Alsop, who was on hand throughout. But being (like Alsop) a Vann admirer and a pretty much unreconstructed hawk who thinks we might just end up "winning" the Vietnam War, the Bellicose Ear takes pleasure in recording at least a paraphrase:

The President spoke quietly and with obvious personal feeling both for the man being honored and for what the man had come to stand for. He used the words "dedication and selflessness" in characterizing John Vann's service as a military and civilian leader. He never asked more of his men than he was willing to do himself, RN said, "which is why he was in that helicopter."

RN said he had known Vann since his '65, '66, and '67 visits to the war zone. Most vivid personal recollection of their last visit "when we said goodbye right here in front of these flags"—aside from substance of conversation, which RN said in open portion of ceremony had been Vann's continued faith in a favorable war outcome—was Vann's firm grip as they shook hands.

"The totality of his service in Vietnam, beyond the call of duty as a military man, and far, far beyond it as a civilian adviser," surely merited the Congressional Medal of Honor, RN said, "and I want you in the family to know I would have given it to him if the law permitted." Instead we gave [the] Medal of Freedom, the highest decoration a civilian can receive.

This country is in his debt, RN said, and so is South Vietnam, whose chance of avoiding Communist tyranny when this long war ends will be in good measure to Vann's credit. Long in the future, the President concluded, South Vietnamese children may well read about him with the same gratitude that Americans feel for Lafayette—"as the citation says, he was that kind of hero."

Ron Ziegler has indicated his disinclination to give out any of this to the press, but I feel that at least the touches about the handshake and the Medal of Honor should be slipped out, inasmuch as Alsop was privy to all of it.

POF89

JUNE 16, 1972

TO: **H. R. Haldeman**

FROM: **John Dean**

RE: **Impeachment Advertisement in *New York Times***

This is to bring you up to date on the status of the counterattack against the "impeachment" advertisement that appeared in the *New York Times* on May 31. As you undoubtedly know, the Committee for the Re-Election of the President has added its protest to complaints already filed by the Schuchman Foundation's Center for the Public Interest. On June 9, Glenn Sedam, General Counsel of the Committee, filed a formal complaint with the Comptroller General and the Clerk of the House and requested an investigation of the circumstances surrounding publication of the ad. On the same date, John Mitchell also wrote to John Gardner suggesting that Common Cause investigate the ad. Copies of their letters are attached at Tab A.

On June 7, the Schuchman Foundation followed up its complaints with letters to all Congressmen listed in the ad's "honor roll" asking whether they had provided the National Committee for the Impeachment with the certifications required under the Federal Election Campaign Act. A copy of one of these letters is attached at Tab B. So far, Representatives Conyers, Chisholm and Abzug have replied. Each denies issuing any certification or authorizing the use of his name in the ad. Copies of these responses, attached at Tab C, are being forwarded to the Comptroller General.

The General Accounting Office has also sent copies of the complaints to the *New York Times* and the listed sponsors of the ad and has requested that the charges be answered. No replies have yet been received. The *New York Times*, however, is apparently feeling the heat as it partially responded in an editorial today which piously stated the paper's policy of keeping advertising columns open to all comers. The editorial carefully refrained from any discussion of the charge that the impeachment ad, aside from being in very poor taste, violated the Federal Election Campaign Act.

We have investigated the sponsors listed in the ad and discovered that three of these individuals—Alfred Hassler, Corliss Lamont and Robert Bobrick—have close ties to the Communist Party and communist front organizations. Interestingly enough, Hassler and Ron Young, another person listed as a sponsor, in a letter to the editor of the *Times* published today denied having ever given permission for use of their names in connection with the ad and asked that they not be connected with the impeachment campaign. Another sponsor, William Stringfellow, was arrested and indicted for knowingly harboring Daniel Berrigan, who was captured at Stringfellow's house. However, we do not believe that this information can be usefully exploited to discredit this ad due to the fact that antiwar activists have long been publicly known to have close ties to communist organizations without any significant impact on their effectiveness.

Confidential information recently received also reveals that the Peoples Coalition for Peace and Justice (PCPJ) and the War Resisters League (WRL) are working on their own drive to impeach the President. PCPJ is the group that brought us May Day while WRL is a branch of a worldwide pacifist organization. Both organizations are reported to have adopted this strategy in reaction to their failure to launch a successful Spring 1972 antiwar offensive. It is significant to note in this regard that one of the sponsors of the ad, David McReynolds, is an active leader of WRL.*

*Memo withdrawn from JFB5 because release would constitute a clearly unwarranted invasion of privacy or libel of a living person or would disclose investigatory information for law enforcement purposes.

JWD5

JUNE 16, 1972

TO: **H. R. Haldeman**

FROM: **John Dean**

RE: **McGovern War Record**

As I am sure you are aware, following the release of the attached article and a reiteration of the same charges by William Loeb, McGovern has asked DOD to release his military "201" personnel file.

Arrangements have been made to insure that if and when the Army does release copies of the contents of this file to McGovern, a public announcement of the same will be made which will indicate the number of documents in the file. This should reduce the chances that McGovern will only release selected and favorable documents.

You should also be aware that there is nothing in McGovern's file which directly substantiates the allegation about his cowardice. We are advised that there is only one paragraph in one of the documents which is not complimentary to the Senator. Also, the file lists the number of combat missions McGovern flew, and although no additional notations are made the reviewer stated that the number seemed somewhat low by comparison to other pilots flying in combat at that time. The file also contains the citations for McGovern's decorations, including his Distinguished Flying Cross, and reflects his various promotions during his military career.

The party reviewing the file also advised that there is no evidence that any documents have been removed heretofore, or that there had been any tampering with the file.

cc: Chuck Colson

CWC79;
21 SENATE HEARINGS 9894

JUNE 16, 1972

TO: **John Dean**

FROM: **Chuck Colson**

Has anyone run any checks or investigations on the key McGovern staffers? I was told yesterday that Gordon Weil has some very questionable things in his background. He is apparently one of the chief brain trusters who travels with McGovern.

cc: Pat Buchanan

CWC13;
10 SENATE HEARINGS 4247;
21 SENATE HEARINGS 9896

JUNE 16, 1972

TO: **Joanne Gordon**

FROM: **Charles Colson**

Would you please have Signal rerun the first McGovern-Humphrey debate from California. I would like to know how McGovern refers to Russia; what precise phrases he uses throughout the program—specifically, does he simply say "The Union."

CWC13

ACTION MEMORANDUM

JUNE 19, 1972

Get the Lincoln Amnesty point researched. McGovern is saying that he is for amnesty just as Lincoln was, or in the Lincoln tradition. The President's view, based on Sandburg's report, is that Lincoln did not in effect provide true amnesty. He permitted the deserters to rejoin their units and serve and thereby escape the penalties of desertion. In any event, we need a clear-cut statement as to what Lincoln did do, and then a plan for use of this to shoot down McGovern's contention.

HRH

HRH112

ACTION MEMORANDUM

JUNE 19, 1972

Look for a range of beach possibilities for the President's use at Rehoboth or other close-by areas where he can commute by helicopter from Washington at times when the weather in Florida is not satisfactory.

    We need, of course, the same degree of seclusion and security that we have to have anyplace else. The prime requirements would be an adequate house and hopefully a private beach area with ocean swimming.

HRH

HRH112

JUNE 19, 1972

TO: **John Dean**

FROM: **Charles Colson**

RE: **Howard Hunt**

Dick Howard just discovered the attached in his chron file; this is a copy and Bruce Kehrli is looking for the original. I think it can be flatly and clearly said that his services here terminated on March 31, 1972. There is also attached a report of a conversation which Joan Hall had with Howard Hunt approximately 6 or 8 weeks ago.

CWC131;
3 SENATE HEARINGS 1157

JUNE 19, 1972

TO: **Charles Colson**

FROM: **Joan Hall**

RE: **Discussion with Howard Hunt**

For the record, approximately 6 or 8 weeks ago in a casual conversation, I asked Howard Hunt why he had not turned in any time sheets. He replied, "That is being taken care of elsewhere." I did not inquire any further and the subject was dropped. (Note: I had initialed his time sheets each month and was merely curious why I had not received one.)

CWC131;
3 SENATE HEARINGS 1159

JUNE 19, 1972

TO: **Bruce Kehrli**

FROM: **John Dean**

RE: **Donation of Tennis Court: Camp David**

In response to your inquiry, the Secretaries of the respective military departments are each specifically authorized by statute to accept gifts for the installations under their command. Thus, there is no legal impediment in regard to Mr. Kendall's offer to donate and install a tennis court at the Camp David facility.

Procedurally, the offer should be made in the first instance to the local commanding officer having jurisdiction over Camp David, who should then refer it to his Secretary for approval. While under some circumstances conditions for maintenance, etc., are imposed on the donor, such is highly unlikely in the instant case and in any event we can effectively deal with that problem if it should arise.

By way of further information, it would appear that the donating corporation will be eligible to take a charitable deduction for the value of this gift. We are seeking confirmation of this opinion by IRS and will give you a definitive answer on this in the immediate future.

JFB2

[*The following is an excerpt from the President's News Summary of June 20, 1972, which markings show that he read.*]

Politics

With 40% in, Sen. Smith led challenger Monks 19,500 to 8,100. Porteous scored a landslide win over Young for 1st Dist. GOP House nomination while Bangor Mayor Cohen narrowly led Abbott Greene in early returns.

VP Agnew told the Jaycees that the "elitists of the new left and their renegade followers," and not the "system," are due for a shakeup in Nov.

DNC BREAK-IN

Dole on film on NBC said he was "surprised and dismayed" and in favor of wide-open investigation to put the facts on the table. On CBS/ABC Dole said he could see no reason for the break-in. What was to be gained by such a "despicable" act? NBC reporter said that tho no one has proved GOP is behind it, Dems are instituting court action anyway. . . . After report on Court's wire tap decision, Cronkite said illegal bugging was apparently 1 of aims of break-in. O'Brien on CBS/ABC film said he'd "never seen such a crass violation of individual rights." On ABC Larry began his speech to mayors by also addressing "John Mitchell—wherever you're bugging me." Rest of speech, said new ABC man Kaplow, was standard political oratory w/O'Brien trying to take credit from RN's foreign policies by rapping domestic programs. Dole followed on ABC calling O'Brien's response straight partisan and posturing reaction.

ABC noted McCord was hired on recommendation of Al Wong, head of Secret Service technical security branch. ABC only net to note McCord was fired Mon. by Comm. to Re-Elect and by RNC which had been paying $3400/month to his 6 man firm.

NBC noted WH denounced raid as a "3rd rate burglary attempt," and a mar to the nation's political process. (RZ said RN had made no personal inquiries because "it's nothing he'd be involved with, obviously." RZ said Att. Gen. would investigate without RN's prompting, and, says UPI, hinted Dems were trying to exploit the incident.)

ABC used AP's story on WH reaction which said "RN was depicted as taking no interest in the break-in, ignoring the incident."

On film on all nets, McG denounced DNC break-in and called it one of [the] most shocking actions in a long time and the "legacy of years of snooping" encouraged by Mitchell and his subordinates. On CBS, he said trend of snooping leads to quasi-fascism. But he said he had no evidence of GOP involvement altho on NBC he said when Dole and Mitchell are together, you have to raise an eyebrow.

On CBS, HHH said RN and his Cabinet "owe the country an apology and an explanation for this incredible act" and he said he hadn't the "slightest idea" if GOP was behind the incident. HHH said it's "an indication of the kind of things that can happen in US politics." He discounted a Dem investigation on grounds that it'd be labeled politically motivated and said Justice would have to be trusted.

Also on CBS, Muskie said action was symptomatic of tendency of this Admin. to use this kind of surveillance to invade privacy. . . . Mansfield said: "I don't think the RNC had anything to do with it." He said both Mitchell and Dole had denied a role and "I think they are speaking the truth." He added: "What happened at DNC could happen to the RNC."

Scott said: "Whoever did it, it was unconscionable and inexcusable." He also said it was "unconscionable and inexcusable for the media to tie this to the GOP."

Proxmire asked Burns to provide the name of the bank that issued the $100 bills including the $6,300 police confiscated from the suspects. Prox also asked who purchased the bills and "other pertinent details." D.C. police refused to disclose the serial numbers of the bills which might be used at trial. . . . Burns later said the Fed. couldn't trace the bills until agencies working on the case informed it of the serial numbers. Prox regarded the answer unsatisfactory and thought a "cover-up" was in the making.

U.S. Atty Titus announced a Federal Grand Jury will be empaneled to take evidence.

Rep. Waldie asked Fair Campaign Practices Comm. to conduct an investigation of the incident. . . . Rep. Van Deerlin revised what he described as an old political ditty: "Mother's only a shoplifter; sister picks pockets with me; brother prowls only the pawn shops; but Dad's with the GOP." . . . Another Calif. Cong., Rees, said: "To think we were such a threat that we had to be bugged."

HANDWRITTEN MARGINAL NOTE FROM THE PRESIDENT TO MR. COLSON AND MR. BUCHANAN: "Haven't there been some other break-ins in political and govt'al offices[?] Where were the cries of anguish when the *Times* and *Anderson* [emphasis in original] got prizes for publishing *stolen* [emphasis in original] top secret govt documents?"

POF40

ACTION MEMO

JUNE 20, 1972

What's happened to the project to collect all of the worst smear materials on Nixon and the development of a counterattack available to charge the opposition with this smear program? This would include the things such as the books, movies, the *Village Voice* columns, etc.

HRH

HRH112

JUNE 20, 1972

TO: **Mr. Chuck Colson**

FROM: **Bruce Kehrli**

RE: **McGovern**

The June 20 News Summary contained the following note from *U.S. News* on George McGovern:

Mag also notes he voted in '56 against the "Eisenhower doctrine" resolution which authorized use of U.S. forces to prevent Soviet Union penetration of Middle East.

Referring to the above, it was noted that this would be very powerful for Jewish constituents.

cc: H. R. Haldeman
    Alexander P. Butterfield

POF40

w/RN from ss83

JUNE 20, 1972

TO: **The File**

FROM: **Charles W. Colson**

RE: **Howard Hunt**

The last time that I recall meeting with Howard Hunt was mid-March. According to my office records, the date was March 15. At that time I was under the impression that Hunt had left the White House and was working at the Committee for the Re-election of the President.

I may have seen Hunt once or even possibly twice subsequent to that time. These were (or this was), however, a chance encounter. I do recall seeing him outside of my office during a day this Spring; I recall inquiring about his health since he had told me in March he had bleeding ulcers. During the brief conversation in the corridor, nothing was discussed of any of Hunt's work or his areas of responsibility. As I recall, he merely told me that he had been very busy and that after getting some rest, his health had been restored.

I also talked to him on the telephone the night Governor Wallace was shot simply to ask him for his reactions on what he thought might have been the cause of the attempted assassination. (Hunt was known [as] something of an expert [on] psychological warfare and motivations when in the CIA.)

The only other communication I can recall subsequent to March 15 was a memo I sent to Howard in connection with what I thought his duties were at 1701, i.e., security at the Republican Convention. Steve Bull told me he had a friend in Miami who had been stationed in the White House but was now in the Miami office of the Secret Service who wanted to be of help to whoever was handling security for the convention. I merely sent Hunt a note suggesting that he get in touch with Bull's friend.

To the best of my recollection, Hunt came to me during the month of January and said he had no work to do here and no one was giving him any assignments and that this was the only campaign year he would ever probably have a chance to participate in, that he cared only about one thing, the re-election of the President, and that he wanted to be of help in any way he could, for pay or not for pay. I told him I had nothing in my office, but that I thought once the Committee was organized and Mitchell was in charge, there would be work for him to do at the Committee. I told him that I would be sure the Committee was aware of his desire to help. I did nothing further.

A few weeks later Hunt dropped by my office with Gordon Liddy, from the Committee. I believe this was in February, possibly early in the month, although my office records do not show the visit. Hunt said he was in the building and just wanted to talk briefly. Both he and Liddy said that they had some elaborate proposals prepared for security activities for the Committee, but they had been unable to get approval from the Attorney General. I explained that Mitchell would soon be at the Committee and that they should be persistent and see him because he was the only one who could authorize work they would be doing. I have a vague recollection that Liddy said, "We (referring to Hunt and himself) are now over at the Committee working and we are anxious to get started but can't find anyone who can make a decision or give us the green light" or words to that effect. While Liddy and Hunt were in my office, I called Jeb Magruder and urged them to resolve whatever it was that Hunt and Liddy wanted to do and to be sure he had an opportunity to listen to their plans. At one point, Hunt said he wanted to fill me in and I said it wasn't necessary because it was of no concern to me, but that I would be glad to urge that their proposals, whatever they were, be considered. There was no discussion that I can recall of what it was that they were planning to do other than the fact that I have the distinct impression that it involved security at the convention and/or gathering intelligence during the Democratic National Convention.

In March, Hunt sent me a memo explaining that when he retired from the CIA he had failed to designate survivor benefits for his wife and in view of the fact that he had had severe ulcer attacks, he wondered if this could be changed in view of his present government service. I told him to take the matter up with Dick Howard, which he did. Dick's memo to Kehrli, copy attached, was the result. I assume Dick Howard discovered at this time that Hunt was still on the rolls even though not working for us.

I had assumed throughout Hunt's tenure in the White House that he was charged to someone else's budget. I signed the original request for him to be a consultant because everyone else was in California at the time it was decided to bring him in. Shortly after he came on board, however, he was assigned to David Young and Bud Krogh and I didn't consider at any time after that that Hunt was under my supervision or responsibility.

From time to time after Hunt had come on board, he did talk to me, normally to express his frustrations in being unable to get things through the David Young operation. Of course, on occasion also we talked socially and about politics, something Howard and I had done from time to time over the years.

3 SENATE HEARINGS 1170

JUNE 20, 1972

TO: **Mr. Pat Buchanan**

FROM: **Bruce Kehrli**

RE: **DNC Break-in**

Referring to the following note from the June 20 News Summary, a report
was requested on previous break-ins in political or governmental offices.

On film on all nets, McGovern denounced DNC break-in and called it one of the
most shocking actions in a long time and the "legacy of years of snooping" encour-
aged by Mitchell and his subordinates.

Please forward this report to the Office of the Staff Secretary by
June 23.

cc: H. R. Haldeman
    Alexander P. Butterfield

POF40, ss81

JUNE 21, 1972

TO: **Steve Karalekas**

FROM: **Chuck Colson**

I would like from you this morning an opinion as to whether I have any
cause of action for libel against the *Washington Post*. The general rule, as
you well know, is that public figures do not have any standing to sue for
libel although in my opinion the article on page 7 of the *Post* this morning
may stretch the general rule. If there are categories of any exception, I
can't imagine this one not being in them. All of yesterday's publicity is
fine—legally, that is, mere McCarthyism guilt by association but the article
on page 7, "Cast of Characters Involved in Democratic Office Bugging
Case"—I am not involved in the case in any way.

There is an implication here that goes way beyond the fact [of]
anything that has been reported thus far. I would argue that to the average
person it would appear that I am being investigated along with all the
thugs arrested at the Watergate.

Do not rely on your own opinion. I would suggest that you call
Morry Leibman in Chicago [phone number] or Tom Evans in New York
[phone number] and ask who in their firms are their libel experts. If there
is even a shred of a case, I would like to sue the *Post*.

P.S. Isn't there some rule about malice which does give public figures a
right to sue? As a matter of fact, how did the Alioto suit against *Life* turn
out?

cwc131

[Transcript of a recording of a meeting between the President and H. R. Haldeman, the Oval Office, June 23, 1972, from 10:04 A.M. to 11:39 A.M.]

HALDEMAN: O.K.—that's fine. Now, on the investigation, you know, the Democratic break-in thing, we're back to the—in the, the problem area because the FBI is not under control, because Gray doesn't exactly know how to control them, and they have, their investigation is now leading into some productive areas, because they've been able to trace the money, not through the money itself, but through the bank, you know, sources—the banker himself. And, and it goes in some directions we don't want it to go. Ah, also there have been some things, like an informant came in off the street to the FBI in Miami, who was a photographer or has a friend who is a photographer who developed some films through this guy, Barker, and the films had pictures of Democratic National Committee letterhead documents and things. So I guess, so it's things like that that are gonna, that are filtering in. Mitchell came up with yesterday, and John Dean analyzed very carefully last night and concludes, concurs now with Mitchell's recommendation that the only way to solve this, and we're set up beautifully to do it, ah, in that and that . . . the only network that paid any attention to it last night was NBC . . . they did a massive story on the Cuban . . .

PRESIDENT: That's right.

HALDEMAN: . . . thing.

PRESIDENT: Right.

HALDEMAN: That the way to handle this now is for us to have Walters call Pat Gray and just say, "Stay the hell out of this . . . this is, ah, business here we don't want you to go any further on it." That's not an unusual development . . .

PRESIDENT: Um huh.

HALDEMAN: . . . and, uh, that would take care of it.

PRESIDENT: What about Pat Gray, ah, you mean he doesn't want to?

HALDEMAN: Pat does want to. He doesn't know how to, and he doesn't have, he doesn't have any basis for doing it. Given this, he will then have the basis. He'll call Mark Felt in, and the two of them . . . and Mark Felt wants to cooperate because . . .

PRESIDENT: Yeah.

HALDEMAN: . . . he's ambitious.

PRESIDENT: Yeah.

HALDEMAN: Ah, he'll call him in and say, "We've got the signal from across the river to, to put the hold on this." And that will fit rather well because the FBI agents who are working the case, at this point, feel that's what it is. This is CIA.

PRESIDENT: But they've traced the money to 'em.

HALDEMAN: Well, they have, they've traced to a name, but they haven't gotten to the guy yet.

PRESIDENT: Would it be somebody here?

HALDEMAN: Ken Dahlberg.

PRESIDENT: Who the hell is Ken Dahlberg?

HALDEMAN: He's, ah, he gave $25,000 in Minnesota and, ah, the check went directly in to this, to this guy Barker.

PRESIDENT: Maybe he's a . . . bum. . . . He didn't get this from the committee though, from Stans.

HALDEMAN: Yeah. It is. It is. It's directly traceable and there's some more through some Texas people in—that went to the Mexican bank which they can also trace to the Mexican bank . . . they'll get their names today. And (pause)

PRESIDENT: Well, I mean, ah, there's no way . . . I'm just thinking if they don't cooperate, what do they say? They, they, they were approached by the Cubans. That's what Dahlberg has to say, the Texans too. Is that the idea?

HALDEMAN: Well, if they will. But then we're relying on more and more people all the time. That's the problem. And, ah, they'll stop if we could, if we take this other step.

PRESIDENT: All right. Fine.

HALDEMAN: And, and they seem to feel the thing to do is get them to stop?

PRESIDENT: Right, fine.

HALDEMAN: They say the only way to do that is from White House instructions. And it's got to be to Helms and, ah, what's his name? . . . Walters.

PRESIDENT: Walters.

HALDEMAN: And the proposal would be that Ehrlichman (coughs) and I call them in . . .

PRESIDENT: All right, fine.

HALDEMAN: . . . and say, ah . . .

PRESIDENT: How do you call him in, I mean you just, well, we protected Helms from one hell of a lot of things.

HALDEMAN: That's what Ehrlichman says.

PRESIDENT: Of course, this is a, this is a Hunt, you will—that will uncover a lot of things. You open that scab, there's a hell of a lot of things and that we just feel that it would be very detrimental to have this thing go any further. This involves these Cubans, Hunt, and a lot of hanky-panky that we have nothing to do with ourselves. Well, what the hell, did Mitchell know about this thing to any much of a degree?

HALDEMAN: I think so. I don't think he knew the details, but I think he knew.

PRESIDENT: He didn't know how it was going to be handled though, with Dahlberg and the Texans and so forth? Well, who was the asshole that did? (Unintelligible) Is it Liddy? Is that the fellow? He must be a little nuts.

HALDEMAN: He is.

PRESIDENT: I mean he just isn't well screwed on, is he? Isn't that the problem?

HALDEMAN: No, but he was under pressure, apparently, to get more information, and as he got more pressure, he pushed the people harder to move harder on—

PRESIDENT: Pressure from Mitchell?

HALDEMAN: Apparently.

PRESIDENT: Oh, Mitchell, Mitchell was at the point that you made on this, that exactly what I need from you is on the—

HALDEMAN: Gemstone, yeah.

PRESIDENT: All right, fine, I understand it all. We won't second-guess Mitchell and the rest. Thank God it wasn't Colson.

HALDEMAN: The FBI interviewed Colson yesterday. They determined that would be a good thing to do.

PRESIDENT: Um hum.

HALDEMAN: Ah, to have him take a . . .

PRESIDENT: Um hum.

HALDEMAN: An interrogation, which he did, and that, the FBI guys working the case had concluded that there were one or two possibilities, one, that this was a White House, they don't think that there is anything at the Election Committee, they think it was either a White House operation and they had some obscure reasons for it, nonpolitical . . .

PRESIDENT: Uh huh.

HALDEMAN: . . . or it was a . . .

PRESIDENT: Cuban thing—

HALDEMAN: Cubans and the CIA. And after their interrogation of, of . . .

PRESIDENT: Colson.

HALDEMAN: . . . Colson, yesterday, they concluded it was not the White House, but are now convinced it is a CIA thing, so the CIA turnoff would . . .

PRESIDENT: Well, not sure of their analysis, I'm not going to get that involved. I'm (unintelligible).

HALDEMAN: No, sir. We don't want you to.

PRESIDENT: You call them in. . . . Good. Good deal. Play it tough. That's the way they play it and that's the way we are going to play it.

HALDEMAN: O.K. We'll do it.

PRESIDENT: Yeah, when I saw that news summary item, I of course knew it was a bunch of crap, but I thought, ah, well, it's good to have them off on this wild hair thing because when they start bugging us, which they have, we'll know our little boys will not know how to handle it. I hope they will though. You never know. Maybe, you think about it. Good!

HALDEMAN: Mosbacher has resigned.

PRESIDENT: Oh yeah?

HALDEMAN: As we expected he would.

PRESIDENT: Yeah.

HALDEMAN: He's going back to private life (unintelligible). Do you want to sign this or should I send it to Rose?

PRESIDENT: Ah, yeah (scratching noise).

HALDEMAN: Do you want to release it?

PRESIDENT: O.K. Great. Good job, Bob.

HALDEMAN: Kissinger?

PRESIDENT: Huh? That's a joke.

HALDEMAN: Is it? Ah, O.K.

PRESIDENT: I don't know, maybe it isn't worth going out and talking (unintelligible). Maybe it is.

HALDEMAN: Well, it's a close call. Ah, Ehrlichman though[t] you'd, you probably, he, he . . .

PRESIDENT: What?

HALDEMAN: Well, he said you probably didn't need it. He didn't think you should, now at all. He said he felt fine doing it.

PRESIDENT: He did? The question, the point is, does he think everybody is going to understand about the busing?

HALDEMAN: That's right.

PRESIDENT: And, ah, well, Lonzo says no.

HALDEMAN: Well, this, the fact is somewhere in between, I think, because I think that is missing some . . .

PRESIDENT: Well, if the fact is somewhere in between, we better do it.

HALDEMAN: Yeah, I think Mitchell says, "Hell yes. Anything we can hit on at any time we get the chance . . . and we've got a reason for doing it . . . do it."

PRESIDENT: When you get in these people . . . when you get these people in, say: "Look, the problem is that this will open the whole, the whole Bay of Pigs thing, and the President just feels that" . . . ah, without going into the details . . . don't, don't lie to them to the extent to say there is no involvement, but just say this is sort of a comedy of errors, bizarre, without getting into it, "the President believes that it is going to open the whole Bay of Pigs thing up again. And, ah, because these people are plugging for, for keeps and that they should call the FBI in and say that we wish for the country, don't go any further into this case," period!

HALDEMAN: O.K.

PRESIDENT: That's the way to put it, do it straight (unintelligible).

HALDEMAN: Get more done for our cause by the opposition than by us at this point.

PRESIDENT: You think so?

HALDEMAN: I think so, yeah.

PRESIDENT: Still (unintelligible) moves (unintelligible) very close election (unintelligible) he keeps saying if he moves a little—

HALDEMAN: They're all . . . that's the whole thing. The *Washington Post* said it in its lead editorial today. Another "McGovern's got to change his position," and that that would be a good thing, that's constructive. Ah, the whitewash for change.

PRESIDENT: *Post* prints the news so they'll say that is perfectly all right.

HALDEMAN: 'Cause then they are saying . . . on the other hand . . . that maybe we're not so smart. We have to admire the progress he's made on the basis of the position he's taken and maybe he's right and we're wrong.

PRESIDENT: To be very (unintelligible) (laughs).

HALDEMAN: Sitting in Miami played into our hand a little bit.

PRESIDENT: No.

HALDEMAN: They, ah, eliminated their law prohibiting male homosexuals from wearing female clothing, now the boys can all put on their dresses . . . so the gay lib is going to turn out 6,000 fags to (laughs). I hope they (unintelligible) them.

PRESIDENT: How did they (unintelligible)?

[*Transcript of a recording of a meeting between the President and H. R. Haldeman, the Oval Office, June 23, 1972, from 1:04 P.M. to 1:13 P.M.*]

PRESIDENT: O.K. (unintelligible) and, ah, just, just postpone the (unintelligible, with noises) hearings (15 seconds unintelligible, with noises) and all that garbage. Just say that I have to take a look at the primaries (unintelligible) recover (unintelligible) I just don't (unintelligible) very bad, to have this fellow Hunt, ah, you know, ah, it's, he, he knows too damn much and he was involved, we happen to know that. And that it gets out that the whole, this is all involved in the Cuban thing, that it's a fiasco, and it's going to make the FB—ah, CIA look bad, it's going to make Hunt look bad, and it's likely to blow the whole, uh, Bay of Pigs thing which we think would be very unfortunate for CIA and for the country at this time, and for American foreign policy, and he just better tough it and lay it on them. Isn't that what you . . .

HALDEMAN: Yeah, that's, that's the basis we'll do it on and just leave it at that.

PRESIDENT: I don't want them to get any ideas we're doing it because our concern is political.

HALDEMAN: Right.

PRESIDENT: And at the same time, I wouldn't tell them it is not political . . .

HALDEMAN: Right.

PRESIDENT: I would just say, "Look, it's because of the Hunt involvement," just say (unintelligible, with noise) sort of thing, the whole cover is, uh, basically this (unintelligible).

HALDEMAN: (Unintelligible) Well, they've got some pretty good ideas on this need thing.

PRESIDENT: George Shultz did a good paper on that, I read it . . . (Unintelligible voices heard leaving the room)

[*Transcript of a recording of a meeting between the President and H. R. Haldeman in the EOB office on June 23, 1972, from 2:20 P.M. to 2:45 P.M.*]

HALDEMAN: Well, it's no problem. Had the . . . two of them in, uh, state of health (unintelligible) but it's kind of interesting. Walters said that, uh, make a point. I didn't mention Hunt at the opening. I just said that, that, uh, this thing which we give direction to we're gonna create some very major potential problems because they were exploring leads that led back into, to, uh, areas it will be harmful to the CIA, harmful to the government (telephone rings). But, didn't have anything to with, with, with (unintelligible) kind of thing.

PRESIDENT: (Answers telephone) Hello? Chuck, I wondered if you would, ah, give John Connally a call. He's on his trip. I don't want him to read it in the papers before Monday about this quota thing and say, "Look, uh, he met, uh, we're gonna do this, but, but, I checked, uh, I asked you about the situation, and you personally checked your calendar and made, have an understanding. It's only temporary (unintelligible). It won't affect (unintelligible) people (unintelligible)." O.K. I didn't want him to read it in the papers. Good. Bye. (Hangs up telephone)

HALDEMAN: (Unintelligible).

PRESIDENT: (Unintelligible) He said . . .

HALDEMAN: I think Helms did, too. Helms said well, uh, I've had no contact (unintelligible) and, uh, Gray called and said, uh, yesterday, and said uh, that he thought—

PRESIDENT: Who had, Gray?

HALDEMAN: Gray had called Helms, which we knew, and said, uh, uh, I think we've run right into the middle of a CIA covert operation.

PRESIDENT: Gray said that?

HALDEMAN: Yeah, and Helms said, "Nothing, nothing we've got at this point," and, uh, uh, Gray said, "Sure looks to me like that's what we did." Some damn thing where he had—(unintelligible).

We can do about it—this would require at all and, uh, that was the end of that conversation. You can fix it so (unintelligible) we don't, so (unintelligible) we don't think (unintelligible). Said, well, the problem is that it tracks back to the Bay of Pigs. It tracks back to some other—if their leads run out to people who had no involvement in this except by the contacts or connections, but it gets to areas that are at the (unintelligible) to be raised. The whole problem of this, this fellow Hunt, uh . . .

So at that point Helms's kind of got, the picture, kind of like the picture (unintelligible).

. . . he, he said, he said, "We'll be very happy to be helpful to, ah, you know, and we'll handle everything you want. I would like to know the reason for being helpful." And it may have appeared when he wasn't gonna get it explicitly but was gonna get it through generality. So he said fine, and uh, Walters. I don't know whether we can do it. Walters said that (laughs). Walters is gonna make a call to Gray.

(Unintelligible) that's the way we put it, that's the way it was left, and, uh, (unintelligible).

PRESIDENT: How would that work though? How would—for example, if they're desperate (unintelligible) got somebody from Miami bank to be here to count the inventory.

HALDEMAN: (Unintelligible) they can do that (unintelligible). Somebody (unintelligible). But, the point John made was the Bureau doesn't, the Bureau is going on, on this because they don't know what they're uncovering. (Unintelligible) say should continue to pursue it, uh, they don't need to because they've already got their case as far as the, uh, charges against these men, (unintelligible) and, uh, as they pursue it because they're uncovering some (unintelligible).

Sure enough, that's exactly what—but we didn't in any way say we had any political—

. . . interest or concern or anything like that, uh, (unintelligible). One thing Helms did raise is he said that, that Gray, he asked Gray why he felt they're going into a CIA thing and Gray said, "Well, because of the characters involved and the amount of money involved." Said there's a lot of dough in this someone and, uh, (unintelligible) here is the possibility that one of our guys—that probably has some significance to the question (unintelligible).

PRESIDENT: (Unintelligible) Well, we'll cross that bridge.

HALDEMAN: Well, I think they will 'cause our, see, there isn't any question.

PRESIDENT: If it runs back to the bank—so, what the hell, they, who knows, maybe Dahlberg's contributed to the CIA (unintelligible).

HALDEMAN: CIA gets money as we know 'cause, I mean their money moves in a lot of different ways, too.

PRESIDENT: Yeah. However we thought that it did a lot of good (Unintelligible)

HALDEMAN: Right.

PRESIDENT: Can you imagine what Kennedy would have done with that money?

JUNE 23, 1972

Dear Elmer:*
    Thanks for your good note of the 22nd. You are absolutely correct that I have nothing to do with the preposterous events you read about, but it is nice to know that good friends realize that without having to be told. Keep the faith!
    Best personal regards.

Sincerely,

Charles W. Colson
Special Counsel
to the President

P.S. When I leave the White House they will legitimately have grounds for a felony charge against me because I intend to blow up the *Washington Post*.

*[Letter to Elmer W. Raba, general agent, Ohio National Life Insurance Company, Washington, D.C.]

cwc131

JUNE 25, 1972

TO: **Chuck Colson**

FROM: **Pat Buchanan**

I have a better idea. Rather than pimp the *Washington Post*, let's wait for McGovern to say something about this, as he will. At that point in time, we should fall all over McGovern—who gives a damn about the *Post*—and say, this SOB is raising hell about a couple of Cubans stealing papers from Larry O'Brien's office, when George McGovern himself personally urged Daniel Ellsburg [sic], the thief of secret Government documents, to fence those documents with the *New York Times,* who published them. McGovern is a hypocrite. To him stealing Government documents and publishing them to undermine his own Government is just fine—but a couple of screwballs stealing Larry O'Brien's documents is immoral. McGovern is a hypocrite.

Let's let the little fish go by and troll for the Big Fellow.

PJB5

DRAFT

[JUNE 26, 1972]

Dear Mr. O'Brien:

This will acknowledge receipt and thank you for your letter of June 24, 1972 to the President, which has been forwarded to me for response.

You may be assured that the recent incident involving the breaking and entry of the headquarters office of the Democratic National Committee is being fully and thoroughly investigated by the Federal Bureau of Investigation, and that this Department will prosecute violators of the Federal law to the fullest extent.

Sincerely,

Richard G. Kleindienst

JWD5;
3 SENATE HEARINGS 1163, 1167

DRAFT

[JUNE 26, 1972]

Dear Mr. O'Brien:

The President has asked me to respond to your letter of June 24, 1972, requesting that he direct the Attorney General to appoint a special prosecutor in connection with the recent breaking and entry of the headquarters office of the Democratic National Committee. The President is confident that this matter is being fully investigated by the FBI and that the Department of Justice will prosecute all violators of the federal law in a manner consistent with the high integrity and traditions of that Department and the American judicial system.

Sincerely,

John W. Dean, III
Counsel to the President

JWD5;
3 SENATE HEARINGS 1164, 1168

JUNE 26, 1972

TO: **Ken Clawson**

FROM: **Charles Colson**

I am utterly appalled after reading the two news magazines' reports on the Watergate incident. *Newsweek* reports that I "roared guilt by association." Since I talked to no reporters last week of any kind and since I don't ever recall roaring guilt by association, where in God's name did *Newsweek* get such an utter fiction? *Time* is even worse. It reports in full the whole question of the FBI checking telephone records and reports that I, indeed, talked to the FBI. I cannot conceive that the Bureau would put out this kind of information and I would be fascinated if you can shed any light on how this information got to *Time*. The way the story is written it would appear that Gray talked with *Time*. In fact, there is a direct quote which would appear to be attributed to the FBI. The two agents that I talked to assured me that our discussion would not end up in the newspapers. In fact, they kept trying to tell me that during the interview, which interview, by the way, I asked for so as to put on the record the fact that neither I nor anyone else here had any knowledge of this idiocy.

The latter point about the FBI troubles me the most and I am asking John Dean by copy of this memo to find out what is going on. It certainly shakes my confidence in the Bureau considerably.

cwc131

JUNE 27, 1972

TO: **Mr. John W. Dean, III**

FROM: **Alexander P. Butterfield**

RE: **Review of White House-OEOB Access Lists**

I ordered a complete review of the 1972 White House-OEOB access lists and found that Mr. Howard Hunt, a Consultant during the first three months of the calendar year, had only three (or possibly four) outside visitors. The record—as it pertains to Mr. Hunt's visitors—appears below:

Month and Day	Name of Visitor	Time of Entry
January	None	
February	None	
March 2	Williams, Jaye	2:30 P.M.
2	Kilby, Sheldon	2:30 P.M.
29	Kilcullen, John	* —
April 10	Rash, Thomas	1:20 P.M.
May	None	
June	None	

*[Since no entry was recorded, it is probable that Mr. Kilcullen did not keep his appointment.]

ss82

JUNE 28, 1972

TO: **H. R. Haldeman**

FROM: **David C. Hoopes**

RE: **Overdue Memoranda for the President's File**

According to our records, you have not yet turned into this office Memorandum for the President's File on the event(s) listed below. In that the President has asked specifically that this important personal file be complete at all times, to within 2–3 days of the current date, I would like to ask you to take a few minutes today—while your memory of the facts is still fresh—to prepare a summary of what transpired, what commitments were made (if any) and what kind of mood or atmosphere prevailed.

As you are probably aware, these papers need not be lengthy. Write as much or as little as you think appropriate keeping in mind the historical significance of the total file, and the fact that it will increase greatly with time.

Thank you.

The President's meeting with Former Attorney General John N. Mitchell on Wednesday, April 12, 1972, at 3:29 P.M.

POF88

JUNE 30, 1972

TO: **Shelley Buchanan**

FROM: **Charles W. Colson**

Would it be possible to get 4 tickets to *Jesus Christ Superstar* for any evening. Would prefer the whole box but understand there is quite a demand for this show. Many thanks for anything you can do.

cwc131

JULY 1, 1972

TO: **Mr. Henry Kissinger**

FROM: **Bruce Kehrli**

RE: **Sony**

The July 1 News Summary contained the following note.

Japan's Sony Corp. claimed it was not aware U.S. planes were using its TV sets in

electronically guided bombs in raids over North Vietnam and protested that its
products were being used in war.

Referring to the above, it was suggested that perhaps we can discreetly
cut back on all defense purchases from Sony.

cc: H. R. Haldeman
    Alexander P. Butterfield

SS85

JULY 1, 1972

TO: **Mr. Henry Kissinger**

FROM: **Bruce Kehrli**

RE: **Swedish Ambassador**

The July 1st News Summary contained the following note.

The Swedish Ambassador to North Vietnam, Oebey, said: "I've seen with my own
eyes how U.S. planes have bombed dikes and dams in the Red River Delta." He
added: "If RN doubts this is correct, he can send his own officials."

Referring to the above, it was requested that this statement be
knocked down as coming from a stooge of Palme.

Please follow up and submit a report on actions taken to the Office
of the Staff Secretary by July 7, 1972.

cc: H. R. Haldeman
    Alexander P. Butterfield

ss85

JULY 1, 1972

TO: **The President**

FROM: **H. R. Haldeman**

RE: **Six Crises Information / Al Moscow Whereabouts**

I checked both Rose Woods and Chuck Lichenstein concerning which
chapters Moscow and Lichenstein did the basic work on for *Six Crises*.
Below are their reports:

Chapter	Lichenstein Report	Rose Woods Report
The Hiss Case	Lichenstein	Lichenstein with strong backup of Moscow
The Fund	Not sure	Al Moscow with strong backup of Mazo
The Heart Attack	Woods and the President	The President
Caracas	Mazo	Mazo
Khrushchev	Mazo and Lichenstein	Mazo with assistance of Moscow and Lichenstein
The Campaign of 1960	Lichenstein	Lichenstein—but this was one that was really worked on by many people—Mazo, Finch, Waldron, etc.

Al Moscow is now living in Stamford, Connecticut, finishing up a book on the Rockefeller brothers which he hopes to have published late this summer. He is strongly in support of the President and his policies, and has wanted to write to him on many occasions, but did not want to bother him.

HRH162

SENSITIVE

JULY 6, 1972

TO: **The President's File**

FROM: **H. R. Haldeman**

RE: **Meeting in the President's Western White House Office, July 6, 1972. Participants: Ehrlichman, MacGregor, Malek and Timmons**

This meeting was to review the general political situation. The first part of the meeting covered legislative points with Bill Timmons, who was in for about 20 minutes. Bill reviewed the specifics on our legislative program and did so for the press when he left the meeting. The President instructed him to signal our veto strategy and to hit the Democratic tactic of overloading on many of the bills now coming up. The President will veto these bills regardless of the worthy purpose of them if they are overloaded. He feels we have to stop the reckless course of exceeding budget requests.

The President considers more important than all the legislative proposals, the need to hold down the cost of living and avoid a tax increase, so he will examine each bill with this in mind. It's time to call a halt with the support of the responsible members of Congress who will not push these cynical election year proposals.

There will be no compromise on H.R. 1 under any circumstances.

The purpose between the conventions is to get a vote up or down to avoid putting partisan politics above the public interest. Congress owes it to the country to vote the President's proposals up or down. On the top of the list is the bussing proposal. Any Congressman or Senator who votes for any increase over the budget must assume the responsibility for raising prices, and which could lead to a tax increase.

Timmons then left the meeting and it got down to a basic political discussion.

There was a review of the question regarding relations with John Mitchell. It is important not to embarrass him, but we need great decisiveness in the campaign organization. The President questioned Magruder's role—felt strongly he should not be the chief of staff and MacGregor assured him that he would not be—that that was going to be Malek's position and Magruder would handle the areas he had already been handling.

There was discussion of the Democratic organization, first as a front to tie in big names, and secondly as a legitimate instrument for enlisting Democrats in the key states. This would, of course, have to vary state by state. For example, Paul Ziffren in California is a real possibility. Maybe this whole approach should be pluralized for several different organizations.

It was emphasized that the Colson operation must be gotten under control, but in doing so, MacGregor must let all the various people think they are running their sections.

Regarding women, the President questioned the use of Pat Hutar and Malek said they are using her only as a recruiter, they are looking for a woman as co-chairman.

On surrogates, the problem is to give them worthwhile things to do. It was suggested we use the Cabinet and White House wives to do telephoning of the networks and that sort of thing and to work the small states, emphasizing the importance of getting women on television.

The President urged the group to maintain low visibility at the Democratic Convention. There should be no truth squad or anything of that sort.

He told MacGregor he should not be tied to the office running details—he should use Malek to do that—that he should concentrate on the big plays. He said that very few people can make the move on to the national scene effectively because they think parochially and it's important for Clark to guard against that. He should build up some personal surrogates to cover the small states and handle personal contacts for him.

As far as the President's time is concerned there will be no appearances with other candidates unless that helps us. There will be no effort to get Senate seats and so forth. Others will have to do this.

It was agreed that the Vice President posed a sensitive problem and that Mitchell should be used to work on that, but that Haldeman should work out arrangements for the Vice President's schedule planning.

It was agreed that word should be gotten out to all speakers that no one is to hit McGovern during the Democratic Convention week.

The President told MacGregor to use Finch's judgment regarding California problems, but to keep him out of operations in the state.

The meeting ended with assurances from MacGregor and Malek that they were in good shape on putting all of these things together and the President seemed to be satisfied that that was the case.

POF89

[JULY 7, 1972]

Demonstrations Scheduled for the Democratic Convention

July 8	Youth International Party Senior Citizens Rally 7:00 P.M., Flamingo Park, Miami Beach
	National Tenants Organization Rally, 4:00 P.M., Convention Center
	Workers Action Movement Picket various hotels
July 9	ZIP (Zippies) Marijuana Smoke-in Bay Shore Golf Course, Miami Beach
	Workers Action Movement Picket various hotels
	Southern Christian Leadership Conference Rally, Manor Park, Miami
July 10–14	Cuban refugee groups Demonstrations, Convention Center
July 10	National Welfare Rights Organization March, 7–10:00 P.M. Flamingo Park to Convention Center
July 11	Students for a Democratic Society March to Convention Hall, 4:30 P.M.
	Gay Liberation Front Demonstration, Convention Hall
July 12	Gay Activist Alliance "Kiss-in," Convention Center

JWD5

JULY 10, 1972   5:30 P.M.

TO: **Mr. H. R. Haldeman**

VIA: **Dwight L. Chapin**

FROM: **Ronald H. Walker**

RE: **Miami Beach**

July 10, at approximately 9:30 this morning, we departed the Jockey Club
en route to the Miami Convention Center. We went across the 79th Street
Causeway and picked up Collins Boulevard and paralleled Collins on
Indian Creek which runs one street over. The traffic was, I would consider,
unusually light. There seemed to be no problem moving onto Indian
Creek and from what we could see on the cross streets, there was just as
little problem running down Collins Avenue.

We drove past the various hotels along Miami Beach and again
there were no problems. There were no crowds. Some occasions there
were traffic jams but there were sufficient police along the routes to expedite the movement of vehicle traffic.

When we arrived at the Miami Beach Convention Center, we could
hear the demonstrators coming from Flamingo Park. They were approximately two blocks away. At that point in time, we stopped in front of the
Convention Center and I was surprised to see only one large television
tower at the north end of the Convention Center area where they had
proposed demonstrators to be. There is an unusual amount of lighting,
flood lights, and spot lights, obviously done by the network themselves, to
cover these various events.

As I looked up at the octagon tower which is 17 floors, obviously the
tallest building in the immediate vicinity, I noticed an unusual amount of
electronic apparatus and in discussing this with Dick Keiser of the Secret
Service, he told me that those belong to the networks, contrary to what
I initially thought they belonged to, the FBI, Security, and other official
government agencies.

We drove down to watch the demonstrators come down Washington Boulevard and at approximately 15th Street, which is the intersection
next to the Jackie Gleason Hall, they were moving on the right hand side
of the street. There were approximately 500, on the outside 700. They
were dressed in their usual attire which is short cut-off pants, T-Shirts, girls
with no bras on. This is the same group, same type of slogans that were
heard across the country in recent years. In my mind there was an unusual
amount of Vietnam Veterans type persons dressed in military attire and
also a great deal of chanting about "Victory for the Vietnamese," "Victory
for the Viet Cong," "Victory for the Cambodians," "Victory for the people
of Laos," and moving into the crowd they were very quiet, not as boister-
ous as I had seen other crowds.

There were a lot of still photographers moving in the groups and some of them weren't any better than the demonstrators. There was a mounted camera power pack moving in front of the delegation, and some large banners, but not many. There were very few signs. There was a mobile truck moving about 25–30 yards down Washington Boulevard in front of the demonstration. They moved out and when they had passed the Jackie Gleason Hall, they fanned out to cover all four realms of Washington Boulevard moving down in front of the Convention Center. They stopped directly on the lawn area in front of the Convention Center about 200 yards away from the camera which was on the platform. They immediately sat down on the ground and started talking. They did have a bullhorn capacity but the range of the bullhorn, diameter wise, could not have been more than about 25 yards. It was not a very good system at all. They stayed for about 30 minutes and then the speaker asked them if they could get up without killing one another and they would march back to Flamingo Hall [sic]. The basic thrust of the speeches that were given, although limited, was to end the war, to support McGovern and to give the convention delegates a rough time. They then packed up and moved out, back to Flamingo Park.

After moving to Flamingo Park, it was not as bad as I had personally thought it would be. They had given them a large area and in that area they had broken it down into various elements of the demonstration— SCLC, Vietnam Veterans, Hippies, Yippies, and the zippies.

The smell in the area was bad. Obviously a lot of pot, obviously very few baths and with the heat and mugginess of the climate here in Miami, I am sure that contributed to the immediate vicinity. There seemed to be an awful lot of young people either loaded or sick. The sun had apparently taken a lot out of them because there were many running around with sunburn lotion on their faces, especially foreheads and noses, and in the medical tent there were an awful lot of people lying on the ground and being administered to by medical people.

The SCLC is an area where they have pitched pup tents and have roped it off. That is where the blacks are gathering. The other areas are as sporadic—ranging from old buses that have American flags hanging out of them, to other makeshift tents, many of them just lying around underneath the trees. There were an awful lot of old people that were moving around, and I would say just as many sightseers as there were people at the park itself. I would imagine the number of people at the park was approximately 600.

One thing that disturbs me is that I have just learned that the Democratic National Committee has just issued press credentials to not only the press area but floor passes to both Abbie Hoffman and Jerry Rubin. I don't know what it is in the background up there but someone might want to look into it.

There are a number of nicely dressed people, I would say anywhere in the vicinity of about 30 to 40 age bracket, that are carrying our type of radios, the HG 220, and monitoring the various activities. I was not able to determine what activities they were monitoring; however, Dick Keiser of the SS tells me that they are [a] religiously oriented group of young ministers from around the country. I believe the initials are RCALC. Somebody might want to look into that but they are obviously keeping control and trying to keep control of the activities that are transpiring in Flamingo Park.

Of course, it is very obvious that they have not received the numbers they had talked about and I do not anticipate that they will. Of course this evening we will be able to know much more when the first session of the convention begins and we can see what activities they have planned.

They don't seem to have much spirit behind them at this point. Shortly after that we moved down to Collins Avenue because we heard that Muskie had called for a meeting with Larry O'Brien, and of all the candidates. We parked the car at the Seasons Hotel and then walked down to the Doral, which is the McGovern headquarters, and spent considerable time there. It was extremely confusing, the parking outside was horrendous, the traffic was not moving very well in front of the hotel. McGovern was in his suite on the top floor. There was a lot of security, Secret Service, around and a lot of well-known national press. None of them saw me, but I saw a lot of them. The press facilities are nothing like we have. It is just an awful lot of enthusiastic convention attenders, an awful lot of youth, and an awful lot of black. Everything that you go for on the table, whether it be bumper stickers or anything else (buttons, hats, etc.) you have to pay for with prices ranging from $0.10 to $4.00 per item. Nothing is free.

There is a great deal of enthusiasm as I would expect for any candidate at this point.

After spending some time there, and seeing what the flow of activity was, the elevator bank was not as good as I had expected. Even with five elevators they were not moving as rapidly as I had thought they would when I was down there my last time. The flow to the hotel was no problem and the lobby was big enough. The hallways are big enough. They had an awful lot of delegate and democratic convention doors, hospitality suites. There were Congressman and Governor and Senator suites on the main floor itself, and a large press center as I indicated before.

We moved down the beach to the Fountainbleau and at the Fountainbleau we watched some of the Presidential candidates arriving for the Muskie meeting at 1:00. McGovern did not show. At this point I have a question mark as to whether Humphrey showed, but I am sure you will know by the time you get this memorandum. It was just total bedlam. You could not move, there was no control in the lobbies or anything else, maybe that is by design. The Democratic National Committee again was having people pay for their soft drinks in the lobby. Abernathy at this point with the SCLC came in with about 25 people and they began to sing "We Shall Overcome." They had press coverage, a number of cameras inside, an awful lot of lights, awful lot of reporters—not well-known reporters, mostly just young people that are running around with cameras trying to get stories.

At this point that is about the best we have been able to do up to

4:00 P.M. this afternoon. We will be in a series of meetings during the rest of the afternoon and then observing the convention during the course of the evening.

I will have another one of these reports, either late this evening or first thing tomorrow morning.

DLC20

JULY 24, 1972

TO: **Secretary Connally**

FROM: **The President**

Right after our conversation today I called President Johnson and reached him at the Ranch. I told him that I did not want to embarrass him in any way, but that since you had announced that you were undertaking to organize a Committee of Democrats to Support Nixon a number of contacts had been made with people who were close to him and that several of them had indicated a desire to join you, but naturally they would not want to do anything that would be embarrassing to President Johnson.

I told him that I knew and respected his position with regard to supporting the nominees of his Party as a former President but that I would greatly appreciate it if when individuals who were in his Administration or who were supporters of his asked him about joining you in Democrats for Nixon that he might take the position of neutrality.

He responded by reading me a letter that was being sent out, he said, in answer to literally thousands of letters and wires and calls that had come in to the Ranch in the period immediately before the Democratic Convention, during the Convention and since the Convention. He said that except for about a half a dozen of these calls and letters all indicated total disenchantment with the McGovernites and many indicated a desire to support us in the campaign. The letter signed by his secretary made these points: (1) That as one who had had every honor that his Party could give him over a period of forty years he, as a Democrat, would support the Democratic ticket at all levels. (2) However, he had always taken the position that what an individual did in a Presidential campaign was a matter of conscience and that he under no circumstances would try to interfere with that decision.

He then went on to say that he had agreed with most of the positions that I had taken during my tenure in office and that he found himself in sharp disagreement with the nominees of his Party. He said that he did not want to do anything that would make my job harder and would therefore not discourage any of his friends who wanted to join you in the Democrats for Nixon organization. He said, as a matter of fact, he had a very difficult problem with his own family, particularly his two daughters and sons-in-law, all of whom had expressed a desire to oppose McGovern. Naturally, he said that he felt that he had to keep them from doing that because it would be broadly misinterpreted.

I told him that among those we had talked to were George Christian, Dwayne Andreas and Marvin Watson. He then told me about Temple and several others who had already talked to him indicating their desire to join the Democrats for Nixon group. He said that he had not discouraged any of them and would under no circumstances do so.

I told him that you planned to come to see him sometime later this week and he said he would be delighted to see you and have a good talk with you.

The upshot of the conversation is that he feels he cannot be in a position of jumping the traces and leaving his own Party on the Presidential nomination. On the other hand, he actually if anything indicated that he welcomed the actions of his friends and supporters in supporting the Democrats for Nixon group.

Under the circumstances, I think the real problem we have here is what he does when McGovern comes to see him. For him to make a flat statement after McGovern sees him that he supports McGovern and to have a picture taken I think could be harmful to us. On the other hand, if after McGovern sees him he could simply remain silent and make no comment at this time and then at a later time give a pro forma endorsement to the Democratic ticket, this would allow us the time we need to gather in the sheaves.

PPF4; HRH162, 230

JULY 24, 1972

TO: **Tricia and Julie**

FROM: **The President**

It occurs to me that from time to time you may be asked for anecdotes which would relate to some of the political events that have occurred over the years.

One of the best ones is a Churchill quote which could well be used by each of you when the question is raised as to how you felt after the 1960 campaign. As you will recall, Churchill in 1945, after the allies had won the war came up for election. To the great surprise of the whole world and of everybody concerned, the Labor Party won and Churchill lost. Churchill's wife, the next day, said to him, "This may be a blessing in disguise." Churchill's response was, "If this was a blessing it was very *well* disguised." You might say that that is the way that both of you felt after the election defeat in 1960.

Another line that is very useful is with regard to the comeback after the defeat in California. You could tell of how President de Gaulle gave a luncheon for your mother and me, and that after the luncheon he told some of his very close associates that he thought your father had a position of political leadership ahead of him despite what had happened in the 1960 and 1962 elections. You can also point out that in his informal toast that he gave at the luncheon he surprised everybody concerned by referring to his past friendship for your father and said that he felt that there was more responsibility for leadership in the years ahead.

Of course, de Gaulle had his ups and downs as well. After leading the French resistance forces to victory in World War II and serving as the head of government in France for a period, he lost the election and went into total retirement. He then came back many years later when France needed him to hold the country together and to give a new spirit to the French people.

Also, on a personal side, you might mention some of our Christmas parties where I played the piano for group singing, etc., always by ear. In fact, one particularly interesting anecdote was an occasion in New York when Tom Dewey was there and Monsignor Ahearn as well as Bishop Cooke, who later became Cardinal. Ahearn had a beautiful tenor voice and Dewey was an excellent baritone. I played the piano and the two of them sang a duet to the delight of 75 to 100 of our guests who were present.

You can say that these kinds of events are not publicly known but they have been part of the Nixon story that is to you most heartwarming. And also point out that when you had your own birthday parties, etc., that I from time to time played a happy birthday song for you.

I think another personal note that could be made is that when I come in to dinner at the White House—before dinner I will often make telephone calls. I call people who may be sick, who have had hard luck like losing an election or not getting a promotion in business that they expected, or sometimes the mother of someone who has been killed in action. These calls never, of course, are publicized because they are personal in nature, but I feel this is one of the responsibilities of the President. As a matter of fact, one of the most rewarding things about the position is to be able to call people, not only when they have been very successful and to congratulate them, but also when they have fallen on hard times or had bad luck one way or another. To me these personal calls never given to the press are the most rewarding ones I make from a personal standpoint. Everybody, of course, calls an individual when he does well and when he is successful. I know from experience that you receive very few letters or calls when you suffer a defeat. It is in that period that you find out who your real friends are, and a President should always be the first one to recognize this fact—to stick by people or to remember them on those occasions when they have reason to believe that everyone else has forgotten them.

HRH230

W/RN from PPF4

JULY 24, 1972

TO: **Charles Colson**

FROM: **Max M. Kampelman**

Have you thought of the possibility that a student at the University of Indiana may register at Bloomington, vote there and also register and vote in his home town in New Jersey? I know it's illegal but most difficult to enforce.

JULY 25, 1972

TO: **Fred Malek**

FROM: **Charles Colson**

The attached was sent to me by one of our Democrats for Nixon. It's a hell of a valid point. We should have some system for guarding against this. I have thought of it in connection with my own son being able to vote twice, which, of course, is fine, but we must not let the Democrats do it!

ACTION MEMORANDUM

JULY 26, 1972

RE: **The Vice President**

The Vice President should knock off golf and use of the White House tennis courts. We should not look leisurely as we go into the campaign.

HRH

EYES ONLY

[JULY 28, 1972]

TO: **The President's File***

FROM: **George Shultz,** Secretary of the Treasury

RE: **Report on Golf Game**
      Friday, July 28, 1972 (3:00 P.M.)
      Burning Tree Club

PARTICIPANTS: The President   Secretary Shultz
               Secretary Rogers   George Meany

The game was arranged as a way of giving the President a chance to talk individually with George Meany. Meany had been reluctant to have a breakfast meeting or some other officially scheduled meeting in the White

House on the grounds that such a meeting would become public knowledge to the detriment of both men. He suggested the golf game, recognizing that it, too, probably would become public knowledge, but that it did not look quite so official.

The President and George Meany rode together in a golf cart and talked a great deal in the process, often delaying taking a shot while they completed whatever thread of conversation they were on.

The President arranged a match with himself and Meany against Secretary Rogers and me, and then rearranged the handicap at the end of the first nine. The President and Meany won the second nine, and George Meany commented that the President not only played well but bargained well, too.

We sat for about an hour on the porch at Burning Tree. Meany did most of the talking, almost exclusively on two topics—his utter contempt for McGovern and the way the Labor Movement worked at national politics.

Meany spent some time on his policy differences with McGovern but the underlying theme of his talk was about McGovern's lack of character and tendency for double dealing.

On the policy side, Meany takes it as beyond argument that McGovern's approach to defense spending and foreign policy is disastrous and ridiculous. On this score, he kept emphasizing that this was a case where the Labor Movement had to look beyond labor issues and oppose McGovern as being "bad for America and bad for the world."

Meany went into considerable detail, however, on McGovern's record on 14(B). First there was McGovern's vote against the repeal of 14(B) in 1966. This was followed by a letter to Reed Larson, head of the National Right to Work Committee, in September 1968, reiterating his opposition to repeal of this section of the Taft-Hartley Law. Meany noted, with a laugh, that now that McGovern is running for President, he says he made a mistake in his vote and he has changed his mind. (I believe that Meany would have respected McGovern more if he had stuck to his position, even though that position is repulsive to organized labor.)

This was one of Meany's many examples of why you can't trust McGovern.

George Meany also went through in great detail the history of negotiations over a sale of wheat to the Russians in 1965. McGovern backed the sale. According to Meany, he did, too. The sticky point had to do with whether or not it would be 50 percent in American bottoms. Meany feels he had a deal to this effect with President Kennedy. As Meany sees it, the sale and the price were agreed on so that, from the standpoint of the farmers, they had what they wanted. McGovern, however, completely supported breaking the 50 percent-American-bottoms deal, the point being that changing this requirement would mean more profits for the grain companies at the expense of jobs for American seamen. Meany notes with emphasis that McGovern's speech on this was taken directly from statements being put out by the big grain companies.

Meany promised to supply me with materials on both the 14(B) and wheat sale events. On both of these things, Meany's principal point of emphasis was McGovern's double dealing, both times at the expense of labor.

Meany regards McGovern's performance at the convention as ridiculous and again emphasized how it showed McGovern's inability to stand up to pressure. He cited McGovern's cutting off of Pierre Salinger when the McGovern staff objected. As an example, he said that Larry O'Brien had been used by McGovern and that he, Meany, would not be conned by O'Brien.

Meany described at length the organization of the AFL-CIO for political work. He pointed out that the policy of nonendorsement by the parent AFL-CIO meant that the State Federations and City Centrals would not endorse a Presidential candidate, though constituent international unions could do so. He said he expected some 27 individual unions out of a total of more than 100 would endorse McGovern but that the part of the labor movement organized for political action would not make any endorsement.

Meany justified his position on the basis that most of the constituent unions would not endorse McGovern and that he felt a good many of the building trade unions would endorse the President. He will offer no objection to this course of action.

Meany feels that McGovern will be beaten and beaten badly. He thinks that, even if he were so inclined, money spent by labor on McGovern would be wasted and there are much better things to spend their money on, such as state and local contests. Meany talked about the implications of various Presidential pluralities in different states. It was clear from his detailed comments that he had thought this matter through carefully. It was also clear that Meany would not change his mind about McGovern under any circumstances. He really despises the man and what he feels McGovern has done to the Democratic party. On the way out, the President inquired about Mrs. Meany and their daughters. Meany responded by telling the President that he would be doing "all right with the Meany family, which always votes Democratic." Mrs. Meany would vote for the President, the oldest daughter would vote for the President, and the youngest daughter would. The in-between child would follow the "old man and not vote for anybody." Then, just as we were about to leave, Meany put his hand on the President's shoulder and said, with a smile, "Just so you don't get a swelled head, you ought to know that Mrs. Meany really hates McGovern."

After the President had gone and Meany and I had showered and were leaving, Meany thanked me warmly for arranging the game, said that he enjoyed it tremendously and that, even though he would not vote for the President, he had to admit that he liked him.

*[Report by Shultz dated 8/8/72]

POF89

ACTION MEMORANDUM

JULY 31, 1972

The President would like a film print of *Sunrise at Campobello* sent down to Governor Wallace so that he can see it. Our film man should take the film down and run it for them and then bring it back.

Make arrangements to get a print of the film immediately. Let me know when we've got it; I will call Governor Wallace's staff to make arrangements for getting it down there and setting up a showing. Paul Fisher probably should handle this himself.

HRH

HRH112

AUGUST 1, 1972

TO: **Mr. Henry Kissinger**

FROM: **Bruce Kehrli**

RE: **UN**

The July 31 News Summary contained the following note:

The NY News *features a report describing Waldheim as "stung" and "angry" over RN's charge that the UN Chief used a "hypocritical double standard" on the war. . . . The* Times *says the "normally ebullient and forthright" Bush "appeared subdued and troubled" following his talks with Waldheim.*

Referring to the above, it was requested that you work with Pat Buchanan to take a hard line on this issue.

Please follow up and submit a report on actions taken to the Office of the Staff Secretary by August 4.

cc: H. R. Haldeman
    Alexander P. Butterfield
    Pat Buchanan

ss85

AUGUST 2, 1972

TO: **Dick Howard**

FROM: **Joanne Gordon**

RE: **McGovern/American Peace Crusade**

McGovern's name did appear on the HUAC report of April 1, 1951, as a sponsor of the American Peace Crusade. (See attached copy.)

In 1958 McGovern brought a $250,000 libel suit against Glenn Martz, Editor of the *Lowdown on Farm Affairs,* because Martz' newsletter mentioned the then-Congressman McGovern in connection with HUAC's report on Communist fronts. McGovern denied that he was not then and never [sic] a sponsor or a member of any Communist or Communist front organization. Martz apologized to McGovern and McGovern dropped the suit. (See Argus 12/2/60 attached.)

McGovern *may* have written then HUAC Chairman Francis E. Walter disassociating himself from the American Peace Crusade. We have tried to find out and have not succeeded. HUAC's files concerning Members of Congress are sealed—even to one of my contacts there.

Ken Khachigian has also been working on this. He has [the] impression that CWC has a contact at HUAC—perhaps he can do some checking into the 1951 files for us????

Unless we can find out whether McGovern did disassociate himself from Crusade soon after his name appeared in the HUAC 1951 report, we cannot use this one.

The feeling of the people I had look into this is that if Martz could have proved McGovern's involvement or sponsorship with the Crusade he certainly would have and would not have allowed the suit to be dropped.

cwc79

AUGUST 3, 1972

TO: **Dr. Henry A. Kissinger**

FROM: **Alexander P. Butterfield**

RE: **PRC Visit by Waldheim**

The President noted on page 5 of today's News Summary that Kurt Waldheim plans to go to Peking around mid-August. (I have just learned that it will be a 4-day stay, August 11–15.) He wants you to keep an eye on the visit and ensure that we react *quickly and strongly* should the Secretary General do or say anything, however subtly, to undermine our fence-mending efforts or impair even slightly the current U.S.-PRC relationship.

Please report on this matter, through the office of the Staff Secretary, on or before August 16.

ss85

AUGUST 5, 1972

TO: **Ken Clawson**

FROM: **Charles Colson**

Can we get a set of press credentials for Clem Stone's son-in-law at the Republican Convention? This one is like Lou Harris, just a favor to a good guy.

cwc132

AUGUST 5, 1972

TO: **Ken Clawson**

FROM: **Charles Colson**

Couldn't we do better than this? It is incredible to me that this is all we have gotten out of Charleton Heston!

cc: Mickey Gardner

cwc132

AUGUST 7, 1972

TO: **Maurice Stans**

FROM: **Charles Colson**

Per our conversation, Charles Francis Adams would like to talk with you about contributing to the President's campaign. It occurs to me that he could also be very helpful to you in raising large sums from other fellow Bostonians if you can get him involved.

cwc113, 132

AUGUST 7, 1972

FROM: **RNC Research Division**

[RE:]   **Robert Sargent Shriver, Jr.**

Biography

BORN:	November 9, 1915, in Westminster, Maryland.
EDUCATION:	Yale College, B.A., Cum Laude, 1938. Yale Law School, LL.B., 1941.
FAMILY:	Married Eunice Mary Kennedy, 1953; five children: Robert Sargent III, Maria, Timothy, Mark, Anthony.
RELIGION:	Roman Catholic.

CAREER:	1940–1941	Winthrop, Stimson, Putnam and Roberts, law firm.
	1945–1946	Assistant Editor, *Newsweek.*
	1947–1948	Joseph P. Kennedy Enterprises, associate.
	1948–1961	Merchandise Mart, Chicago, assistant general manager.
	1961–1966	Peace Corps, director.

1964–1968	Office of Economic Opportunity, director.
1968–1970	U.S. Ambassador to France.
1970	Organized Congressional Leadership for the Future.
1971–Present	Freid, Frank, Harris, Shriver and Jacobson, law firm.

CIVIC AFFAIRS· President, Chicago Board of Education, 1955. Chicago Council of Foreign Relations.

MILITARY: U.S. Navy, Lt. Comdr., 1940–45.

AUTHOR: *Point of the Lance,* 1964.

Public Career

1961–1966 PEACE CORPS DIRECTOR

After the election of his brother-in-law, John F. Kennedy, Sargent Shriver was asked to head the fledgling Peace Corps. After the appointment John Kennedy reportedly said, "It's easier to fire a relative if it flops." As head of the Corps, Shriver was praised by his fellow Democrats for his administrative capabilities and his success in lobbying Congress for funds.

1964–1968 OFFICE OF ECONOMIC OPPORTUNITY

Shriver's success with the Peace Corps led President Johnson to name him to head up the Great Society's war on poverty as head of the Office of Economic Opportunity. Shriver's tenure at OEO was more [blank space]

In 1968 a rising crescendo of protests against OEO waste, maladministration, payroll-packing and political meddling required Shriver's appearance before various congressional committees. Representative Edith Green (D-Ore.), sponsor of the Women's Job Corps legislation, said at the time,

*Outside of the outrageous costs for this program, the additional tragedy is we are reaching so very few who need help. (*Indianapolis News, *August 31, 1967.)*

In 1967, GAO probers researched the Job Corps center in Pleasanton, California, and found that after two years of operations the estimated cost of the center had jumped from $12.8 million to $25.5 million, the dropout rate was 55 percent and only eight percent of the enrollees were placed in jobs related to their training.

Political Career

1968–1970 AMBASSADOR TO FRANCE

In March, 1968, Shriver was saved from the OEO and appointed Ambassador to France. Pundits viewed the appointment as a master political stroke by President Johnson. It appeared to be a move to "neutralize" Shriver in brother-in-law Bobby Kennedy's attempt at the Democratic presidential nomination. What LBJ forgot to tell Shriver was that he would not seek re-election. When Shriver did not return to campaign for Senator Kennedy, it created some ill-will within the family.

OFFICE SEEKER

Although Shriver has never held an elective office he has made several attempts. Shriver, however, was unable to find a state suitable or receptive to his candidacy.

1968

In late 1967 Sargent Shriver was mentioned as a possible opponent to Senator Everett Dirksen. At that same time Shriver also talked over the possibility of running for governor of Illinois with several Daley lieutenants. In both instances Shriver received little support from the White House.

1970

In 1970, after leaving his post as Ambassador to France, Shriver traveled throughout Maryland in an attempt to ignite a Shriver for Governor movement. That also fizzled. That same year Shriver's name was mentioned as a possible opponent for Governor Nelson Rockefeller in New York. That assignment went to Arthur Goldberg, leaving Shriver somewhat of a frustrated office seeker.

VICE PRESIDENTIAL HOPEFUL

This year makes the third presidential year in a row that Shriver has been on the list of vice-presidential possibilities. In 1964 there was talk about a Johnson-Shriver ticket, that is, until LBJ ruled out choosing anyone in the Cabinet. In 1968 Shriver appeared on Hubert Humphrey's list, but the Kennedy family discouraged that. Each time Shriver was mentioned for vice-president, including this year, the argument was made that his Kennedy ties would help.

CONGRESSIONAL LEADERSHIP FOR THE FUTURE

Forever a loyal Democrat, Sarge Shriver paid his party dues in 1970 by heading up an organization called the "Congressional Leadership for the Future." Shriver campaigned for Democratic candidates in 24 states and raised $95,000 in the process. The effectiveness of his crusade is questionable, however. In New York, for example, he campaigned for Arthur Goldberg (candidate for governor), Richard Ottinger (candidate for senator), and seven other congressional candidates. Out of that lot only two incumbent congressmen were able to retain their seats. Shriver did make a lot of friends nevertheless, and he will probably collect those I.O.U.'s this year.

On the Issues

VIETNAM

"If we disengaged there tomorrow, we'd gain stature in most of the world." —*Buffalo Evening News*, September 17, 1970

"[The] time for us to get out is now."

"What we went out there to do has actually been achieved . . . at a terrible cost in life. The basic issue is that the Vietnamese people . . . are now in a position where they can sink or swim on their own." —*Washington Post*, April 6, 1970

WAR ON POVERTY

Asked whether eliminating poverty would take closer to 10 or 30 years (Shriver) said:
"I think it will be closer to ten, but it depends a great deal on the amount of money . . . the Congress appropriates for this purpose, the amount of support we are able to get Nation-wide." —*Washington Post*, March 1, 1965

Shriver told his questioners on "Face the Nation" that he had proposed to President Johnson that the poverty budget be increased until it was eventually comparable to spending for the Vietnam war. —*Washington Post*, August 21, 1967

One of Shriver's chief lieutenants described OEO as a "sad shop" that will get even sadder unless President Johnson replaces Shriver with a "magical name." —*Washington Post*, February 11, 1968

ECONOMY

"Nixon believes you can cure unemployment by putting people out of work. He thinks the most disposable product we have is the worker. We Democrats believe in human beings, not dollar bills and ABM's." —*Hartford Courant*, September 26, 1970

ABORTION

"As a Catholic I'm opposed to abortion," but Shriver added that if he were governor he would have signed Maryland's new, liberal abortion law. —*Washington Post*, April 7, 1970

"I believe that if you repeal the abortion laws, at the same time you should add a new statute to provide psychiatric guidance, for example, and counseling, to provide better family planning information, to provide better child care clinics, to provide better education across the board about child health and human development, so that young men and women have a better understanding of their responsibilities as citizens and what it means to be a parent, what it means to raise a family."

—"Meet the Press," April 5, 1970

GUN CONTROL

"The firearms problem in cities is very different from that in Maryland's rural areas. I think there should be strict control laws in urban areas and different, much softer laws in rural areas."

—*Baltimore News-American*, April 17, 1970

DRUGS

Shriver said that marijuana is no worse than alcohol or nicotine and has been viewed "with a double standard." Hard drugs, however, are frightening.

"I hate to say this about myself, but if I saw a pusher giving heroin to my boy I'd want to kill the pusher."   —*Baltimore Sun*, April 15, 1970

SHRIVER—THE POLITICS OF HATE

"The Nixon-Agnew strategy is to draw attention to the campuses this autumn and to stir up anger towards the students. They want demonstrations. They want hecklers. They jump at them with glee."

—*Newark News*, September 29, 1970

"Spiro Agnew has become this nation's great divider . . . (he) appeals to everything low and mean and bitter in the American character."

—*Hartford Courant*, September 23, 1970

"Maybe Agnew and Ky could go around the country together. . . . It could be a very good tour. . . . It would be interesting for Americans to see the kind of allies we have in Southeast Asia. Of course, he is exceptional," Shriver said, noting that Ky is an admirer of Adolf Hitler.

—*Hartford Courant*, September 23, 1970

"He (Agnew) attacks young people because he lives for today not for the future. He thinks they're all bad because of a few kooks."

—*Hartford Courant*, September 26, 1970

"While Mr. Agnew may speak very tough about law and order," Mr. Shriver said, he is "offering American resentment, division and anger."

—*New York Times*, September 20, 1970

A short time after Rawlings made the comment about putting "the Greek from Baltimore" on a leash, Shriver said: "I might just add a thought that if they (high elected officials) don't like (young people) here, maybe they can go back to Greece with the young people there—not just to Baltimore, but all the way back to Greece." —*Washington Post*, October 8, 1970

CWC79

AUGUST 9, 1972

TO: **H. R. Haldeman**

FROM: **The President**

This memorandum is one that you can discuss with Ehrlichman, but on a totally confidential basis. I mentioned the fact that O'Brien's name had popped up in the investigation by IRS of Hughes Tool Company. Connally feels very strongly that any information we get in this matter should not be held, but should pop out just as quickly as possible. I have mentioned it to Ehrlichman and Ehrlichman says that unless O'Brien responds to the request that he submit to a voluntary IRS interrogation that he would be subpoened. I think that this should not be handled on that basis until at least a telephone call is made by the head of IRS to O'Brien. Before O'Brien then stonewalls it, a subpoena should follow.

The most important factor, however, is urgency. Connally strongly urged that in addition to following through on the $190,000 that was paid to O'Brien and Associates and $120,000 that was paid to Joe Napolitan we should follow up on the Napolitan returns in 1968 and O'Brien's as well. According to Connally, while there was approximately 9 million dollars unpaid bills after Humphrey's unsuccessful campaign, all of the bills which have been submitted to Napolitan were paid. O'Brien at that time, of course, was making a great deal out of the fact that he was an unpaid National Chairman. Connally believes that following up there may bring us some pay dirt. The point here is that Connally's very strong conviction is that dropping something on O'Brien will have far more effect now than at a later time and will keep all of our Democratic opponents a little loose. The longer we let it go, the more possibility the charge will be made that it was a last minute smear. I consider it of the highest priority to have John Ehrlichman, if he has the time, or you personally, to ride IRS on this matter until we get a decision one way or another. Be sure to emphasize to John and all concerned, that we are not concerned, that we are not trying to develop a legal case that is airtight. The very fact that O'Brien and Associates received any money at all from Hughes, when it is firmly established, it should be put out. What is most important is that the IRS audit of O'Brien begin Thursday—that means tomorrow— at the very earliest. This means that today, Wednesday, the call must be made by the head of IRS to O'Brien so that the stage can be set for a subpoena in the event that O'Brien does not show up voluntarily. Don't let him delay.

HRH179, 230

AUGUST 11, 1972

TO: **The President's File**

FROM: **John F. Evans,** Assistant Director, Domestic Council

RE: **Meeting with Don Johnson**
Friday, August 11, 1972, 11:30 A.M. (actual commencement, 12:20 P.M.)

When Don Johnson entered the room, the President sat him down beside the desk for a photo opportunity saying, "we don't have to worry about you being in the picture, you're big enough." During the photo opportunity, the President asked Johnson about his plans to attend the various veterans organizations' conventions being held in late August, and Johnson told him that he would be at all of them and was looking forward to the President's attendance at the American Legion Convention in Chicago on August 24.

The President told Johnson, "I'm delighted to have you as a member of the Domestic Council and I want you to make sure you get appropriate publicity about it in the veterans press. You might mention that this appointment puts the V.A. Administrator at 'Cabinet status.' "

Johnson said he was personally honored to be made a member of the Domestic Council and thought that this was a great recognition for the Veterans Administration which has interest in many areas.

The President said to Johnson, "You have to be my broker in making sure we get good legislation. There are two things I can't veto: one is social security and the other is veterans legislation. Don't put us in a bad bargaining position. I want you to talk to Tiger (Congressman Teague, D., Texas), as a matter of fact, both Teagues. Make sure we get the best possible bill."

Johnson gave a status report on pending veterans legislation and said there is one bad bill that is a Teague favorite called the "Instant Medical School" Bill. The President said, "What can we do?" Johnson said, "Well, Teague wants something for Temple, Texas." The President said, "Give him Temple, Texas, as a pilot. Look at the payoff we gave to Otto Passman. I want you to say to Teague that we'll give him a pilot. On second thought, maybe I better not get into this. You handle it. I will say that Teague is always right (on voting) on national security matters." Don Johnson added that Teague was working with John Connally on the "Democrats for Nixon" Program.

The President said to Johnson, "I want you to start scheduling yourself"—then as an aside—"you aren't 'hatched' are you?" Johnson indicated he wasn't. The President went on, "Schedule yourself between the Convention and Election into the major States—New York, Pennsylvania, Michigan, California, Ohio, Texas. Find forums, and not just veterans forums, but labor organizations. Don't just talk about veterans, but talk about honoring the men who have served in the armed services. Kill the hell out of them on amnesty and talk about national defense. All that matters between now and November is making our case. I want you to do T.V. talk shows. You are a natural politician and you know how to handle these things. Be sure to talk about national defense."

The President reached over and pulled out a file and opened it and said to Johnson (explaining that it was quotations from McGovern), "Listen to a couple of these beauts." The President said, "This fellow Ramsey Clark, have you heard what he says?" Saying that he didn't want Johnson just to do routine things, the President read from the file a quote from McGovern stating after J. Edgar Hoover was dead that McGovern thought Hoover was a "menace to justice." The second quote of McGovern which the President read stated that McGovern thought Ramsey Clark would be perfect as head of the FBI. The President said, "Here is a man (Ramsey Clark) who has been giving aid and comfort to the enemy—to the Communists—and McGovern wants him to be head of the FBI. What do you think about that?" Another quote was McGovern's position on amnesty and the relief to be afforded those who have "avoided an immoral war as a matter of conscience." The President said, "What about the 50,000 Americans who went through that lousy war and got their asses shot off?"

Don Johnson went on to say that he had already been to 10 State veterans conventions, and two things are particularly well received. First, that he thanks them for their support of the President on national defense. The President interjected, "You mean the mining and bombing in my May 8 statement?" Johnson agreed and went on to say that the other point was the amnesty question to which the President responded, "You mean it hits a raw nerve with them?"

Johnson recited his recent appearances and the President said, "It's time, instead of showing concern about staying in the war, that people showed concern over honoring those who have served. My position on amnesty is clear, I am against it, I won't consider it, now or after the war; I think those who avoided the draft should be penalized because we have got to consider those who have paid with their life."

John Ehrlichman asked Don Johnson whether he talked about jobs for veterans, suggesting that program should also be a major focus of his speaking tour. The President said, "We got you (Johnson) and the retired Chairman of Equitable Life to get a program going to get jobs for veterans and we have made it work."

Don Johnson said that he expected the President would want to hear a report on Governor George Wallace. He said that the veterans had all their equipment and staff at the Governor's mansion and everything would be ready to go on August 16. The President said to Johnson, "When you leave this meeting I want you to call Wallace or if he isn't available, talk to Mrs. Wallace. Say that you have just talked to the President and you give him a report on what the veterans are doing and that the President said that Don Johnson is at their command. You say that to Governor Wallace or Mrs. Wallace. He will appreciate it. Tell them that I send my best and use the White House operator. As a matter of fact, in your travels, why don't you drop in to see him. He will appreciate it and it will be good therapy for him."

The President gave Don Johnson a new set of cuff links and a new pin for his wife at the end of the meeting.

POF89

AUGUST 11, 1972

TO: **Mr. Chuck Colson**

FROM: **Bruce Kehrli**

RE: **Watergate Caper**

The August 11 News Summary contained the following note:

The Watergate caper "isn't funny any more," says James Kilpatrick. "The thing is beginning to smell to high heaven. MacGregor and RN himself have to do more than they've done so far. The affair has to be exposed fully and promptly. . . . More than indignant denials are now required." Kilpatrick emphasizes that "RN, himself, above all others, must demand swift and public disclosure" to explain the $25,000 check.

Referring to the above, it was requested that you note that our friends are beginning to nip on this issue.

cc: H. R. Haldeman
     Alexander P. Butterfield

ss83

AUGUST 12, 1972

TO: **H. R. Haldeman**

FROM: **The President**

Covering some odds and ends, Milton Pitts, the Barber, has indicated on a couple of occasions that he would be very glad to go to Florida during the period of the campaign at his own expense. Apparently he has a brother who lives in Miami and he would like to go down and visit him for a few days. My guess is that this is probably for personal purposes as much as anything else, but it occurred to me that, having taken his predecessor down, and if we have the room, that you might have it arranged for him to go down on one of the planes, not mine, but with the understanding that he should not indicate that he is going down for the purpose of providing any services for me, but that we have simply invited him to come down to the Convention because of his loyal service to the President and the White House staff. If by some long chance I find that I might need him while I am there, of course we could use him although I have no expectation whatever that that will be the case. Follow this up any way you want. Don't discuss it with me further.

Also, with regard to Ehrlichman, would you indicate to him that I think that in handling the Romney matter, that he, Ehrlichman, might discuss the Van Dusen case with Romney. It would certainly ease Romney's going in the event that Romney felt that we were going to have continuity in the Department by having his Under Secretary fill out the balance of his term. Ehrlichman, however, should make the decision. He doesn't need to discuss it with me. I will respect whatever his judgment turns out to be.

I have noted that in McGovern's New England swing that the Press has played up fairly heavily the fact that he has been challenging to debate. I was curious as to whether my directive of several weeks ago that someone in the Press and, lacking that, someone writing him a letter or some friendly Press man putting in a questioning the members of his staff, would confront him with how he voted in 1964 on the Mansfield motion which opposed the repeal of 315 on the ground, as Mansfield put it, that "no President should debate his opponent."

This point has not been made in any public forum that I know of. Colson has been so busy with the Democrats for Nixon that he has not followed up on it even though I indicated that I thought it was quite important in terms of destroying the McGovern credibility to show how he has turned 180 degrees around on this. I want you to follow up on Colson and in any other way you see fit. The purpose here is to nail McGovern on being purely political in making the debate challenge and, in effect, dishonest since he had taken exactly the other position in 1964 when Johnson was the candidate and also the President. I, too, have changed my position but I will flatly say that I have changed it because, having come into the Presidency, I realize that, particularly at this time with all the sensitive information and all of the sensitive issues that we are discussing with foreign powers, it would be injurious to the national interests for the President to debate his opponent. I would like a report from you on what happens in following up on this project.

Also, Haldeman to discuss with Ehrlichman. One of Romney's recommendations was that I go to Wilkes-Barre. This seems to me to be a very stupid suggestion as of this time. I will simply run into what Romney ran into in spades. However, after the Convention, and particularly after we have appointed Carlucci in the event that we go forward with that plan, the possibility of an unscheduled drop-by in the area could well be considered. However, I would withhold a decision on it until we see how things go at a later time after the Convention.

On another subject, in the discussions that you have with Ehrlichman and later on that you have with Ehrlichman and MacGregor and Mitchell, I think that it is vital that we set up immediately the program that I have been advocating for the past two years—the assignment of one top Nixon man from either the White House staff or the Campaign Committee to oversee each major State. We already have a start. Mitchell is responsible for New York and New Jersey and nothing should be done in either of those States without going through Mitchell. Connally is responsible for Texas. Perhaps Malek or Haldeman should have the responsibility for California with, of course, constant recognition of the necessity to check with Mitchell on his relations with Reagan and checking with Finch in the fields in which he is particularly competent. At the moment, I would think that Ehrlichman should have Michigan because of the overriding importance of busing as an issue. If Mitchell has the time, he could handle Missouri. This leaves Ohio, Pennsylvania and Illinois. Colson is particularly effective in Western Pennsylvania and Ehrlichman has some stroke with Rizzo in Philadelphia. It is important that one man—I don't know whether it should be Ehrlichman or Colson or somebody else—should be in charge of the whole State to see that it doesn't come apart and to see that we do what is necessary to strengthen our position there.

Illinois is vitally important because of the operation with Daley. Connally has some stroke with Daley but of course should not be in charge of the State. Under no circumstances do we want someone to take Illinois who is going to be too close to Ogilvie. Ohio also presents a special problem because of the bickering among the various Ohio factions. Give me a memorandum as to how you have followed up on these major States.

I would also add that Wisconsin probably needs some specific man in charge of it. Minnesota I think should be given specifically to MacGregor. Let Colson have whatever effort we decide is worth the making in Massachusetts.

In the southern States, I feel strongly that Harry Dent has demonstrated, by the way the Virginia matter has been handled, his enormous capabilities. The Virginia pattern is a model for what could be done in other southern States, particularly in the border States like North Carolina and even Georgia. When Jack Marsh gets more active, it might be that he could be a man with special responsibility for some of the southern States. Florida, of course, ought to have one man in charge. The same is true of Arkansas as well as Tennessee and Kentucky.

I can't emphasize too strongly here that simply having a regional director for a whole region is not adequate. We tried that in '60 and '68 and it was a flop. I don't object to having the regional directors but what I want added on to that for each major State and each critical State where we are going to have a fight, there should be one man who is responsible directly to me and to the campaign organization for that State. I would like to see this plan as soon as possible. It probably can't be developed before the Convention although you should try to do so. You should try to have something underway before that, but I would like to discuss it at the first time available when we get to California. I want to see it in memorandum form and then I will sit down with you, MacGregor and possibly Mitchell to go over it State by State.

HRH162, 179

W/RN from HRH230

AUGUST 14, 1972

TO: **Bob Haldeman**

FROM: **The President**

I would like for you to discuss with Haig, in Henry's absence, on a totally confidential basis, the idea you have suggested of attempting to announce an end of the draft. I feel that announcing that the draft has ended prior to the election is probably not in the cards. On the other hand, I think moving the date up from June 1st to January 1st might be doable. As you will well understand, Haig will be the one that will lean the hardest against it in Henry's shop. On the other hand, you can point out that making such a flat announcement in the campaign could have a very significant effect. As a matter of fact, it would be my view that we could make the announcement around the 15th of September or perhaps shortly after the 15th of September. I know that you feel that announcing the draft will end at a date in the future may not be credible. I think this is true if Laird were to make the announcement. On the other hand, I think that if I say that the draft is going to end on January the 1st, at the beginning of the new term, it would be both credible and very, very effective.

HRH162

W/RN from HRH230 and PPF4

AUGUST 14, 1972

TO: **Bob Haldeman**

FROM: **The President**

With regard to the various requests we have for interviews, like the AP, UPI, Hearst and *U.S. News,* I would offer them the option of written answers. You can tell them that if they will submit questions I will dictate answers to them. If they say they don't have a chance to follow up, tell them that they can take my written answers and if they have follow-up questions they can submit some more and I will dictate answers to them. You can simply point out that time is the factor and that I can work in dictated answers to fit my own schedule, consistent with my primary responsibilities to carry on the Presidential activities in the period of the campaign.

Whether we go a step further and have personal interviews with the Hearst team and others I think is seriously open to question. If we can avoid it at all we should because once we do it for one we will have to do it for others. The written answers, of course, pose no problem at all because with our research staff we should be able to make some very effective points using this device.

HRH162

W/RN from PPF4 and HRH230

AUGUST 14, 1972

TO: **Bob Haldeman**

FROM: **The President**

With further reference to the discussion I have had with you on Agnew's schedule, I think it is very intriguing to explore the possibility of his following McGovern, not in every appearance McGovern makes, but once or twice a week in major cities that McGovern may visit. As I have pointed out, Agnew is undoubtedly going to draw a bigger crowd and it would give him an opportunity to hit McGovern hard on points that he may have made that need to be corrected.

In addition, the reverse twist here is to schedule Agnew in the day before or two days before McGovern goes in. Here again, we can get a good crowd comparison and Agnew, using this tactic, could ask searching questions and say that he believes the people have a right to know what McGovern's answers are to those questions. In fact, this latter tactic may be preferable to the first, but both could be tried. The more we can get Agnew engaged in a debate with McGovern the better.

It is also very important to emphasize to Agnew again that he should ignore Shriver. I realize that when he has a Q & A there may be instances when he will have to respond to a question on Shriver, but he should brush it off as quickly as possible so that we do not have a national debate between Agnew and Shriver rather than a national debate between Agnew and McGovern.

With regard to Shriver, what should be developed is a truth squad operation in which some of our better speakers follow him into the key areas that he goes into. As a matter of fact, you might sandwich him, having someone go in before and ask a few questions which they want him to answer and someone following him. The sandwich operation could also be used on McGovern with someone going in before and then Agnew going in afterwards, or vice versa.

PPF4; HRH162
W/RN from HRH230

ACTION MEMO

AUGUST 21, 1972

RE: **San Clemente Celebrities Party**

We should not use the Mariachi band at this dinner, we should find some other music, something very special, maybe the best orchestra or party group in California, or some star like Les Brown with a combo, or Henry Mancini.

The dinner should be catered by Chasens if it's using any outside caterers. It should not be Spanish food. Actually it's not a dinner, I guess it's a reception, but there should be a very substantial buffet.

We should use the very best brands of Scotch and Bourbon, not the ordinary stuff that we've used in the past and at the Teamsters' thing.

There should be plenty of good Mosel wine for the ladies who in Hollywood drink white wine. When this is served, it should be pointed out that it's the President's favorite and that he especially selected it for the occasion.

Overall, this should be planned as a very high-level, special occasion and we should look for whatever fancy touches we can supply, although we cannot use military personnel, etc.

HRH

HRH112

AUGUST 28, 1972

TO: **The Staff**

FROM: **Charles Colson**

There are 71 days left between now and the election. Every single one of these is a campaign day and for those of you who have not been reminded of this lately, every day has 24 hours.

I hope that it will be possible for each one of us to have some time during the campaign occasionally to recharge the batteries; an occasional Sunday afternoon may be possible but don't count on it.

There should be no necessity for this kind of a memo and in the case of most of you there is not. Just so there is no misunderstanding, however, I want to make it perfectly clear what the policy will be for the next 71 days. No one should plan any trips anywhere without my express approval. No one should ever be out of reach of the telephone. The White House Switchboard must know at all times where everyone is; each individual member of the staff should insure that he or she can be reached at any time of the day or night, either by phone or by pageboy. No speaking engagements should be accepted, no trips should be planned without my knowing and approving in advance.

Many of you have been through political campaigns before. For those who have not, a campaign is a 24 hour a day, 7 day a week job. Do not be lulled into a sense of false security by the polls which show the President well ahead at the moment. They will change. Make every day count. Think to yourself at the beginning of each day, "what am I going to do to help the President's re-election today?" and then at the end of each day think what you did in fact do to help the President's re-election.

I will be expecting maximum output from every member of the staff for whom I have any responsibility. I will be very intolerant of less than maximum output. I am totally unconcerned with anything other than getting the job done. If I bruise feelings or injure anyone's morale, I will be happy to make amends on the morning of November 8, assuming we have done our job and the results are evident.

I can well understand that many of you may have gotten the wrong impression of me since so many erroneous things have found their way into print lately. Just so you understand me, let me point out that the statement in last week's UPI story that I was once reported to have said that "I would walk over my grandmother if necessary" is absolutely accurate.

cwc13

AUGUST 31, 1972

TO: **Chuck Colson**

FROM: **Ken Khachigian**

Have worked up a brief line on Shriver's Confederate ancestors, and also included a note from *Post* story indicating that Shriver's family were slaveholders.

Gave it to Stan Scott and he is trying to get the story fed into certain segments of Black media and will give it to Black surrogates.

cc: Buchanan
    Stan Scott

PJB5

1972

SEPTEMBER–DECEMBER

SEPTEMBER 1, 1972

TO: **Charles W. Colson***

FROM: **Joanne L. Gordon**

RE: **Gary Hart Press Conference**

As you requested, attached are the highlights of Gary Hart's press conference of today.

Gary Hart Press Conference

Attached release "Kennedy Letter Spurs Million Member Club Drive."
  Hart arrived late, in blue denim jacket, no tie, open shirt—
  Purpose of conference was to bring press to date on McGovern
campaign.
  He said this is "turning point" in campaign and opened with statement that McGovern campaign, unlike Nixon's, is open, as is building they
are in.
  He immediately referred to "the Nixon secret plan Number 2"
dealing with tax reform. For 3½ years we have been told about the
Number 1 secret plan . . . dealing with the war. . . . The tax plan may or
may not be revealed prior to the election. According to one RN campaign
spokesman tax plan would be some sort of national sales tax, it is all
information we can get. . . .

Organization

In 5–6 weeks since Democrat Convention:
opened 758 offices in all of 50 states
selected 50 best state coordinators

formed state steering committee for each state in effort of massive involvement of citizens—efforts won't be apparent for 1–2 weeks prior to election.

GOAL

To get on streets 1 million citizen volunteers to contact their neighbors for Democrat ticket.

Watergate

"I don't think it's any more—as I indicated a few days ago—any more legitimate to hold George McGovern accountable for organizations' problems in the campaign than to hold Richard Nixon directly accountable for the burglary in the Watergate."

"Political espionage"—a great deal of attention still has to be focused on it since people across country don't know all that has been exposed here in D.C. He didn't know that Rothblatt objected to Mitchell giving deposition this morning—he said Administration should clear up whole matter—it may be hiding a major scandal.

Time has come for common standards to be set up for both candidates—either both be held accountable for organizational and what is going on in their campaigns or both accept responsibility for issues, themes and overall conduct, but not day-to-day operation.

O'Brien

He is playing key part in McGovern organization and Democrat Party "confident he will stay"
"there is some value and legitimacy" to his criticisms—every effort is being made to tighten up and coordinate.

Coordinate in 2 areas: issue development and timing of issues by candidate and spokesmen.

O'Brien was briefed this week on financial and structural matters.

O'Brien is #1 man on campaign—National Campaign Chairman—valuable for his assistance and advice and experience—liaison with Democrat Party—working with state leaders.

Hart is #2 man—Campaign Director—in charge of day-to-day operation.

KEY ISSUES

war, tax reform, defense spending, especially credibility in government.

BUDGET

will be ½ of Republicans—expect to spend approx. 20 million.

Campaign will be won or lost on 2 major levels:

1. candidate and issues—if RN emerges from hiding, superiority of McGovern and Shriver will emerge.

2. political organization—Democrats are decentralized with emphasis on state organizations to which time, media, and all funds are going.

POLLS

Now only reflect that there is lack of familiarity with McGovern and details of where he stands.

Their own information shows: they are better off in the states where they campaigned intensely during primary time.

"When Nixon appears, if he does, he will repeat his dramatic tendency to blow substantial leads in the polls."

O'Brien tells Hart that at this point in campaign Demos are 6 weeks ahead of Demo campaign in 1968.

Hart predicts:
by Sept. 20–25 McGovern will close in to 18–20 points difference
by 2nd week in Oct. will close in to 10 points difference
by 3–4 weeks of Oct. will close in to 5 points difference
Election will be a toss-up!

*[Markings on memorandum indicate Mr. Colson briefed the President verbally on the contents.]

cwc18

SEPTEMBER 4, 1972

TO: **John Dean**

FROM: **Charles Colson**

There is one item of unfinished business from my deposition and that is Edward Bennett Williams asked if I would obtain from you a copy of Hunt's letter to me of August 9. He then asked if it could be made available to him. The request of me was that I try to obtain it from you. Please advise.

cwc132

SEPTEMBER 5, 1972

TO: **Ken Clawson**

FROM: **Charles Colson**

Whoever put the UPI-13, attached, on the wires deserves a bonus from the McGovern headquarters. It is a masterful classic innuendo. "Despite his protests he knows nothing about it, John Mitchell today was to resume secret court order testimony." Good God, where will these fellows ever stop? The use of the word "despite" is very artful in this instance to, of course, convict Mitchell publicly.

cwc132

SEPTEMBER 6, 1972

Washington, D.C.

Dear Murray and Dan:*

I appreciate very much your telegram of this date. I don't know anybody who needs defense more! My only problem is that Chotiner has an obvious conflict of interest since he can only gain by further discrediting of Colson and I am afraid that despite his enormous skills, Hofgren couldn't raise the money needed!

Thanks for the thought.

Sincerely,

Charles W. Colson
Special Counsel
to the President

*[Letter to Murray Chotiner and Daniel Hofgren, co-chairmen, Friends of Charlie Colson Committee, Washington, D.C.]

cwc132

SEPTEMBER 12, 1972

Dear Mr. Monette:*

Your letter and copy of your testimony before the Select Committee on Elections, addressed to our Comptroller, have come to me for reply because of my responsibility in this area of our business.

The Democratic National Committee has an outstanding debt of $1.5 million to the various operating companies in the Bell System, for telephone service for the 1968 convention and associated campaigns. However, I must stress that we have been far from silent, as you assume, about this matter. We have and will continue to press vigorously for full payment of this debt from the Committee.

For your information, the bill is largely for service, long since disconnected, to individual Democratic candidates whose obligations the National Committee has explicitly assumed. About 1500 telephone bills, some for campaign services of only a day or two in duration, were accumulated in the few months preceding the 1968 election.

Further, we have obtained the Democratic National Committee's acknowledgement in writing of the full amount of the debt and a promise to pay as soon as the funds are available. Mrs. Jean Westwood, recently appointed head of the Committee, has stated that top priority will be given to paying the debts owed to the Telephone Companies and the airlines. The Democrats have always met their obligations to us in the past and we expect them to do so this time as well.

In the past it was not unusual for both major political parties to take some time to pay their bills due to the cyclical nature of their operations and incomes. However, having experienced these extended delays in payment we have changed our policy to strictly pay-as-you-go for all conventions and candidates. In line with this, both the Democrats and the Republicans paid in full in advance for service at their 1972 Conventions in Miami.

Since you are recommending in your testimony that corporations be permitted to make limited contributions to political parties, let me emphasize that we do not subsidize or contribute to any political party and we have never done so. We have always been scrupulous in treating all parties and candidates alike.

Thank you for writing and giving me the opportunity to explain our position on this matter.

Sincerely,

[s/E. G. Greber]

*[Letter from Edward G. Greber, vice-president, American Telephone & Telegraph Company, to V. H. Monette, Smithfield, Virginia, who corresponded periodically with the White House]

JFB5

SEPTEMBER 15, 1972

TO: **Nancy Kennedy**

FROM: **Fred Fielding**

Per your inquiry, if a President is impeached and removed from office he is not entitled to receive the compensation, office staff and space, and similar benefits provided by law for "former Presidents." See 3 U.S.C. 102, note (P.L. 85-745, as amended).

The statute authorizing Secret Service protection of former Presidents (18 U.S.C. 3056) does not address the question of whether removal by impeachment negates the right to receive this protection. Obviously, there is no case law or judicial interpretation of this provision, but we would conclude that such protection would still be available, at the direction and discretion of the Secretary of the Treasury. If a more definitive opinion is needed on this subject, please advise.

JFB2

SEPTEMBER 19, 1972

If President Wins Nobel Peace Prize:*

Three Options

     1. Allies trip ending in Norway to accept award. November 27 to December 10.

     2. Accept award in Norway; then make Allies tour. December 7 to December 18.

     3. Fly to Norway to accept award and return to USA. December 6 to December 10.

PLAN 1:

Nov. 27–28	Japan
Nov. 29	Korea
Nov. 30	Thailand
Dec. 1–3	Australia
Dec. 4	Ethiopia
Dec. 5	Turkey
Dec. 6–7	Brussels (European Summit)
Dec. 8	Norway
Dec. 9	Washington, D.C.

PLAN 2:

Dec. 7	Ireland
Dec. 8	Norway
Dec. 9–10	Brussels (European Summit)
Dec. 11	Turkey
Dec. 12	Ethiopia
Dec. 13–15	Australia
Dec. 15	Thailand
Dec. 16	Korea
Dec. 17–18	Japan (Cross Date Line)
Dec. 18	Washington, D.C.

PLAN 3:

Dec. 6–8	Ireland
Dec. 8–10	Norway
Dec. 10	Washington, D.C.

*The identity of the author of this memorandum is not certain.

DLC17

SEPTEMBER 20, 1972

TO: **John Ehrlichman**
       H. R. Haldeman
       Charles Colson

FROM: **Pat Buchanan**

My understanding is that the anti-Nixon weasel John Pemberton is now being politically cleared—once again—this time for the job of Deputy

General Counsel at EEOC. Repeatedly, about a year ago, it was pledged that Pemberton would be "on the street" in two or three weeks because of his anti-Nixon activities. This promise was conveyed to the Hill as well. Now it turns out that Jim Buckley's office has been asked to "clear" the clown again—for appointment for Deputy General Counsel. The White House is being made to look like an incompetent ass on the matter.

My recommendation is that we call the General Counsel and the head of that Agency and simply tell them that if Pemberton is not permanently removed from the list of employees, come November, there will be a house-cleaning of the entire Agency.

PJB5

SEPTEMBER 20, 1972

TO: **John Dean**

FROM: **Charles Colson**

I hope you're following the enclosed. If we can trace any of this to McGovern or even to his low level supporters, we have a perfect offset to the Watergate.

cwc132

SEPTEMBER 29, 1972

TO: **Mr. John Dean**

FROM: **Bruce Kehrli**

RE: **Elizabeth Manning**

The September 29 News Summary contained the following note:

A drive is underway to obtain a nomination for RN for the Nobel peace prize next year. "This is very unique," said Elizabeth Manning, a magazine editor who is running the effort. "The Nobel people said nobody had ever tried anything like this before."

Referring to the above, it was noted that this effort should be turned off.

I understand that you are already working on this particular case— please forward a report on actions taken to the Office of the Staff Secretary by October 2.

cc: H. R. Haldeman
    Alexander P. Butterfield

ss86

PERSONAL AND CONFIDENTIAL

SEPTEMBER 30, 1972

Dear Bebe:*

George McGovern has a powerful group working for him here in Washington. In fact, they are having a fund-raising party for him tomorrow. You and perhaps Bob Abplanalp might enjoy reading the flyer that is being handed out on the streets here in Washington.

It would appear that McGovern will do well with the blacks, the poor and now the fags. I hope there aren't more around than we think.

Best personal regards.

Sincerely,

Charles W. Colson
Special Counsel
to the President

*[Letter to Bebe Rebozo, Key Biscayne, Florida]

CWC 132

OCTOBER 2, 1972

TO: **Ziegler, Moore, Safire, Colson, Chapin, Ehrlichman, Buchanan**

FROM: **Bruce Kehrli**

RE: **Presidential Posture During Next Six Weeks**

The following are some comments and suggestions on the President's posture during the next six weeks. Your comments and recommendations have been requested by noon on Wednesday, October 4.

The only thing McGovern has going for him is when he puts on his ministerial robes. When he talks defense, budgets, economics, etc., he unravels. But when he puts on his ministerial robes, and jumps on us about Watergate or the wheat deal, when he talks honesty, integrity, etc., he registers.

There is a "vague feeling" that the President would help himself if he would put on his "ministerial robes" and give an "uplifting" kind of speech—not about taxes or the budget or Vietnam, but "I think that a President, when he gets things flopping around under him like the Watergate, has to let people know that he personally is for honesty, integrity, etc. That kind of uplift speech would be a good thing."

It's not at all a necessity that the speech should directly address Watergate, etc. (though it would have been better to have jumped in immediately, and declared, in effect, that that's the sort of thing "up with which I will not put," to borrow Churchill's famous phrase—anyone who runs a big organization is going to have things like that happen, but the important thing, when they do, is to get on the side of the angels, quick).

This might be handled not in a speech but rather in a press conference, with the TV cameras.

In general, the only thing the campaign needs now is "a little spiritual uplift"— something that shows a real concern for people, for the future, for integrity— something that goes beyond the programmatic and gets to ideals, to principles, and again, to deep concern.

ss86

W/RN from SS81, 84

OCTOBER 2, 1972

TO: **Ken Clawson**

FROM: **Charles Colson**

I thought you might be interested that the quote in the *Washington Post* attributed to John Mitchell, "if you print that crap, Katherine Graham will find herself in a wringer" was not exactly accurate. What Mitchell said was that she would find her tit in a wringer. Apparently McGovern was told about this story and the actual quote on the airplane this week and his response was "based on Katherine Graham's figure, there's no danger in that." I just thought you might like to pass this along to her at the appropriate time.

CWC132

ACTION MEMORANDUM

OCTOBER 2, 1972

We need a leaflet for Defense plants that should be used in the last week that would say, for instance, if at McDonnell Douglas: "Save the B-1; Save your job; vote for Nixon." It should be done on a positive approach although we should also take a look at the negative side of the same thing, which would be "Don't let McGovern take your job away by canceling the B-1."

HRH

HRH112

OCTOBER 2, 1972

TO: **Bob Brown**

FROM: **Charles Colson**

One of our political analysts whose judgment is quite good has suggested that we carefully, quietly, on a low-key basis, spread the word throughout the black community that McGovern now favors white flight schools. His aid to parochial schools speech did not distinguish, as our proposal does, white segregationalist academies from non-public schools generally. He spoke merely of aiding non-public schools, specifically parochial schools. We have made quite a distinction of the fact that the aid would go only to those schools that have IRS eligibility, which of course excludes the Southern white academies.

Naturally we cannot do this in a big visible way,, but I would think some articles in black publications, perhaps some leaflets and perhaps some talk from the pulpit would get the message through the black community that McGovern in this proposal and in his attempt to win votes in the Northeast, has really sold out the blacks in the South. A word-of-mouth campaign could be very devastating on him in this regard and, of course, won't hurt us a bit because of the nature of our bill and the fact that the blacks aren't really expecting us to be on their side on all of these issues, whereas they do expect it from McGovern.

CWC132
W/RN from CWC13

OCTOBER 2, 1972

TO: **Bob Teeter**

FROM: **Charles Colson**

Lou Harris has volunteered to spend a day with us going over his data, giving you some suggestions on specific areas where he believes we should be concentrating our polling efforts, areas that he describes as those that would show movement if any movement is taking place. In short, Lou has volunteered to give us a day in which we could pick his brains, you and I together.

I strongly recommend we take him up on this—perhaps not for a day, but at least a few hours just to see if he has some thoughts that we would like to explore. It's up to you to call the shot on this one; whenever you have the time we'll set it up.

CWC48, 132

OCTOBER 3, 1972

TO: **Bruce Kehrli**

FROM: **Bill Safire**

RE: **Final Six-Week Posture Comment**

Most people think all politicians are a little crooked. Therefore, I do not think a speech by the President wearing "ministerial robes" is appropriate. Nothing would be worse from our point of view than a ringing protestation of honesty and integrity, because it would be defensive and show that McGovern's getting to us. We would then be keying the campaign to his battleground.

We should press our strength and his weakness. The central speech of the campaign should be on the peace theme: Nixon's view of how to build the peaceful world order, the need for strength of arms and strength of character, how to keep the peace in the next generation, and then—interestingly—the domestic meaning of peace. Peace will mean less inflation, which means more freedom of the paycheck. More tax money spent on services rather than arms, which means no new taxes needed. More freedom for young people no longer under the shadow of draft. More and better jobs and business as, for the first time, we show what peacetime prosperity can mean.

Very hopeful speech, which people need, and quite credible, as Nixon is considered surefooted in foreign affairs.

ss84

OCTOBER 4, 1972   6:30 P.M.

TO: **Pat O'Donnell**

FROM: **Dwight L. Chapin**

We want to route Father McLaughlin around the country with Shriver as much as possible, day after day after day. On those occasions when we cannot get McLaughlin there or when the opportunity is prime, we should work in Myles Ambrose. As I stated in another memorandum, we've got Blatchford available and he should bang away also.

We have good solid evidence that Shriver was extremely disturbed that Blatchford was in Des Moines, Iowa, when he was and got so much media attention. That just proves our whole thing's working.

cc: Chuck Colson

DLC17

SENSITIVE/EYES ONLY

OCTOBER 6, 1972

TO: **Bill Gifford**

FROM: **Charles Colson**

George Wallace is reportedly very upset at us for withholding $47 million in highway funds that he is keenly interested in. I have no more facts than that, but can get them for you if you need them. I needn't spell out the political implications here. This has very *high priority*. Please get back to me with whatever information you have and whatever encouragement we can possibly give.

Thanks.

---
cwc13

OCTOBER 10, 1972

TO: **Pat Buchanan**

FROM: **Charles Colson**

The line building in the liberal media is that McGovern's going to be soundly defeated because of his own ineptness—the Eagleton affair, mistakes he has made, internal squabbling in the McGovern camp, etc. etc. Note what Mary McGrory has been doing. She has been eviscerating McGovern personally. The liberal media cannot possibly allow this election to be interpreted as the plebiscite that it is. John Roche did a neat column on what this election is all about, very much taking our line that it is really a referendum on the major issues of the day and that Nixon's views represent the views of the vast majority of the American people and that McGovern has simply, as Yankelovich pointed out, misjudged the mood of the country. I think it is important that our side of this case be told. What about a Buchanan op ed piece? What is really the issue here is the establishment and its views. The Eastern Establishment is about to be repudiated by the American people. You could write this brilliantly and I'm sure that some of your friends on the conservative side would love to be talking about this and writing about it. In fact, Phillips could do a magnificent piece on this.

What do you think?

---
cwc132

W/RN from cwc5

OCTOBER 16, 1972

TO: **H. R. Haldeman**
Charles Colson

FROM: **Pat Buchanan**

Say it ain't so.

HANDWRITTEN REPLY FROM COLSON TO BUCHANAN: "Lock the doors and bar the windows— we're O.K.—Congress has to do it."

PJB5

OCTOBER 16, 1972

TO: **Dick Howard**

FROM: **Charles Colson**

Get a speech drafted as soon as possible pointing out the sheer hypocrisy of George McGovern claiming as he did on his TV Q & A last night, that ITT money has gone into the Nixon campaign and that was the way in which they bought a favorable settlement. Go back and dig up some of the speech material we had during the ITT affair to get the basic answer to that. First of all, the charge is totally untrue, but secondly and more important is the fact that the only ITT money that is reported to have gone into the campaign anywhere, has gone into McGovern's. Somebody by the name of Border in Ohio, either an ITT officer or a member of the board of directors, has given large sums to McGovern. Let's get a speech put together that is a tough one that makes the point of how ludicrous it is for McGovern to be talking about this while he apparently is the only known beneficiary of ITT money. He should be hit very, very hard on this. This is a speech that Hruska could give and I'll get some press out of it. If not Hruska, then Dole could do it.

I think we could really score some political points here. Also if pressed, the ITT people are prepared to say they have given nothing to the Nixon campaign, but have given to McGovern. It's a nifty story.

cwc132

OCTOBER 18, 1972

TO: **Pat Buchanan**

FROM: **Chuck Colson**

If we need to detail the horrors of the McGovern campaign which the press have glibly neglected, we might very well consider using the attached which got very little media play. There is a McGovern worker threatening to kill the President and naturally that is nowhere near as shocking as sending 200 pizzas to a Muskie fund raiser.

cwc132

OCTOBER 19, 1972

TO: **Pat Buchanan**

FROM: **Charles Colson**

Some of the press comments in recent days suggest to me that the establishment is going down for its last dying gasp; as one of our better analysts put it, the last "burp" of the establishment, as they are trying to digest McGovern.

Maybe we could get some columns started through the Buckleys and Kilpatricks along the lines of how this is the establishment's last-ditch effort to put their views through their hand-picked candidate, McGovern, across to the American people. They are about to be soundly repudiated and they are giving it their last breath, but it's too late.

I think it is terribly important to the President that in the second term it be made clear that he won on the issues and because of his record and leadership. It is also important to the country because we may at long last have a chance to strip the establishment of the power that it has had for so long.

Can you do something in this area?

PJB5

W/RN from CWC5, 132

OCTOBER 23, 1972

TO: **Dave Gergen**

FROM: **Charles Colson**

In the veto message on all these bills or in the radio address, let's get a phrase in "it is about time that politicians began to talk straight to the American people and tell them the truth."

cwc132

FOR IMMEDIATE RELEASE*
WEDNESDAY, OCTOBER 25, 1972

McGovern Says Chain of Scandal Runs to White House

Following are excerpts from remarks made today by Senator George McGovern in Cleveland, Ohio:

> *We have learned today that the chain of scandal and corruption runs to the very heart of Mr. Nixon's White House operation.*
>
> *What a shocking revelation it is that Mr. Nixon's closest personal advisor, H. R. Haldeman, controlled the Republican fund that was used to hire undercover agents, to forge letters and documents, to wiretap and bug, and to burglarize the private offices of the Democratic party.*
>
> *This places the whole ugly mess of corruption, espionage and sabotage squarely in the lap of Richard Nixon.*
>
> *Next to Mr. Nixon himself, Haldeman is the most powerful man in the White House. He is the White House chief of staff. He is closer to Richard Nixon than any other man.*

I say that Richard Nixon owes the American people an explanation.

In 1952, General Eisenhower ordered candidate Nixon to answer for an $18,000 slush fund, and that scandal rocked the country.

Now the issue is a $700,000 fund for criminal activity and political subversion, run from deep inside the White House.

These activities demean the public trust and they disgrace the Presidency.

I will discuss these matters in a nationwide television broadcast tonight. But I say today, to Mr. Nixon, it is time for you to come out of hiding and to come clean with the American people.

*[News release from "McGovern/Shriver '72" campaign]

cwc80

OCTOBER 27, 1972

TO: **Alex Butterfield**

FROM: **H. R. Haldeman**

The President has raised the question about whether we are getting the new picture out. Apparently the old picture was at some place where he was last night and he's very disturbed that it was there. Is the campaign organization using the new one?

HRH125

ACTION MEMO

OCTOBER 27, 1972

The President wants a small press facility built just outside the gate at Camp David—possibly where the press shack is now. It should be a modest cabin that provides a press lounge and briefing room facility, with light, electricity, heat, tables, chairs, lavatory facilities, and perhaps a refrigerator and hot plate for coffee, etc. Plans should be drawn up on this immediately with no action taken, of course, until after the election.

HRH

HRH112, 125

OCTOBER 27, 1972

TO: **Pat O'Donnell**

FROM: **Chuck Colson**

Please check for me when any of the *Washington Post* television station licenses are up for renewal. I would like to know what the upcoming schedule is.

cwc132

OCTOBER 31, 1972

TO: **John Dean**

FROM: **Charles Colson**

Attached is the page out of *Newsweek* which has always been, in my mind, the most libelous article involving me. The *Post*, of course, owns *Newsweek*; the *Post*'s lawyer knew I was not involved.

One should not only look at the fine print, but the clear implication of a page like this and, of course, the reaction of the readers of the magazine, who don't stop to draw fine distinctions that might be drawn, but get the impression of a guilty person. It is the juxtaposition of the photographs on this page which is particularly offensive.

cwc132

NOVEMBER 7, 1972

TO: **Maurice Stans**

FROM: **Charles Colson**

The faucet is still running.

cwc132

NOVEMBER 8, 1972

TO: **Maurice Stans**

FROM: **Charles Colson**

A few more dribbles from the faucet.

cwc132

NOVEMBER 10, 1972

TO: **The President**

FROM: **Patrick J. Buchanan**

My own "plans and preferences" for the second Nixon Administration cannot be divorced from my own ideas and hopes for that Administration. Thus, the extended recommendations—prior to my personal suggestions for PJB. First, a bit of history.

In a historical context, the President's victory in 1968, narrow though it was, was the first major defeat inflicted in ten years upon the political and intellectual regime that dominated life in the United States throughout the past decade. Consider what the Left controlled in 1968— before the President's November victory.

Their candidate, though anti-Left, was in the White House, a landslide victory over Mr. Conservative. Their political instruments, the Kennedys and the liberals, were the dominant forces in both Houses of Congress. Their philosophy and appointees held a conclusive majority of the United States Supreme Court. Their voices dominated the major networks and newspapers and news magazines. They controlled all the major socially active and intellectual foundations and think tanks across the country. Liberalism, and the Left, was master of all it surveyed on the great campuses of the country. They controlled the best publishing houses—and the most significant intellectual journals and reviews without exception. In a sentence, the American Liberal Left dominated the cultural, social, intellectual and political life of the United States to an unprecedented degree—and their hegemony left us a nation in social chaos and endless war.

The Nixon Counter-Revolution

But what has happened in four years?

First, the White House has now gone, for a second time and in an incredible landslide, to a political figure whom the American Left views as an archenemy.

Second, the Congress, however, still rests in the control of the Left; little has changed in its composition in four years; this has been one of our shortfalls.

Third, the Supreme Court is another story. The President has all but re-captured the institution from the Left; his four appointments have halted much of its social experimentation; and the next four years should see this second branch of government become an ally and defender of the values and principles in which the President and his constituency believe.

Fourth, while we failed to move decisively to exercise control of the bureaucracy in the first crucial months of 1969—that error seems to be on the way to correction, if one is to believe news reports from the first days after the election of 1972.

Fifth, with the Vice President's pre-emptive strike at Des Moines, the elite and liberal media have been driven onto the defensive, and have suffered an unprecedented and justified loss in the confidence and esteem of their fellow citizens.

Sixth, because of their manifest cowardice in the face of the depredations of student mobs, the elite colleges and universities have suffered a loss of confidence with the American people—even exceeding that of the liberal journalists. They caved under pressure—and in front of the whole country and the fact that Harvard went overwhelmingly for McGovern shows how much further the academic elite is from the views and values of the American majority.

Seventh, as for their foundations and think tanks, we have done little or nothing either to expose their inter-connections and anti-Administration bias or toward developing competing institutions of our own.

The Republican Roosevelt

Our primary objective in the second term should be making of the President, the Republican FDR, founder and first magistrate of a political dynasty, to dominate American politics long after the President has retired from office.

In 1932, the nation went to the polls and repudiated Hoover and the Depression; in 1964, they repudiated Goldwater and the "radical right." They did not vote for the "100 Days," or the "Great Society," but that is what they got because strong leaders grabbed an ambiguous mandate and translated it into sweeping social reform. In 1972, the nation has repudiated McGovern and McGovernism, and the President should use the mandate to impose upon the nation his own political and social philosophy.

The Supreme Court

The President's four appointments to the Supreme Court were among the most significant and far-reaching decisions of the first term. Fifty years from now, liberals will say: "what we have to do is turn the Supreme Court in our direction—the way President Nixon did." In my judgment, the President should (a) begin quietly now the selection process for the next two seats on the Supreme Court; (b) ascertain who in the Federal and State Judiciary are the most brilliant strict constructionists; and (c) select from among these men ethnics and Catholics so that the next appointment will not simply further the President's convictions about the judiciary, but help to cement the New American Majority.

Beyond this, a study should be made of the most outstanding jurists and attorneys in every sector of the country who are strict constructionists—and through their ongoing appointments to the Federal Bench, the President can re-make not only the Supreme Court, but the entire Federal Judiciary.

But the "search" should be undertaken now—so that problems associated with a public search, i.e., when a member of the High Court dies or steps down, are avoided. One of the most serious problems the nation faces is the assumptions by Federal jurists of the broader role of judicial legislators and agents of social reform and social change.

The Media

The President will be the beneficiary of considerable advice to "try to get along" with the media in the second term. It will be argued, we have to live with them—so let us follow a policy of live-and-let-live.

With regard to the major networks, that situation in the national media is not simply occasionally hostile to the President and his purposes—but endemically hostile. The Nixon White House and the national liberal media are as cobra and mongoose—the situation extends beyond the traditional conflict between democratic government and free press. For what it obtains is this:

A small, ideological clique has managed to acquire monopoly control of the most powerful medium of communication known to man; and they regularly use threat unrivaled and untrammeled power to politically assault the President and his Administration. This is not a question of free speech, or free press—it is a basic question of power.

Shall we acquiesce forever in left-wing control of communications media from which 50%–70% of the American people derive their information and ideas about their national government? The interest of this country and the furtherance of the policies and ideas in which we believe demand that this monopoly, this ideological cartel, be broken up. Already the Sevareids, before their captive audience of this world, are doing dirt on the President's victory. We are being told "racism" played a major role in the landslide, that "backlash" was a dominant factor.

Before these characters are finished they will be having us apologize for the tremendous victory the President won. And anyone who thinks that any temporary "détente"—which was to our tactical advantage—represents permanent co-existence does not understand the nature of their dislike and distrust and hostility toward this Administration and its philosophical point of view is rooted in their guts.

Again, this must be viewed as a question of "power"—there are strong arguments that can be made—and made publicly—against their monopoly. We should move against it the way TR moved against the financial monopolies. Our timing should be right, but we should be unapologetic about what we are doing.

What I would like to do in this area is work with those of a similar cast of mind to develop, quietly, a media strategy for dealing with the Left com[b]ination of the networks—and other powerful organs of opinion. It would include our defenses against the network, a strategy against their monopoly control, and a thought-out program for cleaning out public television of that clique of Nixon-haters who have managed to nest there at taxpayer expense.

The New American Majority

If the President is not to enter the history books as a second political Eisenhower—a Republican Regent between Democratic Magistrates—then we have to begin to make permanent the New Majority that returned the President to office. That new majority essentially consists of the Republican base nationally, the Nixon South, the ethnic, blue collar, Catholic, working class Americans of the North, Midwest and West.

The danger I see is that the silent majority, which spoke out loud and clear November 7th, fell silent again on November 8th. And whose voices are again dominant? Those of the liberal media. And the pressure they will place upon us will be the same as in the past, to advance the political and social interests of the "fashionable minorities"—principally blacks, women—and to ignore the ethnics and working class Americans who voted Republican for the first time. If we accede to these pressures— for example, for a higher percentage of blacks and women in top-level positions, etc.—we will be wasting our energies on a politically sterile and foolish game. Our future is the Democratic working man, Southern Protestant, and Northern Catholic—and ethnic. And people whose primary interest in political plums and patronage for these Democrats should be structured directly into the personnel shops of every department of Government, including the White House. We already have a "women's department" in our personnel shop—we need an "ethnic" man in there, who will be on the lookout for Italians and Poles and Irish Democrats who stood with the President, and who are the backbone of this new majority. The same principle should apply to the handout programs of HEW, OEO and other giveaway agencies. If we are going to continue to give away tax dollars at bureaucratic discretion, then the dough should start going as well to those who are our friends.

Fordham and Whittier and Brigham Young and Kansas State should be getting the swag from OEO—Harvard, Yale, Princeton and the other Left institutions should be cut back. If we do not dis-establish OEO— which I recommend—then OEO poverty grants should be shifted from exclusively black and Spanish-speaking and Puerto Rican communities to poor Jewish and Italian neighborhoods.

But the central point is that the "fashionable minorities" didn't give the President the greatest landslide in history. We did our worst with Women's Libbers and black activists, and Mexican-American poverty concessionaires.

We owe them justice—but we owe our friends more. My fear is that media pressure will become so intense that we will return to the discredited political game of spending the resources of Nixon taxpayers to benefit McGovern bureaucrats.

The Great Society R.I.P.

Our pressing domestic need is stabilization of the American economy, and an end to inflation. Perhaps the greatest ongoing threat to that stability is the pressure of the burgeoning Great Society programs upon the federal budget. As many of these programs as politically possible should be eliminated—even the agencies abandoned—and it should be done almost immediately.

The President's landslide of November will have evaporated on Capitol Hill by June, if not before. If we do not eliminate these programs now, they will never be eliminated, and President Nixon and all his successors will be wasting the annual increment in Federal revenues, funding inefficacious programs for the greater honor and glory of Lyndon Johnson.

This would be a tragedy. If RN has to pay the political price of raising taxes to pay for LBJ's schemes—it would be an act of political generosity, unmatched in history, one we should not make. One the other hand—if the Great Society programs are cut and dropped, it may mean an avoided tax increase this year—and possibly tax cuts in the next few years—or programs that have upon them nothing but the RN Brand.

And the country is ready and waiting for the ax to fall upon these programs. In the sophisticated sociology circles, it is recognized that these programs have always created greater problems than anticipated—and never matched the promise of their inception. Invariably, while they have been paid for in either inflated prices or working people, or the taxes of Nixon voters, their principal beneficiaries have been poverty conces-sionaires, liberal beaucrats, social workers, university professors and teach-ers—and other assorted anti-Nixonites. The Great Society can be looked at many ways. One of them is that it represented an enormous increase in power and influence and income for the "public sector" at the expense of the private sector. Another is that it represented a national rip-off of the working class that brought enormous prestige, power and money to the upper-middle-income professional class. The Moynihan article on this de-velopment is brilliant.

My specific recommendation here would be to employ at once the services of Edward Banfield—the best man in the field—of Harvard, have him identify what programs and agencies to drop over the side—and to get on with it—before our political adversaries have time to dig out from under the avalanche.

As with the removal of recalcitrant bureaucrats, the elimination of wasteful and unsuccessful programs should be done all at once—in a brief span of time. Otherwise, the dropping of each program or each bureaucrat has its own special set of headlines—creating its own separate political and journalistic backlash. If they all go at once, and soon, they will be forgotten before they can be adequately protested.

The Bureaucracy

The call for resignations from all political appointees has likely, in a stroke, regained a measure of discipline over the bureaucracy that had badly dissipated over four years. Frankly, conspicuous removal, first, of all ap-pointees who resisted the philosophical direction of the Administration would be perhaps the single most beneficial act we could perform—to guarantee a successful four years in domestic policy. With the names Toby Moffit, Leon Panetta, Wally Hickel and Busing Jim Allen, one recalls that it was our own appointees and indeed some of our own agency shops—that inflicted upon the President some of the most serious damage in the first four years. A house-cleaning of the bureaucracy, coupled with the massive transfer of politically disloyal civil servants, it seems to me [is] essential for a successful second Administration.

Beyond the purging of the disloyal and recalcitrant and the infusing of new blood, there is an over-riding need for this Nixon Administration to create a new "cadre" of Republican governmental professionals who can survive this Administration and be prepared to take over future ones. One of the recurring problems of the first term, in my judgment, was "credentialitis," the insistence that our appointees have credentials and extensive experience in respective fields. Whenever we start at credentials, however, we find that people politically sympathetic and loyal to the President can rarely match professional bureaucrats and liberals—because they won their credentials in Democratic years.

Political and philosophical loyalty to the President and Administration should be the first criteria of appointments. Very few of these types of appointments have embarrassed the Administration. However, of those with credentials who were never with us in heart, we have had many embarrassments.

Again, one of the valid criticisms of our first assumption of office was that we gave away the franchise to Cabinet officers who, in cases such as the Department of State, did not "clean house" as we had promised, but were in effect captured by the bureaucracy.

This mistake should not be repeated—we should clean house in every Department; we should bring in new blood; we should seek out leaders of the New Majority; and bring them into positions of influence and power. Instead of being an Ivy League Paradise, the State Department might do with a few more FSOs from the middle class that gave the President this victory.

Foundations & Institutes

Along these lines, if we are to build an enduring Republican Majority, then we need to construct institutes that will serve as the repository of its political beliefs. The Left has the Brookings Institution, tax-exempt, well-financed and funded—sort of a permanent political government-in-exile for liberal bureaucrats and Democratic professionals.

Conservative thinkers and Republican professionals need the same kind of institution here in Washington. The AEI is not the answer. What is needed is something new, initiated in the coming year sometime, and funded both by Government contracts and contributions from American business—and other pro-Republican foundations. This could serve many purposes: (a) a talent bank for Republicans in office; (b) a tax-exempt refuge for Republicans out of office to stay at work and stay together; (c) a communications center for Republican thinkers the nation over.

An institution of this character—with an imaginative leadership—could provide Republican Administrations for decades with policy ideas and programs, that would present a realistic and principled alternative to those now issuing forth from an essentially liberal-left bureaucracy and places like the Brookings Institution.

We should not leave office without such an Institution in being.

With regard to other Foundations—our political interests dictate public exposure of the ideological bias of the Ford Foundation—and circumscription of its manifold efforts to fund the political activism of the American Left.

With its $3.5 billion in assets and its hundreds of millions in annual allocation, the Ford Foundation has become both Exchequer and Command Post for the entire American Left. Groups as diverse as Brookings, the Fund for the Republic, NPACT TV and the Southern Christian Leadership Conference—all depend for survival upon the financing of Bundy and his friends.

A public exposure of Ford's record, and repeated political attacks could sensitize the nation to what they are doing, frighten Ford back away from "social activism," and perhaps produce a cornucopia of Ford funds for Republican and Conservative causes—to spare Ford from being taken apart by the Congress at some future tax reform hearings. Despite the appearance of power and solidity and confidence, the Ford Foundation, like the American Left, is a paper tiger.

This is another area in which I have some knowledge and understanding and in which I would like, with others of a similar kind, to develop and create a strategy of neutralizing their institutions and power centers, and helping to build our own.

Cultural Leader

One of the findings of a recent poll was that President Nixon, unlike President Kennedy, was not viewed as a "cultural leader" by most Americans. Yet, in modern politics, the meshing of culture and politics is taking place on the Left—and the political clash of 1972 was mirrored in the cultural clash between, for lack of better terms, Middle America and the "adversary culture" written of by Lionel Trilling.

My strong belief is that one of the functions of the President is the celebration—through the use of the powers and honors at his disposal—of traditional American values and their exponents and defenders.

The President should have put together in his behalf an ad hoc White House staff group to generate and sift ideas—for this kind of association of the President's name and office with men and women who are the reflections of traditional values, and adornments of American culture. A splendid example here would have been a Freedom Medal for the late and great American writer John Dos Passos, a giant of our time, who was wholly out of favor with the liberal left.

Beyond this, the idea of White House dinners with distinguished academicians, journalists and artists in attendance—from which the paragons of the Left are conspicuously absent—is an example of what we have in mind.

There is a deep fissure in American society—that goes beyond the political into the realm of the social and cultural. As the President was clearly Middle America and McGovern the candidate of the counterculture—we should pay tribute and honor to those who carry the body of our traditions, just as McGovern would have celebrated the Robert Lowells and Arthur Millers.

Racial and Social Activism

Though the nation is more at peace with itself than four years ago, there are still bitter and rancorous social and racial troubles—as manifest in the busing situation in Detroit, the Forest Hills and Canarsie situation in New York.

Social peace, the basis of any progress, seems to me to dictate that the Government at the national level get out altogether of the business of mandating the racial composition of either neighborhoods or schools. While there is no indication that forced integration has advanced the cause of education, there are manifest signs that it has injured the cause of racial harmony and social peace. The integrationist philosophy of the fifties is proving a prescription for social chaos in the seventies. The moral capital of the U.S. Government is being expended in a fruitless endeavor. HEW, an agency that gives away fifty billion dollars a year, is a hated term in many American communities.

To me it would be a tragedy for the President to fritter away his present high support in the nation for an ill-advised governmental effort to forcibly integrate races.

Far better, it seems to me, for the President to preach the positive thrust of an open society that contains both integrated communities and ethnic communities—and indicate the unwisdom of Government's massive intrusion to change the racial topography of the nation. Such a speech could be done—it would be one as well that goes directly against the philosophical underpinnings of the "quota" system, which needs not only to be condemned, but removed from Government policy in its present "affirmative action" manifestation.

Those people including Mr. Pottinger and other similarly well-intentioned souls in the Government should be removed. For four years the Administration was plagued by zealots at Justice and HEW who took their policy cues not from the President—but from a rejected ideology.

Beyond this, the President should move to get political control of IRS—in particular the tax-exempt division. Today, social activism, outside the purview of the code, is being financed with tax exemptions; and the elimination of tax exemption from some conspicuous offenders would have a decidedly cooling effect upon the other organizations which utilize their tax-exempt status for political raids and assaults upon the larger community.

Conclusion and Buchanan Interests

From the President's interview and actions of the past three days, the coming year promises to be one of the most crucial in the political history of the last two decades. The issue of reduced government and reduced taxes, versus more government and higher taxes is a *re-aligning issue*—one on which, if the President draws the sword and holds his ground, the nation will be politically divided, and on which we can cement a New Majority.

As this is what the President has in mind in the next six months, I would want to remain here in the White House to assist in the undertaking and the defense of the decision.

My principal complaint of the last four years is not that I have been required to do too much, but that I have been asked to do too little, and have been involved too late in decisions which I feel could have been influenced for the better. In the next Administration I would like to be structured into the decision-making process, in such a fashion as to influence the direction of domestic and political and social policy—as well as the defense of it once made. If the President is going to move after the ineffectual programs and recalcitrant bureaucrats, there are few in here with greater aptitude and enthusiasm for the task, or willingness to help research and carry it out than yours truly.

In terms of specific area of assignment, this is difficult to say, as I do not know who will stay or who will leave, what is going to be structured in and what structured out.

But if, as reported, Herb Klein is leaving, I would want to be considered for the position.

First, it would provide regular access to the decision-making process where I think I can help the Administration; the job would require the kind of knowledge and information of the news which we already have in my shop, because of the news summary. Third, it would provide me with the opportunity to articulate and defend Administration positions against attack, with some spirit, and too, in turn, better carry out the attack assignments which the President has from time to time, some of which I could then undertake myself, rather than persuading some recalcitrant Cabinet or sub-Cabinet officer to deliver what we have written. Beyond that, the office could be re-structured, and re-staffed, to bring in individuals who were editorial writer types who could by-line pieces, articulating or defending Administration positions.

If the President is moving hard in the direction of the *Star–News* interview, then that is the kind of direction, kinds of decisions, that I am uniquely qualified to support and defend.

Briefly, that position would but enhance my present assignment of presidential press conferences; it would enable me to continue overall supervision of the news summary operation; it would not inhibit my writing the major addresses which the President from time to time requests. Beyond that, it would provide that access to information, a measure of influence in policy decisions that I think would benefit the White House, and also an opportunity to defend and articulate the President's decision, which I feel qualified to defend.

If that is not open or not a possibility, I would still want, as first choice, to remain inside to help with what I have outlined above and what the President is doing. Greater involvement in the decision process does not preclude, but would enhance my ability to do what we are already doing in this shop. If the President is interested in my staying on in the White House and lending a hand with what he is doing, I am at his disposal and would happily settle for a title and amenities commensurate with others of like ability, contributions and responsibilities.

Finally, if the President does not see a significant role for me in any new staff structure, I would then like his consideration for the USIA Directorship—if Frank Shakespeare is vacating it. That is in the world of communication; at this juncture in time, I would imagine no great difficulty in confirmation; the appointment of an individual of 34, a presidential loyalist, to the job should reflect well, not badly on the Administration.

Above are but a few thoughts, which are difficult in the absence of knowledge of what staff structure is now being put into place.

HRH162

ACTION MEMO

NOVEMBER 12, 1972

Julie Eisenhower wants a paying job until April or whenever David gets out of the Navy. She is very much interested in working on documentary films which she has had some academic training in.

A plan should be worked out for employing Julie as a consultant on review and preparation for production of first-term documentaries—not campaign films but long-range, historical documentaries.

HRH

HRH125

NOVEMBER 13, 1972

TO: **Gordon Strachan**

FROM: **L. Higby**

As I indicated you are to take full responsibility for checking every day for any leaks within the Administration and following up directly with a phone call on behalf of HRH to ask the agency head or department head to track down the leak.

You should then follow up on a daily basis, ruthlessly, to make sure that we don't let up or don't give the appearance that we are letting up. We need to keep banging hard.

HRH14

NOVEMBER 14, 1972

TO: **The President**

FROM: **Peter Flanigan**

Dow Jones closed above 1,000 for the first time today at 1,003.17 with a volume of 20,000,000 shares, up 6.10.
    Congratulations!

HRH14

NOVEMBER 14, 1972

TO: **H. R. Haldeman**

FROM: **Charles Colson**

RE: **Bob Dole**

Bob Dole called me today to say that he would like to see me and review with me appointments he is about to make as Chairman of the Republican National Committee. The obvious point of the call was to fish around and see if he is remaining as Chairman because he said, "no one has told me that I am not going to be Chairman, so I am assuming I am staying on." He then said he would like to review with me people he would like to appoint to various committees within the RNC. Needless to say, I said nothing, but apropos our discussion yesterday regarding the RNC in general and its general counsel in specifics, I think very shortly someone should talk to Bob Dole. I don't mind being the one if you want, but I need to know what to say to him. Or obviously it would be better if someone like you were to talk to him.
    Bob also called me yesterday about the attached and then sent the letter over. I think either you or I should talk to the President about it. Bob is, as we both know, overly sensitive about these things. Maybe what we need is a nice letter from the President to Bob which he can publicize, but I thought rather than put that in the works we should settle what Dole is going to be told and when as a first step.
    What this all adds up to is there is a problem that ought to be met head on fairly fast before we discover that the thing is out of control.

CWC132

NOVEMBER 15, 1972

TO: **H. R. Haldeman**

FROM: **The President**

I would like for you to discuss with Buchanan the contents of this memorandum, but I do not want copies made and distributed because I wouldn't want anything to get out to the press on matters of this nature.

I think it is necessary that we have first a monograph prepared with regard to or which might be entitled "Things They Would Like to Forget." In this area would be to go back to what the commentators and columnists wrote and said at the time of Cambodia when they predicted World War III, and also what they wrote and said at the time of the May 8 decision when they predicted the cancellation of the Soviet Summit. Secondly, this piece should go back and pick up all of the predictions that were made in 1971, and particularly after the '70 Cambodia decision with regard to RN's inevitable defeat in 1972. In addition, the predictions that were made with regard to McGovern's inevitable appeal to youth, the prairie populist, and all that sort of thing, and finally, the predictions that were made during the course of the campaign that McGovern was closing the gap, that RN would blow the lead, etc.

The second monograph should be entitled "Dirtiest Campaign in History Against a President." Here you could pick up the worst of the McGovern/Shriver quotes and even some from other of the Democratic partisans. You might go back and pick up some of the smears on RN through the years. You might also use this as a method of demolishing again, the myth of RN's rough campaigns in the past. Go back and read Earl Mazo and his quotes with regard to the Douglas campaign and the Harry Truman lines, all of which hit on issues and all of which were cases where RN hit hard on the issues, but never questioned, as a matter of fact, made it clear, that he never was raising questions about motives or patriotism, only about judgment. In this respect there should also be the counter-side of it to the effect that RN (one of the cleanest campaigns in history) not only did he never attack the opponents, but as far as surrogates and everybody else were concerned, they stuck to the issues and never engaged in name calling. Also, in terms of the campaign tactics, while we were unmercifully heckled and our meetings sometimes disrupted by violent demonstrators, orders were put out and pretty thoroughly carried out, which avoided any heckling of McGovern or Shriver and of course, no violence whatever.

With regard to the media, perhaps a good way to get at that problem is to praise the writing press generally, for their relative objectivity, with the exception of the *Washington Post,* the *New York Times,* and in the television field, CBS. It is better to praise some and pick out a few deserved opponents as targets of justifiable criticism for terribly biased campaign coverage.

Another monograph should deal with the subject that "RN Won It." This would answer the line of Semple et al. that it was a question of simply tenacity and being "lucky." Here you could point out that RN for four years was up against overwhelming odds—a Congress in control by the other party, the candidate of a minority party with the Republicans only 25% of the voting population whereas it was around 35% when Eisenhower ran in 1952 and 1956.

The fact that RN made some very tough decisions—November 3rd, Cambodia, August 15, May 8, and, of course, the decision on China which was really one of the tough decisions.

Then, in terms of RN winning it, you might point out that he refused to be drawn into the battle despite provocation not only from the press and McGovernites, but from within his own party. The point should be made that he resisted even the advice of his friends like the *New York Daily News,* Kilpatrick, etc., that he should get in the ring and slug it out. Incidentally, in reading over the memoranda that were prepared right after the Democratic convention in this respect, I note that a number of our own people, including Bill Safire on one extreme, and John Whitaker on the other, felt that we should not have an above the battle position, but should get in and fight hard to win the election.

Also on this score, we should point out that RN's Southern Strategy, his opposition to busing, his appointments to the Supreme Court, his standing firm on the patriotic theme, his opposition to expanded welfare programs, his support of the work ethic, and his refusal, even after the Meany episode at Miami Beach, to get into a battle with labor. These were all decisions that were enormously important in fashioning the victory. It should be pointed out, for example, that many of his own staff felt that on aid to parochial schools, amnesty, pot, etc., where RN took a strong position, he turned out to be right and some of the staffers turned out to be wrong.

These are just some thoughts which you might pass on to Buchanan. You can tell him, of course, that Colson has done a lot of work in his shop on this through Schurz, but that Buchanan may be able to do some of the writing and may have some suggestions as to how we can get these themes across in the months ahead.

In sum, we want to get across the truth which is that it wasn't just the case of McGovern losing it, it was the case of RN winning the election. Here you go back to the Lubell and Sidlinger ideas that the election was really won on May 8 when RN made this tough decision, and when, from there on, it was probably not possible for any Democrat to win.

HRH179

ACTION MEMO

NOVEMBER 21, 1972

Knock off Kissinger's proposed trip to China before the Inauguration. That cannot be done.

HRH

HRH14,112

ACTION MEMO

NOVEMBER 21, 1972

We must physically move all of the memoranda from and to the President, especially the handwritten stuff, originals, and so forth, from the Kissinger office files into the President's files. This is all the material for the first term.

HRH

HRH112

NOVEMBER 21, 1972

TO: H. R. Haldeman

FROM: L. Higby

RE: Colson Position as General Counsel of the RNC

Colson in his conversation with me this morning mentioned one thing that needs to be covered with Bush is the fact that the President's desire is to have Colson serve as General Counsel for the RNC. He indicated that while this is being locked up with Bush, you should make this point to him.

HRH14

TALKING PAPER—COLSON

NOVEMBER 22, 1972

The idea of you functioning as RNC Counsel is not a good one after all. You should be free to move on the Connally matter and also your concentration should be on the New Majority, not the National Committee.

Instead, you should pick a good Republican lawyer friend that you can trust and have some ties to and that you can work with and we'll have him put in instead.

HRH

HRH14

TOP SECRET   SENSITIVE/EYES ONLY

NOVEMBER 22, 1972   (CABLE)

TO: Dr. Henry Kissinger, Paris
      (Through Colonel Kennedy, White House—Washington, D.C.)

FROM: H. R. Haldeman, Camp David

The President is very disappointed in the lack of progress in the negotiations to date. Under the circumstances, unless the other side shows the same willingness to be reasonable that we are showing, I am directing you to discontinue the talks and we shall then have to resume military activity until the other side is ready to negotiate. They must be disabused of the idea they seem to have that we have no other choice but to settle on their terms. You should inform them directly without equivocation that we do have another choice and if they were surprised that the President would take the strong action he did prior to the Moscow summit and prior to the election, they will find now, with the election behind us, he will take whatever action he considers necessary to protect the United States' interests.

HRH14

ACTION MEMO

NOVEMBER 30, 1972

Check with Al Haig—Bob Hope is very distressed because he's had no invitation to China. He's especially mad because he read that Dave Mahoney did get one.

Hope very much wants to go to China and do a film of a show there as he did in Russia some years back which was a great thing for the Russians. We should see that this is followed up at the President's highest level of concern.

HRH

HRH112, 125

DECEMBER 4, 1972

TO: **Buchanan**

FROM: **Khachigian**

Colson called this morning with a project that the President wants done. They want an article, magazine length, on the worst things the *Washington Post* has said about RN. The ad hominem stuff.

It should go back as far as the fifties to point out their vicious opposition to RN. The story line would be that the *Post*'s 1972 vendetta was the ultimate frustration. After years and years of heaping scorn and abuse on RN, the public was overwhelmingly supporting RN—something the *Post* simply could not stand; thus the increasing stridency from them and the irresponsibility on Watergate.

It was suggested that we point out the double standard used by the *Post*—e.g., the Carswell case. The *Post* used one standard on Carswell that they did not use on Thurgood Marshall. Colson says it ought to be a "butcher piece"—perhaps for the *New York Times* magazine.

How do you want to work it out?

PJB5

ACTION MEMORANDUM—L. HIGBY

DECEMBER 5, 1972

We should go ahead on the boat acquisition project—give me a progress report right away.

HRH

HRH112

DECEMBER 16, 1972

TO: **Dr. Henry Kissinger**

FROM: **The President**

Here are some further reflections on your briefing today, Saturday, having in mind the need to strengthen the portions which might be interpreted as meaning that we were willing to go along with the present pace of negotiations without taking some action to stop the ominous enemy buildup, an action that would bring the negotiations to a quicker conclusion.

Since October 8th and since you made your "peace is at hand" statement, we have been patiently trying to work out technical details so that there will be no misunderstandings. The clarifications and changes that we have insisted upon have had only one purpose—after a very long war we don't want to end it with a settlement which will bring only a short peace.

But now the remaining differences can be settled within the matter of a few hours by an exchange of messages between the two sides and without a further meeting, provided there is a serious intent on both sides to negotiate a real and lasting peace rather than to try to gain some advantage which will enable one side or the other to renew the war.

We have been talking with the enemy for over four years. During that four years ———— thousand Americans, North Vietnamese and South Vietnamese have lost their lives. The time has come now to bring the talking and the war to an end. Reluctantly you would have to say that, for the past 30 days, the way the other side has gone up the hill and down the hill on various proposals would indicate a filibuster rather than a serious intent to reach a settlement and end the fighting.

We want a rapid settlement for three basic reasons.

First, from a personal standpoint, our POWs—we want the release of our POWs, some of whom have been incarcerated for over five (or six) years.

Second, we want to stop the fighting because, while our U.S. casualties are minimal with several weeks in which there have been no killed-in-action, South Vietnamese and North Vietnamese are dying in battle by the thousands every week.

574   FROM: THE PRESIDENT

And third, we want a settlement now because we will not tolerate allowing the peace talks to be used as a cover for a military buildup which could mean a step-up in the war in the future.

Both the North Vietnamese and the South Vietnamese must share responsibility for the delay in reaching a settlement. Each side wants to gain advantages at the peace table it has not and cannot gain on the battlefield. It is time to have the ceasefire and let the people of South Vietnam decide at the ballot by their votes what kind of government they want for South Vietnam. It is time (pick this up from the previous memorandum) that we move this conflict from the battlefield to the ballot box.

Consequently, we are going to step up our pressure on both sides for a faster settlement. In taking this course, we are doing it in the interests of both sides. Neither side can gain from continuing the war—from prolonging the war. Neither side can gain from prolonging the peace talks. We are ready to resume the talks and to reach a rapid settlement whenever the enemy is ready to do so.

In the meantime, the President will continue to order whatever actions he considers necessary by air and sea to prevent what now appears to be an ominous buildup in North Vietnam for the purpose of launching a new offensive against South Vietnam.

HRH230

DECEMBER 19, 1972

TO: **Mr. Herbert Klein**

FROM: **Bruce Kehrli**

RE: **Circulation of** *Time*

The December 19 News Summary contained the following note:

Steinem's Ms *has become the talk of the mag trade, says* Time, *with its circulation at* 395,000 *and headed to* 530,000. *It's ending its 1st 6 months in the black—"almost unheard of."*

Referring to the above, especially the portion [set in roman type in line 2], the question was asked—how influential is this?

Please follow up and submit a report, comparing this circulation to the circulation of other prominent magazines, and submit the report to the Office of the Staff Secretary by December 21, 1972.

Thank you.

cc: H. R. Haldeman
Alexander P. Butterfield

ss85

DECEMBER 19, 1972

TO: **Mr. Bill Timmons**

FROM: **Bruce Kehrli**

RE: **Bush**

The December 19 News Summary contained the following note:

Human Events *says Hill politicos are "furious" with the "shabby" treatment given Dole by the WH. After working very hard for RN, Dole was "unceremoniously booted out" of his job.* HE *adds many believe Bush will be less likely to squawk about WH decisions.*

Referring to the above, it was noted that you should get some positive material out on Bush.

cc: H. R. Haldeman
    Alexander P. Butterfield

                                                        ss86

_____

DECEMBER 22, 1972

TO: **Larry Higby**

FROM: **Charles Colson**

My staff has informed me that still another potential OEO director has refused the job. The list of candidates is somewhere in the mill and may be in your office right now. Once again we have an opportunity to place a director at the head of OEO who knows what the President wants and knows how to execute political orders.

The President needs politically astute loyalists throughout the government, but he needs them most in old line liberal agencies that are going to be taking the most heat. It is essential that we name a director to OEO who is willing to be a human bomb and walking target. Howie Phillips wants to kill the agency and has a loyal staff capable of doing it. He does not want a job, he wants to do a job. He has now served under two directors who either would not or could not do that which the President wants. I strongly recommend that Howie Phillips be named OEO's new director before he decides to leave the government. Conditions have never been more favorable for doing what the President wants to do.

                                                        cwc132

_____

JANUARY 2, 1973

TO: **John Dean**

FROM: **Charles Colson**

Now what the hell do I do?

3 SENATE HEARINGS 1233

JANUARY 8, 1973

TO: **Bruce Kehrli**

FROM: **John Dean**

RE: **Presidential Yacht**

Through a highly trusted intermediary, Jim Ryder's personal attorney will approach his client to ascertain whether there is any interest and receptivity in donating the yacht "Jardell." The inquiry will be postured as very preliminary.

    We expect to have a response late this afternoon or tomorrow, and I will contact you immediately.

JFB2

ACTION MEMO

JANUARY 11, 1973

Be sure all the orchestras at the Inaugural Concerts are prepared to play Hail to the Chief. Also, all the orchestras at the Balls so that they can do

Ruffles and Flourishes and Hail to the Chief properly when the President comes in.

HRH

HRH179

ACTION MEMO

JANUARY 19, 1973

We need to check out burial opportunities at Yorba Linda as well as Rose Hill and then update that whole plan.

HRH

HRH179

JANUARY 22, 1973

TO: **Bruce Kehrli**

FROM: **John Dean**

RE: **Presidential Yacht**

We are advised that Mr. Ryder cannot donate his yacht to the Government, as it is under a binding contract of sale. Therefore, all further contact with him will be terminated.

With regard to the Levitt yacht, we have been unable to make the right contact to him, and therefore I am going to talk to Bebe Rebozo, who might have some ideas since the yacht is moored in Miami.

I'll keep you advised.

JFB2

ACTION MEMO

JANUARY 23, 1973

We should consider Lady Bird for an Ambassadorial appointment or replacement on the UN Delegation if that's open.

I need a recommendation on each of those two.

I should call Connally and get his view on whether this is a good move.

HRH

HRH112

[JANUARY 25, 1973]

RN approaches his second inauguration with true peace of mind—because he knows that by his actions, often in the face of the most intense sort of criticism, what he is bringing to the world is a "peace of mind"—that is, a peace formed by the exercise of hard reason and calm deliberation, and durable because its foundation has been carefully laid.

Those who think with their hearts, not with their heads, would have established a "peace of the heart"—one which, like so many affairs of the heart, would have ended broken.

The "peace of mind," on the other hand, will last, and by lasting will allow a peace of the heart to take root.

HANDWRITTEN NOTE FROM THE PRESIDENT TO MR. HALDEMAN: "An excellent lesson for—Safire—Klein—et al."

HRH230

FEBRUARY 9, 1973

TO: **The President**

FROM: **Charles Colson**

RE: **Walter Cronkite Interview**

Lest anyone have any doubt about where Walter Cronkite stands, the attached is a rather interesting interview. In my view, this totally destroys Cronkite's credibility. He can't by any stretch of the imagination contend that he is objective. Nor is he a Dr. Jekyll and Mr. Hyde who can report the news objectively and in his after broadcast hours describe the Administration as an evil influence on society.

HRH109

ACTION MEMO

FEBRUARY 12, 1973

The President wants a letter drafted from him to the Nobel Committee saying in effect that it is his practice as President not to accept honors and awards for doing what he considers to be his duty. He therefore requests that he not be considered this year for the Nobel Peace Prize, and wants the committee to know that he would not be able to accept the award if it were to be given to him.

He wants Price to take a stab at a draft on this. It should not be widely discussed, however.

HRH

HRH179

FEBRUARY 13, 1973

TO: **David Young**

FROM: **John Dean**

RE: **Declassification of Presidential Papers**

Prior to the deaths of Eisenhower, Truman and Johnson, the White House received a number of requests to assist in projects to declassify their Presidential papers to facilitate their working with these documents in publications and memoirs and other writings. In an effort to avoid this problem with President Nixon, we should develop a plan immediately to expedite declassification of his papers. For example, a special team of declassifiers might be assembled and commence on this project immediately.

Would you please prepare a proposal setting forth how this can best be done, who should be involved, how long it will take, etc. If you have any questions, please give me a call.

cc: H. R. Haldeman
John Ehrlichman
John Nesbitt
Trudy Brown

HRH109

MARCH 4, 1973   CAMP DAVID

TO: **Bob Haldeman**

FROM: **The President**

In talking to Sammy Davis this morning, he expounded on the idea that he broached at the "Evening at the White House" with regard to a possible Gala honoring the POWs. He suggests the proceeds could be used for the families of those who were killed in action or are missing in action. The idea, of course, is a very appealing one but one that will require a tremendous amount of planning if we are to go forward with it.

What I would have in mind is not that it would be tied in with the reception and dinner we have at the White House for the POWs—that should be a separate function. My view, incidentally, is that that should be a function that should not be televised in its entirety although a part of it might be—but we can think about that later.

In any event, whatever is done at the White House should be something that all the people could look in on and not something people would have to pay to see on closed circuit television. Perhaps the Bob Hope last Vietnam show would be a pretty good answer, provided we could get Bob to de-emphasize some of the girlie stuff and go for some of the more high-powered entertainers for that occasion. The problem with the Bob Hope show, incidentally, that I would see in holding it outside would be the acoustics. This would be particularly true if we were to televise it because, as you know, the applause factor is almost totally eliminated when the show is held outside. However, let us go forward and explore that affair at the White House as quickly as possible so that we can get our plans lined up and the date selected, etc.

Sammy Davis' idea which I explored with him at breakfast this morning could be considered along these lines:

First, as far as the beneficiaries are concerned, possibly we should think of it in terms of setting up a scholarship fund for the children of those who were killed in action or missing in action. I would not provide a total . scholarship—perhaps one of a thousand dollars because my guess is that most of these young people will probably be eligible for loans in the Federal program in any event. This way it could be spread further and could benefit a greater number.

It would be necessary to set up a foundation for the purpose of administering the fund.

What Sammy suggests is that there be a closed circuit affair shown in major cities throughout the country with tickets—perhaps for dinners at $1,000 a plate. I would guess that if we could pick up five million dollars for Republican fund-raising closed circuit dinners we could do even better with this kind of a dinner if we got the proper promotion on it in view of the fact that the contributions would be tax deductible and corporations could buy tables without any legal complications.

What could be done would be to have a celebrity in each one of the cities and possibly a representative group of POWs as well.

The show could probably best be originated from Los Angeles—most of the talent will be there and you could take some place like the Century Plaza and probably get excellent acoustics and a good television picture. I would attend the Los Angeles dinner—or whatever one was the originating affair.

He suggests that Paul Keyes be the producer. Naturally, Sammy wants to participate in the production as well and I suppose here you would have problems because other people, like Hope, would think that they should be in on the production. The idea of Keyes producing it is most appealing because we could work with him and he has excellent contacts with so many people in show business who might participate in the Gala. It probably ought to be about an hour and a half show—possibly with the number of celebrities we would have to put it to two hours but this should pose no particular problem. After all, plays and movies are now two hours or more and people would be fascinated to sit there and see the greatest Hollywood production ever of superstars.

Sammy is taking on himself the responsibility of checking with unions to see that they would cooperate.

I am not making a decision now that we should go forward with this. However, I think it should be explored because I think the idea has a great deal of potential if we could get a decision made soon that we would go forward if we can get the right producer and the right people here to follow up.

What you might do is to have Caruthers check the thing out from the standpoint of cooperation of everybody involved—with Paul Keyes, of course, being the ideal man to do the production and direction. I think it would be better to have Caruthers explore the thing on our part rather than anybody else from the White House staff since he is familiar with show business and also with the many legal problems which would be involved with various television personalities, the bands, etc., that might participate.

If Caruthers is not available to do it, we would have to select somebody else from the staff. The only one I can think of would be Len Garment but, as he would admit, organization is not his strong suit. He is great with the ideas. In any event, if you would get in touch with Keyes and, if you think well of it, with Caruthers, et al., and give me a recommendation on this I would like to have it as soon as possible. Obviously Sammy is hot for the idea and will be doing a lot of promoting on it and since he did mention it at the Evening at the White House last night there will be considerable press interest until we decide either to do it or not to do it.

PPF4; HRH162

W/RN from HRH230

DRAFT

MARCH 10, 1973

TO: **Mr. Stephen Bull**

FROM: **The President**

I think we should be pretty generous with regard to requests by Congressmen for photos with constituents and so forth. You could work this in these morning periods that you have available. What is important is that under no circumstances must we have anybody in if he's going to talk substance.

Talk to Timmons about this, not for the purpose of soliciting business but for the purpose of telling him that when it would be helpful to his operation to have somebody drop in with the Snow Queen or what-have-you that I will be glad to undertake it. Doing a few of these will get around the Hill and will help us. One thing, however, that must be avoided is doing more than one for a Congressman or Senator. We have too often in the past concentrated on friends, doing three or four for them, over a period of time, and doing nothing for others. Obviously this kind of appointment should be granted primarily for those who support us in the

Congress but, now and then, someone who does not support us all the time should be brought in just to keep the proper balance from a PR standpoint.

PPF4

W/RN from HRH230

MARCH 12, 1973

TO: **Bob Haldeman and Henry Kissinger**

FROM: **The President**

It has occurred to me that perhaps the most effective individual we could find to write about our record on bringing the war in Vietnam to an end on a responsible basis would be Sir Robert Thompson. He wrote a book in 1968 or '69 called *No Exit from Vietnam,* which was a brilliant analysis of the mistakes we had made there and which really pointed the way for some of the steps we have taken to get our policy on the right track.

I don't know how this could be programmed, but if a publisher like Hobe Lewis or someone else could be found, Thompson could do a book which would set the historical record straight in an objective way better than almost anybody I know. We, of course, have to assume that his critique would not be totally favorable but this will make it far more credible.

Explore the situation and see what can be done.

HRH162, 230

W/RN from PPF4

RN TAPE

MARCH 12, 1973

TO: **John Dean**

(This is one where you will make only one copy for my file and deliver the other copy to him—it is private.)

I noted the story in the *Post* this morning with regard to some college student who had been hired to get some information with regard to demonstrators which might be useful in keeping those activities from developing into violence or have other unpleasant consequences.

It is difficult for me to understand why we have not done an adequate job of getting the facts out chapter and verse on the massive activities of McGovern and so-called peace groups in funding demonstrations against me, members of the family and others during the campaign. As you are aware, there were virtually no demonstrations whatever on our part against their meetings. This I had ordered at the beginning of the year. On the other hand, I cannot recall a meeting in which I participated where there were not demonstrations, including the non-political-type meetings like the one at the Statue of Liberty. There was hard evidence of the McGovern people supporting and inciting the violent demonstration in San Francisco which resulted in several thousand dollars in property damage. There was also hard evidence of the McGovern headquarters inciting the demonstration in Los Angeles the following day. And it would be hard for me to believe that the fire bombing of our Phoenix headquarters with a loss of $100,000 was done by one of our own people.

It would seem to me that the facts on such activities should be accumulated and that somebody—perhaps the only man who has the guts to do it, Goldwater—should blast the McGovernites for their vicious activities. Needless to say, it would be helpful if Hruska or someone on the Ervin Committee on our side could see that at a time they are investigating our campaign activities they also investigate the charges that have been made against their actions. I have raised this point to no avail on previous occasions. Perhaps you now can follow through and see that something is done.

Give me a report at your convenience.

(RMW—rather than your taking the file copy bring it back to me because until I get the report I want to keep the file copy in my briefcase so that I can check on whether there has been a follow-up.)

PPF4;
3 SENATE HEARINGS 1100

MARCH 14, 1973

TO: **John Ehrlichman**

FROM: **The President**

As I read again the article in *Philadelphia* magazine I felt even more strongly that we need a list of 10 or 15 "horrible examples" of how money has been wasted in model cities, community action, etc.

As a matter of fact, there was even a story, to my amazement, in the *Washington Post* this morning pointing up how the operators of an OEO program had loaned $225,000 to themselves. Just a few of these horrible examples, well scattered among the Congress and among our surrogates, will do far more good than tons of lofty rhetoric which we are spewing out in such volume.

I hope you put one of our brighter people on this job and dig out good, sharp anecdotes that can be distributed among members of Congress and appropriate speakers.

PPF4; HRH162

[MARCH, 1973]*

Potential matters for discussion with Sen. Baker
Meeting to be totally off the record
Time: 30 Min.
Staff: Timmons and Dean

General

—Take Baker's pulse and find out how much he wants to help keep this from becoming a political circus.
—Baker can be assured that no one in the White House had any knowledge that there was going to be a break-in and bugging of the DNC.
—If Baker appears to be truly desirous of cooperating—and the fact he is seeking guidance may so indicate—he might be told that there are matters unrelated to the bugging incident per se (e.g., Segretti, Kalmbach) that could be embarrassing and tarnish good people whose motives were the highest. Surely he can appreciate that things which occur at the White House have a degree of sensitivity that occurs nowhere else in government.

1968 Bugging

—Tell Baker that J. Edgar Hoover personally informed the President shortly after taking office that his campaign had been bugged. Presently seeking to obtain documentation and evidence of the 1968 incidents.

Appearances of White House Staff Members before Senate Committee

—Statement coming out shortly on the matter of Executive privilege (Draft attached).
—Cannot state at this time if such witnesses will be provided to Committee. Must wait to determine how the issue develops.
—A possible resolution of the problem may be that when the Committee believes a White House staff member is essential as a witness, we can compromise and agree upon a sworn written interrogation.

General Guidance

—Seek to get hearings over as quickly as possible because they really are a witch hunt. The President can note that hearings of this type damage all government officials and the institutions of government. The public wants to believe the worst about all politicians, and hearings of this type are going to damage all elected officials.

—Committee procedures should protect the rights of minority members to information, calling its own witnesses, notice of meetings, etc.

—Minority Counsel should be tough, aware of the way things operate in Washington, and able to handle a fellow like Sam Dash who has been selected as Majority Counsel. Dash is a partisan.

—Wally Johnson should be initial contact point, but if Baker feels he wants to raise something that he chooses not to discuss with Wally, then arrangements can be made to meet with Dean. (Note: Frankly, the naming of Dean as the man who deals with the President on such matters preserves our posture on Executive privilege should Dean be called as a witness.)

NOTE: Have just learned that Baker has publicly announced the appointment of Fred Thompson as Chief Minority Counsel. Timmons has recommended George Webster as our candidate.

*[A handwritten note by the President on this undated and unsigned meeting suggestion says "file John Dean." Mr. Dean was named by the President as his liaison on Watergate matters on or before 3/7/73. James McCord, one of the Watergate burglars, sent a letter to Federal District Court Judge John Sirica on 3/21/73. White House records say that the first substantive meeting between Mr. Nixon and Senator Howard Baker in 1973 was on 5/3. They met again on 5/8 to discuss Soviet Jews, records show.]

PPF7

APRIL 25, 1973

GRANT COUNTY PRESS   Petersburg, West Virginia

"When the President's in Trouble, We're All in Trouble"

> *Because of the rapidity with which the Watergate story is unfolding, anything that comes out in your Press this week may be obsolete before you see it. Each day brings with it a new angle which, from the most optimistic point of view, doesn't look great. But to avoid the inevitable accusation that because we're Republican, publishing a Republican newspaper, we're going to look the other way, we want our readers to know that we strongly disapprove of the involvement of our party in anything that hints of deception and Watergate is certainly no exception.*

> *To say that it's been a difficult time for the Republican constituency would be a gross understatement. And, admittedly, it's getting increasingly difficult for us to keep the faith. But in all fairness to President Nixon, we feel that we should withhold our judgement until all of the facts are in. Heaven only knows that he needs all the support he can muster about now!*

> *Monday noon, when we switched on our television set to see what was new with Watergate, we were pleased to note that not only was our Senator Robert Byrd a guest on Washington's Panorama, but that his comments regarding the investigation were obviously carefully studied and stated.*

> *His statement that "When the President is in trouble, we're all in trouble" was very profound. We agree with him in this statement, as well as his suggestion that the President should immediately "reconstitute" his staff to maintain people who have integrity and unload the rest. Senator Byrd pointed out that "although*

he did not believe Nixon had prior knowledge of the Watergate incident, he felt that he could not absolve himself from the responsibility for the scandal." And while this is sad, nevertheless we believe it's true.

And so it goes. But one thing's for certain—the American public wants the story and they mean to have it in its entirety. The matter has now moved beyond political lines out into the realm of trust.

MAY 2, 1973

GRANT COUNTY PRESS Petersburg, West Virginia

Editorial Comment

More on Watergate

Tuesday morning finds us in as much confusion as we were a week ago regarding the Watergate caper. And the President's talk Monday night contributed little toward alleviating our frustration to the end that we could make any kind of constructive editorial comment. We listened carefully to his speech, we heard news analysts take it apart and put it back together again, we considered the resignations Monday of top-level men, and heard opinions of a panel of Republican Senators, all of which finds us still at sea. And it goes without saying that this feeling is the consensus among Americans everywhere.

More than anything we want to believe in our President and we are trying very hard to do just that. To assume that he had prior knowledge of or involvement in the Watergate scandal is not fair because he certainly deserves the same consideration that is accorded others of a lesser stature whom the system says is [sic] innocent until proven guilty.

Trite though it may sound, the fact remains that Nixon is our duly elected commander-in-chief, that by virtue of this fact he should command our respect and loyalty and that as of this moment, we'll cast our lot with him. He has brought us through some of the country's most troubled waters by exercising great leadership qualities in the face of unprecedented opposition and it is our devout hope that in due process he will be vindicated from any involvement whatsoever in this scandal that has practically immobilized governmental operations.

Sure, there's a credibility gap—sure there are many doubts and unanswered questions. But until all the facts are in, we'll continue to reserve our judgment. And it goes without saying, there's more to come.

MAY 9, 1973

GRANT COUNTY PRESS *Petersburg, West Virginia*

Editorial Comment

Eternal Vigilance is the Price of Liberty

Forgery, sabotage, bribery, conspiracy, thievery and discreditability are some of the more unpleasant words in the vocabulary, yet they have become commonplace in today's news.

The Watergate episode, which continues to make Page 1 headlines in all newspapers and takes precedence over all other news on the television newscasts, becomes more involved and complicated with each passing day. So much so that we marvel at the ability of newsmen to keep abreast of the situation and yet retain some semblance of coherence.

And it is to the news aspect of the Watergate scandal that we wish to address ourself this week.

Monday's announcement that the Washington Post *had won the 1973 Pulitzer Prize for meritorious public service for its coverage of the Watergate scandal will bring with it mixed emotions for it has been no secret that neither the* Post *nor the* New York Times *have been among the Nixon Administration's favorite newspapers. And, we must admit, though access to both newspapers for us is quite limited, there have been times when we felt that both were extremely biased in reporting matters pertaining to the President.*

But with the exposé that began some ten months ago and which has grown to proportions undreamed of in the last few weeks by the ordinary American citizen, we have to commend these newspapers and their reporters for dedication to digging out the facts and more importantly, for "telling it like it is." This type of assignment takes a special kind of person with a dedication that far exceeds that of other professions for certainly it's not a pleasant task.

The circumstances leading up to the big explosion about Watergate cannot leave even the most mediocre newspaper editor without some serious thoughts in the matter regarding his role. No matter how small or seemingly unimportant the newspaper, there's hardly any one of us who has not been asked upon occasion to withhold or alter news and most of us have been guilty of compliance at some time or other.

The determination of the Washington Post *and the* New York Times *reporters to call the shots as they saw them should serve as a mandate to all newspaper editors to rededicate themselves to honest and objective reporting at any cost and to concentrate solely on telling it like it is, rather than reporting what someone else says it is.*

The Watergate caper has made us more aware today than ever before that Jefferson knew what he was talking about when he said as far back as 1787:

"The basis of our government being the opinion of the people, the very first object should be to keep that right, and were it left to me to decide whether we should have a government without newspapers, or newspapers without a government, I should not hesitate to prefer the latter."

MAY 30, 1973

GRANT COUNTY PRESS   Petersburg, West Virginia

Press Has Many Roles

Hundreds of editors of the nation's dailies gathered a couple of weeks ago in Washington to attend [the] 50th convention of the American Society of Newspaper Editors. And, as would have been expected, the nation's capital was the last place in the world they would escape from talk of the Watergate scandal which has rocked the Nixon administration and indeed the nation that elected it.

Many prominent persons addressed the ASNE, from Senators to Editors, but the outstanding observations, according to our way of thinking, came from noted playwright, diplomat, politician and Republican Claire Booth Luce who expressed her thoughts on Watergate at a luncheon address.

While hailing the Watergate story as a "triumph of investigative reporting," Mrs. Luce pointed out that the press may wrongly look on the scandal as vindication of their many clashes with the Chief Executive ranging from their opposition to his Vietnam policy to his challenge of their right to publish the purloined Pentagon Papers.

On this last point, Mrs. Luce took the press to task for making the Pentagon Papers burglary seem justified and the Watergate affair unjustified. Both in her mind were equally wrong.

"On the evidence, the demons of suspicion that drove Ellsberg and Russo to burglary were the same demons that entered into the Watergate conspiracy," she told ASNE.

In conclusion, Mrs. Luce called upon the press to pick up the gauntlet the Nixon administration has dropped. ". . . I know that if the press has the power to hurt, even to ruin, it has also the power to heal and restore," she said. "What Watergate may have made impossible for the President to do—the Press now must do—try to bring us together.

"Considering what is at stake not just for Mr. Nixon but for all Americans will the Press try to help us out of this painful and dangerous hour?"

MAY 31, 1973

TO: **Len Garment**

FROM: **Fred Fielding**

RE: **Presidential Appearance—Grand Jury**

"Are men of the first rank and consideration—are men in office—men whose time is not less valuable to the public than to themselves—are such men to be forced to quit their business, their functions, and what is more than all, their pleasure, at the beck of every idle or malicious adversary, to dance attendance upon every petty cause? Yes, as far as it is necessary, they and everybody. . . .

"Were the Prince of Wales, the Archbishop of Canterbury, and the Lord High Chancellor, to be passing by in the same coach, while a chimney-sweeper and a barrow-woman were in dispute about a half-penny-worth of apples, and the chimney-sweeper or the barrow-woman were to think proper to call upon them for their evidence, could they refuse it? No, most certainly."[*]

[*]. . . . 4 *Works of Jeremy Bentham* 320–321 (1843) (cited with approval by the Court in *Branzburg v. Hayes*, 408 U.S. 665, 688 [1972] to illustrate the breadth of Grand Jury powers)

JFB2

JUNE 13, 1973

TO: **Bruce Kehrli**

FROM: **Paul Barrick***

RE: **Legal Fee**

I am sorry to return this to your office but Mr. Colson was employed by the White House at the time of this expenditure. It does not appear to be anything the Finance Committee was involved in, and your office handles all White House expenses; therefore, I believe it would be to your advantage to get the answers from Mr. Colson.

*[Memorandum written on Finance Committee to Re-elect the President letterhead]

JFB2

JUNE 26, 1973

Dear Bill:*

Enclosed are pertinent portions of letters received from a constituent of mine, Mr. James F. Foster, who is interested in obtaining certain information relative to the political financial contribution made by the dairy industry to the Finance Committee to Re-elect the President and the series of events surrounding the announced increase in dairy support prices in April, 1970.

I have contacted the Comptroller General of the United States to obtain the information regarding the contribution. However, I will appreciate being furnished a detailed scenario of the following events: (1) Date the dairy industry requested an increase in support prices; (2) date this request was rejected and by whom; (3) date the group of dairymen met with President Nixon; and (4) the date the Secretary of Agriculture (Hardin, I believe) reversed himself and announced an increase in dairy support prices.

Your assistance in providing this information necessary to respond to Mr. Foster's inquiry will be very much appreciated.

Sincerely yours,

Bob Dole
U. S. Senate

*[Letter to William E. Timmons, assistant to the President]

JFB2

JULY 7, 1973   THE WESTERN WHITE HOUSE, SAN CLEMENTE

TO: General Alexander Haig

FROM: The President

Over the past few days, we have discussed a number of projects which require a considerable amount of follow-up. The purpose of this memorandum is simply to reinforce some of the views I have previously expressed to you and to add some other ideas that have occurred to me since our talks.

In general, I think one of our major deficiencies has been that we have tried to get a point across using only one bullet. Our opponents have been enormously effective in getting three or four rides out of the same story. I realize they have a much easier job than we have because they have the cooperation of the press. On the other hand, we must redouble our efforts to use a number of forums, individuals and other devices to get out a story. Throughout this memo I will keep referring back to this basic point. It is one that you should emphasize strongly to Ziegler and all others who are working on trying to get out our stories.

Of immediate importance is to build up a drum beat for the Committee to hear Haldeman, Ehrlichman and Colson at the earliest possible time. It is, of course, not in our interest at all to have Haldeman and Ehrlichman not appear until September or even October. The strategy of both the Committee and Cox is clear—they want to drag on these hearings and maintain public interest in them as long as they can. They realize that when they put the big names on that interest will soon evaporate. Consequently, it is necessary that there be an all-out offensive starting with the press, using where we can our friendly commentators and columnists, with the party people, with the Congress—if possible with a member of the Committee like Guerney and even Baker if he is willing, and with the individuals concerned themselves. Haldeman, Ehrlichman and Colson.

Demands should be made in every forum for the Committee to hear these men and call them so that they can have a chance to answer the vicious libels that have been levelled against them at the earliest possible time. Charges should be made that the Committee and Cox are deliberately delaying and dragging out—the hearings in the one instance and the Grand Jury proceedings in the other—for political purposes. This is a major project and one that must be undertaken by everybody concerned. Elliot Richardson, for example, should speak to this point and every member of the Cabinet who has an opportunity to do so. This is one area where a statement from the White House—perhaps by Buzhardt—might be in order. But the most important thing is not simply to rely on one person to do it or one commentator—spread the story in a planned way over a number of people and possibly it will get through one of them—if we are lucky two or three may pick up this line and then we will have it made.

An example of our failure to follow through on a story was when Scott went out after a meeting in the Oval Office and put out the fact that there were twice as many taps in the Kennedy Administration as there were in ours. We all cheered around the White House for 24 hours after he had done this but there was no follow-up whatever and the story died without a blip. We must not let this happen again if we can possibly avoid it.

With regard to Haldeman and Ehrlichman, it would seem to me that their counsel would be urging that they be heard as soon as possible. Of course, they must follow whatever advice their counsel gives them on this particular point. Colson, of course, is already banging on the door and trying to be heard but is not getting much press on it. Mitchell, for other reasons of course, is not pressing for an early hearing. But our interests will be greatly served by getting the major figures heard by the Committee at the earliest possible time and by getting the Grand Jury either to indict or to fold up at the earliest possible time.

This brings me to a point that Richardson should emphasize with Cox and a point also that should be emphasized by all of our spokesmen with regard to Cox. He was appointed as Special Prosecutor for the particular purpose of investigating Watergate. The Grand Jury has been meeting for months. Instead of following up on the Watergate investigation and either bringing indictments or indicating that there is no ground for indictment, he is deliberately going into extraneous issues. He cannot be allowed to get away with this. Richardson should take him to task on it but we know, of course, that Richardson will be a relatively weak reed in this respect. But—here, members of the Senate, the press and whatever other spokesmen we can enlist should hit him hard on the fact that as Special Prosecutor he is derelict in his duties in trying to conduct a partisan political vendetta rather than to do the job he was appointed to do—bring the Watergate defendants to trial at the earliest possible time.

A second area in which we need a triple threat approach is with regard to getting out the story on the Kennedy Administration's use of the

FBI for wire tapping. What we want to do here is not to put out names but to put out categories and to re-emphasize the point that Scott made that there were twice as many taps in the Kennedy Administration for national security purposes as during our Administration. Again, every possible forum must be used and every individual we can enlist must be used. A concerted public relations campaign should be developed on this case as on the one I have mentioned previously.

I think, incidentally, that we may be putting too much of a load on Buzhardt. He has the responsibility for virtually all of these matters and he simply isn't able to wheel them. What we need is to give each one of these projects probably to one individual or at most two to one individual and to have follow-up from you at the top and then possibly we can get some action.

A similar case involves the paper that was in the Dean locked box. I think it would be a mistake simply to rely on one bullet in this instance— Guerney, for example, to use it in the Committee. Here, again, there should be a calculated leak in advance, Guerney should be enlisted and perhaps somebody on the Senate Floor and somebody following up in the Cabinet as well. By using all of these bullets—one may hit. By relying on just one, we may miss the target altogether.

Another case along the same lines is a result of the IRS study of the so-called enemy list. Here it is important that we not let the IRS drag out their investigation. I realize that it will necessarily take a lot of time but you should ask them to give you a deadline as to when they can finish it without pressing them to do anything that would result in less than an adequate investigation. When it is completed, however, I would not just rely on Shultz to get the story out. You should use Shultz and again the whole galaxy of other stars to hammer this thing home—recognizing that Shultz is usually not too effective in getting out a story.

Another area where there should be more than one bullet approach is with regard to Buchanan's paper on the campaign tactics of the Democrats in 1972. A game plan should be worked out now to get this paper out—not just by having it presented to the Committee but to have parts of it leaked to people—again from the Senate, the House, the Cabinet, etc.—have these people demand that the Committee go into this matter and, of course, build it up in every possible way before it is dropped before the Committee by a member of the Committee.

With regard to the matter we discussed this morning, I think you might give to Ziegler your round-up of members of the Cabinet, members of the staff, and of course Congressional types that I have seen since the first of the year. While this is not a major issue we are getting a bad rap on the President being isolated. As you well know, the schedule has been very, very heavy in terms of seeing people. In fact, too heavy insofar as doing the job of the Presidency adequately on issues that really matter. Looking to the future in this respect, I think Ziegler should try each day to get out more names of people on the staff, etc., whom I see so that we do not have a build-up develop as it did over the last four years along the lines that the President's top staff people keep him from seeing members of the Cabinet, members of the Congress, and members of his own staff.

We, of course, are aware that this is purely a press line and that what they are really after is that they want the President to have cozy little chats with them. This we will never do. On the other hand, we should not let them get away with giving us a bad time on the general issue of the availability of the President on an almost unprecedented basis to talk to members of the Congress, etc.

Another area where we need perhaps a broader than one shot approach is with regard to the decision I made early in the Administration to discontinue the use of the armed services for domestic intelligence. As you know, this was common practice in the Johnson Administration and my recollection is that it was also used in the Kennedy Administration. Someone should be able to develop a pretty good paper on that point as to the number of people who were involved in that activity from the armed services—the scope of the activity and how this Administration has discontinued it.

In fact, what we have here if we combine the facts that we know are true with regard to our limited use of the FBI is a very positive story rather than a negative one. This Administration has never used the FBI for purely political purposes—both Kennedy and Johnson did. This Administration discontinued the use of the armed services in domestic intelligence and if our IRS study turns out as we hope and expect it to, this Administration has not used the IRS for political partisan purposes. In other words, rather than being the most repressive Administration in these areas it is perhaps the least repressive Administration despite the fact that we had a massive problem to deal with in terms of domestic violence and, therefore, had much more justification than either Johnson or Kennedy had for enlisting all agencies of the government to deal with that violence.

PPF4

JULY 17, 1973

Dear Mr. President:
    Today the Select Committee on Presidential Campaign Activities met and unanimously voted that I request that you provide the Committee with all relevant documents and tapes under control of the White House that relate to the matters the Select Committee is authorized to investigate under S. Res. 60. I refer to the documents mentioned in my letter to Mr. Leonard Garment of June 21, 1973, and the relevant portions of the tapes alluded to by Mr. Alexander Butterfield before the Committee on July 16, 1973.

If your illness prevents our meeting to discuss these issues in the next day or two, I should like to suggest that you designate members of your staff to meet with members of the Select Committee staff to make arrangements for our access to White House documents and tapes pertinent to the Committee's investigation.

I should like respectfully to relate that the Committee's investigation is on-going and that access to relevant documents should not be delayed if the Committee is to perform its mission. May we hear from you at your earliest convenience?

The Committee deeply regrets your illness and hopes for you a speedy recovery.

Sincerely,

Sam J. Ervin, Jr.
Chairman, Select Committee on
Presidential Campaign Activities
United States Senate
Washington, D.C.

AMH13

JULY 23, 1973

Dear Mr. Chairman:*

I have considered your request that I permit the Committee to have access to tapes of my private conversations with a number of my closest aides. I have concluded that the principles stated in my letter to you of July 6th preclude me from complying with that request, and I shall not do so. Indeed the special nature of tape recordings of private conversations is such that these principles apply with even greater force to tapes of private Presidential conversations than to Presidential papers.

If release of the tapes would settle the central questions at issue in the Watergate inquiries, then their disclosure might serve a substantial public interest that would have to be weighed very heavily against the negatives of disclosure.

The fact is that the tapes would not finally settle the central issues before your Committee. Before their existence became publicly known, I personally listened to a number of them. The tapes are entirely consistent with what I know to be the truth and what I have stated to be the truth. However, as in any verbatim recording of informal conversations, they contain comments that persons with different perspectives and motivations would inevitably interpret in different ways. Furthermore, there are inseparably interspersed in them a great many very frank and very private comments, on a wide range of issues and individuals, wholly extraneous to the Committee's inquiry. Even more important, the tapes could be accurately understood or interpreted only by reference to an enormous number of other documents and tapes, so that to open them at all would begin an endless process of disclosure and explanation of private Presidential records totally unrelated to Watergate, and highly confidential in nature. They are the clearest possible example of why Presidential documents must be kept confidential.

Accordingly, the tapes, which have been under my sole personal control, will remain so. None has been transcribed or made public and none will be.

On May 22nd I described my knowledge of the Watergate matter and its aftermath in categorical and unambiguous terms that I know to be true. In my letter of July 6th, I informed you that at an appropriate time during the hearings I intend to address publicly the subjects you are considering. I still intend to do so and in a way that preserves the Constitutional principle of separation of powers, and thus serves the interests not just of the Congress or of the President, but of the people.

Sincerely,

[s/Richard Nixon]

*[Letter to Sam J. Ervin, Jr., chairman, Select Committee on Presidential Campaign Activities, United States Senate]

AMH13

JULY 23, 1973

Dear Senator:*
In view of the intervening events since our telephone conversation on July 12, I know of no useful purpose that would be served by our having a meeting at this time. If you feel otherwise, please have Mr. Edminsten contact Mr. Timmons, and he will arrange a time for a meeting.

Sincerely,

[s/Richard Nixon]

*[Letter to Sam J. Ervin, Jr., chairman, Select Committee on Presidential Campaign Activities, United States Senate]

AMH13

AUGUST 2, 1973

TO: The President

FROM: Alexander M. Haig, Jr.

Attached is a copy of a letter from Charles L. Black, Jr., the Luce Professor of Jurisprudence at Yale University, outlining his views on the matter of executive privilege on tapes and documents. It is strongly supportive of your position and is especially significant in view of Black's normally liberal stance on most issues. It is also significant that Bob Bork has reversed his originally skeptical attitude on our position.

AMH13

SEPTEMBER 13, 1973

Dear Mr. President:*

Fred Buzhardt has, I trust, explained to you the circumstances behind the current dilemma I face with the Ervin Committee.

My inability to testify—if that is the ultimate disposition—will be one of the great disappointments of my life. Beginning in June, I asked the Committee to hear me. I asked for equal time to answer John Dean. I wanted only the opportunity to state the truth and answer the vicious charges made against you.

It is now obvious why the Ervin Committee turned down my repeated requests. It wanted no more pro-Nixon testimony; but more importantly, I now have reason to believe that some Committee members realized that by delaying my appearance, other circumstances could intervene either to prevent me from appearing altogether or at the very least, drastically impair my credibility.

The Committee's position with respect to me underscores the double standard with which you and all those around you have had to contend. In the case of Dean, he was given immunity to testify. In my case, the Committee has refused an identical request for immunity, obviously because my testimony—unlike Dean's—would be favorable to you.

I am not in the slightest concerned about my own guilt or innocence. My conscience is clear; I feel I have done my duty for my country and that when we have seen all of this through, the truth will prevail. What grieves me beyond words, however, is that I may be denied the opportunity to tell the American people what a travesty it has been to try you in the way they have before this Committee.

I hope you know that my loyalty to you is unswerving; it is my sense of devotion to you that makes my inability to testify so painful to me personally. As I told you the last time we talked in your office, the proudest moments of my life have been spent serving you and our country. I hope and pray that in some small way I can continue to do so and, I should add, serve the truth as well.

The greatness of your place in history has been assured, Watergate notwithstanding. What happens to those of us who served with you is of little consequence. I am confident we will be vindicated, but whatever happens we have the satisfaction of having helped you in some small measure—and we have the hope we may in our own ways continue to do so.

Respectfully Yours,

Charles W. Colson

*[Letter from Charles Colson, Colson & Shapiro, Washington, D.C.]

HANDWRITTEN NOTE FROM THE PRESIDENT TO MS. ROSE MARY WOODS: "Call him—tell him 'RN completely understands—and believes he will be off in the end. The irony is that Ellsberg is a hero and those who tried to protect the nation's security are now under attack.'"

PPF7

OCTOBER 17, 1973

GRANT COUNTY PRESS   *Petersburg, West Virginia*

Editorial Comment

Sad But True

A commentator last Wednesday evening signed off his newscast with this wish, "May You Live in Interesting Times" and then asked the question, "Who would have ever thought that 1973 would have been as interesting as it has been?"

To us, the word "interesting" is hardly apropos. In its place, we would term this year as having been the most chaotic, frustrating and demoralizing in our memory. And the farewell address of Spiro T. Agnew Monday evening did little to ease any of the tensions we've been feeling.

When private citizen Agnew bade public life farewell, he did so with denials of wrongdoing, and surely no one who sat before his television screen would have been devoid of feelings of compassion and deep regret. Here was a man who, rather than the self-assured and confident vice president of the United States, was visibly shaken by what he termed in his address as "a nightmare come true." During his five years in the nation's second highest office, he had attracted an entourage of followers that was unprecedented for holders of this position. Here was a man who, on the surface, had everything going for him. But Monday night, he was wearing another mask that didn't become him.

Stating that his plea of "no contest" before the Courts last Wednesday which preceded his resignation later that day was made to "still the raging storm," he reiterated in his address Monday evening denials of bribery and extortion charges against him.

Concluding his address with the statement that "God reigns" and the Government in Washington still lives, [he] left most of us with the feeling that it is well that God does reign. Where else could one go for the wisdom, the courage and the strength to weather these chaotic days in which we are living?

If there's [a] lesson to be learned at all from this experience, and there usually is, we should hope that there will be an awakening of the public to the need for more personal interest in governmental processes, not only at the national level, but all the way down through state, city and county agencies. Our opinions do count, but they must be heard!

OCTOBER 24, 1973

GRANT COUNTY PRESS   *Petersburg, West Virginia*

Editorial Comment

This Is Our Country, Land That We Love!

Who among us wasn't stunned when we learned via special news bulletin Saturday night that a nation which has done a magnificent job of keeping the faith, had once again had the rug pulled out from under it? Who among us wasn't torn by emotions of fear, despair, resentment, anger and most of all—distrust?

The bulletin that prompted these reactions told of the firing by President Nixon of special Watergate prosecutor Archibald Cox and his assistant, William Ruckelshaus, and the accompanying resignation of Attorney General Elliott Richardson.

Dismissals, resignations and firings have become very commonplace in Washington, the most recent having occurred just about ten days prior to the tragic news Saturday night when Vice President Spiro Agnew tendered his resignation from the nation's second highest office. They have been so commonplace that one would think that by now we would be accustomed to them. But what took place Saturday evening seemed to be the straw that broke the camel's back. It's simply expecting too much of the American people to continue to keep the faith in the midst of the nation's greatest constitutional crisis.

As this is written Tuesday morning, we confess to mounting feelings of hostility and distrust. But as these feelings well up within us, so does the determination that we'll be darned if we'll bury our heads in the sand and do nothing. There's too much at stake for us to sit idly by and "let George do it." Whatever your mood, we implore you not to sink to the apathetic level. Be mad, hurt, frustrated or whatever you're capable of feeling, but above all, do not be apathetic!

Now you may ask, "what can we do?" You can write or wire your Congressman and express your feelings—you can tell him whether you think the President should be impeached or whether he should be given another opportunity to vindicate himself. Thousands of telegrams poured into Washington on Monday of this week in which the mood of the country was indicated to the Congress. It's not too late for you to be heard. Just address your letter or telegram to Representative Harley O. Staggers, House Office Building, Washington, D.C. He's there to work for you—let him know what you want him to do.

Finally, you may ask, "what are we going to do?" The answer is this: We want to hear a report on Elliott Richardson's press conference held later today, as well as to what the President will say in his defense which reportedly will come later this week via press conference. It's doubtful, however, that it will change our feeling that he should resign. But we shall see.

Meanwhile, whatever your mood, remember with us that "This Is Our Country, Land That We Love." It is far bigger than any one person or vested-interest group; it goes beyond political boundaries, and even though circumstances through the past months have caused us to wonder, it does belong to us. Let's unite now to protect it as we do all things that are precious to us. Let's replace distrust with awareness and apathy with action.

OCTOBER 31, 1973

GRANT COUNTY PRESS Petersburg, West Virginia

The President and the Press

No one can entertain any doubts about who our Chief Executive will be for the next three years following President Nixon's news conference last Friday evening. He made it "crystal clear" that he had no notion of resigning and it appears that the prospect of instituting impeachment proceedings is dim indeed.

Now that we know where the President stands with the news media, we'd like to make a suggestion. We would like to recommend that something be done to improve relations and thereby better enable the news media and the White House to communicate. It would seem to us that once he has Foreign Affairs under control, this might be a good assignment for Secretary-of-State Henry Kissinger, who seems to be able to reestablish communications in situations where there has been a complete break-down.

Frankly, the problem is too knotty for us to even suggest a solution. And, we know that we should not criticize unless we have a workable alternative. But when one considers the complexities of today's world, there seem to be fewer and fewer applicable alternatives to most situations.

In any event, it seems an elementary conclusion that something will have to be done to bring the President and the press together.

OCTOBER 31, 1973

TO: **Al Haig**

FROM: **Leonard Garment**

RE: **Transfer of Property—Committee to Re-elect the President**

We are advised that CRP is officially terminating its existence as of midnight tonight. As you may be aware, the Committee's files—including an extensive film collection—are currently being held in courtesy storage at the Archives. Jack Nesbitt's office has asked what steps should be taken at this time in regard to the deeding of such materials.

Although there are several possible alternatives, since the materials will ultimately be turned over to the Presidential Library, I would recommend that a Deed of Gift be executed *today,* which would provide as follows:

—Transfer to Archives for ultimate inclusion in the Nixon Library collection

—Disclosure of contents to be restricted consistent with Archives policy and not be opened for research or public review until the Nixon Library is opened for such purposes, except pursuant to subpoena or at the direction of the President or his designee

—The gift is conditioned on the right of attachment by creditors of the Committee to satisfy any judgments against the Committee if no other assets are available.

Presuming this is agreeable to the donor, what do you think?

Agree _____
Disagree _____
Comment _____

cc: Jack Nesbitt

(Handwritten note to Haig from LG—Bryce Harlow has approved this)

_____ JFB3

RN TAPE

NOVEMBER 6, 1973

TO: **Judge Sirica**

I have been concerned, as I am sure the Court has, by the impression that has been created in recent days that in the process of my complying with the decision of the Circuit Court of Appeals by turning over the tape recordings of my conversations which have been subpoenaed by the Special Prosecutor that there are "two missing tapes."

I have no doubt but that the technical evidence which has been presented to date and will be presented during the continuing investigation of this matter will demonstrate to the Court's complete satisfaction that there are no missing tapes.

The two conversations in question were a 5-minute telephone conversation with John Mitchell on the evening of June 20 and a conversation with John Dean in the EOB on the evening of April 15. These conversations were not recorded for purely mechanical reasons which have already been testified to in Court and which I will briefly recap again below.

The only telephone calls which were recorded in the Residence of the White House were those which were made in the Lincoln Sitting Room which, as the Court knows, I use as an office. Telephone conversations in the family quarters have never been recorded during this Administration. The telephone call in question was one that I made on the telephone in the family quarters just before going in to dinner.

Turning now to the conversation with Mr. Dean which occurred between 9:00 and 10:00 P.M. on Sunday evening, April 15, it was not recorded simply because of the technical reason that the tape box because of my very use of the EOB on Saturday and Sunday, April 14 and 15, was completely full. In fact, the tape ran out during the course of my conversation with Mr. Kleindienst which occurred in the afternoon of that day. At   (the hour is to be found as to when the tape did run out). The Secret Service operators who were in charge of the recording equipment were in no way responsible for this happening. It had been their normal practice to take off on Friday for the weekend and to come back on Monday morning, and to leave enough tape in the machines to record six hours of conversation. Normally this would have covered all conversations I would have made on a weekend. In this case, they had no reason to believe that I might use the EOB office that much over a weekend and consequently at that time did not know that all the conversations which occurred over the weekend had not been recorded.

On September 29, after the Circuit Court opinion came down, I decided to review the tapes for the purpose of finding a means to comply with the Circuit Court decision. It was then, for the first time, that the technicians reported that they were unable to find the telephone tape of the Mitchell conversation of June 20 or the recording of the Dean conversation of April 15.

As the Court knows, all other tapes have been found and will be turned over to the Court in a manner in compliance with the Circuit Court's decision. The tape recordings which will be turned over to the Court, incidentally, include six [sic] conversations in which Mr. Dean participated—September 15, March 13, two on March 21, and one on March 22. It should be noted that the Senate Committee did not subpoena the Mitchell telephone conversation or the Dean conversation of April 15. The conversations which they considered vital in which Dean participated of September 15, March 13 and two on March 21 were all recorded and will be turned over to the Court in compliance with the Circuit Court decision.

The conversation with Mr. Dean on the 15th which was not subpoenaed by the Senate Committee occurred after he had gone to the prosecutors and he came in to tell me what he had already told the prosecutors.

While the technical proof therefore is clear that no tape recordings exist of these two conversations, I want to make every effort to be cooperative with the Court in providing information that the Court considers necessary for the Grand Jury proceedings and also I believe that it is in the national interest that simply because tape recordings do not exist, neither the Court nor the Nation will be informed as to what occurred in those conversations.

Consequently, I have been conducting a search of my personal diary to see what information I could find which would be of an evidentiary nature with regard to the discussions which took place in these two conversations.

To assist the Court in this matter I have examined the contents of my personal diary for those two days.

It has been my practice to dictate on a somewhat regular basis—usually once a week and more often when time permits my recollections and observations on highlights of events which have occurred as I recall them. When I have dictated such memoranda they are put in my private file with a notation at the beginning of the dictation that they are not to be transcribed. None of them, incidentally, have ever been transcribed.

In addition to these dictated on those occasions, when I made notes during the course of a meeting I put them in my private diary file for that date. In those cases when I have made notes during the course of a meeting it was not my practice [to] dictate recollections with regard to that particular meeting, since I considered the notes to be adequate for historical and other purposes.

Turning now to the two conversations in which no tape recordings were made I find that on June the 20th at 8:30 P.M. I dictated a memorandum for file which covered personal matters. In the course of that memorandum I made a brief reference to the five-minute telephone call I had had with John Mitchell. The following is an exact transcript of my reference to that call taken directly from the IBM dictabelt which I dictated on that date.

I also talked to John Mitchell late in the day and tried to cheer him up a bit. He is terribly chagrined that the activities of anybody attached to his committee should have been handled in such a manner and he said that he only regretted that he had not policed all of the people more effectively in his own organization.

It is of interest to note that this is substantially what John Mitchell testified to before the Ervin Committee when he was asked about this conversation. There is no further reference to the John Mitchell conversation on the tape that I dictated for that day.

Turning now to the Dean conversation of April 15, I made notes of the conversation while it occurred. I also made notes during the meeting I had had earlier in the day with Attorney General Kleindienst and Mr. Petersen. Following my usual practice I did not dictate any memorandum for the file on that date but put the notes in my personal diary file for April 15.

Because there is no tape recording available covering that meeting and because of my desire to remove any impression that there is something to hide I am turning over with this memorandum to the Court for inspection in camera and use before the Grand Jury under the same ground rules of the subpoenaed tapes, my notes of the conversations I had with Kleindienst, Petersen and Dean on April 15. Because I want no doubt whatever to exist as to the authenticity of these notes I am providing the originals to the Court, and after the Court has examined them and had the opportunity to make photostats of them, I would appreciate it if the Court would return the originals to me for my personal diary file. There has been, understandably, some confusion with regard to what recordings might be available for the April 15 meeting for which I must assume the responsibility.

And then, Fred [Fielding], put in here, but in a more condensed way, the business about Henry Petersen.

PPF4

NOVEMBER 7, 1973

GRANT COUNTY PRESS   *Petersburg, West Virginia*

Editorial Comment

To Err Is Human

    The tumultuous public demands for resignation or impeachment of President Nixon become increasingly loud and more deafening with each passing day. And pollsters are reporting that his ability to govern and his credibility are plummeting with as much rapidity as the demands for termination of his Presidential tenure.

    Amid all of this frenzied activity, much of which is motivated by sheer frustration and feelings of helplessness, we believe we should pause to ask this question: "Who would replace President Nixon if he did comply with what seems now to be the wishes of the majority and did tender his resignation? Is there anyone next in line with the wisdom and experience that would be required to deal effectively with foreign and domestic affairs?"

    We've got to admit—Watergate or no, the President's record is not a defunct one by any manner or means. Just one year ago he was the most popular guy in the country. Granted, a lot has happened in the interim, but can we completely lose sight of the good things that have happened to this nation during the Nixon regime? We believe not!

But back to a replacement. At this time, there's no vice-president, but even if there were, would the designate, Gerald Ford, possess the necessary qualities to assume all the demands of the Presidency? Next in line is Speaker of the House Carl Albert who, it seems to us, is less than interested in the possibility of becoming President Nixon's replacement.

All of this brings us to this point which we ask you to consider. Perhaps it's a mark of naivete and even ludicrous to think of it, but over the weekend we wondered what would happen if President Nixon chose to make available all Watergate-related material?

The worst, as we see it, would be a continuation of demands for resignation and possible acceleration of impeachment proceedings.

The other thing that could happen, however, deserves consideration, we believe. People for the most part want to believe in their president. It's important to them that they can and it's important to the country. If given all the facts and an opportunity to weigh them, isn't it conceivable that American people might be forgiving enough to want the President to complete his term of office? We believe so! We believe that Americans are not only forgiving, but that they are understanding of the human frailities [sic] from which each of us suffer.

Granted, we expect the President to epitomize the highest standards in morality and honesty, and justly so. But aren't we being terribly idealistic when we disallow for any humanness in an individual and aren't we, by so doing, placing him or her in a position where there's really no possible way to measure up?

We've been as disenchanted and frustrated as any of you. Matter-of-fact, we believe even more so because we've had to defend our profession against attacks by the President, and yet try to retain some degree of loyalty and respect for him. If you will recall, two weeks ago we said editorially that we felt the President "should probably resign." And certainly the events that have followed that editorial have done nothing to improve the Presidential image.

But we refuse to believe that there isn't another way out. We still believe that Mr. Nixon will rally to the wishes of the people who, one year ago, proclaimed loud and clear at the ballot box that they believed in him. We believe that he will come forward and make available records that are necessary to unravel this tangled web that is undermining public morale.

If this should happen, if he should say to the country of which he is chief executive, and to the world at large, "I am human—I have erred," we believe it could be one of the greatest turning points in history.

Finally, we believe that the nation would rejoice in the humanness of one so great and would find a strength and unity in this quote: "To err is human—to forgive is divine!"

NOVEMBER 12, 1973

Dear Mr. President:

Some time ago I mentioned to you on the phone the Trueblood

book on Lincoln. I have read a number of Lincoln books, but this is in many ways the most revealing.

I can't help but feel as I read through this that, relatively speaking, his ordeal in 1862 was very similar to that which you are now enduring. Yet with faith he survived it and, of course, earned a singular place in history. I am convinced that you will do the same thing; in the end it will be the trial that you have withstood that will add to, rather than detract from, your greatness.

Respectfully yours,

Charles W. Colson*

*[Colson & Shapiro, Washington, D.C.]

PPF7

[*Markings indicate the President saw the following handwritten letter.*]

NOVEMBER 16, 1973

Dear President Nixon,

I was at the Georgetown hospital in little Teddy's room when you phoned him this morning. It was so wonderful. He had been told about one hour earlier that he would lose his leg the next day. His father and mother were all trying to be cheerful and then Big Teddy left the room but quickly returned smiling and said, "The President wants to talk with you, Teddy." Little Teddy spoke. "No he doesn't. I don't believe he is calling me up." Then you came on the phone and Teddy talked with assurance and pride. Afterwards we all laughed and tried to guess what you said and who would be the first to find out, etc. Everybody's spirits were picked up and the rest of the day seemed so much easier.

I know you carry many burdens and yet find time to cheer a boy and his family. That is a gesture of unselfishness and nobility.

I thank you very very much.

Sincerely,

[s/Eunice Kennedy Shriver]

PPF10

NOVEMBER 26, 1973

TO: **Al Haig**

FROM: **Pat Buchanan**

Am uncertain if I conveyed the measure of my concern at not having my own papers restored to my own files, and I hope this memo will do so.

a. No other loyal active senior staff member has been placed in this position, and few others would have tolerated it this long.

b. Those are my papers, from my files, surrendered over *temporarily* and *voluntarily,* and the refusal of the lawyers to return them constitutes, in my judgment, a breach of faith.

c. If the lawyers' refusal is based on some fear of what will happen to the lawyers should they give them back, that fear is certain to enlarge rather than diminish as the crunch comes so the time for resolution is now.

d. If our own team is unwilling to take even the minuscule risk of minor embarrassment, involved in turning my own papers back over to me, then the hell with it, we can pack it in right now.

Let me repeat the situation. Jaworski has not subpoenaed my files; we have already beaten Ervin in Court; I have already testified; the most flamboyant of my political papers, which Ervin had subpoenaed, are already in the public sector.

Cannot believe the President would endorse this dog-in-the-manger posture, given his own willingness to go to the brink on this question. In any event, if the "lawyers" refuse the return of those papers, when asked, I want to take the matter up in my next conversation with the President.

Realize the lawyers are busy, they have other great concerns—but what is of insignificance to them has assumed great importance to me. All I want is those five boxes out of the Bomb Shelter and back where they belong.

AMH13

DECEMBER 3, 1973

TO: **Fred Buzhardt**
Leonard Garment

FROM: **Fred Fielding**

RE: **Hoffa Pardon**

This afternoon Larry Traylor, the Pardon Attorney, called to advise me of a telephone conversation in regard to the Hoffa pardon.

He stated that he met this morning with a Mr. Lawrenceson, who identified himself as Executive Director of the National Association for Justice, and on behalf of Mr. Hoffa he requested a copy of the White House memorandum to the Pardon Attorney directing that a condition be imposed upon Mr. Hoffa's pardon. Mr. Traylor advised him that no such memorandum exists.

Mr. Lawrenceson told Mr. Traylor that they are taking the position that the President did not personally sign the warrant granting Mr. Hoffa's commutation of sentence; rather, Mr. Lawrenceson said his experts had looked at the signature and concluded that it was a forgery. In this regard, it is interesting to note that Mr. Lawrenceson has a copy of the Master Warrant in question, which is signed but undated—the only such copies that I have ever seen that were undated are in the White House files.

Mr. Lawrenceson said that his organization is seeking to have the condition of Mr. Hoffa's commutation removed by administrative action, rather than going into court. They feel the President is vulnerable on this matter because of the alleged forgery, and also because of their claim that the condition was added by the intervention or maneuvering of Charles Colson as a condition of an agreement between him and the International Brotherhood of Teamsters that Colson would get the IBT as a client once he left the White House.

JFB3

w/RN from JFB3 [sic]

1974

Looking back, I probably should have pardoned them. I'm not sure that the country would have taken it at that time. It was a little stirred up, as you might imagine . . . It was a tragic situation; I wish I could have, but I didn't.

—RICHARD M. NIXON IN RESPONSE TO A QUESTION ABOUT H. R. HALDEMAN AND JOHN EHRLICHMAN ON NBC'S "MEET THE PRESS," APRIL 10, 1988

FEBRUARY 2, 1974

Dear Mr. President,

I am deeply grateful for the privilege of riding with you from the White House to attend the Prayer Breakfast at the Hilton Hotel, and riding back.

I was delighted to see the enthusiastic reception that you got when you arrived back.

I was also delighted to see the enthusiastic reception you received from the 3,000 attending the Prayer Breakfast, from all over the world. Your remarks concerning the spiritual life of Lincoln were deeply appreciated. I had rather hoped that you would go from the wonderful expression about Lincoln's dependence on the Lord in times of crisis, to your own personal experience. I think everyone was waiting for it and expecting it. As one Senator said to me afterward, "he went to the brink and backed away." In any event, everyone was appreciative. While I know you have a personal and private commitment, yet at some point many are hoping and praying that you will state it publicly as Harold Hughes and Chuck Colson are now doing. In taking such a stand you would find the deepest personal satisfaction in your own life.

To be President is a great and thrilling attainment. However there is one thing far greater than being President—and that is being a committed child of God. There is a thrill, a joy, an adventure, an excitement, a

609

satisfaction, awaiting you in that direction, no matter what the circumstances around you, that is indescribable.

I agree with Senator Percy that your State of the Union Address was one of the greatest addresses that you have ever delivered. In my judgment you scored many points!

The events of the next few weeks will be dramatic and historic. I am sure that millions of Americans will be in prayer that God's will shall be done. I especially will be praying for you and the family.

With warmest personal affection, I am

Cordially yours,

[s/Billy]*

*[Letter from Billy Graham, Montreal, North Carolina]

MAY 13, 1974

Dear Rose Mary,*

I am sure that you must be aware that I have no sympathy whatsoever with the latest editorial spasm of the *Chicago Tribune,* a paper I was once proud to serve, but can no longer respect.

The action was not the paper's but the editor's, which may be something of a paradox. However, the editor, Clayton Kirkpatrick, cannot write and cannot think and has no grounding in history—past or present.

He is a constant reader of the *Washington Post.* This reading has moved him to bring the *Tribune* into the eastern establishment and, like most converts, he is out-liberalling the liberals.

Don't misunderstand me, I like Kirkpatrick, indeed, I am saving him for the role of donner [sic] in a heart transplant, because I have never known him to use his heart or his head, for that matter.

I do not see the paper, because he does not choose to send it to me, which makes him a far more generous man that I had expected him to be. He has saved me much anguish, but some of his blunders and stupidity reach me.

If failure should be a legitimate reason for calling for resignation, I can only wonder that he doesn't adopt his own advice since the paper is losing circulation and advertising to say nothing of influence.

Cordially,
[s/Walter]

P.S. Need I say that no small reason for refusing to resign is that the new *Tribune* must not be victorious.

*[Letter to Rose Mary Woods from Walter Trohan, Newmarket-on-Fergus, County Clare, Ireland]

OPPOSITE LETTERHEAD IS HANDWRITTEN RN COMMENT: "Haig note!"

PPF188

[Handwritten letter]

JUNE 3, 1974

Dear Chuck,

    I know what a terribly sad and difficult day this must be for you and your fine family.

    I want you to know that in a very personal way it is an equally sad day for me.

    You must however keep your faith in the fact that as time goes on your dedicated service to the nation will be remembered long after this incident has become only a footnote in history.

Always—your friend,

RN

PPF7

JUNE 8, 1974

TO: **Rose**

FROM: **The President**

I would like for you to call Charlie Rhyne and ask him to prepare over a period of time, because there is no urgency on it, a three-thousand-word speech, and it must not be more than that, that he would recommend that I make with regard to how world law can contribute to world peace. He has talked to me often about this and I have in the past not felt that the time was right to make such a statement. I don't have in mind a forum at the moment—my guess is that a national radio broadcast would probably get the most news coverage combined, of course, with a very heavy mailing—to his mailing list and others interested in this subject.

    I have in mind that such a speech might be made in perhaps early September or perhaps during the month of August if we are in a position to get any kind of an audience at that time. Impress upon him that there is no urgency on this, but I would like to see a draft which he would recommend would be appropriate for the President to issue, either as a speech or statement or what have you.

PPF4

[Handwritten letter]

JUNE 8, 1974

Dear Gerry—

    This is just a note to tell you how much I have appreciated your superb and courageous support over these past difficult months.

How much easier it would be for you to pander to the press and others who desperately are trying to drive a wedge between the President and the Vice President.

It's tough going now but History will I am sure record you as one of the most capable, courageous, and honorable Vice Presidents we have ever had—

RN

PPF8

JUNE 8, 1974

Dear Walter:*

I greatly appreciate your letter of May 13, but, believe me, I was sure before that you had no sympathy whatsoever with the latest editorial spasm of the *Chicago Tribune*.

Your letter, as a matter of fact, gave us all a good chuckle because you can say a lot of things that we would like to!

I hope that you are enjoying life more each day in Ireland and that you will continue to keep in touch with us.

I know the President would want me to extend his very warmest personal regards to you and Mrs. Trohan.

Sincerely,

Rose Mary Woods
Executive Assistant
to the President

*[Letter to Walter Trohan]

PPF188:
MATERIALS REMOVED
FROM PRESIDENT'S DESK

THIRD DRAFT*

AUGUST 5, 1974

FROM: [Raymond] **Price**

Statement by the President

I have today instructed my attorneys to make available to the House Judiciary Committee, and I am making public, the transcripts of my June 23, 1972, conversations with H. R. Haldeman. I have also turned over the tapes of these conversations to Judge Sirica, as part of the process of my compliance with the Supreme Court ruling.

On April 21, in announcing my decision to make public the original set of White House transcripts, I stated that "as far as what the President personally knew and did with regard to Watergate and the cover-up is concerned, these materials—together with those already made available—will tell it all."

Shortly after that, in May, I made a preliminary review of some of the 64 taped conversations subpoenaed by the Special Prosecutor.

Among the conversations I listened to at that time were those of June 23. Although I recognized that these presented a problem, I did not inform my staff or my counsel of it, or those arguing my case, nor did I amend my submission to the Judiciary Committee in order to include and reflect it. As a result, those arguing my case, as well as those passing judgment on the case, did so with information that was incomplete and in some respects erroneous. This was a serious act of omission, which I now regret, and am sorry for. I did not then realize the extent of the implications which that conversation might now appear to have.

Since the Supreme Court's decision 12 days ago, I have ordered my Counsel to analyze the 64 tapes, and I have listened to a number of them myself. This process has made it clear that the tape of the June 23 conversation is at variance with certain of my previous statements. Therefore, I have ordered it made available immediately to the Judiciary Committee so that it can be reflected in the Committee's report, and so that it will be included in the record to be considered by the House and Senate.

In a formal written statement on May 22 of last year, I said that shortly after the Watergate break-in I became concerned about the possibility that the investigation might lead to the exposure either of unrelated covert activities of the CIA, or of sensitive national security matters that the so-called "plumbers" unit at the White House had been working on, because of the CIA and plumbers connections of some of those involved. I said that I therefore gave instructions that the FBI should be alerted to coordinate with the CIA, and to ensure that the investigation not expose these sensitive national security matters.

That statement was based on my recollection at the time—some eleven months later—plus documentary materials and the sworn testimony of those involved.

The June 23 tapes clearly show, however, that at the time I gave those instructions I did discuss the political aspects of the situation, and that I was aware of the advantages this course of action would have with respect to limiting possible public exposure of involvement by persons connected with the re-election committee.

My review of the additional tapes has, so far, shown no other major inconsistencies with what I have previously submitted. While I have no way at this stage of being certain that there will not be others, I have no reason to believe that there will be. In any case, the tapes in their entirety are now in the process of being furnished to Judge Sirica. He has begun what may be a rather lengthy process of reviewing the tapes, passing on specific claims of executive privilege on portions of them, and forwarding to the Special Prosecutor those tapes or those portions that are relevant to the Watergate investigation.

It is highly unlikely that this review will be completed in time for the House debate. It appears at this stage, however, that a House vote of impeachment is, as a practical matter, virtually a foregone conclusion, and that the issue will therefore go to trial in the Senate. In order to ensure that no other significant relevant materials are withheld, I shall voluntarily furnish to the Senate everything from these tapes that Judge Sirica rules should go to the Special Prosecutor.

I recognize that this additional material I am now furnishing may further damage my case, especially because attention will be drawn separately to it rather than to the evidence in its entirety. In considering its implications, therefore, I urge that two points be borne in mind.

The first of these points is to remember what actually happened as a result of the instructions I gave on June 23. Acting Director Gray of the FBI did coordinate with Director Helms and Deputy Director Walters of the CIA. The CIA did undertake an extensive check to see whether any of its covert activities would be compromised by a full FBI investigation of Watergate. Deputy Director Walters then reported back to Mr. Gray that they would not be compromised. On July 6, Mr. Gray reported to me, and, as the record shows, I then told him to press ahead vigorously with his investigation—which he did.

The second point I would urge is that the evidence be looked at in its entirety, and the events be looked at in perspective. Whatever mistakes were made in the handling of Watergate, I remain firmly convinced that the record does not justify the extreme step of impeachment and removal of a President. I trust that as the Constitutional process goes forward, this perspective will prevail.

*[First draft is in PPF186.]

AMH24

AUGUST 14, 1974

GRANT COUNTY PRESS *Petersburg, West Virginia*

Editorial Comment

Hail to the Chief

Ascension of Gerald Ford to the Presidency of the United States last Friday will be remembered as one of the most significant turning points in the history of this nation. This is true because with it we see a resumption of the basic philosophies which are absolute necessities if this nation is to survive.

In place of deception and exploitation, we see honesty, integrity and candor. We see a vulnerability and an openness in the new President that has revolutionized the lives of thousands of individuals who have made these attributes an important part of their lifestyle in the past six or eight years and which has replaced frustrations and anxieties with a feeling of strength and serenity which can come from only one source.

We believe that President Ford will not rely exclusively on his own strengths nor those of the people with whom he surrounds himself. We believe that he will consult often the never-failing provider of comfort and strength and this makes us feel good. Too long those in the top echelons of government have relied on their own instincts and strengths, only to bring us to where we were last week this time.

But today, for the first time in more than two years, many things seem right with the world. What a welcome change!

IMPEACHMENT OF RICHARD M. NIXON, PRESIDENT OF THE UNITED STATES*

August 20, 1974—Referred to the House Calendar and ordered to be printed

---

Mr. Rodino, from the Committee on the Judiciary, submitted the following

REPORT

together with

SUPPLEMENTAL, ADDITIONAL, SEPARATE, DISSENTING, MINORITY, INDIVIDUAL AND CONCURRING VIEWS

The Committee on the Judiciary, to whom was referred the consideration of recommendations concerning the exercise of the constitutional power to impeach Richard M. Nixon, President of the United States, having considered the same, reports thereon pursuant to H. Res. 803 as follows and recommends that the House exercise its constitutional power to impeach Richard M. Nixon, President of the United States, and that articles of impeachment be exhibited to the Senate as follows:

RESOLUTION

Impeaching Richard M. Nixon, President of the United States, of high crimes and misdemeanors.

*House Calendar #426, House of Representatives, 93d Congress, 2d Session.

Resolved, That Richard M. Nixon, President of the United States, is impeached for high crimes and misdemeanors, and that the following articles of impeachment be exhibited to the Senate:

Articles of impeachment exhibited by the House of Representatives of the United States of America in the name of itself and of all of the people of the United States of America, against Richard M. Nixon, President of the United States of America, in maintenance and support of its impeachment against him for high crimes and misdemeanors.

Article I

In his conduct of the office of President of the United States, Richard M. Nixon, in violation of his constitutional oath faithfully to execute the office of President of the United States and, to the best of his ability, preserve, protect, and defend the Constitution of the United States, and in violation of his constitutional duty to take care that the laws be faithfully executed, has prevented, obstructed, and impeded the administration of justice, in that:

On June 17, 1972, and prior thereto, agents of the Committee for the Re-election of the President committed unlawful entry of the headquarters of the Democratic National Committee in Washington, District of Columbia, for the purpose of securing political intelligence. Subsequent thereto, Richard M. Nixon, using the powers of his high office, engaged personally and through his subordinates and agents, in a course of conduct or plan designed to delay, impede, and obstruct the investigation of such unlawful entry; to cover up, conceal and protect those responsible; and to conceal the existence and scope of other unlawful covert activities.

The means used to implement this course of conduct or plan included one or more of the following:

1. making or causing to be made false or misleading statements to lawfully authorized investigative officers and employees of the United States;

2. withholding relevant and material evidence or information from lawfully authorized investigative officers and employees of the United States;

3. approving, condoning, acquiescing in, and counseling witnesses with respect to the giving of false or misleading statements to lawfully authorized investigative officers and employees of the United States and false or misleading testimony in duly instituted judicial and congressional proceedings;

4. interfering or endeavoring to interfere with the conduct of investigations by the Department of Justice of the United States, the Federal Bureau of Investigation, the Office of Watergate Special Prosecution Force, and Congressional Committees;

5. approving, condoning, and acquiescing in the surreptitious payment of substantial sums of money for the purpose of obtaining the silence or influencing the testimony of witnesses, potential witnesses or individuals who participated in such unlawful entry and other illegal activities;

6. endeavoring to misuse the Central Intelligence Agency, an agency of the United States;

7. disseminating information received from officers of the Department of Justice of the United States to subjects of investigations conducted by lawfully authorized investigative officers and employees of the United States, for the purpose of aiding and assisting such subjects in their attempts to avoid criminal liability;

8. making false or misleading public statements for the purpose of deceiving the people of the United States into believing that a thorough and complete investigation had been conducted with respect to allegations of misconduct on the part of personnel of the executive branch of the United States and personnel of the Committee for the Re-election of the President, and that there was no involvement of such personnel in such misconduct; or

9. endeavoring to cause prospective defendants, and individuals duly tried and convicted, to expect favored treatment and consideration in return for their silence or false testimony, or rewarding individuals for their silence or false testimony.

In all of this, Richard M. Nixon has acted in a manner contrary to his trust as President and subversive of constitutional government, to the great prejudice of the cause of law and justice and to the manifest injury of the people of the United States.

Wherefore Richard M. Nixon, by such conduct, warrants impeachment and trial, and removal from office.

Article II

Using the powers of the office of President of the United States, Richard M. Nixon, in violation of his constitutional oath faithfully to execute the office of President of the United States and, to the best of his ability, preserve, protect, and defend the Constitution of the United States, and in disregard of his constitutional duty to take care that the laws be faithfully executed, has repeatedly engaged in conduct violating the constitutional rights of citizens, impairing the due and proper administration of justice and the conduct of lawful inquiries, or contravening the laws governing agencies of the executive branch and the purposes of these agencies.

This conduct has included one or more of the following:

1. He has, acting personally and through his subordinates and agents, endeavored to obtain from the Internal Revenue Service, in viola-

tion of the constitutional rights of citizens, confidential information contained in income tax returns for purposes not authorized by law, and to cause, in violation of the constitutional rights of citizens, income tax audits or other income tax investigations to be initiated or conducted in a discriminatory manner.

2. He misused the Federal Bureau of Investigation, the Secret Service, and other executive personnel, in violation or disregard of the constitutional rights of citizens, by directing or authorizing such agencies or personnel to conduct or continue electronic surveillance or other investigations for purposes unrelated to national security, the enforcement of laws, or any other lawful function of his office; he did direct, authorize, or permit the use of information obtained thereby for purposes unrelated to national security, the enforcement of laws, or any other lawful function of his office; and he did direct the concealment of certain records made by the Federal Bureau of Investigation of electronic surveillance.

3. He has, acting personally and through his subordinates and agents, in violation or disregard of the constitutional rights of citizens, authorized and permitted to be maintained a secret investigative unit within the office of the President, financed in part with money derived from campaign contributions, which unlawfully utilized the resources of the Central Intelligence Agency, engaged in covert and unlawful activities, and attempted to prejudice the constitutional right of an accused to a fair trial.

4. He has failed to take care that the laws were faithfully executed by failing to act when he knew or had reason to know that his close subordinates endeavored to impede and frustrate lawful inquiries by duly constituted executive, judicial, and legislative entities concerning the unlawful entry into the headquarters of the Democratic National Committee, and the cover-up thereof, and concerning other unlawful activities, including those relating to the confirmation of Richard Kleindienst as Attorney General of the United States, the electronic surveillance of private citizens, the break-in into the offices of Dr. Lewis Fielding, and the campaign financing practices of the Committee to Re-elect the President.

5. In disregard of the rule of law, he knowingly misused the executive power by interfering with agencies of the executive branch, including the Federal Bureau of Investigation, the Criminal Division, and the Office of Watergate Special Prosecution Force, of the Department of Justice, and the Central Intelligence Agency, in violation of his duty to take care that the laws be faithfully executed.

In all of this, Richard M. Nixon has acted in a manner contrary to his trust as President and subversive of constitutional government, to the great prejudice of the cause of law and justice and to the manifest injury of the people of the United States.

Wherefore Richard M. Nixon, by such conduct, warrants impeachment and trial, and removal from office.

Article III

In his conduct of the office of President of the United States, Richard M. Nixon, contrary to his oath faithfully to execute the office of President of the United States and, to the best of his ability, preserve, protect, and defend the Constitution of the United States, and in violation of his constitutional duty to take care that the laws be faithfully executed, has failed without lawful cause or excuse to produce papers and things as directed by duly authorized subpoenas issued by the Committee on the Judiciary of the House of Representatives on April 11, 1974, May 15, 1974, May 30, 1974, and June 24, 1974, and willfully disobeyed such subpoenas. The subpoenaed papers and things were deemed necessary by the Committee in order to resolve by direct evidence fundamental, factual questions relating to Presidential direction, knowledge, or approval of actions demonstrated by other evidence to be substantial grounds for impeachment of the President. In refusing to produce these papers and things, Richard M. Nixon, substituting his judgment as to what materials were necessary for the inquiry, interposed the powers of the Presidency against the lawful subpoenas of the House of Representatives, thereby assuming to himself functions and judgments necessary to the exercise of the sole power of impeachment vested by the Constitution in the House of Representatives.

In all of this, Richard M. Nixon has acted in a manner contrary to his trust as President and subversive of constitutional government, to the great prejudice of the cause of law and justice, and to the manifest injury of the people of the United States.

Wherefore Richard M. Nixon, by such conduct, warrants impeachment and trial, and removal from office.

MEET THE PRESS

[The conclusion of NBC's program of April 10, 1988]

TOM BROKAW: What about when you are self-critical of your personal style or how you treat people or how you look at the world? Do you see anything that you might have done differently?

RICHARD NIXON: Well, I suppose I could have treated the press better.

TOM BROKAW: Well, I wasn't looking for that necessarily.

RICHARD NIXON: But then they might have treated me better. No, I think under the circumstances it's very difficult for one to psychoanalyze himself. You know I don't go much for this psycho-history. I don't go much for psycho-TV shows, either. I think they're rather revolting. And as far as sitting down and psychoanalyzing myself and saying, now, how could I have been a better person, it's just not my bag.

JOHN CHANCELLOR: . . . Write me a paragraph that might be written about the turn of the century or the next century about Richard Nixon.

RICHARD NIXON: . . . History will treat me fairly. Historians probably won't because most historians are on the left, and I understand that. I would say as people look back on the Nixon administration they're probably most likely to remember 50 years from now, 100 years from now, that it made a difference on a very major issue. We changed the world. If it had not been for the China initiative, which only I could do at that point, we would be in a terrible situation today with China aligned with the Soviet Union and with the Soviet Union's power. The China initiative hasn't brought peace to the world. We can't be sure that will happen. But without it, we would be in terrible shape.

CHRIS WALLACE: . . . Do you have thoughts about what you could have accomplished in the rest of the second term, and how, flowing from that, America would have been so different?

RICHARD NIXON: My priorities were these. One, interestingly enough, one of the first ones, was the Mideast. I talked about it over and over again with Henry Kissinger in February and March of 1973. Second was [that] we would not have lost the war in Vietnam. I would have seen to it that we would have forced the North Vietnamese to keep the Paris peace agreement. And that would have meant that we wouldn't have had basically what happened in all the places around the world, Cambodia, Laos, even what happened in Africa and even in Nicaragua. The other part is that we—I think we would have done something at home. There was an area particularly I was interested in, and that was to have a real welfare program. I am concerned about the fact that when you look at blacks, they are worse off today, generally speaking, on an average, than they were in 1966 when the Great Society program started, and the problem is the family. We've got to do something about that, and our family assistance program was the right way to go. . . .

APPENDIX

The following is the law passed by Congress in 1974 and signed by President Gerald Ford, which seized the papers, recordings, and other materials of President Richard M. Nixon. Its constitutionality was upheld by the Supreme Court of the United States in 1978.

44 U.S.C. 2111 Note
PRESIDENTIAL RECORDINGS AND MATERIALS
PRESERVATION ACT

Delivery and Retention of Certain Presidential Materials

SEC. 101. (a) Notwithstanding any other law or any agreement or understanding made pursuant to section 2111 of title 44, United States Code [this section] any Federal employee in possession shall deliver, and the Archivist of the United States (hereinafter in this title referred to as the "Archivist") shall receive, obtain, or retain, complete possession and control of all original tape recordings of conversations which were recorded or caused to be recorded by any officer or employee of the Federal Government and which—

(1) involve former President Richard M. Nixon or other individuals who, at the time of the conversation, were employed by the Federal Government;

(2) were recorded in the White House or in the office of the President in the Executive Office Buildings located in Washington, District of Columbia; Camp David, Maryland; Key Biscayne, Florida; or San Clemente, California; and

(3) were recorded during the period beginning January 20, 1969, and ending August 9, 1974.

(b)(1) Notwithstanding any other law or any agreement or understanding made pursuant to section 2111 of title 44, United States Code [this section], the Archivist shall receive, retain, or make reasonable efforts to obtain, complete possession and control of all papers, documents, memorandums, transcripts, and other objects and materials which constitute the Presidential historical materials of Richard M. Nixon, covering the period beginning January 20, 1969, and ending August 9, 1974.

(2) For purposes of this subsection, the term "historical materials" has the meaning given it by section 2101 of title 44, United States Code [section 2101 of this title].

Availability of Certain Presidential Materials

SEC. 102. (a) None of the tape recordings or other materials referred to in section 101 shall be destroyed, except as hereafter may be provided by law.

(b) Notwithstanding any other provision of this title, any other law, or any agreement or understanding made pursuant to section 2111 of title 44, United States Code [this section], the tape recordings and other materials referred to in section 101 shall, immediately upon the date of enactment of this title, be made available subject to any rights, defenses, or privileges which the Federal Government or any person may invoke, for use in any judicial proceeding or otherwise subject to court subpoena or other legal process. Any request by the Office of Watergate Special Prosecution Force, whether by court subpoena or other lawful process, for access to such recordings or materials shall at all times have priority over any other request for such recordings or materials.

(c) Richard M. Nixon, or any person whom he may designate in writing, shall at all times have access to the tape recordings and other materials referred to in section 101 for any purpose which is consistent with the provisions of this title, subsequent and subject to the regulations which the Archivist shall issue pursuant to section 103.

(d) Any agency or department in the executive branch of the Federal Government shall at all times have access to the tape recordings and other materials referred to in section 101 for lawful Government use, subject to the regulations which the Archivist shall issue pursuant to section 103.

Regulations to Protect Certain Tape Recordings and Other Materials

SEC. 103. The Archivist shall issue at the earliest possible date such regulations as may be necessary to assure the protection of the tape recordings and other materials referred to in section 101 from loss or destruction, and to prevent access to such recordings and materials by unauthorized persons. Custody of such recordings and materials shall be maintained in Washington, District of Columbia, or its metropolitan area, except as may otherwise be necessary to carry out the provisions of this title.

Regulations Relating to Public Access

SEC. 104. (a) The Archivist shall, within ninety days after the date of enactment of this title [Dec. 19, 1974] submit to each House of the Congress a report proposing and explaining regulations that would provide public access to the tape recordings and other materials referred to in section 101. Such regulations shall take into account the following factors:

(1) the need to provide the public with the full truth, at the earliest reasonable date, of abuses of governmental power popularly identified under the generic term "Watergate";

(2) the need to make such recordings and materials available for use in judicial proceedings;

(3) the need to prevent general access, except in accordance with appropriate procedures established for use in judicial proceedings, to information relating to the Nation's security;

(4) the need to protect every individual's right to a fair and impartial trial;

(5) the need to protect any party's opportunity to assert any legally or constitutionally based right or privilege which would prevent or otherwise limit access to such recordings and materials;

(6) the need to provide public access to those materials which have general historical significance, and which are not likely to be related to the need described in paragraph (1); and

(7) the need to give Richard M. Nixon, or his heirs, for his sole custody and use, tape recordings and other materials which are not likely to be related to the need described in paragraph (1) and are not otherwise of general historical significance.

(b) The regulations proposed by the Archivist in the report required by subsection (a) shall not take effect until the expiration of the first period of 60 calendar days of continuous session of the Congress after the date of the submission of such regulations to each House of the Congress. For the purposes of this subsection, continuity of session is broken only by an adjournment of Congress sine die, but the days on which either House is not in session because of an adjournment of more than three days to a day certain are excluded.

(c) The provisions of this title shall not apply, on and after the date upon which regulations proposed by the Archivist take effect under subsection (b), to any tape recordings or other materials given to Richard M. Nixon, or his heirs, pursuant to subsection (a)(7).

(d) The provisions of this title shall not in any way affect the rights, limitations or exemptions applicable under the Freedom of Information Act, 5 U.S.C. §552 et seq.

Judicial Review

SEC. 105. (a) The United States District Court for the District of Columbia shall have exclusive jurisdiction to hear challenges to the legal or constitutional validity of this title or of any regulation issued under the authority granted by this title, and any action or proceeding involving the question of title, ownership, custody, possession, or control of any tape recording or material referred to in section 101 or involving payment of any just compensation which may be due in connection therewith. Any such challenge shall be treated by the court as a matter requiring immediate consideration and resolution, and such challenge shall have priority on the docket of such court over other cases.

(b) If, under the procedures established by subsection (a), a judicial decision is rendered that a particular provision of this title, or a particular regulation issued under the authority granted by this title, is unconstitutional or otherwise invalid, such decision shall not affect in any way the validity or enforcement of any other provision of this title or any regulation issued under the authority granted by this title.

(c) If a final decision of such court holds that any provision of this title has deprived an individual of private property without just compensation, then there shall be paid out of the general fund of the Treasury of the United States such amount or amounts as may be adjudged just by that court.

Authorization of Appropriations

SEC. 106. There is authorized to be appropriated such sums as may be necessary to carry out the provisions of this title.

(End of note)

§ 2112. PRESIDENTIAL ARCHIVAL DEPOSITORY

(a) When the Archivist considers it to be in the public interest he may accept, for and in the name of the United States, land, buildings, and equipment offered as a gift to the United States for the purpose of creating a Presidential archival depository, and take title to the land, buildings, and equipment on behalf of the United States, and maintain, operate, and protect them as a Presidential archival depository, and as part of the national archives system; and make agreements, upon terms and conditions he considers proper, with a State, political subdivision, university, institution of higher learning, institute, or foundation to use as a Presidential archival depository land, buildings, and equipment of the State, subdivision, university, or other organization, to be made available by it without transfer of title to the United States, and maintain, operate, and protect the depository as a part of the national archives system.

The Archivist shall submit a report in writing on a proposed Presidential archival depository to the President of the Senate and the Speaker of the House of Representatives, and include—

a description of the land, buildings, and equipment offered as a gift or to be made available without transfer of title;

a statement of the terms of the proposed agreement, if any;

a general description of the types of papers, documents, or other historical materials proposed to be deposited in the Presidential archival depository so to be created, and of the terms of the proposed deposit;

a statement of the additional improvements and equipment, if any, necessary to the satisfactory operation of the depository, together with an estimate of the cost; and

an estimate of the annual cost to the United States of maintaining, operating, and protecting the depository.

The Archivist may not take title to land, buildings, and equipment or make an agreement, until the expiration of the first period of 60 calendar days of continuous session of the Congress following the date on which the report is transmitted, computed as follows:

Continuity of session is broken only by an adjournment sine die, but the days on which either House is not in session because of an adjournment of more than three days to a day certain are excluded.

(b) When the Archivist considers it to be in the public interest, he may deposit in a Presidential archival depository papers, documents, or other historical materials accepted under section 2111 of this title, or Federal records appropriate for preservation.

(c) When the Archivist considers it to be in the public interest, he may exercise, with respect to papers, documents, or other historical materials deposited under this section, or otherwise, in a Presidential archival depository, all the functions and responsibilities otherwise vested in him pertaining to Federal records or other documentary materials in his custody or under his control. The Archivist, in negotiating for the deposit of Presidential historical materials, shall take steps to secure to the Government as far as possible, the right to have continuous and permanent possession of the materials. Papers, documents, or other historical materials accepted and deposited under section 2111 of this title and this section are subject to restrictions as to their availability and use stated in writing by the donors or depositors, including the restriction that they shall be kept in a Presidential archival depository. The restrictions shall be respected for the period stated, or until revoked or terminated by the donors or depositors or by persons legally qualified to act on their behalf. Subject to the restrictions, the Archivist may dispose by sale, exchange, or otherwise, of papers, documents, or other materials which the Archivist determines to have no permanent value or historical interest or to be surplus to the needs of a Presidential archival depository. Only the first two sentences of this subsection shall apply to Presidential records as defined in section 2201(2) of this title.

(d) When the Archivist considers it to be in the public interest, he may cooperate with and assist a university, institution of higher learning, institute, foundation, or other organization or qualified individual to further or to conduct study or research in historical materials deposited in a Presidential archival depository.

(e) When the Archivist considers it to be in the public interest, he may charge and collect reasonable fees for the privilege of visiting and viewing exhibit rooms or museum space in a Presidential archival depository.

(f) When the Archivist considers it to be in the public interest, he may provide reasonable office space in a Presidential archival depository for the personal use of a former President of the United States.

(g) When the Archivist considers it to be in the public interest, he may accept gifts or bequests of money or other property for the purpose of maintaining, operating, protecting, or improving a Presidential archival depository. The proceeds of gifts or bequests, together with proceeds from fees or from sales of historical materials, copies or reproductions, catalogs, or other items, having to do with a Presidential archival depository, shall be paid into the National Archives Trust fund to be held, administered, and expanded for the benefit and in the interest of the Presidential archival depository in connection with which they were received, including administrative and custodial expenses as the Archivist determines.

§ 2113. DEPOSITORY FOR AGREEMENTS BETWEEN STATES

The Archivist may receive duplicate originals or authenticated copies of agreements or compacts entered into under the Constitution and laws of the United States, between States of the Union, and take necessary actions for their preservation and servicing.

§ 2114. PRESERVATION OF MOTION-PICTURE FILMS, STILL PICTURES, AND SOUND RECORDINGS

The Archivist may make and preserve motion-picture films, still pictures, and sound recordings pertaining to and illustrative of the historical development of the United States Government and its activities, and provide for preparing, editing, titling, scoring, processing, duplicating, reproducing, exhibiting, and releasing for non-profit educational purposes, motion-picture films, still pictures, and sound recordings in his custody.

§ 2115. REPORTS; CORRECTION OF VIOLATIONS

(a) In carrying out their respective duties and responsibilities under chapters 21, 25, 29, 31, and 33 of this title, the Archivist and the Administrator may each obtain reports from any Federal agency on such agency's activities under such chapters.

(b) When either the Archivist or the Administrator finds that a provision of any such chapter has been or is being violated, the Archivist or the Administrator shall (1) inform in writing the head of the agency concerned of the violation and make recommendations for its correction; and (2) unless satisfactory corrective measures are inaugurated within a reasonable time, submit a written report of the matter to the President and the Congress.

§ 2116. LEGAL STATUS OF REPRODUCTIONS; OFFICIAL SEAL; FEES FOR COPIES AND REPRODUCTIONS

(a) When records that are required by statute to be retained indefinitely have been reproduced by photographic, microphotographic, or other processes, in accordance with standards established by the Archivist the indefinite retention by the photographic, microphotographic, or other reproductions constitutes compliance with the statutory requirements for the indefinite retention of the original records. The reproductions, as well as reproductions made under regulations to carry out chapters 21, 29, 31, and 33 of this title, shall have the same legal status as the originals.

(b) There shall be an official seal for the National Archives of the United States which shall be judicially noticed. When a copy or reproduction, furnished under this section, is authenticated by the official seal and certified by the Archivist, the copy or reproduction shall be admitted in evidence equally with the original from which it was made.

(c) The Archivist may charge a fee set to recover the costs for making or authenticating copies or reproductions of materials transferred to his custody. Such fee shall be fixed by the Archivist at a level which will recover, so far as practicable, all elements of such costs, and may, in the Archivist's discretion, include increments for the estimated replacement cost of equipment. Such fees shall be paid into, administered, and expended as a part of the National Archives Trust Fund. The Archivist may not charge for making or authenticating copies or reproductions of materials for official use by the United States Government unless appropriations available to the Archivist for this purpose are insufficient to cover the cost of performing the work.

§ 2117. LIMITATION ON LIABILITY

When letters and other intellectual productions (exclusive of patented material, published works under copyright protection, and unpublished works for which copyright registration has been made) come into the custody or possession of the Archivist, the United States or its agents are not liable for infringement of literary property rights or analogous rights arising out of use of the materials for display, inspection, research, reproduction, or other purposes.

§ 2118. RECORDS OF CONGRESS

The Secretary of the Senate and the Clerk of the House of Representatives, acting jointly, shall obtain at the close of each Congress all the noncurrent records of the Congress and of each congressional committee and transfer them to the National Archives and Records Administration for preservation, subject to the orders of the Senate or the House of Representatives, respectively.

B

APPENDIX

Following is the text of the Presidential Records Act of 1978, signed by President Jimmy Carter, which has governed the handling and disposition of presidential records since 1981.

PRESIDENTIAL RECORDS

(44 U.S.C. Chapter 22)

§ 2201. DEFINITIONS

As used in this chapter—

(1) The term "documentary material" means all books, correspondence, memorandums, documents, papers, pamphlets, works of art, models, pictures, photographs, plats, maps, films, and motion pictures, including but not limited to, audio, audio-visual, or other electronic or mechanical recordations.

(2) The term "Presidential records" means documentary materials, or any reasonably segregable portion thereof, created or received by the President, his immediate staff, or a unit or individual of the Executive Office of the President whose function is to advise and assist the President, in the course of conducting activities which relate to or have an effect upon the carrying out of the constitutional, statutory, or other official or ceremonial duties of the President. Such term—

(A) includes any documentary materials relating to the political activities of the President or members of his staff, but only if such activities relate to or have a direct effect upon the carrying out of constitutional, statutory, or other official or ceremonial duties of the President; but

(B) does not include any documentary materials that are (i) official records of an agency (as defined in section 552(e) of title 5, United States

Code); (ii) personal records; (iii) stocks of publications and stationery; or (iv) extra copies of documents produced only for convenience of reference, when such copies are clearly so identified.

(3) The term "personal records" means all documentary materials, or any reasonably segregable portion thereof, of a purely private or non-public character which do not relate to or have an effect upon the carrying out of the constitutional, statutory, or other official or ceremonial duties of the President. Such term includes—

(A) diaries, journals, or other personal notes serving as the functional equivalent of a diary or journal which are not prepared or utilized for, or circulated or communicated in the course of, transacting Government business;

(B) materials relating to private political associations, and having no relation to or direct effect upon the carrying out of constitutional, statutory, or other official or ceremonial duties of the President; and

(C) materials relating exclusively to the President's own election to the office of the Presidency; and materials directly relating to the election of a particular individual or individuals to Federal, State, or local office which have no relation to or direct effect upon the carrying out of constitutional, statutory, or other official or ceremonial duties of the President.

(4) The term "Archivist" means the Archivist of the United States.

(5) The term "former President," when used with respect to Presidential records, means the former President during whose term or terms of office such Presidential records were created.

§ 2202. OWNERSHIP OF PRESIDENTIAL RECORDS

The United States shall reserve and retain complete ownership, possession, and control of Presidential records; and such records shall be administered in accordance with the provisions of this chapter.

§ 2203. MANAGEMENT AND CUSTODY OF PRESIDENTIAL RECORDS

(a) Through the implementation of records management controls and other necessary actions, the President shall take all such steps as may be necessary to assure that the activities, deliberations, decisions, and policies that reflect the performance of his constitutional, statutory, or other official or ceremonial duties are adequately documented and that such records are maintained as Presidential records pursuant to the requirements of this section and other provisions of law.

(b) Documentary materials produced or received by the President, his staff, or units or individuals in the Executive Office of the President the function of which is to advise and assist the President, shall, to the extent practicable, be categorized as Presidential records or personal records upon their creation or receipt and be filed separately.

(c) During his term of office, the President may dispose of those of his Presidential records that no longer have administrative, historical, informational, or evidentiary value if—

(1) the President obtains the views, in writing, of the Archivist concerning the proposed disposal of such Presidential records; and

(2) the Archivist states that he does not intend to take any action under subsection (e) of this section.

(d) In the event the Archivist notifies the President under subsection (c) that he does intend to take action under subsection (e), the President may dispose of such Presidential records if copies of the disposal schedule are submitted to the appropriate Congressional Committees at least 60 calendar days of continuous session of Congress in advance of the proposed disposal date. For the purpose of this section, continuity of session is broken only by an adjournment of Congress sine die, and the days on which either House is not in session because of an adjournment of more than three days to a day certain are excluded in the computation of the days in which Congress is in continuous session.

(e) The Archivist shall request the advice of the Committee on Rules and Administration and the Committee on Governmental Affairs of the Senate and the Committee on House Administration and the Committee on Government Operations of the House of Representatives with respect to any proposed disposal of Presidential records whenever he considers that—

(1) these particular records may be of special interest to the Congress; or

(2) consultation with the Congress regarding the disposal of these particular records is in the public interest.

(f)(1) Upon the conclusion of a President's term of office, or if a President serves consecutive terms upon the conclusion of the last term, the Archivist of the United States shall assume responsibility for the custody, control, and preservation of, and access to, the Presidential records of that President. The Archivist shall have an affirmative duty to make such records available to the public as rapidly and completely as possible consistent with the provisions of this Act.

(2) The Archivist shall deposit all such Presidential records in a Presidential archival depository or another archival facility operated by the United States. The Archivist is authorized to designate, after consultation with the former President, a director at each depository or facility, who shall be responsible for the care and preservation of such records.

(3) The Archivist is authorized to dispose of such Presidential records which he has appraised and determined to have insufficient administrative, historical, informational, or evidentiary value to warrant their continued preservation. Notice of such disposal shall be published in the

Federal Register at least 60 days in advance of the proposed disposal date. Publication of such notice shall constitute a final agency action for purposes of review under chapter 7 of title 5, United States Code.

§ 2204. RESTRICTIONS ON ACCESS TO PRESIDENTIAL RECORDS

(a) Prior to the conclusion of his term of office or last consecutive term of office, as the case may be, the President shall specify durations, not to exceed 12 years, for which access shall be restricted with respect to information, in a Presidential record, within one or more of the following categories:

(1)(A) specifically authorized under criteria established by an Executive order to be kept secret in the interest of national defense or foreign policy and (B) in fact properly classified pursuant to such Executive order;

(2) relating to appointments to Federal office;

(3) specifically exempted from disclosure by statute (other than sections 552 and 552b of title 5, United States Code), provided that such statute (A) requires that the material be withheld from the public in such a manner as to leave no discretion on the issue, or (B) establishes particular criteria for withholding or refers to particular types of material to be withheld;

(4) trade secrets and commercial or financial information obtained from a person and privileged or confidential;

(5) confidential communications requesting or submitting advice, between the President and his advisers, or between such advisers; or

(6) personnel and medical files and similar files the disclosure of which would constitute a clearly unwarranted invasion of personal privacy.

(b)(1) Any Presidential record or reasonably segregable portion thereof containing information within a category restricted by the President under subsection (a) shall be so designated by the Archivist and access thereto shall be restricted until the earlier of—

(A)(i) the date on which the former President waives the restriction on disclosure of such record, or

(ii) the expiration of the duration specified under subsection (a) for the category of information on the basis of which access to such record has been restricted; or

(B) upon a determination by the Archivist that such record or reasonably segregable portion thereof, or of any significant element or aspect of the information contained in such record or reasonably segregable portion thereof, has been placed in the public domain through publication by the former President, or his agents.

(2) Any such record which does not contain information within a category restricted by the President under subsection (a), or contains

information within such a category for which the duration of restricted access has expired, shall be exempt from the provisions of subsection (c) until the earlier of—

(A) the date which is 5 years after the date on which the Archivist obtains custody of such record pursuant to section 2203(d)(1); or

(B) the date on which the Archivist completes the processing and organization of such records or integral file segment thereof.

(3) During the period of restricted access specified pursuant to subsection (b)(1), the determination whether access to a Presidential record or reasonably segregable portion thereof shall be restricted shall be made by the Archivist, in his discretion, after consultation with the former President, and, during such period, such determinations shall not be subject to judicial review, except as provided in subsection (e) of this section. The Archivist shall establish procedures whereby any person denied access to a Presidential record because such record is restricted pursuant to a determination made under this paragraph may file an administrative appeal of such determination. Such procedures shall provide for a written determination by the Archivist or his designee, within 30 working days after receipt of such an appeal, setting forth the basis for such determination.

(c)(1) Subject to the limitations on access imposed pursuant to subsections (a) and (b), Presidential records shall be administered in accordance with section 552 of title 5, United States Code, except that paragraph (b)(5) of that section shall not be available for purposes of withholding any Presidential record, and for the purposes of such section such records shall be deemed to be records of the National Archives and Records Administration. Access to such records shall be granted on nondiscriminatory terms.

(2) Nothing in this Act shall be construed to confirm, limit, or expand any constitutionally-based privilege which may be available to an incumbent or former President.

(d) Upon the death or disability of a President or former President, any discretion or authority the President or former President may have had under this chapter shall be exercised by the Archivist unless otherwise previously provided by the President or former President in a written notice to the Archivist.

(e) The United States District Court for the District of Columbia shall have jurisdiction over any action initiated by the former President asserting that a determination made by the Archivist violates the former President's rights or privileges.

§ 2205. EXCEPTIONS TO RESTRICTED ACCESS

Notwithstanding any restrictions on access imposed pursuant to section 2204—

(1) the Archivist and persons employed by the National Archives and Records Administration who are engaged in the performance of normal archival work shall be permitted access to Presidential records in the custody of the Archivist;

(2) subject to any rights, defenses, or privileges which the United States or any agency or person may invoke, Presidential records shall be made available—

(A) pursuant to subpoena or other judicial process issued by a court of competent jurisdiction for the purposes of any civil or criminal investigation or proceeding;

(B) to an incumbent President if such records contain information that is needed for conduct of current business of his office and that is not otherwise available; and

(C) to either House of Congress, or, to the extent of matter within its jurisdiction, to any committee or subcommittee thereof if such records contain information that is needed for the conduct of its business and that is not otherwise available; and

(3) the Presidential records of a former President shall be available to such former President or his designated representative.

§ 2206. REGULATIONS

The Archivist shall promulgate in accordance with section 553 of title 5, United States Code, regulations necessary to carry out the provisions of this chapter. Such regulations shall include—

(1) provisions for advance public notice and description of any Presidential records scheduled for disposal pursuant to section 2203(f)(3);

(2) provisions for providing notice to the former President when materials to which access would otherwise be restricted pursuant to section 2204(a) are to be made available in accordance with section 2205(2);

(3) provisions for notice by the Archivist to the former President when the disclosure of particular documents may adversely affect any rights and privileges which the former President may have; and

(4) provisions for establishing procedures for consultation between the Archivist and appropriate Federal agencies regarding materials which may be subject to section 552(b)(7) of title 5, United States Code.

§ 2207. VICE-PRESIDENTIAL RECORDS

Vice-Presidential records shall be subject to the provisions of this chapter in the same manner as Presidential records. The duties and responsibilities of the Vice President, with respect to Vice-Presidential records, shall be the same as the duties and responsibilities of the President under this chapter with respect to Presidential records. The authority of the Archivist with respect to Vice-Presidential records shall be the same as the authority of the Archivist under this chapter with respect to Presidential records, except that the Archivist may, when the Archivist determines that it is in the public interest, enter into an agreement for the deposit of Vice-Presidential records in a non-Federal archival depository. Nothing in this chapter shall be construed to authorize the establishment of separate archival depositories for such Vice-Presidential records.

C

APPENDIX

The National Archives in 1987 formally notified attorneys for Mr. Nixon of its intention to release in January 1989 several dozen hours of taped conversations which were subpoenaed and transcribed by the Watergate Special Prosecutor but never used in court. The Archives also informed Mr. Nixon's attorneys that the first portions of the tapes that had not been subpoenaed will be ready for public listening by January 1991. The log of these taped conversations is some 27,000 pages long. Here is a brief history of the tapes compiled by the National Archives.

The White House taping system under President Nixon consisted of a network of seven stations maintained and operated by agents of the Technical Security Division of the Secret Service.

The system was installed in several segments. In February 1971 seven microphones were placed in the Oval Office—five in the President's desk and one on each side of the fireplace. Two others were placed in the Cabinet Room under the table near the President's chair. All nine devices were wired directly to Sony 800B recorders in an old locker room in the White House basement.

Two months later four microphones were installed in the President's hideaway office in the Old Executive Office Building (EOB). Three were concealed under the top of the President's desk and the fourth in the knee well below. The devices were wired to machines in an adjacent room. The President's telephones in the Oval Office, the EOB, and the Lincoln Sitting Room in the White House were linked to another recorder in the White House basement.

In May 1972 the Secret Service set up a system in the President's study in Aspen Lodge at his Camp David retreat. A microphone hidden in the room and others connected to two telephones on the President's desk and his table were wired to Sony 800B recorders in a room under the residence.

The recorders used five-inch reels with an average tape length of about 1,800 feet. Each ran at a speed of 15/16 of an inch per second, allowing approximately six hours of recording per reel. In the two and a half years the system was in operation, 950 tapes were created.

The systems in the Oval Office, the EOB, and the Camp David study were sound-activated. The telephone systems were engaged each time a call was placed. The Cabinet Room system was designed to be operated manually by switches located on each side of the President's chair or by a switch controlled by the President's appointment secretaries, Alexander P. Butterfield and, later, Stephen B. Bull.

The quality of the recording was relatively poor. Frequent mechanical malfunctions, volume fluctuations, inferior equipment and tape quality, extraneous noise, and the system's sound-activated properties added to the problem. The Nixon Project has corrected some of these failings by the use of complex sound enhancement equipment, which filters out some interfering noises and increases the volume. No one on the White House staff conducted periodic reviews of sound quality after the system was installed, and the Secret Service technicians who set up the system were not permitted to listen to the recordings.

Added to the quality problem is the fact that the majority of the conversations on the tapes are unstructured, free-flowing, and spontaneous. In other words, they are normal exchanges, consisting of frequent interruptions, sentence fragments, unclear enunciation, and unknown allusions.

The Camp David study microphone was disconnected on March 18, 1973. The Camp David telephones and the other systems were shut down on July 18, 1973, two days after their existence was revealed by Alexander Butterfield to the Senate Select Committee on Presidential Campaign Activities.

The White House tapes available for public listening (through 1988) consist of the 31 conversations that were played to the juries as evidence in *United States v. John B. Connally* and *United States v. John D. Ehrlichman, Harry R. Haldeman, Robert Mardian, John N. Mitchell and Kenneth W. Parkinson.*

Both cases were prosecuted by the Watergate Special Prosecution Force (WSPF) and tried in the United States District Court for the District of Columbia in Washington, D.C. Secretary of the Treasury John Connally was indicted by a grand jury in July 1974 for conspiring to commit perjury and obstruct justice and for accepting illegal contributions for the 1972 campaign from three large dairy cooperatives in exchange for obtaining administration support for increased milk support prices. Connally was tried on the charges of accepting illegal payments and found not guilty on April 17, 1975; the other charges were dropped the next day. Ehrlichman, Haldeman, Mardian, Mitchell, and Parkinson were indicted by a grand jury on October 1, 1974, on various charges of perjury, conspiracy, and obstruction of justice. On January 1, 1975, the trial jury found Ehrlichman, Haldeman, Mardian, and Mitchell guilty and acquitted Parkinson.

The WSPF originally obtained approximately 100 tape-recorded conversations for use in its investigations. In addition to recordings from the White House, this number included two telephone conversations recorded on dictabelt in the offices of Charles W. Colson and John D. Ehrlichman. The recordings were transcribed and the transcripts were reviewed by the WSPF. From this body of materials the WSPF introduced as Government exhibits and played in open court one tape-recorded conversation in the Connally trial and 30 in the *U.S. v. Mitchell, et al.* trial, a total of approximately 12½ hours of conversation. The transcripts were provided to the jurors as listening aids.

In July 1978 Judge John J. Sirica gave the National Archives the set of copies of the 30 conversations that were introduced as evidence in the Mitchell trial. Another set of copies, a copy of the conversation used in the Connally trial, and a copy of the transcripts which had been kept by the WSPF had been turned over previously, in June 1977, to the Judicial and Fiscal Branch of the National Archives.

INDEX

Beatles, the, 194
Becker, 173
BeLieu, Ken, 60
Bell, George, 235, 369, 370
  memos to
    from Colson, 201–2, 279, 309
    from Huston, 207–8
Bell, J. Raymond, communications
    from Colson to, 425, 460
Bennett, Robert, xxx, xxxii, xxxvi,
    xxxix, 186, 202–3, 209–10, 293, 308
Benton, Thomas Hart, 432
Bentsen, Lloyd, li, 169, 392
Bernstein, Leonard, 298
Berrigan, Daniel, 323, 493
Berry, Loren, 142
Biafra, 89–90
Biemiller, Andy, 187, 208
Black, Charles L., Jr., 596–97
Blackmun, Harry A., 114–15
Black Panthers, 89, 98, 219, 221
Black United Front, 270
Blake, Lord Robert, lxvi, 358
Blatchford, 553
Bobrick, Robert, 493
Bobst, Elmer, 105, 142, 243, 244
Boeschenstein, Harold, 97
Bond, Julian, 96
Boone, Pat, 334
Bork, Robert H., 153, 597
  letter from Colson to, 153
Borman, 73
Borsch, Fred, 222
  letter from Colson to, 222
Bradley, Ben, 429
Bradshaw, David, 96, 176, 285
  letter from Colson to, 96
Brady, Thomas A., 165, 166
  memos to F. Donald Nixon from,
    165
Bremer, 445, 446
Brennan, 323
Brennan, J. V.
  memo to Woods from, 124–25
Brennan, Peter, 158, 161
Brennan, William, xliii-xliv, 327
Brezhnev, Leonid, 308–9, 442, 482
Brinkley, David, 428
Brokaw, Tom, 484–85, 621
Brooke, Edward W., 96, 97, 182,
    453–54

Brookings Institution, xxi, xxii, 29, 146,
    148, 208, 435
Brown, Bob, memos from Colson to,
    551–52
Brown, Clarence, 20
Brown, Edgar W., Jr., 142
Brown, Gertrude, memo from
    Butterfield to, 311
Brown, John R., III
  memos from
    to Butterfield, 111
    to Ehrlichman, 88, 92–94, 96–97,
      109, 156–57, 161
    to Finch, 156–57
    to Haldeman, 95, 98, 116, 117, 141,
      152, 156–57, 162–63, 212
    to Kissinger, 89–90, 90, 96–98,
      109, 111
  memos to
    from Colson, 180
    from Haldeman, 30
    from Higby, 159
    from Dub O'Neill, 40
Brown, Pat, xiv, xv
Bryant, Anita, 116
Buchanan, Patrick J., xvin, xviin, xliii,
    36–38, 44, 54, 148, 171, 172, 202,
    243, 306–7, 313, 323, 367, 419,
    480, 483, 526, 569
  communications from
    to Abel, 221
    Assault Strategy, 463–73
    to Chapin, 195–96, 203
    to Cole, 42
    to Colson, 313, 368, 422, 434,
      509–10
    to Dean, 238
    to Ehrlichman, Haldeman, and
      Colson, 548–49
    to Erhlichman and Krogh, 346
    to Haig, 606–7
    to Haldeman, 78–79, 211, 239–40,
      303, 304, 320–22, 326–28,
      341–44, 345
    to Haldeman and Colson, 554
    to Hyde, 262
    to Kehrli, 318–19, 328–29
    to Kissinger, 323
    to Kissinger and Haldeman, 229,
      314–15
    to Magruder, 113

Buchanan, Patrick J. *(cont'd)*
  to Nixon, 37, 146, 217–18, 287, 310,
    311, 317–18, 324–26, 340–41,
    401–2, 558–68
  to Warren, 207
  memos to
    from Cole, 42
    from Colson, 328, 341, 368, 490,
      554–58
    from Haldeman, 41–42, 88–89,
      219–20
    from Huntsman, 243
    from Kehrli, 501, 550–51
    from Khachigian, 344, 573
    from Nixon, 77, 175, 474–76
Buchanan, Shelley, memos to
  from Colson, 512
  from Joan Hall, 358
Buckley, William F., 304, 338
Bull, Stephen, 119, 499
  memo from Nixon to, 582–83
Bundy, McGeorge, 17, 259
Bundy, William, 400
Burch, Dean, xviii, 150, 151, 170,
  171–73, 232, 245, 380
Burger, Warren E., xliii, 191–92
  letter from Nixon to, 257
  letter to Nixon from, 254–55
Burke, Elizabeth, 54
Burning Tree golf course, 46–47
Burns, Arthur F., 3, 61–62, 101, 147,
  196, 227, 498
Burton, 168
Burum, Miss (Nixon's 5th grade
  teacher), 19
Bush, George, xlvi, xlviii, xlix, li, lii,
  43, 163, 169, 302, 333, 526, 572,
  576
Butterfield, Alexander P., 119,
  594
  memos from
    to Gertrude Brown, 311
    to Dean, 511
    to Dent, 34
    to Ehrlichman, 327
    to Haldeman, 22, 288–89, 305
    to Harlow and Klein, 22
    to Hughes and Haig, 306
    to Kissinger, 527
    to Nixon, 54, 59–60, 61–63, 65–69,
     287

memos to
  from John R. Brown, III, 111
  from Dean, 259, 268
  from Haldeman, 55, 215, 221, 557
  from Nixon, 180, 335, 421
Buzhardt, Fred, 592, 593, 597
  memo from Fielding to, 607–8
Byrd (senator), 586–87
Byrnes, Jimmy, 4, 4

Calhoun, J. M., 158
Cambodia, 138, 139, 143, 144, 181
Capp, Al, 174
Carlucci, Frank, 537
Carmichael, Stokely, 141
Carswell, Harrold, 30–31, 114,
  573
Caruthers, 582
Case, Clifford, 182, 423
Casey, Thomas, 370–71
  communications from Colson to,
    371, 377–78
Casey, William J., 142, 228
Cash, Johnny, 95
Cashen, Henry, 371
  memos from Colson to, 162, 225
Caulfield, Jack, 209, 300
  memos from
    to Dean, 212
    to Haldeman, 214–15
Cavett, Dick, 267, 288
CBS, 139–40, 165, 171, 172, 216, 230–34,
  245, 289, 292, 296–97, 298–99,
  301, 329–30, 357
Cecil, Lord D., 358
Central Intelligence Agency (CIA),
  35, 141, 143, 179, 448–49, 502, 504,
  506–9, 613
Chamberlain, Neville, 130
Chancellor, John, 333, 429, 621
  letter from Colson to, 350
Chapin, Dwight L., 46–47, 71
  memos from
    to Haldeman, 43, 192–3, 204–5
    to Nofziger, 218
    to O'Donnell, 553
  memos to
    from Buchanan, 195–96, 203
    from Colson, 186, 216–17, 226, 260
    from Haldeman, 149, 185, 319–20,
     442

Edson, Peter, xxvii
Edwards, Willard, xii, xiii
Efron, Edith, 304, 328
Ehrlich, Ev, 288
Ehrlichman, John, xxxvii, xxxix, xl-xli,
    19, 48, 58–59, 99, 127–28, 173, 196,
    221, 412, 433, 450, 503, 505, 533,
    535, 537, 538, 591, 592
  communications from
    to Graham, 223
    to Krogh, 8–11
    to Nixon, 272–73, 315–16, 323,
      459–60
  communications to
    from John R. Brown, III, 88,
      92–94, 96–97, 109, 156–57, 161
    from Buchanan, 346, 548–49
    from Butterfield, 327
    from Cole, 53
    from Colson, 234–35, 289–90, 293,
      299–301, 424–25, 437
    from Dean, 302–3, 360, 364–65
    from Graham, 223
    from Haldeman, 36–37, 38, 145,
      147
    from Helms, 360
    from Hughes, 43–44
    from Huntsman, 345
    from Kehrli, 374, 550–51
    from Nixon, 2, 4, 12–14, 16–20,
      23–24, 32, 33, 35, 51, 69–70, 73,
      99–102, 179, 214, 242–44, 260–61,
      406–11, 450–51, 584
    from Patterson, 223–24
Eisenhower, David, 108–9, 175
Eisenhower, Dwight D., 28, 46–47,
    105
Eisenhower, Julie Nixon, lxv, 72,
    108–9, 175, 320–22, 359, 383, 392,
    393, 398, 568
  memo from Nixon to, 521–22
Ellender, 440, 441
Elliott, Roland, memo from Colson to,
    369
Ellsberg, Daniel, xxi-xxiii, 280–81,
    283–84, 286, 293, 299–300, 472,
    510
Enthoven, Alain, 211
Epstein, Edward, 221

Ervin, Sam J., Jr., 145
  letters from Nixon to, 595–96
  letter to Nixon from, 594–95
Ervin Committee, 584, 585–86,
    591–97, 603, 607
Evans, Bud, memo from Colson to,
    140–41
Evans, Richard, memos to Nixon
    from, 534–36
Evans, Rollie, 350
Evans, Tom, 501
  memo to Colson from, 403–4

Federal Bureau of Investigation (FBI),
    xxii, xxxv, 141, 163, 255, 256, 293,
    323, 445, 461, 502, 504, 506, 508,
    510, 511, 618
Federal Communications Commission
    (FCC), 150, 151, 152, 171, 173, 233,
    245, 380
Felt, Mark, 445–46, 502
Field, Clark, 107
Fielding, Fred, 604
  memos from
    to Buzhardt and Garment, 607–8
    to Dean, 255–56, 405
    to Garment, 589–90
    to Nancy Kennedy, 547
    to Khachigian, 489–90
    to Stephanie Wilson, 291
  memos to
    from Dean, 262, 277
    from Howard, 440
Fielding, Lewis, 618
Finch, Robert, 63–64, 324
  memo from Dean to, 356–57
Findley (senator), 423
Fisher, Max, 142
Fisher, Paul, 526
Fitzsimmons, Frank, 157–58, 260,
    303
Flanigan, Peter, 160, 290, 334, 336,
    450
  memos from, to Nixon, 63–64, 569
  memos to
    from Colson, 249–50, 330–31
    from Haldeman, 60, 64, 87, 94–95
    from Nixon, 51–52, 73, 182–83
Fonda, Jane, 262–63, 266–67
Ford, Benson, 142

Haig, Alexander *(cont'd)*
  from Harris, 308–9
  from Nixon, 261–2, 591–94
Haldeman, H. R. (Bob), xvi*n*, xxvii,
    xxviii, xxix, xxx, xxxii, xxxv,
    xxxvii-xxxix, xli, xlviii, lxii, 309,
    367, 490, 502–9, 556, 591, 592, 612
  communications from, 93–94, 312,
    391
    Action Memos, 220, 373, 375,
      377, 386–87, 426, 437, 495,
      498, 523, 526, 540–41, 551, 557,
      568, 571–73, 577–78, 578–79
    to John Brown, 30
    to Buchanan, 41, 41–42, 88–89,
      219–20
    to Butterfield, 55, 215, 221, 557
    to Chapin, 149, 185, 319–20, 442
    to Cole, 29
    to Colson, 157–59, 178, 237–38
    to Dean, 152, 210
    to Dent, 98–99
    to Ehrlichman, 38, 145, 147
    to Ehrlichman, Ziegler, Klein,
      Kissinger, and Harlow, 36–37
    to Flanigan, 60, 64, 87, 94–95
    to Higby, 28, 38, 63, 574
    to Gen. Hughes, 25–28, 113–14, 156
    to Huston, 201
    to Kissinger, 138, 572–73
    to Kissinger and Buchanan, 88
    to Klein, 89
    to Krogh, 106
    to Magruder, 80–81, 87
    to Nixon, 110, 334, 513–14, 514–16
    political strategy papers, 482, 483
    to Gen. Schulz, 55
    to Constance Stuart, 65
    to Whitaker, 29
    to Winchester, 40
    to Mrs. Winchester, 173–74
  memos to
    from John R. Brown, III, 95, 98,
      116, 117, 141, 152, 156–57, 162–63,
      212
    from Buchanan, 78–79, 211, 229,
      239–40, 303, 304, 314–15,
      320–22, 326–28, 341–50, 548–49,
      554
    from Butterfield, 22, 288–89, 305

  from Caulfield, 214–15
  from Chapin, 43, 192–3, 204–5
  from Chotiner, 108
  from Colson, 97, 163, 164, 170–73,
    176, 189, 190, 200, 205, 211,
    218–19, 220, 235, 245, 257–60,
    267, 271–72, 274, 279–85,
    290–93, 295–299, 301, 306–7,
    310, 313–14, 325, 329–30, 351,
    367–68, 372, 373, 402–3, 430,
    569
  from Dean, 184, 208–10, 238–39,
    266, 297, 302–3, 308, 360–62,
    395–96, 463, 492–94
  from Higby, 98, 142, 572
  from Hoopes, 461, 512
  from Huntsman, 225–26
  from Huston, 38–39, 56, 141, 143,
    145, 147–48
  from Kehrli, 357, 484–85
  from Magruder, 81
  from Nixon, 1–7, 11–17, 23, 31–32,
    34, 35, 38, 44–49, 53, 58–59,
    65, 69–77, 83, 85, 86, 90–92, 95,
    99–109, 113–16, 120, 125–40, 160,
    175–78, 181–82, 191–92, 202–4,
    213–14, 227, 250–54, 261, 270–71,
    354, 359, 382–89, 392–93,
    396–99, 405–6, 412–15, 417–21,
    430–31, 433–34, 440–41, 448–50,
    480, 533, 536–40, 569–71,
    580–83
  from Safire, 150
  from Walker, 517–20
  from Woods, 120, 417, 438
Hall, Joan, 495
  memos from
    to Shelley Buchanan, 358
    to Colson, 496
Hallett, Douglas, xxxi, 351
  memos from Colson to, 291–92, 372,
    422, 488
  memos to Colson from, 305, 355,
    425
Halperin, Morton H., 137
Harlow, Bryce, 3, 22, 46, 55, 102, 109
  memos to
    from Butterfield, 22
    from Haldeman, 36–37
    from Nixon, 69–70

Strachan, Gordon, xxv, xxxix
   memos to
      from Colson, 419
      from Dean, 200, 330, 442
      from Higby, 568
Stringfellow, William, 493
Strolling Strings, 420
Stroud, Candy, 288, 289
Stroul, 484
Stuart, Constance (Connie), 125,
   156
   memo from Haldeman to,
      65
Student Mobilization Committee,
   106
Students for a Democratic Society
   (SDS), 39, 106, 329, 361, 516
Subversive Activities Control Board,
   98, 104
Suffridge, James, 157, 218
Swanson, Gloria, 178
Swearingen, John, 144
Sweden, 90
Swim, Dudley, 142

Taiwan, 332–33
Taylor, Bob, 8
Taylor, Marty, 259
Teague (congressman), 534
Teague, James, 390
Teamsters Union, 260
Teeter, Bob, memos from Colson to,
   552
Thimmesch, Nick, 163, 189
Thomas, E. Parry, 177
Thomas, Helen, 354
Thomas, Jane, 394
Thompson, Fred, 586
Thompson, Sir Robert, 583
Thornton, 228
Thrower, Randolph W., 118, 147
   memo to Nixon from, 121
Time, Inc., 205–7
Timmons, William E., 226, 514, 582,
   596
   letter from Dole to, 590–91
   memos to
      from Colson, 247–48
      from Kehrli, 576

Titus, 498
Toland, Jack, letter to Conrad from,
   42–43
Toland, John S., xvi–xviin
Tolson, Clyde, 120
Tower, John G., 78, 79
Traylor, Larry, 607
Trilling, Lionel, 319, 565
Trohan, Walter, 94
   letter from, to Woods, 610
   letter to, from Woods, 612
Trowbridge, Sandy, 224
Tuchman, Barbara, 63
Tunney, 423, 485
Turck, Nancy, 54
Turkey, 51
Turner, Wallace, xxxv
Tydings, 171

Udall, Moe, 486
Udall, Stewart, 261
Ukrainian Congress Committee of
   America, 443
UPI, 275
Urban Affairs Council, 77–78
Usery, Bill, 158, 219
USIA, 35

Valenti, Jack, 27
Van Arsdale, Harry, 222
Vance, Cyrus, 136
Van Deerlin (congressman), 498
Vanderbilt University, 436
Vann, John, 73, 428, 491–92
Vanocur, Sandy, 288, 473
Veterans of Foreign Wars (VFW), 396
Vidler, Barbara Ann, 394
Vietnam Veterans Against the War
   (VVAW), 395
Vietnam War, 44–45, 50, 62, 64,
   66–68, 72, 73, 79, 96–98, 136,
   138–39, 167, 189, 199, 270–86,
   378–79, 422–23, 427–29, 432–33,
   574–75, 583, 621
Vinson, Mrs., 423
VISTA, 109
Volcker, Paul, 335
Volpe, John, memo from MacGregor
   to, 389